D1754596

Archive for Reformation History

An international journal
concerned with the history of the Reformation and its significance in world affairs,
published under the auspices of the Verein für Reformationsgeschichte and
the Society for Reformation Research

North American Editors

Ute Lotz-Heumann – Marjorie Elizabeth Plummer

European Editors

Thomas Kaufmann – Martin Keßler

Advisory Board – Wissenschaftlicher Beirat

Michael Driedger, St. Catharines/Ontario – Renate Dürr, Tübingen – Birgit Emich, Frankfurt a. M. – Mark Greengrass, Sheffield – Brad S. Gregory, Notre Dame/Indiana – Scott Hendrix, Princeton/New Jersey – Mack P. Holt, Fairfax/Virginia – Susan C. Karant-Nunn, Tucson/Arizona – Thomas Kaufmann, Göttingen – Martin Keßler, Bonn – Yves Krumenacker, Lyon – Ute Lotz-Heumann, Tucson/Arizona – Janusz Małłek, Toruń – Marjorie Elizabeth Plummer, Tucson/Arizona – Silvana Seidel Menchi, Pisa – Carla Rahn Phillips, Minneapolis/Minnesota – Heinz Schilling, Berlin – Ethan H. Shagan, Berkeley/California – Christoph Strohm, Heidelberg – James D. Tracy, Minneapolis/Minnesota – Alexandra Walsham, Cambridge – Randall C. Zachman, Notre Dame/Indiana

Vol. 113 · 2022

Gütersloher Verlagshaus

Archiv für Reformationsgeschichte

Internationale Zeitschrift
zur Erforschung der Reformation und ihrer Weltwirkungen,
herausgegeben im Auftrag des Vereins für Reformationsgeschichte und
der Society for Reformation Research

Europäische Herausgeber

Thomas Kaufmann – Martin Keßler

Nordamerikanische Herausgeberinnen

Ute Lotz-Heumann – Marjorie Elizabeth Plummer

Wissenschaftlicher Beirat – Advisory Board

Michael Driedger, St. Catharines/Ontario – Renate Dürr, Tübingen – Birgit Emich, Frankfurt a. M. – Mark Greengrass, Sheffield – Brad S. Gregory, Notre Dame/Indiana – Scott Hendrix, Princeton/New Jersey – Mack P. Holt, Fairfax/Virginia – Susan C. Karant-Nunn, Tucson/Arizona – Thomas Kaufmann, Göttingen – Martin Keßler, Bonn – Yves Krumenacker, Lyon – Ute Lotz-Heumann, Tucson/Arizona – Janusz Małłek, Toruń – Marjorie Elizabeth Plummer, Tucson/Arizona – Silvana Seidel Menchi, Pisa – Carla Rahn Phillips, Minneapolis/Minnesota – Heinz Schilling, Berlin – Ethan H. Shagan, Berkeley/California – Christoph Strohm, Heidelberg – James D. Tracy, Minneapolis/Minnesota – Alexandra Walsham, Cambridge – Randall C. Zachman, Notre Dame/Indiana

Vol. 113 · 2022

Gütersloher Verlagshaus

Mitarbeiter der Redaktion – Editorial Assistant
Dr. Ellen Yutzy Glebe

Das *Archiv für Reformationsgeschichte* ist eine jährlich erscheinende Zeitschrift mit einem anonymisierten Begutachtungsverfahren. Manuskripte in deutscher, französischer und italienischer Sprache werden per E-Mail erbeten an Prof. Dr. Dr. h. c. Dr. h. c. Thomas Kaufmann, Universität Göttingen, thomas.kaufmann@theologie.uni-goettingen.de, und Prof. Dr. Martin Keßler, Schlegel-Professur für Kirchengeschichte mit dem Schwerpunkt Reformation und Aufklärung, Rheinische Friedrich-Wilhelms-Universität Bonn, Martin.Kessler@uni-bonn.de. Manuskripte in englischer Sprache werden per E-Mail erbeten an Prof. Dr. Ute Lotz-Heumann, Heiko A. Oberman Chair, und Prof. Dr. Marjorie Elizabeth Plummer, Susan C. Karant-Nunn Chair, University of Arizona, ArcRefHist@arizona.edu. Es werden nur Original-Beiträge im *ARG* aufgenommen. Es wird empfohlen, rechtzeitig vor Abschluss des Manuskripts bei den jeweiligen Herausgebern Merkblätter zur formalen Gestaltung der Beiträge anzufordern.

The *Archive for Reformation History* is a double-blind peer reviewed journal that appears annually. Manuscripts in English should be sent by e-mail to Ute Lotz-Heumann, Professor of History and Heiko A. Oberman Chair, and Marjorie Elizabeth Plummer, Professor of History and Susan C. Karant-Nunn Chair, University of Arizona, ArcRefHist@arizona.edu. Manuscripts in German, French, and Italian should be sent by e-mail to Prof. Dr. Dr. h. c. Dr. h. c. Thomas Kaufmann, University of Göttingen, thomas.kaufmann@theologie.uni-goettingen.de, and Prof. Dr. Martin Keßler, Schlegel Professor of Church History, University of Bonn, Martin.Kessler@uni-bonn.de. The *ARH* only accepts original manuscripts. Please contact the editors for guidelines for the preparation of manuscripts.

Klimaneutral*
Druckprodukt
ClimatePartner.com/14044-1912-1001

Penguin Random House Verlagsgruppe FSC® N001967

Auch als Online-Ausgabe erhältlich: www.degruyter.com/view/j/arg
ISBN 978-3-579-08479-4
Print-Ausgabe: ISSN 0003-9381
Online-Ausgabe: ISSN 2198-0489
Copyright © 2022 by Gütersloher Verlagshaus, Gütersloh,
in der Penguin Random House Verlagsgruppe GmbH,
Neumarkter Straße 28, 81673 München

Die Zeitschrift und alle in ihr veröffentlichten Beiträge sind urheberrechtlich geschützt. Kein Teil dieser Zeitschrift darf ohne schriftliche Genehmigung des Verlages in irgendeiner Form reproduziert, digitalisiert oder gesendet werden.
Sollte diese Publikation Links auf Webseiten Dritter enthalten, so übernehmen wir für deren Inhalte keine Haftung, da wir uns diese nicht zu eigen machen, sondern lediglich auf deren Stand zum Zeitpunkt der Erstveröffentlichung verweisen.

Satz: SatzWeise, Bad Wünnenberg
Druck und Einband: PB Tisk, a. s., Pribram
Printed in Czech Republic
www.gtvh.de

Inhalt

Finn Schulze-Feldmann
Der Versuch einer spirituellen Erneuerung abseits der Reformation:
Das freie weltliche Stift Gernrode unter Elisabeth von Weida, 1504–32   7

Terence McIntosh
The Words of Forgiveness: Luther, *The Keys*, and the Nuremberg
Absolution Controversy 36

Daniel Gehrt
Pictorial Renaissance Bookbindings and the Domestication of Lucas
Cranach's Iconography:
An Overlooked Medium of the German Reformation 70

Brandt Klawitter
Omnis utriusque's Conflicted Reordering: Pastoral Theology and
Admission to the Lord's Supper in View of Wittenberg-Related Church
Orders (1523–1528) 109

Ulrich Gäbler
„Tut um Gottes willen etwas Tapferes". Ermutigt Zwingli mit diesem
Aufruf die Zürcher zum Krieg? 137

Esther Chung-Kim
Pious City: Community and Charity in Calvin's Geneva 168

Christine Christ-von Wedel
Beredtes Schweigen. Basler Theologen und der Hexenwahn 198

Saskia Limbach und Martin Christ
Möglichkeiten und Grenzen konfessioneller Koexistenz. Briefwechsel,
Studien- und Druckorte Oberlausitzer Geistlicher in der zweiten Hälfte
des 16. Jahrhunderts 233

Andrew J. G. Drenas
"Holy Handkerchiefs!" A Study of St. Lawrence of Brindisi's Eucharistic
Spirituality and Mass Handkerchiefs 265

Miscellanea

Wolfgang Huber
„der erst, der das Euangelium den von kitzingen zu den letzten Zeiten bracht": Der Weg des Christoph Hoffmann (um 1495–1553) vom Promovenden Karlstadts zum kursächsischen Hofprediger 291

Thomas Gerhard Wilhelmi
Brieffunde in einer Sammelhandschrift aus dem Hamburger Geistlichen Ministerium 313

Der Versuch einer spirituellen Erneuerung abseits der Reformation: Das freie weltliche Stift Gernrode unter Elisabeth von Weida, 1504–32

Von Finn Schulze-Feldmann

EINLEITUNG

„Als erste in der Region nahm Elisabeth von Weida die wahre Lehre des Evangeliums 1521 unter verschiedenen Schwierigkeiten, Drohungen und Hinterhalten von Feinden an."[1] Dieses Narrativ des Stiftschronisten Andreas Popperodt (aktiv 1532–1564), dass Äbtissin Elisabeth von Weida (1460/61–1532) die reformatorische Lehre 1521 im freien weltlichen Stift Gernrode eingeführt habe, hat spätestens seit Matthäus Merian d. Ä. die Geschichtsschreibung des Stifts geprägt.[2] Nachdem es Otto von Heinemann aufgriff, bestimmt es auch

---

1. Der vorliegende Beitrag entstand im Rahmen des Dietrich-Moderhack-Stipendiums der Historischen Kommission für Anhalt-Sachsen. Der Autor dankt insbesondere Cornelia Linde und Andreas Pečar sowie den Mitarbeiter_Innen des Landesarchivs Sachsen-Anhalt, der Anhaltischen Landesbücherei, des Pfarramts in Gernrode und des Gernröder Kulturvereins.
Andreas Popperodt, „Annales Gernrodenses", in: *Johann Christoph Beckmann* (Hg.), ACCESSIONES HISTORIAE ANHALTINAE. Von unterschieden Das Hoch=Fürstl[iche] Hauß Und Fürstenthum Anhalt Belangenden Materien sampt dazu gehörigen Documenten: Wobei zugleich Eine CONTINUATION Der Hoch=Fürstl[ichen] Anhaltischen Geschichte von A[nno] 1709 biß 1716. Ingleichen Eine Beschreibung Etlicher Adelicher zu dem Fürstenthum Anhalt gehörigen Geschlechter / Auch einiger andern daselbst vorgegangenen Veränderungen, Zerbst 1716, VD18 90025164, Fol. [D 2ʳ]-Lᵛ, hier 67: „Elisabetha de Wida Abbatissa [...] prima in hac regione Anno 1521. veram Evangelii doctrinam, inter varias difficultates, minas, & insidias hostium complexa est".
2. *Matthäus Merian d. Ä.* (Hg.), TOPOGRAPHIA Superioris Saxoniæ Thüringiæ / Misniæ Lusatiæ etc: Das ist Beschreibung der Vornehmsten vnd Bekantesten Stätt / vnd Platz in Churfürstenthum Sachsen / Thüringen / Meissen, Ober vnd NiderLaußnitz vnd einverleibten Landen; auch in andern Zu dem Hochlöblichsten Sächsischen Craiße gehörigen Fürstentumen (außer Brandenburg vnd Pommeren), Graff: vnd Herrschafften etc., Frankfurt 1650, VD17 3:659998U, 87. Siehe auch *Johann Christoph Beckmann*, Historie Des Fürstenthums Anhalt Von dessen Einwohnern und einigen annoch verhandenen Alten Monumenten / Natürlicher Gütigkeit / Eintheilung / Flüssen / Stäten / Flecken und Dörfern / Fürst[licher] Hoheit / Geschichten der Fürstl[ichen] Personen / Religions=Handlungen / Fürstlichen Ministris, Adelichen Geschlechtern / Gelehrten / und andern Bürger=Standes Vornehmen Leuten, 2 Bde., Zerbst 1710, Bd. 2, VD18 90024516, 38; *Julius Bernhard von Rohr,*

den modernen Diskurs um die Reformation in Gernrode.³ Nur vereinzelt finden sich Einwände wie in einer Biographie Elisabeths, in der Franke aufgrund brieflicher Quellen und altkirchlicher Praktiken einen späteren Anschluss an die Wittenberger Reformationsbewegung im Jahr 1525 annimmt.⁴ Diese Argumentation wurde in der Geschichtsschreibung lokalpatriotischer Prägung bis 1918 allerdings vehement verworfen.⁵ Mit dem Verweis auf Popperodts tendenziöse Darstellung der Reformation griff Hans K. Schulze in der jüngsten Monographie über Gernrode dennoch Frankes These auf, ohne aber eine schlüssige Analyse der Ereignisse anzubieten.⁶

So vielversprechend und verlockend es auch sein mag, die Einführung der reformatorischen Lehre im Stift Gernrode exakt zu datieren, so wenig ertragreich erscheint dieses Unterfangen. Tatsächlich verbietet sich aufgrund Elisabeths starker Orientierung an kirchlichen Traditionen eine vorschnelle Charakterisierung als lutherischer Akteurin.⁷ Ihrem in der Gernröder Stiftskirche

---

Geographische und Historische Merckwürdigkeiten des Vor= oder Unter=Hartzes, Welche von denen Fürstenthümern Blanckenburg und Hartzgerode, dem Stifft Quedlinburg, den Grafschafften Manßfeld, Stollberg und deren Städten, Flecken, Schlössern, ehemaligen Clöstern, alten Ruderibus, Bergwercken, notablen Bergen, Flüssen, Seen auch andern Naturalibus, sowohl in Ansehung derer ehemaligen als itzigen Zeiten mancherley besonders in sich fassen, Frankfurt und Leipzig 1736, VD18 11364211, 414–416.

3. *Otto von Heinemann*, Die Stiftskirche zu Gernrode und ihre Wiederherstellung, Bernburg 1865, 20.

4. *Franke*, „Elisabeth von Weida und Wildenfels, Äbtissin des freien weltlichen Stiftes Gernrode: 1504–1532", in: Mittheilungen des Vereins für Anhaltische Geschichte 8 (1902), 313–335, hier 325.

5. *Hermann Suhle*, „Die Reformation im Stift Gernrode 1521", in: Unser Anhaltland 2.42 (1902), 489–493, hier 492–93; *Friedrich Winfrid Schubart*, „Stephan Molitor, der Reformator des Stiftes Gernrode", in: Zerbster Jahrbuch 2 (1906), 7–19, hier 10–11; *Rudolf Bahn*, Geros Gründung: Die Reichsabtei Gernrode: Ein Beitrag zur Kulturgeschichte des Mittelalters und der Reformationszeit, Köthen 1908, 50–53; *Hans Hartung*, Zur Vergangenheit von Gernrode, Quedlinburg 1912.

6. *Hans K. Schulze*, Das Stift Gernrode, Köln, Graz 1965, 64–67.

7. Dieser Beitrag folgt Irene Dingels Unterscheidung zwischen der frühen Reformationsbewegung als einer personenbezogenen Identität und der späteren lutherischen Konfession. Dingel führt dazu folgendes aus: „Wenn Luther selbst die Bezeichnung ‚Lutherani' und ‚Wittenbergenses' als Synonym verwandte, wie ebenfalls jüngst herausgearbeitet wurde, belegt dies im Grunde nur, dass für Luther der Referenzpunkt für das ‚Lutheraner-Sein' oder ‚Lutherisch-Sein' ein personen- und gruppenbezogener war. Natürlich verband sich damit auch die Parteinahme für die neue reformatorische Lehre dieser Person oder Gruppe. Ein Konfessionsbezug aber liegt nicht zugrunde." Wird hier die Bezeichnung „lutherisch" verwendet, bezieht sie sich spezifisch auf die später vollzogene Konfessionszuschreibung. Siehe *Irene Dingel*, „Wie lutherisch war die Wittenberger Reformation? Von vorkonfessioneller Vielfalt zu theologischer Profilierung", in: *Irene Dingel, Armin Kohnle, Stefan Rhein, Ernst-Joachim*

materialisierten Reichsverständnis der fortwährenden *unio imperii et ecclesiae* entsprechend reformierte sie das Stift zwar unter Berücksichtigung der Wittenberger Reformationsbewegung. Selbst als Gernrode zu einem reichsweit beachteten Damenstift protestantischer Frömmigkeit avanciert war, verblieb es aber sowohl religiös als auch politisch auf Distanz zu dieser. Um diese Komplexität zu erfassen, setzt sich der vorliegende Beitrag daher zum Ziel, die historiographische Fokussierung auf die reformatorischen Ereignisse seit 1517 zu durchbrechen und stattdessen die Amtszeit Elisabeths von Weida als Gernröder Äbtissin in ihrer Gesamtheit zu betrachten. Der Zeitraum von 1504 bis 1532 soll so weniger als einschneidende Epochenwende begriffen werden, sondern als eine diachron über die vermeintliche Zäsur der Reformation verlaufende Zeit einer graduellen Transformation.

Obwohl die Verengung auf den Betrachtungszeitraum seit 1517 und die Beibehaltung diskursiver Muster der Geschichtsschreibung des frühen 20. Jahrhunderts zu einer vereinfachten Darstellung geführt haben, ist Gernrode punktuell als Beispiel für die frühe Reformation in die Forschung eingegangen.[8] Dabei stellt sich der gegenwärtige Forschungsstand zu der spätmittelalterlichen und frühneuzeitlichen Geschichte reichsunmittelbarer Frauenstifte generell als ausgesprochen disparat dar. Auch wenn vermeintlich bedeutsamere Stifte wie das benachbarte Quedlinburg jüngst mehr Aufmerksamkeit erfahren haben, bleibt das monastische Spezifikum Frauenstift trotz der zahlreichen Studien zu Frauenklöstern in der Frühen Neuzeit nach wie vor ein Kuriosum.[9] Neue, auch für Gernrode relevante Impulse setzen derweil Publikationen um Themenkomplexe wie der landesherrlichen Reformation im lange Zeit vernachlässigten mitteldeutschen Raum.[10] Wie der biographische Eintrag zu Eli-

---

Waschke (Hg.), Initia Reformationis: Wittenberg und die frühe Reformation, Leipzig 2017, 409–428, hier 413–414.

8. *Merry E. Wiesner,* „Ideology meets the Empire: Reformed Convents and the Reformation", in: *Merry E. Wiesner* (Hg.), Gender, Church and State in Early Modern Germany: Essays by Merry E. Wiesner, London 1998, 47–62, hier 57; *Antje Rüttgardt,* Klosteraustritte in der frühen Reformation. Studien zu Flugschriften der Jahre 1522 bis 1524, Gütersloh 2007, 15.

9. Siehe beispielsweise *Teresa Schröder-Strapper,* Fürstäbtissinnen: Frühneuzeitliche Stiftsherrschaften zwischen Verwandtschaft, Lokalgewalten und Reichsverband, Köln, Weimar, Wien 2015; *Ute Küppers-Braun,* Frauen des hohen Adels im kaiserlich-freiweltlichen Damenstift Essen (1065–1803): Eine verfassungs- und sozialgeschichtliche Studie, zugleich ein Beitrag zur Geschichte der Stifte Thorn, Elten, Vreden und St. Ursula in Köln, Münster 1997; *Peter Kasper,* Das Reichsstift Quedlinburg (936–1810): Konzept – Zeitbezug – Systemwechsel, Göttingen 2014; *Gerrit Deutschländer, Ingrid Würth* (Hg.), Eine Lebenswelt im Wandel: Klöster in Stadt und Land, Halle 2017.

10. *Tobias Jammerthal, David Burkhart Janssen* (Hg.), Georg III. von Anhalt: Abend-

sabeth von Weida in Eva Labouvies Lexikon bedeutender Frauen in Sachsen-Anhalt zeigt, haben diese bisweilen jedoch nicht zu einer Neubewertung geführt.[11] Zurecht resümierte Eike Wolgast in seiner umfassenden Untersuchung zum Verhältnis der Klöster im Reich zur Reformation, dass Gernrode unzulänglich erforscht sei.[12]

Im Fokus der folgenden Betrachtungen sollen die Wechselwirkungen von Ausdrucksformen weiblicher Frömmigkeit und der Artikulation und Durchsetzung politischer und ökonomischer Interessen des Stifts stehen. Diese gilt es sowohl mittels der materiellen Umgestaltungen des Stifts als auch anhand der in archivalischen Quellen evidenten liturgisch-theologischen Neuorientierung sowie den erhaltenen Korrespondenzen nachzuzeichnen. Zunächst ist aufzuzeigen, dass die vermeintlich reformatorischen Ereignisse der frühen 1520er Jahre weder dem Muster von Fürstenreformationen folgten, noch Luthers frühe Kirchenkritik und theologischen Reformimpulse konsequent umgesetzt wurden; die Bezeichnung als lutherische Reformation ist somit zu verwerfen. Die anschließende Betrachtung der Reformaktivitäten Elisabeths seit ihrem Amtsantritt 1504 verdeutlicht vielmehr, dass die Reform der Stiftsliturgie am Ende eines langwierigen Reformprozesses stand, der auf die strukturelle und wirtschaftliche Konsolidierung sowie die geistliche Stärkung des Stifts abzielte. Nicht so sehr theologische Erwägungen, sondern der externe Mediatisierungsdruck seitens geistlicher und weltlicher Reichsfürsten waren hierfür ursächlich. In der Tat hielt dieser Mediatisierungs- und Säkularisierungsdruck bis über die Zeit von Äbtissin Elisabeth von Weida an. Dass Elisabeth trotzdem als erste lutherische Äbtissin des Stifts Gernrode gilt, resultiert aus der sich seit etwa 1527 durchsetzenden Wahrnehmungsveränderung. Während es vielmehr eine gewisse Passivität Elisabeths war, die nun Freiräume für weitere reformatorische Veränderungen schuf, wurden sie und ihr Stift als Teil der Reformationsbewegung bezeichnet, eine Sicht, die sich bis heute durchgesetzt hat.

---

mahlsschriften, Leipzig 2019; *Christoph Volkmar*, Reform statt Reformation: Die Kirchenpolitik Herzog Georgs von Sachsen 1488–1525, Tübingen 2008; *Armin Kohnle, Siegfried Bräuer* (Hg.), Von Grafen und Predigern: Zur Reformationsgeschichte des Mansfelder Landes, Leipzig 2014; *Susan Richter, Armin Kohnle* (Hg.), Herrschaft und Glaubenswechsel. Die Fürstenreformation im Reich und in Europa in 28 Biographien, Heidelberg 2016; *Christoph Volkmar*, Reform statt Reformation: Die Kirchenpolitik Herzog Georgs von Sachsen 1488–1525, Tübingen 2008.

11. *Erik Richter*, „Weida und Wildenfels, Elisabeth von (Äbtissin von Gernrode)", in: *Eva Labouvie* (Hg.), Frauen in Sachsen-Anhalt: Ein biographisch-bibliographisches Lexikon vom Mittelalter bis zum 18. Jahrhundert, Köln, Weimar, Wien 2016, 371–372.

12. *Eike Wolgast*, Die Einführung der Reformation und das Schicksal der Klöster im Reich und in Europa, Gütersloh 2014, 243.

GRADUELLE TRANSFORMATION

Im Heiligen Römischen Reich entschieden die Territorialfürsten, einschließlich der geistlichen Reichsstände, über die Einführung der reformatorischen Lehre in ihrem Herrschaftsgebiet. Um das Narrativ der Chronik Popperodts genauer zu überprüfen, ist es daher unausweichlich, die Ereignisse in Gernrode anhand der Parameter zu untersuchen, die für das jüngst wieder vermehrt betrachtete Konzept der Fürstenreformation als konstitutiv erachtet werden[13]: Zum einen ist dies die Einführung der neuen Lehre mittels eines symbolträchtigen Akts, der mit altkirchlichen Praktiken bricht. Als eines der frühsten Beispiele kann hier Andreas Karlstadt (1486–1541) herangezogen werden, der 1521 die Weihnachtsmesse in der Wittenberger Stadtkirche auf Deutsch feierte und das Abendmahl in beiderlei Gestalt reichte.[14] Spätestens nachdem Georg Spalatin (1484–1545) Kurfürsten Friedrich III. von Sachsen (der Weise, 1463–1525) als Wegbereiter der Reformation inszenierte, indem er explizit darüber berichtete, dass sein Landesherr den Laienkelch auf seinem Sterbebett empfangen hatte, etablierte sich dieser Akt rasch als Zeichen einer Abkehr von der römischen Kirche.[15] Zum anderen legte der Erlass einer Kirchenordnung die normative Grundlage dafür, die neue Theologie in die Alltagserfahrung der jeweiligen Kirche zu übertragen und das Kirchenwesen rechtlich neu zu verfassen. Stilprägend hierfür war die von Luther 1523 verfasste *Ordnung eines gemeinen Kasten* für die Stadt Leisnig.[16]

---

13. *Armin Kohnle*, „Die ernestinischen Fürsten Friedrich der Weise und Johann der Beständige und ihr Verhältnis zu Martin Luther in den Anfangsjahren der Reformation", in: *Dingel, Kohnle, Rhein, Waschke* (Hg.), Initia Reformationis (wie Anm. 7), 391–408, hier 391–93. Die Fürstenreformation als Forschungsfeld wurde seit den 1970er Jahren wesentlich von Eike Wolgast geprägt. Hier seien lediglich zwei seiner Werke exemplarisch angeführt. *Eike Wolgast*, Die Wittenberger Theologie und die Politik der evangelischen Stände. Studien zu Luthers Gutachten in politischen Fragen, Gütersloh 1977; *Wolgast*, Einführung (wie Anm. 12). Für jüngere Beiträge zur Fürstenreformation, siehe *Richter, Kohnle*, Herrschaft (wie Anm. 10).

14. *Charlotte Methuen*, „Luther's Life", in: *Robert Kolb, Irene Dingel, L'Ubomír Batka* (Hg.), The Handbook of Martin Luther's Theology, Oxford 2014, 7–27, hier 17.

15. *Saskia Jähnigen*, „,im rechten erkenntnis des Euangelij[...] verschieden': Tod und Memoria Kurfürst Friedrichs des Weisen zwischen spätmittelalterlicher Tradition und reformatorischem Wandel", in: *Heiner Lück, Enno Bünz, Leonhard Helten, Armin Kohnle, Ernst-Joachim Waschke* (Hg.), Das ernestinische Wittenberg: Residenz und Stadt, Petersberg 2020, 283–296, hier 285–286.

16. D. Martin Luthers Werke: Kritische Gesamtausgabe, 73 Bde., Weimar 1883–2009 (im Folgenden: WA), 12.1–30.

Betrachtet man die vermeintlich reformatorischen Ereignisse in Gernrode, fällt zunächst auf, dass keine zeitgenössischen Quellen einen wie auch immer gearteten symbolischen Akt des Bekenntniswechsels für die Äbtissin Elisabeth von Weida bezeugen. Erst zwecks ihrer Memoralisierung findet sich ein solches auf ihrer Grabplatte und in der eingangs zitierten Stiftschronik, mit der Popperodt im Geiste der Magdeburger Centurien das Stift als Hort der frühen Reformation und Elisabeth als erste „lutherische" Reichsfürstin zu inszenieren versuchte.[17] Tatsächlich aber wurden noch im Herbst 1520 Luthers Reformideen als allgemeine Kirchenkritik abgetan und selbst das Wormser Edikt schien ihm in einigen Punkten Zugeständnisse zu machen[18]; ein eigenständiges Bekenntnis, dem sich Elisabeth hätte anschließen können, existierte dergestalt noch nicht. Politisch hätte eine im symbolträchtigen Jahr des Wormser Reichstags erklärte Anhängerschaft an den nunmehr unter der Reichsacht stehenden Luther Elisabeth von Weida zudem schwer beschädigt. Solch ein Akt kann also ausgeschlossen werden.

Popperodts Datierung ist allerdings dahingehend beachtlich, als das Jahr 1521 auf die Rückkehr Stefan Molitors, des einstigen Diakons und seit 1521 Pastors der Stiftskirche, nach Gernrode verweist.[19] Popperodt und nachfolgende Historiker haben ihm eine elementare Rolle in der Gernröder Reformation zugewiesen. Mehr als fraglich bleibt jedoch, ob Elisabeth, wie von Schubart und Wäschke argumentiert, Molitor spezifisch wegen seiner Kenntnisse der lutherischen Kirchenkritik, die er sich bei einem möglichen Studium in Wit-

---

17. *Friedrich Winfrid Schubart*, „Gernröder Inschriften und Denksteine", in: Mitteilungen des Vereins für Anhaltische Geschichte und Altertumskunde 9.1 (1901), 33–41, hier 35; *Popperodt*, „Annales" (wie Anm. 1), 67. Noch von Heinemann hatte Elisabeth von Weida als erste lutherische Äbtissin bezeichnet. *Von Heinemann*, Gernrode (wie Anm. 3), 20. Zu den Magdeburger Centurien und ihrem Geschichtsverständnis, siehe *Harald Bollbuck*, Wahrheitszeugnis, Gottes Auftrag und Zeitkritik: Die Kirchengeschichte der Magdeburger Zenturien und ihre Arbeitstechniken, Wiesbaden 2014. Im Falle Popperodts ist die verklärende Interpretation der Stiftsvergangenheit außerdem darauf zurückzuführen, dass ihm mit dem ehemaligen Stiftsherren Caspar Scharffe, seinem qua seiner zweiten Frau Apolonia Schwiegervater, und Molitor zwei Männer zur Hilfe standen, die aktiv am Reformationsprozess beteiligt gewesen waren. *Suhle*, „Reformation" (wie Anm. 5), 490–491; *Popperodt*, „Annales" (wie Anm. 1), 67–68.

18. *Eike Wolgast*, „Die deutschen Territorialfürsten und die frühe Reformation", in: *Bernd Moeller, Stephen E. Buckwalter* (Hg.), Die frühe Reformation in Deutschland im Umbruch, Gütersloh 1998, 407–434, hier 413–414.

19. *Herrmann Graf*, Anhaltisches Pfarrerbuch: Die evangelischen Pfarrer seit der Reformation, Dessau 1996, 184, 358. Für Molitor finden sich auch die Namensvarianten Mylius und Müller.

tenberg angeeignet haben könnte, nach Gernrode zurückholte.[20] Des Weiteren hat sich das Narrativ, dass Elisabeth sich aufgrund des Auftreten Luthers auf dem Wormser Reichstag zur Reformierung ihres Stiftes entschloss, bis heute verfestigt, obwohl weder ein Treffen zwischen ihr oder Molitor mit Luther belegt ist, noch andere Quellen dies nahe legen.[21] Dass sie sich intensiv mit der neuen Lehre beschäftigte, nachdem Molitor von der regulären Bestätigung der Stiftsprivilegien auf dem Wormser Reichstag zurückgekehrt war, belegt jedoch eine nur archivalisch erhaltene Ordnung, die liturgische Neuregelungen enthält.

Ohne den externen Druck, wie er für die oft erzwungene Reformierung von Frauenkonventen üblich war, sondern mit der für Fürstenreformationen so wichtigen Freiwilligkeit wurde diese Ordnung also von Elisabeth von Weida zusammen mit Molitor geschaffen.[22] Sie nimmt explizit Bezug auf Luthers *Von ordenung gottis diensts ynn der gemeyne* von 1523 und folgt dieser in Struktur und ihren zeitlichen Anweisungen.[23] Da aber die drei Jahre später von Luther veröffentlichte Schrift *Deutsche Messe und ordnung Gottis diensts* unberücksichtigt blieb, kann die Gernröder Ordnung auf den Zeitraum zwischen 1523 und 1526 datiert werden. Der früheren Ordnung Luthers gleich stellt sie die Bibel ins Zentrum der Stiftsliturgie. So wird die Messfeier durch die Lesung des Evangeliums oder einer Epistel ersetzt und die Predigt in ihrer Bedeutung hervorgehoben[24]: „Darnach will mein g[nädige] f[rau] das die priester an stadt der

---

20. Die von Molitor während seines Studiums in Wittenberg genutzten Bücher sind im Zweiten Weltkrieg verloren gegangen, sodass über diese Korrespondenz und seine Studien wenig bekannt ist. Molitors sechs Quartbände von Lutherschriften aus den Jahren 1518 bis 1520 waren hastig annotiert und jeweils mit den Initialen SM auf der Titelseite versehen. Dass die mit einem E gekennzeichneten Marginalien allerdings auf eine Korrespondenz mit Elisabeth von Weida verweisen, ist eher fraglich, da keine Briefe erhalten bzw. erwähnt worden sind, die eine solche Hypothese bestätigen könnten. Nach der Abreise Luthers nach Worms scheint auch Molitor Wittenberg verlassen zu haben. *Schubart*, „Molitor" (wie Anm. 5), 8–10; *Hermann Wäschke*, „Geschichte Anhalts im Zeitalter der Reformation", in: ders. (Hg.), Anhaltische Geschichte, 3 Bde., Köthen 1912–1913, Bd. 2 (1912), hier 108.

21. Siehe beispielsweise *Rüttgardt*, Klosteraustritte (wie Anm. 8), 15.

22. Eine vergleichende Autopsie mit zeitnahen Handschriften Molitors zeigt, dass es sich hier um ein Manuskript aus seiner Hand handelt. Es liegt also nahe, dass diese schriftzentrierte Ordnung von Elisabeth und Molitor verfasst wurde. Siehe Landesarchiv Sachsen-Anhalt (im Folgenden: LASA) Z 6, Nr. 418 (2) und beispielsweise Z 3, Nr. 108. Zum Aspekt der Freiwilligkeit in Fürstenreformationen, siehe *Eike Wolgast*, „Formen landesfürstlicher Reformation in Deutschland", in: *Leif Grane, Kai Hørby* (Hg.), Die dänische Reformation vor ihrem internationalen Hintergrund, Göttingen 1990, 57–90, hier 60.

23. LASA Z 6, Nr. 418 (2), Fol. 5^v.

24. WA: 12.35–37; LASA Z6, Nr. 418 (2), Fol. 5^v. Hervorzuheben sei hier, dass beispielsweise die Lesungen, Predigt und Gesänge übernommen wurden. Schubart datiert das Schrei-

messe das Euangeliu[m] oder die epistel (wie der doctor in seiner ordnung hat angezeiget) fur dem altare leße vnd dar auff die freuchen ein fein responß gesungen das der priester mit eine[m] vater vnser vnd collecten beschliesßen sollen."[25] Obwohl diese Ordnung trotz Luthers Kritik an der Rolle der Frau im zeitgenössischen Klosterwesen die liturgische Sonderrolle der Stiftsdamen in wesentlichen Zügen beibehielt, führte sie mit dem Gebrauch der deutschen Sprache Elemente der Lehre Luthers ein, die ein noch am 22. Januar 1522 an umliegende Fürsten geschicktes Mandat des Reichsregiments untersagt hatte.[26] Elisabeth schien zumindest partiell Anschluss an die Wittenberger Reformbewegung zu suchen.

Darüber, ob diese liturgische Ordnung tatsächlich Verwendung fand, liegen allerdings keinerlei Hinweise vor. Frankes Argument, dass der Rekurs auf die Heiligen in einem Treueeid von 1525 auf einen Verbleib beim alten Ritus verweist und somit die Ordnung lediglich als Reformvorschlag zu verstehen ist, kann jedoch abgelehnt werden.[27] Nicht nur die Heiligenverehrung, der später im 21. Artikel der *Confessio Augustana* eine positive Funktion zugewiesen wurde, sondern auch weitere Praktiken des altkirchlichen Heiligenkults bestanden trotz des innerreformatorischen Dissenses hierüber fort, wie beispielsweise Bridget Heal eindrucksvoll für die Marienverehrung im 16. Jahrhundert aufgezeigt hat.[28] Dass die Pfarreien im Gernröder Stiftsgebiet zeitgleich mit reformorientierten Pastoren besetzt wurden, suggeriert hingegen, dass sich mit der Gernröder Ordnung eine Öffnung zu Luthers Reformgedanken im Stift vollzog. Die erste Ernennung vollzog sich laut einem Brief vom 6. November 1527 in der Waldauer Eigenkirche, da der dortige Priester seine pastoralen Pflichten vernachlässigt hatte und die Pfarre, nachdem er sich auf seine Vikarie in Magdeburg zurückgezogen hatte, verwaist lag.[29] Diesbezüglich schrieb der Anwalt der Fürsten Wolfgang von Anhalt-Köthen (1492–1566) und Johann IV. von Anhalt-Zerbst (1504–1551), „daß ehebenannte Äbtissin zu

---

ben auf das Jahr 1523. *Schubart*, „Molitor" (wie Anm. 5), 10. Zu der Frage der reformatorischen Umgestaltung des Stundengebets, siehe *Andreas Odenthal*, „'… matutinae, horae, vesperae, completorium maneant …': Zur Umgestaltung der Offiziumsliturgie in den Kirchen des frühen Luthertums anhand ausgewählter liturgischer Quellen", in: Jahrbuch für Liturgik und Hymnologie 46 (2007), 89–122.

25. LASA Z 6, Nr. 418 (2), Fol. 5ᵛ.
26. *Wolgast*, „Die deutschen Territorialfürsten" (wie Anm. 18), 415.
27. *Franke*, „Elisabeth" (wie Anm. 4), 325; Schulze, Gernrode (wie Anm. 6), 64–65.
28. *Bridget Heal*, The Cult of the Virgin Mary in Early Modern Germany: Protestant and Catholic Piety, 1500–1648, Cambridge 2007.
29. *Wäschke*, „Geschichte" (wie Anm. 20), 313–314; *Suhle*, „Reformation" (wie Anm. 5), 492–493; Franke, „Elisabeth" (wie Anm. 4), 325.

Gernrode am Tage Thomae im 1512ten Jahre nach der Geburt Christi angezeigte Pfarre zu Waldal einem Priester, Hermann Hennze genannt, geliehen und dazu präsentiert und lassen instituiren, der sie viele Jahre werweset, bestellt, besessen und inne gehabt bis ungefähr vor zwei Jahren, da die Äbtissin die Lutherische Religion und Lehre an sich selber genommen und von demselben Pfarrer gesonnen und haben wollen, daß er die Ceremonien und Messehalten, wie das Alles von der Kirche eingesetzt, solle fallen lassen und gäntzlich davon abstehen".[30] Während Franke diesen Brief als Beleg dafür ansieht, dass Elisabeth selbst lutherisch geworden sei, geht Hermann Suhle noch einen Schritt weiter und behauptet, dass dies schon vorher geschehen sein müsse und hier die darauffolgende Durchsetzung der Reformation im Stiftsgebiet belegt sei.[31] Tatsächlich scheint sich zeitnah zu der Gernröder Ordnung seit 1525 eine graduelle Erneuerung der Priesterschaft im Stiftsgebiet vollzogen zu haben, wie auch aus den handschriftlichen Aufzeichnungen Friedrich Winfrid Schubarts, die im Pfarramt Gernrode erhalten sind, hervorgeht.[32] In diesen heißt es, dass Elisabeth 1528 den reformatorischen Pfarrer Anders Henckel in die Pfarre in Sudendorf bei Gröningen entsandte[33]; auch dessen Nachfolger, Johann Hildebrandt, war Lutheraner.[34] Gleichwohl diese personellen Veränderungen, wie für Reformprozesse üblich, mit den liturgischen Neuerungen nicht exakt koinzidiert haben mögen, kann aufgrund der Berufung lutherischer Pfarrer davon ausgegangen werden, dass die Gernröder Ordnung mit ihrer schriftzentrierten Liturgie nicht nur ein Reformvorschlag war, sondern tatsächlich im Stift Anwendung fand.[35] Elisabeth von Weida nahm somit die einzigartige Position einer reichsunmittelbaren Äbtissin ein, die anders als anfangs mit spezifischen Reformideen Luthers sympathisierenden Fürstbischöfen diese, wenn auch nur partiell, in das religiöse Leben ihres Stifts integrierte.

Dieses scheinbar eindeutige Bild, dass Elisabeth von Weida die reformatorische Lehre spätestens seit 1525 für das Stift Gernrode annahm, ist aufgrund zweier Beobachtungen aber in Frage zu stellen. Während ein öffentlicher Bekenntniswechsel, wie oben dargelegt, auszuschließen ist, legt das Fehlen wei-

---

30. Pfarramt Gernrode (im Folgenden: PAG).
31. *Suhle*, „Reformation" (wie Anm. 5), 492–93; *Franke*, „Elisabeth" (wie Anm. 4), 325.
32. PAG.
33. PAG. *Uwe Grieme*, „Gröningen", in: *Werner Paravicini* (Hg.), Höfe und Residenzen im spätmittelalterlichen Reich: Ein dynastisch-topographisches Handbuch, 4 Bde., Ostfildern 2003–2012, Bd. 1.2 (2003), 235–237, hier 235.
34. *Graf*, Pfarrerbuch (wie Anm. 19), 180, 287.
35. *Johannes Wolfart*, „Why Was There Even a Reformation in Lindau? The Myth and Mystery of Lindau's Conflict-Free Reformation", in: Renaissance and Reformation 40.4 (2017), 43–72, hier 49–51.

terer Quellen nahe, dass selbst die liturgische Reform von 1523–25 unter Zeitgenossen wenig Beachtung fand. Erst für die späten 1520er Jahre ist überliefert, dass Elisabeth als lutherische Reformatorin charakterisiert wurde.[36] Tatsächlich existieren für den Zeitraum nach der Reform des Stiftsgottesdiensts zwischen 1523 und 1525 und der Einsetzung lutherischer Geistlicher im Stiftsgebiet keine Quellen für weiterführende, das religiöse Leben der Stiftsdamen betreffende Reformen. Dies ist angesichts der Vielzahl an Schriften Luthers, insbesondere der *Deutsche Messe und ordnung Gottis diensts* von 1526, die gänzlich unberücksichtigt geblieben zu sein scheint, verwunderlich.[37] Schwerer wiegt allerdings noch, dass das Stift Gernrode, obwohl es die Weisungen im Mandat des Reichsregiments von 1522 missachtete, Luthers Kirchenkritik trotz der Reformen in wesentlichen Punkten widersprach. Wie schon in *De votis monasticis* 1521 erörtert, bescheinigte Luther Klöstern und Stiften, dass sie sich von ihrer biblischen Grundlage entfernt hatten und in ihrer damaligen Form nicht legitimiert seien.[38] Während er 1520 in *An den christlichen Adel deutscher Nation* zur Rückkehr zu ihren Ursprüngen im apostolischen Zeitalter mahnte, rief er seit 1522 vehement zur Schließung dieser auf.[39] Er betrachtete sie als eine institutionalisierte Form der altkirchlichen Werkgerechtigkeit, die den Stiftern und Stiftsangehörigen zugunsten kommen sollte, dabei aber die Güte Gottes in Zweifel zöge.[40] Mit Verweis auf das Vorbild der heiligen Agnes und das Stift Quedlinburg hob Luther für Frauenstifte, aus denen die Stiftsdamen aufgrund eines fehlenden Gelübdes jederzeit austreten konnten, die Armenfürsorge und Bildungsarbeit als erhaltenswert hervor, eine Vorstellung, die eng mit der lutherischen Beschränkung des weiblichen Geltungsbereiches auf den Haushalt und der weiblichen Rolle als Ehefrau und Hausmutter verbunden ist.[41] Weder mit der Fortschreibung der liturgischen Sonderrolle der

---

36. D. Martin Luthers Werke. Briefe. Kritische Gesamtausgabe, 18 Bde. Weimar 1883– (im Folgenden: WA BR), 5.84.

37. WA: 19.44–113.

38. WA: 6.48, 441; 8.578–80; $10^{I.1}$.351; 10^{II}.129; 10^{III}.332; 11, 441; 17^{II}.51; *Christoph Burger*, Tradition und Neubeginn: Martin Luther in seinen frühen Jahren, Tübingen 2014, 55; *Jane E. Strohl*, „The Framework for Christian Living: Luther on the Christian's Callings", in: *Robert Kolb, Irene Dingel, L'Ubomír Batka* (Hg.), The Handbook of Martin Luther's Theology, Oxford 2014, 365–382, hier 372–373.

39. WA: $10^{I.1}$.253, 662, 681, 684, 687; $10^{I.2}$.29–30, 44, 144, 176–177; 10^{II}.111, 149; 11.40, 445; 12.11–12; 17^{II}.53.

40. WA: 6.257, 375, 439, 444, 451; 7, 36–37; $10^{I.1}$.111–112, 251, 287, 318, 327, 333, 359, 403, 489–493; $10^{I.2}$.38, 65, 79–81, 102, 122, 130, 143, 185; 10^{II}.155, 258; 11.451; 12.36, 63–65, 271, 430, 644, 658, 669–670, 679; 13.40; 14, 47; 15.183, 687, 754; 17^{II}.120.

41. WA 13.53; 14.50; 6.439–440; *Lyndal Roper*, The Holy Household: Women and Morals in Reformation Augsburg, Oxford 1989, 7–55; WA: 6.452. Für Luthers Ansichten über

Stiftsdamen in der liturgischen Ordnung von 1523–25 noch mit dem in Gernrode praktizierten Totengedenken, das, wie zu zeigen sein wird, um 1521 erneuert worden und essentiell für die Stiftsidentität war, sind diese früheren Forderungen Luthers vereinbar. Diese Missachtung wesentlicher Bestandteile der lutherischen Kirchenkritik verbieten es, die Ereignisse bis 1525 als die Einführung der Lehre Luthers zu klassifizieren. Die Gernröder Ordnung als lutherische Kirchen- oder Gottesdienstordnung zu bezeichnen, greift der späteren Reformation des Stifts voraus.

SPÄTMITTELALTERLICHE REFORMEN DES STIFTS GERNRODE

Betrachtet man Elisabeths Amtszeit als Gernröder Äbtissin in seiner Gesamtheit, so hat sie zusätzlich zu den liturgischen Neuerungen Reformen insbesondere auf drei Gebieten vorangebracht: Miteinander verwoben waren die Schließung des zusehends verfallenden Tochterstifts in Frose und die Verbesserung der desolaten wirtschaftlichen Lage des Stifts, die eine drohende Mediatisierung verhindern sollten. Dank dieser konnte seine unabhängige Existenz gesichert und schließlich das geistliche Leben zu neuer Blüte gebracht werden. Hierzu wurde seine ursprüngliche Memorialfunktion neu formuliert und inszeniert nicht zuletzt, um die Eigenständigkeit des reichsunmittelbaren Stifts aus seiner historischen Bedeutung für das *sacrum imperium* abzuleiten.

Aufgabe des Tochterstifts in Frose. Nach ihrem Amtsantritt 1504 bestand eine der dringlichsten Aufgaben Elisabeths darin, der Verwahrlosung des Froser Tochterstifts, das seit dem 10. Jahrhundert dem Stift in Gernrode unterstellt war, entgegenzuwirken. Bereits 1499 forderten die Anhalter Fürsten Waldemar VI. (1450–1508), Georg III., Ernst (1454–1516) und Rudolf IV. (um 1466–1510) ihre Untertanen dazu auf, dessen Wiederaufbau zu unterstützen.[42] Dass diese Instandsetzung 1519 nicht in einem befriedigenden Maße fortgeschritten war, bezeugt die Beschreibung Heinrich Basses in seinem *Panegiricos Genealogiarum Illustrium Principum dominorum de Anholt*. Die Froser Stiftskirche, so schrieb er, sei „mehr als heruntergekommen und in seinem

---

die Ehe, siehe *Merry E. Wiesner-Hanks*, „Lustful Luther': Male Libido in the Writings of the Reformer", in: *Scott H. Hendrix, Susan C. Karant-Nunn* (Hg.), Masculinity in the Reformation Era, Kirksville 2009, 190–212, hier 209; *Strohl*, „Christian Living" (wie Anm. 38), 372–373.

42. LASA Z 2, Nr. 1537.

Mauerwerk teilweise verfallen".[43] Fünf Jahre zuvor, am 9. März 1514, hatte Elisabeth die Übersiedlung der Froser Stiftsdamen nach Gernrode beurkundete, da diese „darjnne verlickeyth vnde vast vele beschweru[n]nge dulden musten dardurch andere Junffern darhene nicht beko[m]men mochten."[44] Die unmittelbaren Gefahren („verlickeyth") und Einschränkungen („beschweru[n]nge"), die der Zustand des Stifts für die Damen bedeuteten, hatten zudem dazu geführt, dass die Anzahl der Stiftsdamen wegen fehlender Beitritte auf drei zurückgegangen war.[45] Den Gernröder Kanonissen in Rechten und Pflichten gleich wurden die Froser Dekanin Elisabeth Guthmans sowie die Stiftsdamen Magdalena von Brachstedt († 1534) und eine aus dem Geschlecht der Kamburg, über die sonst keinerlei Quellen existieren, 1514 ins Mutterstift aufgenommen.[46] Die Identifizierung der Froser Stiftsdamen mittels ihrer ehemaligen Affiliation sowohl in Popperodts *Annales* als auch in einer Urkunde vom 1. März 1515, in der Magdalena von Brachstedt als „vnnßers Stiffts zu Froßenn Korjunferr" bezeichnet wurde, suggeriert, dass diese Übersiedlung zunächst nur temporär war.[47] Erst die Belehnung des Amtsmannes Hans Limerstadt mit dem Klosterhof, durch die das Stift 1530 seine wirtschaftliche Existenzgrundlage verlor, besiegelte das Schicksal des Froser Stifts[48]; es wurde schließlich 1531 formal aufgelöst.[49] Um das Wohl der Stiftsdamen bemüht, hatte Elisabeth von Weida mit der faktischen Schließung des Tochterstifts in Frose eine drastische strukturelle Reform eingeleitet, die wiederum das Gernröder Mutterstift in seiner Existenz stärkte.[50]

---

43. *Heinrich Basse*, Panegiricos Genealogiarum Illustrium Principum dominorum de Anholt, Leipzig 1519, VD16 B 732, Sig. [Cv^r]: „Inuenit itaq[ue] ecclesiam illam plusq[uam] satis desolata[m] et dissoluta[m] muris parit[er]."
44. LASA Z 3, Nr. 58. Walter Elliger datiert die Schließung Froses auf ebendieses Jahr. *Walter Elliger*, Thomas Müntzer: Leben und Werk, Göttingen 1975, 40
45. LASA Z 3, Nr. 58. Siehe auch *Popperodt*, „Annales" (wie Anm. 1), 67.
46. LASA Z 3, Nr. 58. Für Fragestellungen zu den Lebensverhältnissen der Kanonissen mag interessant sein, dass „Darzu eyner yehigen alle zuko[m]mende Jare vff wynachten funffh golden s zurhulffe yrer kleidungk geben vnde reihen wollen." (LASA Z 3, Nr. 58) Zusätzlich zu der Zusicherung, die Stiftsdamen adäquat zu versorgen und unterzubringen, erhielten sie finanzielle Zuwendungen. In diesem Kontext wären ebenso das Testament von Magdalena von Brachstedt, das im Pfarramt Gernrode erhalten ist, relevant.
47. LASA Z 3, Nr. 62; *Popperodt*, „Annales" (wie Anm. 1), 81.
48. *Popperodt*, „Annales" (wie Anm. 1), 67.
49. LASA Z 3, Nr. 114; *Popperodt*, „Annales" (wie Anm. 1), 81. Von den ehemaligen Lehnsherrinnen zeugt heute noch ein von Äbtissin Anna von Kittlitz (1488–1558) 1555 installiertes Wappen an einem Gebäude des Klosterhofes. *Schubart*, „Inschriften" (wie Anm. 17), 37.
50. Diese Beobachtungen zur Auflösung des Froser Stifts erlauben Rückschlüsse auf die dortige Anstellung des späteren Reformators Thomas Müntzer (ca. 1489–1525), die sich

Finanzielle Konsolidierung. Wenngleich die wirtschaftlichen Rahmenbedingungen und Veränderung im Stift nicht unmittelbar Ausdruck einer religiösen Reformaktivität waren, führen sie doch diverse Handlungsebenen zusammen und stellen die intendierten Neuerungen geistlicher und profaner Natur heraus.[51] So spielten nicht religiöse Beweggründe bei der Schließung des Froser Stifts

---

nach wie vor weitreichend unserem Wissen entzieht. Sein Aufenthalt ist durch einen Brief von Klaus Winkeler vom 25. Juli 1515 und einen weiteren des Aschersleber Bürgers Matthäus Volmar vom 28. August 1516 belegt. *Manfred Kobuch*, „Thomas Müntzer in Aschersleben und Frose", in: Zeitschrift für Geschichtswissenschaft 38.4 (1990), 312–334, hier 318; *Ulrich Bubenheimer*, Thomas Müntzer: Herkunft und Bildung, Leiden, New York, Kopenhagen, Köln 1989, 243–247; *Thomas Müntzer*, Schriften und Briefe: Kritische Gesamtausgabe, *Günther Franz, Paul Kirn* (Hg.), Gütersloh 1968, 347, 349. Während Müntzer in ersterem als *prefecti* bezeichnet wird, findet sich in einem dritten undatierten Brief von Ludolf Wittehovet die Amtsbezeichnung *prepositus*. *Kobuch*, „Müntzer" (wie oben), 318–319; *Bubenheimer*, Müntzer (wie oben), 241–46; *Müntzer*, Schriften (wie oben), 349–350. Laut Ulrich Bubenheimer ist letzterer Titel aus rechtsgeschichtlicher Perspektive mehr als fragwürdig, da die einem Stiftspropst traditionell anvertraute Erledigung der Rechtsgeschäfte in Frose von Kanonissen bzw. in Fällen, die einen männlichen Vertreter erforderten, von dem Präfekten (*praefectus*) verrichtet wurde. *Bubenheimer*, Müntzer (wie oben), 90–91. Für die Zeit, zu der Müntzer das Amt des Propstes innehatte, kann allerdings, wie oben ausgeführt, davon ausgegangen werden, dass keine Stiftsdamen in Frose residierten. Da mit dem Abzug der Dekanin, die ihren Titel zumindest nominell behielt, die Leitung des Stifts vor Ort vakant war, kann das Amt des Propstes nur dahin gehend verstanden werden, dass Müntzer die Verantwortung für das wohl auch von Kanonikern verlassene Stift möglicherweise samt seinen liturgischen Verpflichtungen übernommen hatte. *Eike Wolgast*, Thomas Müntzer. Ein Verstörer der Ungläubigen, Göttingen 1981, 11. Der allein für Müntzer belegte Titel des Propstes (*praepositus*) ist also nicht Beleg dafür, dass Mitte der 1510er Jahren noch Stiftsdamen in Frose residierten, sondern ist vielmehr Ausdruck des Gegenteils und des daraus resultierenden rechtlichen Vakuums in Frose. Außerdem könnte er anzeigen, wann die Überführung der Froser Besitztümer und Einkommen nach Gernrode erfolgte. Da nämlich die Anstellungen Müntzers sowohl in rechtlichen als auch in liturgischen Angelegenheiten von dem Verbleib der Einkommen und der mit Stiftungen und dergleichen priesterlichen Pflichten abhingen und die Abschaffung des Froser Propsttitels nur mit der Abwanderung des Einkommens erklärt werden, würde die von Popperodt erwähnte Übertragung grob auf das Jahr 1516 fallen; zudem legt diese These nah, dass zu der Zeit Müntzers tatsächlich keine Kanoniker in Frose anwesend waren. Ob Elisabeth Müntzer wegen seiner Kirchenkritik einstellte, ist eine interessante Überlegung, die allerdings aufgrund mangelnder Quellen rein spekulativ ist und hier nicht weiter Beachtung finden soll. *Peter Matheson* (Hg.), The Collected Works of Thomas Müntzer, Edinburgh 1988, 6–7. Ebenso wenig nachgewiesen ist die häufig bemühte Vermutung, dass die beiden sich in Quedlinburg kennengelernt haben. *Siegfried Bräuer, Günter Vogler*, Thomas Müntzer: Neu Ordnung machen in der Welt: Eine Biographie, Gütersloh 2016, 55.

51. Für derartige Untersuchungen, siehe *Wolfgang Brandis*, „Quellen zur Reformationsgeschichte der Lüneburger Frauenklöster", in: *Falk Eisermann, Eva Schlotheuber, Volker Honemann* (Hg.), Studien und Texte zur literarischen und materiellen Kultur der Frauenklöster im späten Mittelalter, Leiden, Boston 2004, 357–398; *Gudrun Gleba, Ilse Eberhardt*, Summa

eine Rolle, sondern, gleichwohl diese nicht explizit angeführt wurden, wirtschaftliche; eine Instandsetzung schien wohl nicht finanzierbar. Bezeichnend für die desaströse Lage des im Mittelalter reich ausgestatteten Stifts Gernrode ist, dass die 1504 neugewählte Äbtissin Margarethe von Warberg wegen dessen existenzieller wirtschaftlicher Not das Amt der Äbtissin nicht antrat, sondern Gernrode verließ; an ihrer statt wurde Elisabeth von Weida aus dem unweit gelegenen Stift St. Servatius in Quedlinburg als neue Äbtissin in Gernrode installiert.[52] In der Tat verfügte das Stift Gernrode nur noch über einen Bruchteil seiner einstigen Besitzungen. Rudolf Bahn beziffert sie auf Grundlage einer Akte von 1509 auf insgesamt 20 Dörfer, während laut Reinhold Specht 1544 siebeneinhalb Flecken und Dörfern, drei Vorwerken und fünf wüste Marken zu dem Stift gehörten.[53] Laut Franke wurden weder die wüsten Marken noch die Vorwerke kostendeckend betrieben, sodass von dem jährlichen Einkommen nur ein geringer Teil zur freien Verfügung blieb.[54]

Von entscheidender Bedeutung in der Konsolidierung der Stiftsfinanzen war die Beendigung eines Rechtsstreits mit dem Bistum Halberstadt. Der Konflikt war an einem See entbrannt, den ein Mönch aus dem Bistum 1446 angestaut hatte.[55] Da das geflutete Gebiet sich auf Teile der Froser Flur erstreckte,

---

Summarum: Spätmittelalterliche Wirtschaftsnachrichten und Rechnungsbücher des Osnabrücker Klosters Gertrudenberg: Transkription und Kommentar, Münster 2011.

52. LASA Z 6, Nr. 418 (1). Zusammen mit Elisabeth sollen auch ihre Schwester Brigitta und die Dienerinnen Katharina von Breitenbach und Margarete von Bünau nach Gernrode übergesiedelt sein. *Popperodt*, „Annales" (wie Anm. 1), 65. Brigittas Anwesenheit in Gernrode ist in einer Urkunde vom 22. März 1529 belegt. LASA Z 3, Nr. 110. Über das Leben Elisabeths im Stift Quedlinburg oder ihre Kindheit ist wenig bekannt. Laut Popperodt müsste sie 1479/80 geboren worden sein. *Popperodt*, „Annales" (wie Anm. 1), 68. Franke führt außerdem einen Brief an, gemäß dem Elisabeth von Weida zusammen mit Friedrich III. und Ernst von Sachsen (1464–1513) erzogen wurde. *Franke*, „Elisabeth" (wie Anm. 4), 315.

53. *Bahn*, Geros Gründung (wie Anm. 5), 51. Reinhold Specht edierte dieses Dokument 1938. Obschon fehlende archivalische Verweise eine Identifizierung erschweren, scheint es sich bei diesem Schriftstück um die Signatur LASA Z 10, Nr. 36 zu handeln. *Reinhold Specht*, Die anhaltischen Land- und Amtsregister des 16. Jahrhunderts, 3 Bde., Magdeburg 1935–1940, Bd. 2, 180–187.

54. *Franke*, „Elisabeth" (wie Anm. 4), 317. Das jährliche Einkommen betrug 270 Gulden an Zinsen, 12 1/2 Wispel Weizen, 3 1/2 Wispel Roggen, 1 1/2 Wispel Gerste und 1 1/2 Wispel Hafer; die Pröpstin und das Kapitel nahmen ungefähr 314 Gulden, 31 Wispel Weizen, 21 Wispel Gerste, 6 Wispel Hafer ein. LASA Z 10, Nr. 36. Für einen detaillierte Betrachtung des wirtschaftlichen Zustands des Stifts, siehe LASA Z 9.

55. Laut Jakob Friedrich Reimmann, und hierin folgte ihm Beckmann, irrte sich Popperodt in der Behauptung, dass der See 1486 angelegt worden sei. Beckmann vermutete, dass sich Popperodt sich dabei auf dessen Fertigstellung bezog. *Jakob Friedrich Reimmann*, IDEA HISTORIÆ ASCANIENSIS CIVILIS, ECCLESIASTICÆ, NATURALIS, LITERARIÆ In qua ea, quæ ad quadruplex hoc punctum faciunt, ὡς ὸν Τύπῳ quidem tantum; Sed tamen

kam es 1486 zu einem Prozess um die Rechtmäßigkeit und Nutzung des Sees.[56] Aufgrund seiner wachsenden Kosten drohte der Rechtsstreit bald das Stift finanziell zu ruinieren. Der nahgelegenen und später mediatisierten Grafschaft Mansfeld ähnlich drohte Gernrode in die wirtschaftliche Abhängigkeit vom Bistum Halberstadt zu rutschen.[57] Erst durch die Vermittlung des päpstlichen Kommissars Levin von Veltheim konnte am 10. Dezember 1510 ein Vergleich erreicht werden: Zugunsten des Bistums Halberstadt und der Stadt Aschersleben verzichtete Elisabeth auf alle Rechte an dem See. Der damalige Erzbischof von Magdeburg und Administrator von Halberstadt verpflichtete sich wiederum zu einer einmaligen Zahlung von 3.000 Gulden und einer jährlichen Lieferung von zwei Zentnern Hechte oder dem monetären Gegenwert von acht Gulden.[58] Mit dieser Einigung hatte Elisabeth von Weida eine Überschuldung vorerst abwenden können.

Zur Erhöhung ihrer Einnahmen war Elisabeth darauf bedacht, ihre landesherrlichen Rechte konsequent einzufordern, sei es, dass sie dazu Reichsinstitutionen oder, wie im Falle des unrechtmäßig angestauten Sees, den Papst bemühte.[59] Franke berichtet beispielsweise, dass Elisabeth 1507 Einspruch dagegen erhob, dass Waldemar VI. von Anhalt-Köthen einen Weinberg verkaufte, obwohl der verstorbene Besitzer mit diesem vom Stift Gernrode belehnt worden war.[60] Besonders zu betonen sei hier der lang anhaltende Konflikt mit dem Magdeburger Erzbischof und Halberstädter Administrator, Kardinal

---

in Typo ejusmodi delineata sunt, uti res omnes Ascaniensium ex veris merisque M[anu]sc[ript]is & monumentis ἀνεκδότοις excerptæ & nova prorsus, atque adhuc non usitata methodo digestæ & ita ad umbratæ sunt, ut universa hujus antiquissimæ Civitatis ἐγκυκλοπαιδεία Historica uno quasi obtutu à φιλισοροῦσι conspici & sic facillima ratione hæc specialissima particula cum Historia universali connecti & copulari queat. Accessit in fine INDEX CHRONOLOGICUS Omnium Monasteriorum, Collegiorum Fraternitatum & Congregationum quæ vel ab Halberstadensibus institutæ sunt vel ad diœcesin Halberstadensem spectaverunt, Quedlinburg 1708, VD18 15069214, 21; *Beckmann*, Historie (wie Anm. 2), Bd. 2, 109; *Popperodt*, „Annales" (wie Anm. 1), 66–67.

56. *Franke*, „Elisabeth" (wie Anm. 4), 320.
57. Uwe *Schirmer*, „Die Lehnsbeziehungen der Grafen von Mansfeld (1215–1539/40)", in: *Kohnle, Bräuer*, Grafen (wie Anm. 10), 13–44, hier 36–38.
58. LASA U 5, IX Nr. 226. Für weitere Teile des Vertragswerks, siehe LASA Z 3, Nr. 44. Beckmann berichtet zudem noch von einem Vergleich zwischen Elisabeth und den betroffenen Dörfern Frose und Nachterstedt. *Beckmann*, Historie (wie Anm. 2), Bd. 1, 110. Noch 1506 war eine Einigung daran gescheitert, dass örtliche Fischer diese missachteten. *Franke*, „Elisabeth" (wie Anm. 4), 321; LASA Z 6, Nr. 912.
59. Laut Franke forderte Elisabeth in ähnlicher Manier die standesgemäße Ansprache ein, wie aus einem Brief an den Merseburger Bischof Adolf II. von Anhalt-Zerbst (1458–1526) hervorgeht. *Franke*, „Elisabeth" (wie Anm. 4), 322–323.
60. *Franke*, „Elisabeth" (wie Anm. 4), 318.

Albrecht von Brandenburg (1490–1545), um dessen fortwährende Missachtung von Elisabeths Hoheitsrechten und wirtschaftliche Ausnutzung des Stifts Gernrode. Unstimmigkeiten begannen, als Albrecht Stiftsgut aus Gernrode entwenden ließ und dies trotz päpstlicher Intervention nicht unterließ.[61] Außerdem sah der Verweser Albrechts, Botho zu Stolberg (1467–1538), der auch als Schutzherr vom benachbarten Quedlinburg seine dortigen Rechte fundamental erweitert hatte, nicht davon ab, Steuern in den Gernröder Dörfern Alsleben, Alickendorf, Frose und Nachterstedt zu erheben, obwohl Elisabeth ihm dies untersagt und eine schriftliche Bestätigung des Verbots 1516 eingefordert hatte.[62] Der Konflikt eskalierte 1527, als Elisabeth erreichte, dass Kaiser Karl V. (1500–1558) Albrecht von Brandenburg wegen der fortwährenden Steuererhebung zu einer Zahlung von 20 Goldmark verordnete.[63] Auch diese Intervention verfehlte jedoch ihr Ziel, da Albrecht von Brandenburg auch in den drei Folgejahren an der Besteuerung festhielt und zusätzlich eine Wiese auf dem Stiftsgebiet verpfändete.[64] Da weder ein kaiserliches Mandat vom 4. November 1531 noch eine Ermahnung zu dessen Einhaltung Abhilfe bereiteten, entsandte Elisabeth schließlich ihren Anwalt Friedrich Reifstock im selben Jahr zum Reichskammergericht.[65]

Diese Konflikte verdeutlichen, in welchem Maße die wirtschaftliche Eigenständigkeit des Stifts Gernrode von Schlichtungsversuchen zunächst vonseiten des Papstes und später ausschließlich des Kaisers und anderer wichtiger Reichsinstitutionen abhing. Zwecks seiner Sanierung scheute Elisabeth von Weida nicht davor, diese anzurufen, um ihre Rechte gegen so mächtige Kontrahenten wie Kardinal Albrecht von Brandenburg durchzusetzen. Ihre Position als Reichsprälatin war dabei von essentieller Wichtigkeit für die unabhängige Existenz des Stifts Gernrode. Der Eintrag in der Reichsmatrikel 1521, das Reichsmandat 1529 und die damit verbundenen Zusagen im Kampf gegen das Osmanische Reich sind gerade wegen der finanziellen Zumutung angesichts der strapazierten Stiftsfinanzen als eine Demonstration und Manifestierung der

---

61. Elisabeths Gesuch nachkommend, rief dieser im März 1514 die benachbarte Geistlichkeit zur Mithilfe in dieser Sache auf. Weil ebendiese jener Veräußerungen schuldig waren, stellte sich dieses Vorgehen aber als wenig effektiv heraus. *Franke*, „Elisabeth" (wie Anm. 4), 319.
62. PAG; *Kasper*, Quedlinburg (wie Anm. 9), 103.
63. LASA A 13, Nr. 4 (1).
64. LASA A 13, Nr. 4 (2), Fol. 2^r; A 13, Nr. 4 (5), Fol. 6^v; Z 3, Nr. 100.
65. Das Mandat ist in einer Kopie vom 13. Dezember 1531 erhalten. LASA A 13, Nr. 4 (7), Fol. 10^r; (6); (4). Über den Stillstand in den Verhandlungen schrieb Georg III. von Anhalt-Plötzkau am 14. Januar 1532 an Wolfgang von Anhalt-Köthen. LASA A 13, Nr. 4 (8); (9).

Reichsunmittelbarkeit des Stifts und der traditionellen Macht der Reichstifte im Reichskirchenwesen, das trotz konfessioneller Differenzen integraler Bestandteil in der konstitutionellen Balance blieb, zu verstehen.[66] Im Bewusstsein dieses traditionellen Konstrukts stellte sich Elisabeth von Weida einer schleichenden Mediatisierung des Stifts Gernrode durch wirtschaftliche und legale Unterminierung vehement entgegen.

Florieren des geistlichen Lebens. Von dem Erfolg dieser finanziellen Konsolidierung zeugt eine rege Bautätigkeit in der Stiftskirche, die Ausdruck der geistlichen Erneuerung des Stifts ist. 1519 wurde ein repräsentatives Grabmal des Stifters, Markgraf Gero († 965), vor dem zentralen Kreuzaltar in der Vierung installiert und 1521 folgte ein neuer Hochaltar. In beiden wurde ein neues Selbstverständnis des Stiftes artikuliert.[67] Wesentlich für dieses war das Totengedenken des Stifters Geros, aus dem Elisabeth eine gewisse geistliche Bedeutung und politisch-repräsentative Autorität für das Stifts ableitete.

Nicht zuletzt weil der benannte Hochaltar im Bildersturm von 1616 zerstört wurde, ist wenig über ihn, seine Entstehung und Rezeption bekannt.[68] Schubart vermerkt lediglich, dass Pröpstin Ursula von Kittlitz 1519 einen neuen Hochaltar in Auftrag gab und ein „wertvoller Bilderaltar" nach zweijähriger Schaffenszeit 1521 aufgestellt wurde.[69] Als Fokus des liturgischen Geschehens in Gernrode ist davon auszugehen, dass der alte Cyriakusaltar dem neuen wich und die Armreliquie des Heiligen, des Stiftspatrons, hier verwahrt wurde.[70]

Die neue Tumba für Markgraf Gero wurde, wie der Inschrift auf ihrer nördlichen Stirnseite zu entnehmen ist, 1519 errichtet. Dieser ist auf der Deckplatte mit Schwert, Fahnenstange und einer für das 16. Jahrhundert typischen Rüstung zu sehen. Gestiftet wurde das Grabmal ebenfalls von Ursula von Kittlitz,

---

66. Deutsche Reichstagsakten: Jüngere Reihe: Deutsche Reichstagsakten unter Karl V., Gotha 1893–, Bd. 2, 433; *Wiesner*, „Ideology" (wie Anm. 8), 57.

67. Bei der Restaurierung der Stiftskirche im 19. Jahrhundert durch Ferdinand von Quast ließ dieser das Grab auf seinen heutigen Standort umsetzen. *Klaus Voigtländer*, Die Stiftskirche zu Gernrode und ihre Restaurierung 1858–1872, Berlin 1980, 108. Für den ursprünglichen Ort des Grabmals vor dem Kreuzaltar in der Vierung, siehe *Beckmann*, Historie (wie Anm. 2), Bd. 1, Sig. [Y 4ᵛ].

68. *Voigtländer*, Stiftskirche (wie Anm. 67), 112, 138–139, 141; *Hermann Suhle*, „Ältere Nachrichten des Kirchenbuches der Marienkirche zu Bernburg", in: Mitteilungen des Vereins für Anhaltische Geschichte und Altertumskunde 6 (1893), 258–277, hier 274.

69. *Friedrich Winfrid Schubart*, „Versuch einer Gegenreformation im Stift Gernrode", in: Zerbster Jahrbuch 4 (1908), 40–51, hier 44.

70. *Voigtländer*, Stiftskirche (wie Anm. 67), 138–139. Für die Reliquien in Gernrode, siehe *Reinhold Specht*, „Reliquien in Anhalt", in: Zeitschrift des Vereins für Kirchengeschichte der Provinz Sachsen und des Freistaates Anhalt 26.1/2 (1929), 52–66, hier 57–58.

deren Wappen sich zwischen den Relieffiguren der Apostel Philipp und Thomas an der Ostseite des Hochgrabs befindet.[71] Die hochwertige Steinmetzarbeit des modischen Haupthaars und der Äderung der Hände, die der Nürnberger Schule zuzuschreiben sind, reflektiert die wiedergewonnene Stärke des Stifts, die eine solche Anschaffung finanziell ermöglichte.[72] Mit dieser Erneuerung des Totengedenkens untermauerte das Stift primär seine Bedeutung für das Reich als dem liturgischen Zentrum der memoria Geros, der sich um die östliche Expansion und Stabilisierung des Reichs im 10. Jahrhundert verdient gemacht hatte. Die Heiligenreliefs am Gesims des Grabmals, je fünf an den Längs- und zwei an den Schmalseiten, verknüpfen diese mit der damaligen Renaissance des Stifts. So zeigt die zweite Relieffigur an der Südseite die heilige Elisabeth, die mittels eines Wappenschilds der von Weida zu ihrer Rechten als Äbtissin Elisabeth identifiziert werden kann.[73] Ihr Pendant auf der anderen Seite der zentralen Marienfigur bildet die heilige Hedwig, eine Referenz auf die erste Äbtissin Hathui (um 939–1014). Mit dieser Gegenüberstellung wird Elisabeth als der bedeutenden Äbtissin Hathui ebenbürtig dargestellt und somit als diejenige, die es vermocht hat, das in seiner Existenz bedrohte Stift zu erhalten und es in seiner liturgischen Bedeutung als Stätte des Totengedenkens eines herausragenden Reichsfürsten zu stärken.

Dieser in dem Grabmal formulierte Geltungsanspruch spiegelt sich auch in einem undatierten Tafelbild Geros wider, um dessen Entstehung, Bedeutung und Funktion sich eine Debatte entzweit hat. So etablierte von Heinemann die Abhängigkeit des Bildnisses von einer ursprünglichen Grabplatte, die dem neuen von 1519 hatte weichen müssen.[74] Da Begräbnisplatten allerdings nicht für die Zeit vor dem 11. Jahrhundert belegt sind, zweifelte Hans Jantzen diese These an und argumentierte stattdessen für eine Anlehnung des Bildes an das Gero-Siegel, dessen Darstellung samt der Sockelplatte, des Hundes, Schwertes

---

71. *Schulze*, Gernrode (wie Anm. 6), 126–127; *Voigtländer*, Stiftskirche (wie Anm. 67), 107. Das Wappen, das der zu den Füßen Geros ruhende Löwe in seinem Maul hält, konnte bislang nicht identifiziert werden. Es zeigt zwei gegen den Rücken aufgerichtete und gekrönte Löwen mit verschlungenen Schweifen.

72. Die Werkstatt der Tumba ist unbekannt, gleichwohl sie in Verbindung mit der Tilman Riemenschneiders (um 1460–1531) gebracht worden ist. *Schulze*, Stift Gernrode (wie Anm. 6), 127.

73. Aufgrund dieser Darstellung kann Elisabeth von Weida als zweite Stifterin gelten. *Schulze*, Gernrode (wie Anm. 6), 126; *Voigtländer*, Stiftskirche (wie Anm. 67), 107.

74. *Otto von Heinemann*, Geschichte der Abtei und Beschreibung der Stiftskirche zu Gernrode, Quedlinburg 1877, 54. Dieser Ansicht folgten auch *August Fink*, Die figürliche Grabplastik in Sachsen von den Anfängen bis zur zweiten Hälfte des 13. Jahrhunderts, Diss. Berlin, Wolfenbüttel 1915, 5–6; *Ludwig Grote*, Die Stiftskirche in Gernrode, Burg 1932, 28.

und Schildes auf die sächsische Grabplattentradition des 13. Jahrhunderts verweist.[75] Diesem folgt Klaus Voigtländer, der bezüglich der Entstehung vermutet, dass das Tafelbild im Zusammenhang mit der Galerie der Gernröder Äbtissinnen, die Elisabeths Vorgängerin, Scholastica von Anhalt-Zerbst (1451–1504), anfertigen ließ, entstanden sei.[76] Dieser These widerspricht jedoch die Datierung des Bildes mittels der frühhumanistischen Majuskel, in der die Bildüberschrift geschrieben worden ist; sie legt eine Entstehung im Zeitraum zwischen 1505 und 1515, also unter der Ägide Elisabeths, nahe.[77] Dies würde zudem erklären, weshalb das Tafelbild das brandenburgische Wappen mit dem roten Adler und nicht den im Grabmal verwendeten Wappenschild zeigt. Mit diesem verbildlicht das Tafelbild die ruhmvollen Verdienste seines Stifters Geros bei der Etablierung Brandenburgs als Teil des Reiches. Dieser Bezug auf die historische Bedeutung Geros der Mark formuliert einen gewissen Autoritätsanspruch über das damals dort herrschende Haus der Hohenzollern, das erst 1415 in die Ränge der vornehmsten Herrschaftshäuser des Reiches aufgestiegen war. Diese mediale Demonstration des traditionellen Mächtegewichts der beiden Reichsfürsten richtete sich an Kardinal Albrecht von Brandenburg, der wiederholt Elisabeths Hoheitsrechte verletzt hatte. Die visuelle Artikulation der historischen Abhängigkeit Brandenburgs von Gernrode und der daraus resultierenden Ebenbürtigkeit des Stifts suggeriert eine Entstehung des Tafelbildes, nachdem Albrecht von Brandenburg das Bistums Halberstadt 1513 übernommen hatte; dies entspräche zudem der von der frühhumanistischen Majuskel nahegelegten Entstehungszeit.[78] Viel stärker noch als das Grabmal, dessen Erneuerung notwendig gewesen sein mag, zeigt das Tafelbild eine humanistische Rückbesinnung und Verankerung Gernrodes in seiner Geschichte als Stiftung des bedeutsamen Markgrafen Geros, aus der wiederum seine Me-

---

75. *Hans Jantzen*, Ottonische Kunst, München 1947, 131–132. Für einen ähnlichen Standpunkt siehe *Hubert Schrade*, „Zur Frühgeschichte der mittelalterlichen Monumentalplastik", in: *Westfalen* 37 (1957), 44–45; *Günter W. Vorbrodt*, „Die Stiftskirche in Gernrode. Ein kunstgeschichtlicher Beitrag", in: *Schulze*, Gernrode (wie Anm. 6), 91–129, hier 108, 123–124.

76. *Voigtländer*, Stiftskirche (wie Anm. 67), 105–6; *Franz Kindscher*, „Scholastica, Äbtissin von Gernrode 1469 bis 31. August 1504", in: Mitteilungen des Vereins für Anhaltische Geschichte und Altertumskunde 6 (1893), 186–194, hier 187. Von der Ahnengalerie ist lediglich eine Kopie der Darstellung Scholasticas erhalten. *Franz Kugler, Carl Ferdinand Ranke*, Beschreibung und Geschichte der Schloßkirche zu Quedlinburg und der vorhandenen Alterthümer, Berlin 1838, 105.

77. *Vorbrodt*, Stiftskirche (wie in Anm. 75), 123.

78. *Voigtländer*, Stiftskirche (wie Anm. 67), 107; *Vorbrodt*, Stiftskirche (wie Anm. 75), 123.

morialtradition und der aus ihr erwachsene zeitgenössische Bedeutung im politischen Gefüge des *sacrum imperium* abgeleitet wird.

Vor diesem Hintergrund erscheint die Gernröder Ordnung, wie sie Elisabeth und Molitor zwischen 1523 und 1525 erarbeitet haben, in neuem Licht. Die Integration von Luthers Reformideen in die Stiftsliturgie steht am Ende eines langwierigen Reformprozesses, der einerseits entgegen dem Mediatisierungsdruck insbesondere durch den Magdeburger Erzbischof und Halberstädter Administrator das wirtschaftliche und politische Überleben des Stifts sichern sollte. Andererseits intendierte Elisabeth mit den Reformen das religiöse Leben des Stifts zu stärken. Tatsächlich griff sie dabei die von Äbtissin Scholastica geäußerte Kirchenkritik auf. So entspricht die Fokussierung der Liturgie auf die Heilige Schrift zweifelsohne dem lutherischen Prinzip *sola scriptura* und liegt zugleich in der Rückbesinnung auf die ursprüngliche Kirche im apostolischen Zeitalter gemäß humanistischer Ideale begründet. Dass diese Einzug in Gernrode gehalten hatten, suggeriert sowohl die Erneuerung der Memorialfunktion des Stifts in der Errichtung des Gero-Grabmals als auch die Bestände der einstigen Stiftsbibliothek, unter denen sich zahlreiche, bei Humanisten populäre Schriften antiker und patristischer Autoren, wie Dionysius von Halicarnassos, Johannes Chrysostomos und Isidor von Sevilla, finden lassen.[79] Noch vor der Konsolidierung der Reformation als konfessioneller Bewegung berichtete Basse 1519 in seinen *Panegiricos*, dem ersten Werk der anhaltinische Hofgeschichtsschreibung des Hauses Anhalt, aus dem auch Scholastica stammte, dass sie sowohl den Verfall der Sitten als auch die Kirche mit ihrer Vielzahl an Bräuchen, die jeglicher schriftlicher Grundlage entbehren, bemängelt hatte.[80] Sie missbilligte, dass „es desgleichen viele in den Gebräuchen der Kirche gab, von denen sie sagte, dass sie Eid schwören, obwohl sie man dennoch nirgends in der heiligen Schrift, in den Lehren der Kirchenväter oder den Kanonikern geschrieben findet."[81] Während über die darauffolgende Unterredung

---

79. *W. Gröpler*, „Verzeichnis derjenigen Bücher, welche aus der Gernroder Stiftsbibliothek in die frühere Bernburger Landesbibliothek und aus letzterer in die gegenwärtige Anhaltische Behördenbibliothek zu Dessau übergangen sind", in: Mitteilungen des Vereins für Anhaltische Geschichte und Altertumskunde 3 (1883), 772–776, hier 772.

80. *Basse*, Panegiricos (wie Anm. 43), Sig. D ij^r; *Wäschke*, „Geschichte" (wie Anm. 20), 42. Zur Bedeutung von Basses Werk für die anhaltische Erinnerungskultur, siehe *Angela Damisch*, „Repräsentation des Hauses und der Familie", in: *Eva Labouvie* (Hg.), Adel in Sachsen-Anhalt. Höfische Kultur zwischen Repräsentation, Unternehmertum und Familie, Köln, Weimar, Wien 2007, 181–206, hier 186.

81. *Basse*, Panegiricos (wie Anm. 43), Sig. D ij^r: „Item essent plurima in ecclesie illius consuetudinibus q[ui]bus se etiam iuramento coactam submitti dixit que tamen nusq[uam] in scripturis sanctis/in doctrinis partum vel canonibus ecclesiasticis expressa inuenirentur."

mit ihrem Vettern Wilhelm von Anhalt, einem Franziskaner, nichts bekannt ist, lassen sich direkte Verbindungslinien zur liturgischen Ordnung von 1523–25 ziehen.[82] So dient das Fehlen einer biblischen Grundlage dort als Argument, Teile der Heiligenverehrung abzuschaffen und die Bibel in das Zentrum der Liturgie zu rücken.[83] Diese ideengeschichtlichen Kontinuitäten verbieten, die liturgischen Ordnung von 1523–25 und die zeitnahen Neubesetzungen der stiftseigenen Kirchen mit lutherischen Pfarrern einzig der Wittenberger Reformation zuzurechnen. Vielmehr hatte Elisabeth das Stift mittels innovativer und sogleich systemkonformer Neuerungen in seiner Form als ottonischer Memorialinstitution im Reich zu stabilisieren erhofft.[84]

REFORMATION UND MEDIATISIERUNGSDRUCK

Dieser eigenständige Reformweg, der auf institutioneller Kontinuität, historischer Tradition und liturgischer Innovation beruhte, war eng mit Elisabeths Kampf um die Autonomie und gegen eine Mediatisierung ihres Stifts verbunden. Diese komplexe Gemengelage vermögen zwei Konflikte zu illustrieren, die zwischen Elisabeth und den Anhalter Fürsten Johann IV. und Wolfgang über die Pfarre Waldau und die Schutzvogtei von Gernrode und Badeborn entbrannten. Nachdem Elisabeth 1525 den lutherischen Pfarrer Goth in Waldau eingesetzt und damit die Verbreitung der reformatorischen Lehre in ihrem Stiftsgebiet begonnen hatte, ließ Wolfgang am 28. Mai 1526 das dortige Kirchengut unrechtmäßig inventarisieren und auf das unweit gelegene Bernburger Schloss überführen.[85] Zeitgleich nahm Johann IV. Anstoß daran, dass der Pfarrer Goth nicht in seiner infolge von Vernachlässigung unbewohnbar gewordenen Pfarrei, sondern in Bernburg Quartier bezog; 1526 wurde er aus der Stadt

---

Zur humanistische Kirchenkritik, siehe hierzu auch *Wolf-Friedrich Schäufele*, „Die Kirchenkritik des Hoch- und Spätmittelalters und ihre Bedeutung", in: *Dingel, Kohnle, Rhein, Waschke*, Initia Reformationis (wie Anm. 7), 67–82, hier 77–79.

 82. Bei diesem mag es sich um den Vetter von Margarethe von Münsterberg (1473–1530), der zwischenzeitlich in dem Franziskanerkonvent in Halle lebte, handeln. Siehe *Gerrit Deutschländer*, „Briefe aus dem Franziskanerkloster zu Halle: Augustinus Alveldt an die Fürstin Margarethe von Münsterberg", in: *Deutschländer, Würth*, Lebenswelt (wie Anm. 9), 192–224, hier 196–198.

 83. LASA Z 6, Nr. 418 (2), Sig. 5ᵛ.

 84. *Schäufele*, „Kirchenkritik" (wie Anm. 81), 71.

 85. *Studium Hallense* (Hg.), Geschichte Anhalts in Daten, Halle 2014, 264; *Graf*, Pfarrerbuch (wie Anm. 19),150, 261.

vertrieben.[86] Der Gernröder Einspruch hiergegen am Reichskammergericht zeitigte erste Erfolge, als Karl V. am 21. Mai 1527 Johann IV. dazu ermahnte, die Rechte der Äbtissin, ihre Pfarrer zu benennen, nicht zu unterwandern. Nachdem Goth 1528 wiedereingesetzt worden war, wurde auch das Kirchengerät am 26. März 1529 wieder ausgehändigt.[87] Auch wenn theologische Differenzen diese Konflikte augenscheinlich provoziert haben, sind sie doch in erster Linie Beispiele für das fortwährende Ringen um die Hoheitsrechte des reichsunmittelbaren Stifts Gernrode. Anders als im Streit um die Entwendung kirchlichen Eigentums durch Kardinal Albrecht von Brandenburg, zu dessen Beilegung sie den Papst angerufen hatte, wandte sich Elisabeth nun an Reichsinstitutionen, um einer direkten Einflussnahme durch benachbarte Reichsfürsten entgegenzuwirken.

Tatsächlich stand der Konflikt um die Pfarre Waldau vor dem Hintergrund früherer Einmischungen von Landesfürsten in klösterliche Angelegenheiten. Nachdem beispielsweise Äbtissin Magdalene von Anhalt-Köthen-Zerbst († 1515) aufgrund wiederholter Konflikte mit ihrem Schutzvogt Herzog Georg von Sachsen (1471–1539) 1514 aus dem Stift Quedlinburg ausgeschieden war, beschleunigte der deutsche Bauernkrieg von 1524–25 noch die Säkularisation und Mediatisierung von Klöstern. Insbesondere Wolfgang von Anhalt-Köthen, der sich als einer der ersten Reichsfürsten Luther angeschlossen hatten, nutzte den Bauernkrieg, um das unweit von Gernrode gelegenen und in seiner Schutzvogtei stehende Benediktinerkloster Ballenstedt zu säkularisieren.[88] Wie einem bei Hans Peper transkribierten Revers zu entnehmen ist, verständigte er sich mit Abt Mathias Ribke am 9. Oktober 1525 auf eine wohl einvernehmliche Schließung und Übertragung des ehemaligen Klosters; tatsächlich hatten die mit der Lehre Luthers sympathisierenden Mönche es bereits am

---

86. *Studium Hallense*, Geschichte (wie Anm. 85), 264; *Graf*, Pfarrerbuch (wie Anm. 19),150, 261; *Franke*, „Elisabeth" (wie Anm. 4), 330. Dass dieses Vorgehen ohne die Zustimmung der Gernröder Äbtissin geschehen sein muss, geht aus einem Brief, den Reifstock Elisabeth am 12. Oktober 1527 schrieb, hervor. PAG. Es scheint, dass er hier, genau wie aus Briefen vom 13. Dezember 1527 und 1. Dezember 1531 hervorgeht, als ihr Anwalt am Reichskammergericht tätig war. LASA A 13, Nr. 4 (4); Z 6, Nr. 435 (5).

87. *Studium Hallense*, Geschichte (wie Anm. 85), 267; *Franke*, „Elisabeth" (wie Anm. 4), 330; *Suhle*, „Reformation" (wie Anm. 5), 492; *Graf*, Pfarrerbuch (wie Anm. 19), 150, 261.

88. Von einem regen theologischen Austausch zeugen beispielsweise Büchergeschenke des Ballenstedter Priors Basse an den Gernröder Peter Balistarius 1516 und die Ausführungen über Scholastica von Anhalt-Zerbsts Bedenken zum Stand der Kirche im *Panegiricos*. Supplementum, 1488, Anhaltische Landesbücherei Dessau BB 24680, Gesamtkatalog der Wiegendrucke M26238, Titelblatt; *Basse*, Panegiricos (wie Anm. 43), Sig. Cvj^v–v^v.

28. Mai 1525, noch vor der Plünderung durch Bauern, verlassen.[89] Auch der Aufstand in Gernrode am 5. Mai 1525 ist in diesem Kontext zu betrachten. Nachdem Elisabeth die Erhebung gewaltfrei kontrolliert hatte, erneuerte der am 21. Dezember desselben Jahres geleistete Eid das Treueverhältnis zwischen ihr und ihren Untertanen. Dies versetzte sie in die Lage, dass sie jedwede militärische Einmischung, die selbst im Falle ihres zur Hilfe eilenden Bruders Heinrich die Gefahr eines Eingriffs in die Unabhängigkeit des Stifts bedeutet hätte, ablehnen konnte.[90] Tatsächlich wirkt dessen Position prekär, da Wolfgang von Anhalt-Köthen selbst vor dem Status der Reichsunmittelbarkeit nicht zurückschreckte und die von Kaiser Otto II. (955–983) zum Reichskloster erhobene Benediktinerabtei Nienburg nach jahrzehntelangem Druck 1563 säkularisierte.[91] Nachdem das Stift Gernrode zu Beginn des 16. Jahrhunderts finanziell in seiner Existenz bedroht gewesen war, gestaltete sich die Annahme einiger Reformimpulse aus Wittenberg zu einem zusätzlichen Faktor, der wegen Luthers Ablehnung klösterlicher Gemeinschaften die Mediatisierung oder gar Säkularisierung des Stifts zu beschleunigen drohte.

Um zu verhindern, dass ihr Schutzvogt Wolfgang unter dem Deckmantel der Reformation das Stift mediatisierte, kündigte Elisabeth von Weida am 22. Februar 1528 die Schutzvogtei über Gernrode und Badeborn zum Martinstag desselben Jahres auf und bemühte sich konsequent um deren Rück-

---

89. *Wäschke*, „Geschichte" (wie Anm. 20), 227–228; *Hans Peper*, „Stift, Kloster und Schloß. Stift und Kloster bis zu seiner Zerstörung", in: *Bernhard Heese, Hans Peper* (Hg.), Ballenstedter Chronik: Eine Geschichte des Schlosses und der Stadt in Einzeldarstellungen: Von den Anfängen bis 1920, Ballenstedt 1919, ND Ballenstedt 1993, 9–10. Bei dem von Peper abgedruckten Schreiben mag es sich um das verlorene Dokument LASA Z 4 II, 391b Nr. 20 handeln.

90. *Popperodt*, „Annales" (wie Anm. 1), 68. Als wesentlichen Grund für den Aufstand identifiziert Franke steigende Abgaben und das neue Verbots, im Wald zu holzen. *Franke*, „Elisabeth" (wie Anm. 4), 325–327. Zur Bestrafung der Aufständischen überführte Elisabeth das Gernröder Brauhaus in ihren Besitz und forderte zwei Strafzahlung von je 50 Gulden an Pfingsten und Weihnachten der kommenden zwei Jahre. *Wäschke*, „Geschichte" (wie Anm. 20), 249–250.

91. *Erich Vogel*, Chronik des Nienburger Klosters, Teil 2: 1004 bis 1563, Nienburg/Saale 2000. Die mit dem Bauernkrieg zusammenhängenden Unruhen in Nienburg waren auch Thema in der Korrespondenz zwischen Wolfgang von Anhalt-Köthen und Elisabeth von Weida. Siehe LASA Z 6, Nr. 435 (3). Weitere von Wolfgang mediatisierte Klöster umfassen das Nonnenkloster in Mehringen, das, nachdem es 1525 im deutschen Bauernkrieg Schaden genommen hatte, von ihm gegen den Widerstand der Nonnen 1528 säkularisiert wurde, sowie das Kloster Coswig, mit dessen Nonnen er sich am 30. August 1527 vertraglich auf eine zukünftige Versorgung und Unterbringung einigte. *Wäschke*, „Geschichte" (wie Anm. 20), 227–228, 247, 307–308.

kauf.⁹² Die von Elisabeth betriebene finanzielle Konsolidierung des Stifts erlaubte diesen am 18. Mai 1531.⁹³ Nachdem sie ihre Autorität mit ihrer von lutherischen Reformimpulsen angeregte religiöse Erneuerung des Stifts untermauert hatte, zeugt ihre Reaktion auf die Einmischung in konfessionelle Angelegenheiten seitens Johanns IV. und Wolfgangs sowie die Entziehung der Möglichkeit politischer Einflussnahme mittels der Aufkündigung der Schutzvogtei des Letzteren von ihrer Determinierung zur politischen Selbstbehauptung. Elisabeth von Weida präsentierte sich nicht nur als regional unabhängig agierende Landesherrin, die die territoriale Hoheit ihres Stifts gegen andere Reichsfürsten zu wahren wusste, sondern auch als Vorsteherin eines humanistisch geprägten und sich reformierenden Stifts, in dessen Zentrum die liturgische Kontinuität des Totengedenken und die Memorialkultur eines bedeutenden ottonischen Reichsfürsten stand.

DIE REFORMATORISCHE ÄBTISSIN ELISABETH VON WEIDA

Ein weiterer Faktor, der zu der Stilisierung Elisabeths von Weida als lutherischer Reformäbtissin geführt hat, ist eine sich zum Ende der 1520er-Jahre wandelnde Wahrnehmung. Das erste Zeugnis hierfür ist die Beschreibung des Anwalts von Wolfgang von Anhalt-Köthen und Johann IV. von Anhalt-Zerbst vom 6. November 1527, dass Elisabeth sich der „Lutherische[n] Religion" angeschlossen hätte.⁹⁴ Dass diese Einschätzung über den regionalen Kontext hinweg Geltung gewann, bezeugt ein Brief Luthers an den sächsischen Kurfürsten Johann (der Beständige, 1468–1532) vom 25. Mai 1529, in dem er Elisabeth als „fromme Fürstin" bezeichnete.⁹⁵ Sie diente ihm als Beispiel, um dem Fuldaer Koadjutor Johannes III. von Henneberg-Schleusingen (1503–1541) zum Verbleib im Kloster zu raten, sodass er es Elisabeth gleich als dessen Vorsteher reformieren könnte. Dass die in der Gernröder Ordnung festgeschriebene liturgische Reform 1529 bereits nicht mehr Luthers Vorstellungen entsprach, erscheint hierbei sekundär. Elisabeth von Weida galt fortan im Reich als lutherisch.

---

92. LASA Z 3, Nr. 103, 103a, 108, 124–26; Z 6, Nr. 435 (4).
93. LASA Z 3, Nr. 124–25. Diese Wiedereinlösung wurde am 28. Mai 1531 bestätigt. LASA Z 3, Nr. 126. Das Dokumente LASA Z 4 V, 458 Nr. 5 gilt als verloren.
94. PAG.
95. WA BR: 5.84.

Für ebendiesen Zeitraum sind jedoch keinerlei Reformaktivitäten vonseiten Elisabeths überliefert. Vielmehr schuf ihre Passivität Freiräume für weitere Veränderungen, die zwar die Stiftsgeistlichen, nicht aber direkt das religiöse Leben oder den Stiftsverband der Kanonissen betrafen. Dies mögen die Eheschließungen ersterer kurz nach dem Ableben des Stiftspriesters Keusel 1529 verdeutlichen. Nachdem Caspar Scharffe aufgrund seiner ersten Ehe noch sein geistliches Amt in Gernrode hatte verlassen müssen, heiratete er nun die Witwe von Andreas Popperodt d. Ä. und trat erneut in den Stiftsdienst ein; auch Molitor nahm eine gewisse Agnes zur Frau.[96] Aufsehen erregte laut Popperodt d. J. jedoch, dass auch Stiftsdamen sich 1531 verheirateten. Entgegen den Willen der Gernröder Pröpstin und des Kapitels gingen Dorothea und Agnes von Kittlitz Ehen ein und verließen – „ihre Keuschheit und jungfräuliche[n] Anstand missachtend" („pudicitiam & decus virginales non observantes") – das Stift.[97] Nicht allein weil ein solcher Schritt Stiftsdamen traditionell offenstand, sind diese Geschehnisse verwunderlich, sondern auch weil sie Luthers Ermutigung widersprachen, dass Nonnen aus ihrem Kloster austreten sollten, um ihrer Natur entsprechend in ehelichen Gemeinschaften Familien zu gründen.[98] Diesem Gebot folgend waren im Zeitraum von 1529 bis 1534 im nahen ernestinischen Sachsen eine Vielzahl an Klosterordnungen erlassen und Visitationen durchgeführt worden, die die Kanonissen wie im Fall des Augustiner-Chorfrauen-Stifts Brehna 1531 explizit zum Austritt zwecks einer Verehelichung aufriefen, so dieser vom Kapitel gewährt worden war.[99] In Gernrode allerdings scheinen die Eheschließungen der Stiftsdamen als Bruch des für die Existenz des Stifts zentralen Personenverbands angesehen worden zu sein.[100] Dass sich Popperodt der Verehelichung und anschließenden Flucht dieser noch in den 1560er Jahren empörte, suggeriert sowohl den Bedeutungsgrad, dem das kontemplative Leben zugeschrieben wurde, als auch eine gewisse Nervosität darüber, ob die institutionelle Integrität des Stifts trotz seiner Reformierung oder gerade wegen des damit einhergehenden Autoritätsverlusts, der sich in der Bevorzugung lutherischer Theologie über der traditionellen Unterordnung unter dem Stiftskapitel manifestierte, Bestand haben könnte. Die Phase der von

---

96. *Popperodt*, „Annales" (wie Anm. 1), 68.
97. *Popperodt*, „Annales" (wie Anm. 1), 68.
98. WA BR: 3.326–328.
99. Siehe „18. Parochie Brehna", in: Geschichtsquellen der Provinz Sachsen und angrenzender Gebiete, Halle, Berlin 1870–1925, Bd. 41, 308–342, hier 312.
100. *Popperodt*, „Annales" (wie Anm. 1), 68.

Luther inspirierten Reformen Elisabeths schien einer Phase der Neutralität und abwartenden Haltung zu der Reformationsbewegung zu weichen.[101]

Dass Gernrode zeitgleich reichsweite Anerkennung als Hort reformatorischer Frömmigkeit gewann, zeigt ein für reformorientierte Geistliche ungewöhnliches Gesuch. 1530 erbat Ursula von Münsterberg (1491–1534) die Aufnahme in das Gernröder Stift, nachdem sie zusammen mit zwei Nonnen im Oktober 1528 aus dem Kloster der Heiligen Maria von der Buße im sächsischen Freiberg geflohen war.[102] Noch im selben Jahr veröffentlichte sie eine Schrift, die ihren Klosteraustritt rechtfertigen sollte.[103] In dieser bediente sie sich dem lutherischen Argument der *sola fide*, wobei sie ebenso Erasmus' Klosterkritik, dass die persönliche Vervollkommnung nicht nur innerhalb sondern auch außerhalb der Klostermauern erreicht werden könne, aufgriff.[104] Nach längeren Aufenthalten bei Luther und protestantischen Verwandten in Sachsen und Preußen wandte sich die mittellose Ursula 1530 an Elisabeth von Weida und erbat, mit ihrer Mitstreiterin Dorothea Tanbergin in das Stift Gernrode aufgenommen zu werden.[105] Friedrich II. von Liegnitz (1480–1547), bei dem Ursula wegen dessen Sympathien für die Lehren Huldrych Zwinglis (1484–1531) und Kaspars von Schwenkfeld (1490–1561) nicht länger unterkommen wollte, sicherte Elisabeth diesbezüglich auf dem Augsburger Reichstag Unterstützung zu.[106] Auch wenn es aufgrund fehlender Belege unklar ist, ob es tat-

---

101. *Wolgast*, „Die deutschen Territorialfürsten" (wie Anm. 18), 414–428.

102. *Deutschländer*, „Briefe" (wie in Anm. 82), 201; *Hubert Emisch*, „Herzogin Ursula von Münsterberg: Ein Beitrag zur Geschichte der Reformation in Sachsen", in: Neues Archiv für sächsische Geschichte und Alterthumskunde 3 (1882), 290–333, hier 305, 307; *Rüttgardt*, Klosteraustritte (wie Anm. 8), 49–56.

103. *Ursula von Münsterberg*, Der Durchleüchtigen hochgebornen F. Vrsulen/Hertzogin zu Mœnsterberg etc., Grefin zu Glotz etc. Christlich vrsach des verlassen klosters zu Freyberg, Wittenberg 1528, VD16 M 6729 und 6730; siehe auch *Monika Rössing-Hager*, „Reformatorische Nonnen rechtfertigen ihre Kloster- Flucht: Florentina von Oberweimar und Ursula von Münsterberg", in: Heidemarie Wüst (Hg.), Frauen der Reformation: Texte, Wittenberg 1999, 103–129. Die Nürnberger Neuauflage dieser Schrift im folgenden Jahr zeugt von ihrer raschen Verbreitung; siehe *Ursula von Münsterberg*, Der Durchleüchtigen hochgepornen F. Vrsulen/Hertzogin zu Mönsterberg [et]c. Gräffin zů Glotz [et]c. Christlich vrsach des verlassen Klosters zů Freyberg, Nürnberg 1529, VD16 M 6731.

104. *Ursula von Münsterberg*, Vrsach des verlassen klosters (wie Anm. 103). Siehe auch *Deutschländer*, „Briefe" (wie Anm. 82), 201–202. Auf ihrer in dieser Schrift sichtbaren umfangreichen Kenntnis der Bibel und reformatorischer Schriften sowie ihrer überzeugenden Rhetorik beruht Ursulas Ruf als einer der Vorkämpferinnen gegen das klösterliche Leben. *Emisch*, „Ursula" (wie Anm. 102), 311–312.

105. *Emisch*, „Ursula" (wie Anm. 102), 321.

106. Des Markgrafen Georg zu Brandenburg Bedenken seinen Räthen zu Augsburg gegeben, in: *Karl Eduard Förstemann* (Hg.), Urkundenbuch zu der Geschichte des Reichstages

sächlich zu einer Aufnahme in das Stift kam, demonstriert dieses Ersuchen, dass es Elisabeth gelungen war, Gernrode als Gegenentwurf zu katholischen Nonnenklöstern zu gestalten. Sie hatte sie es vermocht, das Stift unter Beibehaltung der Privilegien für die Stiftsdamen und dennoch in Übereinstimmung mit der lutherischen Reformation, zu der sie sich politisch zu distanzieren wusste, zu reformieren.

Am 11. April 1532 verstarb Elisabeth von Weida. Sie wurde im nördlichen Seitenschiff der Stiftskirche beigesetzt.[107] Auf ihrem Grabstein wurden ihre Errungenschaften mit folgender Inschrift gewürdigt: „Elisabeth aus der edlen Familie von Weida, die berühmte Äbtissin dieser Kirche, welche als erste das Evangelium Christi durch Gottes Gnade angenommen und trotz vieler Anfeindung auf ihre eigenen Kosten einzuführen Sorge getragen hat, beschloss ihre Lebenstage im Alter [unleserlich] im Glauben an den Sohn Gottes und in gutem Frieden am 11. April im Jahre des Herrn 1532".[108] Die Inschrift, die insbesondere auf die Einführung der Reformation und nicht auf andere Verdienste wie die Erhaltung des Stifts Bezug nimmt, reflektiert die massiven Umwälzungen, die sich im Stift nach Elisabeths Ableben vollzogen.[109] Gernrode geriet zusehends in den Einfluss des regional dominierenden Geschlechts der Askanier, was sich auch in der Wahl der jungen Anna von Plauen (1506–1548), einer Nichte eines der ärgsten Widersachers Elisabeths, Wolfgangs von Anhalt-Köthen war, zur neuen Äbtissin zeigt. Noch kurz vor ihrem Tod hatte Elisabeth von Weida die Einhaltung ihrer Reformen angemahnt, womit sie wohl eine spätere Unterordnung unter die Lehre Luthers oder beispielsweise die noch zu ihren Lebzeiten verabschiedeten *Confessio Augustana* ausschließen und einen Bruch mit Traditionen der Kirche und des Reichs verhindern wollte.[110] Bereits 1533 wurde diese Mahnung ignoriert, als die Exklusivität

---

zu Augsburg im Jahre 1530, 2 Bde., Halle 1835, Bd. 2, 729–735, hier 733; *Emisch*, „Ursula" (wie Anm. 102), 321.

107. *Franke*, „Elisabeth" (wie Anm. 4), 331.

108. Elisabet ex nobili fa[m]ilia de Wyda clara h[uius] ecclesie abb[atiss]a q[ue] pri[m]a evang[elium] c[h]risti p[er] Dei gra[tiam] a[m]plexa hucq[ue] suis i[m]pe[n]sis i[n]vectu[m] m[u]lto[rum] i[n]vidia curauit [et] die [verloren] i[n] fide filii Dei paceq[ue] *bona* II aprilis clausit a[nn]o d[omini] 1532. Siehe auch *Schubart*, „Inschriften" (wie Anm. 17), 35.

109. Für einen Vergleich mit dem Totengedenken des zeitnah verstorbenen Friedrich III. von Sachsen, siehe *Jähnigen*, „„im rechten erkenntnis des Euangelij[…] verschieden'" (wie Anm. 15).

110. *Popperodt*, „Annales" (wie Anm. 1), 68: „[…] ut & studium veræ pietatis & religionis, ad quam ab ipsa instituti essent, ardenti pectore colerent ac omnibus humanis rebus anteferrent".

der Stiftskirche abgeschafft wurde;[111] mit dieser Degradierung zur Parochialkirche und dem Verlust wesentlicher Stiftsprivilegien wurde laut Schulze der Einzug der reformatorischen Lehre in Gernrode abgeschlossen.[112] Nicht nur die Stiftsdamen verloren infolgedessen ihre liturgischen Privilegien, sondern auch das Stift büßte mit der Einstellung des späteren Chronisten Popperodt als Lehrer in der neu eingerichteten Elementarschule seine essentielle Bildungsaufgabe ein. Die Sonderstellung im protestantischen Lager, die Elisabeth von Weida für das Stift errungen hatte, war verwirkt. Dieser Autoritätsverlust setzte sich in den Folgejahren fort: Ab 1565 wurde das Stift von zumeist minderjährigen Töchtern aus dem Hause Askanien geleitet, ehe das Amt der Äbtissin seit 1614 vakant blieb und das Stift nur noch nominell fortbestand.

ZUSAMMENFASSUNG

Das Narrativ, Elisabeth von Weida habe die lutherische Lehre 1521 im freien und weltlichen Stift Gernrode eingeführt, ist weder für diesen noch für einen späteren Zeitpunkt zutreffend. Ihre seit 1504 betriebenen Reformen sind umfänglicher und primär auf den externen Mediatisierungsdruck vonseiten benachbarter Reichsfürsten zurückzuführen. Die wirtschaftliche und politische Konsolidierung beruhte dabei maßgeblich auf ihrem traditionellen Verständnis der fortwährenden *unio imperii et ecclesiae*, das ihr als Rechtfertigungsgrundlage diente, um ihre Hoheitsrechte mittels der Schlichtungsmechanismen von Kirche und Reich einzufordern. Visuell demonstrierte sie die Bedeutung des Stifts als geistlicher Institution im Reichsgefüge in der Neugestaltung des Gero-Grabmals. Dieses, für die Stiftsidentität elementare Totengedenken stellt einen signifikanten Bruch mit der Lehre Luthers dar, an der sich Elisabeth spätestens seit 1525 zwecks der Reformierung des Stifts orientierte. Der kirchenkritische Diskurs, der seit ihrer Amtsvorgängerin Scholastica überliefert ist, resultierte so in der liturgischen Ordnung von 1523–25, die mit humanistischen Idealen kompatible Prinzipien Luthers wie *sola scriptura* aufgriff. Diese Kombination diverser Reformimpulse sollte daher nicht als Anschluss an eine sich zunehmend politisierende und mit Reichstraditionen brechende Bewegung gesehen werden, sondern als innerkirchlicher Verhandlungsprozess neuer Frömmigkeitsmodi. Auf diese Weise wandelte sich das Stift Gernrode graduell zu einem Ort reichstreuer reformatorischer Frömmigkeit, der mit seinem en-

---

111. *Popperodt*, „Annales" (wie Anm. 1), 68.
112. *Schulze*, Gernrode (wie Anm. 6), 66; *Schubart*, „Molitor" (wie Anm. 5), 12.

gen Stiftsverband derart anerkannt war, dass Ursula von Münsterberg, eine Kritikerin des altkirchlichen Klosterwesens, um Aufnahme in dieses bat. Erst nach Elisabeths Ableben wurden diese Bemühungen mit kirchlichen Reformen, die gleichzeitig eine Anbindung an die Regionalmacht der Askanier gleichkam, zunichtegemacht. Der Versuch einer spirituellen Erneuerung abseits des reformatorischen Lagers war gescheitert und schlussendlich der Fortbestand des Stifts als unabhängig agierender Reichsinstitution unmöglich gemacht.

Dr. Finn Schulze-Feldmann
London
United Kingdom
finn.schufe@gmail.com

ABSTRACT

Elisabeth von Weida, abbess of the Imperial Abbey of Gernrode, has long been considered one of the first to introduce Luther's teachings in her principality, thereby establishing it as an early center of Lutheranism. Methodological inconsistencies and the lack of evidence have recently led scholars to be more cautious about this conclusion. By shifting the focus to Elisabeth's abbacy as a whole, rather than her supposedly Lutheran reforms, this article rejects this view of a drastic Reformation as a turning point in Gernrode's history. Instead, it argues for a gradual transformation which not only predates Luther's movement, but also maintains a cautious distance to the increasingly politicized Lutheranism. In addition to the reforms securing the abbey's economic existence, Elisabeth's liturgical innovations and the refurbishment of the abbey's church were designed to reinforce imperial traditions and invoke the abbey's historical significance as she was relying on imperial institutions to fend off attempts by powerful princes to exploit her vulnerabilities. The institutional framework of the Empire and its principles—which Elisabeth knew how to call upon for protection against a pending mediatization—also enabled her to transform Gernrode into a well-respected center of female Protestant piety.

The Words of Forgiveness: Luther, *The Keys*, and the Nuremberg Absolution Controversy

By Terence McIntosh

In composing a bevy of theological writings in 1530 while residing in the Veste Coburg, Martin Luther sought in large measure to construct an adamantine and insuperable defense of his core Reformation teachings.[1] He did so in order to discourage the Lutheran party from misrepresenting them at the Diet of Augsburg in the vain hope of negotiating a compromise with the Catholic party. For Luther, these theological writings served a largely preservative function, protecting the original purity of his Reformation doctrine. One of them, however, *The Keys*, not only vigorously reaffirmed earlier teachings but arguably also left a significant mark on the subsequent development of the Reformation and German Lutheranism. This mark is first discernible in the mid-1530s during the Nuremberg absolution controversy, which can thus serve as a register of the reception and impact of Luther's work soon after its publication. Moreover, through the controversy's outcome, *The Keys* helped to prepare the ground for subsequent debates about the use of Lutheran private confession as an instrument of church discipline.

At the center of the affair stood Andreas Osiander, the imperial city's most prominent evangelical reformer. He and Johannes Brenz, the reformer in

---

1. An earlier version of this article was presented at the Triangle Intellectual History Seminar (Research Triangle Park, NC, August 2017). The author is grateful for the helpful comments received at this presentation as well as from his colleagues Daniel J. Sherman, Jay M. Smith, and Molly Worthen at the University of North Carolina at Chapel Hill and from two anonymous readers. Abbreviations – *BC*: Robert Kolb and Timothy J. Wengert, eds., *The Book of Concord: The Confessions of the Evangelical Lutheran Church* (Minneapolis: Fortress Press, 2000); *BSELK*: Irene Dingel, ed., *Die Bekenntnisschriften der Evangelisch-Lutherischen Kirche: Vollständige Neuedition* (Göttingen: Vandenhoeck & Ruprecht, 2014); *LW*: Jaroslav Pelikan and Helmut T. Lehmann, eds., *Luther's Works*, 55 vols. (St. Louis: Concordia Publishing House / Philadelphia: Fortress Press, 1955–1986); *MBDS*: Robert Stupperich et al., eds., *Martin Bucers deutsche Schriften*, 19 vols. (Gütersloh: Gütersloher Verlagshaus Mohn, 1960–2016); *MBW*: Heinz Scheible et al., eds., *Melanchthons Briefwechsel: Kritische und kommentierte Gesamtausgabe*, 29 vols. (Stuttgart-Bad Cannstatt: Frommann-Holzboog Verlag, 1977); *OGA*: Gerhard Müller and Gottfried Seebaß, eds., *Andreas Osiander d. Ä. Gesamtausgabe*, 10 vols. (Gütersloh: Gütersloher Verlagshaus Mohn, 1975–1997); *WA*: *D. Martin Luthers Werke: Kritische Gesamtausgabe*, 73 vols. (Weimar: Böhlau, 1883–2009); *WA Br*: *D. Martin Luthers Werke: Briefwechsel*, 18 vols. (Weimar: Böhlau, 1930–1985).

Schwäbisch Hall, together had written the final version of the church ordinance that Nuremberg and the margraviate of Brandenburg-Ansbach-Kulmbach introduced jointly in January 1533. Although the ordinance indisputably reflected Lutheran teachings and practices, including those for private confession and absolution, the new liturgy from Brenz and Osiander did not include a rite of general confession and absolution. This rite—in which the pastor, either after the sermon or before communion, urged all the churchgoers to humble themselves, confess their sins, and forgive their neighbors in order to receive his absolution—had featured in Nuremberg's evangelical services since December 1525 or one of the following months. Because of protests from churchgoers in the city, the magistrates requested from Osiander an explanation for the omission and, in late April, ordered the reinsertion of the rite after receiving counsel from Luther and Philipp Melanchthon. Osiander soon found himself in a heated dispute with the magistrates and many of Nuremberg's other evangelical pastors, and, by August 1533, he had preached defiantly on four occasions to defend the omission and denounce general confession and absolution. In September, at the height of the controversy, he submitted a long and sharply reasoned apologia, *On the Power of the Keys* (*Von schlusseln bekanntnus Osiandri*), which provides the fullest account of his views on the different forms of confession. Written three years after the publication of Luther's *The Keys*, Osiander's work, portions of which first appeared in print in the eighteenth century, cites the Wittenberg reformer extensively.[2] Significantly, in trying to fathom *The Keys* and apply its lessons to Nuremberg's young evangelical church, Osiander focused on critical issues in Luther's theology concerning the means by which God forgives and justifies sinners who have faith. Maintaining emphatically that the formula of general absolution—the words of forgiveness spoken by the pastor during the rite and heard by all the congregants—contradicted the Wittenberg reformer's conviction that a faithful believer, at the mo-

---

2. Ronald K. Rittgers, *The Reformation of the Keys: Confession, Conscience, and Authority in Sixteenth-Century Germany* (Cambridge, MA: Harvard University Press, 2004), 83–88, 92, 121–122, 131–136, 138–150; Gottfried Martens, "'Ein uberaus grosser unterschiedt': Der Kampf des Andreas Osiander gegen die Praxis der allgemeinen Absolution in Nürnberg," in *Festhalten am Bekenntnis der Hoffnung: Festgabe für Professor Dr. Reinhard Slenczka zum 70. Geburtstag*, ed. Christian Herrmann and Eberhard Hahn (Erlangen: Martin-Luther-Verlag, 2001), 145–164, here 146–160; Gunter Zimmermann, *Prediger der Freiheit: Andreas Osiander und der Nürnberger Rat 1522–1548* (Mannheim: Palatium-Verlag, 1999), 310–325; Bernhard Klaus, *Veit Dietrich: Leben und Werk* (Nuremberg: Selbstverlag des Vereins für bayerische Kirchengeschichte, 1958), 148–155. Nuremberg had been using other evangelical forms of the rite of general confession and absolution since 1524. Catholic masses in Germany in the High and Late Middle Ages included versions of the rite in the vernacular.

ment of absolution, would feel absolutely certain that forgiveness had occurred, Osiander saw himself as upholding fundamental evangelical teachings. Since 1518, Luther had steadfastly asserted that God forgives one's sins, be it in the sacrament of penance or, later, in the evangelical rite of private confession, only if one most firmly believes in the spoken words of absolution. But the same firm belief, Osiander averred, could not attach itself to Nuremberg's formula of general absolution. In October 1533, Luther and Melanchthon dealt him a setback by rejecting many of the arguments in his apologia. The controversy persisted, however, and in 1540, Luther and Melanchthon implicitly recognized the validity of Osiander's criticism of the formula of general absolution. Examining in detail the significant twists and turns that led to this outcome not only illuminates a variety of factors that, during the early Reformation, affected the translation of Luther's teachings into acceptable church practice but also suggests new paths for exploring subsequent disputes about Lutheran private confession in early modern Germany.

Although several authors have discussed the Nuremberg absolution controversy in various contexts, they have not sufficiently plumbed the tensions and relations between Osiander and the Wittenberg reformers. While some authors did not consult *The Keys* and did not have easy access to sources published only in the 1980s, including the complete texts of Osiander's apologia and an important sermon in August 1536, others did not study the pertinent material closely enough.[3] In attempting to gauge the reception and impact of Luther's

---

3. Klaus, *Veit Dietrich* (see note 2), 119–121, 147–168; Dietrich Stollberg, "Osiander und der Nürnberger Absolutionsstreit: Ein Beitrag zur Geschichte der Praktischen Theologie," *Lutherische Blätter* 17 (1965): 153–168. For a discussion of absolution, see Martens, "'Ein uberaus grosser unterschiedt'" (see note 2), 159; Zimmermann, *Prediger der Freiheit* (see note 2), 325–338; Gottfried Seebaß, *Das reformatorische Werk des Andreas Osiander* (Nuremberg: Verein für bayerische Kirchengeschichte, 1967), 254–262; Emanuel Hirsch, *Die Theologie des Andreas Osiander und ihre geschichtlichen Voraussetzungen* (Göttingen: Vandenhoeck & Ruprecht, 1919), 48n36; Rittgers, *Reformation of the Keys* (see note 2), 138–169; Rittgers, "Luther on Private Confession," in *The Pastoral Luther: Essays on Martin Luther's Practical Theology*, ed. Timothy J. Wengert (Minneapolis: Fortress Press, 2017), 211–230; Rittgers, "Penance, Confession, Forgiveness, and Reconciliation in Martin Luther's Context and Writings," in *Oxford Research Encyclopedia of Religion* (DOI: 10.1093/acrefore/9780199340378.013.361). In discussing the apologia, Martens only briefly considered Osiander's objections to the wording of the formula of general absolution in relation to Luther's *The Keys*. Zimmermann did not address the issue at all, and Seebaß did not examine the reformer's theological rationale for rejecting general absolution. The remarks in Hirsch's work are outdated. By contrast, Rittgers drew on both *The Keys* and the sources published in the 1980s. But one of Rittgers's conclusions is suspect (see note 39 below), and his work does not accord sufficient attention to the formula of absolution, the focus of the present article.

The Keys in the years immediately after its publication, one should examine how this work informed Osiander's positions during the absolution controversy and the extent to which the Nuremberg reformer had correctly understood and properly applied Luther's writing.

The present article begins by highlighting the considerable importance that Luther, in several writings before 1530, and Melanchthon, in the Augsburg Confession, attached to the words of absolution. Only by recognizing this importance can one appreciate the significance of some of Osiander's major arguments during the controversy in Nuremberg. Luther's *The Keys* also receives close attention, for in presenting new charges about the deficiencies of the sacrament of penance in the Roman church, the reformer implicitly posited new standards that Lutheran private confession and absolution should meet. These standards also had their place in the controversy. Part II turns to Osiander's *On the Power of the Keys* and carefully examines two separate issues, corresponding roughly to the work's two halves. The first concerns the Nuremberg reformer's implicit rejection of Luther's and Melanchthon's initial judgment of the Nuremberg absolution controversy and the question of whether a pastor's preaching of the gospel can effect the forgiveness of an individual's sins. Although not related specifically to the formula of general absolution, this issue reveals the tremendous weight that the spoken words of forgiveness possessed for Osiander. The second issue deals with the reformer's objections to the formula. A careful reading of *The Keys* and *On the Power of the Keys* shows the important ways in which Osiander developed his criticism by drawing meaningfully and accurately from Luther's work. Part III examines the controversy's subsequent development, focusing particularly on Osiander's sermon of 1536 and the Nuremberg preacher Veit Dietrich's appraisal of its arguments. The portion of the sermon that pleased Dietrich confirms the formula of absolution's crucial significance. In 1540, Luther and Melanchthon themselves implicitly validated Osiander's criticism, thereby silently confirming, one might argue, its connections to major arguments in Luther's *The Keys*. Finally, Part IV contends that, as a result of the Nuremberg absolution controversy, *The Keys* created some of the conditions that would lead to later disputes in German Lutheranism about the effectiveness of private confession as an instrument of church discipline.

I.

For Martin Luther, the words of absolution in the sacrament of penance and later in the evangelical ecclesiastical rite of private confession were inextricably tied to Christ's promise of forgiveness in Matt. 16:19. Here, the Lord gave Peter not only the keys to the kingdom of heaven but also the assurance that what Peter either binds or looses on earth shall be bound or loosed in heaven. A sinner, Luther concluded, would certainly receive the remission of both sin and the guilt over it if he or she possessed a fervent, unshakable faith in the truthfulness of Christ's promise, heard as the spoken words of absolution. The reformer affirmed his conviction repeatedly, and it implied that the words of absolution should not deviate in meaning from the Lord's promise to loose in heaven what is loosed on earth.

Luther's *For the Investigation of the Truth and for the Comfort of Troubled Consciences* (*Pro veritate inquirenda et timoratis conscientiis consolandis conclusiones*), which appeared in the early summer of 1518 and which some scholars regard as his first purely reformational text, highlights the importance of the words of absolution in three lapidary statements. Theses 31, 32, and 33 propose that in the sacrament of penance, the priest truly forgives sins and absolves guilt; that as he offers the word of Christ, an apparent reference to John 20:23 and Matt. 16:19, he simultaneously exercises, or provokes, the faith by which the sinner is justified from within; and that nothing except faith alone justifies, for which the priest's administration, or pronouncement, of the word is necessary. According to Oswald Bayer, Luther claimed here, as well as in his account of his hearing in October before Cardinal Cajetan, that only the words of absolution, spoken to the confessant in a specific situation and with pressing needs, could call forth without delay the absolute faith necessary for the forgiveness of sins.[4]

In *The Sacrament of Penance* (*Ein Sermon von dem Sakrament der Buße*), published in October 1519, Luther expanded his claim. After stressing that penance's sacramental effects depend entirely on the confessant's faith, he

---

4. WA 1:632.11–16; Martin Luther, "For the Sake of Investigating the Truth and Terrified Consciences," trans. Sarah Hinlicky Wilson, *Lutheran Forum* 44, no. 4 (2010): 34–35, here 35; Oswald Bayer, *Promissio: Geschichte der reformatorischen Wende in Luthers Theologie*, 2nd ed. (Darmstadt: Wissenschaftliche Buchgesellschaft, 1989), 1–7, 165–202, esp. 192–198. See also Oswald Bayer, *Martin Luther's Theology: A Contemporary Interpretation*, trans. Thomas H. Trapp (Grand Rapids, MI: William B. Eerdmans Publishing Company, 2008), 44–54, esp. 53. I am most grateful to the anonymous reviewer who brought to my attention Bayer's works.

stated that even when, in the absence of a priest, one Christian tells another that God forgives the latter's sins, the latter is certainly absolved by accepting with an unshakable faith the words of absolution as if God himself had spoken them. An irrefragable certainty also exists when the priest absolves. Christ's promise of forgiveness cannot be a lie.[5] Significantly, whoever utters the words of absolution, the confessant should in effect hear God's voice and respond accordingly.

Since everything hinges on the confessant's faith, Luther's sermon asserts emphatically that God's forgiveness depends neither on the confessant's contrition—a sincere remorse for having sinned—nor satisfaction—the performance of penitential acts. This assertion suggests a narrowing of the function of the priest, who, departing from the implied practice in the Roman church, no longer needed to judge a person's contrition. The reformer acknowledged this narrowing by insisting that a priest is bound to grant absolution even though he always possesses only uncertain knowledge about a sinner's contrition. Pointing to theologians who contended that the priest, due to this uncertainty, "cannot at once assign appropriate penance," and thus the confessant "should, and must necessarily" doubt the efficacy of the sacramental absolution, Luther warned: "Be on guard against these misleading and un-Christian gossips. The priest is necessarily uncertain as to your contrition [*rew*] and faith, but this is not what matters. To him it is enough that you make confession and seek an absolution. He is supposed to give it to you and is obligated to do so. What will come of it, however, he should leave to God and to your faith."[6] Later in the sermon Luther insisted that "[t]he priest [...] has sufficient evidence and reason to grant absolution when he sees that one desires it from him. Beyond that, he is not obligated to know anything."[7] Not being obligated to know anything about the quality of one's contrition, the priest should proceed without hesitation to grant absolution, which, if the confessant's faith is genuine, will bestow peace of conscience. The two passages are not proscriptions, however. The reformer did not object if a priest wishes to inquire about the confessant's contrition and, even more importantly, about his or her faith in the truthfulness of Christ's promise of absolution. But Luther warned against the false belief that one could receive absolution on account of one's contriteness.[8] Everything depends on faith.

---

5. WA 2:715.28–716.7, 716.9–10, 716.25–32, 717.6–12.
6. WA 2:716.1–3, 718.1–9 (quote in *LW* 35:14–15).
7. WA 2:719.26–28 (quote in *LW* 35:17).
8. WA 2:720.15–29.

In the decade following the publication of *The Babylonian Captivity of the Church* (*De captivitate Babylonica ecclesiae praeludium*), Wittenberg and then electoral Saxony replaced penance, which Luther no longer regarded as a sacrament, with the ecclesiastical rite of private confession and absolution.[9] At various points in this development, Luther reiterated unequivocally his earlier appraisals of the words of absolution. In September 1521, while residing secretly at the Wartburg, he published *On Confession, Whether the Pope Has the Power to Require It* (*Von der Beicht, ob die der Bapst macht habe zu gepieten*). Primarily an attack on the obligation established by the Fourth Lateran Council in 1215 that Christians obedient to Rome needed to confess their sins to the appropriate clergyman once each year before receiving Easter communion, the work also stresses the comfort and assurance received by a Christian who hears the spoken words of absolution and does not doubt in the least Christ's promise to bind and to loose. Even if a Christian should confess to a layperson and not a priest, the bestowal would still occur.[10] In Luther's eighth Invocavit sermon in the spring of 1522, after his return to Wittenberg, he recommended private confession highly and was unwilling to trade it for all the treasure in the world. Private confession (understood in an evangelical sense) had given him enormous "comfort and strength" as he struggled with his *Anfechtungen*—occasions of intense fear, dread, and despair of Christ's judgment at the end of time—and other individuals would benefit similarly. The comfort and strength stemmed from Luther's receiving "a sure absolution as if God himself spoke it, so that I may be assured that my sins are forgiven." Thus, the reformer concluded, "confession must not be despised."[11] In his eyes, it fortified the confessant spiritually.

The following year, in a sermon on Maundy Thursday, Luther again affirmed that the confessant must hear the spoken words of absolution in private confession with the proper faith and not doubt that God himself speaks through them. "For God has humbled and lowered himself thus, that he placed his holy divine word in the mouth of man so that he should not doubt at all

---

9. For the latest scholarship on this topic, particularly in the context of the Wittenbergers' controversies with the Sacramentarians during the 1520s, see Amy Nelson Burnett, *Debating the Sacraments: Print and Authority in the Early Reformation* (New York: Oxford University Press, 2019), 61, 250–254, 257–258, 262–263, 267–268.

10. WA 8:178.8-30 (assurance); 182.23–28 (layperson); 183.26–27 (layperson).

11. WA 10/III:61.7–64.9 (quotes in *LW* 51:98–99). See also Rittgers, *The Reformation of the Keys* (see note 2), 81–82; Kurt Aland, "Die Privatbeichte im Luthertum von ihren Anfängen bis zu ihrer Auflösung," in *Kirchengeschichtliche Entwürfe: Alte Kirche, Reformation und Luthertum, Pietismus und Erweckungsbewegung* (Gütersloh: Gütersloher Verlagshaus Gerd Mohn, 1960), 452–519, here 462–463.

that [God] himself is saying it. For this reason, we should thus also receive it as if he himself were speaking it [*alls thete ers selbs*]."[12] In 1526, in *The Sacrament of the Body and Blood of Christ—Against the Fanatics* (*Sermon von dem Sacrament des leibs und bluts Christi, widder die Schwarmgeister*), Luther again affirmed the near equivalence of the pastor's spoken absolution and God's pronouncement of forgiveness: "[T]he absolution, in which your neighbor [or priest] absolves you in God's stead, is just as if God himself were speaking, and that should indeed be comforting to us. [...] Such absolution he has put into the mouth of man [or the priest]."[13] Similarly, in "A Brief Exhortation to Confession," which appeared in 1529 in the second edition of *The Large Catechism*, Luther averred that the pastor's words serve as the medium for God's forgiving word: "Note, then, as I have often said, that confession consists of two parts. [...] The second is a work that God does, when he absolves me of my sins through the Word placed on the lips of another person. This is the surpassingly grand and noble thing that makes confession so wonderful and comforting."[14] Surely the spoken words of absolution matter, since forgiveness works through them.

In 1530, when Melanchthon synthesized Luther's various statements about God's absolution and the pastor's words of absolution for incorporation into the Augsburg Confession, he used lofty language and powerful imagery that could stir the faithful deeply. Perhaps intending to channel the confessant's ocular and auricular senses, Melanchthon compared the words of absolution to an awesome pronouncement coming from the firmament:

> At the same time, the people are diligently instructed how comforting the word of absolution is and how highly and dearly absolution is to be esteemed. For it is not the voice or word of the person speaking it, but it is the Word of God, who forgives sin. For it is spoken in God's stead and by God's command. Great diligence is used to teach about this command and power of the keys [...]. It is also taught how God requires us to believe this absolution as much as if it were God's voice resounding from heaven and that we should joyfully find comfort in the absolution, knowing that through such faith we obtain forgiveness of sin.[15]

One year later, in the *Apology of the Augsburg Confession*, Melanchthon expanded on these ideas by calling attention to what the confessant hears when the minister pronounces the words of forgiveness: "[Absolution] is the true

---

12. WA 12:493.5–8. I am most grateful to the anonymous reviewer who referred me to Luther's sermon.
13. WA 19:520.16–22 (quote in *LW* 36:359).
14. *BSELK*, 1160.5–10 (quote in *BC*, 478.15).
15. *BSELK*, 146.27–148.9 (quote in *BC*, 72.2–4).

voice of the gospel. [...] '[F]aith comes from what is heard,' as Paul says [Rom. 10:17]. [...] [W]hen absolution is heard, the conscience is uplifted and receives consolation. [...] [T]he keys truly forgive sins before God according to [Luke 10:16], 'Whoever listens to you listens to me.' Therefore we must believe the voice of the one absolving no less than we would believe a voice from heaven."[16] The confessant needs to believe the pastor's voice as if it were God's. For this reason, the specific words that the pastor utters and the confessant hears would become extremely important.

In the summer of 1530, the months immediately following the presentation of the Augsburg Confession to Emperor Charles V, Luther wrote *The Keys*, in which he contrasted from several angles his evangelical understanding of the power of the keys with the Roman church's alleged misunderstanding and misuse. In the work, he referred only in passing and somewhat obliquely to the words of absolution, insisting that "[y]ou must never doubt what the keys say and give you, at the risk of losing both body and soul. It is as certain as if God himself were saying so, which indeed he does. It is his own Word and command. But if you doubt the same you make God a liar."[17] Striking, of course, is Luther's warning: one makes God a liar and risks damnation by doubting what the keys say and give. He repeated the admonition just a few pages later, but now directed it also to the pastor who utters the words of absolution:

> The greatest honor you can bestow on God and his keys is to trust in them. It is for that reason we teach our people that he who is bound or loosed by means of the key, let him rather die ten deaths than doubt their efficacy. No greater dishonor can be done to God's Word and judgment than lack of faith in the same. For this means as much as to say: God, you are a liar. It is not true what you say. I do not believe it. Hence God must be a prevaricator. He who binds and looses must be equally certain, otherwise he is guilty of similar abominations.[18]

The reasoning behind these warnings appears earlier in the text, in the section describing Rome's second chief abuse of the keys.[19] Luther charged Rome with

---

16. *BSELK*, 447.20–26 (quote in *BC*, 193.39–40).
17. WA 30/II:496.31–35 (quote in *LW* 40:364).
18. WA 30/II:500.11–18 (quote in *LW* 40:368); see also WA 30/II:499.33–500.2.
19. Luther used roughly three-fourths of *The Keys* to accuse Rome of four chief abuses, and the section on the second is by far the longest. The third and fourth abuses do not focus closely on absolution and thus do not require consideration here. For a discussion of the first abuse, which relates to Article 28 of the Augsburg Confession, see Terence McIntosh, "Luther, Melanchthon, and the Specter of Zwinglianism during the Diet of Augsburg in 1530," *Archiv für Reformationsgeschichte/Archive for Reformation History* 111 (2020): 78–108, here 94–96, 104–105, the companion piece to the present article.

having turned the key to loose into a *"clavis errans*, that is to say, a wrong or erring key." After illustrating the problem of the wrong key through an extended fictitious dialogue between a Romanist and a German Lutheran on indulgences, Luther asserted that the pope had attached to the key's efficacy a condition—the sufficiency of the confessant's repentance before God—and that the Romanists now consequently "say, teach, and confess openly that absolution in confession is uncertain. And if repentance [*rew*] before God is insufficient, absolution is not effective."[20] Luther noted, however, that the proof texts in chapters 16 and 18 of Matthew do not hedge the power to bind and loose with any conditions: "These are clear, lucid, and plain words which admit of no *clavem errantem*, of no wrong key. God says it shall be certain and it shall not err. What they bind and loose shall be bound and loosed."[21] But by attaching to penance the condition of sufficiency of repentance, the pope had, in effect, impudently stated that God's word is uncertain: "Thereby he flatly flies in the face of what God says. God says, if it is loosed on earth it must be loosed in heaven. The pope says, it must not necessarily be loosed in heaven, although it is loosed on earth. It is possible for the key to err. Does that not mean as much as if he said to God: Lord, you are a liar."[22] In failing to profess that absolution is certain, the pontiff had committed an abomination.[23]

Luther's stern judgment is a brutally uncompromising extension of arguments from his sermon in 1519, in which he contended that the granting of absolution does not depend in any way on the priest's knowledge of the confessant's contrition and faith. Uncertainties about a person's repentance, worthiness, and fear of God do not matter because of the adamantine certainty that God will fulfill the promise to loose in heaven what his ministers have loosed on earth—provided that the confessant acknowledges through faith the truthfulness of the words of absolution. In *The Keys*, however, Luther attached to the arguments a damnatory sting: the pope, pastor, or confessant who doubts the

---

20. WA 30/II:475.23–24 (quote in *LW* 40:337).
21. WA 30/II:480.14–16 (quote in *LW* 40:344).
22. WA 30/II:481.33–482.4 (quotes in *LW* 40:346).
23. One finds the earliest version of the argument, it seems, in *On Confession* (1521), where Luther asserted that pope and bishop concede that they often loose and bind without effect. A less explicit version appeared in 1529 in the revised edition of Luther's *Large Catechism*. "Where the confession was not made perfectly and in complete detail, we were told that the absolution was not valid, and the sin was not forgiven. Thereby the people were driven to the point that everyone despaired of confessing that purely (which was, of course, impossible), and no conscience could feel at peace or have confidence in the absolution." WA 8:161.16–24; *BSELK*, 1160.13–18 (quote in *BC*, 478.16–17).

unerring efficacy of the words of absolution calls God a liar and faces perdition.[24]

In the treatise's final pages, Luther again discussed the wrong key, which he now dubbed the "conditional key," thereby pinpointing how the Roman church had distorted the meaning of Matt. 16:19. The pope's absolution is nugatory because it is yoked not to faith but to the satisfaction of a condition —the sufficiency of one's repentance—which leads the confessant away from establishing the proper relation to God, who is prepared to forgive:

> But so they understand, teach, and observe concerning the pope's wrong key: The key itself can err, even though a person would like to accept and rely on it. For it is a *conditionalis clavis*, a conditional, a vacillating key which does not direct us to God's Word, but to our own repentance [*rew*]. It does not say candidly and boldly that you are to believe that I most certainly loose you. But it says that if you are repentant [*berewet*] and pious, I loose you, if not, then I fail. That is the *clavis errans*, the erring key. It cannot with any assurance say that I know for certain that I have loosed you before God, whether you believe it or not, as St. Peter's key can say. But it must say something like this, that I loose you on earth, but I really and truly do not know whether you are loosed before God.[25]

The implication of Luther's description of the conditional key could not be clearer. The absolver should not say to the confessant anything about satisfying a condition of repentance and piousness or anything that conveys uncertainty about the absolution's effectiveness before God. This implication also carried enormous force because of Luther's and Melanchthon's earlier assertions that the pastor's voice in absolution was the virtual equivalent of God's word. If the pastor were to attach a condition to his absolution, he would truly make God a

---

24. The manner in which Luther discussed the words of absolution in *The Keys* supports my claim that the reformer wanted to rebut Ulrich Zwingli's charge that Luther's earlier writings on penance and private confession were misguided. *The Keys* refers to the spoken words of absolution only obliquely because they had been the principal target of Zwingli's attack. By highlighting the damnatory sting, however, *The Keys* seeks to prove that Luther could demolish papal teachings more thoroughly than his rival could. McIntosh, "Luther, Melanchthon, and the Specter of Zwinglianism" (see note 19), 86–96.

25. WA 30/II:499.16–25 (quote in *LW* 40:367); see also 481.30–482.17. See Martin Brecht, *Martin Luther*, vol. 2, *Shaping and Defining the Reformation, 1521–1532*, trans. James L. Schaaf (Minneapolis, MN: Fortress Press, 1990), 401–402; Rittgers, *Reformation of the Keys* (see note 2), 154–157. In discussing *The Keys* briefly, Brecht hardly mentions the wrong key. In focusing foremostly on the differences between Luther's and Andreas Osiander's understandings of private confession, Rittgers does not mention the wrong key at all. Instead of requiring the sinner to repent and confess properly, Luther required the sinner to possess faith. In both instances, however, a requirement existed, thus making confession conditional. That both views of confession rested on conditions is in and of itself not problematic.

liar. Andreas Osiander certainly drew this conclusion from his reading of *The Keys* and decided to act upon it.

II.

The following discussion of Osiander's *On the Power of the Keys* focuses on two broad issues that correspond roughly to the work's two halves. The reformer contended vigorously in the first half that a pastor's preaching of the gospel cannot effect the forgiveness of an individual's sins; in the second, he argued that the words in Nuremberg's formula of general absolution could also not effect this forgiveness and the city should thus not reintroduce the rite. To understand Osiander's motive for discussing the first issue requires a brief consideration of the circumstances behind Luther and Melanchthon's early intervention in the Nuremberg absolution controversy.

On 3 April 1533, two magistrates met with Osiander and seven other clergymen to thrash out their conflicting views on general absolution. During the discussions, he reportedly insisted that the rite possesses no value because of the following dilemma: When a large number of worshippers are involved, either the pastor does not and cannot discriminate between those who should receive absolution on account of their faith and repentance and those who should not, or the pastor discriminates by using a conditional formula of absolution, which the New Testament prohibits. It is the formula's wording that troubled Osiander, for the minutes of the meeting read: "[T]he words of absolution, that is the words of remission, must be understood conditionally, thus that a part [of the congregation] was absolved and the other [part] not absolved, which, however, the New Testament does not tolerate or permit at all, for there must be certainty and no baseless hope." Luther himself, Osiander continued, had recognized this prohibition.[26] Five days later the Nuremberg Council appealed to the Wittenberg reformers for advice about settling the troublesome dispute, asking them specifically to decide whether general absolution does more harm than good.[27]

---

26. *OGA* 5:342.12–343.11, quote on 343.3–6.
27. WA Br 6:446–447 (no. 2008, 8 April 1533). Tendentiously, the letter does not mention the dilemma that Osiander had detected. On 4 April 1533, however, he sent accounts of the previous day's meeting with the magistrates and clergymen to Luther and Brenz; only the letter to the latter survives (Zimmermann, *Prediger der Freiheit* [see note 2], 317). In his letter to Brenz, Osiander explained concisely the dilemma that arguably undermines general absolution's validity (*OGA* 5:350.19–26). Presumably Luther received a similar letter; thus he and

In replying to the council, the two reformers concluded that one should not reject the rite of general absolution for two principal reasons. First, it does not differ fundamentally from the public preaching of God's word concerning the forgiveness of sins before an assembly of people, and this preaching is also an absolution. Second, the presence of churchgoers who lack the requisite faith to benefit from absolution does not constitute grounds for rejecting general absolution. Just as one understands that the New Testament proclaims the Lord's forgiveness to everyone throughout the world but does not benefit those whose faith is deficient, so too should one understand that absolution, whether private or general, also fails to benefit those wanting in faith.[28] With the second reason, Luther and Melanchthon grappled with both horns of Osiander's dilemma. They held that the pastor does not need to discriminate between those who should and those who should not receive absolution because one should understand that absolution itself in effect is conditional on faith. But they inadvertently left room for future disputes because they did not comment specifically on the formula of absolution's wording, which Osiander regarded as a crucial issue. Moreover, the reformers acknowledged that private absolution provides a special comfort to the confessant because "each conscience [*gewisen*] struggles by itself over whether this enormous forgiveness that Christ offers belongs to him."[29] They did so to dispel Osiander's fear that the availability of general absolution would lead to a complete collapse of the need for private confession and absolution.[30]

Apparently latching onto Luther and Melanchthon's acknowledgment about the struggling soul, Osiander argued tenaciously in roughly the first half of the apologia that a pastor's preaching could not absolve a Christian's sins.[31] In doing so, he maintained in effect that general absolution, a form of such preaching, could not substitute for the remission of sins in private confession and absolution. In proclaiming the gospel, Osiander affirmed, a pastor can instill in a Christian essential knowledge about God's promise to forgive sins on account of Christ's sacrifice. But a Christian listens to the sermon not in isolation but in the company of many other Christians and knows that at least

---

Melanchthon had a more complete account of the controversy than that which came from the Nuremberg Council.

28. WA Br 6:454.4–19 (no. 2010, 18 April 1533). See also Rittgers, *Reformation of the Keys* (see note 2), 143–144; Zimmermann, *Prediger der Freiheit* (see note 2), 317–318.

29. WA Br 6:454.26–27 (no. 2010, 18 April 1533).

30. Osiander expressed this fear in the meeting of 3 April 1533. See *OGA* 5:336n13; 342.15–19; Rittgers, *Reformation of the Keys* (see note 2), 140.

31. *OGA* 5:422.4–444.14.

some of them will not receive God's gift of forgiveness and salvation. Because the sermon addresses the auditors in general, it cannot indubitably assure anyone in particular that he or she numbers among the saved. Thus, a Christian's faith is uncertain and insecure, unless God lets the pastor say personally to the Christian in the three sacraments—in baptism, private absolution, and the Lord's Supper—that the promise and gift apply specifically to him or her.[32] Immediately after citing Romans, chapter 10, to confirm that faith comes only from hearing God's word, Osiander tied this pointedly to the audible pronunciation of the Christian's name: "[W]hoever should believe that he is by name [the person] whom Christ also wants to make holy with others, God must beforehand let it be said just so to him by name, and he must clearly [*verstendtlich*] hear it." General absolution, which does not include the audible pronunciation of any names, does not convey certainty of absolution, and without this certainty the Christian does not possess the faith required for justification.[33]

Osiander's deft argument did not impress Luther and Melanchthon, who would continue to affirm that the pastor, when publicly preaching the gospel,

---

32. In the apologia, Osiander vigorously defended his view that absolution is a sacrament (*OGA* 5:482.28–490.15). The nature of absolution and private confession in sixteenth-century Lutheranism is fraught with ambiguity. Although Luther himself after 1520 never explicitly referred to them as a sacrament, he stated in *The Large Catechism* (1529) that baptism "comprehends also the third sacrament, formerly called penance, which is really nothing else than baptism" (*BSELK*, 1130.8–15 [quote in *BC*, 465–466.74]). Philipp Melanchthon, however, affirmed unambiguously in the *Apology of the Augsburg Confession* (1531), a work that he prepared in close consultation with Luther and other theologians in Wittenberg, that absolution is the sacrament of penance (*BSELK*, 429.13–18, 447.20–27, 513.3–19 [*BC*, 186.3, 193.39–41, 219.3–220.5]). Roth argues that Luther regarded private confession to all intents and purposes as a sacrament (Erich Roth, *Die Privatbeichte und Schlüsselgewalt in der Theologie der Reformatoren* [Gütersloh: C. Bertelsmann Verlag, 1952], 71–101, esp. 94, 98–101; cf. Rittgers, *Reformation of the Keys* [see note 2], 271n83). Fagerberg comments on the ambiguity (Holsten Fagerberg, *A New Look at the Lutheran Confessions [1529–1537]*, trans. Gene J. Lund [St. Louis, MO: Concordia, 1972], 162–163, 173–174, 206, 207–208, 217, 220). Fagerberg's broader discussion of penitence notes additional complexities regarding the nature of absolution and private confession (206–225). After 1550, Lutheran theologians, with few exceptions and qualifications, denied that absolution is a sacrament (Ernst Bezzel, *Frei zum Eingeständnis: Geschichte und Praxis der evangelischen Einzelbeichte* [Stuttgart: Calwer Verlag, 1982], 21, 28–30, 52–54; Laurentius Klein, *Evangelisch-lutherische Beichte: Lehre und Praxis* [Paderborn: Verlag Bonifacius-Druckerei, 1961], 50–57, 81–85, 97–98).

33. *OGA* 5:425.25–426.3, 426.9–427.4, quotes on 426.29–31. See also Zimmermann, *Prediger der Freiheit* (see note 2), 326–327; Claus Bachmann, *Die Selbstherrlichkeit Gottes: Studien zur Theologie des Nürnberger Reformators Andreas Osiander* (Neukirchen-Vluyn: Neukirchener, 1996), 162–164. The discussion of Osiander's apologia in Bachmann's study (166–170) limits itself to only a few theological topics and purposely does not consider the absolution controversy as a whole.

offers absolution to many people. Nevertheless, the argument shows that Osiander clearly accepted and even broadened the Wittenberg reformers' views regarding the tremendous importance of the spoken words of absolution. Luther and Melanchthon held that the confessant derived comfort and assurance from hearing the spoken words of absolution as if they came directly from God and faithfully believing their truthfulness. Osiander went further, insisting that the comfort and assurance came also from the pastor's personal address to the confessant, who would thereby hear that he or she specifically would receive God's forgiveness. This conviction spirits the rest of the work.

The second half of the apologia presents the scriptural and theological grounds for Osiander's opposition to the reintroduction of general absolution in Nuremberg and his insistence that one can receive the remission of sins only through private confession and absolution. Threaded through the plethora of arguments are several references to the formula of absolution. To bring their significance into relief and to consider the full extent to which Osiander's thinking cleaved to and departed from Luther's, the following pages present first the problem of the unworthy confessant—one who should not receive absolution—which exercised both reformers. Examining their different perspectives and responses to this problem reveals how each reformer assessed the potency of the words of forgiveness in private confession. The focus then shifts to the issue at the heart of the controversy—the words of forgiveness in general absolution; on this particular matter Osiander repeatedly and rightly affirmed a strong affinity between his views and those from Wittenberg.

Matt. 16:19, in which Jesus gave Peter not only the keys to the kingdom of heaven but also the assurance that what Peter bound or loosed on earth would be bound or loosed in heaven, presented Luther and Osiander with an exegetical teaser. The truthfulness of God's word and thus this verse could admit no doubt or qualification of any sort; moreover, the passage provided an immensely important scriptural foundation for the evangelical practice of private confession and absolution. The pastor's authority to forgive sins derived from this verse, and the confessant's faith that Christ fulfilled his promise of forgiveness through the pastor's words of absolution touched also on the passage. So, too, did the Augsburg Confession, which affirms that God's forgiving word mysteriously accompanies the pastor's audible words of absolution as long as the confessant firmly believes that the latter truly expresses God's promise of forgiveness. The puzzle for both theologians was how to interpret Matt. 16:19 in relation to private confession and absolution so as to preserve the verse's unqualified truthfulness and yet avoid the undesirable suggestion that a pastor, by uttering the words of absolution, could remit the sins of someone who would fail to receive God's forgiveness. Such a person would be, above all others, someone who denied the truthfulness of God's promise of forgiveness, who in effect lacked faith and, tautologically, the capacity to receive absolution. Such a person had become an unworthy confessant.

In *The Keys* Luther basically offered two solutions to the teaser.[34] First, he interpreted Matt. 18:18 in a singularly bold and striking manner that suggested that the pastor's absolution itself was one and the same with Christ's absolution:

> But [Christ] speaks in this fashion, If you bind and loose on earth, I will also bind and loose right along with you in heaven. When you use the keys, I will also. Indeed, if you do it, it shall be done, and it is not necessary that I do it after you. What you bind and loose (I say) I will neither bind nor loose, but it shall be bound and loosed without my doing so. It shall be one single action, mine and yours, not a twofold one. It shall be one and the same key, mine and yours, not a twofold one. While you do your work, mine is already done. When you bind and loose, I have already bound and loosed.[35]

Unlike the previously discussed remarks by Luther that a confessant should believe the pastor's words of forgiveness as if they were God's, this passage breaks new ground, proposing in effect that the pastor's use of the keys is joined together in such a manner with Christ's that only one indivisible act of binding or loosing occurs. It is not twofold, whereby one act can precede the other or be distinguished from the other. But this conception of binding and loosing also logically implied that the pastor could not possibly absolve an unworthy confessant, since Christ cannot err.

Luther's second solution complements the first by indicating how the pastor avoids absolving someone Christ would not absolve. As Ronald K. Rittgers has shown, the Wittenberg reformer argued in *The Keys* that God's loosing is an offer of absolution, which truly forgives sins, but the unworthy confessant rejects this offer and the sins remain unforgiven.[36] But since the pastor's use of the keys is inseparable from Christ's, it follows that the confessant is also rejecting the pastor's offer, which truly forgives. As Rittgers has also pointed out, Osiander described the pastor's use of the keys with an unworthy confessant

---

34. The argument in this paragraph and the next two differs in a few respects from that in Rittgers's study but reaches the same conclusion (Rittgers, *Reformation of the Keys* [see note 2], 153–156).

35. WA 30/II:497.10–18 (quote in *LW* 40:365). See Bayer, *Promissio* (see note 4), 186–189. Bayer spotlighted this passage and two others in *The Keys* to show that Luther held, from 1518 to 1530, that the sacrament of penance and, later, private confession work *ex opere operato*.

36. Rittgers, *Reformation of the Keys* (see note 2), 155–156; WA 30/II:498.34–499.8.

as a twofold process, although not quite the type that Luther had decried. In the first part, the pastor's utterance of the words of absolution truly effects the remission of sins both on earth and in heaven. Later, in the second, God alone condemns the confessant because of his or her hardness and lack of faith.[37] One cannot harmonize at all Osiander's notion of a twofold process with Luther's understanding of the use of the keys.

But on another important matter concerning the unworthy confessant one finds the two reformers in close agreement. To assist pastors in determining whether or not to absolve a confessant, Osiander offered a simple rule of thumb: Matt. 18:15–18. In these verses, Jesus, speaking to his disciples, referred not only to the loosing and binding of sins in heaven and on earth but also to the three steps of admonition. Translated into the practice of evangelical church discipline, the three steps required the pastor to admonish a known sinner first privately and then, if necessary, in the presence of one or two witnesses. If these two reproofs did not lead to amendment, then the entire congregation would rebuke and, if necessary, ban the incorrigible sinner. Only by referring to the steps of admonition, Osiander insisted, could a pastor truly and properly forgive a congregant's sins. Thus, absolution would be withheld from anyone who had been reproved but did not accept the correction and express in private confession the willingness to renounce the rebuked sin by saying, "I am sorry."[38] The pastor did not need any extraordinary capacities because Osiander yoked private confession to a system of evangelical church discipline that possessed an indisputable scriptural foundation, involved the wider community—neighbors and the congregation—and used only modestly intrusive methods to censure semipublic and public sins.[39]

---

37. Rittgers, *Reformation of the Keys* (see note 2), 153–154. The pertinent passages in Osiander's apologia read: "Entbindet man yemandt von seinen sunden auff erden, so ist er warlich embunden auch im himel, und ob ers schon nit glaubt, so ist er dennoch entbunden. Er wirdt aber darnach umb den unglauben als umb eine neue sunde verdampt werden" (*OGA* 5:431.28–31). Also, "Darumb, wann der, so da absolvirt wirdt, schon nit genugsame reue hat oder nicht glaubet, so liegen und triegen dennoch darumb die schlussel nicht, sunder es ist gewißlich im himel gelöst, was hienieden auff erden gelöst wirdt. Bleibt aber der gelöset on reu und an glauben, so wirt er umb seiner hertigkeyt und unglaubens willen, die er auch nach der absolutio behelt oder widerumb einwurtzeln lesst, verdampt. Aber die sund, davon er ist entbunden worden, sein im warlich vergeben" (*OGA* 5:448.30–449.2). Whether Osiander thought that a similar twofold process applied to worthy confessants or to binding is not clear.

38. *OGA* 5:449.15–451.2, 465.26–34. The significance that Osiander attached to the phrase "I am sorry" comes principally from Luke 17:1–4, which he regarded as another proof text. See *OGA* 5:453.2–7, 453.18–27.

39. Rittgers did not discuss the three steps of admonition at all. He also did not cite a single line from the apologia to support his claim that Osiander ascribed to the pastor hearing

In recommending Matt. 18:15–18 as a reliable guideline, Osiander was following Luther's lead. In *The Keys*, the Wittenberg reformer explained how to loose and bind sins in a manner acceptable to God by noting first that Matthew's verses provide "a definite text in which Christ himself describes the office of the keys. You cannot go wrong if you follow his instructions. But if you do not, and instead take a novel and peculiar path of your own, you can be sure that you will err and that you are not in possession of the true keys." Luther then discussed the applicability of the verses in assessing the procedure used to ban a member of the congregation.[40] When Osiander explained in his apologia how the verses applied to private confession and absolution, he was obviously heeding Luther's warning about ignoring Christ's instructions.[41]

Luther and Osiander were also in close agreement regarding one of Osiander's principal objections to general absolution, namely that it included, explicitly or implicitly, a conditional formula of forgiveness. Perhaps partly to avoid suggesting to Sunday worshippers that they all received remission indiscriminately through general absolution, Nuremberg's pastors had since 1525 used a formula that stated several basic conditions required for reception—humbling one's heart before God, confessing and repenting [*bereuhet*] one's sins with heartfelt longing for God's grace and help and with firm faith and trust in his promise, and forgiving one's neighbors from one's heart.[42] As noted earlier, Osiander objected in April 1533, at the start of the absolution controversy, to the formula of absolution's wording, which expresses a condition. He returned to the issue in his apologia, which records the entire formula of gen-

---

private confession an extraordinary capacity to gain insight into God's will and thus discriminate between worthy and unworthy confessants (Rittgers, *Reformation of the Keys* [see note 2], 157–158). One should treat this claim with utmost skepticism.

40. WA 30/II:501.10–503.2 (quote in *LW* 40:369–370).

41. The use of the three steps of admonition would have prevented, in theory, many unworthy confessants from receiving absolution, thereby reducing the likelihood of adverse pastoral consequences sprouting from Osiander's notion of absolution as a twofold process. This consideration can perhaps explain why Luther and Melanchthon never bothered to criticize this notion specifically. It had no bearing on subsequent developments in the Nuremberg controversy.

42. In discussing liturgical innovations introduced in 1525 and 1526, Rittgers did not translate the original formula as recorded by Osiander in his apologia but a version from 1664 that omits the words "and repent" from the original phrase "confess and repent your sins and transgressions" (Rittgers, *Reformation of the Keys* [see note 2], 92). The German reads, "bekennt und bereuhet eure sund und gebrechen" (*OGA* 5:444.25; see also 335n8). The original formula appears also in the draft of the Brandenburg-Nuremberg Church Order that Osiander completed in January 1530 (*OGA* 3:528.17–25).

eral absolution.[43] Many pages later, in elaborating on several reasons for general absolution's inability to remit sins, he referred to the conditions—humility, repentance [*reuhe*], heartfelt longing, faith, trust, and forgiveness—in the formula and isolated its most troublesome phrase, a single conditional sentence: "If you [the Sunday worshipper] do that, then I [the pastor] loose you." Even if one were to scratch out the phrase "[i]f you do that, [then I loose you]," Osiander claimed, conditionality would still persist.[44] In concisely stating his objections to the formula of absolution, he insisted emphatically that it differed in no way from the papal key that errs as Luther had described three years earlier in *The Keys*.[45] Several more references to the conditional formula, the papal erring key, and Luther's work soon followed.[46] In the final one, Osiander mentioned once more the formula's conditions of contrition, forgiveness, and faith and the pastor's pronouncement: "If you do that, then I loose you." But, the reformer continued, "that is not correct," and the theologians in Wittenberg have not approved of such an erring key.[47]

Why did Osiander focus particularly on the formula's wording? Drawing from the analysis presented here, one can point to three principal explanations. First, he did so partly because the wording exemplified the inherent uncertainty in sermons that the first part of the apologia had limned. The conditional formula—if you do that, then I loose you—divided the worshippers effectively into two groups, those who did what the conditions required and those who did not, but the specific individuals belonging to each group remained unclear. Thus, the formula of general absolution gave the anxious worshipper no assurance one way or the other. Unable to comfort the believer with the certainty of forgiveness, the formula aggrieved Osiander mightily. In all likelihood, the condition concerning repentance with heartfelt longing offended him the most because it apparently collided head on with Luther's strenuous and compelling insistence in both *The Sacrament of Penance* and *The Keys* that absolution did not depend on the sufficiency of one's repentance.

---

43. *OGA* 5:444.23–32.

44. *OGA* 5:465.12–17, 466.18–20.

45. *OGA* 5, 465.7–10. Rittgers quoted nearly a dozen important lines from Osiander's critique of the formula of absolution but did not mention Osiander's explicit reference to Luther's *The Keys* and substituted ellipses for the three critical lines that include the sentence, "If you [the Sunday worshiper] do that, then I [the pastor] loose you" (Rittgers, *Reformation of the Keys* [see note 2], 153).

46. *OGA* 5:466.34–467.9, 467.21–24, 468.24–25, 469.16–19, 476.19–24. Osiander also referred once to "ein falscher dietrich," which is an oblique reference to the erring key (*OGA* 5:470.34–37).

47. *OGA* 5:481.37–482.14, quote on 482.4–5.

In denying this dependency, Luther was attacking the Roman church's teaching that a valid confession required the complete enumeration of one's sins. Osiander simply extended Luther's argument to its logical conclusion.

His resolute rejection of the formula related also to his understanding of the function of a pastor's voice and words in a valid absolution, one in which the recipient possessed the required faith and trust in the truthfulness of God's promise. In such a case, the pastor's voice became the virtual equivalent of Christ's voice, as asserted in the Brandenburg-Nuremberg church ordinance of 1533, which Osiander and Brenz had written. In private absolution, the sinner, who expected the pastor to "comfort him with God's word and, by the power of the ordained office and the authority that Christ attached to it, free him from his sins and pronounce absolution [*ledig sprechen*], [...] should not doubt at all that his sins are definitely forgiven, as if Christ himself had personally spoken the words. For Christ, who had promised us this, can neither lie nor deceive."[48] Here, Osiander and Brenz merely restated what Luther and Melanchthon had affirmed for years. Through the pastor's voice, God's word was expected to deliver utmost certainty about the remission of sin—certainty that would comfort the confessant. But if the pastor uttered a conditional formula, then the confessant heard uncertainty. Under this circumstance, how could he or she feel confident that the absolution had succeeded? Instead of receiving assurance, the confessant would sense doubt and insecurity and thus risk making God a liar.

Finally, the formula exercised Osiander for a reason that pertained to the absolver. The pastor who uttered the ambiguous formula of general absolution was using the erring key and making God a liar ("der feelschlussel lugstrafft Got").[49] Thus, Osiander accepted fully the assertion in Luther's *The Keys* that the pastor needed to say confidently that he knew for certain that his absolution had loosed the sinner before God. Derived primarily from Matt. 16:19 and 18:15–18, this confidence did not require the pastor's acquisition of any special knowledge about the sinner's confession. But the uncertainty in the formula used in Nuremberg could not express this assurance and would manifest the pastor's own lack of faith in the power of the keys and God's word. The pastor who added a condition to his absolution was committing blasphemy.

---

48. *OGA* 5: 144.8–13. In his apologia, Osiander claimed that "as truly as the minister addresses the absolved and touches him physically [*mit seinem leyb*], as truly does God address and touch the [absolved] with his word and Holy Spirit precisely in and with the absolution and the laying of the hand" (*OGA* 5:489.28–30).

49. *OGA* 5:467.3–11.

III.

In early October 1533 and less than a month after the submission of Osiander's apologia to the magistrates of Nuremberg, Luther and the other theologians in Wittenberg had read the work and issued their opinion.[50] They disappointed Osiander, who had expected them to confirm his assertion that a conditional formula was not correct. Instead, the Wittenberg reformers adhered to Luther and Melanchthon's basic position in April 1533 and affirmed that the word of God proclaims absolution both generally, for all men and women, and specifically, for particular individuals. If faithfully and properly received, sermons could remit a person's sins.

Consequently, the theologians in Wittenberg could not condemn general absolution, which served to remind churchgoers that they should accept the gospel.[51] Furthermore, the theologians noted that the preaching of the word not only looses the sins of the faithful but also binds the sins of the unfaithful. Thus the commingling of the two groups does not diminish general absolution's efficacy in any way.[52] Finally, the reformers stated with unmistakable clarity that absolution, both private and general, is conditional, as is the sermon, and does not benefit worshippers who lack faith.[53] Astonishingly, however, the specific words in Nuremberg's formula of general absolution receive no comment at all. In passing over one of the apologia's most salient topics, did Luther and his colleagues perhaps regard absolution's conditionality and the wording of the formula as two sides of the same coin, thereby obviating the need to treat each issue separately? Nothing in their counsel supports such a supposition, and the theologians almost certainly understood that Osiander

---

50. Klaus, *Veit Dietrich* (see note 2), 121; Georg Theodor Strobel, *Nachricht von dem Leben und den Schriften Veit Dietrichs eines um die Evangelisch-Lutherische Kirche unsterblich verdienten Theologen als ein geringer Beitrag zur Reformations-Geschichte aus gedruckten und ungedruckten Quellen* (Altdorf, 1772), 41; Philipp Melanchthon, *Christliche Berathschlagungen vnd Bedencken: Auch andere nützliche vnd heylsame Erinnerungen vnd Antworten deß weylandt hocherleuchten gelehrten Manns Philippi Melanchthonis, so er in Teutscher Spraach von vielen fürnemmen ReligionsSachen gestellt*, ed. Christoph Pezel (Neustadt an der Hardt, 1603), 127–128. Klaus repeated the false claim in Strobel's work that Melanchthon had also drafted a formula of absolution in October 1533. Strobel did not realize that the text printed in Melanchthon's *Christliche Berathschlagungen vnd Bedencken* is the formula of absolution of 1540 (see below).

51. WA Br 6:528.29–38, 528.50–529.68 (no. 2052, 8 October 1533).
52. WA Br 6:529.69–79 (no. 2052, 8 October 1533).
53. WA Br 6:529.79–84 (no. 2052, 8 October 1533).

viewed the matter differently. He knew that absolution depends on faith, but nevertheless contended that the words matter.

Despite deciding not to confirm any of the crucial arguments in Osiander's apologia, the Wittenberg theologians sought to heal the divisions in Nuremberg by proposing a Solomonic compromise: While every clergyman in the city would continue to recommend to his flock private absolution, whose value no one disputed, Osiander, unlike the others, would not have to use the rite of general confession and absolution in his church services. Moreover, each party would refrain from faulting the other over the issue.[54] The acceptance of this compromise led to an eighteen-month lull in the controversy, but in early 1535, Osiander began to criticize again the practice of general absolution. Developments culminated in August 1536, when he preached on four occasions about the power of the keys. Because several churchgoers complained about the fourth sermon, the Nuremberg magistrates asked him to submit it as a manuscript, which he did in short order.[55] Osiander had addressed a variety of issues in the fourth sermon. In its longest section, he assured his listeners that, under a proper system of evangelical church discipline in Nuremberg, the ministers would not require any of the jurisdictional authority that German bishops in the past had amassed and abused through the power of the keys. He then spoke about the distinction between Christians who need absolution and those who do not and described the ministers who can truly loose and bind sins.[56] But none of these issues would matter as much as the discussion of general absolution.

In the last major part of the sermon, Osiander repeatedly referred to general absolution as an abuse (*mißbrauch*) for four principal reasons. He began by noting that the rite has no foundation in scriptures and the practices of true Christian churches. Second, he remarked derisively that in general absolution the worshippers themselves decide whether they have been loosed or not and the minister decides nothing.[57] Third, by slightly rewording Luther's crucial passage in *The Keys* on conditional absolution, Osiander stressed the rite's inherent uncertainty: "Moreover the absolver [minister] still does not know if he binds or looses, indeed he does not know if he does anything or only pretends.

---

54. WA Br 6: 529.93–530.100 (no. 2052, 8 October 1533).
55. *OGA* 6:166–168; Klaus, *Veit Dietrich* (see note 2), 156. Cf. Rittgers, *Reformation of the Keys* (see note 2), 160–162, with the following discussion of the fourth sermon.
56. *OGA* 6:171.12–176.8 (no jurisdictional authority), 176.9–179.29 (Christians who need absolution), 180.1–181.18 (ministers who can loose and bind).
57. *OGA* 6:179.30–180.1, 181.19–182.9 (no foundation in scriptures), 182.19–35 (worshippers absolve themselves).

For he places it in doubt and a condition and says: If you do that, then I loose you, that is: If you do not do it, then I do not loose you. Now he never knows if they do it or not, therefore he also does not know if he looses or not." In addition, Osiander emphasized, the absolver's uncertainty infects those who hunger for absolution, "[a]nd how can the distressed souls [*gewissen*] be comforted and quieted by such a legerdemain (*gauckhlerey*)? When the absolver does not know what he does, how should they know it?"[58] Osiander still hammered on the words of absolution—what the absolver says—and the troubling consequences that would follow if that utterance is conditional. Finally, Osiander warned that general absolution would undermine private confession.[59]

The magistrate Hieronymus Baumgartner, to whom Osiander had submitted his manuscript, gave it first to Veit Dietrich, asking him to assess the sermon's contents. Dietrich, a native son of Nuremberg, had received a preachership there only in late 1535, at the age of twenty-nine. He was an extraordinary young theologian who had studied in Wittenberg from 1522 to 1529, had lived as a guest in Luther's house from about 1528 to 1535, and had served as Luther's personal secretary for fourteen years.[60] Having been the amanuensis in the Veste Coburg in the summer of 1530, Dietrich knew that Luther did not compose *The Keys* facilely but instead had completed two versions of the text, rejecting the first one as unsatisfactory.[61] Thus, one should assume that Dietrich was intimately familiar with Luther's thinking on absolution and enormously qualified to assess Osiander's sermon. Dietrich's judgment matters.

No more than three days after receiving the sermon, Dietrich submitted his written evaluation. He disagreed with several of Osiander's arguments, but none pertained to the sermon's final section, which specifies the abuses in general absolution. Regarding these abuses, he fully applauded Osiander's contention that the condition in general absolution means that the minister does not know whether his words have any effect.[62] Dietrich quickly added that the condition of faith is also present in private absolution and noted that the sermon's conclusion seemed not to square with the charges that preceded it.

---

58. *OGA* 6:182.35–183.22, quotes on 182.35–183.3, 183.18–21. Cf. WA 30/II:499.22–25.

59. *OGA* 6:183.23–30.

60. Klaus, *Veit Dietrich* (see note 2), 56–57, 60–63, 125–126.

61. WA 30/II:435–464, for the first version, which Luther gave to Dietrich after the completion of the second. See also Klaus, *Veit Dietrich* (see note 2), 71–72.

62. "Illud sane plausibile est, ministrum nescire quid agat, dicere, quod absolvat, & tamen addere conditionem." Quoted in Klaus, *Veit Dietrich* (see note 2), 157.

Nevertheless, unable to deny the abuses that stemmed from the formula used in general absolution, he ended his evaluation by recommending that Nuremberg's other preachers accept Osiander's criticism of the rite and henceforth abide by the church ordinance of 1533, which did not allow for general absolution.[63] Implicitly rejecting the Wittenberg theologians' compromise from three years earlier, Dietrich justified his recommendation by accepting some of the sermon's arguments, and the most salient, in his mind, was that the absolver who utters a condition does not truly know whether he absolves.[64] Luther had drawn the same conclusion in *The Keys*.

Highlighting Dietrich's startling advice raises once again the question why the Wittenberg theologians, in October 1533, did not comment on the words of absolution. Of course, it would be unwise to suppose that Dietrich's perspicacity with respect to Osiander's critique exceeded that of the theologians. Instead, one should critically examine the historical context that frames Luther and Melanchthon's letter of 18 April 1533 and the judgment in October. Knowing apparently nothing in April about Osiander's specific objections to Nuremberg's formula of absolution, Luther and Melanchthon commented authoritatively on the equivalence between absolution and the preaching of the word—a doctrinal point corresponding closely to an important passage in Melanchthon's *Apology of the Augsburg Confession*.[65] After reading Osiander's apologia, which details the objections with exceptional clarity, the Wittenberg theologians, in all likelihood, concluded that they should nevertheless affirm unequivocally Luther and Melanchthon's original position. To have done otherwise and acknowledged the legitimacy of even some of Osiander's contentions could have aggravated the theologians' disagreements with the south German Sacramentarians over absolution. These disagreements persisted in the early 1530s in cities like Frankfurt am Main, whose clergy still remained sympathetic toward Zwingli's teachings and drew support for their position from Martin Bucer's recent writings. Partly in response to the city's dismissal of a Lutheran preacher a few months earlier, Luther published in January 1533 an

---

63. Klaus, *Veit Dietrich* (see note 2), 156–158; these pages include the complete evaluation in Latin and a German translation.

64. Not having critically analyzed Osiander's sermon or Luther's *The Keys*, Klaus could not discern the precise reasons for Dietrich's wish for a complete halt in the use of general absolution (*Veit Dietrich* [see note 2], 158). Rittgers's claim that Dietrich, "in spite of his support of Osiander's position, […] did not subscribe to his colleague's theological justification for it" is inaccurate (Rittgers, *Reformation of the Keys* [see note 2], 158).

65. *BSELK*, 446.27–38 (German), 447.20–26 (Latin); *BC*, 193.39–40. The German version expresses the equivalence more sharply than the Latin.

open letter in which he not only rebuked Frankfurt's pastors for their dissimulation of their Zwinglian understanding of the Lord's Supper but also defended vigorously private confession, which, he claimed, they had rejected. In this defense, he affirmed tersely the doctrinal point that absolution amounts to "nothing other than God's Word."[66]

In March the pastors' response, an apologia, appeared. Regarding its tone and contents, the pastors had followed closely Bucer's advice, which they had received in a letter toward the end of February. Indeed, the apologia emanates "Bucer's spirit" to such a degree that contemporaries and some modern historians concluded that the Strasbourg reformer himself had written the apologia.[67] Significantly, the pastors drew on the language in Luther's open letter to describe the Sacramentarians' understanding of absolution in terms quite similar to those that Luther and Melanchthon would soon use in their letter to Nuremberg's magistrates. The response describes absolution as the proclaiming, or preaching, of God's grace.[68] Moreover, to underscore this conviction, the authors pointed to the rite of general absolution used in worship services in Frankfurt. At the end of sermons, pastors "inform the faithful from God's Word that their sins are forgiven, and the unfaithful [that their sins are] retained."[69] Walther Köhler, who regarded Bucer as the author, held that the pamphlet and Bucer's slightly earlier letter to Frankfurt's ministry were a conciliatory gambit for the purpose of nudging the Lutherans and the south Ger-

---

66. WA 30/III:565.15–570.40 (defense of private confession), (quote in Martin Luther, "An Open Letter to Those in Frankfurt on the Main, 1533," trans. Jon D. Vieker, *Concordia Journal* 16 [October 1990]: 333–351, here 345). Rittgers does not mention the open letter, which clearly bears upon Luther's understanding of absolution in 1533 (Rittgers, *Reformation of the Keys* [see note 2]).

67. Peter Fabisch's careful comparison of the apologia, the letter to Frankfurt's pastors, and Bucer's "Ein Bericht, was zu Frankfurt am Main geleret" from 1533 casts significant doubt on Bucer's authorship of the apologia. See *MBDS* 4:465–475, quote on 467 (introduction by P[eter] Fabisch). Cf. *MBDS* 4:309 (introduction by Robert Stupperich). I am most grateful to the anonymous reviewer who called to my attention Fabisch's discussion.

68. The similarity is striking. The pastors wrote, "So leren wir von der Absolution oder entbindung der sünd, das dieselbig, in kürtz davon zu reden, die verkündigung der gnad Gottes oder des Euangelii sei, es geschehe gleich der menge oder eim und etlichen, das mann mit den schlüsseln des Götlichen worts den glaubigen verkündigt vergebung ihrer sünd, den unglaubigen, das der zorn Gottes über ihn bleib, warum solten wir dann die predig der gnad Gottes (das ist) die Absolution, verachten?" (*MBDS* 4:317.11–17). Luther and Melanchthon stated, "Denn auch die predig des heiligen Euangelii selb ist im grund vnd eigentlich ein absolutio, darinn vergebung der sunden verkundiget wirt vielen personen in gemein vnd offentlich oder einer personen allein offentlich oder Heimlich." (WA Br 6:454.6–9 [no. 2010, 18 April 1533]).

69. *MBDS* 4:317.22–24.

mans to resolve their theological differences over the Lord's Supper and absolution.[70] The Strasbourg reformer had been trying to achieve a compromise since 1530, but success would arrive only in 1536 with the signing of the Wittenberg Concord. Although no negotiations occurred in 1533, Melanchthon was contemplating their resumption. On the issue of absolution, an apologia that strongly reflects Bucer's spirit could serve well as a stepping stone toward compromise as long as the rite of general absolution in south German cities did not become a new bone of contention.[71] But if Osiander's trenchant criticism of Nuremberg's formula of absolution began to circulate more widely, then the likelihood of difficulties in future negotiations would increase. Consequently, one plausible explanation for the apparent decision by the Wittenberg theologians, in October 1533, to withhold comment on Osiander's criticism is that they wanted to forestall its dissemination.[72] When Dietrich hastily prepared his evaluation in early September 1536, however, similar considerations did not weigh on him. The Wittenberg Concord had been signed three months earlier.

On 19 October 1536, Dietrich's close friend Melanchthon, who was returning to Wittenberg after a month-long sojourn in southwest Germany, arrived in Nuremberg for a short visit. Immediately drawn into the controversy, he

---

70. Walther Köhler, *Zwingli und Luther: Ihr Streit über das Abendmahl nach seinen politischen und religiösen Beziehungen*, vol. 2, *Vom Beginn der Marburger Verhandlungen 1529 bis zum Abschluß der Wittenberger Konkordie von 1536*, ed. Ernst Kohlmeyer and Heinrich Bornkamm (1953; repr., Gütersloh: Gütersloher Verlagshaus, 2017), 298–302. Burnett does not discuss the letter and pamphlet (Amy Nelson Burnett, *The Yoke of Christ: Martin Bucer and Christian Discipline* [Kirksville, MO: Northeast Missouri State University, 1994]).

71. Besides Frankfurt am Main, other south German cities used the rite of general absolution; for Strasbourg, see François Wendel, *L'église de Strasbourg, sa constitution et son organisation, 1532–1535* (Paris: Presses universitaires de France, 1942), 209. In a discussion with Luther a few days before the signing of the Wittenberg Concord, Bucer mentioned the practice. South German cities could not compel a believer to confess privately before receiving the Eucharist, he reportedly explained, "weil wir kein wort haben von solcher besonderer absolution, denn man vns der absolution halben entgegen werffen mäg, Wir hören predig, werden vnserer sünden vermanet, beichten die gott vnd begeren gnad, So absoluiert jhr vns in der gemeinen absolution, der selbigen glauben wir, also seind wir dann absoluiert vnd getröstet. Also hören wir auch im predigen allen vndericht des glaubens, fehlet vns etwas daruber, wöllen wir selbst kommen, raht vnd trost süchen" (*MBDS* 6/I:158.21–159.6). On the possibility of resuming negotiations, see Martin Brecht, *Martin Luther*, vol. 3, *The Preservation of the Church, 1532–1546*, trans. James L. Schaaf (Minneapolis, MN: Fortress Press, 1993), 42.

72. Cf. Rittgers, *Reformation of the Keys* (see note 2), 159. It is worth noting that the section of the Wittenberg Concord on absolution makes no reference to the utterance of the absolver (*MBDS* 6/I:132.14–20 [Latin]; 133.16–23 [German]; Burnett, *The Yoke of Christ* [see note 70], 87–88). Another plausible but less interesting explanation for the absent comment is that the Wittenberg reformers did not read Osiander's apologia in its entirety.

heard one of Osiander's sermons and had several conversations with him. On 22 October, Melanchthon gave the magistrates his report, in which he noted with relief that Osiander now acknowledged that the preaching of the word can absolve the sins of some listeners. But the rest of the report's discussion of Osiander focuses heavily on the formula of absolution. Melanchthon contended vigorously that the gospel's promise implies the same condition, namely repentance and faith [*conditio poenitntiae et fidei*], that the formula expresses explicitly; thus, he continued, the conditional formula absolves the sins of those who have true faith. In brief, Melanchthon rejected Osiander's claim that the formula of absolution is a legerdemain (*gauklerey*).[73] Conceding, however, that one could not dismiss Osiander's objection to administering general absolution to the undeserving, he also urged the magistrates to consider the possible benefits of changing the formula. The report ends with ten detailed questions in Latin about absolution; Melanchthon urged the magistrates to send them, plus Osiander's sermon and the formula, to Lutheran theologians for some definitive answers. They, he assumed confidently, would confirm his arguments and undermine Osiander's.[74] But just as important as the contents is the report's stark contrast with the Wittenberg theologians' astonishing silence about the formula of absolution three years earlier. Now Melanchthon addressed the issue head on. According to the editors of Osiander's sermon, the Nuremberg theologian had finally succeeded in initiating a thorough theological discussion of his criticisms of general absolution.[75]

---

73. *MBW* T7:258.25–259.54 (no. 1799, 22 October 1536). Melanchthon's use of the term *gauklerey* is an unmistakable reference to Osiander's argument that the absolver does not know if he binds or looses, in which variations of the term appear six times (*OGA* 6:182.35–183.22).

74. *MBW* T7:259.55–59, 259.67–73, 260.82–96 (no. 1799, 22 October 1536); Klaus, *Veit Dietrich* (see note 2), 159–160. Cf. Rittgers, *Reformation of the Keys* (see note 2), 163–64.

75. *OGA* 6:169. See also Martens, "'Ein uberaus grosser unterschiedt'" (see note 2), 160–161; Stollberg, "Osiander und der Nürnberger Absolutionsstreit" (see note 3), 163. The discussion stuttered, however. In mid-November the magistrates asked Wittenberg's theology faculty to evaluate Osiander's sermon and to answer the ten questions that Melanchthon had given them (WA Br 7:590.25–37 [no. 3104, 13 November 1536]). Responding in late November, Luther and his colleagues affirmed that the sermon, the word of God, can effect absolution in a listener. On this point, however, Melanchthon and Osiander had already agreed in October (*MBW* T7:258.25–29 [no. 1799, 22 October 1536]). Regarding specifically general absolution and Osiander's objections to it, the letter states that a "somewhat longer" report is necessary, which the theologians would write when they had an opportunity (WA Br 7:594.11–595.26 [no. 3108, 28 November 1536]). But they were already deeply involved in the preparations for a possible church council in Mantua in the spring of 1537, and the report never materialized. See Rittgers, *Reformation of the Keys* (see note 2), 164; Klaus, *Veit Dietrich* (see note 2), 161–162.

The controversy ended in 1540, after Luther and Melanchthon had each written a new formula of general absolution for use in Nuremberg.[76] Although the proximate cause for their doing so is not entirely clear, the current formula pleased neither of them, Melanchthon avowed in a letter to Dietrich, because of its foolish wording.[77] Their displeasure amounted in effect to an acknowledgment of the validity of Osiander's objection that the utterance of a condition during general absolution means that the pastor knows not the effect of his absolution. Thus, the new formulas composed by Luther and Melanchthon are nothing less than attempts to expunge all references to a condition. In this regard, Melanchthon's effort falls noticeably short, for its prolixity, which Luther criticized, cannot mask the fact that a key passage still bears a whiff of a condition:[78] "So I admonish all of you to amend yourselves, as Christ the Lord himself preached and commanded you to amend yourselves. And to all who fear God's wrath and earnestly seek to amend themselves, and ask him for forgiveness of their sins, I proclaim forgiveness of their sins and loose them."[79] Only those who, fearing God's punishment, earnestly want to reform themselves can receive forgiveness. But Luther's succinct statement, just one-fourth as long as his colleague's, does not include such a condition, but refers only to faith and repentance:

> Dear friends, because we are mortal and at no time safe from death, humble yourselves before God, and confess in your hearts, that all we poor sinners need his grace and forgiveness at all times.
> And if God would call one of you today or tomorrow from this vale of tears, so I, as a pastor (preacher) by his command, absolve of all sins all who are here now and hear God's Word and, with proper sorrow of their sin, believe in our

---

76. Klaus's claim that the absolution controversy began again to flare up in 1539 is untenable (Klaus, *Veit Dietrich* [see note 2], 163–164; see also Seebaß, *Osiander* [see note 3], 260). Rittgers concurred, but, unlike Seebaß, stated unwarrantedly that "Dietrich and Osiander did apparently disagree over the wording of the Nürnberg formula for general absolution" (Rittgers, *Reformation of the Keys* [see note 2], 277n1). Rittgers's work also wrongly states that the city's carnival parade, the *Schembartlauf*, that mocked Osiander for his objections to general absolution occurred in 1539. The error is partly understandable because the caption of one of the late sixteenth-century illustrations of the parade reproduced in the work begins with the words "Anno 1539" (Rittgers, *Reformation of the Keys* [see note 2], 164–169). As explained in Klaus, the correct year is 1541 (Klaus, *Veit Dietrich* [see note 2], 166–167).

77. *MBW* T9:111.10–11 (no. 2369, 12 February 1540).

78. *MBW* T9:117.15–16 (no. 2373, 15 February 1540) (Luther's criticism).

79. *MBW* T9:118.11–15 (no. 2374, 15 February 1540).

Lord Jesus Christ, in the name of the Father, Son, and Holy Spirit, amen. Go forth in peace, be it to live or die.[80]

Whether Osiander ever saw the two formulas, which were never used in Nuremberg's church services, is not known.

IV.

The present article has outlined a complex triangular connection between Luther's *The Keys* and Osiander's criticisms of Nuremberg's rite of general absolution. One leg of the triangle is that Osiander borrowed heavily from Luther's notion of the erring key (*clavis errans*), or conditional key (*conditionalis clavis*), to argue that the words spoken during the rite vitiated its effectiveness. The formula of general absolution uttered by an evangelical preacher, whose voice one should believe as if it were God's, cannot express the utmost certainty of absolution, Osiander insisted, if the formula includes conditions. Churchgoers earnestly seeking spiritual comfort through the rite would not know if they had received absolution and would thus be left in spiritual danger. Osiander also warned of dire consequences for the preacher, who, by verbalizing uncertainty, made God a liar. In his meeting with Melanchthon in October 1536, Osiander tacitly dropped his point about the churchgoers' uncertainty when he conceded that the public preaching of the gospel can indeed absolve the sins of some listeners. His concern about the preacher remained, however.

The triangle's second leg is that Veit Dietrich flagged this concern for special attention. In his evaluation of Osiander's sermon from 1536, he praised specifically the argument that the pastor who uses Nuremberg's formula of general absolution does not know what his words accomplish, which leads to various abuses. Dietrich undoubtedly defended his judgment of the argument in October during Melanchthon's visit, which at least partly explains why Melanchthon's report to the magistrates focuses primarily on the formula of absolution. The third leg is Luther's and Melanchthon's composing of formulas of general absolution that were more or less free of conditions. In addition to marking the Wittenberg reformers' implicit recognition, after seven years, of the potency of some of Osiander's criticisms of Nuremberg's rite, the new formulas indicate also that Luther's *The Keys*, a searing polemical attack on the papacy's teachings

---

80. WA Br 12:299 (no. 4275, 15 February 1540). Cf., Klaus, *Veit Dietrich* (see note 2), 164–166.

concerning the sacrament of penance, had become also a touchstone for testing the congruity between the doctrine and practice of Lutheran absolution.

This last point suggests that the full historical significance of *The Keys* and the Nuremberg absolution controversy may not yet have received its proper due. Luther's and Melanchthon's concerns in the 1530s about preventing the unworthy from partaking in the Lord's Supper are the pivotal issue here. The Augsburg Confession is important in this regard, for Article 12 refers to the good fruits of repentance, namely that the recipients of private absolution would become less sinful and exhibit moral improvement.[81] Article 25 states that Lutheran preachers administer communion only to those who have been examined and have received absolution.[82] Given that the confessor could not reasonably scrutinize anyone's faith or repentance, the examination of the confessant's intentions regarding amendment provided the most practical means of assessing moral worthiness and would remind the confessant that good fruits should follow absolution—the claim in Article 12.[83]

The importance of the examination and amendment hovered in the background of the Nuremberg absolution controversy. Luther suggested in his open letter to the clergy of Frankfurt am Main in 1533 that confessants needed to indicate in the examination during private confession whether they intended to forsake the sins they repeatedly committed.[84] In October 1536, Melanchthon mulled over the merits of having the confessant affirm his or her intention not to sin; of the ten questions at the end of his report to Nuremberg's magistrates, the eighth asks "[w]hether it is necessary for someone who desires private absolution to promise beforehand to amend his ways?"[85] With his formula from

---

81. *BSELK* 106.10–12 (German), 107.8–9 (Latin); *BC* 44.6, 45.6. The *Apology of the Augsburg Confession* expands on the tenet (*BSELK* 489.6–8, 507.25–509.9; *BC* 209.131, 217–218.174).

82. Luther introduced a precommunion examination in Wittenberg in 1524 and occasionally referred to examinations within private confessions and private confessions within examinations. He regarded the examination as a means to determine whether prospective communicants understood the most basic evangelical teachings about faith and communion. See Burnett, *Debating the Sacraments* (see note 9), 250–254; Brecht, *Martin Luther* (see note 25), vol. 2, 125; Bezzel, *Frei zum Eingeständnis* (see note 32), 12–14; Aland, "Die Privatbeichte im Luthertum" (see note 11), 463–465; Rittgers, *Reformation of the Keys* (see note 2), 82–83; WA 19:520.24–28; 521.10–12; WA 26:220.7–9. Only in the Augsburg Confession, however, were examinations and private confessions formally tied together (*BSELK* 146.25–27 [German], 147.21–22 [Latin]; *BC* 72.1, 73.1).

83. In other words, the examination's purpose would stretch beyond its original function of confirming that the confessant rightly understood the nature of the Sacrament.

84. WA 30/III:567.10–13, 567.21–24.

85. The eighth question, together with the fifth and seventh—"[w]hether the condition

1540, Melanchthon suggested that only those who earnestly want to amend themselves would benefit from general absolution. But Luther apparently thought that mention in the formula of any condition about betterment would be inadmissible.

It is perhaps significant that the first post-Augsburg Confession church ordinance that explicitly describes the examination as a means of determining the confessant's intention to amend himself or herself appeared in Brandenburg in 1540—less than a year after the conclusion of the Nuremberg absolution controversy. Luther, Melanchthon, and Justus Jonas had critically examined drafts in 1539 and given their approval.[86] Other church ordinances with similar descriptions followed after 1555.[87] But the authors of the church ordinances and liturgical agendas did not compose formulas of absolution that reflect strongly the importance of the examination and warn emphatically that forgiveness depends on the sincerity of the confessant's intention.[88] The pastor's words of

---

of faith and sorrow makes either general or private absolution uncertain?" and "[w]hether the power of the keys is rendered useless if the servant does not distinguish with certainty between whom he should bind or loose?"—relates most closely to Osiander's contention that the preacher who utters Nuremberg's formula of general absolution does not know if his words have any effect (*MBW* T7:260.89–93 [no. 1799, 22 October 1536]). The translations are from Rittgers, *Reformation of the Keys* (see note 2), 275n146.

86. Emil Sehling, ed., *Die evangelischen Kirchenordnungen des XVI. Jahrhunderts*, vol. 3, *Die Mark Brandenburg, die Markgrafenthümer Oberlausitz und Niederlausitz, Schlesien* (Leipzig: O. R. Reisland, 1909), 6, 50, 60, 61. The church ordinance of 1535 for Pomerania that Johannes Bugenhagen prepared lacks a similar description (Sehling, ed., *Die evangelischen Kirchenordnungen des XVI. Jahrhunderts*, vol. 4, *Das Herzogthum Preussen, Polen, die ehemals polnischen Landestheile des Königreichs Preussen, das Herzogthum Pommern* [Leipzig: O. R. Reisland, 1911], 330). There are references before 1530 to the willingness to amend oneself as a mark of one's worthiness to receive communion. See ducal Prussia's church ordinance of 1525 in Sehling, *Die evangelischen Kirchenordnungen des XVI. Jahrhunderts*, vol. 4 (see above), 36. Luther's so-called "Exhortation to the Communicants," an enclosure to his letter to Nikolaus Hausmann, includes a similar reference (WA 19:47; WA Br 3:463.23–30 [no. 847, 26 March 1525]). However, the letter and enclosure were first published in 1565 (WA Br 14:581).

87. See, for example, the Württemberg church ordinance of 1559 in August Ludwig Reyscher, *Vollständige, historisch und kritisch bearbeitete Sammlung der württembergischen Gesetze*, vol. 8 (Stuttgart, 1834), 192–193. In Albertine Saxony, the description of the examination evolved from the so-called Celle church ordinance of 1545 (named after the Cistercian monastery in Altzella) to electoral Saxony's church ordinances of 1557 and 1580 (Emil Sehling, ed., *Die evangelischen Kirchenordnungen des XVI. Jahrhunderts*, vol. 1, *Sachsen und Thüringen, nebst angrenzenden Gebieten: Erste Hälfte* [Leipzig: O. R. Reisland, 1902], 297, 318, 428).

88. A comprehensive account of the formulas of absolution used after 1540 lies beyond the scope of the present article. In general, however, a small number of formulas appear repeatedly. First, many were modeled on Luther's formula of private absolution in the *Small Catechism* of 1529 (WA 30/I:387.4–8). They include the formulas in the lordship of Schön-

absolution, which one was to believe as if God were proclaiming them from heaven, silently skirted a condition for absolution that the confessant needed to satisfy. This silence is arguably an outcome of *The Keys* and the Nuremberg absolution controversy—a problematic outcome, for the formulas did not echo fully the descriptions of private confession and absolution in the church ordinances and thus could limit private confession's usefulness as an instrument of church discipline.

The silence did not sit well with some seventeenth- and early eighteenth-century theologians. Thus, Paul Tarnow, who taught at the university of Rostock from 1597 to 1633, unequivocally rejected the notion that the formula of absolution should not contain a condition. He maintained, "The formula of absolution and the [grammatical] mood should always be conditional. Because absolution belongs only to the sincerely repentant, who are known to God alone, the examiner of hearts, concerning which the pastor can only infer from the confessants' words and actions, and therefore private absolution cannot be formed and understood except conditionally, just as in public sermons the forgiveness of sins is announced and imparted to no one except the true be-

---

burg's church ordinance of 1542, in the Hochstift Merseburg's synodal instructions of 1545, in the Kurland's church ordinance of 1570, and in the county of Henneberg's church ordinance of 1582 (Sehling, *Die evangelischen Kirchenordnungen des XVI. Jahrhunderts*, vol. 1 [see note 87], 178, 269; Sehling, ed., *Die evangelischen Kirchenordnungen des XVI. Jahrhunderts*, vol. 2, *Sachsen und Thüringen, nebst angrenzenden Gebieten: Zweite Hälfte* [Leipzig: O. R. Reisland, 1904], 18, 172, 306; Sehling, ed., *Die evangelischen Kirchenordnungen des XVI. Jahrhunderts*, vol. 5, *Livland, Estland, Kurland, Mecklenburg, Freie Reichsstadt Lübeck mit Landgebiet und Gemeinschaftsamt Bergedorf, das Herzogthum Lauenburg mit dem Lande Hadeln, Hamburg mit Landgebiet* [Leipzig: O. R. Reisland, 1913], 84). Second, the formulas in Veit Dietrich's *Agendbüchlein* of 1545 and, with slight variations, two of the three formulas in the Electoral Palatine's church ordinance of 1556 appeared originally in Brandenburg-Nuremberg's church ordinance of 1533, which Brenz and Osiander had composed (Sehling, ed., *Die evangelischen Kirchenordnungen des XVI. Jahrhunderts*, vol. 11/1, *Bayern: Franken* [Tübingen: J. C. B. Mohr (Paul Siebeck), 1961], 187, 531; Sehling, ed., *Die evangelischen Kirchenordnungen des XVI. Jahrhunderts*, vol. 14, *Kurpfalz* [Tübingen: J. C. B. Mohr (Paul Siebeck), 1969], 146). Third, the formula in Mecklenburg's church ordinance of 1552 and one of the two formulas in the principality of Wolfenbüttel's church ordinance of 1569 appeared originally in Brandenburg's church ordinance of 1540 (Sehling, *Die evangelischen Kirchenordnungen des XVI. Jahrhunderts*, vol. 3 [see note 86], 62–63; Sehling, *Die evangelischen Kirchenordnungen des XVI. Jahrhunderts*, vol. 5 [see above], 207–208; Sehling, ed., *Die evangelischen Kirchenordnungen des XVI. Jahrhunderts*, vol. 6/1, *Niedersachsen: Die Welfischen Lande, Die Fürstentümer Wolfenbüttel und Lüneburg mit den Städten Braunschweig und Lüneburg* [Tübingen: J. C. B. Mohr (Paul Siebeck), 1955], 167). The formula in Frankfurt an der Oder's *Agenda* of 1600, however, clearly implies that absolution depends on satisfying the condition of amendment (Sehling, *Die evangelischen Kirchenordnungen des XVI. Jahrhunderts*, vol. 3 [see note 86], 214).

liever."⁸⁹ By the late seventeenth century, Philipp Jakob Spener was endorsing conditional absolution,⁹⁰ and German Pietist theologians, lamenting the shortcomings of private confession in the first half of the eighteenth century, were citing Tarnow approvingly.⁹¹ By fits and starts the issue of conditional absolution generated considerable discussion for well over two centuries. Luther's *The Keys* and the Nuremberg absolution controversy mark the beginning of this long-term engagement.

---

89. "Forma autem & modus semper sit conditionalis. quia enim solis verè poenitentibus tantùm impertiri potest & debet absolutio: quinam autem sint verè poenitentes, soli Deo cordium scrutatori certò constat, de quo minister ecclesiae tantum probabiliter ex dictis & factis confitentium colligit; ideoq[ue] non nisi conditionaliter formari intelligiq[ue] absolutio privata & peculiaris potest, quemadmodum etiam in communi & publica concione nemini nisi verè credenti remissio peccatorum annunciatur & imperitur." Paul Tarnow and Nicolaus Croll, *Disputatio de clavibus regni coelorum, solvente et ligante, eorumque usu legitimo; sub praesidio Pauli Tarnovii* [...] *respondebit M. Nicolaus Crollius* (Rostock, 1617), B3v–B4r; Paul Tarnow, *De sacrosancto ministerio libri III, in quibus de Ministero evangelico* [...] *agitur* (Rostock, 1623), 829. Regarding Tarnow's career, see Theodor Mahlmann, "Tarnow, Paul," in *Biographisch-Bibliographisches Kirchenlexikon*, vol. 11 (Herzberg: Verlag Traugott Bautz, 1996), col. 526–540.

90. See my discussion of Spener's letters before mid-1686 on conditional absolution in Terence McIntosh, "Pietists, Jurists, and the Early Enlightenment Critique of Private Confession in Lutheran Germany," *Modern Intellectual History* 12, no. 3 (2015): 627–656, here 633–636. For subsequent letters, see Philipp Jakob Spener, *Briefe aus der Dresdner Zeit 1686–1691*, 4 vols. (Tübingen: Mohr Siebeck, 2003–2017), vol. 2, *1688*, ed. Johannes Wallmann and Klaus vom Orde (2009), 83.149–84.196 (no. 19, 27 February 1688); 549.107–550.136 (no. 130, 1688); vol. 4, *1690–1691*, ed. Udo Sträter, Johannes Wallmann, and Klaus vom Orde (2017), 559.7–561.51 (no. 122, 1690); 583.274–278 (no. 125, 1690). See also Spener, *Theologische Bedencken und andere Briefliche Antworten* (Halle, 1700; reprinted Hildesheim: Olms, 1999), 1/II:208–210, 265–266; Spener, *Letzte Theologische Bedencken und andere Briefliche Antworten*, ed. Carl Hildebrand von Canstein (Halle; reprinted Hildesheim: Olms, 1987), 3:470 (23 November 1698).

91. Ernst Christian Philippi, *Wohl-gegründetes Zeugniß der Wahrheit von denen Vornemsten und gemeinesten Mängeln bey dem Beicht-Wesen in der Evangelischen Kirche, samt deroselben angewiesener höchst-nöthigen und auch gar wohl möglichen Verbesserung* [...] (Halle, 1720), 41–42. This includes a translation of the passage from Tarnow. See also [Anonymous], "Bedencken eines Evangelisch-Lutherischen Gottesgelehrten, über die von einer gewissen Obrigkeit an ihn erlassene Frage: Wie das Beichtwesen sowol, als die Ausspendung des heiligen Abendmahls dergestalt einzurichten und zu handeln sey, daß rechtschaffene Knechte GOTTes dabey ohne Quaal und Verletzung ihres Gewissens bestehen können?" *Theologia Pastoralis Practica 2, no. 15 (1740)*: 757–780, here 768.

Professor Terence McIntosh
Department of History
CB# 3195, Hamilton Hall
The University of North Carolina at Chapel Hill
Chapel Hill, NC 27599–3195
USA
terence_mcintosh@unc.edu

ZUSAMMENFASSUNG

Luthers 1530 veröffentlichte Schrift „Von den Schlüsseln" warf wichtige Fragen zur Sündenvergebung auf, die sich zentral auf das spätere Verständnis der Privatbeichte im deutschen Luthertum der frühen Neuzeit auswirkten. Diese Fragen traten erstmals in den 1530er Jahren in einer öffentlichen Kontroverse um die Absolution in Nürnberg zutage. Im Mittelpunkt dieser Kontroverse standen Andreas Osianders Bemühungen, den Ritus der Allgemeinen Beichte und Absolution in der Stadt abzuschaffen. Osiander wandte sich vor allem gegen die Formel der Generalabsolution, also die Worte, die der Pfarrer bei der Durchführung des Ritus sprach. Diese Formel enthielt mehrere Bedingungen, die die Gläubigen erfüllen mussten, damit ihre Sünden vergeben werden konnten. Im Gegensatz dazu behauptete Luther, der seit 1518 wiederholt betont hatte, dass ein Mensch, um Gottes Vergebung zu empfangen, den vom Priester oder Pfarrer gesprochenen Worten der Absolution festen Glauben schenken müsse, in „Von den Schlüsseln", dass die Vergebung der Sünden an keine anderen Bedingungen als den Glauben geknüpft sei. Diese beiden Argumente lieferten Osiander die Grundlage für seine Einwände gegen die Nürnberger Formel der Generalabsolution. Obwohl Luther und Melanchthon sich 1533 weigerten, die Gültigkeit von Osianders Einwänden anzuerkennen, taten sie dies 1540 stillschweigend. Offenbar war eine langfristige Folge dieser Situation, dass die lutherischen Territorialkirchen keine Absolutionsformeln verwendeten, die den Gläubigen Bedingungen auferlegten, was Theologen des 17. und frühen 18. Jahrhunderts wie Paul Tarnow und Philipp Jakob Spener verunsicherte.

Pictorial Renaissance Bookbindings and the Domestication of Lucas Cranach's Iconography: An Overlooked Medium of the German Reformation

By Daniel Gehrt

I. AN OVERLOOKED MEDIUM

In the sixteenth century, the Saxon university town of Wittenberg on the Elbe River was not only an innovative and flourishing center in the German Empire for church and educational reforms, book publishing, painting, and engraving, but also for bookbinding design.[1] The dynamic interplay between theologians, humanists, artists, form cutters, and bookbinders of the town catalyzed the nascent transition of bookbinding design in the early sixteenth century from a chiefly ornamental style to a distinctly pictorial style. It combined decorative Renaissance elements with biblical and mythical figures and scenes, well-known ancient personalities, allegorical personifications, portraits of contemporary reformers, scholars, and princes, and corresponding emblems and coats of arms. Many of the most widespread motifs were derived from the iconography that the innovative and highly versatile Renaissance court artist Lucas Cranach the Elder (1472–1553) had developed specifically to foster the Wittenberg Reformation.

It is well known that Cranach was crucial in giving a face to this profound and sweeping reform movement. As Andrew Pettegree recently pointed out, the artist's first groundbreaking advancement to this end comprised introducing pictorial title-page borders to publications of the prolific best-selling author Martin Luther (1483–1546) in the 1520s.[2] Within the large central space framed by these portrait format woodcuts, typesetters could display title, au-

---

1. I am deeply grateful to Steven Rhode and the two anonymous peer reviewers for helping me to enhance this paper. Abbreviations—CDA: Cranach Digital Archive: The Research Resource, https://lucascranach.org/; EBDB: Einbanddatenbank, https://www.hist-einband.de; FB Gotha: Forschungsbibliothek Gotha. VD16: Verzeichnis der im deutschen Sprachbereich erschienenen Drucke des 16. Jahrhunderts, https://www.bsb-muenchen.de/sammlungen/historische-drucke/recherche/vd-16/.

2. Andrew Pettegree, *Brand Luther: 1517, Printing, and the Making of the Reformation* (New York: Penguin Press, 2015), 143–163.

thor, and place and year of publication.³ The woodcuts were often used repeatedly for various writings and print editions. In the earliest borders, Cranach depicted various Renaissance motifs that generally did not exhibit any correlation to the content of the books. These included, for example, stags, lions, bears, dolphins, putti, architectural elements reminiscent of antiquity, and scenes from Greek mythology. As Pettegree argues, they nevertheless contributed to marketing the Wittenberg Reformation as a unique "brand." The decorative elements enhanced the aesthetic appeal of these mass-produced prints and subsequently promoted their sales. Unequivocally, Cranach and his workshop contributed to Wittenberg's upsurge in the sixteenth century as one of the leading print centers in Europe by also creating handsome graphics to illustrate the contents of books.⁴

In general, the popularization of graphic images in print had a significant effect on bookbinding design. In the 1520s, the practice of embossing leather bookbindings predominantly with figures and scenes modeled after graphics began to burgeon in central Europe.⁵ Like Cranach's title-page borders, the corresponding changes in technique and design were intended to economically enhance the aesthetic appeal of books and to thereby increase profits. Although overlooked by Pettegree and most historians, this practice was another development in the book trade with significance for the propagation of the Wittenberg Reformation. Humanistic values and interests as well as Renaissance design had provided the earliest impulses for the new pictorial program emerging in Basel, Prague, Cracow, Breslau, Augsburg, Nuremberg, Heidelberg, Wittenberg, Leipzig, Halle, and other printing centers. Later, however, the Reformation made an indelible impact on book cover design. Motifs of this sort were derived almost exclusively from Cranach's iconography.

Bringing figures and scenes to the fore constituted a turn from the chiefly decorative leather binding styles prevalent in the fifteenth century.⁶ Binders

---

3. Figure 6 is a later example of a pictorial title-page border designed in Cranach's workshop.

4. For a visual display of the rise of Wittenberg among the ranks of the print centers in Europe, see Graeme Kemp, "Off to the Bar Chart Race(s): the Largest Print Centres Through Time (1450–1650)," *VisualizingHistory* (blog), 18 March 2020, https://www.visualisings_leer;history.org/posts/the-largest-print-centres-through-time-1450–1650.

5. Konrad von Rabenau, "Reformation und Humanismus im Spiegel der Wittenberger Bucheinbände des 16. Jahrhunderts," in *Von der Macht der Bilder: Beiträge des CI.H.A.-Kolloquiums "Kunst und Reformation,"* ed. Ernst Ullmann (Leipzig: Karl-Marx-Universität, 1983), 319–328, here 320.

6. Edith Diehl, *Bookbinding: Its Background and Technique* (New York: Dover Publication, 1980), 1:137; Hellmuth Helwig, *Handbuch der Einbandkunde: Bio-Bibliographie der*

continued to impress dark, so-called "blind" lines into the leather with tools that were either heated or dabbed in ink to visually compartmentalize the cover. Instead of filling in these enclosed spaces solely with small stamps that could be impressed into the leather individually by hand, central European binders began to employ rolls and panels. The former—metal cylinders whose narrow edges were engraved from end to end with two or more motifs—could be rolled out to impress a continuous series of images in one pass. Panels were considerably larger than the stamps typical for the Middle Ages and required the use of a relief press. These metal plates were frequently engraved on both sides with corresponding motifs, for example, a prince's portrait and coat of arms or Christ's crucifixion and resurrection.[7] In many cases, the images were accompanied by inscriptions, which was relatively novel. Sometimes these texts identified the person or allegorical figure pictured, or they linked the image to a biblical verse, motto, or aphorism. Rolls, too, were frequently engraved with figures and scenes that related to each other and were occasionally furnished with short inscriptions. These new tools not only saved the artisans time and labor, but they were also instrumental in ushering in a predominantly pictorial design that became a hallmark of German Renaissance bookbinding.[8] Whereas in Catholic and iconoclastic Calvinist cultures ornamental decorations remained prevalent, this new style became especially pronounced in the Lu-

---

Buchbinder Europas bis etwa 1850; Topo-Bibliographie der Buchbinderei: Verzeichnis der Supralibros (Hamburg: Maximilian-Gesellschaft, 1953), 1:56–76.

7. Rabenau, "Reformation und Humanismus" (see note 5), 319; Konrad von Rabenau, "Die doppelseitig gravierte Einbandplatte der Reformationszeit," *Einbandforschung* 21 (2007): 35–50.

8. For examples, see the EBDB, the online database hosted by the State Library of Berlin for fifteenth- and sixteenth-century bookbinding in German speaking areas. See also Konrad Haebler, *Rollen- und Plattenstempel des XVI. Jahrhunderts*, 2 vols. (Leipzig: Otto Harrassowitz, 1928–1929), 1:1–10; Helwig, *Handbuch* (see note 6), 1:74–78; Max Joseph Husung, *Bucheinbände aus der Preussischen Staatsbibliothek zu Berlin in historischer Folge erläutert* (Leipzig: Hiersmann, 1925), 18–22. For an international comparison see, for example, Mirjam M. Foot, ed., *The Henry Davis Gift: A Collection of Bookbindings*, 3 vols. (London: British Library, 1978–2010); Otto Mazal, *Europäische Einbandkunst aus Mittelalter und Neuzeit: 270 Einbände der Österreichischen Nationalbibliothek* (Graz: Akademische Druck- und Verlagsanstalt, 1970); Otto Mazal, *Europäische Einbandkunst aus Mittelalter und Neuzeit: Ausstellung der Handschriften- und Inkunabelsammlung der Österreichischen Nationalbibliothek; Prunksaal, 22. Mai–26. Oktober 1990* (Graz: Akademische Druck- und Verlagsanstalt, 1990). For an overview of European and North American projects dedicated to cataloging bookbindings, see the Consortium of European Research Libraries (CERL), https://www.cerl.org/collaboration/work/binding/main. In other parts of Europe and, of course, in the iconoclastic Arab sphere, abstract or ornamental styles continued to predominate.

theran printing centers that dominated the book market.⁹ The Wittenberg bookbinders, organized into a guild since 1534, were pivotal in this change. They characteristically adorned covers with a central panel framed by rolls.¹⁰ This type of book cover design had structural parallels to the graphically embellished title pages of Wittenberg prints; both exhibited an outer pictorial framework and a dominant central focal point.

The relationship between graphics and bookbinding design has often been overlooked. In the first issue of the journal *Jahrbuch der Einbandkunst* (Yearbook of Bookbinding Art), published in 1927, two essays investigated how woodcuts produced by Cranach's workshop were adapted to rolls and panels.¹¹ Both focused on motifs that had emerged in connection with the Reformation, such as the portraits of Luther and Philip Melanchthon (1497–1560) or the visualization of theological teachings. These and similar essays have been seminal within the field of bookbinding research.¹² However, they have not cap-

---

9. See, for example, Ilse Schunke, *Die Einbände der Palatina in der Vatikanischen Bibliothek* (Leipzig: Insel-Verlag, 1943), esp. 1:58–73, 105–118.

10. The book cover shown in figures 3–4 represents a classical example of the "Wittenberg style." On this style, see Haebler, *Rollen- und Plattenstempel* (see note 8), 1:1–3; Helwig, *Handbuch* (see note 6), 1:74–75; Rabenau, "Reformation und Humanismus" (see note 5); Konrad von Rabenau, *Deutsche Bucheinbände der Renaissance um Jakob Krause, Hofbuchbinder des Kurfürsten August I. von Sachsen* (Brussels: Bibliotheca Wittockiana, 1994), section A of the unpaginated introduction; Konrad von Rabenau, "Wittenberger Einbandkunst im 16. Jahrhundert: Vier Beobachtungen," in *700 Jahre Wittenberg: Stadt—Universität—Reformation*, ed. Stefan Oehmig (Weimar: Verlag Hermann Böhlaus Nachfolger, 1995), 365–384, here 365–366; Konrad von Rabenau, "Leipziger Einbandkunst im 16. Jahrhundert," in *Das Gewand des Buches: Historische Bucheinbände aus den Beständen der Universitätsbibliothek Leipzig und des Deutschen Buch- und Schriftmuseums der Deutschen Bücherei Leipzig*, ed. Roland Jäger (Leipzig: Universitätsbibliothek, 2002), 26–41, here 32–36.

11. Hildegard Zimmermann, "Holzschnitte und Plattenstempel mit dem Bilde Luthers und ihre Beziehungen zur Werkstatt Cranachs," *Jahrbuch der Einbandkunst* 1 (1927): 112–121; Joseph Theele, "Die Spes-Platte der Meister IB und IP: Ein Beitrag zur Beziehung zwischen Graphik und Einbandkunst," *Jahrbuch der Einbandkunst* 1 (1927): 122–128, here 122–123.

12. The following studies represent the status of research in this field that has not yet begun to flourish: Regine Boeff, "'zum ansehen, zum zeugnis, zum gedechtnis, zum zeychen': Reformatorische Ikonographie auf den Büchern der Kölner Evangelischen Gemeindebibliothek und der Bibliothek des Stadtkirchenverbandes," in *"das auch die guten bücher behalten und nicht verloren warden": Die Evangelische Bibliothek in der Universitäts- und Stadtbibliothek Köln*, ed. Wolfgang Schmitz (Cologne: Universitäts- und Stadtbibliothek Köln, 2007), 139–183; Christian Herrmann, "Reformation als Motiv auf Bucheinbänden," *WLB-Forum* 19 (2017): 32–42; Christine Porr, *Die Historische Bibliothek in Quedlinburg und ihre Sammlung lutherisch geprägter Bucheinbände des 16. Jahrhunderts*, 2 vols., Diss. University of Western Australia 2017); Konrad von Rabenau, "Bildnisse von Philipp Melanchthon und Fürst Georg

tured the interest of such related disciplines as art, church, and media history.[13] Surprisingly, bindings have also been seriously neglected in book and material history.[14] Bookbinding research traditionally revolves around identifying workshops and reconstructing their repertoire of tools.[15] Representatives of this and other fields of history have, if at all, only marginally examined the significance of pictorial book covers as a powerful medium.[16] Relatively few attempts have been made to determine the provenance of various volumes and the intentions

---

von Anhalt auf den Büchern der Reformationszeit," *Dessauer Kalender* 42 (1998): 2–19; Rabenau, "Die doppelseitig gravierte Einbandplatte" (see note 7).

13. See Carl C. Christensen, *Princes and Propaganda: Electoral Saxon Art of the Reformation* (Kirksville, MO: Sixteenth Century Journal Publishing, 1992); Julia Carrasco, ed., *Bild und Botschaft: Cranach im Dienst von Hof und Reformation* (Heidelberg: Morio, 2015); Roland Enke, Katja Schneider, and Jutta Strehle, eds., *Lucas Cranach der Jüngere: Entdeckung eines Meisters* (Munich: Hirmer, 2015); Wolfgang Holler and Karin Kolb, eds., *Cranach in Weimar* (Dresden: Sandstein Verlag, 2015). For example, Christensen examines various forms of visual imagery, including paintings, engravings, medals, and sculpture, but not bookbindings in his highly insightful monograph on the propaganda of the Saxon electors in relation to the Reformation. In addition, book covers were not displayed among other media of the Reformation at the major exhibitions in Gotha, Kassel, and Wittenberg commemorating the 500th anniversary of the birth of Lucas Cranach the Younger in 2015 (Carrasco, Schneider, and Strehle). Thanks to the efforts of Matthias Hageböck, book conservator and author of several essays and articles pertaining to historical bookbinding, the cover of one book was presented at the local Cranach exhibition in Weimar (Holler, Kolb, 55, no. 30).

14. See David Pearson, "Bookbinding History and Sacred Cows," *The Library* 21 (2020): 498–517; Nicholas Pickwoad, "An Unused Resource: Bringing the Study of Bookbindings out of the Ghetto," in *Ambassadors of the Book*, ed. Raphaële Mouren (Berlin: De Gruyter Saur, 2012), 83–93.

15. See, for example, Pearson, "Bookbinding" (see note 14), 515. This focus can easily be observed in the central German journal for historical bookbinding research, *Einbandforschung*, published since 1997 in Berlin. The names of most bookbinders remain in obscurity.

16. Johannes Ficker, "Die Bildnisse Luthers aus der Zeit seins Lebens," *Lutherjahrbuch* 16 (1934): 103–161, here 104, 150–153, nos. 386–427. For the inattention to bookbindings in more recent handbooks and anthologies dealing expressly with mediality and the Reformation, see, for example, Johanna Haberer and Berndt Hamm, eds., *Medialität, Unmittelbarkeit, Präsenz: Die Nähe des Heils im Verständnis der Reformation* (Tübingen: Mohr Siebeck, 2012); Helga Schnabel-Schüle, ed., *Reformation: Historisch-kulturwissenschaftliches Handbuch* (Stuttgart: J. B. Metzler Verlag, 2017), 298–352; Klaus Fitschen, Marianne Schröter, Christopher Spehr, and Ernst-Joachim Waschke, eds., *Kulturelle Wirkungen der Reformation / Cultural Impact of the Reformation: Kongressdokumentation Lutherstadt Wittenberg August 2017*, 2 vols. (Leipzig: Evangelische Verlagsanstalt, 2019); Helmut Puff, Ulrike Strasser, and Christopher J. Wild, eds., *Cultures of Communication: Theologies of Media in Early Modern Europe and Beyond* (Toronto: University of Toronto Press, 2017). In Ficker's catalogue of contemporary portraits of Luther, he took all media into account, including bookbinding tools.

of their commissioners.¹⁷ More attention needs to be directed at the materiality, aesthetics, and symbolism of book covers and edges, and their relationship to the written contents they enclothe. Research into the origins and evolution of roll and panel motifs widely used by bookbinders is also a desideratum.¹⁸ In general, the process of adapting images and motifs created originally for paintings and engravings to a multitude of media merits more research. This necessity also holds true for the interplay between the various media.¹⁹ An intermedial, multidisciplinary, and hence more holistic approach is therefore crucial for fully exploiting the significance of pictorial bookbinding design.²⁰

In commemoration of the 550th anniversary of the birth of Lucas Cranach the Elder, this essay provides a broad spectrum of insights into the potential of this promising field of research. The first section examines an array of visual media the artist's chief patrons, the electors of Saxony, employed for their self-fashioning strategies in political and religious contexts. This comparison unequivocally reveals that the princes recognized at a very early stage the efficacy of transmitting Cranach's iconography to the newly burgeoning art of pictorial

---

17. For a recent study on church and educational history testifying to the importance of taking such inquiries into account, see Daniel Gehrt, "Die religiöse Erziehung Herzog Friedrich Wilhelms von Sachsen-Weimar im Spiegel seiner Bibliothek," *Zeitschrift für Thüringische Geschichte* 67 (2013): 75–115, here 77, 100, 105–107. This research reveals how specific portrait panels were used to gain influence on the religious education of a young prince caught in the middle of an inner-dynastic tug-of-war and to cultivate the memory of a deceased Saxon ruler who embodied the confessional stance of one of these two parties.

18. Nadezda Shevchenko, *Eine historische Anthropologie des Buches: Bücher in der preußischen Herzogsfamilie zur Zeit der Reformation* (Göttingen: Vandenhoeck & Ruprecht, 2007), 66–91. Shevchenko investigates several aspects of bookbindings in a section on materiality, including the significance of portrait panels, symbols of power, and the quality and value of materials for strategies of princely representation and the social distinction practiced by scholars when presenting princes copies of their writings.

19. Studies on intermediality in the Reformation and the early modern period have been recently published, but they, too, neglect book cover design. See, for example, Birgit Emich, "Bildlichkeit und Intermedialität in der Frühen Neuzeit: Eine interdisziplinäre Spurensuche," *Zeitschrift für Historische Forschung* 35 (2008), 31–56; Andrew Pettegree, *Reformation and the Culture of Persuasion* (Cambridge: Cambridge University Press, 2005); Louise Vermeersch, "Mennonite Martyrs and Multimedia: On the Form and Function of Intermediality in Reformation Communication," *Archive for Reformation History* 111 (2020): 194–216.

20. Mirjam M. Foot, ed., *Eloquent Witnesses: Bookbindings and their History: A Volume of Essays Dedicated to the Memory of Dr Phiroze Randeria* (London: Oak Knoll Press, 2004). In this anthology, Foot, one of the leading British researchers on historic bookbindings, proves what abundant fruits a broadened approach to this field can yield. The essays examine various social and economic issues as well as aspects related to educational history and material culture. However, they make little or no reference to pictorial bookbindings of the Renaissance and Reformation.

bookbinding design. They not only had portrait panels of themselves produced, but also of Luther and later of Melanchthon as the magisterial reformers at their university. Such initiatives quickly triggered a self-propelled dissemination of similar images through book covers, including those that Cranach created independently of the Saxon court. Capitalizing on this and other media led to the widespread popularization and domestication of Cranach's iconography. This phenomenon is explored in the second section. The third section pursues central questions of the transmission process itself. How, for example, was the iconography, originally created for paintings and engravings, scaled down to the limited space of embossing tools? How was it adapted to the specifications and design trends of this visual medium? What did motifs or elements of compositions convey when they were placed into new frameworks and constellations or furnished with new inscriptions? The study concludes with general observations on the mediality of pictorial bookbindings.

II. THE MULTIMEDIA PORTRAIT STRATEGY OF THE SAXON ELECTORS

In 1502, Elector Frederick III of Saxony, called the Wise (1463–1525), founded the University of Wittenberg and endowed it ten years later with an extensive library, the so-called Bibliotheca Electoralis.[21] These were two of many ambitious projects aimed at transforming the town that he had chosen as his primary seat of power into a political, religious, educational, and cultural hub in central Germany.[22] In addition, he had the court palace in Wittenberg magnificently rebuilt from 1490 to 1515. The church, forming the north wing of the palace complex, was designed by one of the leading late Gothic architects of the time, Conrad Pflüger (ca. 1450–1506/7). It was furnished with prestigious altarpieces and sculptures from such renowned masters as Albrecht Dürer (1471–1528), Hans Burgkmair (1473–1531), Tilman Riemenschneider (ca. 1460–1531), and Conrad Meit (1470/85–1550/51).[23] The palace church

---

21. Ernst Hildebrandt, "Die kurfürstliche Schloß- und Universitätsbibliothek zu Wittenberg 1512–1547: Beiträge zu ihrer Geschichte," *Zeitschrift für Buchkunde* 2 (1925): 34–42, 109–129, 157–188; Sachiko Kusukawa, *A Wittenberg University Library Catalogue of 1536* (Cambridge: LP Publications, 1995).

22. Heiner Lück, "Wittenberg," in *Handbuch kultureller Zentren der Frühen Neuzeit*, ed. Wolfgang Adam and Siegrid Westphal (Berlin: De Gruyter, 2012), 3:2201–2248, here 2206.

23. On these and other forms of Frederick's patronage of the arts, see Christensen, *Princes* (see note 13), 5–7.

housed the elector's renowned collection of over nineteen thousand holy relics, attracting droves of pilgrims from near and far.[24] These institutions, grand architectural works, and extraordinary collections symbolically communicated the elector's rank, power, and affluence as well as his generosity, piety, and patronage of the arts, scholarship, and learning.

In 1505, the thirty-three-year-old artist and entrepreneur Lucas Cranach became a key protagonist in this flourishing environment. He had lived and worked in Vienna for three years before Frederick persuaded him to become his court artist in Wittenberg. Among his multifarious obligations and private business activities, Cranach was responsible for the portraiture of the elector. He designed images that could be broadly disseminated through various visual media. The earliest known portraits of this kind originated in 1507. In this year, Emperor Maximilian I (1459–1519) appointed Frederick imperial general governor (*Reichsgeneralstatthalter* or *imperii locum tenens generalis*) before leaving for Italy. The Saxon prince thus became the official representative of the emperor during Maximilian's absence. To visually demonstrate his advancement in power, Frederick had medals and coins with his profile bust and new title minted (fig. 1).[25] Unlike earlier portraits of Frederick created by other artists, Cranach did not depict the elector with his hair falling freely to his shoulders. Instead, it was bound in a wire mesh calotte.[26] Frederick had silver and gold medals with this image repeatedly minted until the death of Emperor Maximilian I in 1519. He appeared similarly in 1509 in the copperplate engraving on the title page of the illustrated catalog of relics displayed in the palace church in Wittenberg and in several paintings and graphics.[27] In this portraiture Cranach did not strive to produce a realistic likeness of his subject. Instead, he reduced the individual physiognomy to its essential features and

---

24. Stefan Laube, *Von der Reliquie zum Ding: Heiliger Ort—Wunderkammer—Museum* (Berlin: Akademieverlag, 2011), 199–264.

25. Paul Grotemeyer, "Die Statthaltermedaillen des Kurfürsten Friedrich des Weisen von Sachsen," *Münchner Jahrbuch der bildenden Kunst* 21 (1970): 143–166.

26. See the online overview of painted portraits of Elector Frederick, in Corpus Cranach, https://cranach.ub.uni-heidelberg.de/wiki/index.php/CorpusCranach:Friedrich_der_Weise.

27. For images of the relics, see the copperplates and woodcuts by Lucas Cranach the Elder in *Dye zaigung des hochlobwirdigen hailigthums der Stifftkirchen aller hailigen zu wittenburg* (Wittenberg: Symphorian Reinhart, 1509 [VD16 Z 250]). On this work, see Christensen, *Princes* (see note 13), 19–21; Ulinka Rublack, "Grapho-Relics: Lutheranism and the Materialization of the Word," in *Relics and Remains*, ed. Alexandra Walsham (Oxford: Oxford University Press, 2010), 144–166, here 145–147. On his image in paintings, the Dessau altarpiece painted around 1510 is a well-known case in point (CDA, https://lucascranach.org/DE_AGGD_7a).

sharply outlined these to endow the image with an emblematic character. He initially developed this unique style as court artist in Wittenberg and later applied it to other princes and the Wittenberg reformers, making it possible to easily recognize the person portrayed without the aid of inscriptions, coats of arms, attributes, or other symbolic forms of identification.[28] Once established, such stereotypes remained essentially unaltered for several years or decades and were used in all media in order to maintain a high level of recognizability. Other artists who produced works commissioned by Frederick also employed this stereotype. Miniatures of the elector painted in liturgical manuscripts in Nuremberg in 1507 and in Flanders around 1520 are prime examples of this.[29]

In 1522, five years after the outset of Luther's challenge to the papacy, Cranach developed a new image for Frederick.[30] The wire mesh calotte was replaced with a fashionable beret. A mustache complemented his beard. Whereas, in the previous image, Frederick had been endowed with a serene meditative countenance gazing off in the distance, in the new image he appeared stern and resolute with his eyes focused straight ahead. Moreover, he no longer held a rosary in his hands—a devotional device that had become obsolete in Luther's new theology.[31] The Saxon electors continued to employ this image embody-

---

28. On this skillfully developed strategy for advancing the visual presence of the electors of Saxony, see Berthold Hinz, "Die Bildnisse der drei letzten Ernestinisch-Sächsischen Kurfürsten: Entdeckung und Gebrauch des öffentlichen Porträts," in *Lesarten der Geschichte: Ländliche Ordnungen und Geschlechterverhältnisse: Festschrift für Heide Wunder zum 65. Geburtstag*, ed. Jens Flemming (Kassel: Kassel University Press, 2004), 199–220, here 199–200; Hanne Kolind Poulsen, "Between Convention, Likeness and Iconicity: Cranach's Portraits and Luther's Thoughts on Images," in *Lucas Cranach d. Ä.: Zum 450. Todesjahr*, ed. Andreas Tacke (Leipzig: Evangelische Verlagsanstalt, 2007), 205–218, here 211, 214–216; Hanne Kolind Poulsen, "Cranachs Bildsprache und der neue lutherische Glaube," in *Bild und Botschaft: Cranach im Dienst von Hof und Reformation*, ed. Julia Carrasco (Heidelberg: Morio, 2015), 63–71. This phenomenon is discussed specifically for Frederick and his nephew John Frederick respectively in Andreas Tacke, "Marketing Frederick: Friedrich der Weise in der Bildenden Kunst seiner Zeit," in *Kurfürst Friedrich der Weise von Sachsen: Politik, Kultur und Reformation*, ed. Armin Kohnle, Uwe Schirmer, Heiner Lück, Margit Scholz, Thomas Seidel, and André Thieme (Leipzig: Steiner Verlag, 2015), 329–342; Edgar Bierende, "Demut und Bekenntnis—Cranachs Bildnisse von Kurfürst Johann Friedrich I. von Sachsen," in *Johann Friedrich I.—der lutherische Kurfürst*, ed. Volker Leppin, Georg Schmidt, and Sabine Wefers (Gütersloh: Gütersloher Verlagshaus, 2006), 327–357.

29. Irmgard Kratzsch, *Schätze der Buchmalerei: Aus der Handschriftensammlung der Thüringer Universitäts- und Landesbibliothek Jena* (Gera: Druckhaus Gera, 2001), 81–88, 98–104.

30. A painted portrait of Frederick in this fashion, dated 1522, was once part of the art collections of the Palace Museum of Gotha (CC-POR-160–009). See image and information under the URL: https://cranach.ub.uni-heidelberg.de/wiki/index.php/CorpusCranach:Friedrich_der_Weise. The painting has been missing since the Second World War.

31. Rachel King, "The Reformation of the Rosary Bead: Protestantism and the Perpetu-

ing boldness and power after Frederick's death in 1525. When Frederick's brother John assumed power, he had Cranach produce woodcuts of Frederick and himself in a very similar style.[32] When shown facing each other, at a fleeting glance they resemble a mirrored reflection.

This new image was part of a larger self-fashioning campaign. In 1522, Frederick and his brother John also issued a new motto for their dynasty.[33] Of those proposed by the court chaplain and secretary George Spalatin (1484–1545), the princes agreed upon the verse "Verbum Domini manet in aeternum" (The word of the Lord endures forever), derived from Isaiah 40:8 and I Peter 1:25. In and of itself, it was, of course, a statement to which all Christians would subscribe. At the same time, it implied that the word could be obscured. If this were the case, it had to be revealed anew. Moreover, selecting a verse focusing on the word, which Luther upheld as the decisive authority in all religious matters, was significant. In these implied senses, the motto affirmed the princes' commitment to the controversial reform movement of the Wittenberg professors. A colored pen drawing documenting the officially prescribed costumes worn at the electoral Saxon court in the winter of 1522 verifies that these allusions were intentional (fig. 2).[34] The motto was sewn in its abbreviated form "*VDMIÆ*" on the upper right sleeves of the garments. The text accompanying the drawing explains that the motto was used for the first

---

ation of the Amber Paternoster," in *Religious Materiality in the Early Modern World*, ed. Suzanna Ivanič and Andrew Morrall (Amsterdam: Amsterdam University Press, 2019), 194–210, here 195.

32. Printed in Max Geisberg, ed., *The German Single-Leaf Woodcut: 1500–1550* (New York: Hacker, 1974), 2:600, no. G.634 (Frederick) and 2:601, no. G.635 (John). See also Hinz, "Bildnisse" (see note 28), 212–213.

33. Christensen, *Princes* (see note 13), 28–29; Ingetraut Ludolphy, "VDMIAE: Ein Reim der Reformationszeit," *Jahrbuch der Hessischen Kirchengeschichtlichen Vereinigung* 33 (1982): 279–282; Ingetraut Ludolphy, *Friedrich der Weise: Kurfürst von Sachsen 1463–1525* (Göttingen: Vandenhoeck und Ruprecht, 1984), 383; Frederick John Stopp, "'Verbum Domini Manet in Aeternum' : The Dissemination of a Reformation Slogan, 1522–1904," in *Essays in German Language, Culture and Society,* ed. Siegbert Salomon Prawer, Richard Hinton Thomas, and Leonhard Forster (London: University of London, 1969), 123–135; Wilhelm Ernst Tentzel, *Sächsisches Medaillen-Cabinet/ Von Gedächtnüß-Müntzen und Schau-Pfenningen/ Welche Die Durchlauchtigsten Chur- und Fürsten zu Sachsen Ernestinisch- und Albertinischer Haupt-Linien seint zweyhundert Jahren haben prägen und verfertigen lassen* (Gotha: Christian Wermuth, 1705), 1:29–32.

34. "Diese Löbliche Chur: vnd Fursten zue Sachßen, haben zum ersten mahl inn dieser Kleidung diesen Rheim gefuhrt, VERBVM DOMINI MANET IN ÆTERNVM. Funff Jahr vor dieser Zeit, hadt ahngefangen zuschreiben vnd zu predigen der Ehrwurdige Herr Doctor Martinus Lutherus zu Wittenberg, und hadt wied[er] das heilige Göttliche wortt an tag bracht." FB Gotha, Chart. A 233, fol. 8r.

time in this winter and that five years ago, i. e., in 1517, Martin Luther began to write and preach and once again unveiled the divine word. The elector's representatives at the imperial diet convening in Nuremberg in the winter of 1522–1523 presumably wore these newly designed clothes. In the following years, the motto became the rallying cry of the Protestant imperial estates. For the Diet of Speyer in 1526, Elector John of Saxony and Landgrave Philip of Hesse had this phrase demonstratively sewn on the banner in front of their quarters and on the sleeves of the members of their entourages.[35]

No paintings or engravings of Frederick with this inscription are known to have been produced during his lifetime. However, the Saxon elector had a coin minted in Nuremberg bearing his newly created image on its obverse and the motto on the reverse.[36] This provides the most compelling proof that both elements arose in connection with each other. Between May 1522 and January 1523 over fifteen thousand schreckenbergers and approximately six hundred golden groschens were minted, securing a widespread circulation of the coin and the combination of text and image it bore. The gold-plated coins and those minted in pure gold may have been intended as diplomatic gifts for the imperial estates and their representatives at the aforementioned Diet of Nuremberg and for other influential members of society.[37]

Preceding this assembly, pressure from the emperor, the pope, and a powerful fraction of the estates was mounting against Frederick to take action against Luther as prescribed in the Edict of Worms.[38] Emperor Charles V (1500–1558) had issued this decree at his prerogative on 25 May 1521, declaring Luther a heretic and calling for his apprehension so that proceedings could be taken up against him. It also banned Luther's writings. At the same time, the emperor shied away from a head-to-head confrontation with Frederick. This allowed the Saxon elector to elusively thwart the edict's implementation. However, starting in early 1522, Duke George of Saxony (1471–1539) adamantly demanded the execution of the edict. For his own territory, he issued repressive measures against those abandoning their religious orders and casting aside their vows of celibacy to begin a life in wedlock as well as against others who were

---

35. Ludolphy, "VDMIAE" (see note 33).
36. Christensen, *Princes* (see note 13), 28–29; Sina Westphal, *Die Korrespondenz zwischen Kurfürst Friedrich dem Weisen von Sachsen und der Reichsstadt Nürnberg: Analyse und Edition* (Frankfurt am Main: Peter Lang, 2011), 134–142.
37. Tentzel, *Medaillen-Cabinet* (see note 33), 1:29–30.
38. On the following imperial politics, see Armin Kohnle, *Reichstag und Reformation: Kaiserliche und ständische Religionspolitik von den Anfängen der Causa Lutheri bis zum Nürnberger Religionsfrieden* (Gütersloh: Gütersloher Verlagshaus, 2001), 85–380.

publicly supporting evangelical preaching and liturgical practice. The political front spearheaded by George strove to incorporate the Edict of Worms into the recess of the Diet of Nuremberg (1522–1523) to better ensure its enforcement throughout the empire. Elector Frederick's new image and motto were apparently a response to this political challenge.

Duke George first achieved his goal at the Diet of Nuremberg in 1524. However, the state of affairs remained undulant in the following years. Whereas the estates promoting the church reform movement were granted concessions at the Diet of Speyer in 1526, a special committee constituted to resolve the problem of religious disunity drafted a proposal three years later to suspend these. This aroused the protest of six princes under the leadership of Elector John of Saxony and representatives of fourteen imperial cities.

Evidently in connection with the Diet of Speyer in 1529, John had portrait panels made to transmit Cranach's images of him and his brother and their dynastic motto through book covers (figs. 3 and 4).[39] The portrait panels of the two Saxon electors were framed within a Renaissance-style arch. The electorate and Saxon coat of arms were placed in the pendentives of the arch. In the panel depicting John, they are held by putti. The year 1529 was engraved directly below each portrait. This referred to the date both panels, likely two sides of one plate, were produced.[40] Inscriptions followed: Frederick's read "VERBVM DOMINI || MANET IN ETER[NVM]" and John's "IVSTVS QVASI LEO CO[N]FI||DENS ABSQ[VE] TERRO[RE] ERIT." The latter is the second half of Proverbs 28:1 which reads in full: "A wicked person flees though no one pursues, but a righteous person is as bold as a lion." More strikingly than the medal from 1522, the panel portraying John, especially juxtaposed to Frederick's, served to fashion him as a fearless and resolute champion of the Wittenberg Reformation. Presenting both brothers symbolized the continuity of this patronage and protection policy.

As the religious conflict escalated at the imperial level, negotiations to form a defensive military alliance of Protestant cities and territories and efforts to formulate a common confessional stance were intensified.[41] Faced with the imminent threat of the Ottoman Turks after they had besieged Vienna in the

---

39. For the panel portraying Frederick, see Haebler, *Rollen- und Plattenstempel* (see note 8), 1:188, no. III; EBDB p000319. For the panel portraying John, see Haebler, *Rollen- und Plattenstempel* (see note 8), 1:188, no. IV; EBDB p000317.

40. On double-sided plates with corresponding motifs, see Haebler, *Rollen- und Plattenstempel* (see note 8), 1:9; Helwig, *Handbuch* (see note 6), 1:75; Rabenau, "Die doppelseitig gravierte Einbandplatte" (see note 7).

41. Kohnle, *Reichstag* (see note 38), 381–394.

fall of 1529, Emperor Charles V reopened negotiations over the religious differences at the Diet of Augsburg in 1530. The princes of electoral Saxony, Hesse, Brandenburg-Ansbach, Brunswick-Lüneburg, and Anhalt and the imperial cities of Nuremberg and Reutlingen presented the emperor with a confessional statement on 25 June 1530, defending their protest in 1529.[42] This, the so-called "Augsburg Confession," became the consensual theological basis for the Protestant churches in Germany and the defensive military alliance of the Smalkaldic League chartered in 1531.

In the framework of the study at hand, three books using the portrait panels of the two Saxon electors could be identified in historical libraries in Gotha, Frankfurt am Main, and London.[43] Strikingly, all of them adorn copies of the first German version of the Augsburg Confession and the corresponding apology authorized by the confession's chief author, Philip Melanchthon.[44] Furthermore, all three were bound in dark brown calfskin and embossed identically by a bookbinder with the initials I. H. On the front and back cover, the portrait panels are framed by two rolls: the first is a biblical[45] and the second a putto roll.[46] Frederick's portrait was placed on the front and John's on the back. The viewer's attention is drawn immediately to the portraits due to their size, central position, and brilliance. In contrast to the rest of the embossing, both

---

42. Christensen, *Princes* (see note 13), 36–37. In connection with this diet, Elector John had a medal minted in 1530 that once again underscored the steadfastness of his dynasty. On the obverse side of the medal is a double profile of him and his son John Frederick. In the circumscription both are referred to as "EVANGE[LII] CONFESS[ORES] INVICTIS [SIMI]" (invincible confessors of the gospel). On the reverse of the medal, the Apostles Peter and John are depicted before the Jewish high priests. The circumscription reads "ET LOQVEBANTVR SERMONEM DEI CV[M] FIDVCIA." This statement is the last part of Acts 4:31, which reads in full: "After they prayed, the place where they were meeting was shaken, and they were all filled with the Holy Spirit and spoke the word of God boldly."

43. FB Gotha, Druck 8° 14; Johann Christian Senckenberg University Library in Frankfurt am Main, Einband-Slg. 575; British Library, C.48.d.2. For the description of the book cover in Gotha, see Kathrin Paasch, ed., *"… so über die massen sauber in rothen Leder eingebunden": Bucheinbände aus der Forschungsbibliothek Gotha* (Gotha: Forschungsbibliothek Gotha, 2010), 52–53, no. 20.

44. Philip Melanchthon, *Confessio Fidei exhibita inuictiss. Imp. Carolo V. Caesari Aug. in Comicijs Augustae, Anno M.D.XXX. Addita est Apologia Confessionis. Beide/ Deudsch vnd Latinisch* (Wittenberg: Georg Rhau, 1531 [VD16 C 4736]), parts III–IV. On this edition, see Helmut Claus, *Melanchthon-Bibliographie 1510–1560* (Gütersloh: Gütersloher Verlagshaus, 2014), 1:421–423.

45. "SALVATOR"—"PAVLVS"—Moses: "LEX ET PRO[PHETAE] VSQ[VE AD] IOAN[NEM BAPTISTAM]"—John the Baptist: "ECCE AGN[VS DEI]." Dated 1528. Haebler, *Rollen- und Plattenstempel* (see note 8), 2:4, no. 2; EBDB r000094.

46. EBDB r000091.

portraits and the two rosettes directly above and below them were impressed with gold leaf. This represents an early example of gold tooling in German bookbinding.[47]

Considering that the overwhelming majority of prints produced centuries ago have perished over time and that no modern databases exist for systematically searching for specific bookbindings worldwide, identifying three surviving copies suggests that a great number of copies were bound in like fashion. They were most likely commissioned by Elector John of Saxony to symbolically communicate his patronage of this confession and to politically endorse its authority. Just as covers fundamentally served to protect the body of the book from wear and damage, the Saxon electors portrayed on the covers guaranteed the integrity of the Augsburg Confession.

These handsome bindings were conspicuously ostentatious. Typically, dark brown calfskin and gold embossing were reserved for select volumes in distinguished libraries. Books in scholarly collections were generally bound in less costly material, such as vellum, parchment, pigskin, or sheepskin, and blind tooling was predominantly used.[48] If intended for princely libraries, no traces of such provenance can be found in the three existing volumes. In the seventeenth and eighteenth centuries, two were in the possession of influential bourgeois in the imperial town of Frankfurt am Main.[49] This finding gives some ground for speculation that these copies of the Augsburg Confession and Melanchthon's apology were part of a customized ready-bound stock produced to be sold at the Frankfurt book fair. At any rate, these bindings were designed to stand out in library collections of wealthy bourgeois and the nobility.

After John's death in 1532, his son John Frederick, later called the Magnanimous (1503–1554), became elector of Saxony. Cranach also created an iconic image of this prince. His beard and mustache resembled those in the images of his father and uncle. Like the earlier image of Frederick, he was endowed with a pious countenance. Instead of a wire mesh calotte, he was portrayed with short hair. The multimedia portrait strategy of the Saxon electors reached a new

---

47. See Diehl, *Bookbinding* (see note 6), 1:140. This technique became widespread in Germany first in the 1540s.

48. Holger Nickel: "Bucheinbände der Cranachzeit in der Dessauer Bibliothek," in *Cranach in Anhalt: Vom alten zum neuen Glauben*, ed. Norbert Michels (Petersberg: Imhof, 2015), 87–91, here 87–86.

49. The ex libris of the Frankfurt councilman Johann Maximilian Zum Jungen (1596–1649) is pasted to the inside front cover of one of these volumes (Johann Christian Senckenberg University Library in Frankfurt am Main, Einband-Slg. 575). The ex libris of the Frankfurt physician and book collector Georg Kloß (1787–1854) is pasted to the inside front cover of the other (British Library, C.48.d.2).

culmination point under his rule.[50] Alongside his political rival Emperor Charles V, he became the most frequently portrayed prince on German Renaissance book covers.[51]

This brief survey of the unprecedented multimedia portrait strategy of the Saxon electors presents just a few prominent examples. Similar efforts to gain such widespread visual presence are commonly associated with later centuries in which images could be reproduced more readily by technical means.[52] The Saxon electors repeatedly proved to be forerunners in this field. Frederick was, for example, one of the earliest Renaissance princes north of the Alps to skillfully implement medals as a means of disseminating his portrait with an unambiguous political message.[53] He was also innovative in fashioning himself as an extraordinarily pious prince through paintings and engravings. He commissioned numerous paintings in a stereotype composition, and his catalog of relics was the first of its kind to memorialize a ruler on the title page instead of depicting a patron saint.[54] John made further inroads by implementing broadsheet woodcuts and the relatively new medium of roll- and panel-tooled pictorial bookbindings to reach a broader group of recipients.[55] Unlike the costly medals and paintings reserved particularly for the nobility, famed men of erudition, and other influential members of society, these woodcuts and bookbindings were presumably not just intended as special gifts but also distributed on the open market.[56] They thus reached countless scholars, bourgeois, and other consumers, and extended the visual presence of the princes into private homes. John Frederick pressed further ahead by having diptychs of his father and uncle painted in a truly serial manner.[57] The emblematic ster-

---

50. For images of the prince in various media, see Michael Enterlein and Franz Nagel, "Katalog der Darstellungen Johann Friedrichs des Großmütigen," in *Verlust und Gewinn: Johann Friedrich I., Kurfürst von Sachsen*, ed. Joachim Bauer and Birgitt Hellman (Weimar: Hain Verlag, 2003), 119–292. The catalog is by no means exhaustive. It lists, for example, just one panel stamp (254–255, no. 4.1).

51. Haebler, *Rollen- und Plattenstempel* (see note 8), 2:444–447. Haebler identified well over thirty portrait panels for each.

52. Hinz, "Bildnisse" (see note 28), 220.

53. Grotemeyer, "Statthaltermedaillen" (see note 25), 157–158.

54. Rublack, "Grapho-Relics" (see note 27), 145–147.

55. Hinz, "Bildnisse" (see note 28), 212–213.

56. Grotemeyer, "Statthaltermedaillen" (see note 25), 157.

57. For printing and interpretion of these images, see Hinz, "Bildnisse" (see note 28), 213–216; Holler and Kolb, *Cranach* (see note 13), 109, no. 68; Christian Schuchardt, *Lucas Cranach des Älteren Leben und Werke* (Leipzig: Brockhaus, 1851), 1:88–90; Timo Trümper, "Inszenierungsstrategien der Ernestiner: Die Cranachs als Diener des Hofes," in *Bild und Botschaft: Cranach im Dienst von Hof und Reformation*, ed. Julia Carrasco (Heidelberg: Morio,

eotypes fabricated by Cranach facilitated such large-scale manual copying.[58] Through countless reproductions in various media the portraits of the Saxon princes became iconic.

III. DOMESTICATING LUTHERAN ICONOGRAPHY

Not only bookbinders commissioned by the electors of Saxony used panel stamps with portraits of territorial lords of this lineage. Others, notably adherents of the evangelical movement, were apt to replicate panels of the Saxon princes and their coats of arms for their own workshops. This led to a dramatic increase in the dissemination of these and other images, particularly into domestic domains.[59] This phenomenon can be lucidly exemplified by examining panels portraying John Frederick with the facial wound that he had sustained in the momentous defeat of the Protestant military defense alliance at the end of the Schmalkaldic War in 1547. Although the antagonists primarily pursued gains in political power, pamphlets manipulating the perception of military events often interpreted the war from a religious standpoint. With fierce partisanship, Protestants interpreted the emperor's contention with the Schmalkaldic League as a conspiracy in collaboration with the pope aimed at suppressing the "true religion." After capitulating, John Frederick was imprisoned, and he and his sons lost their entitlement to the electoral dignity connected with the duchy of Saxe-Wittenberg and a significant portion of their territory. In pamphlets, poems, folk songs, paintings, engravings, medals, and bookbinding tools of Protestant provenance, John Frederick was portrayed as a martyr.[60]

2015), 17–28, here 21–22. For the payment for this work on 10 May 1533, see Landesarchiv Thüringen—Hauptstaatsarchiv Weimar, Ernestinisches Gesamtarchiv, Reg. Bb 4361, fol. 44r, https://lucascranach.org/archival-documents/DE_ThHStAW_EGA_Reg-Bb_43 61_44r. After John Frederick's accession to power in 1532, he commissioned Cranach's workshop to paint sixty such diptychs as part of his campaign to legitimize his claim to the Saxon electorship that Emperor Charles V had not immediately acknowledged.

58. See, for example, Sabine Fastert, "Die Serienbildnisse aus der Cranach-Werkstatt: Eine medienkritische Reflexion," in *Lucas Cranach d. Ä.: Zum 450. Todesjahr*, ed. Andreas Tacke (Leipzig: Evangelische Verlagsanstalt, 2007), 135–157.

59. Adolf Schmidt, "Bildnisse auf deutschen Bucheinbänden des sechzehnten Jahrhunderts," *Jahrbuch der Einbandkunst* 4 (1937): 16–36, here 17.

60. Christensen, *Princes* (see note 13), 92–101; Daniel Gehrt, "Kurfürst Johann Friedrich I. und die ernestinische Konfessionspolitik zwischen 1548 und 1580," in Leppin, Schmidt, Wefers, *Johann Friedrich I.* (see note 28), 307–326, here 310–315; Daniel Gehrt, *Ernestinische Konfessionspolitik: Bekenntnisbildung, Herrschaftskonsolidierung und dynastische Identitätsstiftung vom Augsburger Interim 1548 bis zur Konkordienformel 1577* (Leipzig: Evan-

His war wound, a scar running across his left cheek, became a distinctive emblem—like the attribute of a saint—symbolizing the sacrifices he had made to champion a divine cause in the eyes of his sympathizers. Well over twenty panels of the stigmatized war hero with the inscription "Victus eras acie fidei constanti a tandem victorem ante homines fecit et ante Deum" (You who were conquered by the sword were nevertheless made victorious before men and God through steadfastness of faith) are known to have been used in various bookbinding workshops in southern and central Germany (fig. 5).[61] This specific text, with its unambiguous message, was transmitted together with John Frederick's portrait solely through book covers. They were thus an essential part of the masterful multimedia campaign of the German prince to capitalize on his own political losses. His initiative triggered bookbinders in Protestant towns to have similar panels made. This self-propelled dissemination process contributed significantly to the popularization of this image and the message it carried. Considering the many panels identifiable today, thousands of book covers must have been adorned with these texts and images, thus reaching an enormous audience. Preserved in countless private libraries, they served in the subsequent years, decades, and centuries to perpetuate John Frederick's memory and the dynastic myth of his own fashioning.

This is just one of numerous motifs created by Cranach, the dissemination of which developed its own momentum in bookbinding. Martin Luther's portrait, the most prolific iconic image of the Wittenberg Reformation, is another compelling example of this dynamic transmission process. Like the electors of Saxony, the earliest known portrait panel of Luther was engraved in 1529.[62] It was made for the workshop of the Wittenberg court bookbinder Joachim Linck.[63] The common date of origin is undoubtedly no mere coincidence. It suggests that all the panels were part of a larger strategy of Elector John to employ pictorial bookbinding design for his political and religious aims. By

---

gelische Verlagsanstalt, 2011), 75–77; Gabrielle Haug-Moritz, "Zur Konstruktion von Kriegsniederlagen in den frühneuzeitlichen Massenmedien—das Beispiel des Schmalkaldischen Krieges (1547–52)," in *Kriegsniederlagen: Erfahrungen und Erinnerungen*, ed. Horst Carl (Berlin: Akademie-Verlag, 2004), 345–374.

61. Haebler, *Rollen- und Plattenstempel* (see note 8), 2:446–447. Haebler identified a total of twenty-three panels with this inscription. The bookbinding database in Berlin (EBDB) provides information on seven such panels used at workshops in Augsburg (p001643), Halle (p001320), Jena (p000066), the Lower Rhine (p003410), Magdeburg (p000967), Wittenberg (p003607), and an unknown place (p003403).

62. Rabenau, "Bildnisse" (see note 12), 4.

63. On Linck's biography, see Fritz Juntke, "Die hallische Buchbinderfamilie Linck," *Gutenberg-Jahrbuch* 38 (1963): 301–308.

deliberately combining portrait panels, numerous book covers in the 1530s and the following decades expressed Luther's intrinsic relationship to the Saxon electors and Melanchthon.[64] The earliest known portrait panel of the latter was crafted in 1536 for Linck's workshop.[65] The inscription read: "CONATVR PARVAS ARTES || ORNARE MELAN[CHTHON] NEC TAMEN || HOC MERTIVM DVXERIS ESSE LEVE" (Melanchthon attempted to embellish the lesser arts. Nevertheless, you may not make light of this achievement). This was a reference to his exceptionally influential academic reforms, especially in the faculties of philosophy and theology, that greatly contributed to the Leucorea's success in becoming the most frequently attended university in the German Empire.[66] Linck had a corresponding panel of Luther made in the same year.[67] The inscription read: "ISTA REFERT VIVI FACIEM PI||CTVRA LVTHERI QVI PVRO || CHRISTI DOGMATA CORDE DO[CET], 1536" (This picture represents the appearance of the living Luther. He teaches the dogmas of Christ with a pure heart, 1536). This panel pair reflected the complementary interaction of the two professors. The efforts of the Saxon electors stimulated bookbinders in Protestant towns across the empire to have similar tools produced for their workshops. In effect, Luther and Melanchthon were depicted more frequently on sixteenth-century book covers than any other person.[68]

Cranach created numerous works in cooperation with the Wittenberg reformers.[69] A close and dynamic interaction can be assumed especially for those visually conveying theological thought, such as the artist's well-known allegorical composition generally referred to as "Law and Gospel."[70] Cranach developed several versions of this composition throughout his life, the earliest dating

---

64. See, for example, Rabenau, *Krause* (see note 10), no. 17, 32, 39; Rabenau, "Bildnisse" (see note 12), 8.

65. Haebler, *Rollen- und Plattenstempel* (see note 8), 1:266, no. XIV. See also Rabenau, *Krause* (see note 10), no. 17; Rabenau, "Bildnisse" (see note 12), 8.

66. Lück, "Wittenberg" (see note 22), 2211–2212.

67. Haebler, *Rollen- und Plattenstempel* (see note 8), 1:181, no. III.

68. Haebler, *Rollen- und Plattenstempel* (see note 8), 2:448–451. Haebler identified well over 110 portrait panels for each.

69. See, for example, Ikonka van Gülpen, *Der deutsche Humanismus und die frühe Reformations-Propaganda 1520–1526: Das Lutherporträt im Dienst der Bildpublizistik* (Hildesheim: Olms, 2002); Benjamin D. Spira, "Lucas Cranach, der Maler Luthers: Der Hofmaler und der Reformator—Bindung, Bilder und Bedeutung," in *Bild und Botschaft: Cranach im Dienst von Hof und Reformation*, ed. Julia Carrasco (Heidelberg: Morio, 2015), 51–62, here 52–56.

70. On the development of this composition and the myriad of versions that were produced, see Miriam Verena Fleck, *Ein tröstlich Gemelde: Die Glaubensallegorie "Gesetz und Gnade" in Europa zwischen Spätmittelalter und Früher Neuzeit* (Korb: Didymos-Verlag, 2010).

to the late 1520s. Typically, the picture is divided in the middle by a tree. Old Testament scenes and figures representing divine law and the old covenant are depicted to the left and those from the New Testament illustrating divine grace and the new covenant to the right. The intricate composition not only imparted Luther's understanding of righteousness through faith and grace alone (*sola fide* and *sola gratia*) but also his characteristic Christocentric theology. In addition, it represented the two most fundamental exegetical categories in the emerging hermeneutical culture of Lutheranism. This was clearly expressed in the earliest surviving guideline to studying theology, written by Melanchthon around 1529, and the humanistic *loci* or commonplace method that he had ingeniously adapted to biblical studies in 1520.[71] For this reason it is not surprising that variations of the composition were designed especially to illustrate title-page borders of Bibles, sermons collections, and Melanchthon's *Loci communes theologici*.[72] One of the most prominent examples embellished the second edition of Luther's Bible translation printed in 1541 (fig. 6).[73]

Like Cranach's iconic portraits, this allegorical composition was modified for various media, significantly advancing its popularization and domestication. Miriam Verena Fleck explored the origins and development of "Law and Gospel" and its transmission throughout Europe in twenty-seven different media ranging from wood, stone, and glazed stove tile reliefs over enamel and glass painting to tooled leather bookbindings.[74] By cataloging more than three hundred pertinent objects, she has made the entry of Cranach's iconography into the private domestic realm and everyday material culture of the sixteenth century tangibly clear. Cranach's composition was not only adapted to altar, epitaph, and wall paintings, and pulpit reliefs, tombs, stained glass windows, bells, and tapestries for churches, but also to a wide variety of household items, including ovens, chimneys, chests, ceramic tableware, and painted enamel plates. Variations of this motif could also be found in private libraries in the form of single-leaf engravings, book illustrations, or bookbinding rolls and panels. It

---

71. *Melanchthons Briefwechsel: Kritische und kommentierte Gesamtausgabe*, ed. Heinz Scheible (Stuttgart-Bad Canstatt: Fromman-Holzboog, 1977), vol. 1: *Regesten*, 363, no. 854; vol. 3: *Texte* (2000), 665–677. See also Robert Kolb, "Luther's Hermeneutics of Distinctions: Law and Gospel, Two Kinds of Righteousness, Two Realms, Freedom and Bondage," in *The Oxford Handbook of Luther's Theology*, ed. Robert Kolb, Irene Dingel, and L'Ubomír Batka (Oxford: Oxford University Press, 2014), 168–184, here 169–175.

72. See the numerous examples in Fleck, *Glaubensallegorie* (see note 70), 442–477.

73. VD16 B 2712.

74. Fleck, *Glaubensallegorie* (see note 70), 196–208, 600–612 (catalogue of rolls and panels).

was adapted in a few rare instances to miniatures in manuscripts and in one known case to a cast, embossed, and engraved silver book cover.[75]

In comparison to other media facilitating the infiltration of Cranach's iconography into homes, book covers were generally less conspicuous, since the rolls and panels were relatively small and most bindings were not, for example, embossed with gold leaf or colored with lacquer paint (fig. 7). Brightly painted ceramic tableware was visually more prominent if displayed or actually used. Tile reliefs of glazed earthenware stoves were often decorated in the second half of the sixteenth century with images created by Cranach, including elements of "Law and Gospel" and portraits of theologians and princes of the Reformation.[76] The tiles were larger than book cover panels and freely visible in rooms. In addition, the heat radiating from the stoves could move those present to draw nearer, inviting them to observe the motifs more closely. When books were placed in shelves, the images were hidden. At the same time, they constituted the first impressions when grasping a book and could arrest the attention of the beholder. Form, binding materials, design, aesthetics, symbolic value, and other properties could be stimulating to this end.

To what extent bookbinders themselves, commissioners, or artistic and consumer trends determined the design of a book cover is a highly elusive and ultimately speculative question in most cases due to the lack of pertinent written documents. Principally, this fundamental aspect to understanding the dynamics of pictorial bookbindings as a medium can only be approached from general knowledge available on conditions and practices of the time. It has been established that books were not just sold unbound but also bound.[77] In

---

75. This book was part of the so-called "Silver Library" of Albrecht (1490–1568) and Anna Maria of Prussia (1532–1568). On this library, see, for example, Shevchenko, *Anthropologie des Buches* (see note 18), 79–87; Ruth Slenczka, "Die preußische Silberbibliothek— ein reformatorischer Staatsschatz," in *Reformation und Freiheit: Luther und die Folgen für Preußen und Brandenburg*, ed. Ruth Slenczka (Petersberg: Michael Imhof Verlag, 2017), 147–154.

76. For Protestant iconography adorning glazed earthenware stove tile reliefs from the second half of the sixteenth century, see, for example, David Gaimster, "Pots, Prints and Protestantism: Changing Mentalities in the Urban Domestic Sphere, c. 1480–1580," in *The Archaeology of Reformation, 1480–1580*, ed. David Gaimster and Roberta Gilchrist (Leeds: Maney Publishing, 2003), 122–144. See essays by Claudia Hoffmann, Julia Hallenkamp-Lumpe, Eva Roth Heege, Kirsi Majantie, and Edgar Ring in Carola Jäggi and Jörn Staecker, eds., *Archäologie der Reformation: Studien zu den Auswirkungen des Konfessionswechsels auf die materielle Kultur* (Berlin: De Gruyter, 2007); Harald Meller, ed., *Mitteldeutschland im Zeitalter der Reformation: Interdisziplinäre Tagung vom 22. bis 24. Juni 2012 in Halle* (Halle: Landesamt für Denkmalpflege und Archäologie Sachsen-Anhalt, 2014).

77. Pearson, "Bookbinding" (see note 14), 502–506. This can be readily observed, for example, in the surviving lists of books delivered to George Spalatin in the Wittenberg palace

the latter case, it is possible that the bookbinder designed the cover in consultation with the publisher and bookseller. All the actors involved were interested in maximizing profits. Publications purchased without a binding could be bound individually or in a single volume. In this scenario, the customer determined what type of binding he or she could afford.[78] Because of the higher costs, most collectors of books did not have every volume bound in leather and elaborately embossed. Even in the collections of sixteenth-century princes, this type of binding was often reserved for books that were personally or conventionally more highly esteemed, such as theological and religious works, whereas those valued less were sometimes bound rather austerely in less expensive materials.[79] The bookbinder may have accommodated special interests and wishes of his customer in respect to design.

Variations were, however, limited to the tools, materials, and skills available to the binder. For this reason alone, it was not possible in many cases to adorn a cover with images corresponding directly to the content of the book.[80] Engraving a roll or panel was a time-consuming artisan craft and only cost-effective if the tool could be repeatedly used over several years.[81] Thus, motifs were selected that appealed to broader consumer interests. In some instances, a weal-

---

in the years 1512 and 1513 (FB Gotha, Chart. B 24, fol. 110r–114r; https://dhb.thulb.uni-jena.de/receive/ufb_cbu_00004162). Presumably, they had been acquired for the Bibliotheca Electoralis. The lists were generally divided into the categories "bound" and "unbound." Most books were unbound. Rabenau makes clear that early sixteenth-century Leipzig binders had more books bound for book dealers than for private customers. See Rabenau, "Leipziger Einbandkunst" (see note 10), 28. Recent research on the well-preserved private library of the early northern German reformer Johannes Block (1470–1545) has revealed that many of the books that he purchased in Tartu (Dorpat) had been previously bound in various German and Dutch printing centers. See Jürgen Geiß-Wunderlich, "Pommern, Livland, Finnland—und zurück: Der Wanderprediger und Reformator Johannes Block im Spiegel seiner Büchersammlung," in *Johannes Block: Der pommersche Reformator und seine Bibliothek*, ed. Jürgen Geiß-Wunderlich and Volker Gummelt (Leipzig: Evangelische Verlagsanstalt, 2018), 125–178, here 135.

78. A blind-tooled folio-size leather binding with rolls and panels could cost around half a taler or large silver coin. This is the price noted, for example, on the front pastedown of volume BP 72 in the library of the Dominican church in Erfurt that was bound in Erfurt in 1577. I thank Dr. Ilsabe Schalldach for granting me access to this collection.

79. See, for example, Gehrt, "Religiöse Erziehung" (see note 17), 77; Shevchenko, *Anthropologie des Buches* (see note 18), 70–73.

80. Helwig, *Handbuch* (see note 6), 1:75.

81. A good example of the long-term use of some bookbinding tools is a roll depicting Christ, David, Isaiah, and John the Baptist that was produced in 1545 for the Wittenberg bookbinder Franz Lindener (EBDB r002401). It was used over thirty years later for the aforementioned volume bound in 1577 (see note 78). On Lindener and the continued use of his tools, see Haebler, *Rollen- und Plattenstempel* (see note 8), 1:260–261.

thy commissioner bore the production costs so that a particular motif could be employed for his own library or for widespread dissemination into the book collections of others. This explains to some degree why—apart from Luther and Melanchthon—Habsburg emperors and Protestant princes dominated sixteenth-century German portrait panels.[82]

The reception of this medium lies largely in obscurity. Practically no sources have survived providing direct insights into how contemporary owners and observers perceived the imagery on book covers or other household items. Recent studies on objects with biblical or other religious motifs in British and Dutch homes from the sixteenth to the eighteenth century have, however, been able to make some inferences by investigating the cultural and ideological contexts of the artifacts' origins as well as discourses and material properties that may have affected their perception and use.[83] These objects served as a means of expressing faith and religious and social identity. Some were designed additionally for moral and religious instruction, social conditioning, or memorial purposes.

Although Cranach's biblically based motifs, such as "Law and Gospel," transcended confessional boundaries from a general perspective, many observers were aware of their origins in Wittenberg, an environment associated with a very specific confessional culture. Thus, pictorial bookbinding tools could take on subtle confessional connotations. The function that reformers and their patron princes assumed as figures of confessional identification gained efficacy

---

82. Haebler, *Rollen- und Plattenstempel* (see note 8), 2:444–452. The portrait panels identified by Haebler are distributed as follows: fifty-five of the Habsburg emperors; five of the princes und princess of Anhalt; one of the duke of Bavaria; seven of the margraves of Brandenburg; eleven of the dukes of Brunswick; two of the king and queen of Denmark; two of landgraves of Hesse; twelve of the counts and countesses palatine of the Palatinate; one of the king of Poland; six of the dukes and duchesses of Prussia; seven of the dukes and duchesses of Saxony; one of the duchess of Silesia; one of the king of Sweden; twelve of the dukes of Württemberg; 122 of Luther; 115 of Melanchthon; and one each of eighteen other private individuals.

83. See, for example, Gaimster, "Pots" (see note 76); Tara Hamling, *Decorating the "Godly" Household: Religious Art in Post-Reformation Britain* (New Haven, CT: Yale University Press, 2010); Tara Hamling, *Culture and Domestic Life, 1500–1700* (New Haven, CT: Yale University Press, 2017); Catherine Richardson, *A Day at Home in Early Modern England: Material*, 133–139; Andrew Morrall, "Protestant Pots: Morality and Social Ritual in the Early Modern Home," *Journal of Design History* 15 (2002): 263–273; Alexandra Walsham, "Domesticating the Reformation: Material Culture, Memory and Confessional Identity in England," *Renaissance Quarterly* 69 (2016): 566–616; Alexandra Walsham, "Eating the Forbidden Fruit: Pottery and Protestant Theology in Early Modern England," *Journal of Early Modern History* 24 (2020): 63–83.

especially through their broad dissemination in various media, including book covers. The massive production of images of Luther reflected the unequivocal veneration of this contemporary theologian so characteristic for Lutheranism. At the same time, most panel stamps of Luther were produced after his death, adding a memorial dimension to their various functions.[84] Thus, Cranach's iconography, transmitted widely through books and their covers, offered several possibilities for expressing or inducing confessional affiliation. This was one of the keys to the astonishing success of the multimedia campaign orchestrated by the Saxon electors, the Wittenberg reformers, and Cranach.

IV. ADAPTING GRAPHIC ILLUSTRATIONS TO BOOKBINDING TOOLS

Cranach's iconography was largely transmitted through graphic illustrations to bookbinding tools.[85] Naturally, modifications had to be made to meet the specifications of this medium and to take account of stylistic trends. To better understand the significance of this transformation a few crucial aspects will be explored in this section, including the influence of ancient Roman architecture on the composition of panels, the miniaturization and simplification of motifs, and the mixing and merging of elements.

German Renaissance bookbinding design was influenced by the widespread humanist interest in imitating architectural forms of antiquity. Thus, when a portrait created by Cranach was engraved in a panel stamp, it was typically incorporated into a new framework. Reminiscent of ancient Roman tomb sculpture and funerary altars, the portraits in the panels were depicted under Renaissance-style arches or pediments supported by columns and often furnished with inscriptions in majuscule. True to the objects they were emulating, panel designers tended to use Latin for inscriptions. This ancient language was

---

84. Haebler, *Rollen- und Plattenstempel* (see note 8), 2:448–450. Of the fifty-seven portrait panels of Luther in the EBDB, only six are dated. The years range from 1562 to 1579. Of the 122 portrait panels of Luther that Haebler identified, four are dated. These include the years 1533, 1556, 1562, and 1567. For cultivating the remembrance of an authoritative circle of Wittenberg reformers through pictorial bookbinding tools, see Daniel Gehrt and Philipp Knüpffer, "Der vergessene Nachfolger von Johannes Bugenhagen und Philipp Melanchthon in Wittenberg: Bericht und Ausblick über die Forschung zu Paul Eber," in *Paul Eber (1511–1569): Humanist und Theologe der zweiten Generation der Wittenberger Reformation*, ed. Daniel Gehrt and Volker Leppin (Leipzig: Evangelische Verlagsanstalt, 2014), 19–42, here 23–25.

85. Helwig, *Handbuch* (see note 6), 1:75.

frequently chosen also for political contexts in which the vernacular would have been more suitable to reach the target audiences. The previously mentioned panel stamps and medals of the electors of Saxony that arose in connection with imperial diets are cases in point. The inscriptions were in Latin, although the negotiations at these assemblies were carried out primarily in German.

As has been shown for the portraits of the electors of Saxony, images transmitted to bookbinding tools were often combined with new inscriptions. Of the hundreds of panels that were engraved with portraits of Luther and Melanchthon, many were inscribed with their personal mottos that could also be found on paintings and engravings.[86] Luther's was taken from Isaiah 30:15 —"In silentio et spe erit fortitudo vestra" (In quietness and trust is your strength)—and Melanchthon's from Romans 8:31—"Si Deus pro nobis, quis contra nos" (If God is for us, who can be against us?). However, most panel inscriptions referred to their writings. Luther's read: "Nosse cupis faciem Lutheri hanc cerne tabellam, si mentem libros consule" (If you wish to become familiar with Luther's visage, then view this picture; if you wish to know his thoughts, then consult his books) (fig. 7). And Melanchthon's: "Forma Philippe tua est sed mens tua nescia pingi nota est ante bonis et tua scripta docent" (Philip, this is your likeness, but your mind remains unknown to good men without the teaching of your writings).[87] These inscriptions, not used in any other media, encouraged the observer to read the books of these prolific authors. They could refer to the prints bound in the volume at hand. However, as already mentioned, many pictorial rolls and panels did not correspond thematically to the content and provenance of the volumes they adorned. The reference could also be more general, for instance, to other books in the collection of which they formed a part. Almost all sixteenth-century libraries of Protestant provenance had at least a few books by both authors. In larger collections, like that of George Spalatin and the Bibliotheca Electoralis, Luther's books could constitute a category of their own in the respective classification system.[88] The panel inscriptions were reminiscent of those used by Albrecht

---

86. Haebler, *Rollen- und Plattenstempel* (see note 8), 2:448–451.

87. The panel of Luther (EBDB p00062) shown in figure 7 was used by the Jena bookbinder Lucas Weischner (1550/55–1609) to adorn a copy of Heinrich Posthumus Reuss's (1572–1635) *Confessionschrifft* (1599: VD16 M 5039). On this copy, see Paasch, *Bucheinbände* (see note 43), 72–73.

88. Hendrikje Carius, "Die 'Bibliotheca Spalatini' als humanistisch-reformatorische Gelehrtenbibliothek," in *Buch und Reformation: Beiträge zur Buch- und Bibliotheksgeschichte Mitteldeutschlands im 16. Jahrhundert*, ed. Enno Bünz, Thomas Fuchs, and Stefan Rhein (Leip-

Dürer and Cranach in the early sixteenth century for engravings of Melanchthon and Luther or by the Dutch artist Quinten Massys (1466–1530) for a medal of Erasmus von Rotterdam.[89] All reflected upon the artist's ability to merely render a representation of the physical appearance of these influential European scholars. However, they could not capture the greatness of their minds. Their works could provide a far more vivid picture of their thoughts. Such engravings, medals, and paintings of famous persons also formed parts of early modern library collections and were sometimes displayed in connection with the corresponding books. Pictorial bookbinding design thus assumed this library tradition and placed references to the books on the covers.[90]

Since shading and other fine details of engravings could not be easily embossed on leather, the emblematic character of Cranach's portrait style with its pronounced contours facilitated the adaption to bookbinding tools. In this process, the motif was significantly reduced in scale und subsequently simplified. Most panels did not exceed the dimensions of 10 × 6 cm—many were

---

zig: Evangelische Verlagsanstalt, 2014), 87–123; Kusukawa, *Library Catalogue* (see note 21), xxxi. Spalatin arranged books under the categories of Luther's Latin (*Lutherana Latina*), German (*Lutherana Germanica*), and Latin-German writings (*Lutherana Latina et Germanica*). He also had individual categories for books by Erasmus (*Erasmica Theologica*), Melanchthon (*D. Phil. Melanchthonis varia in Theologia*), and Johannes Bugenhagen (*Doctoris Pomerani varia*) (Carius, 101). The catalog of the Bibliotheca Electoralis from 1536 listed thirty titles under the category of Luther's Latin works (*Reverendi patris nostrii D. Doctoris Martini Lutheri opera latina*) and seventy-four titles under the category of Luther's works in German (*Germanica Lutheri*) (Kusukawa, xxxi).

89. Martin Warnke, *Cranachs Luther: Entwürfe für ein Image* (Frankfurt am Main: Fischer-Taschenbuch-Verlag, 1984), 36–39.

90. For pictorial portraits, see Carius, "Bibliotheca Spalatini" (see note 88); Babett Forster, "Johann Major im Bildnis an der Universität Jena: 'Ein besseres Gesicht,'" in *Johann Major (1564–1654): Professor der Theologie, Superintendent in Jena und Kirchenpolitiker im Dreißigjährigen Krieg*, ed. Katharina Bracht (Leipzig: Evangelische Verlagsanstalt, 2017), 143–155; Helga Hoffmann, *Das Weimarer Luthertriptychon von 1572: Sein konfessionspolitischer Kontext und sein Maler Veit Thiem* (Langenweißbach: Sandstein Verlag, 2015), 33–34; Sascha Salatowsky, ed., *Im Kampf um die Seelen: Glauben im Thüringen der Frühen Neuzeit* (Gotha: Forschungsbibliothek Gotha, 2017), 183. Included among the inventory of the Bibliotheca Electoralis at the University of Wittenberg in 1536 were portraits of kings, the electors of Saxony, the princes of Anhalt, and many scholars (Carius, 119). Portraits of professors are known to have been hung in the university library of Jena in the seventeenth century. The portraits and books were arranged in the rooms according to the four faculties (Forster, 151–153). Around 1700, the library of the dukes of Saxe-Gotha-Altenburg at Friedenstein Palace was furnished with various portraits of Luther and a series of paintings depicting the pope as Antichrist, thus making a visual reference to its exceptional collections on the history of the Reformation and the dukes' historiographical bent (Hoffmann, 33–34; Salatowsky, 183).

considerably smaller—and the width of a roll ranged from 1 to 2.5 cm. Miniature derivatives of Cranach's iconography were traditionally regarded as aesthetically inferior in the discipline of art history. As a result, studies on the widespread dissemination of Cranach's iconography beyond paintings and engravings and the transformation processes of motifs to other media remains a desideratum up to this day. They are, however, essential for understanding the popularization and domestication of this iconography, as discussed in the previous section.

A panel of creation (123 × 62 mm), used in 1574 for a volume containing an advanced Lutheran catechism and a collection of sixty sermons on Revelations, provides some interesting insights into this transformation process (fig. 9).[91] It was unmistakably inspired by the well-known woodcut designed by Cranach as the opening, full-page illustration for Luther's complete translation of the Bible, first published in 1534 (fig. 8).[92] Subsequently, both have a common structure. God the Father was depicted hovering above his creation with a distinctive dramatic hand gesture and conspicuous wavelike fold on the right side of his wind-blown cape. To fill out the rectangular proportions of the panel better, the earth is not depicted within a circle, but an oval. Nevertheless, the sun and the moon were placed in the same positions in the heavens. The designer of the panel did not attempt to incorporate the detailed landscape of the woodcut with its sea, rivers, mountains, and trees into the stamp. The wide variety of birds, fish, reptiles, and mammals surrounding Adam and Eve was also omitted. Instead, just a few animals having no resemblance to those in the woodcut were introduced: two birds, a deer, a bear with cub, and cattle. The background was left plain, making the three scenes that were not part of the woodcut more discernible. In the middle lower half of the oval, God the Father is creating Eve from Adam's side. In the upper right, Adam and Eve are falling into sin by consuming the forbidden fruit of the tree of the knowledge of good and evil. They are consequently expelled from paradise by an angel with a flaming sword in the upper left. Thus, the characteristic features of the wood-

---

91. EBDB p000666. It adorns the front cover of the volume (FB Gotha, Theol 2° 305/2) containing Simon Musäus (1521–1576), *Catechismus Examen* (1571; VD16 M 5036), and Georg Nigrinus (1530–1602), *Apocalypsis in Sechzig Predigen* (1573; VD16 S 4622). It was originally part of the library of the widowed duchess Dorothea Susanna of Saxe-Weimar (1544–1592). Similar panels are depicted in: EBDB p000650, p000663, p000664; Ilse Schunke: *Die Einbände der Palatina in der Vatikanischen Bibliothek* (Vatican: Biblioteca Apostolica Vaticana, 1962), 1:161.

92. VD16 B 2694. The colored woodcut pictured in figure 8 is from the 1545 edition (VD16 B 2718).

cut were not only condensed to fit within a considerably smaller framework and customized to the different proportions, but new elements were also added to extend the pictorial narrative from the first to the second and third chapter of Genesis. As a counterpart to Creation and the Fall, the back cover was adorned with a panel of the Last Judgment.[93]

It is also revealing to examine how Cranach's various renditions of "Law and Gospel" were adapted to panels. Due to the many scenes it comprised, the composition was rarely transferred in its entirety. The few attempts to integrate all or most elements into the compact framework of a panel were modeled after an engraving similar to the aforementioned title-page border of the Wittenberg Bible published in 1541 (fig. 6).[94] A double-sided plate (154 × 90 mm) produced in 1565, presumably for the workshop of the Wittenberg bookbinder Nicolaus Müller, is a prime example of this.[95] Seven of the eight scenes are represented. Only the annunciation of the birth of Christ to the shepherds was omitted. Viewing the opened book from the back, law was to the left and gospel to the right. The composition underwent a much more radical reduction as it was transferred to a single panel (87 × 50 mm), engraved in 1563 (fig. 10).[96] The two double scenes forming the upper partition of the title-page border of the Wittenberg Bible were left out. Instead, just the four main scenes were pressed into a narrow architectural framework formed by three columns supporting two rib vault ceilings and divided horizontally by a middle floor. Thus, law and gospel were not divided as usual by a tree, but rather by an architectural element, as was typical for Renaissance bookbinding design. At the upper level, Adam and Eve's fall into sin was depicted to the left and the triumph of the resurrected Christ over the devil to the right. Due to the lack of space, the personification of death was left out of the latter scene. At the lower

---

93. EBDB p000667.

94. See Fleck, *Glaubensallegorie* (see note 70), 206–208, 605, 607–608, cat. no. 296, 302.

95. Haebler, *Rollen- und Plattenstempel* (see note 8), 1:299, no. I (gospel panel with crucifixion). The panels were used, for example, for the cover of a copy (Herzog August Bibliothek: 604 Theol.) of Paul Crell (1531–1579), *Euangelion aus allen vier Euangelisten* (1571; VD16 B 4665). For the panels, see Fleck, *Glaubensallegorie* (see note 70), 607–608, cat. no. 302; illustration in appendix.

96. This panel is not catalogued in the EBDB. See Haebler, *Rollen- und Plattenstempel* (see note 8) or Fleck, *Glaubensallegorie* (see note 70). It adorns the back cover of Jacob Heerbrand's (1521–1600) *Compendium theologiae* (Tübingen: VD16 ZV 7522; FB Gotha, Theol 8° 344/5). The volume was once part of the Bibliotheca Gerhardina. Similar panels are depicted in: Porr, *Quedlinburg* (see note 12), 2:13 (Municipal Museum of Quedlinburg, Historical Library, Cc 146), 20 (University Library of Aberdeen, pi 58089 Dod p), 21 (EBDB p003115).

level, Moses with the stone tablets of the law and the personification of death driving the unrighteous man into the flames of hell were depicted to the left and the unrighteous man and John the Baptist standing next to the crucified Christ and the lamb of God to the right. Due to the narrow width of the partition, the gruesome creature commonly accompanying the personification of death was omitted and only one person could be shown suffering the pangs of hell. Whereas the title-page border from 1541 depicted a man and woman, the pope, and a monk in the flames, the only identifiable person engraved in the panel from 1563 was the pope. This panel was part of a double-sided plate. The corresponding side depicted two landscape format scenes with the annunciation of Christ's birth to the Virgin Mary by the angel Gabriel and the conception of Christ in the upper half and the birth of Christ in the stall and the announcement to the shepherds in the lower half.[97] These images were classical renditions of these biblical stories. The annunciation had little resemblance to the corresponding scene in Cranach's composition of "Law and Gospel." However, they compensated for two of the four themes that were not included in the "Law-and-Gospel" panel on the other side of the plate, namely the conception of Christ and the announcement of his birth to the shepherds. Only the bronze snake that miraculously saved Israelites bitten by poisonous snakes in the wilderness (Numbers 21:6–9) and the Last Judgment were not represented.

Curiously, the bronze snake in the panel from Müller's workshop was not placed as usual on the side representing the law or Old Testament, but the gospel.[98] Traditions in bookbinding design can offer a plausible explanation for this peculiar switch. First, it is necessary to take a closer look at the numerous crucifixion rolls and panels incorporating the group of three men at the base of the tree as depicted in an early large-scale painting of "Law and Gospel" that is today part of the collections of the Prague National Gallery.[99] They

---

97. This panel, also exactly 87 × 50 mm, has not been cataloged either. It bears the year 1563 as the date of origin. The inscription for the annunciation was taken from Luke 1:38: "ECCE ANCILLA DOMINI FIAT MIHI" and for the birth of Christ from Isaiah 9:6: "PVER NATVS EST NOBIS ET FILIVS DA[TVS]."

98. A title-page border used for books printed in Amsterdam from 1530 to 1534 provides another rare example of the bronze snake on the gospel side. See Heimo Reinitzer, *Gesetz und Evangelium: Über ein reformatorisches Bildthema, seine Tradition, Funktion und Wirkungsgeschichte* (Hamburg: Christians, 2006), 2:67–71.

99. Fleck, *Glaubensallegorie* (see note 70), 196–208, 600–612 (catalog of rolls and panels). For images of the painting in Prague, see the CDA, https://lucascranach.org/CZ_NGP_O10732. This motif's connection to the composition "Law and Gospel" is not indicated in the standard reference sources for German Renaissance panels and rolls (Haebler, *Rollen- und Plattenstempel* [see note 8]; EBDB). Haebler often just describes it as a crucifixion scene with-

could be engraved particularly well into the relatively narrow rolls and panels since the unrighteous man is not standing as in the famous rendition of this composition in the Gotha Palace Museum.[100] Thus, John the Baptist pointing to the crucified Christ could be shown directly behind this person, who is sitting on a stump or stone block with his legs crossed. An Old Testament prophet—presumably Isaiah, to whom Christian exegetes traditionally attributed prophetic revelations of the death of Christ and its soteriological significance—stood on the other side of the cross. Since the 1550s, this threesome often appeared in combination with the bronze snake (fig. 11).[101] Although this scene was commonly depicted in Cranach's compositions of "Law and Grace," it was not borrowed from them. The scene of Abraham's ultimate test of faith in which he is about to sacrifice his only son Isaac until halted at the final moment by an angel of the Lord (Genesis 22:1–13) was added to the composition in some cases although it was not part of Cranach's "Law and Gospel."[102] Both the bronze snake and the sacrifice of Isaac were among the scenes frequently used in crucifixion rolls that had emerged around 1525.[103] These bookbinding tools were divided into four motifs, beginning with Christ's crucifixion. Usually two persons, either Mary and John or Adam and Eve, stood under the cross. The second and third scenes portrayed the fall into sin and the resurrection of Christ. The fourth partition of the roll was reserved for the motif of the bronze snake or the sacrifice of Isaac. The latter was often inscribed with the attribute *fides* (faith). Individual components of such series were frequently integrated into a single composition without the threesome under the cross, as seen in a panel engraved in 1545 for the workshop of the Leipzig bookbinder Andreas Vicker (fig. 12).[104]

---

out any reference to those below the cross. In the EBDB, it is generally described as "crucifixion with John the Baptist and Moses" although the latter figure is never depicted with horns, Moses's attribute. No reference is made to the naked man sitting below John.

100. See images of the painting, CDA, https://lucascranach.org/DE_SMG_SG676.

101. For example, EBDB, p001385, p001622, p001910, p002505, p002668, p002671, p002792, p002817, p002857, p002865, p002889, p002933, p003063, p003756, and p003801. The example shown in figure 11 adorns the back cover of a volume containing Niels Hemmingsen's (1513–1600) commentaries on Peter (1566; VD16 B 5225) and Hebrews (1568: VD16 B 5200).

102. See, for example, EBDB p001247.

103. Fleck, *Glaubensallegorie* (see note 70), 198–199.

104. Haebler, *Rollen- und Plattenstempel* (see note 8), 1:450, no. I; EBDB p001554. It adorns the front cover of a handwritten copy of Melanchthon's *Confessio Saxonica* from 1551 (FB Gotha, Chart. B 284; Reprinted in *Corpus Reformatorum*, ed. Heinrich Ernst Bindseil [Halle: Karl August Schwetschke, 1855], 28: 327–457). See Daniel Gehrt and Sascha Salatowsky, ed., *Aus erster Hand: 95 Porträts zur Reformationsgeschichte: Aus den Sammlungen der*

Thus, the rolls and panels with the group of the Prague type represent an amalgamation of an element of Cranach's iconography with other scenes traditionally used in bookbinding design since the Reformation to propagate salvation by faith. In this process, the stringent division between law and gospel and Old and New Testament was disbanded. The focus was placed on Christ's work of salvation. Thus, the crucifixion panels were often inscribed with the second half of John 1:29: "Ecce agnus Dei qui tollit peccata mundi" (Behold, the Lamb of God, who takes away the sin of the world) or a similar verse. In addition, they were frequently complemented by a panel on the back cover depicting Christ's resurrection similar to the Prague type.[105] The bronze snake and the sacrifice of Isaac were incorporated into crucifixion panels and rolls as typological prefigurations of this event. However, this long-standing exegetical tradition alone does not explain the extraordinarily profuse propagation of these motifs in sixteenth-century German bookbinding tools. As in the publication of religious tracts, pamphlets, and broadsheets, Protestants dominated pictorial bookbinding design. Thus, this trend was likely motivated by their understanding of justification of the sinner before God as a process occurring solely through faith and grace. A similar impetus probably led to the novel introduction of the naked man on the stone block or wooden stump into pictorial bookbinding compositions. This figure represented the viewer of the book cover. Thus, it drew the observer into the scene and underlined the individual immediacy of salvation, constituting Luther's teaching of the priesthood of all believers.[106] Identifying these trends in bookbinding design helps to explain the shift of the bronze snake to the gospel panel in Müller's workshop. There it was displayed next to the cross as in so many rolls and panels incorporating the Prague group.

Overall, these examples demonstrate the formative influence of Roman architecture on Renaissance bookbinding design. They also prove that transmitting

---

Forschungsbibliothek Gotha (Gotha: Forschungsbibliothek Gotha, 2014), 46–47, no. 23. Other examples include EBDB p000327, p000328, p000336, p000362, p000921, p001280, p001340, p001426, p001432, p001439, p001531, p001554, p001635, p001669, p001754, p001766, p001857, p002004, p002304, p002308, p002325, p002379, p002492, p002501, p002705, p002868, p002809, p002921, p003001, p003100, and p003457.

105. For example, EBDB p000337, p000361, p001248, p001328, p001427, p001555, p001623, p001637, p001638, p002294, p002502, p002670, p002704, p002787, p002818, p002856, p002892, p002934, p003064, p003755, p003802, and p003805.

106. See Caryn D. Riswold, "Priesthood of All Believers," in *Dictionary of Luther and the Lutheran Traditions*, ed. Timothy J. Wengert (Grand Rapids, MI: Baker Academic, 2017), 2:634–635.

Cranach's iconography to the tools was not just a matter of size reduction. It sometimes involved a dynamic mixing and merging of various motifs and artistic styles. Remarkably, there was a tendency in sixteenth-century German bookbinding design to compact several pictorial elements into the already limited space to form compositions with complex symbolic messages or longer narratives. Finally, it can be observed that the front and back panels of bound volumes were often made to complement each other and hence are to be viewed interconnectedly.

V. THE MEDIALITY OF PICTORIAL BOOKBINDINGS

Although examining just a few select aspects of pictorial Renaissance bookbindings in sixteenth-century Germany, this explorative study has established some significant insights into the origins and broad dissemination of iconic images created by Lucas Cranach. As the multimedia portrait strategy of the electors of Saxony outlined here readily proves, contemporaries were aware of the immense potential of pictorial bookbindings for communicating political and religious messages. They did not just enhance the aesthetic appeal but could also serve as tools of persuasion. Bindings were strategically employed to efficaciously augment the dissemination of specific images. They significantly advanced the popularization and domestication of the iconography that Cranach had masterfully developed for the Wittenberg Reformation and contributed to the extraordinarily high visibility of the Saxon electors, Luther, and Melanchthon in public and private realms.

From the findings of this study, some general observations regarding the significance of pictorial bookbindings as a bourgeoning medium in central Europe since the 1520s can be gleaned. This phenomenon is especially associated with leather bindings. Paper, vellum, and parchment could also be embossed, but leather was ideal for making deep and sharp impressions. The introduction of rolls and panels made it considerably easier and economical for bookbinders to furnish covers with various detailed portraits and scenes. This facilitated the broad dissemination of certain motifs. At the same time, leather was more expensive than many other materials and employing embossing tools required time and artisan skill. Due to these cost factors, not every book volume was bound in leather and elaborately embossed. Thus, such volumes could especially be found in institutional libraries and in the private collections of well-off scholars.

The shift from adorning book covers predominately with ornamental or decorative elements to bringing figures and scenes to the fore was especially pronounced in Lutheran cultures. It elevated the possibilities and efficacy of this medium to a whole new level since these visual elements could convey more complex ideas and messages. The interplay of various motifs placed in reference to each other intensified this effect. Rolls themselves were generally engraved with interrelated images, double-sided panel plates with corresponding motifs, and these individual tools could be integrated into various constellations to add further layers of meaning. The novelty of introducing portraits of contemporary persons into the pictorial program, influenced so strongly by humanism and the Wittenberg Reformation, offered points of reference to present times. Furthermore, rolls and panels were generally accompanied by inscriptions. Many did not merely identify the person or scene depicted but instead associated these with selected Bible verses, mottos, and aphorisms or presented an allegorical understanding of the image. Finally, pictorial bookbinding tools could better link the cover to the book content. Such references were seldom, at least partially because of the limited selection of tools available at a single workshop.

Most sixteenth-century pictorial motifs were not created specifically or exclusively for bookbinding tools. Rather, they were generally derived from graphic illustrations. In the transmission and adaption process, elements from different sources were often mixed, merged, and placed into new compositions. Bookbinding design was thus part of an intermedial interaction. This is especially evident in the dissemination of Cranach's iconography related to the Reformation. The various media with their individual properties and characteristics reached different audiences and impacted them in their own ways. Whereas paintings could be especially moving due to their size, aesthetics, vibrant colors, and vitality, they were generally commissioned works reserved for a relatively exclusive audience if not displayed in churches or other public buildings. In contrast, motifs could be readily transferred into countless private homes through engravings, illustrated books, and pictorial bookbindings widely available on the market.

To fully understand the dynamics and efficacy of this process of visual communication it is essential to know who determined the design of the covers, what those involved intended to convey, how the cover was perceived, and what impression it made. Unfortunately, historical sources providing direct answers to these questions are extremely rare. To gain further insights into the intention, function, and reception of certain bookbindings, inferences must be drawn from the design of the cover and the imagery and text it contains, from discourses and material properties that may have affected its perception and use, and from the historical, cultural, and ideological context of these artifacts. By underlying the significance of pictorial bookbindings as a medium of the German Renaissance and Reformation, this article calls for additional studies taking multifaceted approaches to this promising and revealing field of research. It also invites further analysis beyond the masterpieces produced directly by Cranach and his journeymen to the entire range of derivative works through which his iconography found its way into countless homes.

Dr. Daniel Gehrt
Research Library of Gotha
Schloss Friedenstein
99867 Gotha
Germany
Daniel.Gehrt@uni-erfurt.de

ZUSAMMENFASSUNG

Im frühen sechzehnten Jahrhundert wurden ornamentale Bucheinbände zunehmend durch bildliche Darstellungen ersetzt. Dies wurde zu einem Markenzeichen der deutschen Renaissance-Buchbinderei. Biblische Figuren und Szenen, bekannte antike Persönlichkeiten, allegorische Personifikationen, Porträts zeitgenössischer Gelehrter und Herrscher sowie entsprechende Embleme und Wappen waren gängige Motive. Bucheinbände mit Bildern wurden in der Folge zu einem wirksamen Mittel, um unter anderem politische und religiöse Botschaften zu vermitteln. Diesem visuellen Medium wurde jedoch in der Forschung bislang wenig Aufmerksamkeit geschenkt. Anlässlich des 550. Geburtstags von Lucas Cranach dem Älteren (1472–1553) bietet die vorliegende multidisziplinäre und multimediale Studie ein breites Spektrum an Einblicken in das Potenzial dieses vielversprechenden Forschungsgebiets. Der Beitrag untersucht, wie die Ikonographie, die Cranach für die Wittenberger Reformation schuf, für die Gestaltung von Bucheinbänden adaptiert wurde. Dies führte zu einer weitreichenden Popularisierung und Domestizierung der von Cranch geschaffenen Bilder.

Figure 1: Hans Krug the Elder, Medal of Elector Frederick distinguishing him as imperial general governor (1508). Foundation of the Friedenstein Palace in Gotha, inv. no. 2.2./3746.

Figure 2: Lucas Cranach the Elder's workshop, Winter costume for the electoral Saxon court with abbreviated motto on upper sleeve (1522). FB Gotha, Chart. A 233, fol. 8r.

Figure 3: Front cover of Augsburg Confession with portrait panel of Elector Frederick (1531). Johann Christian Senckenberg University Library in Frankfurt am Main, Einband-Slg. 575.

Figure 4: Back cover of Augsburg Confession with portrait panel of Elector John (1531). Johann Christian Senckenberg University Library in Frankfurt am Main, Einband-Slg. 575.

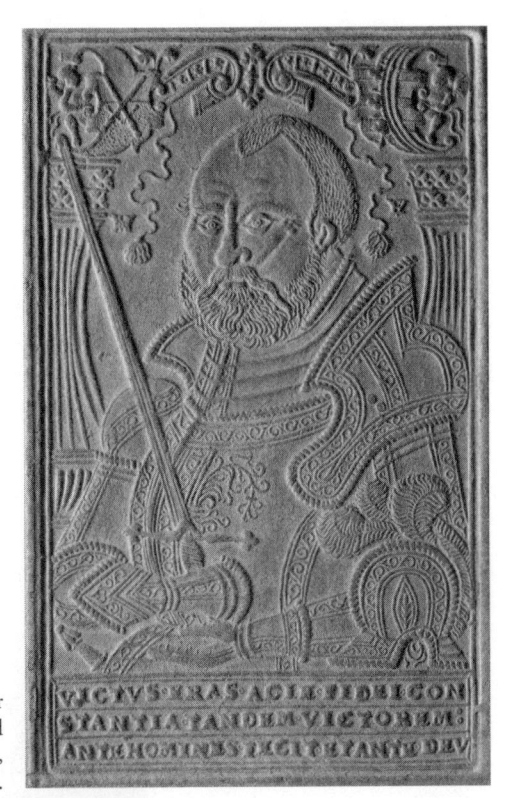

Figure 5: Portrait panel of Elector John Frederick with war wound (used in or after 1579). FB Gotha, Theol 8° 345/2.

Figure 6. Lucas Cranach the Elder's workshop, Title-page border depicting "Law and Gospel" for the 1541 edition of Luther's Bible translation. FB Gotha, Theol 2° 23/7.

Figure 7: Portrait panel of Luther, painted in lacquer colors, with inscription referring to his writings (used in or after 1599). FB Gotha, Theol 4° 502/3, front cover.

Figure 8: Lucas Cranach's workshop, Colored woodcut of creation in Luther's Bible translation (1545). FB Gotha, Theol 2° 23/10 (1), fol. 8v.

Figure 9: Panel of creation (used in 1574).
FB Gotha, Theol 2° 305/2, front cover.

Figure 10: Panel of "Law and Gospel"
(1563, used in or after 1576). FB Gotha,
Theol 8° 344/5, back cover.

Figure 11: Crucifixion panel with John the Baptist, a naked sinner sitting on a stone block, Isaiah, and the bronze snake (used in or after 1568). FB Gotha, Druck 8° 687, front cover.

Figure 12: Crucifixion panel with the sacrifice of Isaac and the bronze snake (1545, used in or after 1551). FB Gotha, Chart. B 284, front cover.

Omnis utriusque's Conflicted Reordering: Pastoral Theology and Admission to the Lord's Supper in View of Wittenberg-Related Church Orders (1523–1528)

By Brandt Klawitter

In 1530 with the presentation of the Augsburg Confession to Emperor Charles V, the Lutheran princes asserted, "confession has not been abolished for it is not customary to administer the body of Christ except to those who have been previously examined and absolved."[1] As Melanchthon's later *Apology* made abundantly clear, the defining words of Lateran IV's *Omnis utriusque* are latent within this text.[2] This text states, in part, that

> all the faithful of both sexes shall after they have reached the age of discretion faithfully confess all their sins at least once a year to their own (parish) priest and perform to the best of their ability the penance imposed, receiving reverently at least at Easter the sacrament of the Eucharist, unless perchance at the advice of their own priest they may for a good reason abstain for a time from its reception; otherwise they shall be cut off from the Church (excommunicated) during life and deprived of Christian burial in death.[3]

---

1. "The Augsburg Confession," Article XXV in *BC*, 73. See also *BSELK*, 147; "Augsburg Confession," Article XXIV, lines 6, 36 (*BC*, 69–71; *BSELK*, 143, 146–147).

Abbreviations—*BC*: Robert Kolb and Timothy J. Wengert, eds., *The Book of Concord: The Confessions of the Evangelical Lutheran Church* (Minneapolis: Fortress Press, 2000); *BSELK*: Irene Dingel, ed., *Die Bekenntnisschriften der Evangelisch-Lutherischen Kirche: Vollständige Neueedition* (Göttingen: Vandenhoeck & Ruprecht, 2014); *LW*: Jaroslav Pelikan, Helmut T. Lehmann, eds., *Luther's Works*, 55 vols. (St. Louis/Philadelphia:, 1955–1986); *WA*: *D. Martin Luthers Werke: Kritische Gesamtausgabe*, 73 vols. (Weimar: Böhlau, 1885–2009); WA Br: *D. Martin Luthers Werke: Briefwechsel*, 18 vols. (Weimar: H. Böhlau, 1930–1985).

2. See "Die Apologie der Confessio Augustana," Article XI, in *BSELK*, 426–433.

3. "Omnis utriusque sexus fidelis, postquam ad annos discretionis pervenerit, omnia sua solus peccata confiteatur fideliter, saltem semel in anno, proprio sacerdoti, & injunctam sibi poenitentiam, studeat pro viribus adimplere, suscipiens reverenter ad minus in Pascha eucharistiae sacramentum: nisi forte de consilio proprii sacerdotis, ob aliquam rationabilem causam ad tempus ab ejus perceptione duxerit abstinendum: alioquin & vivens ab ingressu ecclesiae arceatur, & moriens Christiana careat sepultura." Joannes Domenicus Mansi et al., eds., *Sacrorum conciliorum nova, et amplissima collectio*, vol. 22 (Venice: Antonius Zatta, 1778), cols. 1007–1010 (Canon XXI). For the English translation, see Canon 21, in "Medieval Sourcebook: Lateran IV, Select Canons, 1215," Internet History Sourcebooks Project, https://sourcebooks.fordham.edu/source/lat4-select.asp.

Notably, this canon did much to shape pastoral practice throughout the later Middle Ages by affixing confession of sins to yearly participation in the Eucharist. One might argue, in fact, that in the wake of *Omnis utriusque*, a sort of pastoral theological constellation coalesced to include confession and admission to the Eucharist *and* catechetical practice.

Focusing on this constellation, it is worth asking how these disparate, yet related, elements of pastoral practice would realign—or if they would change at all—with the arrival of the Reformation and Luther's eventual rejection of *Omnis utriusque*'s mandated private confession. To be sure, the various individual elements of this constellation are well-trodden loci within historic and contemporary Reformation scholarship. The intent of this article is not to rewrite their approach. Instead, it poses this question: What happens if one attempts to view this constellation and its constituent elements as an organic whole? This article outlines what might be termed a "conflicted reordering" of the elements within this constellation and their relationship one to another as it explores the legacy of *Omnis utriusque* for Luther and the Reformation that unfolded in Wittenberg. Towards such ends, this study will lean upon relevant sermons and occasional writings by Luther, but will then especially examine the early Wittenberg-related church orders—Luther's *Formula Missae* (1523), *Deutsche Messe* (1525), and Melanchthon's *Unterricht der Visitatoren* (1528). These texts, as will be observed, are relevant on account of their reflection and normative expression of pastoral theological developments for Wittenberg and later Saxon environs, to say nothing of their subsequent influence upon the wider Wittenberg movement.

PASTORAL CARE IN THE WAKE OF LATERAN IV AND THE BIRTH PANGS OF REFORMATION

As noted by Martin Ohst, the precise way priest and penitent, confession and the Mass were related to one another had not been universally prescribed for the Latin church prior to Lateran IV's *Omnis utriusque* (Canon 21) of 1215.[4] *Omnis utriusque*, subsequently incorporated into canon law via *Liber Extra* in 1234, changed this situation. Indeed, this canon decisively mandated that full confession of all (mortal) sins was now required once each year prior to the Easter participation in the Eucharist for everyone having reached the age of

---

4. Martin Ohst, *Pflichtbeichte: Untersuchungen zum Busswesen im hohen und späten Mittelalter* (Tübingen: Mohr, 1995), 14–32.

discernment.⁵ Moreover, it prescribed that confession was to be made to *one's own* priest. Significantly, Ohst highlights this codification of the priest-penitent relationship as a further sharpening of Gratian's position that led to a heightened understanding of the priest's power of the keys.⁶ Indeed, according to Atria Larson, *Omnis utriusque*'s codification of the relationship between the parishioner and his or her own priest, though not entirely novel, was at least as significant as confession's prescription.⁷ Nevertheless, lest the mandated form overshadow the focus, the canon clearly stated that such pastoral care was curative in nature: "that he [the priest] may pour wine and oil into the wounds of the one injured after the manner of a skillful physician."⁸

R. Emmet McLaughlin's essay on the historiography of penance aptly shows that the question of *Omnis utriusque*'s success in effecting improved pastoral care—similar to late medieval innovation within the practice of penance—has been the subject of a good deal of scholarly attention and debate, both along confessional lines as well as within Catholic circles.⁹ Indeed, recent scholarship has readily demonstrated that medieval penance and confessional practice were far from monolithic both in understanding and in actual practice.¹⁰ Nevertheless, *Omnis utriusque* did comprise the first universally binding rule regarding

---

5. On the ambiguity surrounding which sins, see Klaus Harms, *Die gottesdienstliche Beichte als Abendmahlsvorbereitung in der Evangelischen Kirche, in Geschichte und Gestaltung* (Greifswald: Bamberg, 1930), 5–6. For the age of discernment, see Ronald K. Rittgers, *The Reformation of the Keys: Confession, Conscience, and Authority in Sixteenth-Century Germany* (Cambridge, MA: Harvard University Press, 2004), 25; Peter Alan Dykema, "Conflicting Expectations: Parish Priests in Late Medieval Germany" (PhD diss., University of Arizona, 1998), 292–294; Peter Göbl, *Geschichte der Katechese im Abendlande vom Verfalle des Katechumenats bis zum Ende des Mittelalters* (Kempten: Kösel, 1880), 102–104. Rittgers places the age of discernment at between seven and fourteen years, while Dykema refers to the confession and communion of children without elaborating on ages.

6. Ohst, *Pflichtbeichte* (see note 4), 32–36.

7. Atria A. Larson, "Lateran IV's Decree on Confession, Gratian's *De Penitentia*, Confession to One's *Sacerdos Proprius*: A Re-Evaluation of *Omnis Utriusque* in Its Canonistic Context," *Catholic Historical Review* 104 (2018): 415–437.

8. Mansi, *Sacrorum conciliorum* (see note 3), col. 1009–1010.

9. R. Emmet McLaughlin, "Truth, Tradition and History: The Historiography of High/Late Medieval and Early Modern Penance," in *A New History of Penance*, ed. Abigail Firey (Leiden: Brill, 2008), 19–72.

10. In addition to McLaughlin's discussion, see also Anne T. Thayer, *Penitence, Preaching, and the Coming of the Reformation* (New York: Routledge, 2017); Thomas N. Tentler, *Sin and Confession on the Eve of the Reformation* (Princeton, NJ: Princeton University Press, 1977); and Berndt Hamm, *The Reformation of Faith in the Context of Late Medieval Theology and Piety* (Leiden: Brill, 2004), esp. chapters 3 and 4. For an anecdotal discussion of practice, see Mary Mansfield, *The Humiliation of Sinners: Public Penance in Thirteenth-Century France* (Ithaca, NY: Cornell University Press, 1995), 66–91.

frequency for both confession and Eucharist, even conjoining these two sacraments in an inseparable nexus.[11] While Peter Dykema observes that the focus of the priesthood was the administration of the sacraments and especially "to produce the body and blood of Christ," Anne Thayer notes that the sacrament of penance was of foremost significance when it comes to *pastoral* ministry during the later Middle Ages.[12] This role in conducting confession was a reality which would also have been reflected in the minds of parishioners: "Whatever else the preacher stressed, the European laity would know that they were to confess every year, and that they were expected to do it thoroughly."[13]

The latter point is aptly observed in Guido of Monte Rochen's very influential *Handbook for Curates* (*Manipulus curatorum*), a pastoral manual which offers further insight as to the importance of *Omnis utriusque* in the latter Middle Ages.[14] In this work, the sacrament of penance—especially confession—comprises the author's main pastoral focus. Guido goes to great length when instructing priests that they may assist the faithful in making a full confession of sins (*confessio*) from a contrite heart (*contritio*) and that they would impose the proper satisfaction (*satisfactio*) upon the penitent.[15] Guido's treatment of penance is itself reflective of *Omnis utriusque*. Implicitly, it made reference to the skilled physician who applies medicine to his patient.[16] More explicitly, *Handbook for Curates* discussed this canon in connection with the question of "one's own priest," ramifications for not making yearly confession, concern for worthy communication, timing of confession, and the seal of confession.[17]

Guido's *Handbook* also helps to outline the internal bonds within our postulated pastoral theological constellation. For example, we observe that the Eucharist's connection with confession helped to protect those guilty of mortal

---

11. McLaughlin, "Truth" (see note 9), 20n10.

12. Dykema, "Conflicting Expectations" (see note 5), 10, 175; Thayer, *Penitence* (see note 10), 46. See also Alexander Murray, "Counseling in Medieval Confession," in *Handling Sin: Confession in the Middle Ages,* ed. Peter Biller and A. J. Minnis (Suffolk: York Medieval Press, 1998), 63–77.

13. Thayer, *Penitence* (see note 10), 64.

14. Anne T. Thayer and Katharine J. Lualdi, "Introduction," in Guido de Monte Rochen, *Handbook for Curates: A Late Medieval Manual on Pastoral Ministry,* ed. and trans. Anne T. Thayer (Washington D.C.: Catholic University of America Press, 2011), xiii. See also Dykema, *Expectations* (see note 5), 142; Tentler, *Confession* (see note 10), 30–31, 37–38. Thayer and Lualdi note that Guido de Monte Rochen's fourteenth-century handbook (early 1330s) was the eleventh most popular printed work by the turn of the sixteenth century, having appeared in some 122 editions between 1468 and 1501.

15. Guido, *Handbook* (see note 14), 181–244, 164–181, 244–270.

16. Guido, *Handbook* (see note 14), 204, 208.

17. Guido, *Handbook* (see note 14), 196, 185, 195, 188–189, 241–244.

sins from unworthily communing.[18] Guido also stated that confession was necessary in order to prevent scandalous reception. The driving concerns he expressed here were related chiefly to unconfessed mortal sins, pollutions, mental and spiritual aptitude, notorious sin, and excommunication.[19] Similarly, the priest's catechetical activities were themselves ordered towards the larger goal of right confession. Thus, catechetical preaching, while covering the basics of what is to be believed (the creed), what is to be asked (Lord's Prayer), and what is to be hoped for, placed special emphasis on what is to be done and avoided (the Ten Commandments and the seven deadly sins), given that such knowledge was foundational for confession.[20] Basic catechetical knowledge could itself be an element investigated or imparted in the confession.[21] All of which aligns well with the wider findings of scholars regarding the relationship between late medieval catechesis and confession.[22]

Having now roughly sketched the outlines of the pastoral-theological constellation which arose out of *Omnis utriusque*—particularly the systemic relationship between confession, reception of the Lord's Supper, catechesis, and the circumscribed limits of pastoral care—we do well to raise the question as to how any subsequent reform attempts in connection with a given element of this constellation would affect it in its entirety. More concisely stated: as Luther's gospel discovery began to reflect transformative light back towards the individual elements of penance in the later 1510s, and then, towards the sacrament as a whole in the year 1520,[23] what changes would be effected with respect to the wider field of pastoral care?

---

18. Guido, *Handbook* (see note 14), 78.

19. Guido, *Handbook* (see note 14), 77–86. See also Tentler, *Confession* (see note 10), 61–62; Thayer, *Penitence* (see note 10), 57. Tentler notes the seriousness with which this pastoral control was taken in some instances. Thayer makes a similar observation based on Robert Caracciolo's fifteenth-century pastoral manual.

20. Guido, *Handbook* (see note 14), 271–306. See also Thayer, *Penitence* (see note 10), 22–23; Tentler, *Confession* (see note 10), 89; Charles P. Arand, *That I May Be His Own: An Overview of Luther's Catechisms* (St. Louis: Concordia, 2000), 35–39.

21. Guido, *Handbook* (see note 14), 236. See also Tentler, *Confession* (see note 10), 84; Arand, *Overview* (see note 20), 34; Albrecht Peters, *Kommentar zu Luthers Katechismen*, vol. 5, *Die Beichte, die Haustafel, das Traubüchlein, das Taufbüchlein* (Göttingen: Vandenhoeck & Ruprecht, 1994), 78; Göbl, *Katechese* (see note 5), 105–118.

22. Matthew Oseka, "Melanchthon's Contribution to the Art of Catechesis: A Study of *Catechesis Puerilis*," *Theology Today* 73, no. 3 (2016): 263–276, here 264–266; Arand, *Overview* (see note 20), 34, 37, 53n59; Gottfried G. Krodel, "Luther's Work on the Catechism in the Context of Late Medieval Catechetical Literature," *Concordia Journal* 25 (1999): 364–404, here 366.

23. Emil Fischer, *Zur Geschichte der evangelischen Beichte*, 2 vols. (Aalen: Scientia, 1972).

The idea of a sort of dissolution of this constellation seems all but inevitable as one approaches 1520–1521. Regarding penance itself, its historical structure of *contritio, absolutio,* and *satisfactio* had been fundamentally redefined in favor of the new triad of absolution, grace, and faith. Moreover, the new terminology removed any notion of human contribution.[24] Luther could and did still converse with its traditional nomenclature, as he did in *The Babylonian Captivity*.[25] Contrition, that proper sorrow for sin, though not entirely abnegated, was understood to be worked by God in the sinner's heart through faith. As Luther put it, "A contrite heart is a precious thing, but it is found only where there is an ardent faith in the promises and threats of God."[26] As Erik Herrmann highlights, for Luther, confession had furthermore been decoupled from priestly jurisdiction—i.e., *one's own priest*—in view of his understanding of the priesthood of all believers, even if, as Ronald Rittgers notes, the reformer still envisioned confession as taking place primarily between priest and penitent.[27] Along with this distinction, Luther denied any notion of a complete confession of sins as an impossibility.[28] He also rejected the contribution of satisfaction to the working of penance.[29] Furthermore, even if, as Berndt Hamm notes, the conception of divine mercy could extend quite far in pre-Reformation teaching regarding penance, Luther broke with these notions in his assertion that grace was not contingent upon even the slightest human contribution to the various elements of penance.[30] Rather, he now viewed penance as fully and totally reliant on Christ's promise of his gracious absolution addressed to the sinner.[31]

See also Joachim Bauer, Dagmar Blaha, and Stefan Michel, *Der Unterricht der Visitatoren (1528): Kommentar—Entstehung—Quellen* (Heidelberg: Verein für Reformationsgeschichte, 2020), 141–142; Harms, *Abendmahlsvorbereitung* (see note 5); Thayer, *Penitence* (see note 10), chapter 5; Rittgers, *Keys* (see note 5), chapter 3. Fischer provides a thorough study of these developments (1:118–216), and marks the conclusion of this process as manifesting itself in late 1520 with *De captivate Babylonica* and then especially with *Wider die Bulle des Endchrists* (2:1–24).

24. WA 2:715, 21–39; *LW* 35:11; Rittgers, *Keys* (see note 5), 54, esp. 54n31. Rittgers argues that the traditional triad constituting penance was supplanted by "absolution, grace, and faith."

25. See section on penance in which Luther redefines *contritio, confessio,* and *satisfactio*, WA 6:543–549.

26. *LW* 36:84; WA 6:545.

27. WA 6:546–548. See Erik Herrmann, "The Babylonian Captivity (1520)," *Lutheran Quarterly* 34 (2020), 71–81, here 79–80; Rittgers, *Keys* (see note 5), 56.

28. *LW* 36:85. See also Rittgers, *Keys* (see note 5), 53.

29. Rittgers, *Keys* (see note 5), 54.

30. Hamm, *Reformation* (see note 10), chapter 3, particularly 124–125.

31. Rittgers, *Keys* (see note 5), 54–55.

And, in extending outward from the *ex opere operato* view of private confession, which Luther also rejected, he fundamentally attacked the idea of private confession as somehow comprising adequate preparation for reception of the Eucharist.[32] Moreover, with Luther's reinterpretation of confession and renewed focus upon the gospel promise, catechesis would not be long in beginning to experience its own fundamental reorientation.[33]

Luther's revolutionary shifts in understanding, taken as a whole, would strongly seem to portend that *Omnis utriusque*'s constellation of pastoral care could have and should have been abandoned. Its foundational structure had been undermined and the bonds by which its diverse elements cohered had seemingly been rent. Nevertheless, Luther, despite his own strongly worded attacks on the ecclesial reality of his day, was hesitant to cut recklessly. Luther still arguably viewed confession—for the sake of absolution and promise—as sacramental.[34] Concerning private confession, Luther still stated, that "it is useful, even necessary, and I would not have it abolished. Indeed, I rejoice that it exists in the church of Christ, for it is a cure without equal for distressed consciences."[35] Moreover, at least judging by Luther's later reaction to Karlstadt's innovations (see below), obligatory confession, though divested of its former understanding, was apparently still the norm prior to reception of the Lord's Supper. Indeed, catechetical publications up until 1520 continued to serve such confessions.[36] Thus, in its own way, a now very weakened legacy of *Omnis utriusque* remained.

Even as nature is said to abhor a vacuum, so also Wittenberg late in 1521. In the space created by Luther's hesitance, intensified by his polemic writings, and exacerbated by his exile at the Wartburg, Andreas Bodenstein von Karlstadt acted in his stead.[37] During the Christmas celebration that year, Luther's col-

---

32. See *Instructio pro confessione peccatorum* (1518), WA 1:264, 9–16; Tentler, *Confession* (see note 10), 358.
33. Arand, *Overview* (see note 20), 66.
34. See *De captivitate Babylonica*, WA 6:543–549, 572; Ronald K. Rittgers, "Luther on Private Confession," *Lutheran Quarterly* 19 (2005), 312–331, here 313–314.
35. *LW* 36:86; WA 6:546.
36. Arand, *Overview* (see note 20), 65.
37. Fischer, *Beichte* (see note 23); Harms, *Abendmahlsvorbereitung* (see note 5), 38; and Ronald J. Sider, *Karlstadt's Battle with Luther: Documents in a Liberal-Radical Debate* (Philadelphia: Fortress Press, 1978), 3–4. In contrast to the more traditional depiction of Luther's later reaction to Karlstadt's communion innovations found in Fischer, Harms and Sider both depict Karlstadt as being more closely aligned with Luther's criticism against mandated private confession, and thus find Luther's attack upon his colleague as somewhat disingenuous, or at least not entirely justified.

league, shunning traditional priestly garb and making use of the German language, invited the Wittenberg congregation to receive the Lord's Supper in both kinds and without prior confession. The decision to commune, or not, was left up to the parishioner provided one had the necessary, right faith.[38] Moreover, Karlstadt's innovations proved quite popular with the laity and were soon adopted in the areas around Wittenberg.[39]

Notably, Karlstadt's actions were not without support and precursor. Martin Brecht observes that both Justus Jonas and Melanchthon offered tacit approval to Karlstadt's alterations.[40] Additionally, Melanchthon and some of his students had previously been involved with a similar, semiprivate evangelical mass already on 29 September that same year. In connection with this, they had used the German vernacular and distributed the sacrament in both kinds.[41] Though the exact format of the event is not entirely clear, Thomas Kaufmann is reluctant to discount the possibility that, already at that date, customary private confession had been abnegated or that *perhaps* Melanchthon himself had officiated.[42] Whatever the case, what is certain is that by the close of the year 1521, Lateran IV's tightly woven knot, with its practical plaiting of confession, communion, catechesis, and pastoral care, was finally cut. The only question remaining involved the fate of the various strands. In other words, how would

---

38. Bauer, Blaha, and Michel, *Unterricht* (see note 23), 142; Sider, *Karlstadt's Battle* (see note 37), 5–15; Andreas Bodenstein von Karlstadt, *Predig Andresen Boden. von Carolstatt tzu Wittenberg / Von emphahung des heiligen Sacraments* (Wittenberg: Nickel Schirletz, 1522) [VD16 B 6185]. For an analysis of Karlstadt's sermon, see Neil R. Leroux, "Karlstadt's Christag Predig: Prophetic Rhetoric in an 'Evangelical' Mass," *Church History* 72 (2003): 102–137.

39. James S. Preus, *Carlstadt's* Ordinaciones *and Luther's Liberty: A Study of the Wittenberg Movement 1521–1522* (Cambridge, MA: Harvard University Press, 1974), 29. See also Fischer, *Beichte* (see note 23), 2:154–156; Martin Brecht, *Martin Luther: Ordnung und Abgrenzung der Reformation 1521–1532* (Berlin: Evangelische Verlagsanstalt, 1981), 2:46.

40. Brecht, *Luther* (see note 39), 42–43; Johannes Heinrich Bergsma, *Die Reform der Messliturgie durch Johannes Bugenhagen (1485–1558)* (Kevelaer: Butzon & Bercker, 1966), 10–11. Bergsma notes that Johannes Bugenhagen did not share in their support.

41. See Preus, *Carlstadt's* Ordinaciones (see note 39), 9; Wolfgang Simon, "Karlstadt neben Luther: Ihre theologische Differenz im Kontext der 'Wittenberger Unruhen' 1521/1522," in *Frömmigkeit, Theologie, Frömmigkeitstheologie*, ed. Gudrun Litz, Heidrun Munzert, and Roland Liebenberg (Leiden: Brill, 2005), 317–334, here 319; Heinz Scheible, *Melanchthon, Vermittler der Reformation: Eine Biographie* (Munich: C. F. Beck, 2016), 77. There is some disagreement in the literature as to whether this event took place in Melanchthon's home and was conducted by Melanchthon (Preus), in the Augustinian Cloister (Simon), or whether it took place at the town church under the auspices of one of the priests (Scheible).

42. For a helpful discussion of this event and its related sources, see Thomas Kaufmann, *Der Anfang der Reformation: Studien zur Kontextualität der Theologie* (Tübingen: Mohr Siebeck, 2018), 217–218n134.

pastoral care be exercised in relationship to the Lord's Supper, to include the place of confession and catechesis, henceforth?

DEVELOPMENTS IN WITTENBERG AND WITTENBERG-RELATED CHURCH ORDERS (1523–1528)

The turmoil, which had arisen under Karlstadt's direction in December, proceeded further the following month. In February, however, his innovations were decisively checked as the electoral authorities stepped in to overturn much of what had taken place.[43] Nevertheless, the abiding uncertainty and chaos of the situation prompted Luther's hasty return from the Wartburg to his Wittenberg pulpit in early March.[44] Once back, he promptly preached his *Invocavit* sermons in which he sought to diffuse the theological unrest and allow patient teaching to proceed with unforced change, even while at least some of Karlstadt's innovations were retained. Luther's overriding concerns here were pastoral and revolved around his understanding of the freedom of the gospel. Thus, they militated against the alleged legalism of Karlstadt, on the one hand, and *Omnis utriusque*'s compulsory confession and communion practice, on the other. Nevertheless, Luther's preaching also portended that Karlstadt's abandonment of the pastoral oversight of communion was only temporary. In the sixth sermon, while explaining that repentant faith alone constitutes proper preparation for the sacrament, Luther indicated that there is a harmful partaking of the Lord's Supper.[45] Here, it is especially faithless communing done according to the pope's dictates (i. e., *Omnis utriusque*!) which the reformer had in mind.[46] Two days later, he then explained three types of confession which ought to be practiced.[47] First, Luther envisioned a restoration of confession which could deal with public, manifest sins according to the outline of Matthew 18. Second, Luther discussed the heart's private confession before God. Third, and most cherished of all, Luther commended, though did not mandate, that private confession could take place between any two Christians. Luther states, "I will allow no man to take private confession away from me, and I would not give it up for all the treasures in the world, since I know what com-

---

43. Brecht, *Luther* (see note 39), 46–48.
44. Brecht, *Luther* (see note 39), 48–53; Bauer, Blaha, and Michel, *Unterricht* (see note 23), 142.
45. WA 10/III:48–54 (14 March 1522).
46. WA 10/III:50–51.
47. WA 10/III:58–64 (16 March 1522 [Reminiscere]).

fort and strength it has given me."⁴⁸ Here, once again, it was the absolution which Luther especially had in mind: "We must have many absolutions, so that we may strengthen our timid consciences and despairing hearts against the devil and against God."⁴⁹ Scripturally, Luther found the basis for such a private confession in Matthew 18.⁵⁰

While Karlstadt's innovations, particularly the reintroduction of communion under two kinds, would necessitate further theological and pastoral attention from Luther in the weeks and months that followed, Luther focused his energies primarily on instructing that one ought to be able to examine one's own faith.⁵¹ He did, however, make nominal endorsement of pastoral announcement for communion, though this was left temporarily undefined.⁵² He also highly encouraged confession.⁵³ This notwithstanding, as Klaus Harms observes, the relaxation of required confession and announcement with the pastor was the only one of Karlstadt's reforms that Luther allowed to remain in place.⁵⁴

In preaching on Maundy Thursday in 1523, Luther would begin to address this matter more thoroughly. After explaining the importance that the communicant be able to rightly recognize what is received in the sacrament, Luther inveighed against those who dishonor the sacrament by viewing it as a good work. In fact, he continued, offering it to those who view it in such manner would be analogous to giving it to a pig.⁵⁵ Luther thus announced that the reigning practice of communing according to one's own devotion would be allowed one further year. It would, however, then be put back in order so that no one would be allowed to partake of the sacrament without the pastor first inquiring as to his faith (*wie seyn hertz steet*), knowledge, and purpose for desiring to commune. Thus, once more, Luther intoned, the issue would be overlooked, but then, for the sake of the gospel, this inadequacy would need to be improved.⁵⁶

---

48. *LW* 36:98; WA 10/III:61.
49. *LW* 36:99; WA 10/III:62.
50. Matthew 18:19.
51. See *Von beider Gestalt des Sakraments*, WA 10/II:11–41, here 38.
52. "dem priester ansagen und bitten auß geystlichem hunger umbs sacrament." WA 10/II:27.
53. WA 10/II:32.
54. Harms, *Abendmahlsvorbereitung* (see note 5), 38.
55. "Denn es ist nicht vil anders, das du disen das heylig Sacrament gibst, denn wenn du es einer Saw inn hals stost." WA 12:477.
56. WA 12:478, 1–7 (citing from version II, based on the Hagenaw printing of Johannes Secerium); Harms, *Abendmahlsvorbereitung* (see note 5), 39–40. Note that the two different

In Luther's sermon for the second day of Easter, he similarly expressed concern for those who incur harm through rashly communing according to the merits of their own preparations (and not in faith), or who have lost all reverence for the divine in the manner of the contemporary prophets.[57] Similarly, in an October epistle to Nicholas Hausmann, Luther admitted that he had long considered how an order for communion ought to be prescribed, though he had not yet completed this. Nevertheless, it was clear for him that in the future no one should be allowed to commune without first being examined (*auditum*) and having rightly answered for his faith. Others should be excluded.[58] Thus, it is readily apparent that, for Luther, the case for relaxation of pastoral oversight of the sacrament was merely a temporary measure. Allowance for such practice was made out of pressing pastoral concern in a situation confused both by previous practice and Karlstadt's innovations.

Luther's initial works involving worship reform also appeared in 1523. The first of these, *Von Ordenung gottis diensts in der gemeine*, appeared in the spring of 1523 and was connected both to a request from the city of Leisnig and to the reinstatement of weekday worship services in Wittenberg.[59] This initial evangelical order, however, had little to say about pastoral oversight of the sacrament and nothing in connection with the possibility of unworthy eating or drinking. Neither did it mention private confession, liturgical exhortation, or any other typical manner of attempting to exercise pastoral care of those partaking in the sacrament, though, as Bernhard Klaus notes, the liturgical function of the Lord's Prayer prior to the Lord's Supper *could possibly* have served this function for Luther in these earlier liturgies.[60] Concerning the questions of "to whom?" and "by which means?" the Lord's Supper should be distributed, *Von Ordenung* merely notes, "If anyone desires to receive the sacrament at this time, let it be administered at a time convenient to all concerned."[61]

---

versions of this sermon, published in 1523, vary on this point. Hans Lufft's Wittenberg edition (version I) discusses the importance of worthy communing at this juncture, though without mentioning the pending reintroduction of pastoral oversight. The Weimar editors viewed the Hagenaw edition, however, as stemming from Wittenberg and likely under Luther's influence (WA 12:472–475).

57. *Propheten ym landt*, WA 12:496–499, here 499. Luther is referring to Karlstadt and his ilk. See Fischer, *Beichte* (see note 23), 2:171.
58. WA Br 3:182–183; Harms, *Abendmahlsvorbereitung* (see note 5), 41.
59. WA 12:31–32.
60. Bernhard Klaus, "Die Rüstgebete," in *Leiturgia: Handbuch des evangelischen Gottesdienstes*, ed. Karl Ferdinand Müller and Walter Blankenburg (Kassel: Johannes Stauda, 1955), 523–568, here 540–541.
61. *LW* 53:13; WA 12:37.

Luther's Formula Missae (1523). *Formula Missae*, which appeared on 4 December 1523, fulfilled Luther's previous announcement regarding a pending order for worship—to include changes in the administration of the Lord's Supper.[62] While *Von Ordenung* had been silent on matters related to the administration of the Lord's Supper, Luther's *Formula Missae* did much to fill in the blanks with respect to the role pastors were expected to exercise in their spiritual oversight of the communicants at Wittenberg. Broadly speaking, the order was conservative in nature, though simultaneously clear in its break with the Mass as well as in its emphasis on Gospel orientation and proclamation.[63] With respect to pastoral oversight of the Lord's Supper, the pastor was to ensure that those who come to the Lord's Table could answer for their faith and their participation in the Lord's Supper. Luther writes,

> Here one should follow the same usage as with baptism, namely, that the bishop[64] be informed of those who want to commune. They should request in person to receive the Lord's Supper so that he may be able to know both their names and manner of life. And let him not admit the applicants unless they can give a reason for their faith and can answer questions about what the Lord's Supper is, what its benefits are, and what they expect to derive from it. In other words, they should be able to repeat the Words of Institution from memory and to explain that they are coming because they are troubled by the consciousness of their sin, the fear of death, or some other temptation of the flesh, the world, or the devil, and now hunger and thirst to receive the word and sign of grace and salvation from the Lord himself through the ministry of the bishop, so that they may be consoled and comforted; this was Christ's purpose, when he in priceless love gave and instituted this Supper, and said, "Take and eat," etc.[65]

As for the nature of this pastoral interview, Luther resisted the urge to be too dogmatic, advising that it could be yearly or perhaps even just once in a lifetime —or not at all—if it is clear already that the communicant has a proper understanding and faith.[66] Nevertheless, pastoral concern for unworthy communica-

---

62. Harms, *Abendmahlsvorbereitung* (see note 5), 42n19.

63. For discussion of the background and contents of this work, see Brecht, *Luther* (see note 39), 125–129.

64. See WA 12:220n4; Harms, *Abendmahlsvorbereitung* (see note 5), 41. Note that one early Speratus translation (WA 12:202, D) clarifies *Episcopus* with the comment, "Hiein würdt der namen Bischoff für ein yetzlichen seelsorger oder Pfarher genommen."

65. *LW* 53:32; WA 12:215. Luther further provided five *Beichtfragen* for would-be communicants to answer in a 1525 addendum to a republication of his 1523 Maundy Thursday sermon (WA 11:79–80). Regarding dating, see Ferdinand Cohrs, *Die evangelischen Katechismusversuche vor Luthers Enchiridion*, 4 vols. (Berlin: A. Hofmann, 1900–1902), 4:148; Harms, *Abendmahlsvorbereitung* (see note 5), 42n19. Cohrs places the dating for the writing of these questions in 1523.

66. WA 12:215.

tion was not far from his thinking. He continues, "For, by this practice, we want to guard lest the worthy and unworthy alike rush to the Lord's Supper, as we have hitherto seen done in the Roman church."[67] Moreover, "those [...] who are not able to answer in the manner described above should be completely excluded and banished from the communion of the Supper, since they are without the wedding garment."[68] Thus, the overarching concern is for right faith and understanding of the sacrament. The determination was to be made by the pastor.

This position is made clear as Luther shifts his train of thought towards the reality that the sacrament is simultaneously a public confession. He writes that "when the bishop has convinced himself that they understand all these things, he should also observe whether they prove their faith and understanding in their life and conduct."[69] Along these same lines, Luther also states that those who are brazen in their sin ought to be excluded. After all, he continues, participation in the Lord's Supper is part of the confession made by believers before God, angels, and men that they are Christians.[70] Regarding whether those receiving communion ought to be required to confess privately before communion, Luther did not want to make such a requirement. At the same time, he advised that such a practice should not be despised.[71] While there is some uncertainty as to whether *Formula Missae*'s changes were introduced at Christmas (1523) or perhaps Easter the following year, it is clear that the changes were in place by the latter date.[72]

It is worth mentioning that much of Luther's work is reflected in the (pseudo-) Bugenhagen publication, *Ordnung der Euangelischen Messz*, which appeared somewhat later in 1524. Johannes Bergsma offers a compelling argument that this order of worship, though borrowing heavily from Luther's *Formula Missae*, does not provide an entirely accurate depiction of the Wittenberg service, nor is it likely that this service, with accompanying commentary,

---

67. *LW* 53:33; WA 12:215.
68. *LW* 53:33; WA 12:216. Note that the Latin here varies slightly, though not substantively.
69. *LW* 53:33; WA 12:216.
70. WA 12:216; WA 11:210. In Luther's sermon for the second Sunday of Advent (6 December 1523), where, nearly simultaneously with the publication of *Formula Missae*, he brought up the pastor's duty to know those who would go up to the sacrament (*ut nosceremus eos qui accedunt*) and to rebuke (*increpare*) and send away (*abigere*) the impious.
71. WA 12:216.
72. For the later dating, see Harms, *Abendmahlsvorbereitung* (see note 5), 44–45; Rittgers, *Keys* (see note 5), 83. For scholars favoring Christmas as the time of introduction, see Fischer, *Beichte* (see note 23), 2:175–177; Brecht, *Luther* (see note 39), 128–129.

was actually authored by the supposed author.[73] Nevertheless, the service is clearly something of an abbreviated summary of Luther's order. It contains, for example, the recent (re)introduction of pastoral announcement prior to communing.[74] Also of significance, given its use in subsequent church orders and liturgies, is the inclusion of an optional exhortation or admonition to the communicants.[75] The author refers to such an exhortation as a custom in some places and expresses no wish that it be a law. The suggested placement of this admonition is following the sermon—though even that seems flexible. Neither is the general content of such an admonition entirely decided and it is left to the discretion of the pastor.

Taking a step back, we can now summarize developments roughly up to the time of Luther's *Formula Missae*. First, all mandates directed towards private confession and compulsory communion have been dropped. God's word and human need were to awaken desire for their use. Pastoral oversight, now disconnected from the previous requirements of Lateran IV's *Omnis utriusque* and fundamentally reoriented, has begun—at least in nascent fashion—to display its new form. This oversight consists primarily in the requirement that the pastor, to the extent possible, ensures the communicant possesses a basic understanding of the Lord's Supper and requisite faith. It was to safeguard *both* that the sacrament was not disparaged, *and* that the unworthy communicant would not eat and drink to his own judgment. In a broader sense, the pastor was also to teach, preach, and counsel his parishioners so that they would be able to *inwardly* confess their sins and partake in faith. At this point, however, there is no explicit mention of a more general catechetical requirement. Thus, while it is possible that basic catechetical knowledge might have been retained from the pre-Reformation background, it seems more likely that what had become disjointed in the fog of the Reformation has not yet fully been reincorporated.[76] Finally, whereas the essential element of medieval confession had been

---

73. Bergsma, *Reform* (see note 40), 59–60; Anneliese Bieber-Wallmann, "Von der Autorität des Stadtpfarrers zu Wittenberg—Bugenhagen und der Sammeldruck 'Von Der Euangelischen Messz' (1524)," in *Johannes Bugenhagen (1485–1558): Der Bischof der Reformation*, ed. Irmfried Garbe and Heinrich Kröger (Leipzig: Evangelische Verlagsanstalt, 2010), 129–153; WA 19:46. Bergsma notes that Bugenhagen contested the attribution of his name to this order.
74. Bergsma, *Reform* (see note 40), 61.
75. Bergsma, *Reform* (see note 40), 60–61.
76. Luther's sermon for the afternoon of Laetare (1523) (WA 11:66) hints that he may have already had in mind a broader view of questioning as he offers a favorable nod towards the pastor's examination (*scutari/explorare*) of a child's faith. See also, William P. Haugaard, "The Continental Reformation of the Sixteenth Century: Reformation Emphases Significant

the yearly private confession to one's priest, now the essential points of confession have been simultaneously internalized and directed towards absolution. In that sense, we note that there is a latent but recognizable elevation of other means of confession, whether through the words of the Lord's Prayer, conversation with a fellow Christian (in addition to the pastor), or perhaps—as observed in the (pseudo-) Bugenhagen liturgy—even through use of general confession or admonishment in the service.

Luther's Deudsche Messe und ordnung Gottis dienst. While Luther was reticent to become involved in prescribing matters of worship, cries for—and initial attempts at creating—vernacular forms of worship were appearing throughout German-speaking lands during these same years. Given the fact that some of these innovations were implemented by more radical voices, some of which went so far as to bind consciences to specific language and forms of worship, and, given the challenges of matching music and content rightly to the German tongue, Luther kept his distance and hesitated even more. Nevertheless, by Easter 1525, he felt compelled to take up the task of developing a fitting German worship service. By October his work was well under way, as is evidenced by a letter to Nikolaus Hausmann and records of Luther's consultations with musical experts. On 29 October, an initial trial of *Deutsche Messe* took place with the service being officially introduced at Christmas. Early in 1526, Luther's *Deudsche Messe und ordnung Gottis diesnts* appeared in print.[77]

---

for Catechesis," in *A Faithful Church: Issues in the History of Catechesis*, ed. John H. Westerhoff, III and O. C. Edwards Jr. (Wilton, CT: Morehouse-Barlow, 1981), 109–173, here 160; N. S. Tjernagel, "Forerunners of the Catechism: A View of Catechetical Instruction at the Dawn of the Reformation," in *Luther's Catechisms—450 Years: Essays Commemorating the Small and Large Catechisms of Dr. Martin Luther* (Fort Wayne, IN: Concordia Theological Seminary Press, 1979), 47–54, here 53–54; Arand, *Overview* (see note 20), 66; Amy Nelson Burnett, "'Instructed with the Greatest Diligence Concerning the Holy Sacrament': Communion Preparation in the Early Years of the Reformation," in *From Wittenberg to the World: Essays on the Reformation and its Legacy*, ed. Erik Herrmann and Charles Arand (Göttingen: Vandenhoeck & Ruprecht, 2018), 47–66. See also Cohrs, *Katechismusversuche* (see note 65), 4:232–234; Johann Michael Reu, *Dr. Martin Luther's Small Catechism: A History of Its Origin, Its Distribution and Its Use* (Chicago: Wartburg Publishing House, 1929), 8–11. Haugaard views the catechetical requirements as more limited initially, but as gradually expanding throughout and after the late 1520s. Arand states that such a general catechetical requirement was reintroduced in Wittenberg after 1524. Also of interest, and perhaps somewhat in favor of the latter argument, is Burnett's essay, which highlights a genre of catechetical material specifically focused around proper reception of the Lord's Supper which peaked and then waned as the 1520s drew to a close, being subsumed under the emerging evangelical catechisms.

77. WA 19:44–51. See also Brecht, *Luther* (see note 39), 246–249; Heinrich Bornkamm

Regarding our topic, this work did not deal directly with pastoral admission to the sacrament, though the pastoral interview may be assumed by this point.[78] *Deutsche Messe* does, however, cast light on two aspects indicative of an emerging sense of pastoral responsibility, namely, emphasis upon catechesis and the use of liturgical elements to assist in right reception of the sacrament. Turning first to catechesis, it is important to keep in mind that the increased concern for Christian instruction, which had been manifested already in the late Middle Ages, reached something of a fever pitch by the mid-1520s in Reformation Germany.[79] Luther had himself been aware of the need for improved catechetical efforts and had begun working towards those ends already at the outset of the 1510s, both through preaching and publishing.[80] By the beginning of the 1520s, these efforts had morphed into a determined effort which led to further publications,[81] most significantly Luther's influential *Betbüchlein* in 1522.[82] Moreover, we perceive Luther's poignant concern for Christian education in all useful arts—to extend beyond what could be provided in the home —in his letter of 1524, "To the Councilmen of All Cities in Germany that They Establish and Maintain Christian Schools."[83] A similar concern is evident in Luther's letter to the congregation in Dorpat, dated June 1525, where he explains that worship ought to instruct and improve the common people.[84] This is, of course, in addition to the many other contemporary catechetical efforts—some encouraged directly by Luther—which issued forth from Reformation environs.[85]

---

and Karin Bornkamm, *Luther in Mid-Career: 1521–1530* (Philadelphia: Fortress Press, 1983), 466–474.

78. For purposes of illustration, see Bugenhagen's letter of June 1525 to the Christians in Livonia (Dorpat), WA 18:423–425.

79. See Tjernagel, "Forerunners" (see note 76), 50–52.

80. From 1516–1517, Luther preached on the Ten Commandments for the laymen in Wittenberg (published 1518); WA 1:394–521, followed by a series on the Lord's Prayer in Lent of 1517 (published 1519), WA 2:74–130. For an outline of Luther's work on catechetical materials throughout the 1510s and 1520s, see Reu, *Small Catechism* (see note 76), 7–16.

81. Reu, *Small Catechism* (see note 76), 8–9; WA 7:194–229.

82. WA 10/II:331–451. Note that this booklet would later be recommended for use as a basis for instructing the youth in Luther's *Deutsche Messe*. See WA 11:77.

83. *An die Ratherren aller Städte deutsches Lands, daß sie christliche Schulen aufrichten und halten sollen*, WA 15:9–53; *LW* 45:339–378. See also Tjernagel, "Forerunners" (see note 76), 53.

84. *LW* 53:41–50; WA 18:412–421. See also WA 19:48.

85. Contemporary efforts in this trajectory must include the Wittenberg-published *Eyn buchlin fur die leyen vnd kinder* (1525) (VD16 ZV 2192) in Robert Kolb and James A. Nestingen, eds., *Sources and Contexts of the Book of Concord* (Minneapolis: Augsburg Fortress,

Turning now to *Deutsche Messe*, Luther's concern for Christian instruction stands front and center.[86] Following an introduction in which he outlines three variants for public or semipublic worship (Latin, German, and a more informal home gathering), he turns directly to the dire need for basic Christian instruction, or the *Catechismus*.[87]

> First, the German service needs a plain and simple, fair and square catechism. Catechism means the instruction in which the heathen who want to be Christians are taught and guided in what they should believe, know, do, and leave undone, according to the Christian faith. This is why the candidates who had been admitted for such instruction and learned the Creed before their baptism used to be called *catechumenos*. This instruction or catechization I cannot put better or more plainly than has been done from the beginning of Christendom and retained till now, i.e., in these three parts, the Ten Commandments, the Creed, and the Our Father.[88] These three plainly and briefly contain exactly everything that a Christian needs to know. This instruction must be given, as long as there is no special congregation, from the pulpit at stated times or daily as may be needed, and repeated or read aloud evenings and morning in the homes for the children and servants, in order to train them as Christians. Nor should they only learn to say the words by rote. But they should be questioned point by point and give answer what each part means and how they understand it.[89]

As Luther continues, he illustrates his question-and-answer methodology for teaching the catechism in a manner which clearly anticipates his later *Small Catechism*, going first through the petitions of the Lord's Prayer and then the

---

2001), 1–12. See also Agricola's Latin catechism of 1526 (Kolb and Nestigen, 13–30), encouraged by Luther, and any number of other similar works. For a discussion of these efforts, see Arand, *Overview* (see note 20), 70–72; Tjernagel, "Forerunners" (see note 76), 51–52; and, most extensively, Cohrs, *Katechismusversuche* (see note 65).

86. See, Frank S. Senn, "Martin Luther's Revision of the Eucharistic Canon in the Formula Missae of 1523," *Concordia Theological Monthly* 44 (1973): 101–118. Senn notes the didactic emphasis of Luther's *Deutsche Messe* both as one of its chief attributes as well as its greatest weakness (101).

87. Arand, *Overview* (see note 20), 70–71; E. G. Schwiebert, *Luther and His Times: The Reformation from a New Perspective* (St. Louis: Concordia, 1950), 638; Reu, *Small Catechism* (see note 76), 11; Cohrs, *Katechismusversuche* (see note 65), 4:239n2. See also WA 30/I:429–430; WA Br 3:431. Arand observes that "the term 'catechism' as a title for these primers did not come into extensive use until the mid- to late-1520s." Schwiebert notes that Luther first mentioned the *catechismus puerorum*, understood as a booklet and not merely basic instructional content, in a February 1525 letter to Justus Jonas and Johann Agricola.

88. Burnett, "Instructed" (see note 76), 59. Luther does not yet include the sacraments and confession under the term *catechismus*. Nevertheless, it was first in 1525 that print editions of Luther's *Betbüchlein* began to include material on the Lord's Supper and thus began a fusion of what had formerly been *two* separate genres, as observed by Burnett.

89. *LW* 53:64–65; WA 19:76.

creed. Finally, he suggests that the reader look to his *Betbüchlein* from 1522 for additional questioning.[90]

Proceeding to his recommendations for Sunday and weekday services, Luther emphasizes his conviction that "the preaching and teaching of God's Word is the most important part of the divine service."[91] After outlining his ideas for the various services, he begins to discuss the service proper. For the purposes of this article, Luther's instructions following the sermon prove significant. He states, "After the sermon shall follow a public paraphrase of the Lord's Prayer and admonition for those who want to partake of the sacrament."[92] He then proceeds to the congregational prayers, clearly structured around the Lord's Prayer. This, together with the exhortation, filled the historic, liturgical space for the general confession.[93] It is likely that the prayers and exhortation still retained hints of that function in their liturgical placement here, even though Luther's clear intention was to emphasize the gospel message and promise of the sacrament.[94] This gospel-centered, faith-provoking emphasis is perceived by the words of the exhortation to confident faith, which read:

> Secondly, I admonish you in Christ that you discern the Testament of Christ in true faith and, above all, take to heart the words wherein Christ imparts to us his body and his blood for the remission of our sins. That you remember and give thanks for his boundless love which he proved to us when he redeemed us from God's wrath, sin, death, and hell by his own blood. And that in this faith you externally receive the bread and wine, i.e., his body and his blood, as the pledge and guarantee of this. In his name therefore, and according to the command that he gave, let us use and receive the Testament.[95]

Whether such an exhortation should be read from the pulpit or the altar, Luther left a matter of freedom, though he notes that the ancients apparently gave such admonition from the pulpit. Continuing on such a practical note, Luther's instructions emphasize his catechetical, liturgical ideal as he encourages

---

90. WA 19:76–77.
91. *LW* 53:68; WA 19:78.
92. *LW* 53:78; WA 19:95.
93. Klaus, "Rüstgebete" (see note 60), 536–537. According to Klaus, Luther was aware of this historical function but seems to regret that the exhortation had become merely a corporate confession in his exclamation, "Aber die vermanung zu eyner offentlichen beicht worden ist" (WA 19:96–97).
94. Klaus, "Rüstgebete" (see note 60), 539–542.
95. *LW* 53:79–80; WA 19:96.

that the wording be precisely formulated and consistently repeated, thus avoiding confusion and better instructing the people.[96]

It is informative to note what has occurred with this pre-communion exhortation. Liturgically speaking, Luther has replaced the traditional preface with an alternative form of preparation for the sacrament. This is expressive both of his own pastoral theological understanding of confession as well as wider liturgical trends which had become increasingly prevalent in Reformation Germany. On the latter point, we observe with Julius Smend's study, that this liturgical change was reflective of German-speaking liturgical trends during the 1520s.[97] That is not, however, to imply that Luther's changes had emerged without considerable forethought. Earlier in 1525 he had sent Nicolaus Hausmann a suggested German preface (i. e., exhortation) to use instead of the traditional preface.[98] Moreover, this change was likely also reflective of Luther's own opposition to traditional liturgical elements that he viewed as tainted by the accretions of the Mass and which hindered the emphasis and focus on Christ's words of institution.[99]

Zooming out for a moment, what might be said about the pastoral care constellation, "confession-communion-catechesis," at this point in Wittenberg? To begin with, given that penance and confession have been turned towards heartfelt repentance and faith in the merits of Christ, the pastoral and liturgical means for accomplishing their ends also come under reconsidera-

---

96. WA 19:96–97. Further highlighting this catechetical usage is Luther's 1526 release of *Was dem gemeynem volcke nach der predig fur zu lessen* (Wittemberg, 1526) (VD16 ZV10016), which also included the recitation of the remaining chief parts of the catechism in addition to the Lord's Prayer (included in *Deutsche Messe*). See also notes contained in WA 19:52–53.

97. Julius Smend, *Die evangelischen deutschen Messen bis zu Luthers deutscher Messe* (Göttingen: Vandenhoeck & Ruprecht, 1896); Bergsma, *Reform* (see note 40), 58–59; WA 19:47, 58–59. Smend notes several exhortative practices in currency throughout Reformation lands, whether included in the sermon (e.g., Müntzer's service, Smend, 110), as an addendum, prior to the sermon (e.g., Basel, Smend, 214), or even as an element of the communion liturgy (e.g., Nuremberg, Smend, 177), and suggests that Luther's replacement of the preface was reflective of this influence. Bergsma argues that Luther likely had access to the German services from Nördlingen, Allstedt, Strasbourg, Nuremberg, and perhaps others.

98. WA Br 3:462–463.

99. Peter Brunner, *Worship in the Name of Jesus*, trans. M. H. Bertram (St. Louis: Concordia, 1968), 292–293. For Luther's understanding of the *Beichte* as properly contained in the Lord's Prayer, see Peters, *Kommentar* (see note 21), 19; Bergsma, *Reform* (see note 40), 50–51; Klaus, "Rüstgebete" (see note 60), 541; *BSELK*, 1159.

tion.[100] For example, the movement of the sinner to repentance and faith through the preached word now takes much higher priority in pastoral work.[101] Fundamental knowledge of the faith—the basic teachings of law and gospel—also take on increased priority via catechetical teaching and preaching. Additionally, pastoral theological concerns force a reconsideration of liturgical elements. This is, indeed, what has happened in Luther's replacement of the traditional preface with an exhortation.[102] Moreover, while private confession still had a function in this overarching pastoral work, absent its mandate, it had in a certain sense become merely the foremost of several means by which pastoral aims could be carried out.[103] Furthermore, while by 1523 the free nature of confession and simultaneous pastoral responsibility for admittance to the sacrament had tentatively been sketched out, the relationship of catechesis to these elements had not yet been fully formulated and the liturgical expression of evangelical confession in connection with the Lord's Supper still required fine-tuning. Nonetheless, with Luther's *Deutsche Messe*, we have observed premonitions of newfound correspondence between elements in our constellation, even if and even though specific relationships remain slightly in flux. It is as we approach Melanchthon's *Unterricht der Visitatoren* that these various elements, and particularly catechesis, will further harden into a new homeostasis within our proposed Wittenberg pastoral theological constellation.

Unterricht der Visitatoren. The general upheaval to religious life which flowed out of the early years of the Reformation required not only that attention be paid to matters of worship, but also dictated that other practical matters of church life be addressed, ordered, and remedied. The need for this was already felt leading up to the mid-1520s and became increasingly pressing thereafter. It was perhaps in connection with support and payment of the clergy within the territory that problems were discerned most poignantly. There remained, however, two urgent needs. First, addressing these matters was important for ensuring that the Reformation gains connected with Luther's gospel insight would be realized at the parish level. Second, against the recent backdrop of the Peas-

---

100. Thayer, *Penitence* (see note 10), 154–157.
101. Reinhold Seeberg, *Lehrbuch der Dogmengeschichte*, vol. 4/1, *Die Enstehung des protestantischen Lehrbegriffs*, 5th ed. (Basel: Benno Schwabe & Co., 1953), 171–172.
102. For contemporary Reformation developments in Nuremberg, see Rittgers, *Keys* (see note 5). For a wider-angle view, see Klaus, "Rüstgebete" (see note 60), 542–556.
103. See Johannes Bugenhagen, *Ain Sendtbrieff herrn Johan Bugenhagen Pomern* (Augsburg, 1525), Aiiiiv (VD16 B 9256). It is worth noting that Bugenhagen, around this time, apparently practiced a more corporate form of absolution prior to the Lord's Supper.

ants' War and the—both real and perceived—antinomian, anti-authoritarian impulses of so-called *Schwärmer*, it was pressing that such disruptive reformational elements be corrected.[104] Indeed, while Luther was finalizing his *Deutsche Messe*, he was already considering and consulting with Elector John—who had himself previously undertaken visitation efforts in his duchy[105]—regarding a more comprehensive visitation to address the broader needs of the church.[106] Initial organizational efforts for the Saxon visitation were undertaken during Lent the following year (1526), the results of which, among other matters, led Luther to press his case for visitation once again in November that same year.[107] Visitations were subsequently initiated in February (1527) for electoral Saxony and then resumed later that summer in the elector's Thuringian lands.[108] Not to be overlooked is the fact that this Thuringian visitation included Orlamünde and its environs, where Karlstadt, following his departure from Wittenberg, had served as a pastor from 1523 to 1524 and whose influence—also regarding administration of the Lord's Supper—was still felt at the time of the visitation.[109] Records of initial instructions were already present during these early visitations.[110] More developed instructional drafts, most notably Melanchthon's controversial *Articuli de quibus egerunt per visitatores*, appeared thereafter.[111] These instructions, as drafted by Melanchthon, were further re-

---

104. For background information (in addition to standard biographies and sources), see Bauer, Blaha, and Michel, *Unterricht* (see note 23), 11–62; Bauer and Michel, *Der "Unterricht der Visitatoren" und die Durchsetzung der Reformation in Kursachsen* (Leipzig: Evangelische Verlagsanstalt, 2017); Herman A. Speelman, *Melanchthon and Calvin on Confession and Communion: Early Modern Protestant Penitential and Eucharistic Piety* (Göttingen: Vandenhoeck & Ruprecht, 2016), 97–128; Susan Karant-Nunn, *Luther's Pastors: The Reformation of the Ernestine Countryside* (Philadelphia: American Philosophical Society, 1979).

105. See Bornkamm and Bornkamm, *Luther* (see note 77), 487; Bauer, Blaha, and Michel, *Unterricht* (see note 23), 29–30. Already in 1525, the then duke had initiated a visitation effort for his duchy via Nicholas Hausmann in Zwickau and Jakob Strauss in Eisenach.

106. WA 26:177.

107. WA 26:178.

108. WA 26:179–180.

109. Bauer, Blaha, and Michel, *Unterricht* (see note 23), 141. Regarding Karlstadt's activities in Orlamünde, see Ronald J. Sider, *Andreas Bodenstein von Karlstadt: The Development of His Thought, 1517–1525* (Brill: Leiden, 1974), 181–197.

110. See *Anordnungen und Fragartikel der Visitatoren*, dated July 1527, in Bauer, Blaha, and Michel, *Unterricht* (see note 23), 313–314.

111. WA 26:180–182. For Melanchthon's draft (published without his permission in October 1527), see *ARTICULI DE QVIBVS EGERVNT PER VISItatores in regione Saxoniae* (Wittembergae: Schirlenz, 1527) (VD16 M 2590), esp. B4v regarding pastoral examination for the Lord's Supper. For Luther's reference to this *pulcherrima ordinatione* in his 20 August 1527 letter to Nicholas Hausmann, see WA Br 4:232–234. Regarding the controversy with

viewed, revised, and lightly edited by Luther, Bugenhagen, and others throughout the fall and winter.[112] Luther wrote the preface to the document the following January with publication occurring in the latter half of March 1528.[113]

Unterricht der Visitatoren is significant both because of its content as well as on account of the considerable influence it would have on later church orders. In terms of its content alone, there are multiple elements that interact with *Omnis utriusque*'s late medieval heritage and further redefine the Wittenberg reworking of the same. *Unterricht* thus offers testimony to the further refinement of pastoral admittance to the Lord's Supper. Furthermore, its increased emphasis upon catechesis in connection with admittance to the Lord's Supper is noteworthy, though the pastor-parishioner framework and questions of pastoral care in exceptional circumstances also come into discussion.

If we begin by taking *Unterricht* as a whole, its catechetical emphasis comes immediately to the fore. For example, its doctrinal, even catechetical, topical register nearly mimics what one would expect from a catechism.[114] This fact coincides with Susan Karant-Nunn's observation that these instructions were, in themselves, a sort of stopgap measure which offered emergency training for ignorant clergy.[115] The importance placed upon catechesis as a foundational aspect of the school curriculum further highlights the catechetical emphasis of the instructions.[116] Perhaps more importantly, however, is the stress placed upon the pastor's role as an instructor of basic Christian teaching—to include the establishment of time and space for such catechetical preaching, typically Sunday afternoons, but also other times as circumstances dictate.[117] This emphasis merely serves to highlight the reality that, whatever the catechetical assumptions had been earlier in the decade, these became—at least on paper—normative for the Saxon lands via a better organized children's catechetical program.[118] Moreover, the required pastoral interview prior to the Lord's Supper

---

Johann Agricola that arose about Melanchthon's draft, see Timothy J. Wengert, *Law and Gospel: Philip Melanchthon's Debate with John Agricola of Eisleben over Poenitentia* (Carlisle: Paternoster, 1997), 94–138.

112. Johannes Bugenhagen, *Selected Writings*, trans. Kurt K. Hendel (Minneapolis: Fortress Press, 2015), 1:32–33; WA Br 4:265; WA 26:183–184.

113. Bauer, Blaha, and Michel, *Unterricht* (see note 23), 61.

114. WA 26:201.

115. Karant-Nunn, *Luther's Pastors* (see note 104), 24.

116. WA 26:237–238.

117. WA 26:230–231; Cohrs, *Katechismusversuche* (see note 65), 4:259–260.

118. See Laurentius Klein, *Evangelisch-lutherische Beichte: Lehre und Praxis* (Paderborn: Verlag Bonifacius-Druckerei, 1961), 77–78; Gerald Strauss, *Luther's House of Learning: Indoctrination of the Young in the German Reformation* (Baltimore: Johns Hopkins University

almost certainly assumed basic catechetical learning by this time.[119] Any question on this matter would have been clarified, at the very latest, by the time Luther wrote his catechisms the following year.[120]

What did *Unterricht* instruct about the Lord's Supper, though? Under the section "The Sacrament of the Body and Blood of the Lord," Melanchthon instructs that three articles, in particular, be explained to the people.[121] In the first article, driving against the teachings of especially Zwingli and Karlstadt, Melanchthon emphasizes a straightforward understanding of Christ's clear words of institution.[122] The people are to believe that "the true body of Christ is in the bread and the true blood of Christ is in the wine."[123] To merely receive the elements as normal food would be to incur divine judgment, as accords with St. Paul's admonition to the Corinthians (1 Cor. 11:27).

The people should be shown that the sacrament is rightly received in two kinds and also that this is based on Christ's institution.[124] Out of this flows a discussion, written by Luther and reflective of his earlier writings, regarding pastoral practice towards conflicted consciences.[125] In taking on this question, the ground rule is first established that the gospel's proper teaching is proclaimed to all, whether they are strong, weak, or obstinate. The celebration of the sacrament under one kind is, thus, to be condemned as contrary to the

---

Press, 1978), 268–276. Luther's comments in *Sermon von dem Sakrament* (Easter 1526) (WA 19:520–521), indicate that more general catechetical questioning was in place in Wittenberg at that time. Strauss makes the argument that the success of the program such visitations sought to implement was often limited.

119. For parallel developments in other Reformation areas apparent by this time, see Philipp Melanchthon, *Corpus Reformatorum*, ed. Gottlieb Bretschneider (Halle: Schwetschke et filium, 1835), 1:717–719; Heinz Scheible, *Melanchthon* (see note 41), 59–60; Cohrs, *Katechismusversuche* (see note 65), 4:246–247. In 1525, Melanchthon encouraged clergy in the Nuremberg churches to focus energy upon the instruction of youth and examination prior to communion. Cohrs connects this examination with Luther's five *Beichtfragen* (Cohrs, 4:149). By 1527, such a program had apparently been instituted as a replacement for private confession (Cohrs, 4:252–253) and is perhaps reflected in Wenzeslaus Linck's *Unterrichtung der Kinder, so zu Gottes Tisch wollen gehen* (1528) (Cohrs, 3:41–48). As is evident from Linck's instructions, communion attendance required a basic understanding of salvation, law, and gospel, as well as a sufficient understanding of the sacrament.

120. *BSELK*, 854–857 (*Small Catechism*, preface). One suspects that Luther's preface to the Large Catechism also has pastoral questioning in mind (*BSELK*, 928–931).

121. WA 26:213.

122. Bauer, Blaha, and Michel, *Unterricht* (see note 23), 122–127.

123. *LW* 40:289; WA 26:213.

124. WA 26:214.

125. Bauer, Blaha, and Michel, *Unterricht* (see note 23), 327–329. For Luther's removal of this section in the 1538 republication of *Unterricht der Visitatoren*, see *LW* 40:290n18.

Lord's teaching. Right teaching and doctrine must be allowed to reign freely.[126] Nevertheless, given that one must give consideration to weak or confused consciences, some patience is also to be exercised. Thus, as long as right teaching is in no way hindered, Luther counsels that truly weak or uninstructed Christians (regarding communion under two kinds) may be allowed to commune under one kind "for the time being and where they ask for it the pastor or preacher may so administer it."[127] Luther's justification then follows, "In this way the doctrine of both kinds will not be weakened or compromised, but only the application or use of the doctrine will be temporarily postponed through Christian patience and love."[128] Nevertheless, the doctrine must be maintained while love forgives and bears with some slowness in application. The obstinate, however, "those who will neither learn nor practice this doctrine," should be offered neither kind.[129] How was this determination to be made? "The pastor, who knows his people and daily associates with them, must distinguish between the weak and the obstinate. He can easily observe those folk who have a good disposition, who gladly listen to the preaching and gladly want to learn and be rightly guided thereby. But the rough and the perverse who pay no attention to preaching are under no circumstances to be considered weak, however loudly they claim to be so."[130]

Melanchthon then continues to his most fundamental point of pastoral teaching. Namely, "that one teach the reason for the use of the sacrament and how one shall be properly prepared."[131] Under this topic, Melanchthon organizes four points of instruction. First, the pastor should instruct the congregation concerning the magnitude of the sin of dishonoring the sacrament. This is based, once again, on 1 Cor. 11:27–28, but then also tied to Ex. 20:7 and the notion of misusing the Lord's name. Melanchthon writes,

> Undoubtedly also this dishonor to the body and blood of Christ will not go unpunished. This shall be taught the people carefully, so that they may avoid this sin and be urged to reverence, penitence, and improvement. Nor shall such be admitted to the sacrament as are caught in the web of open sin, adultery, gluttony, and the like, and show no contrition.[132]

---

126. WA 26:214.
127. *LW* 40:290; WA 26:215.
128. *LW* 40:290–291; WA 26:215.
129. *LW* 40:291; WA 26:215.
130. *LW* 40:292; WA 26:216.
131. *LW* 40:292; WA 26:216.
132. *LW* 40:292; WA 26:216. In connection with this point, see also Melanchthon's discussion of "Vom rechten Christlichen Bann" (WA 26:233–235).

In the second article, Melanchthon commands that no one "shall be admitted to the sacrament unless he has previously been to the pastor who shall inquire if he rightly understands the sacrament, or is in need of further counsel, etc."[133] Melanchthon will, somewhat remarkably, return to this very point two more times, thus emphasizing the importance of pastoral counsel and pointing out that unworthy communing also impugns the pastor who communes his parishioners carelessly.[134] Why this reiteration and emphasis upon pastoral responsibility for those who would commune, especially given that this topic had not received a similarly heavy focus in the summer of 1527?[135] As noted previously, composition and revision work involving *Unterricht* were partially completed following the findings of the visitors in Thuringia. Included in this was the area which had previously come under Karlstadt's influence around Orlamünde. In the wake of Karlstadt's complete rejection of private confession, it seems probable that corrective measures were being set in place to reinstitute pastoral supervision over the sacrament—perhaps somewhat akin to what had happened in Wittenberg previously that same decade.[136]

A more significant question, however, is perhaps what was sought through this emphasis upon pastoral administration of the Lord's Supper? In terms of pastoral care, the reformers sought a type of care for souls which would correspond with the Wittenberg understanding of faith and the workings of law and gospel. Troubled consciences were to be comforted and weak or ignorant Christians were to be properly instructed lest they sin against the body and blood of the Lord. And yet, as Klaus Harms notes, Melanchthon's language goes quite far in pushing such salutary confession and absolution—perhaps even to a point that, functionally, becomes less free and more reminiscent of *Omnis utriusque*.[137] Moreover, Melanchthon writes, "In examination before the sacrament the people are to be *exhorted* to make confession."[138] In this section, although *Omnis utriusque*'s dictum of recounting all sins is ostensibly being combatted, Melanchthon's wording seems to push confession in a direction that nearly recalls previous confessional requirements.[139] This is even more

---

133. *LW* 40:292; WA 26:216.
134. See WA 26:220; WA 26:232.
135. Bauer, Blaha, and Michel, *Unterricht* (see note 23), 141.
136. Bauer, Blaha, and Michel, *Unterricht* (see note 23), 141–142.
137. Harms, *Abendmahlsvorbereitung* (see note 5), 49–52.
138. *LW* 40:296 (emphasis added); WA 26:220.
139. Kurt Aland, "Die Privatbeichte im Luthertum von ihren Anfängen bis zu ihrer Auflösung," in *Kirchengeschichtliche Entwürfe* (Gütersloh: Gütersloher Verlagshaus, 1960), 452–519, here 466–468. Aland notes this general tension, but also that "die Verpflichtung stärker ist als die Freiheit" (468). Indeed, according to Aland, although Melanchthon claims "Die

the case when one keeps in mind *Omnis utriusque*'s stipulation that confession be made "to one's own priest."[140] If Susan Karant-Nunn is correct, such exhortation to confession could even be (or at least became) quite personal, even prying.[141] Interestingly, while there is no basis for believing that Luther fundamentally disagreed with what was written here, there is reason to think that clarification was in order. In fact, Luther added two such clarifications on the point of confession and pastoral registration in the 1538 republication of *Unterricht*. Here, he emphasized both the *free* nature of confession and the possibility of a pastor not interviewing communicants prior to every communion.[142]

Returning to the discussion of what pastors are to teach their people regarding right reception of the Lord's Supper, Melanchthon arrives at his third article. The people are to be instructed on right repentance and "rough, fearless persons will not be admitted."[143] In other words, if it is kept in mind that Christ's death was brought about on account of the gravity of man's sin, a proper remembrance of this death must necessarily include repentance of sin and the desire for forgiveness—that which, in fact, is promised in the sacrament.[144] Finally, Melanchthon admonishes that the people be taught concerning the implications of Christian fellowship that flow out of the participation in the bread and body of Christ (1 Cor. 10:17). In this respect, Christian love is to be awakened, and all envy and hatred is to be put aside.[145]

CONCLUDING THOUGHTS

In many ways, with Melanchthon's *Unterricht* and its nearly compulsory confession and absolution, we have come full circle. While the winds of change had seemingly been blowing away from *Omnis utriusque*'s ordering of pastoral care in the early 1520s—so much so that Karlstadt's actions at Christmas in 1521 arguably reflect the spirit of Luther's earlier push for reform—it now seems as if the emerging evangelical movement has lurched back into the prac-

---

Bapstische Beicht ist nicht geboten," what is actually being rejected is not confession, but its papal form (467).

140. WA 26:220.

141. Susan Karant-Nunn, *The Personal Luther: Essays on the Reformer from a Cultural Historical Perspective* (Leiden: Brill, 2018), 40–41.

142. See Emil Sehling, ed., *Die Evangelischen Kirchenordnungen des XVI. Jahrhunderts* (Leipzig: O. R. Reisland, 1902), 1:160, col. 2n1; 162, col. 2n2.

143. *LW* 40:292; WA 26:216.

144. WA 26:216–217.

145. WA 26:217.

tice from which it had sought to free itself, a fact only compounded by subsequent church ordinances. As Thomas Tentler observes, "Fifty Lutheran church ordinances between 1525 and 1591 decreed individual confession with the *Verhör* as a precondition of admission to the Lord's Supper: no Lutheran polities failed to adopt it, and many forbade general absolution of the congregation."[146] Indeed, the pastor-parishioner dynamic, the compulsion to confess and be absolved, and the catechism's continued role in this process are all rather reminiscent of days gone by. As Bernd Moeller argued, it seems that Melanchthon was attempting to find something of a middle way between Lateran IV and the Wittenberg rejection of the same.[147] Moreover, in practice, Augustana's almost compulsory "custom," that is, "to examine and absolve," existed quite within the historic space created by *Omnis utriusque*.[148]

The apparent structural similarities, however, obscure several notable, indeed seismic, changes which had taken place within the system. Confession and catechesis had both been inwardly transformed and redirected. Replacing catechesis's general deference to confession during the late Middle Ages, its purpose was broadened and heightened in service to the gospel. Indeed, catechesis vied for the central position that private confession previously had enjoyed and, in certain respects, became a central focus of pastoral attention. Likewise, confession, though retained, had also been transformed in both its form and focus. The inward-focused, detail-oriented, comprehensive confession that had defined Luther's own struggle, was superseded by an acknowledgment of fundamental sinfulness on the part of the penitent. Private confession before the pastor therefore became *one* means, though hardly the sole means, of acknowledging both sinfulness and specific sins. The focus, however, had shifted towards the absolution—no longer contingent on the priest's sole mediation of the keys, but now received directly on the merits of Christ's promise in a variety of formats.

In conclusion, the shape of pastoral care in the early years of Wittenberg's Reformation constituted something of an uneasy tension. Without some sort of ordering—an ordering which ironically conformed to the rough outlines of pastoral practice inherited from *Omnius utriusque*—gospel freedom threated to dissolve into chaos. At the same time, one might fairly raise the question as to

---

146. Thomas Tentler, "Confession," in *The Oxford Encyclopedia of the Reformation*, ed. Hans J. Hillerbrand (Oxford: Oxford University Press, 1996), 1:403.

147. Bernd Moeller, "Das Innocentianum von 1215 in der Confessio Augustana," *Zeitschrift für Kirchengeschichte* 75, nos. 1–2 (1964): 156–158.

148. *BC*, 72–73 ("Augburg Confession," Article XXV, line 1); *BSELK,* 147. See also Harms, *Abendmahlsvorbereitung* (see note 5), 51–52.

whether such a concession was itself a begrudging admittance of a disappointed earlier vision of Reformation.

Dr. Brandt Klawitter
Associate Professor of Chuch History
Department of Theology, Religion, and Philosophy
NLA University College
PB74 Sandviken
5812 Bergen
Norway
brandt.klawitter@nla.no

ZUSAMMENFASSUNG

Aus dem Dekret „Omnis utriusque" des Vierten Laterankonzils ging eine pastoraltheologische Konstellation hervor, die die Privatbeichte und die Spendung der Eucharistie durch den Priester miteinander verband – und auch die Katechese weitgehend einschloss. Obwohl die Vorgaben des Dekrets von den Reformatoren vordergründig abgelehnt wurden, waren sie für das Frömmigkeitsverstädnis der Reformation von Bedeutung. Der Beitrag untersucht diese Entwicklung in den Anfangsjahren der Reformation in Wittenberg. Inwieweit blieben die Verbindungen zwischen Beichte, Katechese, Abendmahlsseelsorge und sogar verschiedenen liturgischen Elementen erhalten? Inwieweit wurden sie verändert? Anhand der frühen Wittenberger Kirchenordnungen kommt dieser Beitrag zu dem Schluss, dass das Erbe des Dekrets „Omnis utriusque", wenn auch nicht in seiner Bedeutung, so doch in seiner äußeren Form bis in die Reformation hinein fortbestand.

„Tut um Gottes willen etwas Tapferes".
Ermutigt Zwingli mit diesem Aufruf die Zürcher zum Krieg?

Von Ulrich Gäbler

Der Erste Kappelerkrieg im Juni 1529 stürzte die Eidgenossenschaft in die tiefste Krise ihrer mehr als 200-jährigen Geschichte.[1] Die religionspolitischen Differenzen drohten in einen Krieg auszuarten. Huldrych Zwingli hatte deshalb Ende Mai 1529 einen detaillierten Feldzugsplan für die Zürcher Truppen entworfen.[2] Den Kern des Konflikts sah Zwingli im Solddienst[3] („Reislauf") bei den papsttreuen Innerschweizer Fünf Orten[4] Uri, Schwyz, Unterwalden, Luzern und Zug. Die Teilnahme von Schweizer Truppen an Kriegen, vor allem südlich der Alpen, nahm zu Anfang des 16. Jahrhunderts enorm zu. Es entwickelte sich ein eigentliches Militärunternehmertum, indem ausländische Mächte einheimische Angehörige der Führungsschicht mit der Rekrutierung von Truppen beauftragten und sie dafür finanziell mit „Pensionen" oder „Jahrgeldern" entschädigten. Die sogenannten „Fremden Dienste" hatten erhebliche Konsequenzen, die im Einzelnen schwer abzuschätzen sind. Sicher trug die militärische Emigration zum Abbau der Überbevölkerung in den ländlichen Gebieten bei. Die eingeführten Geldsummen förderten die Bildung einer

---

1. Einen guten Überblick über die politischen und rechtlichen Aspekte der Reformation in der Schweiz bietet *Leonhard von Muralt* in dem postum erschienenen Beitrag „Renaissance und Reformation", in: Handbuch der Schweizer Geschichte, Bd. I, Zürich 1972, 389–570; eine neuere Zusammenfassung bei *Martin Körner*, „Glaubensspaltung und Wirtschaftssolidarität (1515–1648)", in: Geschichte der Schweiz und der Schweizer, 3. unveränderte Auflage, Basel 2004, 357–446.
2. „Ratschlag über den Krieg", in: Huldreich Zwinglis Sämtliche Werke, hg. v. *Emil Egli* u. a., 21 Bde., Berlin, Leipzig, Zürich 1905–2013 (im Folgenden: Z), Bd. VI/II (1968), 424–440.
3. *Georg Gerig*, Reisläufer und Pensionenherren in Zürich, 1519–1532. Ein Beitrag zur Kenntnis der Kräfte, welche der Reformation widerstrebten, Zürich 1947; *Philippe Henry*, „Fremde Dienste", in: Historisches Lexikon der Schweiz, 13 Bde., Basel 2002–2014 (im Folgenden: HLS), Bd. 4 (2004), 789–796; *Valentin Groebner*, „Pensionen", in: HLS 9, 606f.; *Alain-Jacques Czouz*, „Reisläufer", in: HLS 10, 219f. Zwingli selbst bezog bis 1520 eine päpstliche Pension, s. *Oskar Farner*, Huldrych Zwingli. Seine Entwicklung zum Reformator, 1506–1520, Zürich 1946, 271–276; *Gottfried W. Locher*, Die Zwinglische Reformation im Rahmen der europäischen Kirchengeschichte, Göttingen, Zürich 1979, 67–74; Z VIII 781, Anm. 8.
4. „Ort" ist eine Bezeichnung für einen der selbstständigen Teile der Eidgenossenschaft, heute Kanton.

wohlhabenden Elite, die sich von der übrigen Bevölkerung abhob. Warnende Stimmen fehlten nicht. Angeprangert wurden sowohl die Abhängigkeit vom Ausland sowie luxuriöser Lebensstil, Verweichlichung, Müßiggang, Versuchung zu Verrat und Bestechlichkeit, und die Verleugnung alteidgenössischer Tugenden. Der hohe Blutzoll von Schweizer Kriegsknechten in den verlustreichen Schlachten in Oberitalien verstärkte die Ablehnung der Fremden Dienste.

Zwingli nahm diese Kritik auf und forderte praktische Konsequenzen. Nach seiner Überzeugung widersprechen Söldnertum und Pensionenwesen dem Willen Gottes, gefährden den Bund der Eidgenossenschaft und nötigen deshalb zum Eingreifen. Vor seinem Zürcher Amtsantritt 1519 hatte Zwingli als Pazifist im Geiste des Erasmus die Gräuel eines Krieges gebrandmarkt.[5] Jetzt, im Mai 1529, riet er zu einem Feldzug gegen die Innerschweizer. Im Juni 1529 setzten Friedensverhandlungen ein. Hat er dann mit seinem Aufruf an die Zürcher Obrigkeit „Tut um Gottes willen etwas Tapferes"[6] erneut zum Angriffskrieg ermuntert? Um einer Antwort auf diese Frage näherzukommen, ist es nötig, im Folgenden zuerst die Entwicklung von Zwinglis Anschauungen zu Solddienst und Pensionenwesen seit 1519 zu erörtern. Danach kommt in einem zweiten Teil seine Haltung unmittelbar vor und während des Ersten Kappelerkrieges zur Sprache.

I.

Schon bald nach Zwinglis Ankunft in Zürich begannen die Fremden Dienste zum zentralen politischen Thema der Eidgenossenschaft zu werden. Die anstehende Erneuerung des Soldbündnisses mit dem französischen König stieß auf Kritik. Schließlich blieb im Unterschied zu den anderen eidgenössischen Orten nur Zürich 1521 einem Abkommen fern und erließ im folgenden Jahr ein generelles Verbot des Pensionenwesens und des Reislaufens. Inwieweit Zwinglis Wirken die Entscheidungen der Obrigkeit beeinflusst hat, ist nicht

---

5. „Der Labyrinth", Frühjahr 1516, Z I 59f., Verse 201–212, zur Sache s. *Locher*, „Zwinglische Reformation" (wie Anm. 3), 67; *Olivier Bangerter*, La pensée militaire de Zwingli, Bern etc. 2003.

6. Als typisch für Zwingli und als Maxime christlichen Handelns fand dieser Satz im Zusammenhang mit dem Zürcher Reformationsjubiläum 2019 weite Verbreitung bis hin zur Zitierung auf der Sondermarke der Deutschen und der Schweizerischen Post (https://www.ref.ch/news/deutsche-post-wuerdigt-zwingli-erstmals-mit-einer-briefmarke (Zugriffsdatum: 16. Februar 2022).

mit Sicherheit festzustellen. Selbst schrieb er drei Jahre später, dass allein die Kraft des Wortes Gottes den Umschwung bewirkt habe,[7] ein unmissverständlicher Hinweis auf seine eigene Predigttätigkeit.

Deutlich fassbar wird Zwinglis radikale Absage an Solddienst und Pensionenwesen erstmals im Jahre 1522. Nachdem Schweizer Truppen auf den italienischen Schlachtfeldern große Verluste erlitten hatten, erhoben sich in Schwyz Zweifel an der Sinnhaftigkeit des französischen Soldbündnisses. Um Klarheit zu schaffen, tagte im Mai 1522 die Landsgemeinde von Schwyz. Zwingli lieferte den Gegnern des Vertrages mit einer rasch hingeworfenen Druckschrift Argumente für dessen Ablehnung. „Eine göttliche Vermahnung an die Eidgenossen zu Schwyz"[8] warnt schon im Vorwort die Miteidgenossen vor fremden Herren und weist darauf hin, dass sie gemäß der „göttlichen Schrift"[9] von ihnen befreit werden können. Bei der Analyse der gegenwärtigen Zustände in Schwyz kommt er zum Schluss, die gottgewollte Frömmigkeit habe bei den Altvorderen noch geherrscht, sie hätten deshalb mit göttlichem Beistand ihre Feinde überwinden können. Jetzt aber herrsche Eigennutz und Laster. Solddienst und Pensionenwesen führten zu Verderbnis von Sitten und zum Verfall von Recht und Gerechtigkeit. Gott sei aufgegeben worden. Doch die gerechte Strafe werde folgen. Ebenso wie es dem Volk Israel erging, das Prophetenwarnungen missachtete und deshalb gemäß dem „Willen Gotts" die Babylonische Gefangenschaft erdulden musste.[10] Die alten Eidgenossen hätten sich in siegreichen Schlachten gegen fremde Potentaten durchgesetzt, jetzt drohe der Eidgenossenschaft, durch deren Gold überwunden zu werden.[11] Für fremde Herren an einem Feldzug teilzunehmen, sei verwerflich. Zu einem Christenmenschen passe es überhaupt nicht, in den Krieg zu ziehen.[12] Dem Argument, das Alte Testament bezeuge doch kriegerische Auseinandersetzungen Israels mit seinen Feinden, begegnet Zwingli mit dem Hinweis, es habe sich aus-

---

7. „Der Hirt", 26. März 1524, Z III 11,10–13; *Huldrych Zwingli*, Schriften, hg. v. Thomas Brunnschweiler, Samuel Lutz, 4 Bde., Zürich 1995 (im Folgenden: ZS), Bd. I, 253 f.; s. noch: Johannes Kesslers Sabbata mit kleineren Schriften und Briefen, hg. v. Historischen Verein des Kantons St. Gallen, St. Gallen 1902, 90,28–40.
8. 16. Mai 1522, Z I 155–188; ZS I 75–100; vgl. *Bangerter*, La pensée militaire (wie Anm. 5), 38–64; *Christian Moser, Hans Rudolf Fuhrer*, Der lange Schatten Zwinglis. Zürich, das französische Soldbündnis und eidgenössische Bündnispolitik, 1500–1650, Zürich 2009, 33–37.
9. Z I 166,7.
10. Z I 177,3.
11. Z I 166,14–16.
12. Z I 179,17 f.

schließlich um einen Kampf gegen sündige Völker gehandelt.[13] Die theologische Argumentation Zwinglis in seiner „Vermahnung" geht vom Alten Testament aus und folgt einem Dreischritt: Ein sittenstrenges Leben entspricht dem Willen Gottes,[14] verlässt ein Volk diesen Weg, wird es gewarnt, auf eine Missachtung der Mahnung folgt die verdiente Strafe. In den folgenden Jahren wird der Reformator dieses am Alten Testament gewonnene Beweisverfahren immer wieder aufnehmen und bis 1529 nach verschiedenen Seiten hin vertiefen.

In den kommenden beiden Jahren 1523 und 1524 fielen in Zürich Entscheidungen, die zum Durchbruch der Reformation führten. Zu Anfang des Jahres 1523 ließ der Rat ein Religionsgespräch veranstalten, das sich mit der Rechtmäßigkeit von Zwinglis Wirken auseinandersetzen sollte. Als Ergebnis dieser Disputation stellte die Obrigkeit fest, niemand sei imstande gewesen, Zwinglis Auffassungen zu widerlegen. Deshalb könne er mit seinen Predigten fortfahren, und ebenso sollten die Pfarrer Zürichs wie er in Übereinstimmung mit der Bibel lehren. Nach dieser Klärung der theologischen Grundlage folgte im Oktober desselben Jahres eine zweite Disputation, die den Weg zur Auflösung des traditionellen Kirchenwesens freimachte. Die dominierende Rolle Zwinglis bei diesen Veränderungen schlug sich einmal in einer an der Disputation gehaltenen programmatischen, später gedruckten Predigt über das Pfarramt nieder („Der Hirt") und ebenso im Auftrag der Obrigkeit, eine zusammenfassende Darstellung der reformatorischen Lehre zu veröffentlichen („Eine kurze christliche Einleitung").[15]

Die Vorgänge in Zürich alarmierten die eidgenössischen Bündnispartner. Ohne Beteiligung von Zürcher Abgeordneten tagten sie im Januar 1524 und schickten hernach eine Delegation an die Limmat mit dem Vorwurf, die dortigen Vorgänge brächten Hass und Spaltung in die Eidgenossenschaft. Die Angegriffenen verteidigten sich geschickt mit einer eigenen Druckschrift[16] und konnten auf einer gemeineidgenössischen Versammlung („Tagsatzung") am 1. April 1524 einer Verurteilung durch die Miteidgenossen entgehen. Diese stellten sogar fest, nichts Unfreundliches gegen Zürich im Sinn zu haben.[17] Die Front der Reformationsgegner bröckelte ab. Trotzdem verschärfte sich die

---

13. Z I 177,22–24.
14. S. u. Anm. 163–167.
15. 17. November 1523, Z II 626–663. Zu „Der Hirt" s. Anm. 7.
16. Amtliche Sammlung der ältern Eidgenössischen Abschiede aus dem Zeitraume von 1521 bis 1528, Bd. IV, Abt. 1a, bearb. v. Johannes Strickler, Brugg 1873 (im Folgenden: EA), Nr. 173, zu f, 398–406; Zwingli hat „mehr oder weniger weitgehenden Einfluss auf die Abfassung ausgeübt", *Emil Egli*, in: Z III 70.
17. EA IV/1a, Nr. 173, zu f, 398.

Lage für Zürich im Laufe des Monats April. Die entschiedenen Gegner einer kirchlichen Umgestaltung ergriffen die Initiative. In einer Zusammenkunft am 8. April erklärten die Innerschweizer Fünf Orte, sie wollten das herkömmliche Kirchenwesen bewahren, alle reformatorischen Bestrebungen unterdrücken und bestrafen.[18] Mit Ausnahme von Zürich, Schaffhausen und Appenzell beschloss die eidgenössische Tagsatzung am 28. Juni 1524, an der bewährten christlichen Lehre festzuhalten und Zürich aufzufordern, die ketzerischen Zustände abzustellen.[19] Eine Scheidung der Geister hatte eingesetzt. Obwohl Zürich isoliert blieb, hielt es entschlossen am bisherigen Kurs fest.

Unter den Vorwürfen an die Zürcher Adresse wog am schwersten die Anklage politischer Natur, Zürich gefährde den Bestand der Eidgenossenschaft. Als Entgegnung auf diese Beschuldigung verfasste Zwingli den Aufruf „Eine treue und ernstliche Vermahnung an die Eidgenossen", 2. Mai 1524,[20] und kehrte den Spieß um. Nicht die reformatorische Bewegung bedrohe den Bestand der Eidgenossenschaft, wohl aber der Reislauf. Die Begründung für diese Widerrede lieferte Zwingli ähnlich wie in der „Vermahnung" von 1522 mit politischen, ökonomischen und sozialen Argumenten, allerdings erweiterte er den Kreis der Angesprochenen und wandte sich an alle Eidgenossen. Theologische Erwägungen bleiben jetzt weitgehend beiseite, Beweise aus dem Alten Testament spielen keine Rolle. Um größere Überzeugungskraft zu gewinnen, erschien die „Vermahnung" anonym. Zwinglis Autorschaft ist allerdings unbestritten. Der Verfasser will als ein im Ausland lebender Eidgenosse und Laie erscheinen, leugnet sogar, sich in kirchlich-theologischen Dingen auszukennen, denn er wisse ja nicht, ob die sogenannte „neue Lehre", das heißt die Reformation, ein Irrtum sei oder nicht.[21] Scharf stellt Zwingli wiederum der Zeit der Altvorderen, die beim wahren Gott geblieben seien und nach dessen Willen[22] lebten, das korrupte Heute gegenüber. Durch Gottes Hilfe habe man sich aus der Willkürherrschaft des Adels befreien sowie Recht und Gerechtigkeit herstellen können.[23] Jetzt sei man weit davon entfernt,[24] eine neue Herrschaftsschicht sei am Entstehen,[25] und der überall ausgebreitete Eigennutz füh-

---

18. EA IV/1a, Nr. 175, 410f.
19. EA IV/1a, Nr. 188a, 444f.
20. Z III 97–113; ZS I 313–329, mit Einleitung und Übertragung ins Neuhochdeutsche durch Hans Ulrich Bächtold, auf die ich mich im Folgenden gelegentlich stütze; vgl. *Bangerter*, La pensée militaire (wie Anm. 5), 64–117.
21. Z III 110, 12–15.
22. S. u. Anm. 163–167.
23. Z III 103,1–104,4.
24. Z III 105,31–33.
25. Z III 108,25–28.

re zum Streit.²⁶ Das Eigennutzdenken streicht Zwingli noch stärker hervor als 1522. Nur dessen Beseitigung werde Frieden bringen,²⁷ dann sei noch feste Hoffnung auf Gott.²⁸ Auf doppelte Weise gefährde der Reislauf die Eidgenossenschaft. Zum einen brächten Geschenke fremder Potentaten die Einheimischen dazu, ohne jede Rücksicht auf das Wohl der Eidgenossenschaft alles zu tun, was die ausländischen Herren verlangten.²⁹ Zum anderen hätten aus der Fremde zurückgekehrte Kommandanten ihre Soldaten verlassen und jetzt damit begonnen, wegen der Predigt von Gottes Wort in der Heimat Unruhe zu stiften, und versucht, die Eidgenossen gegeneinander aufzuhetzen.³⁰ Zwingli sorgt sich um die Zukunft der Eidgenossenschaft. Insbesondere befürchtet er wegen der reformatorischen Predigt schwerwiegende Auseinandersetzungen zwischen den Bündnispartnern, womit er unübersehbar Zürichs prekäre Situation im Auge hat.³¹

Die knappen, theologisch geprägten Aussagen bringen ohne ausführliche Erläuterung Grundsätzliches zur Sprache. Abgesehen von dem schon genannten Hinweis auf den „Willen Gottes" widerspricht Zwingli der Meinung, wegen des Soldvertrages mit Frankreich sei schon alles verloren, die Schweiz heillos zerstritten, bald werde sie untergehen. Dem setzt er die Überzeugung entgegen, wer sich bessere, dem verweigere Gott die Gnade nicht.³²

In einer bemerkenswerten Passage³³ spricht Zwingli die eidgenössischen Bündnispartner direkt an. Das gegenseitige Aufhetzen führe nur ins Verderben. Deshalb sollten sie sich in den Streit ihrer Pfarrer um Glauben und Sakrament nicht einmischen. Dies brächte nur Zwietracht. Die Zeit werde lehren, wer recht habe. Zwingli hat scheinbar kein direktes Interesse an kirchlich-theologi-

---

26. Z III 105,6f.
27. Z III 105,5–8.
28. Z III 105,9.
29. Z III 105,16–19.
30. Z III 109,16–29.
31. Zwingli bespricht die Lage Zürichs in seiner Schrift „Plan zu einem Feldzug", Z III 539–583; ZS III 1–29, mit Einleitung und Übertragung ins Neuhochdeutsche durch *Rainer Henrich*, die Datierung ist unsicher (von Mitte 1524 bis Anfang 1526). Darüber hinaus erörtert Zwingli detailliert Plan und Durchführung kriegerischer Aktionen gegen die V Orte. Erstaunlicherweise widmet der Reformator dem Pensionenwesen nicht mehr als einen Halbsatz und begnügt sich damit, die Bestrafung der Pensionenherren zu nennen, Z III 576, 5–7. Vgl. *von Muralt*, „Renaissance und Reformation" (wie Anm. 1), 490f.; *Bangerter*, La pensée militaire (wie Anm. 5), 123–153.
32. Z III 111,7–14.
33. Z III 110,2–15, vgl. dazu *Oskar Farner*, Huldrych Zwingli. Seine Verkündigung und ihre ersten Früchte, 1520–1525, Zürich 1954, 481, und *Bangerter*, La pensée militaire (wie Anm. 5), 77f.

schen Klärungen. Der Schein trügt. Für ihn hat die Neuordnung des Kirchenwesens keine nachrangige Bedeutung. Um die Reformation zu erringen und, wie in Zürich geschehen, zu sichern, bedarf es politischer Veränderungen, nämlich der Abschaffung des unmoralischen Reislaufs. Dieser falle dahin, wenn Gottes Wort ungehindert verkündigt werde. Mit dieser zeitlichen und kausalen Abfolge schließt sich der Kreis: Verkündigung des Wortes Gottes mit dem Anprangern von gesellschaftlichen Missständen, Warnung vor Strafe, Abstellen des Reislaufs, reformatorische Erneuerung.

In den Monaten nach der Zweiten Zürcher Disputation von Oktober 1523 hatte sich Zwingli intensiv mit dem Alten Testament beschäftigt.[34] Diese Studien vertieften sein Verständnis von Geschichte und Gegenwart, brachten ihn zu einer biblisch breiter abgestützten Sicht auf die Aufgaben eines Pfarrers und trugen zur Klärung seiner eigenen Rolle als führender Theologe Zürichs bei. Die Gegenwart charakterisiert Zwingli als eine besondere Zeit, die sich durch die Verkündigung des Wortes Gottes auszeichne. Seit Langem sei es nicht mehr gepredigt worden, jetzt habe Gott das Licht seiner Wahrheit neu angezündet,[35] stärker sei Gottes Wort jetzt hervorgetreten als jemals seit dem Anfang des Christentums.[36] Das Verständnis von „Gottes Wort" in theologischer und anthropologischer Perspektive hatte Zwingli im Jahre 1522 in seiner Schrift „Von Klarheit und Gewissheit des Wortes Gottes"[37] erörtert. Aufgrund seiner alttestamentlichen Lektüre fügt er nun ein wesentliches neues Element hinzu. Er fasst deren Ertrag schärfer und wendet ihn auf die Gegenwart an. Israels Propheten geißelten Unrecht und Machtmissbrauch.[38] Dasselbe geschehe jetzt, Gott schicke rechtzeitig Propheten, um die sündige Welt zu warnen.[39] Sollten die Übeltäter die Warnungen gehört haben, die Zustände allerdings nicht ändern und verbessern, dann werde die Strafe folgen.[40] Zwingli füllt den schon 1522 gewonnenen prophetischen Dreischritt, indem er ihn ins Heute überträgt. Unüberhörbar verknüpft er diese prophetischen Warnungen mit der Notwendigkeit einzugreifen und nicht allein Gottes Gericht abzuwarten: „Doch Gott hat immer auch die gestraft, die den Sündern nicht entgegengetreten sind. Und da einige ihr Unwesen ganz offen betreiben, muß man dies abstellen oder erwarten, daß Gott sein Schwert über das ganze Volk erhebt und

---

34. Z III 5,14–6,2.
35. Z III 60,5–9.
36. Z III 27,28–28,9.
37. 6. September 1522, Z I 328–384.
38. „Wer Ursache gebe zu Aufruhr", Dezember 1524, Z III 432,13–16.
39. Z III 36,17–19.
40. Z III 62,20–22.

gebraucht."[41] Damit ging Zwingli über das hinaus, was er bisher vertreten hatte. Eine aktivere Rolle kündigte sich an. Ein Jahr später war es so weit.

Das Zürcher Reislaufverbot vom Jahre 1522 ließ sich nicht lückenlos durchsetzen.[42] Hunderte Untertanen zogen in fremde Dienste. Mehrmals erneuerte der Rat sein Verbot, setzte Strafen fest, verfügte Todesurteile gegen Begünstiger des Solddienstes und belegte einfache Kriegsknechte mit Geldbußen. Anfang des Jahres 1525 kam es wiederum zu einem massiven Anstieg wegziehender Reisläufer. Die Zürcher Obrigkeit bekräftige am 7. Februar das Verbot und nahm Verdächtige fest.[43] Zwingli sah sich dem Vorwurf ausgesetzt, seine Stimme nicht gegen diesen Missstand in Zürich selbst erhoben zu haben. In einer Predigt stellte er sich dieser Kritik und räumte ein, längere Zeit geschwiegen zu haben.[44] Es sei nicht notwendig gewesen, da der Rat eifrig gegen den fremden Kriegsdienst aufgetreten sei,[45] womit er unausgesprochen dem Rat vorwirft, darin jetzt nachgelassen zu haben. Diese Kritik an den Versäumnissen des Rates verknüpfte der Prediger mit einer scharfen Verurteilung der Pensionennehmer und der Hauptleute, die Kriegsknechte mit Schiffen wegführten.[46] Sie seien Metzgern gleich, die Vieh nach Konstanz brächten, Geld dafür nähmen, um ohne Vieh zurückzukommen. Das trieben sie immer wieder.[47] In seinem Zorn werde Gott strafen. Einen Ausweg gebe es: „Gott hat gesagt: ‚Entferne den Bösen aus deiner Mitte'."[48] Wenn man zur Ruhe kommen wolle, dann „müssen wir die Pensionenherren und Hauptleute unter uns entfernen."[49] Diese radikale Forderung überliefert auch Zwinglis Nachfolger Heinrich Bullinger in seiner Reformationsgeschichte.[50] Unmissverständlich rief Zwingli den Rat

---

41. Z III 111,3–7; Übertragung ins Neuhochdeutsche im Anschluss an Hans Ulrich Bächtold, ZS I 327; vgl. o. Anm. 20.
42. Zum Folgenden s. *Gerig*, Reisläufer (wie Anm. 3), 32–43.
43. *Gerig*, Reisläufer (wie Anm. 3), 45.
44. Von der Predigt hat sich die Nachschrift eines unbekannten Zuhörers erhalten: „Predigt wider die Pensionen", hg. v. *Ernst Gagliardi*, in: Zwingliana 3/11 (1918, Nr. 1), 337–347 mit dem Tagesdatum 5. März 1525. Im Folgenden ziehe ich diese Edition heran. Die Herausgeber der kritischen Zwingliausgabe kannten diese Nachschrift nicht. Sie stützten sich bei ihrem Abdruck (Z III 586–589) auf die Wiedergabe der Predigt in: *J. J. Hottinger, H. H. Vögeli* (Hg.), Heinrich Bullingers Reformationsgeschichte, 3 Bde., Zürich 1838, I, 258–261. Die Nachschrift lag Bullinger vor, doch er brachte am Text erhebliche Änderungen an.
45. „Predigt" (wie Anm. 44), 340.
46. „Predigt" (wie Anm. 44), 344.
47. „Predigt" (wie Anm. 44), 343.
48. „Predigt" (wie Anm. 44), 345. Zwingli bezieht sich auf Bibelstellen wie Deuteronomium 17,2 und 12.
49. „Predigt" (wie Anm. 44), 345.
50. *Bullinger*, Reformationsgeschichte (wie Anm. 44), I, 260.

zu einem harten Vorgehen gegen die Förderer des Reislaufs auf und löste damit den Grundsatz des Vorjahres, man müsse das Unwesen abstellen, mit einem konkreten Appell ein. Eine unmittelbare Reaktion auf Zwinglis Predigt ist nicht bekannt. Allerdings hielt der Reislauf weiterhin an.[51] Doch im nächsten Jahr griff der Rat durch. Zwingli spielte dabei eine entscheidende Rolle.[52] In einer Predigt von Mitte September 1526 hatte Zwingli aufgedeckt, dass in Zürich Pensionenherren ungestraft ihr Unwesen treiben könnten.[53] Daraufhin ließ der Rat Zwinglis Vorwürfe im Einzelnen überprüfen. An zwei Tagen stand der Reformator als Zeuge selbst Rede und Antwort. In einer längeren Eingangserklärung[54] führte er aus, seine Kanzelworte mit Bedacht gewählt zu haben. Denn er habe gesehen, dass alle, die des Pensionennehmens verdächtig seien, dem Evangelium[55] Widerstand leisteten und große Machenschaften erkennen ließen. Er habe seine Stimme erheben müssen, denn vor dem Richterstuhl Gottes würde er sein Schweigen nicht verantworten können. Er wisse, in Zürich würden Pensionen genommen, und auch andernorts gebe es Umtriebe, die gegen Mandate des Rates verstießen. Solange die Obrigkeit diesen Übelstand nicht abstelle und entsprechend strafe, werde er nicht schweigen.[56] Nur wenn der Rat bereit sei, die Angelegenheit gründlich zu untersuchen, wolle er alles, was er über Pensionennehmer wisse, offen darlegen, „doch nicht als Ankläger, sondern als einer, der gefragt wird".[57]

Tatsächlich berichtete der Reformator in einem zweiten Verhör so ausführlich über einzelne Personen, die er als Pensionennehmer verdächtigte, dass der protokollierende Stadtschreiber Wolfgang Mangolt hinzusetzte, die Aussagen des Reformators seien so umfangreich gewesen, dass es unmöglich gewesen sei, alles schriftlich festzuhalten.[58] Das Verfahren endete mit einer aufsehenerregenden Entscheidung. Wegen der Annahme von Pensionen verurteilte der

---

51. Der Rat wies die Gemeinden an, den fremden Kriegsdienst zu verbieten und Verdächtige zu melden, *Bangerter*, La pensée militaire (wie Anm. 5), 119.
52. „Zeugenaussage Zwinglis", 11. und 12. Oktober 1526, Z V 402–415; *Gerig*, Reisläufer (wie Anm. 3), 53–69; *Bangerter*, La pensée militaire (wie Anm. 5), 119–122.
53. Die Predigt ist nicht erhalten. Zwingli erwähnt sie in seiner Zeugenaussage, Z V 406,10–407,2. Siehe das Folgende.
54. Z V 406,8–408,12.
55. Für Zwingli zielt das Evangelium wie das Gesetz auf ein gottgefälliges Leben, denn die Gesetzespredigt sei Teil der Verkündigung des Evangeliums. Siehe Z XV 236,2–6: „Dum praedicatur euangelium, omnes convincantur peccatores esse, nam et euangelii pars est legis praedicacio, poenitentia. Arguit ergo evangelium consciencias, ut erubescant et convertantur." Luthers Kontrastierung von Gesetz und Evangelium liegt Zwingli fern.
56. Z V 407,11 f.
57. Z V 408,11 f.
58. Z V 411,12–14.

Rat den betagten Junker, langjährigen Ratsherren und vielfachen Delegierten der Stadt in auswärtigen Missionen Jakob Grebel (ca. 1460–1526) zum Tode.[59] Das Urteil wurde am 30. Oktober vollstreckt. Die Hinrichtung traf bei Zeitgenossen auf Unverständnis, Zwingli galt ihnen als Anreger und Betreiber des Schuldspruchs. Im Lichte seiner bisherigen Äußerungen zu Reislauf und Pensionenwesen lässt sich eine konsequente Linie feststellen vom prophetischen Dreischritt bis hin zu dem Aufruf: „Entferne den Bösen aus deiner Mitte". Diese Aufforderung schließt Vernichtung ein. Der Reformator hat das Todesurteil zweifellos begrüßt. Weitere Prozesse gegen Pensionenherren endeten mit geringfügigen Strafen oder der Einstellung des Verfahrens.[60]

Verständlich wird Zwinglis verstärktes Eingreifen im Kampf um das Pensionenwesen durch einen Blick auf seine theologische Entwicklung, insbesondere seine intensive exegetische Arbeit am Alten Testament. Mit den erwähnten alttestamentlichen Studien 1523/1524 erarbeitete sich Zwingli die Grundlagen für seine Tätigkeit als Experte für den ersten Teil der Bibel an der sogenannten „Prophezei". Ab September 1523 plante man am Zürcher Großmünster die Einrichtung einer theologischen Ausbildungsstätte.[61] Im Juni 1525 war es dann so weit. Für die Bibelschule bürgerte sich im Anschluss an 1. Korintherbrief 14, 26–33 der Name „Prophezei" ein.[62] Am Beginn diente sie vor allem der Schulung von schon im Amte stehenden Pfarrern der Stadt. Zu Zwinglis Lebzeiten hat man im Chor des Großmünsters nur das Alte Testament behandelt, für das Neue Testament war das Fraumünsterstift auf der anderen Seite der Limmat zuständig. Die kursorische Exegese des Alten Testaments eröffnete jeweils der Hebräischdozent mit der Erläuterung des Urtextes, hernach legte Zwingli den Abschnitt aufgrund des griechischen Bibeltextes der Septuaginta lateinisch aus, hierauf folgte durch einen Pfarrer eine Ansprache zum Text in deutscher Sprache. Die Teilnahme stand jedermann offen. Von der Mehrzahl der Exegesen Zwinglis haben sich Nachschriften erhalten. Seine besondere Wertschätzung für die Propheten Jesaja und Jeremia zeigt sich daran, dass er nur die Erklärungen zu diesen beiden biblischen Büchern selbst herausgebracht hat.[63] Sie sind grundlegend für Zwinglis Verständnis des Alten Testaments. Am

---

59. *Martin Lassner*, „Jakob Grebel", in: HLS 5, 662; *Walter Jacob*, Politische Führungsschicht und Reformation. Untersuchungen zur Reformation in Zürich 1519–1528, Zürich 1970, 173–177.
60. *Gerig*, Reisläufer (wie Anm. 3), 53–69.
61. *Emidio Campi*, „Die Reformation in Zürich", in: *Amy Nelson Burnett, Emidio Campi* (Hg.), Die schweizerische Reformation. Ein Handbuch, Zürich 2017, 71–133, hier: 88f.
62. Z IV 361–365; 393,26–419,6.
63. Ediert in: Z XIII und XIV.

höchsten schätzte er das Jesajabuch, das er in der Prophezei von September 1527 bis Ende Februar 1528 behandelte.[64] Doch ließ ihn der Prophet nicht los, denn schon im Monat darauf legte er dieses Prophetenbuch bis Dezember 1528 seinen täglichen Predigten im Großmünster zugrunde.[65] Beinahe jeden Tag, sechzehn Monate lang, hat sich der Reformator mit Jesaja beschäftigt.

II.

In der zweiten Hälfte der Zwanzigerjahre des 16. Jahrhunderts festigten sich die konfessionellen Gegensätze, und mit ihnen erhöhte sich das politische Konfliktpotenzial zwischen den Bündnispartnern.[66] Die konfessionellen Trennlinien zeichneten sich mit der Badener Disputation vom Jahre 1526 ab.[67] Sie fand unter der Verantwortung der Tagsatzung statt, wohin alle eidgenössischen Stände ihre Delegierten entsandt hatten. Das traditionelle Kirchenwesen verteidigte der Ingolstädter Theologieprofessor Johannes Eck, ihm stand auf der Gegenseite der Basler Reformator Johannes Oekolampad gegenüber. Zwingli selbst nahm an der Disputation nicht teil, da er wie der Rat der Zusicherung freien Geleits nicht traute.[68] Stattdessen äußerte er sich in mehreren, zum Teil auch gedruckten Schriften sowohl zur Ausrichtung der Disputation selbst wie zu den von Eck vorgelegten Thesen.[69] Für unseren Zusammenhang ist von Belang Zwinglis Vorwurf an die Adresse der V Orte, sie würden sich durch die geforderte Anwendung des Wormser Edikts von 1521 mit der Reichsacht über Luther und dessen Anhänger dem deutschen Reichstag unterstellen und damit die altbewährte schweizerische Freiheit beschränken.[70] Zwingli geißelte die Verbindungen zum Ausland und brachte damit einen politisch gewichtigen Vorwurf gegenüber den Innerschweizern ins Spiel, der später eine bestimmende Rolle in der Auseinandersetzung der Religionsparteien spielte. Angesichts der eindeutigen Mehrheitsverhältnisse an der Tagsatzung

---

64. *Edwin Künzli*, „Nachwort zu den Jesaja-Erklärungen", in: Z XIV 411 f.
65. Z XV.
66. Zum Folgenden s. *von Muralt*, „Renaissance und Reformation" (wie Anm. 1), 488–500; *Helmut Meyer*, „Kappelerkriege", in: HLS 7, 91–93.
67. *Alfred Schindler, Wolfram Schneider-Lastin* (Hg.), Die Badener Disputation von 1526. Kommentierte Edition der Protokolle, Zürich 2015.
68. Siehe seine „Antwort über das zugeschickte Geleite", 16. Mai 1526, Z V 155–170.
69. Z V 1–195; 202–271.
70. Z V 179,4–13; 215,5–14; vgl. *Locher*, „Zwinglische Reformation" (wie Anm. 3), 186: In diesen Schriften Zwinglis „wird kräftig das schweizerische Misstrauen gegen die Ausländer geschürt."

konnte die Verurteilung Zwinglis und seiner Anhänger nicht überraschen.[71] Dagegen stimmten die vier Städte Bern, Basel, Schaffhausen und selbstverständlich Zürich. Die von den V Orten angestrebte gemeineidgenössische Verurteilung der Reformation misslang. Der durch die Religionsfrage entstandene Graben zwischen den Bundesgenossen hatte sich weiter vertieft. Bald folgten politische Konsequenzen.

Erst nach der Badener Disputation setzte sich 1528 die Reformation in Bern, dem politisch und wirtschaftlich mächtigsten Stadtstaat der Schweiz, endgültig durch. Diese Klärung beendete die isolierte Stellung Zürichs, weitere Städte wie Basel, Schaffhausen und St. Gallen folgten später dem Beispiel Berns. Als politische Konsequenz begannen diese Städte auf eidgenössischer Ebene geeint zu agieren und sie verpflichteten sich durch einen Bündnisvertrag („Christliches Burgrecht"[72]) zur Verteidigung gemeinsamer Interessen. Sie erstrebten nach außen hin ihre Religionspolitik zu koordinieren und in ihrem Inneren durch enge Kontakte ihrer Prädikanten eine möglichst große Einheitlichkeit in Lehre und Praxis der einzelnen Kirchen zu erreichen.

Die Städte Bern und Zürich schlossen am 25. Juni 1528 ein solches Bündnis. Die beiden Städte unterschieden sich jedoch in mehrfacher Hinsicht voneinander.[73] In Bern fehlte eine Figur wie Zwingli mit ähnlichem theologischem, kirchlichem und politischem Gewicht. Zudem hielten sich in den ersten Jahren nach dem Umschwung in der bernischen Elite ansehnliche reformationskritische Kräfte, welche eine konsequente Religionspolitik erschwerten. Anders als in Zürich gab es in Bern unter den Ratsherren mit Niklaus Manuel (ca. 1484–1530) eine Führergestalt zur Verteidigung der Reformation.[74] Im Jahre 1528 stieg der ehemalige Söldnerführer in französischen Diensten in wichtige zivile und militärische Ämter auf. Diplomatisches Geschick und kluges Durchsetzungsvermögen machten ihn zum Gesicht der bernischen Außenpolitik. Auf zahlreichen Reisen vertrat er Bern an eidgenössischen Konferenzen und als Gesandter zu einzelnen Orten. Allein im Juni 1529 war er dreimal auf Zürcher Boden.[75] Genauso alt wie Zwingli sollte er

---

71. *Schindler, Schneider-Lastin,* Badener Disputation (wie Anm. 67), 181 f.
72. *Heinzpeter Stucki,* „Christliches Burgrecht", in: HLS 3, 376 f.; *von Muralt,* „Renaissance und Reformation" (wie Anm. 1), 491.
73. *Martin Haas,* Zwingli und der Erste Kappelerkrieg, Zürich 1965, 54–60.
74. *Cäsar Menz, Hugo Wagner* (Hg.), Niklaus Manuel Deutsch, Maler Dichter Staatsmann, Bern 1979; 450 Jahre Berner Reformation. Beiträge zur Geschichte der Berner Reformation und zu Niklaus Manuel, Bern 1981; *Rudolf Dellsperger,* „Manuel Deutsch, Niklaus", in: Religion in Geschichte und Gegenwart, 4. Aufl., Bd. V, Tübingen 2002, 773; s. noch u. Anm. 111 f.
75. *Jean-Paul Tardent,* Niklaus Manuel als Staatsmann, Bern 1967, 26.

in der eidgenössischen Religionspolitik zum prominentesten Gegenspieler des Zürcher Reformators werden. Die beiden kannten sich seit der Berner Disputation von Januar 1528, bei der Zwingli als Hauptvertreter der reformatorischen Seite auftrat und Manuel als „Rufer" eine moderierende Funktion innehatte.[76]

Die unterschiedlichen Positionen von Manuel und Zwingli traten erstmals im sogenannten Unterwaldner Handel zutage.[77] Ende Oktober 1528 rebellierten Bauern im Berner Oberland. Die Lage verschärfte sich, als 800 katholische Unterwaldner die Grenze zu Bern überschritten, bernische Dörfer besetzten und bis zum Westufer des Brienzersees vorstießen. Manuel erhielt den Auftrag, mit einem Truppenkontingent die Eindringlinge nötigenfalls mit Waffengewalt zu vertreiben. Dank seines bedachten Vorgehens gelang es ihm, ein Blutvergießen zwischen den Eidgenossen zu vermeiden. Die Unterwaldner zogen ab, doch warf ihnen Bern wegen der Missachtung bernischer Hoheitsrechte und des gewaltsamen Vorgehens den Bruch der eidgenössischen Bünde vor. Unter Vermittlung von Delegierten aus anderen Teilen der Schweiz setzten intensive Gespräche ein, um einen Ausgleich zwischen Bern und Unterwalden zu erreichen. Tatsächlich einigte man sich am 18. März 1529. Allerdings traf das Übereinkommen bei dem mit Bern verburgrechteten Zürich auf harsche Kritik und strikte Ablehnung. Man beschuldigte die Berner der unangebrachten Nachgiebigkeit gegenüber der katholischen Seite. Unter dem Eindruck dieser Vorhaltung zog Bern seine Zustimmung zurück. Zwingli hatte in einem Gutachten vom 20. März 1529 der abschlägigen Reaktion Zürichs vorgearbeitet.[78] Darin geht er über die zwischen Bern und Unterwalden hängigen Rechtsfragen hinaus und fordert, die mittlerweile zwischen den Religionsparteien eingetretenen Auseinandersetzungen auf eidgenössischer Ebene zu lösen. Verantwortlich für die Konflikte machte er die Feindseligkeiten der katholischen Seite mit den „Intrigen der Pensionenherren".[79] Die offizielle Antwort Zürichs ging in wesentlichen Teilen auf Zwinglis „Ratschlag" zurück, übernahm allerdings nicht die Passage zu den Pensionenherren. Die beiden Burg-

---

76. *Hans Rudolf Lavater*, „Niklaus Manuel Deutsch – Themen und Tendenzen", in: 450 Jahre Berner Reformation (wie Anm. 74), 289–312. Der Rufer hatte zur Aufgabe, „diejenigen auf das Rednerpodium zu bitten, die sich als Votanten eingetragen hatten", 305. Zu den Meinungsverschiedenheiten zwischen Manuel und Zwingli, s. u. Anm. 80f., 111, 113, 149.

77. *Tardent*, Niklaus Manuel (wie Anm. 75), 221–240; *Haas*, Zwingli (wie Anm. 73), 48–84; ferner die Einleitungen von Muralts zu den beiden unten erwähnten „Ratschlägen" Zwinglis, Anm. 78 und 83.

78. „Erster Ratschlag betreffend den Frieden zwischen Bern und Unterwalden", 20. März 1529, Z VI/II 318–344.

79. Z VI/II 341,4–6.

rechtsstädte waren sich angesichts der eingetretenen Meinungsverschiedenheit mit der Zürcher Zurückweisung Berns der Gefahr eines schwerwiegenden innerprotestantischen Zwists wohl bewusst. Deshalb begab sich Manuel nach Zürich, um persönlich einen Ausgleich zu suchen. Am 4. April 1529 sprach er fast eine volle Stunde vor dem Großen Rat der Zweihundert,[80] der in Zürich die letzte Entscheidung in allen schwerwiegenden Geschäften zu fällen hatte. Von der Rede sind nur Bruchstücke überliefert. Sicherlich rief er zum Frieden unter den Eidgenossen auf und begründete seine Argumentation mit der Friedensbotschaft des Evangeliums, wie er es zwei Monate später vor demselben Gremium wiederum tat.[81] Es nützte nichts. Zürich blieb bei seiner ablehnenden Haltung. Der Beschluss des Rates lehnt sich an Zwinglis Ratschlag vom 20. März an und übernimmt jetzt verschärfend auch den Passus zum verheerenden Einfluss der Pensionenherren.

Mit diesem Entscheid ist Zwinglis beharrliche Verurteilung des Pensionenwesens in der gesamten Eidgenossenschaft erstmals Bestandteil der Zürcher Politik geworden. Die Berner brachten dieser Haltung Zürichs keinerlei Sympathie entgegen, zumal bei ihnen das Söldnerwesen noch nicht verschwunden war.[82] Die Verhandlungen zu einem Frieden zwischen Bern und Unterwalden gingen weiter, doch Zürich nahm daran nicht mehr teil. Deshalb schickte der Zürcher Rat eine Delegation nach Bern, um einen neuen Friedensvorschlag zu erarbeiten. Die Zürcher Abgesandten erhielten von der zuständigen Ratskommission einen Verhandlungsauftrag („Instruktion"), der sich erneut auf einen Vorschlag Zwinglis mit harten Friedensbedingungen stützte,[83] wiederum forderte der Reformator ein Pensionenverbot. Wohl mit Absicht waren die Forderungen so hochgeschraubt,[84] dass eine Zustimmung Unterwaldens von vornherein als aussichtslos erscheinen musste. Wahrscheinlich wollte man Zeit gewinnen, um die sich ausbreitende Reformation in Territorien der Ost- und Nordschweiz durch einen „eidgenössischen Grundvertrag"[85] rechtlich zu sichern. Tatsächlich verständigten sich die beiden Burgrechtsstädte am 18. April 1529 darauf, den V Orten einen solchen weitreichenden Vorschlag[86] zu ma-

---

80. *Tardent*, Niklaus Manuel (wie Anm. 75), 235–237.
81. S. u. Anm. 111 f.
82. Aktensammlung zur Geschichte der Berner Reformation 1521–1532, hg. v. *Rudolf Steck, Gustav Tobler*, Bern 1923, Nr. 1847, 1956.
83. „Zweiter Ratschlag betreffend den Frieden zwischen Bern und Unterwalden", 12. April 1529, Z VI/II 361–371, s. dazu *Haas*, Zwingli (wie Anm. 73), 77–80.
84. Zum Beispiel sollte es den Unterwaldnern zehn Jahre lang verboten sein, an den eidgenössischen Tagsatzungen teilzunehmen, Z VI/II 370,7.
85. *Von Muralt*, in: Z VI/II 364.
86. *Von Muralt*, in: Z VI/II 364 f.

chen. Vom Pensionenverbot war darin allerdings nicht mehr die Rede, wohl konkretisierte er das andere von Zwingli in seinem Ratschlag vom 20. März 1529 anvisierte Verhandlungsziel, nämlich die Anerkennung der in den sogenannten „Gemeinen Herrschaften" (oder „Vogteien")[87] reformatorisch gewordenen Kirchgemeinden.

Neben den Städten Zürich, Bern, Basel, Schaffhausen und Biel hatte sich die Reformation in den ersten Monaten des Jahres 1529 in den ländlichen Gebieten der Nord- und Ostschweiz ausgebreitet.[88] Die Religionsfrage in den dortigen „Gemeinen Herrschaften" führte zum folgenschwersten Konflikt zwischen den katholischen und reformatorischen Ständen. Die Gemeinen Herrschaften gingen in der Regel auf gewaltsame Erwerbungen aller oder mehrerer Stände zurück. Entsprechend oblag diesen die Regierung in einem solchen Untertanengebiet, das im Namen aller zuständigen Orte ein auf zwei Jahre gewählter Vogt verwaltete. Das Recht, jeweils den Vogt zu bestimmen, lag bei einem der regierenden Stände, die in einer festgelegten Folge an die Reihe kamen. Die Vögte stellten, je nach Zuständigkeit, Uri, Schwyz, Unterwalden, Luzern, Zug, Glarus, Zürich, Bern. Der Streit ging um die Frage, wer in den Gemeinen Herrschaften die Kompetenz zur Einführung der Reformation habe. Die Städte des „Christlichen Burgrechts" nahmen den Standpunkt ein, es liege im Ermessen der einzelnen Gemeinden, durch Mehrheitsbeschluss die Messe abzuschaffen und reformatorische Prediger anzustellen. Wie schon im Burgrecht mit Bern vereinbart, schützte Zürich entstehende Gemeinden in der Grafschaft Baden, in den Freien Ämtern, im Thurgau, im Gaster, im Rheintal und im Untertanenland der Fürstabtei Sankt Gallen. Die V Orte hielten dagegen fest, die jeweils regierenden Stände hätten zusammen über die Religionsfrage ihrer Gemeinen Herrschaft zu entscheiden, und der von ihnen eingesetzte Vogt habe sich danach zu verhalten. Diese Haltung der katholischen Orte ist naheliegend, da sie bei der Verwaltung aller größeren Vogteien die Mehrheit hatten und deshalb dort den Übergang zur Reformation verhindern konnten. Im Unterschied zur Tagsatzung erforderte nämlich ein Beschluss der regierenden Orte keine Einstimmigkeit. Die beiden Parteien gerieten in eine staatsrechtliche Pattstellung.

---

87. *André Holenstein*, „Gemeine Herrschaften", in: HLS 5, 201 f.
88. Zum Folgenden *Haas*, Zwingli (wie Anm. 73), 85–95; *Heinzpeter Stucki*, Bürgermeister Hans Rudolf Lavater 1492–1557. Ein Politiker der Reformationszeit, Zürich 1973, 84; *von Muralt*, „Renaissance und Reformation" (wie Anm. 1), 496–498; *Kurt Spillmann*, Zwingli und die zürcherische Politik gegenüber der Abtei St. Gallen, St. Gallen 1965 (= Diss. phil.I Universität Zürich, 1965), 21–38. Im April 1529 verfasste Zwingli drei „Ratschläge" zur Aufhebung der Abtei und zur Reformation in deren Gebiet, Z VI/II Nr. 133, 135, 136.

Die katholischen Orte sahen sich durch den Fortgang der Reformation in den Gemeinen Herrschaften von Einkreisung bedroht und schlossen deshalb am 22. April 1529 mit dem habsburgischen König Ferdinand I. eine „Christliche Vereinigung" ab,[89] die sich, wie auch das „Christliche Burgrecht", als Vertrag mit defensiven Zielen verstand. Die Religionsfrage durch Verhandlungen zu lösen, schien je länger je mehr aussichtslos zu werden. Weiter verschärfend wirkte die zunehmende Protestantisierung in den Freien Ämtern, weil sich dadurch eine territoriale Brücke zwischen Zürich und Bern erreichen ließ, was in der Innerschweiz die Befürchtung auslöste, von den wichtigen Verbindungen mit den nördlich gelegenen habsburgischen Gebieten abgeschnitten zu werden. Die konfessionellen Spannungen verschärften sich. Schon Anfang April hatten sich Zürich ebenso wie die V Orte auf einen innerschweizerischen Waffengang eingestellt.[90]

Die evangelischen Städte fühlten sich ihrerseits durch die „Christliche Vereinigung" gefährdet, da ihr Gebiet sowohl im Norden wie im Osten an habsburgische Territorien grenzte.[91] Deshalb forderten sie die V Orte auf, das Bündnis mit Ferdinand I. zu widerrufen.[92] Mit diesem Verlangen verknüpften sie das Angebot einer detaillierten, umfassenden Friedensordnung im Sinne des erwähnten Vorschlages der Burgrechtsstädte vom 18. April 1529. Betroffen machte die Evangelischen der Vorwurf der Innerschweizer, sie seien böse Christen, seien vom rechten Glauben abgefallen und lehrten unchristlich sowie aufrührerisch. Darauf antworteten sie mit der Feststellung, sie hielten sich an die zwölf Artikel des christlichen Glaubens. Sicherlich geht diese Behauptung auf Zwingli zurück, denn der Reformator hat sich mehrmals, um von seinem „Glauben Rechenschaft abzulegen",[93] des Apostolikums bedient. Die V Orte

---

89. *Heinzpeter Stucki,* „Christliche Vereinigung", in: HLS 3, 377; *von Muralt,* „Renaissance und Reformation" (wie Anm. 1), 492 f.

90. *Von Muralt,* in: Z VI/II 373 und 407 f.; *Haas,* Zwingli (wie Anm. 73), 123–125.

91. Das Folgende aufgrund von Zwinglis Gutachten „Ratschläge betreffend Verhandlungen mit Bern", 19. bis 22. Mai 1529, Z VI/II 407–423; *Haas,* Zwingli (wie Anm. 73), 129–133; *Tardent,* Niklaus Manuel (wie Anm. 75), 239 f. Martin Haas hat als Erster die chronologische Reihenfolge einschlägiger undatierter Aktenstücke zum Kappelerkrieg rekonstruiert, darauf konnte Leonhard von Muralt mit weiteren eigenen Präzisierungen aufbauen. Diese Zwinglitexte erschienen in der Lieferung 21 von Z VI/II im Oktober 1966.

92. *Von Muralt,* in: Z VI/II 407 f.

93. „Die beiden Predigten Zwinglis zu Bern", 19. und 30. Januar 1528, Z VI/I 443–498. In der ersten Predigt legt er das Apostolikum Artikel für Artikel aus und erklärt am Anfang, er wolle „mines gloubens rechnung geben", Z VI/I 450,4. Vgl. noch den am Apostolikum ausgerichteten Aufbau der beiden apologetischen Bekenntnisschriften „Fidei ratio", 3. Juli 1530, gerichtet an Karl V., Z VI/II 753–817 und „Expositio fidei", Sommer 1531, an Franz I., Z VI/V 1–163.

wiesen die Vorschläge der Städte zurück und bekräftigten, an der „Christlichen Vereinigung" festzuhalten.[94] Statt der Aussicht auf einen Frieden nahmen die Spannungen zwischen den Eidgenossen noch zu. Um sich über das weitere Vorgehen gegenüber den Innerschweizern zu verständigen, luden die Burgrechtsstädte Bern und Zürich zu einem Treffen ihrer Gesandten nach Aarau. In Zürich nahm die Ausarbeitung der Instruktionen mehrere Tage in Anspruch. Zwingli lieferte dazu Vorschläge.[95] Der Reformator erörtert verschiedene Maßnahmen, wie militärische Interventionen[96] oder eine Blockade der Lebensmittelzufuhr namentlich von Brotgetreide und Salz, was man den Schwyzer Untertanen mitteilen sollte, um sie gegen ihre Oberen aufzubringen.[97] Im Zentrum steht allerdings die Bekämpfung des Pensionenwesens. Denn es gehe darum, die Hauptschuldigen, die Pensionenherren, zu beseitigen, wenn das nämlich geschähe, hätten alle miteinander Frieden. Wenn nicht, müsse man mit Gottes Hilfe stets energisch darauf hindrängen,[98] bis man sich des Gesindels entledigt habe und die Angelegenheit zu einem christlichen, ruhigen Ende gebracht sei.[99] In der Endfassung der Instruktion blieb das Pensionenwesen allerdings unerwähnt, im Unterschied zu den Vorschlägen militärischer Natur.

Noch bevor die Gesandten in Aarau zusammentraten, kam es zu einem folgenschweren Zwischenfall.[100] Der Pfarrer im zürcherischen Schwerzenbach, Jakob Kaiser, wirkte daneben noch in einer Kirchgemeinde in der Gemeinen Herrschaft Gaster, die von Schwyz und Glarus regiert wurde. Schwyz protestierte gegen die reformatorische Tätigkeit Kaisers und dessen Schmähungen katholischer Frömmigkeit. Da er seine zwinglianische Predigttätigkeit fortsetzte, ließen ihn die Schwyzer am 22. Mai 1529 gefangen nehmen und auf eigenes Gebiet bringen. In Zürich war man sich der Gefahr für Kaisers Leben bewusst und sandte deshalb den erfahrenen, doch gegenüber Zwinglis politischer Kompromisslosigkeit kritisch eingestellten Ratsherrn Hans Edlibach[101] nach Schwyz, um ein ordentliches Gerichtsverfahren einzufordern. Als die De-

---

94. Tagsatzung von Baden, 7.-13. Mai 1529, s. *von Muralt*, in: Z VI/II 408.
95. Vgl. Einleitung und Kommentar von Muralts zu Zwinglis „Ratschlägen" (Anm. 91).
96. Z VI/II 420,13–422,3, zum Teil lehnt er sich an seinen „Plan zu einem Feldzug" an, s. o. Anm. 31.
97. Z VI/II 420,6–9.
98. Zwingli gebraucht an dieser Stelle das Wort „tringen", dessen Bedeutungsfeld schließt eine militärische Aktion ein, Schweizerisches Idiotikon. Wörterbuch der schweizerdeutschen Sprache, 14. Bd., Frauenfeld 1987 (im Folgenden: SI), 1103f.
99. Z VI/II 420, 1–5.
100. Zum Folgenden: *Haas*, Zwingli (wie Anm. 73), 131f.
101. *Jacob*, Führungsschicht (wie Anm. 59), 145–147.

legierten der beiden Burgrechtstädte in Aarau eintrafen, hatte Zürich seine frühere Instruktion bereits um den aktuellen Fall Kaiser erweitert. Unmissverständlich weist es nun die Gesandten an, die Berner darüber zu informieren, Zürich werde im Falle einer Hinrichtung Kaisers dies unverzüglich mit der Tat an „Leib und Gut" der Schwyzer rächen.[102] Zürich drohte also mit einem Krieg. Das Treffen in Aarau blieb ohne Ergebnis. Die beiden Berner Gesandten Niklaus Manuel und Peter von Werdt reagierten mit Unverständnis auf Zürichs Ultimatum und schrieben noch am selben Tag nach Bern, „die Verbündeten betrachteten den Krieg als unvermeidlich".[103] Jakob Kaiser erlitt als Ketzer am 29. Mai 1529 in Schwyz den Feuertod.

Ehe in Zürich die Debatte über das Vorgehen nach Kaisers Tod einsetzte, hatte Zwingli bereits einen „Ratschlag über den Krieg" verfasst.[104] An den Anfang setzt der Reformator die Hinrichtung Kaisers. Sie könne nicht ungestraft bleiben. Daraufhin rät er zum sofortigen Angriff auf Schwyz, und zwar ohne eine Verständigung mit Bern. Zürich solle allein handeln. Im Einzelnen erörtert er danach, wo und wie die Zürcher Truppen einzusetzen seien, bis hin zu deren Bewaffnung und Versorgung mit Proviant.[105] Wie bei wichtigen politischen Geschäften üblich, nahm eine vorberatende Kommission am 1. Juni 1529 die Arbeit auf, um die Entscheidung des Großen Rates vorzubereiten.[106] Ihr lag Zwinglis „Ratschlag" vor. In der Kommission waren die Meinungen über das weitere Vorgehen geteilt. Wohl übernahmen die Ratsherren Zwinglis Begründung für die Notwendigkeit, Schwyz zu bestrafen, doch lehnten sie den Aufruf des Reformators zum unverzüglichen Losschlagen ab. Im Gegensatz zu Zwingli riet man zur Abstimmung mit Bern. In diesem Sinne entschied der Rat.

In Bern hatten mittlerweile die Gesandten nach der Rückkehr von Aarau mündlich über den festen Kriegswillen der Zürcher berichtet.[107] Als Reaktion darauf sandten die Berner zwei Schreiben an die Limmat, in denen sie eindringlich darum baten, den Frieden zu wahren und es nicht auf einen Krieg ankommen zu lassen. Einen dritten Brief hielten sie für so wichtig, dass sie eine Gesandtschaft beauftragten, ihn nach Zürich zu bringen.[108] Kennzeichnend

---

102. Zitiert in: Z VI/II 416.
103. *Tardent*, Niklaus Manuel (wie Anm. 75), 240.
104. Entstanden zwischen dem 25. und 29. Mai, Z VI/II 424–440; vgl. *Haas*, Zwingli (wie Anm. 73), 133–135.
105. Die militärischen Ausführungen stützen sich zum Teil auf den „Plan zu einem Feldzug", s. o. Anm. 31.
106. Zum Folgenden s. *von Muralt*, in: Z VI/II 425–428.
107. *Tardent*, Niklaus Manuel (wie Anm. 75), 241 f.
108. Aktensammlung zur Geschichte der Berner Reformation (wie Anm. 82), Nr. 2314, 2316, 2318.

für die unterschiedliche Einstellung der Berner Elite zur Reformation ist die Zusammensetzung dieser Delegation: Niklaus Manuel, der die Reformation mit Nachdruck verteidigte, und Anton Bischof, der ihr eher skeptisch gegenüberstand.[109] In dem Brief mahnten die Berner wiederum zum Frieden und versicherten zugleich, Zürich entsprechend den Burgrechtsverträgen beizustehen, falls es mit Waffengewalt[110] angegriffen werde.

Zur Erläuterung des Briefes sprach Manuel am 3. Juni 1529 mehr als eine Stunde vor dem Großen Rat. Der Stadtschreiber Werner Beyel zeichnete die Rede auf.[111] In einem ersten Teil schildert Manuel die Position Berns. Wegen des Konflikts mit Schwyz und den anderen Inneren Orten wolle Bern keinen Krieg beginnen, denn Gottes Wort wisse nichts anderes als Friede und Einigkeit. In Zürich habe die Reformation angefangen, dort habe gütliches Handeln viel erreicht, Bern habe dabei vermittelnd gewirkt, es hätte sonst schon längst Krieg gegeben. Danach geht Manuel auf die konkrete konfessionelle Situation ein und mahnt dazu, die traditionelle Frömmigkeit des einfachen Volkes in den V Orten richtig einzuschätzen. Ein religiös motivierter Krieg bringe nichts. So leicht ließen sich die Innerschweizer nicht von der herkömmlichen Kirche trennen, weil sie treulich am Alten festhielten und das Pensionenwesen keineswegs verurteilten. Mit Spiess und Hellebarde könne man den Menschen den Glauben nicht eingeben. Knapp kommt Manuel in einem zweiten Teil auf die außenpolitischen Bedrohungen zu sprechen. Der Kaiser sei mit seinen Feinden nicht so sehr beschäftigt, als dass er nicht dazu in der Lage wäre, sich des Konflikts in der Eidgenossenschaft anzunehmen. Im Süden hätten die übel gesinnten Walliser ein starkes Heer stehen, und beim Herzogtum Savoyen wisse man

---

109. *Tardent*, Niklaus Manuel (wie Anm. 75), 241 charakterisiert Bischof als „altgesinnt".

110. Aktensammlung zur Geschichte der Berner Reformation (wie Anm. 82), Nr. 2318. Im Brieftext wird von einem „thätlichen" Angriff gesprochen, worunter sowohl „gewaltsam" als auch „kriegerisch" verstanden werden kann, SI 13, 2044f.

111. Vorzüglich ediert von *Hugo Wagner*, „Niklaus Manuel in Dokumenten", in: *Menz, Wagner*, Manuel, 1979 (wie Anm. 74), 121–137, hier: 134f. Eine detaillierte Analyse bietet *Tardent*, Niklaus Manuel (wie Anm. 75), 242–259, in der er Manuels Darstellung der offiziellen Politik Berns von dessen persönlicher Meinung unterscheidet. Bei einer Würdigung der Rede ist zu berücksichtigen, dass die Niederschrift Beyels Themen anreißt, ohne dies näher auszuführen. Die erforderlichen Ergänzungen bleiben naturgemäß unsicher. Da Beyel zudem die aus Zürcher Sicht wichtigeren Punkte notiert haben dürfte, muss offenbleiben, ob aus seinem Bericht ein zutreffender Gesamteindruck der Rede zu gewinnen ist. Zum Inhalt vgl. *Ulrich Im Hof*, „Niklaus Manuel als Politiker und Förderer der Reformation, 1523–1530", in: *Menz, Wagner*, Manuel, 1979, (wie Anm. 74), 92–99, bes. 97–99; *Gottfried W. Locher*, „Niklaus Manuel als Reformator", in: 450 Jahre Berner Reformation, (wie Anm. 74), 383–404, bes. 392–395.

nie, woran man sei. Im Falle eines gegnerischen Angriffs werde man der verbündeten Stadt beistehen. Beschwörend wendet er sich an seine Zuhörer „durch des liden cristi willen" bittend, Zürich solle nicht so hitzköpfig sein und die Eidgenossenschaft dem Wagnis eines Krieges aussetzen.[112] Auf friedlichem Wege gehe die Sache der Burgrechtsstädte voran. Wolle man aber Gewalt anwenden, so werde man Anstoß erregen, denn, so weist Manuel auf ein Jesuswort hin, wer einen Backenstreich empfängt, solle auch die andere Backe hinhalten (Matthäusevangelium 5,39). Abschließend bekräftigt Manuel die Berner Zusage, wenn es nötig sei, werde man Zürich beistehen, doch die Herren von Bern seien überzeugt, jetzt sei eine solche Notlage nicht gegeben.

Am Tag nach Manuels Rede überschlugen sich die Ereignisse.[113] Zwingli musste erkennen, dass Manuels Auftritt direkt gegen ihn und die Seinen mit ihrem unbedingten Kriegswillen gerichtet war. Deshalb ergriff der Reformator die Initiative und forderte, da die V Orte nicht auf die Klagen Zürichs eingegangen seien, den Rat dazu auf, das Heer aufzubieten, um das Unrecht zu strafen und die Verkündigung von Gottes Wort in deren Gebieten sicherzustellen. Der Rat lehnte ab und wollte weiter mit den Innerschweizern verhandeln. Daraufhin kündigte Zwingli seinen Rücktritt an, am nächsten Tag werde er Zürich verlassen. Etwa zur selben Zeit, als man den Reformator zum Bleiben überredete, kam aus Bern eine überraschende Nachricht. Dort hatte eine Zürcher Delegation vorgesprochen und einen Meinungsumschwung bewirkt. Im Gegensatz zu Manuels reservierter Haltung sagte man Zürich sofortige Unterstützung zu. Die Nachricht traf am Abend des 4. Juni in Zürich ein – in dringenden Fällen ritten die Boten einen Tag und eine Nacht von der Aare an die Limmat.[114] Vermutlich unter dem Eindruck von beidem, Zwinglis Rücktrittsdrohung und der wohlwollenden Antwort Berns, beschloss man wahrscheinlich noch in der Nacht vom 4. auf den 5. Juni den Auszug der Zürcher Truppen. Bern hatte bereits am 4. Juni seine Streitmacht mobilisiert.

Eine militärische Auseinandersetzung kündigte sich an.[115] Am 8. Juni erklärte Zürich den V Orten den Krieg in einem sogenannten „Absagebrief".[116] Am Tag darauf zog die Hauptmacht („Banner") aus und lagerte bei Kappel an

---

112. *Tardent*, Niklaus Manuel (wie Anm. 75), 248.
113. *Haas*, Zwingli (wie Anm. 73), 140–144; *von Muralt*, in: Z VI/II 429–431.
114. *Tardent*, Niklaus Manuel (wie Anm. 75), 22 f.
115. Die folgenden Ereignisse zusammengefasst bei *Martin Haas*, Huldrych Zwingli und seine Zeit. Leben und Werk des Zürcher Reformators, 2. Aufl., Zürich 1976, 231–237.
116. Der Absagebrief ist gedruckt in: Z VI/II 444–447, die V Orte erhielten ihn am 11. Juni 1529, Z VI/II 448 f. Zwingli hat einige unbedeutende „Randbemerkungen auf den Absagebrief an die Fünf Orte", 8. Juni 1529, angebracht, Z VI/II 441–447.

der Grenze zwischen Zuger und Zürcher Gebiet.[117] Zwingli begleitete das Banner hoch zu Ross mit einer Hellebarde auf der Schulter.[118] Seine Aufgaben als Prädikant im Felde hatte er in seinem „Plan zu einem Feldzug" beschrieben.[119] Neben dem Hauptmann bedarf es als Mitverantwortlichem eines „dapfren christlichen predicanten … [mit] vil redlichkeit, eerlich kriegen und tugenden, die der houptman nit selbs lert".[120] Tatsächlich verkündete Zwingli im Lager „Gottes Wort", und als man den 10. Juni festgelegt hatte, um in die Schlacht zu ziehen, sollte der Reformator vorher eine Predigt halten.[121] In Kappel wurde ein „Kriegsrat" eingerichtet, dem die militärische Führungsspitze sowie Ratsherren aus Zürich angehörten. Zwingli zog man zu Besprechungen bei. Dieses Gremium konnte zwar bei gewichtigen Entscheidungen nur mit Zustimmung des Großen Rates in Zürich vorgehen, doch gewann es zunehmend an Bedeutung. Da Kappel nur etwa eine halbe Tagesreise von Zürich entfernt lag, konnten Berichte und Entscheide rasch übermittelt werden. Am 9. Juni 1529 zog auch das Berner Banner aus. Zu den militärischen Spitzen gehörten Niklaus Manuel und Peter von Werdt. Später erhielten die beiden Städte noch Zuzug anderer Verbündeter, wie zum Beispiel von Basel, das Zwinglis Politik reserviert gegenüberstand und eher der Berner Linie folgte.[122] Die ersten Innerschweizer Truppen trafen ebenso am 9. Juni in Zug ein, zwei Tage später kam die Luzerner Hauptmacht dazu.[123]

Zürich beschränkte sich nicht darauf, das Banner gegen die Innerschweizer aufzubieten. Vielmehr benutzte es die Gelegenheit, um in den Gemeinen Herrschaften durch militärische Aktionen vollendete Tatsachen zu schaffen.[124] So führte zum Beispiel der leidenschaftliche Zwinglianhänger Hans Rudolf Lavater ein Truppenkontingent („Fähnlein") in die Ostschweiz. Sowohl im Gebiet der Abtei St. Gallen wie in den Gemeinen Herrschaften brachte er mit mehr oder weniger Druck Gemeinden dazu, sich durch Mehrheitsentscheid der Reformation anzuschließen und sich dem Schutz Zürichs zu unterstel-

---

117. Über den Aufmarsch der Truppen s. *Haas*, Zwingli (wie Anm. 73), 146–158.
118. So ein Augenzeuge: *Georg Finsler* (Hg.), Die Chronik des Bernhard Wyss, 1519–1530, Basel 1901, 121,6.
119. Z III 580,4–581,2.
120. Z III 580,4–7; 581,1 f.
121. So ein weiterer Augenzeuge: *Kaspar Hauser* (Hg.), Die Chronik des Laurencius Boßhart von Winterthur, 1185–1532, Zürich 1903, 341 u. 342. Vgl. noch *Haas*, Huldrych Zwingli (wie Anm. 115), 239 zu Zwinglis Predigttätigkeit.
122. *Haas*, Zwingli (wie Anm. 73), 165–167.
123. *Haas*, Zwingli (wie Anm. 73), 156–158.
124. *Haas*, Zwingli (wie Anm. 73), 146–155.

len.¹²⁵ Mit seinen gewaltsamen Aktionen in den gemeinsam regierten Territorien beging Zürich einen eklatanten Bruch eidgenössischer Bünde, da es fremde Hoheitsrechte verletzte.¹²⁶ Zwingli befürwortete dieses Vorgehen.

Auf die Kriegserklärung ließ die Stadt ein gedrucktes Manifest¹²⁷ folgen, das sich auch an die Eidgenossen außerhalb Zürichs richtete und zur Rechtfertigung des Angriffs dienen sollte. Darin heißt es ausdrücklich, man beabsichtige allein die Verursacher der schrecklichen Zustände, nämlich die Pensionenherren, zu bestrafen. Im Absagebrief fand sich dieser Passus nicht. Dagegen nimmt die Nennung des eigentlichen Kriegszieles im Manifest das zentrale Anliegen Zwinglis auf und geht wahrscheinlich auf den Reformator selbst zurück. Es ging Zwingli und den Zürchern weniger um einen „Krieg" als um eine „Strafaktion".

Unmittelbar vor dem Aufbruch nach Kappel ließ Zwingli den Räten eine Erklärung¹²⁸ zukommen, in der er vier Friedensbedingungen nennt, welche die knappe Bemerkung im Manifest erläutern. Sie wiederholen im Wesentlichen, was Zwingli bisher gesagt hatte. Erstens müssten die V Orte Gottes Wort genau gemäß dem Neuen und Alten Testament „frei" predigen lassen. Zur Abschaffung der Messe und zur Beseitigung von Bildern und kirchlichen Zeremonien solle niemand gezwungen werden, Gottes Wort werde dafür sorgen. Die „Christliche Vereinigung" mit König Ferdinand sei aufzulösen. Zweitens müssten für alle Zeiten Pensionen und sonstige Gaben fremder Herren verboten werden. Drittens seien die Empfänger von Pensionen und deren Verteiler an Leib und Gut zu strafen. Seine besondere Schärfe bekommt dieser Artikel durch Zwinglis Forderung, die Bestrafung habe zu geschehen, noch während Zürichs Heer in Kriegsbereitschaft sei. Viertens hätten die V Orte für Zürichs Kriegskosten aufzukommen. Wahrscheinlich schrieb Zwingli diese Zusammenfassung nieder, als er erfahren hatte, dass mehrere eidgenössische Orte sich anschickten, zwischen den Streitparteien zu vermitteln.¹²⁹ Neben der Präzisierung der Kriegsziele diente die Erklärung dazu, die Obrigkeit in

---

125. Zu Lavater s. *Jacob,* Führungsschicht (wie Anm. 59), 208–211; *Stucki,* Lavater (wie Anm. 88), 96–102, der von einem „Ostschweizer Feldzug" spricht, 99.

126. *Spillmann,* Zwingli (wie Anm. 88), 48.

127. „9. Juni 1529", abgedruckt in: EA IV/1b, Nr. 123,3, 225–227, hier: 227. Im gescheiterten sogenannten Alten Zürichkrieg (1456–1460) ging es den Zürchern um Landgewinn auf Kosten von Schwyz, *Martin Illi,* „Alter Zürichkrieg", in: HLS 1, 273f. Im Jahre 1529 lässt sich eine solche Absicht nicht erkennen, deshalb ist im Sinne Zwinglis statt „Krieg" der Begriff „Strafaktion" eher angebracht.

128. „Artikel, ohne die der Friede nicht abgeschlossen werden kann", 9. Juni 1529, Z VI/II 448–453.

129. EA IV/1b, Nr. 122,1, 222.

den kommenden Verhandlungen zur Standhaftigkeit zu ermuntern. Angesichts der Tragweite der Vorschläge wird sie Zwingli selbst kaum als durchwegs realistisch angesehen haben, eher als Zürcher Ausgangsposition für Friedensgespräche.

Als die Berner von Zürichs Angriffsplänen, wie sie in der Kriegserklärung und im Manifest zum Ausdruck kamen, erfuhren, tadelten sie den Bündnispartner in einem harschen Schreiben.[130] Sie hätten erwartet, Zürich begrüße die Vermittlungsbemühungen und enthalte sich jeder Drohung eines Angriffs. Käme es so weit, könnten die Zürcher nicht mit dem Beistand Berns rechnen. Tatsächlich sagte Zürich daraufhin zu, nicht auf gegnerisches Gebiet vorzurücken. Um die Vermittlungsbemühungen voranzutreiben, ergriff Bern die Initiative zu einem Zusammentreffen aller Orte am 12. Juni in Aarau. Den Druck auf ihre Gegner erhöhten die beiden Burgrechtsstädte durch eine Proviantsperre, die es den Innerschweizern unmöglich machte, Nahrungsmittel aus Süddeutschland einzuführen.[131]

Noch vor der geplanten Aarauer Zusammenkunft sandte der Reformator an „Bürgermeister, Kleine und Große Räte zu Zürich" ein umfangreiches Schreiben,[132] in dem er seine Position zu den anstehenden Friedensverhandlungen darlegte und eingehend begründete. Der Brief gliedert sich in drei Teile. Zu Beginn äußert Zwingli seine Sorge, die Auseinandersetzung mit den V Orten werde nicht ordentlich behandelt. Man möge ihm seine „harten" Predigten nicht vorwerfen: Er sei sich sicher, es gebe kein Blutvergießen, denn es gehe nämlich nur um die Beseitigung der Pensionen und des bestehenden Unrechts. Dennoch müsse das Truppenaufgebot aufrechterhalten bleiben, weil er fürchte, der Rat werde sich durch freundliche Worte der Gegenseite für einen Friedensschluss entscheiden, der allerdings ärger sein werde als ein Krieg.[133] Immer habe er es für notwendig erachtet, die Pensionenherren streng zu bestrafen, da sie die Unwissenden verführten und die Gläubigen unterdrückten. Deswegen habe er stets „harte Vorschläge" gemacht, um sie zum Fürchten zu bringen. Zum Besten der Sache könne er wohl auch für Milde eintreten, wie die Ratsherren ja gesehen hätten, als er noch in Zürich gewesen sei. Hierauf folgen die

---

130. „10. Juni 1529", Aktensammlung zur Geschichte der Berner Reformation (wie Anm. 82), Nr. 2348. Vgl. *Tardent*, Niklaus Manuel (wie Anm. 75), 259; *Haas*, Zwingli (wie Anm. 73), 158 f.; *von Muralt*, in: Z VI/II 448–450.
131. *Tardent*, Niklaus Manuel (wie Anm. 75), 260; *von Muralt*, in: Z VI/II 419, Anm. 6.
132. „11. Juni 1529", Z X 152–157; *Haas*, Zwingli (wie Anm. 73), 168 f.
133. Ähnlich heißt es zur selben Zeit in einem undatierten Brieffragment Zwinglis: „Nam ista pax, quam quidam tantopere urgent, bellum est, non pax. Et bellum, cui nos instamus, pax est, non bellum", Z X 147,2–4.

vier Artikel vom 9. Juni 1529 mit einzelnen Erläuterungen, die keine neuen Aspekte beibringen. In einem dritten Teil bespricht Zwingli die aktuelle Situation und skizziert das wünschbare weitere Vorgehen. Den Brief der Berner[134] möge man nicht ernst nehmen, sie seien über die Zürcher Absichten nur unvollständig unterrichtet. Vieles sei bisher noch nicht bedacht worden. Zwingli kommt auf Einzelheiten zu sprechen, doch der Grundtenor dieses Abschnitts ist die Mahnung an die Obrigkeit, „tapfer" zu bleiben im Kampf gegen die Pensionen. Nicht weniger als fünfmal ruft er sie dazu auf.[135] Da die Berner die Auflösung des Bündnisses der V Orte mit König Ferdinand vorantrieben, sei es Aufgabe der Zürcher, weiterhin „tapfer" gegen die Pensionen durchzuhalten, damit werde zwischen den beiden Städten eine völlige Einigkeit im Kirchlichen und im Weltlichen erreicht. Gott werde die Eidgenossenschaft nochmals aufrichten, doch nur, wenn die Zürcher „tapfer" blieben mit der Abschaffung der Pensionen, denn man sehe ja, wie das Evangelium Raum gewinne, aber die „pensiöner betrueben [verwirren] alle ding."[136] Der Gemeine Mann sei zuchtvoll, freundlich und treu. Allerdings gebe es Gegner in den eigenen Reihen, „schwarze Rösser",[137] sowohl in Zürich wie in Kappel. Darum müsse man standhaft bleiben.

Die für den 12. Juni vorgesehene Zusammenkunft in Aarau kam nicht zustande,[138] deshalb begann man direkte Verhandlungen zwischen den beiden Heeren unter Einschaltung von Vermittlern, sogenannten Schiedsleuten. Einen entscheidenden Schritt zur Lösung des Konflikts eröffnete der sich in beiden Feldlagern verbreitende Friedenswille. Mehrere Faktoren trugen dazu bei. Der besonnene Hauptmann des Zürcher Banners, Jörg Berger,[139] wollte jedes Blutvergießen vermeiden und forderte eine friedliche Einigung. Zu dieser Haltung beigetragen haben die Erfahrungen gemeinsamer Feldzüge mit Truppenführern der V Orte auf oberitalienischen Kriegsschauplätzen. Der Luzerner Chronist Johannes Salat berichtet von Verbrüderungen feindlicher Kriegsknechte über die Grenze hinweg. In die Schweizer Nationalgeschichte eingegangen ist die legendenhafte Szene der sogenannten Kappeler Milchsuppe.[140]

---

134. Siehe oben Anm. 130.
135. Z X 156,8 f.; 156,15 f.; 157,1 f.; 157,7–9; 157,15–17.
136. Z X 157,17.
137. Z X 157,5.
138. *Haas*, Zwingli (wie Anm. 73), 170.
139. *Jacob*, Führungsschicht (wie Anm. 59), 127–129; *Heinzpeter Stucki*, „Jörg Berger", in: HLS 2, 225; *Haas*, Zwingli (wie Anm. 73), 167. *Doris Klee*, Konflikte kommunizieren. Die Briefe des Grüninger Landvogts Jörg Berger an den Zürcher Rat (1514–1529), Zürich 2006.
140. *Johannes Salat*, Reformationschronik 1517–1534, bearb. v. *Ruth Jörg*, 3 Bde., Bern

Innerschweizer hätten eine große Schüssel mit Milch auf die Grenze gesetzt und die Zürcher herbeigerufen, die ihrerseits Brot einbrockten. Die beiden Gruppen hätten, jede auf ihrem eigenen Gebiet, die Suppe ausgelöffelt. Die Knappheit an Nahrungsmitteln sowohl im Zürcher[141] als auch im Innerschweizer Heer[142] verstärkte den Friedenswillen bei den einfachen Kriegsknechten.

Der Eindruck des Friedenswillens bei den Angehörigen beider Heere trug möglicherweise zu einem bemerkenswerten Schritt der Vermittler bei. Sie empfahlen, eine Gesandtschaft der V Orte solle im zürcherischen Feldlager auftreten, und am Tag danach sollten die Zürcher zu den Innerschweizern kommen. Tatsächlich erschienen am 14. Juni um 8 Uhr früh die Abgeordneten der V Orte mit etwa 30 Pferden vor den Zürcher Truppen.[143] Anwesend waren auch die Vermittler aus mehreren Orten. Man hatte eine Rednerbühne errichtet, um die sich die Soldaten sammelten. Zuerst sprachen die neutralen Abgesandten. Eindringlich forderten sie eine friedliche Lösung. Scharf prangerte danach ein Zürcher Vergehen der Innerschweizer an, die man nicht länger hinnehmen wolle. Der Luzerner Schultheiss und Truppenkommandant Hans Hug[144] schloss sich den Vermittlern an und warnte davor, sich ins Unglück zu stürzen. Nach mehreren Rednern trat Zwingli auf. Der Reformator rückte Gefährlichkeit und Schaden des Pensionenwesens ins Zentrum, dabei sprach er direkt Hug als dessen Profiteur an. Ohne Abschaffung der Geldzahlungen werde es in der Eidgenossenschaft keinen Frieden geben. Am Morgen des 16. Juni kamen die Zürcher Delegierten in das Lager der V Orte in Baar.[145] Über die

---

1986, Text Band 2: 1528–1534, 579,20–580,9; *Bullinger*, Reformationsgeschichte (wie Anm. 44), II 182f., eine kolorierte Abbildung aus einer Kopie von Bullingers Reformationschronik aus dem Jahre 1605 bei *Meyer*, „Kappelerkriege" (wie Anm. 66), 92; *Georg Kreis*, „Die Kappeler Milchsuppe, Kernstück der schweizerischen Versöhnungsikonographie", in: Schweizerische Zeitschrift für Geschichte 44, 1994, 288–310.

141. EA IV/1b, Nr. 130,1,6, 240; Zürich fragte in Basel nach, ob es dort Getreide kaufen könne, „17. Juni 1529", Aktensammlung zur Geschichte der Basler Reformation in den Jahren 1519 bis Anfang 1534, III. Bd., 1528 bis Juni 1529, hg. v. *Paul Roth*, Basel 1937, Nr. 658 f.

142. Später stellten die V Orte fest, sie hätten wegen Kornmangels Frieden schließen müssen, *Haas*, Zwingli (wie Anm. 73), 158.

143. EA IV/1b, Nr. 131,1 u. 2, 241; *Salat*, Reformationschronik (wie Anm. 140), 580,17–581,20; *Kessler*, Sabbata (wie Anm. 140), 320,1–321,17; *Bullinger*, Reformationsgeschichte (wie Anm. 44), II, 180 (mit chronologischen Irrtümern); *Haas*, Zwingli (wie Anm. 73), 171 f.

144. *Gregor Egloff*, „Hans Hug", in: HLS 6,517.

145. Zum Folgenden s. EA IV/1b, Nr. 135, 253–256; *Salat*, Reformationschronik (wie Anm. 140), 581,21–585,8; *von Muralt*, in: Z VI/II 455 f. Wegen Regenwetters fand die Zu-

Klagen der Gäste berichteten die Innerschweizer an ihre Oberen. Die Zürcher hätten ihnen Vorhaltungen gemacht „mit vil artikeln und einer langen predig, jetz unmüglich ze erzelen; doch so hand sy bsunderlich vil wesens triben mit den pensionen etc."[146] Schließlich kamen die beiden Seiten überein, nichts gegeneinander zu unternehmen und die Vermittler die weiteren Verhandlungen führen zu lassen.

Mittlerweile hatten die Berner die Initiative ergriffen, um den Friedensprozess voranzutreiben. Sie stellten am 14. Juni eine Liste ihrer Friedensbedingungen[147] zusammen und ließen sie Zürich zukommen. Wie schon zu Anfang des Monats schickten sie zudem eine gewichtige Delegation an die Limmat. Als Wortführer trat Niklaus Manuel auf. Am Abend des 15. Juni trafen die Berner in Zürich ein, wo sich auch eine Gesandtschaft aus Basel eingefunden hatte.[148] Noch in der Nacht brachten die Berner ihre Friedensbedingungen vor. Unerwähnt bleiben dabei die zentralen Anliegen Zwinglis und der Zürcher: „Freie" Predigt des Wortes Gottes, Abschaffung des Pensionenwesens, Bestrafung von dessen Profiteuren. Über das Ergebnis dieser nächtlichen Besprechung liegen keine zuverlässigen Nachrichten vor, doch kann als sicher gelten, dass es zu keiner Annäherung der Standpunkte kam, denn die Zürcher hatten bereits am 15. Juni nach Einsicht in die Berner Vorschläge beschlossen, an ihren bisher bekanntgemachten Bedingungen festzuhalten.[149] Zugleich ermächtigten sie den Kriegsrat in Kappel, mit den Bernern weiter zu verhandeln. Sicherlich kannte Zwingli am 16. Juni diese beiden Beschlüsse.

Die Ereignisse der vergangenen Tage ließen den Reformator zweierlei erkennen. Zum einen: Bisher hatte Zürichs Großer Rat seine Position gestützt und durch die Entscheidungen vom 15. Juni bekräftigt. Allerdings kam mit der Übertragung der Verhandlungskompetenz an den Kriegsrat ein Element der Unsicherheit ins Spiel, denn Zwingli war sich bewusst, dass es innerhalb der eigenen Reihen ernst zu nehmende Kritiker seiner Politik gab, „schwarze Rösser", wie er sie nannte. Zum anderen: Eine ähnliche Gefährdung seiner Friedensforderungen musste er im Beschluss von Baar sehen, die Verhandlungen in

---

sammenkunft einen Tag später als geplant statt (EA IV/1b, Nr. 135,1, 254). Baar liegt, etwa eine Wegstunde von Kappel entfernt, im heutigen Kanton Zug.

146. EA IV/1b, Nr. 135,3, 256.

147. EA IV/1b, Nr. 136,38, 267–269. Zu den in den folgenden Tagen auf verschiedenen Ebenen stattfindenden Gesprächen s. *Tardent*, Niklaus Manuel (wie Anm. 75), 260–263; *Haas*, Zwingli (wie Anm. 73), 174–176; *von Muralt*, „Einleitung und Kommentar zu ‚Artikel des Friedens', 16./17. Juni 1529", in: Z VI/II 454–467.

148. EA IV/1b, Nr. 133,1 u. 2, 243 f.

149. *Haas*, Zwingli (wie Anm. 73), 175.

die Hände der Vermittler zu legen, da er von diesen annehmen musste, sie würden seine Vorschläge mit den weitreichenden Maßnahmen ablehnen.

An diesem 16. Juni 1529, zu Mittag um eins, schrieb Zwingli seinen Brief an Bürgermeister und Rat von Zürich mit der Aufforderung: „Tut um Gottes Willen etwas Tapferes".[150] Der Reformator beginnt das Schreiben mit der Mitteilung, soeben seien die „Boten" (aus Baar) zurückgekehrt. Die Herren mögen beachten, was nun Sache sei. Die V Orte redeten gute Worte, sie würden bitten und betteln. Doch dadurch sollten sie sich nicht irremachen oder durch deren „Flennen" beeindrucken lassen, sondern wie schon immer mit allem Ernst handeln, die günstige Situation[151] nicht preisgeben und wirkungsvoll auf einen Frieden drängen. Denn niemand rede freundlicher als diese Leute, doch sobald man das Feldlager verlasse, kämen sie in einem Monat wieder und fingen einen Krieg an. Die Ratsherren mögen „tapfer" sein und sich nicht selbst schaden. In einer kurzen Zwischenbemerkung schlägt Zwingli eine Regelung für das weitere Verfahren rund um die Abtei St. Gallen vor. Unmittelbar danach folgen die beiden Sätze: „Tůnd umb gotzwillen etwas dapfers, ich will üch by minem leben nit verfueren noch hälen.[152] Man kann nit alle ding schreiben."[153] Sie sollen fest im Glauben stehen, das „Flennen" nicht beachten, bis der Friedensvertrag[154] geschlossen ist. Bei der Datumsangabe setzt er zweimal ein „eilends" hinzu. Denn mittlerweile waren neben den Boten aus Baar auch die Berner Delegierten und die anderen Gesandten aus den evangelischen Städten Basel und St. Gallen in Kappel eingetroffen, so dass die Verhandlungen mit dem Zürcher Kriegsrat bevorstanden.[155]

---

150. Zürich Staatsarchiv, E I. 3.1. Nr. 45; Edition in: Z X 164 f.; Faksimile in: Ulrich Zwingli. Zum Gedächtnis der Zürcher Reformation, 1519–1919, Zürich 1919. Abb. 167. Der Brief ist in einem Zug geschrieben, mit einer einzigen Korrektur. Freundlich danke ich Frau Barbara Leimgruber vom Zürcher Staatsarchiv für die Besorgung einer Kopie von Zwinglis Brief.

151. Das von Zwingli verwendete Wort „vorteil" kann präzis „günstige, überlegene Stellung in der Kriegführung" (SI 12, 1500) bedeuten, was er hier durchaus gemeint haben könnte.

152. Übertragung: „nicht ins Unglück führen noch zu etwas verleiten", SI 2, 1131 f. Die Deutung des Wortes hälen verdanke ich einem freundlichen Hinweis von Frau Dr. Ruth Jörg, Zürich.

153. Wahrscheinlich denkt Zwingli dabei an die Kritiker seiner Politik im Kappeler Lager. Namentlich bekannt ist Ratsherr Hans Escher (ca. 1470–1538), der seinerzeit im sogenannten Grebel-Prozess wegen des Pensionenverdachts für ein Jahr seine Mitgliedschaft im Großen Rat verlor, *Haas*, Zwingli (wie Anm. 73), 177; *Jacob*, Führungsschicht (wie Anm. 59), 151 f.; *Gerig*, Reisläufer (wie Anm. 3), 61 f.; s. o. Anm. 60.

154. Zwingli gebraucht hier das Wort „recht" im Sinne von „Vertrag", SI 6, 403 f.

155. EA IV/1b, Nr. 133,1. u. 2, 243 f.

Aus dem Brief spricht die tiefe Betroffenheit des Reformators über den Lauf der Dinge und zugleich die feste Überzeugung, das Richtige vom Rat zu fordern, bekräftigt durch die an eine Eidesformel erinnernde Wendung „bei meinem Leben". Nie zuvor hat Zwingli mit solcher Eindringlichkeit seine Oberen angesprochen und sie vor dem Nachgeben gewarnt.[156]

Die beiden Ausdrücke „etwas Tapferes" und „um Gottes willen" verlangen nach einer Erläuterung. Das Wort „tapfer" ist im Schweizerdeutschen des 16. Jahrhunderts in mehrfacher Bedeutung belegt.[157] Zwingli kann das Wort verwenden in Sinne eines „energischen Handelns", zum Beispiel von einem „tapferen Prediger" sprechen,[158] oder kollektiv, Venedig möge dem Kaiser „tapfer" widerstehen, damit er in Italien vernichtet wird und nicht über die Berge kommt.[159] Mehrfach gebraucht der Reformator das Wort im Zusammenhang mit dem Konflikt zwischen Zürich und den V Orten. Der Begriff „tapfer" wird zum bestimmenden Begriff seiner Erwartungen, Aufforderungen und Mahnungen an die Adresse der Zürcher Obrigkeit, am deutlichsten ausgesprochen im erwähnten Brief vom 11. Juni 1529. Damit zielt das „tapfer sein" vornehmlich auf die Haltung der Oberen in den Verhandlungen mit den Innerschweizern. Als die Spannungen zwischen den beiden konfessionellen Parteien wegen unterschiedlicher Auslegung des sogenannten Ersten Kappeler Landfriedens von Ende Juni 1529 weiter anhielten, mahnte Zwingli unmittelbar vor seiner Abreise zum Marburger Religionsgespräch wiederum die Obrigkeit: „Ihr sollt tapfer sein im Streit um den Frieden und sollt Euch vor nichts fürchten."[160] Aufgrund dieser Stellen kann „etwas Tapferes" gewiss auf Zürichs konsequentes, kompromissloses Bestehen auf den bekannten Friedensbedingungen gemünzt werden. Allerdings lässt sich nicht übersehen, dass Zwingli auch ein kriegerisches Vorgehen im Blick haben könnte. Denn im Kappeler Lager gab es neben den Befürwortern der zurückhaltenden Politik Berns gegenüber den

---

156. Ohne den Brief zu nennen, schreibt von Muralt: „Es war der Augenblick, da Zwingli am dringlichsten vor einem Nachgeben warnte, bevor die Forderungen Zürichs rechtlich festgelegt waren". *Von Muralt*, „Einleitung und Kommentar" (wie Anm. 147), 455. Später, in seinem Festvortrag „Zwinglis Reformation in der Eidgenossenschaft" bei der 450-Jahr Feier der Zürcher Reformation 1969 sagte von Muralt: „Zwingli formulierte seine Kriegsziele oder Friedensbedingungen […] mit den Worten ‚Tůnd umb gotzwillen etwas dapfers'", in: Zwingliana 13/1 (1969/1), 19–33, hier 25.
157. SI 13,970–976.
158. Z III 580,4, s. Anm. 120.
159. Z X 308,15–17, 17. September 1529.
160. Z X 296,11 f., 4. September 1529; ähnlich nochmals am 6. September 1529 von Straßburg aus am Schluss des Briefes: „Hiemit bewar úch gott in allem guten, und sind [seid] dapfer", Z X 301,3.

Innerschweizern gewichtige Stimmen, die trotz fortgeschrittener Friedensgespräche für eine kriegerische Lösung eintraten.[161] Was Zwingli am 16. Juni 1529 dachte, lässt sich nicht sicher feststellen, doch in einer ähnlichen Konfliktkonstellation zwei Jahre später trat Zwingli ausdrücklich für eine gewaltsame Lösung ein. Dabei wiederholte er die Argumentation früherer Jahre, die Eidgenossenschaft sei eine Gemeinschaft, in der es Aufgabe sei, gotteslästerliche Zustände zu bestrafen, da sonst alle dem Gericht Gottes verfallen seien.[162]

Die Redewendung „um Gottes willen" dient Zwingli als Verstärkung einer Ermahnung,[163] dabei ist der substantivische Charakter von „Wille" verblasst.[164] Doch kann er durchaus auch betont von „Gottes Wille" sprechen,[165] womit eine religiöse Komponente ins Spiel kommt, die in Zwinglis Theologie eine zentrale Rolle spielt. Denn für den Reformator ist Gottes Wille das Gesetz und dessen „Inhalt die Lehre von Gottes Wille".[166] Dessen Erkenntnis ist für das christliche Leben unabdingbar. Das kommt in der Zürcher Liturgie von 1528 zum Ausdruck. Den Predigtgottesdienst eröffnet folgendes Gebet: „Lassend unns gott ernstlich bitten, das er sin heylig ewig wort uns armen menschen gnädigklich offnen welle und in erkanntnuß sines willens ynfueren."[167] So dürfte in dieser markanten Passage von Zwinglis Aufruf ein Verweis auf „Gottes Wille" im Sinne eines gesetzestreuen Verhaltens mitschwingen.

Zwinglis eindringlicher Aufruf an seine Oberen blieb ohne Erfolg. Die Berner Position setzte sich durch.[168] Der sogenannte Erste Kappeler Landfrieden

---

161. *Haas*, Zwingli (wie Anm. 73), 180.
162. „Was Zürich und Bernn not ze betrachten sye in dem fünförtischen handel", 17.–22. August 1531, Z VI/V 233, 8–234, 8.
163. Zum Beispiel in der „Ermahnung an die Eidgenossen", 1524 (Z III 113,20), zweimal im Brief an die Gesandten der evangelischen Städte Zürich, Bern, Schaffhausen und St. Gallen, 24. Juli 1529 (Z X 213,2f.; 214,8) oder im Brief an Landgraf Philipp von Hessen, 2. November 1529 (Z X 331,6f.).
164. Siehe Deutsches Wörterbuch von Jacob Grimm und Wilhelm Grimm, Bd. 30, Leipzig 1960, 167: „die grundbedeutung von *um-willen* ist mit dem substantivischen charakter von *willen* schon im mhd. [Mittelhochdeutschen] verblasst [...] die verwendung ist schon sehr frühe völlig die einer präposition"; vgl. SI 13, 1456 und 15, 1287 f.
165. Im „Hirt" (1524) (wie Anm. 7) heißt es: „Dann gheiner lydet den tod umb gottes willen, der nit gottes ist", Z III 40,3 f.
166. *Martin Sallmann*, Zwischen Gott und Mensch. Huldrych Zwinglis theologischer Denkweg im *De vera et falsa religione commentarius* (1525), Tübingen 1999, 200.
167. „Eine kurze gemeine Form, Kinder zu taufen ...", 1528, Z VI/V 431,16–18; siehe auch „Entwurf zu einer Schrift der Prädikanten von Zürich, Bern, Basel und Straßburg an die V Orte", 5. September 1529, Z VI/III 317,7f., am Schluss mit der Anrede an die V Orte: „Hiermit sind [seid] dem allmechtigen herren gott bevolhen, der welle üns alle sines willens underrrichten und nach synem gefallen förmen und gstalten."
168. *Haas*, Zwingli (wie Anm. 73), 176–182.

vom 26. Juni 1529 sicherte als „neues eidgenössisches Recht"[169] den evangelischen Städten wohl die Vollmacht, in den Gemeinen Herrschaften die Reformation nach dem Gemeindeprinzip einzuführen. Es scheiterten allerdings die weitgespannten Pläne Zwinglis mit der Zulassung der reformatorischen Predigt in den V Orten ebenso wie die Beseitigung des Pensionenwesens und die Bestrafung der Pensionenherren. Die konfessionellen Spannungen hielten an[170] und führten schließlich 1531 zum Zweiten Kappelerkrieg, in dem Zürich eine vernichtende Niederlage erlitt, was in den Bestimmungen zum Zweiten Kappeler Landfrieden zum Ausdruck kam. Zwar konnten die einzelnen Orte die Konfession selbst bestimmen, weshalb sich am Konfessionstand der protestantischen Orte nichts änderte. In den Gemeinen Herrschaften aber kam es zu bedeutenden Rekatholisierungen. Die Friedensregelung schrieb die konfessionellen Verhältnisse in der deutschsprachigen Schweiz bis ins 18. Jahrhundert hinein fest.

III.

Die langjährige, unbeugsame Kompromisslosigkeit Zwinglis bei der Verurteilung des Pensionenwesens und bei der Befürwortung einer „Strafaktion" gegen die Innerschweizer Miteidgenossen ruft nach einer Erklärung. Die Antwort lässt sich unschwer geben. Sie führt in das Zentrum von Zwinglis politischer Theologie.[171]

Wenn der Reformator die Eidgenossenschaft in den Blick nimmt, geht er von ihrer Gesamtheit aus. Sie beruht nicht auf dem Zusammenschluss von Teilen, wohl aber ist sie ein vorgegebenes, von Gott errichtetes Gemeinwesen, in Analogie zum Volke Israel.

---

169. *Von Muralt*, „Renaissance und Reformation" (wie Anm. 1), 500.
170. *Helmut Meyer*, Der Zweite Kappelerkrieg. Die Krise der Schweizerischen Reformation, Zürich 1976.
171. *Gottfried W. Locher*, „Das Geschichtsbild Huldrych Zwinglis", in: *Gottfried W. Locher*, Huldrych Zwingli in neuer Sicht. Zehn Beiträge zur Theologie der Zürcher Reformation, Zürich, Stuttgart 1969, 75–103; *Eduard Kobelt*, Die Bedeutung der Eidgenossenschaft für Huldrych Zwingli, Zürich 1970; *Gottfried W. Locher*, „Zwinglis Politik – Gründe und Ziele", in: Theologische Zeitschrift 36, 1980, 84–102, bes. 93 f.; *Walter E. Meyer*, Huldrych Zwinglis Eschatologie. Reformatorische Wende, Theologie und Geschichtsbild des Zürcher Reformators im Lichte seines eschatologischen Ansatzes, Zürich 1987, bes. 235–240; *Ulrich Gäbler*, „Huldrych Zwinglis politische Theologie", in: *Matthias Freudenberg, Georg Plasger* (Hg.), Kirche, Theologie und Politik im reformierten Protestantismus. Vorträge der 8. Emder Tagung zur Geschichte des reformierten Protestantismus, Neukirchen 2011, 9–25.

Zwinglis Selbstverständnis prägt der prophetische Auftrag nach dem Vorbild eines Jesaja oder Jeremia. Zu lernen ist an der Geschichte Israels, wie Gott mit seinem Volk umgeht.

Im eschatologischen Denken Zwinglis gibt es nicht nur ein Gericht Gottes am Ende der Zeiten. Wohl aber immer wiederkehrende Gerichtstage, an denen Gott Ungehorsam gegen sein Wort bestrafen lässt. Der Gedanke legt sich nahe: Zwingli sah in einer „Strafaktion" gegen die V Orte den Vollzug eines Gottesgerichts.

Prof. em. Dr. Dr. theol. h. c. Ulrich Gäbler
Universität Basel
Gatternweg 21
CH-4125 Riehen
Schweiz
ulrich.gaebler@unibas.ch

ABSTRACT

Huldrych Zwingli was convinced that the system of mercenary service in Catholic central Switzerland went against God's will, because the sums foreign powers paid the local ruling classes for recruiting mercenary troops financed a wasteful lifestyle characterized by immorality and godlessness. Believing himself to be bound by the example of the prophets of the Old Testament, Zwingli felt impelled to warn his contemporaries about the impending divine judgement for these abuses. In June of 1529, tensions between the Catholic and Protestant provinces in the Swiss Confederation escalated to a point that made military conflict seem imminent. In the ensuing negotiations to maintain the peace, Zwingli pushed for those who profited from the mercenary service system to incur punishments to life and limb. Should the negotiations fail to achieve this goal, he was likely prepared to repeat his demand that the Zurich City Council should take military action against the central Swiss provinces to abolish mercenary service by force.

Pious City: Community and Charity in Calvin's Geneva

By Esther Chung-Kim

The Reformation in Geneva was not a smooth process.[1] Building a Reformed city meant addressing religious, political, ethnic, disciplinary, and economic tensions, including concerns about charity for community formation. In 1535, an alliance with the free cities of the Swiss confederation led to a revolt against the dukes of Savoy, with Geneva emerging as a free republic. Because the prince-bishop and the Catholic Church had long relied on Savoy for support, many Genevans, including the Children of Geneva faction (*Enfants de Genève*), resisted the rule of the prince-bishop and saw the established church as an inroad for Savoy or other foreign powers to threaten their hard-won liberties.[2] Prior to the Reformation, the magistrates' primary concern was to limit the Catholic Church's economic power because of the Genevan desire for self-rule. With the Reformation, opposition to the prince-bishop became a political and religious revolution that resulted in the creation of new governing councils, the General Hospital, the Company of Pastors, and the consistory.[3] With the shift in political alliances and religious loyalties, the magistrates also transformed former Catholic spaces into the city hospital, a lecture hall, places for Reformed congregations, and the secondary school housed in the former Franciscan monastery at Rive.[4]

The newly independent Geneva adopted Protestantism under the leadership of a French Reformed preacher, William Farel, and the city's General Council

---

1. Abbreviations – *CO*: *Joannis Calvini Opera que supersunt omnia*, 58 vols. (Braunschweig: C. A. Schwetschke, 1863–1900; RC: Registres du Conseil. Archives d'État de Genève, Registres du Petit Conseil, Conseil ordinaire ou Conseil des XXV, du Conseil des LX, du Conseil des CC et du Conseil général de 1409 à 1792; *RCP*: *Registres de la Compagnie des Pasteurs de Genève au Temps du Calvin*, vol. 1, *1546–1553*, ed. Jean-François Bergier (Geneva: Librairie Droz, 1964); *RConsist*: *Registres du Consistoire de Geneve au Temps du Calvin*, 16 vols. (Geneva: Librairie Droz, 1996–2020).

2. William G. Naphy, *Calvin and the Consolidation of the Genevan Reformation* (Louisville, KY: Westminster John Knox Press, 2003), 15–16.

3. Robert M. Kingdon, "The Calvinist Reformation in Geneva," in *Reform and Expansion 1500–1660*, ed. R. Po-Chia Hsia (New York: Cambridge University Press, 2007), 90–103, here 94–95.

4. Scott M. Manetsch, *Calvin's Company of Pastors: Pastoral Care and the Emerging Reformed Church, 1536–1609* (New York: Oxford University Press, 2013), 20.

unanimously approved the creation of the General Hospital as the main institution of poor relief. By reallocating former ecclesiastical revenues, the magistrates took the revenues from smaller ecclesiastical hospitals and former Catholic properties to set up the General Hospital and an education system for the city's children. Since the cost of the Protestant church structure was less than the previous Catholic structure, additional funds went directly into the city's budget.[5] Centralized poor relief in the General Hospital meant that hospital administrators supervised the distribution of charity to needy citizens and residents. The civic leaders and the French pastors wanted to develop a pious city with good governance, an upright citizenry, and communal care.

While scholars have examined various poor relief reforms, this article examines how Geneva's church leaders envisioned community formation and the inclusion of poor relief reform as a major component of a pious city. Poor relief fulfilled the dual purpose of establishing an orderly society and practicing the Christian values of charity and communal care.[6] In addition to the regular poor relief of citizens and residents through the General Hospital, Geneva was one of the first cities to organize a poor relief system for religious refugees during the Reformation through the work of deacons in the church.

The long-term stability and success of the Reformation depended on the effective management of poor relief to care for the needs of the community and the consistent teaching and discipline to reform religious and social culture. With the arrival of John Calvin, the Company of Pastors and the consistory sought to mollify social tensions, reduce disruptive and consumptive behaviors, develop a biblical rationale for expanding poor relief, and encourage individual charity and generosity toward poor relief institutions. Calvin's *Ecclesiastical Ordinances* (1541) created the consistory, which played an important role in educating people to become Reformed Christians. It included the office of lay elders chosen by the magistrates among the three levels of Geneva's government and from each quarter of the city and all the pastors.[7] The city councils and the

---

5. Naphy, *Calvin* (see note 2), 18.

6. See Nicholas Terpstra, *Cultures of Charity: Women, Politics, and the Reform of Poor Relief in Renaissance Italy* (Cambridge, MA: Harvard University Press, 2013); Thomas Max Safley, ed., *The Reformation of Charity: The Secular and Religious in Early Modern Poor Relief* (Boston: Brill, 2003); Timothy G. Fehler, *Protestantism and Poor Relief: The Evolution of Social Welfare in Sixteenth-Century Emden* (Aldershot, UK: Ashgate, 1999); Ole Peter Grell, *Health Care and Poor Relief in Protestant Europe, 1500–1700* (London: Routledge, 1997); Charles H. Parker, *The Reformation of Community: Social Welfare and Calvinist Charity in Holland* (New York: Cambridge University Press, 1990); Robert M. Kingdon, *Control of Morals in Calvin's Geneva* (Columbus, OH: Ohio State University Press, 1972).

7. *Ecclesiastical Ordinances* (1541), *RCP*, 1:7.

Company of Pastors adopted this organization for the city and its nearby territories, "since this ecclesiastical polity was taken from the holy gospel."[8] Formation of a distinct religious identity required the discipline of the consistory and the steady teaching and preaching of educated ministers. Starting with Farel, Geneva's pastors were mostly university-educated foreigners and religious exiles. Because a vast majority of Catholic clergy abandoned the city instead of converting to Protestantism, new recruitment resulted in foreign-born pastors filling many ministerial posts.[9] Almost none of these men had any long-standing ties with either Geneva or traditional clerical training for the priesthood.[10] Calvin, a humanist lawyer by training and a gifted preacher, became their de facto leader. While the city magistrates were careful to protect their civil authority, Calvin sought to protect the church from becoming "annexed by the state as had occurred in other reformed cities, such as Zurich, Basel, Bern, and even Strasbourg."[11] Despite resistance and opposition, Calvin had admirers and supporters in Geneva and even in the surrounding villages.[12]

Unlike other magisterial Protestants, Calvin did not follow the view that ecclesiastical and civil are one entity because he based his church polity on the New Testament, when there had been no Christian rulers. Therefore, the ecclesiastical and civil were necessarily distinct, even if their cooperation was preferred.[13] Unlike the more radical separation of church and state, Calvin promoted two interdependent spheres where the magistrates had the legal prerogative to punish and sentence offenders while the ministers exercised moral authority through their preaching, counsel, and warnings.[14] Although Calvin mostly retained the pastors' prerogative to excommunicate, the magistrates' efforts toward centralization and political control of the church prevailed following Calvin's death.[15] This ultimate removal of the prerogative from the pastors revealed the special role that Calvin and the pastors played in preserving their spiritual authority.

---

8. *RCP* 1:1. For an English translation, see *The Register of the Company of Pastors of Geneva in the Time of Calvin*, ed. Philip E. Hughes (Grand Rapids, MI: Eerdmans, 1966), 35.

9. Manetsch, *Calvin's Company* (see note 4), 44.

10. Elsie Ann McKee, "Worship, Pastorate, and Diaconate in Early Modern Europe," in *John Calvin in Context*, ed. R. Ward Holder (Cambridge: Cambridge University Press, 2020), 119–127, here 126.

11. Manetsch, *Calvin's Company* (see note 4), 27.

12. *RConsist*, 9:xvi.

13. McKee, "Worship" (see note 10), 127.

14. Manetsch, *Calvin's Company* (see note 4), 27.

15. Manetsch, *Calvin's Company* (see note 4), 31.

I. DEFINING THE LIMITS OF COMMUNITY

Amid social tensions in Geneva, building an orderly society meant fostering unity and reconciliation. Calvin and the pastors sought to strengthen unity around a collective Reformed identity and to resolve broken or marred social relationships. Following the waves of refugees into Geneva in the 1550s, the consistory re-engaged in their pedagogical function to teach religious knowledge and the principles of faith. Although many refugees chose to leave Catholic regions and migrate to Protestant cities, they were not necessarily versed or trained in Calvinist doctrine and principles. The religious identity of refugees could be inchoate, yet part of settling in Geneva meant education and formation in a Reformed community. The weekly sermon and catechism were important tools for learning prayers and the confession of faith in the vernacular French; therefore, city officials expected inhabitants to attend worship services. Outsiders seeking to settle in Geneva were expected to be part of the Reformed church and to demonstrate some basic knowledge of the Reformed faith. Some understanding of the Reformed religion was seen as an indication of the resident's acceptance of the Reformed identity of the city. Hence those who could not answer even the most basic religious question ran the risk of a reprimand or a fine to help with the construction of the new school.[16]

In addition to training in the Reformed faith, the pastors saw an efficient poor relief system as a marker of a pious city, since such communal care provided a clear indication that Christian faith bore fruit. Placed at the beginning of the *Register of the Company of Pastors*, the *Ecclesiastical Ordinances* of 1541 declared the importance of a properly maintained church, instruction for the youth, and management of the hospital for the poor.[17] Administrators and managers of the General Hospital made choices about who to admit into the hospital. Implementing poor relief increased the urgency to demarcate the boundaries of a community because once a pious city defined that community, Christian duty included the responsibility of taking care of those in it. Reforming poor relief meant constant negotiation between hoped-for ideals and the realities of limited resources. The strain between Calvinists and other citizens was also noticeable in the consistory's efforts to resolve conflicts and reform immoral behaviors that jeopardized the cohesiveness of the community. In his *Commentary on Psalms*, Calvin asserted that the fruit of a just government would reflect God's special

---

16. *RConsist*, 13–14:xvii.
17. *Ecclesiastical Ordinances* (1541), *RCP*, 1:1; *The Register of the Company of Pastors* (see note 8), 35.

concern for the care of the poor.[18] Calvin expected cooperation between secular and religious authorities because both shared the expectation that unity around common beliefs and values resulted in a stable society.

Defining communities could be complicated because even members accepting the same religious beliefs and authorities might still disagree on other aspects of community formation.[19] An integral part of community dynamics was conflict mediation because "what was common in community was not […] a common understanding so much as a fact that members of the community were engaged in the same argument […] over conflicting goals."[20] Hence, the consistory and the Small Council, both concerned about religious and legal matters, devoted much time and energy to mediating conflicts. Community-building required religious and civic leaders to work consistently toward their goals and ideals of a Reformed community, even as they navigated the complexities of their human communities.[21] The overlapping circles of identity meant that one could be a foreigner outside the civic community and yet a Reformed member inside the church community. In the period when "the religious refugees became a mass phenomenon," the experience of religious exile precipitated a defining moment for many reformers, including Calvin and the French pastors settling in Geneva.[22] A delicate balance between hospitality and xenophobia emerged in the debate over the rights of foreign-born bourgeois. Geneva struggled to define the boundaries between inhabitants (those permitted to live in the city but without the rights to vote or hold office), bourgeois (those who purchased the right to vote and could hold some offices), and citizens (those with the right to vote and hold all political offices).

In the sixteenth century, several shifts affected the definition and boundaries of community. The city as a community required participation, social net-

---

18. Jean Calvin, "Psalm 72:4," in *Commentary on the Book of Psalms*, trans. James Anderson, 5 vols. (Grand Rapids, MI: Baker Books, 2003), 3:129.

19. Michael J. Halvorson and Karen E. Spieling, eds., *Defining Community in Early Modern Europe* (London: Routledge, 2016), 2. See also R. Ward Holder, ed., *John Calvin in Context* (Cambridge: Cambridge University Press, 2020).

20. David Warren Sabean, *Power in the Blood: Popular Culture and Village Discourse in Early Modern Germany* (New York: Cambridge University Press, 1984); Halvorson and Spierling, *Defining Community* (see note 19), 6.

21. Halvorson and Spierling, *Defining Community* (see note 19), 23. See also Philip Benedict, *Christ's Churches Purely Reformed: A Social History of Calvinism* (New Haven: Yale University Press, 2002).

22. Nicholas Terpstra, "Mobility, Community, and Religious Identity in the Early Modern Period: An Alternative Reading of the Long Reformation," in *Early Modern Ethnic and Religious Communities in Exile*, ed. Yosef Kaplan (Newcastle upon Tyne, UK: Cambridge Scholars Publishing, 2017), 1–24, here 3, 23.

works, and support systems. First, the emphasis on one's service to the community often carried with it the exclusion of outsiders because a clear community boundary promoted social responsibility and motivated charity for well-identified insiders or members. Second, in this age of intense piety, a good deal of charitable activity was supported by religious ideals and intent. For Protestants, charity was still linked to piety, because good believers would be generous out of faith and thanksgiving for the grace already given. Acts of charity showed reliance on God rather than money, assurance of election, and obedience to the biblical commandment to love one's neighbor. Third, to keep the community morally upright and minimize crimes meant that discipline and poor relief were often linked.

Religious and war refugees made up the bulk of new inhabitants of Geneva from the middle of the sixteenth century onward, and the city saw large fluctuations in its population as a result. During the 1550s, when persecution increased against the Huguenots in France, Geneva saw its population double from 12,000 to 13,000 to more than 25,000. While some settled in Geneva, many refugees returned to France in the 1560s, when the conditions improved.[23] Persecution prompted more than 250,000 French Protestants to flee to neighboring countries like Holland, England, Geneva, the Swiss cantons, and even Prussia, so that French Protestant movements developed in the diaspora of their exile communities.[24] In many cases, migration reinforced the sense of community and religious identity for those expelled and those who remained behind.[25] Because of the new dynamics brought about by migration and religious refugees, poor relief became a major part of community-building. In his study of Calvinist merchants, Grell noted that the experience of exile shaped the Calvinist collective identity because they understood God's providence as God's chosen people in light of their marginalized and minority status.[26] As opposed to Max Weber's focus on predestination and the accompanying anxiety as promoting a "spirit of capitalism," Grell asserted that many Calvinist exiles expressed little or no doubt about their personal election in

---

23. Jill Fehleison, "Daily Life in Geneva," in *John Calvin in Context* (see note 19), 87–93, here 90.

24. Myriam Yardeni, *Minorité et mentalités religieuses en Europe moderne: L'exemple des huguenots* (Paris: Honoré Champion, 2018), 127–128.

25. Terpstra, "Mobility" (see note 22), 20.

26. Ole Peter Grell, "The Creation of a Calvinist Identity in the Reformation Period," in *Religion as an Agent of Change: Crusades—Reformation—Pietism,* ed. Per Ingesman (Leiden: Brill, 2016), 149–165, here 149.

salvation.²⁷ Instead, Grell emphasized the social and cultural effects of persecution and repeated migrations combined with the insecurity of minority existence within their host communities as the motivation toward worldly success.²⁸ These wealthy merchants, bankers, and highly skilled craftsmen dedicated many hours and resources to serve their foreign churches as elders and deacons who along with the ministers provided leadership for exile Reformed communities throughout Europe.

II. SOCIAL TENSIONS

In Geneva, social tensions arising from political factions threatened the unity of the city until 1541 and then resurfaced in frequent conflicts from 1550 to 1555. The bulk of arguments against the consistory, following its creation in 1541, were not only about the control of morals but also about the scope of authority that the magistrates wanted to "reserve for themselves" without the interference of foreign pastors.²⁹ The consistory records also show citizens who resisted the enforcement of Reformed standards. While the consistory members addressed superstitions and incorrect religious beliefs, they devoted increasing attention to problematic behavior rather than theological disagreements. The consistory rarely summoned people espousing transubstantiation or those denying salvation-by-faith-alone. In 1551, the consistory discussed the trial of Jerome Bolsec, a doctor and former Carmelite who challenged the theology of predestination. Genevan leaders argued that Bolsec's challenge to Calvin's theology of predestination caused people to question the council's decisions, especially after many defended Bolsec's theology and claimed that he did not deserve punishment.³⁰ This conflict raised the question of religious authority since Bolsec's line of reasoning contested Calvin's authority as an interpreter of scripture. The ensuing debate over predestination distressed the consistory because people picked sides, leaving many freewill sympathizers and supporters within Geneva.³¹ Divided public opinion exacerbated social tensions and

---

27. Grell, "Creation" (see note 26), 150.
28. Grell, "Creation" (see note 26), 160.
29. Naphy, *Calvin* (see note 2), 56.
30. *RConsist*, 6:x.
31. *RConsist*, 6:xi. The council requested Basel, Bern, and Zurich to weigh in on the question of predestination to reject Bolsec's teaching. See *CO*, 8:205–208; *CO*, 8:223–234; Wulfert de Greef, *The Writings of John Calvin* (Louisville, KY: Westminster John Knox Press, 2008), 103.

threatened the peace. On 21 December 1551, the council banished Bolsec from Geneva because the divisiveness over predestination disrupted the community. Like many of his contemporaries, Calvin and the council members thought that unity of religion was necessary for political and social stability. While they could overlook private or quiet dissensions, they could not ignore public disputes that weakened the social fabric of the small civic community. The positive side of unity was apparent in the responsibility for the community's well-being, including its neediest members. The negative side of unity was the rejection of those who held dissenting theological opinions, and the exclusion of those theological views that caused social conflict.

By forcing parishioners to admit their faults and refrain temporarily from partaking in the Lord's Supper, the consistory sought to fill the vacuum felt by Protestants after eliminating the sacrament of penance. The consistory aimed to moderate disruptive behavior and guide people to accept a new standard of Reformed belief and practice. The goal of the consistory was to resolve quarrels and encourage reconciliation between conflicting parties, including family disputes. For example, the consistory was willing to overlook some offenses that would normally be punishable if the reconciliation between the offending parties happened at a consistory meeting.[32] The members of the consistory presumed that festering wounds of resentment were incompatible with a pious community and therefore sought to alleviate social tensions by encouraging reconciliation. The consistory believed that their consistent efforts toward conflict resolution among family members, neighbors, citizens, and refugees would promote overall social stability.[33] In addition, the pastors and council members had to deal with the tensions arising from the influx of French and Italian refugees. This social tension was expressed as xenophobic sentiment to foreigners settling in Geneva and resistance to the consistory's discipline imposed for antagonism against the French pastors.

In 1546, anti-French sentiment grew because of the burden of caring for poor refugees and the assimilation of immigrants into Geneva.[34] Persecutions in Provence in 1546 had driven over four thousand strangers to Geneva from Mérindol and Cabrieres alone, thereby overwhelming the travelers' hospital and threatening to tap into the General Hospital's resources originally reserved for Genevans. The tense situation in Europe after Emperor Charles V's victory

---

32. *RConsist*, 8:253.
33. *RConsist*, 8:xxv. See also Watt, "Consistories and Discipline," in *John Calvin in Context* (see note 19), 103–110.
34. Naphy, *Calvin* (see note 2), 123.

over the German Protestant states in the Schmalkaldic War in 1546 and the deteriorating relationship between Genevan magistrates and the French ministers also contributed to growing xenophobic attitudes.[35]

Genevan citizens generally ruled the city along with bourgeois, while inhabitants pledged oaths ensuring their loyalty and obedience to Geneva and its government. Because Geneva had struggled with debt since its revolution for independence in 1535, the bourgeois' and inhabitants' payment of fees and taxes provided the city with the benefit of additional revenue.[36] However, from 1548 to 1554, the council, led by Calvin's opponents, severely limited the purchase of, and proposed limitations to, bourgeois rights. The number of registered French in Geneva had nevertheless increased in 1549. On 5 March 1549, the council decided to create a legal status for these newcomers.[37]

In reaction to the influx of French refugees, the followers of Ami Perrin, an opponent of Calvin, proposed an edict to force new citizens to wait twenty-five years after their admission before gaining the right to participate in the Small Council and the General Council of Two Hundred, the representative governing body of Geneva. The Small Council accepted this proposal, but the Council of Two Hundred did not ratify it.[38] On 7 March 1551, a fight between the French and the Perrinists broke out. Several people were injured, and a servant was killed. When Calvin appeared before the council following this disturbance, he requested that the guilty be punished and protested the behavior of "people who gather themselves and shout everywhere in the streets: kill, kill, pointing to the strangers."[39] The consistory records of 1551 contain numerous examples of this growing social tension between some Genevan citizens and French refugees. This tension had three aspects: political, economic, and socio-religious. First, some Genevans resented the political power of wealthy Frenchmen who had purchased the right of bourgeois in Geneva. Second, some Genevan artisans resisted the economic competition French workers posed. Third, the Children of Geneva faction clashed with the French ministers due to their outward disdain for French influence in Geneva and their resistance to Reformed discipline. Acute tensions among supporters and opponents of the French ministers disrupted any vision of a harmonious Reformed community.

---

35. Naphy, *Calvin* (see note 2), 123.
36. Naphy, *Calvin* (see note 2), 124.
37. Paul-F. Geisendorf, *Livre des abitants de Genève*, vol. 1, *1549–1560* (Geneva: Librairie Droz, 1957), x.
38. *RConsist*, 6:xii.
39. RC, 46:221 (12 March 1551); *RConsist*, 6:xii–xiii.

The Council of Two Hundred sought to monitor and restrict the activities of foreigners.[40] Suspicions about foreigners in the city led the Council of Two Hundred to announce the following mandate regarding strangers on 11 April 1553:

> One may not rent a house to foreigners without notifying their city captains. Likewise, no one should provide lodging in a tavern, hotel, or inn to a foreign person unless he is a citizen or bourgeois, and that nobody is allowed to be taught except citizens and bourgeois. Likewise, the hosts must reveal to the [city] captains those who are staying at their home for at least three days. Foreigners must relinquish all their weapons, etc.[41]

These restrictions limited the number of refugees who could reside long-term in Geneva without permission, since the captain of each city quarter would presumably know where the strangers were renting houses and where any outside guests were staying for more than three days. Knowing where to locate any outsiders would make the enforcement of these laws possible. Such restrictions in the city meant that foreigners also experienced political constraints.[42] The law against carrying arms would be a way to contain possible physical threats, violence, and rebellion, but it also limited the foreigners' self-defense.

Yet Geneva still granted settlement rights in a rural parish to four hundred families from Provence. After much debate, the Council of Two Hundred granted asylum to these refugees at the castles of Peney and Jussy on 10 May 1554, although without conveying any civic or voting rights. While poor refugees frequently burdened Geneva's resources, working refugee residents increased city revenues through taxation.[43] The resettlement of French refugees remained a source of disagreement in Geneva and in many ways pitted the French pastors and the consistory against the Children of Geneva faction who continued to complain about the French pastors' influence.[44] The intensification of conflicts in the 1550s manifested itself in xenophobic remarks against the refugees coming into Geneva and public challenges to the consistory's authority.[45]

---

40. RC, 47:53v–54v /im. 79–80 (11 April 1553); *CO*, 21:539; *RConsist*, 8:xii.

41. *RConsist*, 8:xii.

42. Jae Sung Kim, "Calvin's Doctrine of the Kingdom of God" (master's thesis, Calvin Theological Seminary, 1990), 140.

43. Naphy, *Calvin* (see note 2), 138.

44. *RConsist*, 9:x. See also Heiko Oberman, *John Calvin and the Reformation of the Refugees* (Geneva: Libraire Droz, 2009).

45. *RConsist*, 9:ix.

III. PASTORS AND DISCIPLINE

In addition to resisting foreign influence and the settling of refugees in Geneva since the 1540s, the Children of Geneva faction clashed with the pastors and contested the disciplinary actions of the Genevan consistory. For Calvin and the Company of Pastors, Reformed Christianity was not merely about initial fervor but about training in Reformed doctrine and character formation. In light of the discontent toward refugees, the Children of Geneva faction directed their ire toward the French pastors, particularly Calvin.[46] All the pastors in Geneva except for one were French, and there was therefore an increased resistance directed against the pastors, especially when they tried to exercise their authority. The ministers' efforts to close taverns, to limit the naming of infants after popular Catholic saints at baptism, and to suspend several leading citizens from the communion table resulted in some Genevan citizens, like François Favre and his son-in-law Ami Perrin, claiming that the "city's ministers were usurping traditional rights of the magistrates."[47] Hence, the Perrinists opposed the efforts of French ministers. At the same time, the French ministers who were selected and confirmed by the council to exercise their duty of establishing a Reformed community in Geneva were offended by the Perrinists' attempts to circumvent their authority.

Although Calvin and the consistory were more interested in reconciliation than in punishment, reconciliation could prove elusive when people's honor and reputation were attacked.[48] Consistory cases demonstrated that conflicts arose from the pastors' efforts to discipline unwilling citizens, especially affluent Genevans who often believed that they needed to defend their honor. Defending one's reputation meant a reticence to admit one's faults publicly and to avoid shame and trouble. Adding insult to injury, Calvin was not always discreet in his criticisms, even from the pulpit. In his sermon on the story of Ananias and Sapphira, Calvin warned against impure motives, which was most clearly seen in the common act of lying. He asserted,

> Many come to the sermon only to gain a good reputation. If they were not afraid of being criticized for not being good Christians, they would never set foot in this place. [...] No matter how much we boast of being Christian and put on a good show, we will gain nothing from our efforts unless our actions correspond to our speech. Otherwise, why did God take vengeance on Ananias in this way? [...] Even though he lied to men, he did not escape lying to God. [...] Lying to God is not a

---

46. *RConsist*, 7:xiv.
47. Manetsch, *Calvin's Company* (see note 4), 186.
48. *RConsist*, 7:xx.

difficult thing to do today. How many among us, both men and women, after committing every sin in the book, will confess them if asked? They do not worry about lying impudently before God and his angels, for they think they are scot-free unless there are witnesses to convict them.[49]

For this reason, Calvin recognized the proper role of the consistory in rebuking and reproving transgressions. Much of the work of the consistory seemed to be sorting lies, which may have fueled Calvin's pessimistic view of human nature. He claimed that in less than a year five or six hundred people were called before the consistory, but very few, barely one in a hundred, would confess their transgression unless there were witnesses to convict them, thereby demonstrating "how much perjury we have among us every year."[50] While "it does not occur to them that they are lying to God," as Calvin disclosed, many people seemed more concerned about the judgment of their fellow compatriots than God in the moment of confrontation.[51] After 1555, the consistory convinced the Small Council to recognize lying to the consistory as an act of perjury subject to civil penalty.[52]

1. Politics of Excommunication. The question of authority, a vexing issue for Protestants, hinged on determining who decides who is allowed to participate in the spiritual-social community around the Lord's Supper. In particular, debates emerged about whether suspension from communion should be a theological-religious matter or a political-civic one. For the Children of Geneva faction, suspension was a political issue to be decided by the magistrates. For Calvin and the Company of Pastors, excommunication was a theological question about inclusion in the spiritual body of Christ and partaking in communion as the body of Christ meant reconciliation with other believers. Despite preaching, teaching, admonishing, and advising, excommunication was the most concrete form of discipline for church leaders. The most common form was a minor excommunication, in which the person refrained from receiving the quarterly communion once or twice. When the consistory absolved a person guilty of sinful behavior or wrongdoing, that person was restored to the

---

49. John Calvin, *Sermons sur les Actes des Apostres I-VII 1549–1551*, ed. Willem Balke and Wilhelmus H. Th. Moehn, *Supplementa Calviniana*, vol. 8 (Neukirchen-Vluyn: Neukirchener Verlag des Erziehungsvereins, 1994); for English translation, John Calvin, "Sermon on Acts 5:1–6, June 8, 1550," *Sermons on the Acts of the Apostles, Chapter 1–7*, trans. Rob Roy McGregor (Peoria, IL: Versa Press, 2008), 198–199.
50. Calvin, "Acts 5:1–6" in *Acts of the Apostles* (see note 49), 200.
51. Calvin, "Acts 5:1–6" in *Acts of the Apostles* (see note 49), 200.
52. Émile Rivoire and Victor van Berchem, eds., *Les sources du droit du canton de Genève* (Aarau: Sauerländer, 1933), 3:401.

spiritual community; hence, rejoining the Lord's Supper became the sacramental sign of reconciliation and spiritual unity.

In October 1552, the consistory cleared its schedule to address a case involving the harassment and verbal attack on the pastor, Raymond Chauvet, a French minister known for strict disciplinary standards. Calvin insisted that the council follow up with this case because it concerned the honor of God and religion.[53] The council sentenced the offenders, Berthelier, Bonna, and Sept, to three days of prison, and the consistory prohibited them from the Lord's Supper. On 1 December 1552, when Sept appeared before the consistory, they recorded that they were greatly offended by his rebellion and presented the condition for reconciliation as acknowledgment of his faults.[54] In the ensuing controversy over the power of excommunication, Philibert Berthelier and the Children of Geneva faction held that the magistrates of the city council should have the final say on excommunication and sought to subordinate the ministers, while Calvin and the other ministers argued that the consistory should be able to excommunicate without the approval of the council.[55]

After an ongoing discussion, the Lord's Supper disagreement was resolved in January 1555 with a compromise, when the council decided to stick to the edicts, already promulgated, tacitly confirming Calvin's position. Yet Berthelier, Bonna, and other Perrinists who disagreed with Calvin continued to enjoy some influence in Geneva.[56] Although many Genevan citizens supported Calvinist reform, the Perrinists usually targeted the foreign pastors because they resented their power and authority or perhaps because it was easier to attack unarmed foreigners than Genevan citizens who could carry weapons. Because a cadre of French ministers initiated and sustained the Calvinist reform in Geneva, the resistance to reform often became associated with anti-foreign sentiment. While the most common attacks against the pastors were insults, opponents sometimes used threats of violence or physical assault. On 22 October 1554, Chauvet appeared before the council to report the treatment he had suffered at the house of the apothecary. After he lectured the people for playing music and dancing, someone hit him on the head as he was leaving.[57]

While some Genevans welcomed the strangers, others wanted them to move on. This difference caused tensions between the ministers and magistrates who sought to reduce and manage the downsides of French residents while seizing

---

53. RC, 46:283v / im. 289 (8, 10, 11, 13, 28, 31 October 1552); *RConsist*, 7: xv.
54. *RConsist*, 7:186.
55. *RConsist*, 8:xiii.
56. *RConsist*, 8:xiv.
57. RC, 48:136–136v/im. 143–144 (22 October 1554); *RConsist*, 9:xv.

the benefits.⁵⁸ A core group of Genevan citizens developed business relationships and economic ties with the refugees and supported Calvin and the ministers "for religious and economic reasons" in local politics.⁵⁹ Although the cost of bourgeois admission nearly doubled in 1555, the number of foreigners gaining acceptance as bourgeois increased substantially. Many prominent refugees took an increasing role in the government, thereby helping Calvin to win greater political support.⁶⁰ Bourgeois refugees also helped to elevate one another and regularly donated money to support poor refugees.

In a letter to Bullinger, Calvin acknowledged that the Small Council devised a plan which consisted of admitting new burghers, so that "among the French who had established their home in the city and who were known for their probity, he had chosen nearly fifty to add to the body of the citizens."⁶¹ In three weeks, the council admitted forty-three people to the citizenry compared to the previous year, when it had admitted only seven. By 9 May 1555, the council admitted a total of sixty new burghers. The Perrinists complained about the number of French refugees admitted as bourgeois and insisted that the vote come before the Council of Two Hundred instead of the Small Council, but the Small Council refused this request.⁶²

The mounting political tensions culminated in the riot of 16 May 1555. With intimidating acts toward the French and their Genevan supporters, Perrin sought to overturn the new bourgeois grants, which the council had recently given.⁶³ In the aftermath of their failed violent uprising against the city's leaders, Calvin's main opponents escaped to Bern before their trial and resisted Calvin from a distance. The decisions of the consistory reflected a harshness toward Perrin and his supporters. Calvin and his supporters saw them as unrepentant members of society persisting in immoral or seditious behavior and reacted fiercely against them. For many years after 1555, magistrates saw any local sign of support for the Perrinist exiles as offensive and punishable.⁶⁴ Genevan leaders considered the combination of resistance to discipline, attacks against the French refugees, and violence in the public spaces as endangering communal peace, order, and safety. The sense of communal responsibility was

---

58. Naphy, *Calvin* (see note 2), 137.
59. Naphy, *Calvin* (see note 2), 136, 139.
60. Kingdon, "Calvinist Reformation" (see note 3), 99.
61. Calvin, "Letter 2243, To Bullinger, 15 June 1555," *CO*, 15: 678–679.
62. *RConsist*, 10:xiii–xiv.
63. *RConsist*, 10:xvi.
64. Jeffrey R. Watt, *The Consistory and Social Discipline in Calvin's Geneva* (Rochester, NY: University of Rochester Press, 2020), 33.

deeply entrenched as a religious and social value, but the challenge arose with defining the community that the city was obligated to support and care for. To assist with defining deserving members of the community, the consistory focused on encouraging a standard of moral behavior. If most members were good citizens or residents, then most would qualify for aid or support if needed. Nevertheless, the elusive goal of developing an upright citizenry, even after the departure of the Perrinists, caused Calvin to complain about the lack of discipline in Genevan society.[65]

2. Discipline through Charity, Work, and Moderation. Without extensive financial resources to support all impoverished Genevans, the hospital directors had to make difficult decisions about who would receive poor relief. The General Hospital "used the carrot of alms and the stick of discipline" to ensure that worthy recipients received aid and hospital directors could protect civic resources and the community against potential welfare fraud.[66] The magistrates' definition of the worthy poor allowed them to concentrate their efforts on "those whose poverty they believed to be avoidable and who could be rehabilitated into upstanding community members."[67] The justification for supporting the deserving poor put a high emphasis on morality and religious knowledge. If pastors could maintain the high moral standards of the people, then they could also justify supporting all those people when they needed relief. One would not need to worry about whether they were supporting the undeserving poor. Since it would be easier to justify helping those who were good and deserving, a well-behaved and thus deserving population would make it easier to raise funds, solicit donations, and promote generosity. Effective discipline would improve poor relief for the deserving and increase the validity of a robust system of poor relief.

Since discipline and deserving poor relief went together in Geneva, the specific mechanism for discipline and poor relief was the quarterly visitation of several ministers and the hospital administrators, or procurators (*procureurs*), who were responsible for the finances and administration of the hospital. Hospital directors, or hospitallers (*hopitalliers*), lived at the hospital and managed the daily care of the sick and poor of the General Hospital along with their

---

65. *RConsist*, 10:xxi.
66. Kristen Coan Howard, "'A House Dedicated to God' : Social Welfare and the General Hospital in Reformation Geneva, 1535–1564," (PhD diss., University of Arizona, 2020), 351.
67. Howard, "House," (see note 66), 352.

wives. These hospitallers became a regular presence in the consistory since the Genevan model linked discipline with poor relief.[68] In the *Ecclesiastical Ordinances*, Calvin established a biblical justification for stewards who were procurators and hospitallers. In particular, the consistory members were expected to inquire about and check for any faulty behavior or unruly conduct every three months, and report back to the Small Council.[69] Many church elders who served on the consistory also served on the hospital board. In the period from 1543 to 1558, 77 percent of hospital administrators and 54 percent of hospitallers were church elders serving on the consistory at some point in their career.[70]

The disciplinary and pedagogical role of the consistory was to correct disruptive behavior and to teach Reformed doctrine and practice that helped the community. One of the reasons for the consistory to enforce greater discipline was to reduce poverty. On 23 March 1556, the consistory renewed their efforts to close the taverns. Calvin, accompanied by François Lullin, a lay member of the consistory, complained to the council that "notwithstanding the taverns' expenses, however, they began to come back in waves, especially in Saint-Gervaix, where debauched people [...] should save from day to day, because of their poverty."[71] Religious leaders recognized that discipline was needed to minimize conflict in the community and to reduce the roads leading to poverty.

After the 1555 defeat of the Perrinists, actions against laziness and usury became more common as Calvin and his colleagues expressed their dissatisfaction toward some Genevans who displayed laziness or dissipated their property.[72] For centuries, theologians condemned laziness and considered it a cardinal sin, but the renewed vigor to combat laziness and thus reduce vagrancy was unprecedented as the actions of the consistory and the council against visibly lazy people became more common in the second half of the 1550s.[73] The intensification of discipline coincided with the increasing number of French foreigners accepted as citizens and the full-fledged operational establishment of

---

68. Naphy, "Judges and Shepherds," in *Judging Faith, Punishing Sin: Inquisitions and Consistories in the Early Modern World*, ed. Charles H. Parker and Gretchen Starr-LeBeau (New York: Cambridge University Press, 2017), 104–115, here 113.
69. *Ecclesiastical Ordinances* (1541) in *The Register of the Company of Pastors of Geneva* (see note 8), 43.
70. Naphy, "Judges" (see note 68), 113; Howard, "House" (see note 66), 91.
71. *RConsist*, 11:xix–xx.
72. *RConsist*, 11:xxv.
73. *RConsist*, 11:xxvi.

the *Bourse des pauvres etrangers français,* commonly known as the French Fund.[74]

In April 1556, the consistory summoned the three Cugnard brothers for debauchery, quarreling, blasphemy, and being the source of many scandals. On 11 May 1556, the consistory sent them to the council, which reprimanded them "because they fight violently, swear and blaspheme, and lead dissolute lives without doing anything and without working."[75] The same day, the council rejected vagabonds and pushed them to find work by threatening to make them work on the roofs of the city, an arduous and dangerous task.[76] In November 1556, the Small Council approved several new edicts, including one against laziness. The next day, with the help of Calvin, these edicts were also approved by the Council of Two Hundred. However, when the entire General Council (comprised of all voting Genevan citizens and bourgeois) discussed them, some members, despite Calvin's insistence, opposed them and demanded the revision of the penalties for laziness and blasphemy, because they deemed them too harsh. To Calvin's disappointment, the opposition against such measures prevented the councilmen from passing the edicts on laziness, adultery, and profanity.[77] This example shows that whatever the intentions of Calvin and the Company of Pastors in joint agreement with the Small Council and the Council of Two Hundred, if the General Council did not approve the law, then it would not be accepted in Geneva. This also indicates that the reforms passed or instituted by the initiatives of Calvin and the ruling magistrates had the general or tacit approval of the citizens and bourgeois in Geneva.

As the consistory and the council fought against laziness and vagrancy, they explicitly linked laziness with public begging. On 25 February 1557, the consistory summoned the needler Pierre Guindel, who was accused of laziness and begging. While Guindel denied these charges by declaring that he did not refuse to exercise his profession to earn a living, the testimony of two other men said the opposite. The consistory excluded Guindel from the Lord's Supper and sent him before the council, which forced him to leave the city under penalty of the whip.[78] On the same day, the council discussed the need to expel beg-

---

74. See Jeannine E. Olson, *Calvin and Social Welfare: Deacons and the Bourse française* (Selinsgrove, PA: Susquehanna University Press, 1989).
75. RC, 51:129v (11 May 1557).
76. *RConsist*, 11:xxvi.
77. *RConsist*, 11:xvi.
78. *RConsist*, 12:48, 53 (25 February, 4 March 1557); RC, 53:39 (8 March 1557).

gars, poor vagrants, and troublemakers and to regulate the affairs of the city hospital by limiting freeloaders and driving out those poor "who eat the bread of others."[79] Lazy beggars who were construed as practicing problematic and consumptive behaviors received harsher treatment. Although Geneva was a haven for many Reformed refugees, the city continued to maintain its earlier standards against foreigners and strangers who lingered in Geneva as begging vagabonds without a clear intent to work or earn a living.

In economic dealings, Calvin stressed the importance of finding a balance between personal economic interest on one hand and altruism and charity on the other.[80] On 19 November 1556, the consistory summoned Pierre Penon for borrowing money at usurious rates from Étienne Bandière, who was also called before the consistory on the same day.[81] While the consistory sought to break up a usury network, the purpose of this restriction was to limit desperate artisans from falling into poverty and to protect the vulnerable, including refugees. Penon, a French religious refugee from Meaux who had become a Genevan inhabitant two and half years earlier, found himself short on cash.[82] Bandière, a native Genevan, served as a dealer to this loan and confessed to the crime of usury. Five months earlier, Bandière had caused a scandal because of his angry violent threats against poor foreigners.[83] Now he was caught taking advantage of a foreigner for the sake of financial gain.

The juxtaposition of great wealth to the point of wasteful luxury with the awareness of extensive need and poverty in a small city did not bode well for community harmony and unity. Although the first law against extravagance arose in Geneva over a century before Calvin arrived, Calvin affirmed that wealth could corrupt the soul through the sins of vanity and pride. He urged the authorities to ban expensive accoutrements that were only for ostentation since such uses of wealth focused on self-aggrandizement rather than helping others. An ordinance from 10 March 1550 reflected the city's desire to minimize excessive drinking and gambling, because of the dissipation of goods that went with them.[84] In the sumptuary laws of 1558, the concern of pastors was to reduce conspicuous, extravagant consumption that highlighted the gap be-

---

79. RC, 53:27 (25 February 1557); *RConsist*, 12:xvii.
80. *RConsist*, 11:xxvii.
81. *RConsist*, 11:283–284.
82. Geisendorf, *Livre* (see note 37), 30. Pierre Penon was recorded with his city of origin and profession (draper-clothier) with eight other people on 9 May 1554.
83. *RConsist*, 11:129.
84. *RConsist*, 12:xvi.

tween the rich and poor and exacerbated the problem of poverty.[85] Despite the tendency of Calvin and the council to over-legislate on spending, the purpose of these laws was to cultivate a "climate of thrift" in the effort to meet human needs of citizens and refugees.[86]

The correction of immoral behavior was linked to poor management of money and falling into poverty. In February 1554, when the barber, Pierre Biolley, and the pie maker, Michel Chevalier, were summoned for the vice of gambling, they were both accused of setting a bad example and losing money by betting.[87] One of the reasons for the consistent call for moderation was the connection the pastors saw in indiscriminate spending and resultant poverty. Ultimately, the council agreed with the consistory and sought to prevent the excesses that increased pride, gluttony, and poverty, and promoted moderation instead by disapproving of high consumption of luxury items. By the request of the consistory, in January 1559 the council passed an edict to limit gambling and gaming for gold or money, to increase participation in the catechism classes and communion, and to circumvent the excess and wasting of money at rowdy gaming scenes.[88]

IV. CHARITY AND CARE FOR CITIZENS AND STRANGERS

Calvin summarized the three marks of the church as the proclamation of the word of God, the celebration of the Lord's Supper, and the communion of believers in caring love, which included living in peace and harmony with one's neighbors.[89] Calvin noted that Christ, rather than calling his followers one by one to give each of them a different teaching, called them all together to give them the same word, so that believers "might grow in charity and fraternal love into one body and be joined to the head who is Jesus Christ."[90] The most significant visible marker of the church was the social practice of believers en-

---

85. W. Fred Graham, *The Constructive Revolutionary: John Calvin and His Socio-Economic Impact* (Richmond, VA: John Knox Press, 1971), 110–113.
86. Graham, *Constructive Revolutionary* (see note 85), 114.
87. *RConsist*, 9:xix.
88. *RConsist*, 13–14:xxii.
89. Calvin, "Sermon on Acts 2:41–42, January 26, 1550" in *Acts of the Apostles* (see note 49), 58.
90. Calvin, "Sermon on Acts 2:43–45, February 2, 1550" in *Acts of the Apostles* (see note 49), 74.

gaged in charity toward one's household, including children, relatives, and servants, as well as the orderly poor relief system for the community.

1. Calvin's Sermons on Charity. Calvin's sermons were the most common way people learned about Reformed ethics since Genevans were required to attend the weekly sermon. Calvin demonstrated a concern for people's faith because he believed that true faith produces true love. In his sermon "The Three Marks of the Church," Calvin explained that faith is about perseverance, a lasting kind of trust in God, and an ongoing enthusiasm for hearing God's word. He admits that this kind of faith is difficult since "every day we see many people who wander from it; they initially appear to be followers of the gospel and great advocates of the word, but fall away in the end and become despisers of God."[91] Calvin pointed out the hypocrisy and pretense of those who coveted their neighbor's possessions and seized another's property or cheated one another, yet "wanted to be regarded as great Christians!"[92] He warned,

> If a person boasts of being faithful and does not have pity on the poor, God will disavow him [...]. He must be sufficiently concerned about his neighbors to help them with the wealth God has placed within his hands. [For] Solomon says, if a man has a fountain in his house and can draw as much as he needs from it, he would be an ungrateful man unless he lets it flow out so his neighbors can share it. ... [Hence, the ancients] laid such a great foundation in the church [because] they wanted the poor to be provided for.[93]

To restore the church to its original standard, Calvin cautioned against ingratitude that would hinder such progress. In his sermon "Fellowship of Saints," Calvin pointed out that sincere love should involve actions to help neighbors, not just by sending goods but by getting involved and by being present "in body and in person," so that it is done "sincerely and enthusiastically."[94]

In his sermon on Acts 5, Calvin emphasized three guidelines from the practices of the early church: generosity of the rich, orderly distribution of resources, and meeting people's needs. He noted that "things were not done helter-skelter" because when someone gave his goods haphazardly without a plan for how to do it, he demonstrated that he is not motivated by love but by his ambition to be recognized by others.[95] Balancing the dual concerns of compas-

---

91. Calvin, "Acts 2:41–42" in *Acts of the Apostles* (see note 49), 58.
92. Calvin, "Acts 2:43–45" in *Acts of the Apostles* (see note 49), 77.
93. Calvin, "Acts 2:43–45" in *Acts of the Apostles* (see note 49), 78.
94. Calvin, "Sermon on Acts 4:32–37, June 1, 1550" in *Acts of the Apostles* (see note 49), 181.
95. Calvin, "Sermon on Acts 5:1–6, June 8, 1550" in *Acts of the Apostles* (see note 49), 190.

sion for the poor and good judgment, Calvin called for the use of prudence and discernment to determine how best to distribute the goods fairly, both in the general administration of poor relief and in private giving among individuals.[96] Just as deacons were elected for the purpose of fair administration of poor relief, the wealthy are "the dispensers of the goods which God has placed in their hands."[97] In his sermon "Judged according to our Merits and Demerits," Calvin described that Ananias and Sapphira were likely held in esteem and honored by the faithful since they were very successful people who had enough resources to sell a piece of property and give it up for distributing alms; yet their dishonesty and greed led to their demise.[98] Rooted in the interpretations of biblical and early Christian texts, Calvin's socioeconomic views were meant to be applicable for a new republic that included both the rich and the poor as well as natives and foreigners.

Between 1548 and 1554, the route to full assimilation for eligible refugees was severely curtailed and very few new French bourgeois were admitted.[99] During this period around 1550, Calvin wrote his commentary and sermons on the Acts of the Apostles. This barrier to acceptance for the French might have been on Calvin's mind. For Calvin, equity was first and foremost a virtue within the hearts of believers before it made its appearance as a guide for justice in human social life.[100] The equitable person strove for justice to fulfill the commandment to love one's neighbor. But this perspective required that one viewed all people as one's neighbors.[101] Calvin espoused a freedom in giving, not necessarily in exchange for spiritual benefits, but to address the economic needs of the community.[102]

2. Poor Relief for Citizens: The General Hospital. As Geneva's main poor relief institution since 1535, the General Hospital was "dedicated to a holy purpose," so that all the resources from former churches, monasteries, and convents

---

96. Calvin, "Acts 5:1–6" in *Acts of the Apostles* (see note 49), 192.
97. Calvin, "Acts 5:1–6" in *Acts of the Apostles* (see note 49), 194.
98. Calvin, "Sermon on Acts 5:7–15, June 22, 1550" in *Acts of the Apostles* (see note 49), 204.
99. Naphy, *Calvin* (see note 2), 127.
100. Guenther H. Haas, *The Concept of Equity in Calvin's Ethics* (Carlisle, UK: Paternoster Press for the Canadian Corporation for Studies in Religion, 1997), 50.
101. Haas, *Concept,* (see note 100), 52.
102. See Kathryn Blanchard, *The Protestant Ethic or the Spirit of Capitalism* (Eugene, OR: Wipf & Stock, 2010). Blanchard argues that Calvin's economics is guided by a strong notion of Christian freedom, which rejects former prescriptive forms of giving for religious rituals to gain eternal spiritual merit.

could be centralized for the "most pious use of caring for the poor."[103] Related to the General Hospital but in separate locations, Geneva set up an auxiliary hospital for travelers and another one for plague victims. The *Ecclesiastical Ordinances* of 1541 explained the role and expectations of Geneva's hospital leaders to manage the hospital's income, provide alms to the needy, and oversee a physician and surgeon providing medical care for the poor.[104]

Based on 1 Timothy 3:1–13, Calvin applied the qualifications for overseers and deacons to those who directed the care of the poor. In his commentaries, Calvin emphasized that deacons were required to set a good example with their own families "in an honorable and godly manner."[105] The *Ecclesiastical Ordinances* applied this principle to the hospital, so that the hospital directors would govern not only their own families but also their hospital family as a Protestant "household dedicated to God."[106] The *Ecclesiastical Ordinances* also specified that those in Calvin's category of deacons, including the hospital directors, would assist the minister with the cup in the celebration of the Lord's Supper.[107]

According to the consistory records in the 1550s, the pastors, accompanied by a deacon or a lay elder, visited parishioners' homes during the weeks preceding the celebration of the Last Supper, especially before Easter. While pastors primarily sought to check the degree of religious knowledge among the people and to see if they were able to recite prayers as well as the creed in preparation to receive the Lord's Supper, during these visitations the pastor and accompanying elder or deacon would see firsthand the needs of the people.[108] Although ostensibly they were going to check levels of instruction and spiritual formation, they were also learning about people's living conditions and could assess charitable needs through these visitations.

Hospital administrators played a major role in managing the city's resources and implementing the Reformation, since the hospital directors had to take the Oath of Preachers and Deacons, swearing to serve the church, keep the faith,

---

103. RC 13:351–352 (14 November 1535); *Les sources du droit du canton de Genève* (see note 52), 2:303–304, fol. 683 (14 November 1535). For an English translation, see William C. Innes, *Social Concern in Calvin's Geneva* (Allison Park, PA: Pickwick Publications, 1983), 94.
104. *RCP,* 1:7–8.
105. Calvin, *Commentaries on the Epistles to Timothy, Titus, and Philemon,* trans. William Pringle (Grand Rapids, MI: Baker House Books, 2009), 85–87.
106. Howard, "House" (see note 66), 18; *RCP,* 1:8; *CO,* 10:24; *The Register of the Company of Pastors* (see note 8), 43.
107. Howard, "House" (see note 66), 93.
108. *RConsist* 11:xxi.

and demonstrate allegiance to the authorities.[109] Regarding poor relief, the main criteria for receiving regular support from the city included: "citizenship, ability and willingness to work, and religiosity (and in particular, orthopraxy)."[110] The hospital, which served as a catchall (an orphanage, dormitory, asylum, group home, and assisted living facility), became "a replacement family home that cared for and disciplined poor Genevans" from the cradle to the grave.[111]

At the beginning of 1557, the consistory registers included the list of names of administrators for the hospital immediately followed by the list of assistants to the consistory. It is the first time that hospital administrators were directly mentioned at the start of a consistory register; a similar list also appears in the subsequent volumes for 1558 and 1559. In 1557, three of the hospital administrators were also concurrently serving as members of the consistory. The hospital administrators were beginning to play an important role in establishing the discipline in Geneva. They monitored moral behavior at the hospital and maintained order.[112] The expansion of the list demonstrated the growing reach of the pastors and the consistory as well as the collaboration between hospital directors, who cared for the poor citizens and residents, and the pastors and deacons who cared for poor foreigners and refugees.

3. Deacons. Calvin affirmed civil involvement in poor relief and the religious value of caring for the poor. He supported the existing structure of the General Hospital and understood this organization from the perspective of the biblical models in Acts 6, 1 Timothy 3, and Romans 12. He established the deacons' ministry as second to the elders, and permanently necessary in every rightly ordered church, thus making a distinctive church office of lay ministers.[113] Rather than viewing deacons in their medieval role as assistants in the liturgy, Calvin interpreted the role of the deacon as those engaged in the relief of the poor.

The deacon, as steward or administrator, was responsible for collecting and distributing alms and goods to help the poor, while a second type of deacon was in charge of domestic chores, caring for the sick, and maintaining the

---

109. *Les Sources du Droit du Canton de Genève* (see note 52), 2:392 (16 July 1542); Howard, "House" (see note 66), 53.
110. Howard, "House" (see note 66), 11.
111. Howard, "House" (see note 66), 340.
112. *RConsist*, 12:xiii.
113. McKee, "Worship" (see note 10), 127.

household.[114] Calvin referred to Romans 12 to reiterate that those who care for the poor ought "to be cheerful and pleasant," because the poor person would be sad if someone helped him and grumbled at the same time; "it would be as if the person hit him with one hand and gave him a piece of bread with the other."[115] Calvin recommended that deacons do their work with glad hearts and refrain from berating the poor, so that the poor would be cheered by the deacons' expression of care and affection.[116]

Meanwhile, private charity was still meant to be an integral part of social relationships, especially among family members. Calvin expected individuals to be concerned for the needy people known to them and to help them beyond what they received from the hands of the deacons.[117] Heads of household were responsible for the support of their families, including elderly parents, children, relatives, and servants. However, care for strangers and those outside the family or household were mediated through an institution to prevent abuse. Magistrates and ministers wanted to discourage traveling beggars and ensure aid was dispersed in an orderly manner to the deserving poor. Hence, the purpose of deacons was the orderly administration and supervision of poor relief to avoid the commotion, confusion, and grumbling that inevitably arose among large groups.[118] In his sermon "The Qualifications of Deacons," Calvin asserted that believers have a personal responsibility to use wealth wisely by having a clear procedure for distributing alms fairly.[119] The concern was not whether people would give private charity but about how private giving should not result in a lack of supervision and haphazard giving where some got too much and others received nothing. Calvin also cautioned against stingy deacons who withheld care from the poor and let them languish; instead, he called for continuous improvement of poor relief, since this would follow the apostles' intentions when they chose deacons as a position of honor and responsibility.[120] Calvin sought to follow the pattern of the early church, in which deacons were ordained to minister to the poor who were neglected or overlooked.

---

114. Calvin, "Sermon on Acts 6:1–3, August 10, 1550" in *Acts of the Apostles* (see note 49), 307.
115. Calvin, "Acts 6:1–3" in *Acts of the Apostles* (see note 49), 307.
116. Calvin, "Acts 6:1–3" in *Acts of the Apostles* (see note 49), 308.
117. Calvin, "Acts 6:1–3" in *Acts of the Apostles* (see note 49), 315–316.
118. Calvin, "Sermon on Acts 6:1–6, August 17, 1550" in *Acts of the Apostles* (see note 49), 317.
119. Calvin, "Acts 6:1–3" in *Acts of the Apostles* (see note 49), 303–304.
120. Calvin, "Acts 6:1–3" in *Acts of the Apostles* (see note 49), 309.

In his interpretation of Romans, Calvin recognized that the widows of the early church often served as the second type of deacon. In his *Institutes of Christian Religion*, Calvin stated that "women could fill no other public office than to devote themselves to the care of the poor."[121] Based on his scriptural interpretation, Calvin extended the notion of widows to all women and delineated a public office for women as caretakers of the poor. In a time when there were no public offices open to women, Calvin designated the care of the poor as a public office for women on the basis of "Scripture, the practices of the early Church, and the contemporary role of women in welfare."[122] While caring for the poor in one's community was a well-established concept throughout Europe, Calvin's understanding of true believers being scattered throughout Europe led him to broaden his understanding of community refugees. This perspective extended poor relief to strangers, foreigners, and refugees whose security and well-being could be precarious.

4. Poor Relief of Refugees. As Andrew Spicer noted in his study of French exiles in England, the exile churches established their own systems of poor relief, not only to cope with the general social problems of the time but also in response to specific religious crises such as the St. Bartholomew's Day Massacre. Poor relief was re-sacralized with both a religious and social significance, so that the extent of support given by exile churches could turn out to be much more generous and much more comprehensive than local relief programs.[123] In the face of increased poverty, many cities lacked structural support for migrants, exiles, and refugees.

In the *Ecclesiastical Ordinances* of 1541, under the fourth order of the church (deacons), Calvin included the necessity of the travelers' hospital (*l'hospital des passants*) as a form of special charity in the developing social welfare system.[124] Starting in the late 1540s, French pastors conferred on the matter of providing poor relief for religious refugees and foreigners arriving in Geneva.

---

121. Calvin, *Institutes of Christian Religion*, ed. John T. McNeill, trans. Ford Lewis Battles, 2 vols. (Louisville, KY: Westminster Press, 1960), 2:1061; Jeannine Olson, "John Calvin's Only Public Office for Women, the Care of the Poor: Wet Nurses, Widows, and Welfare among French Refugees and in the Reformed Tradition," *Mythes et réalités du XVIe siècle: foi, idées, images: études en l'honneur d'Alain Dufour*, ed. Bernard Lescaze and Mario Turchetti (Alessandria: Edizioni dell'Orso, 2008), 51–69, here 52.

122. Olson, "Public Office for Women" (see note 121), 51.

123. Andrew Spicer, "Poor Relief and the Exile Communities," in *Reformations Old and New: The Socio-Economic Impact of Religious Change, c. 1470–1630*, ed. Beat A. Kümin (Aldershot, UK: Scholar Press, 1996), 254–255.

124. *RCP*, 1:8.

With the aid of wealthier refugees, they helped to set up a fund for poor French refugees. While the city concentrated on its needy citizens, the French immigrant community sought to accommodate waves of refugees with its own social welfare solution: the French Fund.[125] These refugees were "not simply *passants* (travelers) but sought longer-term shelter until they could return to their homeland; yet the travelers' hospital could not adequately care for the sheer number of French religious refugees."[126] The creation of the French Fund allowed the travelers' hospital to focus exclusively on transients rather than attempting to cater to the large number of immigrants, and especially religious refugees, who settled in the city. Consequently, the French Fund became far more important for the care of outsiders than the travelers' hospital, because the French Fund made it possible for religious refugees to settle in the city's territories, to join the churches, and to reside temporarily or integrate into the society as tolerated outsiders. Subsequent generations of those who stayed in the city often gradually assimilated, especially as they gained bourgeois rights.

The charitable activities of the French Fund included funding dowries, paying monthly stipends to wet nurses, granting regular gifts of money to the needy, lending mattresses and bedclothes, funding medical care, providing temporary room and board to travelers, and underwriting job retraining for refugees whose skills were not applicable in the Genevan economy. Outsourcing the care of the foreign poor to their own immigrant communities allowed the General Hospital to focus on Genevans and to preserve civic resources by limiting its own social welfare disbursements.[127] But this separation did not mean a lack of interest or concern. In fact, the General Hospital administrators, Guillaume Chicand (citizen), Michel Varro (bourgeois), and François de Roches (French immigrant and bourgeois), were all donors to the French Fund.[128]

Foreigners were also subject to the same consistorial discipline as citizens. Advocacy for religious refugees did not mean all foreigners were accepted, since those considered troublemakers, destructive agitators, or unfaithful cheats were called before the consistory and encouraged to change their ways. For further action, the cases would be passed to the Small Council, which could discipline criminal behavior with external restraints, such as imprisonment, punishment, penalty of fines, and banishment. In multiple cases, people left on their own to

---

125. See Jeannine E. Olson, *Calvin and Social Welfare* (see note 74).
126. Howard, "House" (see note 66), 255. For example, in 1545, four thousand refugees fled Merindol and Cabrières and arrived in Geneva.
127. Howard, "House" (see note 66), 261.
128. Howard, "House" (see note 66), 256.

avoid such charges, including foreigners who got in trouble. For example, the French goldsmith, Jacques Le Tessen, opted to voluntarily leave Geneva rather than be obliged by the consistory and council to keep his promise to marry his lover, Isabeau Charbonnière. After their first appearance before the consistory, they were referred to the Small Council, but four days later Charbonnière came alone before the Small Council and reported that Le Tessen had already left the city.[129] Discipline was linked to poor relief in this case because the council ordered Charbonnière to leave the city in three days, since she had followed Le Tessen to Geneva and, with his departure, would likely become dependent on the city's poor relief. This case also revealed that the burden of discipline and the burden of poverty could fall more heavily on women in the case of broken engagements or spousal abandonment.

On 16 November 1556, Calvin appeared before the council. He reaffirmed the need to receive foreigners, coming to Geneva "for the word of God," but at the same time he recognized the need "to prevent the dangers and to remove the abuses," since foreigners could make up stories to be accepted into the city and then cause scandals.[130] Acceptance of refugees did not mean accommodating bad behavior. Hence, consistory members sought to discourage the settlement of those simply seeking to escape from prior responsibilities.

Refugees continued to flock to Geneva mostly from France, but also from Italy and England during the reign of Mary Tudor (1553–1558). The number of Italian refugees had grown to a point where they requested that the consistory hire a preacher who would give a sermon in Italian after the main sermon. To accommodate the growing number of English and Italians, Calvin asked the council to grant them a place of worship to attend sermons and receive the sacraments in their own languages. Therefore, the council earmarked the Notre-Dame-la-Neuve Chapel (Calvin's *Auditoire*, adjacent to St. Pierre's) for the English and Italian communities.[131] By 1557, while Huguenots negotiated a precarious position in France, Calvin and the consistory strengthened their position in Geneva. The reformer's adoptive city continued to welcome many Protestants. In October 1557, the council received hundreds of new inhabitants, mainly French (around two hundred), but also around fifty Englishmen, twenty-five Italians, and even four Spaniards.[132] Upon Calvin's advice, the

---

129. *RConsist*, 5:77; MS Registres du Conseil de Genève, 21 April 1550, 44:367, 368v; Esther Chung-Kim, *Economics of Faith: Reforming Poor Relief in Early Modern Europe* (New York: Oxford University Press, 2021), 148.

130. *RConsist*, 11:xvii–xviii.

131. RC, 50:35v (14 November 1555); *RConsist*, 10:222n1229.

132. *Rconsist*, 12:xi.

council responded to this increased population of religious refugees by rededicating the Church of Saint Germain as the fourth place of worship in the city, and appointing two new pastors, François Morel and Claude Dupont.[133] For Italian, Spanish, English (and Scots), and German immigrants, independent congregations provided the opportunity to worship in their own languages and establish their own systems of social welfare called ethnic funds, such as the Italian Fund or the English Fund.[134]

In December 1557, following the execution of seven Huguenot prisoners in Paris, the council acceded to Calvin's request to secretly come to the aid of Parisian Protestants.[135] Refugees also engaged in mission work back in their home countries, such as France. Although the Reformed religion would remain a minority religion in France even at its height in the 1560s, the work of missionary pastors and the undercover transport of evangelical books into France helped to increase support for the Reformed cause. The French Fund even diverted some funds to help the Reformed cause. The French Fund also provided financial help for refugee families whose main breadwinners—often husbands and fathers—were caught in France while smuggling Reformed books.[136]

V. CONCLUSION

Because Calvin recognized order as the third mark of the church, he viewed discipline as the way to uphold community unity. Increased involvement of lay members of society in poor relief did not automatically translate into charity becoming less religious. Rather, the impact of laicization demonstrated how religious authority expanded into areas beyond specific devotional duties of worship, sacraments, and church order and became more diffused among select lay members. Lay involvement in the discipline of the church community meant that religion exerted its influence in a new, maybe even more powerful way, via the emerging lay civic leaders who would see their work as elders, deacons, hospitallers, and charity workers as a divine calling and ultimately

---

133. *RConsist*, 12:xi.
134. Howard, "House" (see note 66), 237.
135. *RConsist*, 12:xi.
136. Jeannine Olson, "The Mission to France: Nicolas Des Gallars' Interaction with John Calvin, Gaspard de Coligny, and Edmund Grindal, Bishop of London," in *Calvinus clarissimus theologus: Papers of the Tenth International Congress on Calvin Research*, ed. Herman J. Selderhuis (Göttingen: Vandenhoeck & Ruprecht, 2012), 344–357.

accountable to God. Their collective effort to live piously in the world would influence their culture and society.

Geneva became an influential city because of its extensive support for existing poor relief institutions and establishing funds for newly emerging needs, namely the foreigners' relief funds. Calvin and the pastors believed that discipline and charity were necessary for community-building in Reformed cities. Discipline promoted ethical standards for maintaining harmonious social relations and a form of training to understand and internalize Reformed doctrine, practice, and values. Upholding a set of standards, albeit imperfectly, whether around ethical practices, biblical principles, doctrinal stances, communal values, or some combination of these goals, contributed to a collective identity. The foci on discipline and poor relief balanced the stringent and supportive forces of city leaders as Geneva sought to become a pious city. Calvin, the Company of Pastors, and the elders and deacons serving on the consistory, the General Hospital, and the French Fund played a significant role not only in shaping the social values for this community formation, but also in setting the boundaries on the range of acceptable behaviors.

Calvin saw the church as a network of Reformed communities scattered throughout Europe. His views impacted not only Geneva and neighboring Swiss regions, but also various Reformed communities in France, Germany, the Netherlands, England, Scotland, and Eastern Europe.[137] With the spread of Reformed Protestant churches, communal care and poor relief were extended to care for displaced exiles, so that in many cities with Reformed churches, Calvinists established independent diaconates to relieve poor church members, following the Genevan model. Despite conflict and resistance, magistrates, ministers, and lay leaders in sixteenth-century Geneva labored toward strengthening the Reformed community and supporting the hospital and relief funds.

Professor Esther Chung-Kim
Department of Religious Studies
Claremont McKenna College
850 Columbia Avenue
Claremont, CA 91711
USA
echungkim@cmc.edu

---

137. See Benedict, *Christ's Churches* (see note 21).

ZUSAMMENFASSUNG

Der vorliegende Aufsatz befasst sich mit den zahlreichen Versuchen, städtische Gemeinschaftsbildung in Genf zu befördern. Dieser soziale Gestaltungsprozess beruhte vor allem auf Disziplinierung und Armenfürsorge. Die städtischen Räte und die Geistlichen im Genfer Konsistorium arbeiteten zusammen, um Streitigkeiten zu schlichten und die städtische Ordnung aufrechtzuerhalten. Sie disziplinierten Sünder und Missetäter und schufen Systeme der Armenfürsorge für „würdige" Arme, indem sie die städtische Gemeinschaft neu definierten, soziale Spannungen zu lösen suchten, moralische Normen aufstellten und die soziale Fürsorge beförderten. Als die Zuwanderung von Hugenotten aus Frankreich zu einer Flüchtlingskrise führte, gründeten Calvin und die französischen Pfarrer zusammen mit wohlhabenden französischen Spendern die sogenannte „Bourse française", die ausschließlich der Armenfürsorge für Ausländer diente. Calvin betonte Einigkeit und kommunale Verantwortung bei der Lösung von Konflikten und förderte einen hohen moralischen Standard, um das Bild einer „würdigen Gemeinschaft" zu schaffen. Sein Ziel war, damit die Einnahme von Spenden für die Armenhilfe zu befördern. Die Institutionen von Kirche und Staat in Genf unter Calvin erkannten die Rolle der Laien beim Aufbau einer gottesfürchtigen und gläubigen Stadt und schufen ein Modell für die Armenfürsorge und zur Unterstützung von Flüchtlingen, das zum Vorbild anderer reformierter Städte im frühneuzeitlichen Europa wurde.

Beredtes Schweigen. Basler Theologen und der Hexenwahn

Von Christine Christ-von Wedel

EINLEITUNG

Der Glaube an übernatürliche Zauberkräfte wird weltweit und zeitenübergreifend zunehmend interdisziplinär erforscht. Er hat sich bekanntlich in ganz Europa seit der Mitte des 15. Jahrhunderts mit besonderen Merkmalen panikartig ausgebreitet. Für unerklärliches Siechtum, plötzlichen Tod, Unfruchtbarkeit, Viehsterben oder Hagelwetter wurden Hexer oder Hexen verantwortlich gemacht, denen ein Teufelspakt vorgeworfen wurde. In Inquisitionsprozessen mit harter Folter gestanden Tausende das Teufelsbündnis und wurden verbrannt. Zahlreiche regionale Fallstudien belegen, wie vielfältig die Gründe und die Verläufe von Hexenprozessen waren. Mit sorgfältigen Quellenanalysen und Vergleichen konnten aber auch typische regionale, überregionale und gesamteuropäische Merkmale benannt werden. Insbesondere werden in Verbindung mit der damaligen magischen Weltsicht wirtschaftliche, klimatische, politische, gesellschaftliche, rechtliche und konfessionelle Bedingungen hervorgehoben und ihre Bedeutsamkeit breit, aber auch kontrovers diskutiert.[1] Hier interessiert die Diskussion um die konfessionellen Einflüsse.

Keith Thomas hat die viel beachtete Forschungsthese aufgestellt, die Reformation habe in protestantischen Landen die Hexenpanik gesteigert durch das Abschaffen von Wetterglocken, Flurprozessionen, Benediktionen etc., welche

---

1. Vgl. z. B. *Malcolm Gaskill*, Witchcraft, Oxford 2010, bes. 2 f.; *Brian P. Levack*, Hexenjagd. Die Geschichte der Hexenverfolgung in Europa, München 2009. Vgl. auch aus der schier unerschöpflichen Literatur: *Rita Voltmer*, Hexen. Wissen was stimmt, Freiburg im Breisgau, 2008; *Walter Rummel, Rita Voltmer* (Hg.), Hexen und Hexenverfolgung in der Frühen Neuzeit, Darmstadt 2008; *Dieter Harmening*, Zauberei im Abendland. Vom Anteil der Gelehrten am Wahn der Leute. Skizzen zur Geschichte des Aberglaubens, Königshausen 1991; *Kathrin Utz-Tremp*, Von der Häresie zur Hexerei. „Wirkliche" und imaginäre Sekten im Spätmittelalter, Hannover 2008; *Kathryn A. Edwards* (Hg), Werewolves, Witches, and Wandering Spirits. Traditional Belief and Folklore in Early Modern Europe, Kirksville 2012; *Markus Hirte* (Hg.), „Mit dem Schwert oder festem Glauben". Luther und die Hexen, Darmstadt 2017; *Jörg Haustein*, Martin Luthers Stellung zum Zauber- und Hexenwesen, Stuttgart u. a. 1990. *Gerhard Schormann*, Hexenprozesse in Deutschland, Göttingen 1981, und insbesondere die neueste Ausgabe von *Wolfgang Behringer*, Hexen. Glaube, Verfolgung, Vermarktung, München 2009[7] mit einer nachgeführten Literaturliste.

die Kirche zuvor Unglücksfällen und vermeintlicher Zauberei entgegengesetzt habe.² Die spätere, insbesondere englischsprachige Forschung ging noch weiter. Der Kampf von den protestantischen Kanzeln herab gegen abergläubische Praktiken sowie gegen volkstümliche Segnungen und Beschwörungen habe die Bevölkerung geradezu auf den Hexenglauben fixiert. Die beharrlichen Hinweise Martin Luthers sowie Johannes Calvins und ihrer Nachfolger auf ein bedrohliches Wirken des Teufels seien für die in der frühen Neuzeit intensivierte Hexenverfolgung mitverantwortlich, und die verinnerlichte Frömmigkeit und die verlangte reformatorische Sittenstrenge hätten die Bevölkerung überfordert. Sie habe die Schuld für das eigene Versagen angesichts der hohen moralischen Ansprüche auf vermeintliche Hexen projiziert.³

Die These wurde breit rezipiert, obwohl manches dagegen spricht: Hexenprozesse gingen in katholischen wie protestantischen Regionen zurück, als sich die Reformation nach 1520 durchzusetzen begann. Sie flammten erst nach 1560, während der Hungerkrisen und Seuchen der kleinen Eiszeit, in beiden Konfessionen neu auf,⁴ ließen aber schon am Ende des Dreißigjährigen Krieges wieder nach. Sie ebbten also ab in der Zeit der protestantischen Hochorthodoxie, als vermehrt Sittenstrenge durchgesetzt wurde, eine starke Frömmigkeitsbewegung aufbrach und auch protestantische Theologen, anders als die erste und zweite Generation der Reformatoren, ausgefeilte Dämonologien veröffentlichten.⁵ Einzelne Fallstudien zu reformierten Gebieten und ihrer Pfarrerschaft scheinen mir darum dringlich.

Nachdem ich kürzlich Zürich untersucht habe,⁶ sei nun ein Blick auf das reformierte Basel im 16. und 17. Jahrhundert geworfen. Wie in anderen Städten auch wurden die Hexenprozesse in Basel vom Ratsgericht geführt, Geist-

---

2. *Keith Thomas*, Religion and the Decline of Magic, Harmondsworth 1973², bes. 58–89, 763, 588–598.
3. Zusammengefasst bei *Levack*, Hexenjagd (wie Anm. 1), 111–113.
4. *Wolfgang Behringer, Hartmut Lehmann* et al. (Hg.), Kulturelle Konsequenzen der „Kleinen Eiszeit", Göttingen 2005; *Behringer*, Hexen (wie Anm. 1), 48–55.
5. Dabei ist die insbesondere von Jörg Haustein für Luther aufgeworfene Frage, ob Reformatoren der gemäßigteren „Episcopi-Tradition", die Hexenflüge und Sabbate ablehnte, oder der radikaleren „Malleus-Tradition", für die ich im reformierten Basel keine Belege fand, zuzuordnen seien (vgl. *Haustein*, Martin Luthers Stellung (wie Anm. 1), bes. 173), für die Fragestellung dieses Aufsatzes kaum von Belang. Der Glaube an die Hexensabbate dürfte die großen Kettenprozesse ausgelöst haben, die Ablehnung der Hexensabbate änderte aber nichts an der grundsätzlichen Kriminalisierung der vermeintlichen Hexer und Hexen auch unter Protestanten.
6. *Christine Christ-von Wedel*, „Die Zürcher Hexenprozesse und die Reformatoren", in: Zwingliana 48 (2021), 71–114.

liche haben darauf nur indirekt Einfluss nehmen können, durch Anzeigen, Predigten, öffentliche Disputationen, sonstige theologische Publikationen und, sofern sie dazu aufgefordert wurden, durch Gutachten sowie seelsorgerliche Betreuung und auch Befragung[7] der Verhafteten.

Quellen zu den maßgeblichen Theologen der Zeit fließen in Basel reichlich, sind aber kaum erschlossen. Nur zu Johannes Oekolampad liegen Ernst Staehelins Bibliographie und Briefedition vor, zu Oswald Mykonius Rainer Henrichs Briefregesten sowie zu Simon Sulzer Daniel Abendscheins Schriftenliste.[8] Weitere wissenschaftliche Editionen oder gar digitale Werkausgaben fehlen. Ich konnte darum im Rahmen einer kleineren Fallstudie nicht jeweils das Gesamtwerk der Autoren systematisch und abschließend durchsuchen. Ich habe mich darauf beschränkt, in exegetischen Werken und Predigten die Auslegungen zu einschlägigen Bibelstellen nachzuschlagen und unter anderen Veröffentlichungen die durchsucht, in denen ich allenfalls Hinweise auf Hexen und Zauberei vermuten konnte, sowie die bekannten Gutachten und Prozessakten benutzt. Sämtliche Titel von drei dicken Sammelbänden mit Basler theologischen Disputationen zwischen 1570 und 1610 habe ich durchgesehen, ohne allerdings auf irgendwelches Interesse am zeitgenössischen Hexenwesen zu stoßen,[9] was, wie sich zeigen wird, durchaus bedeutsam ist. So kann ich doch wagen, Ergebnisse vorzulegen.

BASLER HEXENPROZESSE

Nach den sehr gründlichen Archivforschungen von Diethegen Guggenbühl setzten Hexenverfahren in Basel früh ein, schon während des Basler Konzils, auf dem Hexentheoretiker wirkten, insbesondere der damals das Basler Dominikanerkloster reformierende Johannes Nider. Zwischen 1433 und 1519 wurden in fünfundzwanzig aktenkundigen Hexenverfahren mit oft mehreren Be-

---

7. Staatsarchiv des Kantons Basel-Stadt (im Folgenden StA Basel), Criminalia 4,8 (15).

8. *Ernst Staehelin* (Hg.), Oekolampad-Bibliographie. Verzeichnis der im 16. Jahrhundert erschienen Oekolampaddrucke, Basel 1918; ders. (Hg.), Briefe und Akten zum Leben Oekolampads, 2 Bde., Leipzig 1927 und 1934; *Rainer Henrich* (Hg.), Oswald Myconius Briefwechsel 1515–1552. Regesten, Zürich 2017; *Daniel Abendschein*, Simon Sulzer. Herkunft, Prägung und Profil des Basler Antistes und Reformators in Baden Durlach, Stuttgart 2019, 549–639.

9. Sammelbände der Universitätsbibliothek Basel: UBH VB M 63; UBH Frey Gryn 3 IV 2; UBH Frey Gryn 3 IV 3. Sogar in den Thesen *De miraculis et signis temporum* von Amandus Polanus, Basel 1608, die signa und praestigia der Dämonen und schlechter Menschen thematisieren, erlaubt sich der Basler Theologe kein Wort zu vermeintlicher Hexerei, § 94.

schuldigten einundzwanzig vermeintliche Hexer oder Hexen sicher verbrannt, sechs freigesprochen und eine ausgewiesen.[10] Schon seit 1519 verurteilte der Basler Rat im 16. Jahrhundert keine der Hexerei Angeklagte mehr zum Tode. Aber er trat, nachdem sich die Reformation 1529 durchgesetzt hatte, noch auf elf Zaubereiprozesse ein, vier endeten mit Verbannung, zwei Frauen mussten wegen geführter Drohreden für die Kosten ihrer Untersuchung aufkommen, ein Mann, der im Rausch behauptet hatte, er habe sich dem Teufel ergeben, durfte keine Waffen mehr tragen, die übrigen wurden bedingungslos freigesprochen. Nach 1564 sind in Basel keine Zauberei- und Hexenprozesse für das 16. Jahrhundert mehr überliefert.[11] Das änderte sich mit einem spektakulären Fall im Jahr 1602, der zu einer Verurteilung, aber nicht zu einer Hinrichtung führte. Die weiteren aus dem 17. Jahrhundert bekannten Basler Zaubereiverfahren endeten mehrmals nicht mit einer Verurteilung der Verdächtigten, sondern mit Verurteilungen ihrer Verleumder, insbesondere verhängte der Rat keine Todesurteile, abgesehen von den Hinrichtungen eines Spekulanten und Ehebrechers im Jahre 1624, bei dem neben Zaubereivorwürfen auch der Verdacht eines Teufelspaktes aufkam, und einer Frau, die 1680 des dreizehnfachen Giftmordes schuldig gesprochen wurde. Der angebliche Teufelspakt spielte bei beiden nur eine untergeordnete Rolle.[12]

WEYERS *DE PRAESTIGIIS DAEMONUM*

Dass der Rat seit Juli 1564 bis ins 16. Jahrhundert hinein nicht mehr auf Hexereiprozesse eintrat und auch nachher zurückhaltend blieb, trifft zeitlich zusammen mit der Herausgabe von Johann Weyers *De praestigiis daemonum* 1563 durch den damals berühmtesten humanistischen Drucker Basels, Johannes Oporin. Das umstrittene Werk erschien bis zu Oporins Tod 1568 gleich viermal – 1563, 1564, 1566, 1568 – und auch nachher druckte es die Offizina Operiana 1577 und 1583 weiter und verlegte auch Weyers eigene Kurzfassung *De lamiis* 1577 und 1582.[13]

---

10. *Dietegen Guggenbühl*, Mit Tieren und Teufeln. Sodomiten und Hexen unter Basler Jurisdiktion in Stadt und Land 1399–1799, Liestal 2002, 124 f.
11. Ibid., 125–130, 225.
12. Ibid., 132–152 und 333; *Albert Schnyder*, Zauberei und Schatzgräberei vor dem Basler Rat. Von der Suche nach besonderen Ursachen und verborgenen Schätzen im 17. und 18. Jahrhundert, Liestal 2003, 121 und 123; vgl. auch *Catherine Huber*, Die Hexenprozesse in Basel im 16. und 17. Jahrhundert, Liz.-arb. phil. I Univ. Basel, 1989, 61.
13. Vgl. für De praestigiis: Verzeichnis der Drucke des 16. Jahrhunderts (im Folgenden:

Weyer, Leibarzt des Herzogs Wilhelm von Jülich-Kleve-Berg und bedeutendes Mitglied des dortigen Erasmuskreises, hielt die angeblichen Teufelsbünde und Flüge zum Hexensabbat der vermeintlichen Hexen für Wahnvorstellungen elender melancholischer Kranker. Der Teufel gaukle ihnen nur allerhand vor. Der Arzt am herzoglichen Hof in Kleve geißelte die grausamen Haftbedingungen und Foltermethoden und appellierte an christliche Milde. Gelehrte Magie, die an Fürstenhöfen grassierte, verpönte auch er als Gotteslästerung und Ketzerei.[14] Die Magier oder Zauberer schadeten durch ihre falschen Versprechungen und Wahrsagereien den Menschen und versetzten ganze Regionen in Unruhe. Sie sollten wie andere Ketzer auch, nur wenn sie hartnäckig auf ihren Lügen und Irrtümern beharrten, bestraft werden, reuige aber straffrei bleiben. Nur Giftmischerei, die ebenfalls als Zauberei galt, nahm Weyer aus. Grundsätzlich aber drängte Weyer darauf, Magie als abschreckend zu bestrafen, allerdings in christlichen Zeiten nicht mit dem Tode, sondern mit Landesverweis, obwohl, wie er ausdrücklich u. a. mit Ex 22,18 ausführte, das Alte Testament die Todesstrafe vorsah.[15] Er versicherte, mit Christi Heilswerk seien Magie und Zauberei überwunden: „Vor zeiten führten die bösen Geister die menschen am narrenseil vmbher/ dieweil sie sich nider liessen vnnd einamen die Brünnen/Flüß/ Stein vnnd Holtz/ vnnd machten sie also mit jhrer verzauberunge gar zuo thoren: Aber nach dem vnnd das wort Gottes erschienen ist/ sind solche triegerische verblendungen verschwinen und vergangen."[16] Weyer befleißigte sich also des erasmischen historischen Ansatzes im Umgang mit dem alttestamentlichen Tötungsgebot: Was damals galt, muss heute nicht mehr gelten.[17] Doch, so Weyer, auch in christlichen Zeiten beherrsche der Teufel die Gewissen und sei sogar in die Kirchen eingedrungen. So hätten sich etwa in den Taufritus allerlei abgöttische Missbräuche eingeschlichen.[18] Insbesondere aber verführe der Teufel die gelehrten Schwarzkünstler, die, anders

---

VD 16), W: 2663–2668; 2677 und 2678, sowie für De lamiis: VD 16 W 2648 (2653) und 2647 (2652).

14. Ich zitiere aus der ebenfalls in Basel erschienenen deutschen Übersetzung: Von verzeuberungen, verblendungen, auch sonst viel vnd mancherley gepler des Teuffels vnnd seines gantzen Heers …: fünff bücher zum andern mal widerumb übersehen, gemehrt und gebessert. Erstlich durch […] Herrn D. Johann Wier […] in Latinischer zungen in Truck verfertigt; Nachmols aber […] durch Johannem Füglinum Basiliensem […] in Teutsche sprach gebracht vnnd an tag gegeben, Basel 1565 (vgl. VD 16 W 2669, http://gateway-bayern.de/VD16+W+2669), bes.+ iiijr-+Vv.

15. Ibid., 979–996 und 1015 f. Vgl. *Johannes Weyer*, De lamiis, Basel 1582, 64.

16. *Weyer*, Von verzeuberungen (wie Anm. 14), 48.

17. Vgl. zu Erasmus' historischem Ansatz u. Anm 114.

18. *Weyer*, Von verzeuberungen (wie Anm. 14), 51.

als die ungebildeten vermeintlichen Hexen, statt Gebet und natürliche Mittel „alle verbottenen/ vngebürlichen mittel und curationes" benutzten, „von dem teufel zu beuestigung seines Reichs erdacht vnd auff die ban gebracht/ so durch ungötliche beschwerungen/ character/ oder wunderbarliche zeichen/ ligaturen/ dz ist ding die man anbindt/ periapta/ oder solche stuck/ welche man an den hals oder andere glieder des leibs anhencket/ fingering/ sigel/ bilder/ vnd andere dergleichen teufels laruen/ zugehn vnd beschehend", aber durch die heilige Schrift und natürliche Argumente widerlegt seien.[19] Weyer kämpfte demnach gegen einen Aberglauben, der Zauberei für möglich hielt und entsprechende Mittel anwandte, erklärte aber die meist alten, armen Frauen, die als Hexen verbrannt wurden, für unschuldig.

FÜGLINS ÜBERSETZUNG VON WEYERS KAMPFSCHRIFT

Bereits 1565 brachte Oporin eine deutsche Fassung heraus. Der Basler Pfarrer Johannes Füglin, damals Helfer an der Peterskirche, später Pfarrer der Leonhardsgemeinde, hatte *De praestigiis daemonum* bereits keine zwei Jahre nach der Erstausgabe ins Deutsche übersetzt und so auch unter Lateinunkundigen verbreitet. Pfarrer Füglin beschreibt in seinem Vorwort die Entstehungsgeschichte: Weyer habe „mich [Füglin] mit rhat/ ja anhalten deß hochgelehrten [...] Herrn D. Simon Sultzers/ meines geliebten Preceptoris vnd der Kirchen zu Basel vorstender vnd Bischoff/ für gut vnnd nützlich angesehen/ [...] solchs buch in Teutsche zungen [...] zuuerdolmetschen. Vnnd das fürnemlich auß dem grund vnd vrsach das Teutscher alt vnd weitberümbter Nation Fürsten/ Herrn/vorstender vnd Oberkeiten/ beide Geistliche vnd auch Weltliche auch beide hoch vnd nider stands im verkehrten vrtheil deß verzeubern vnd Hexengümpelmarckts/ so gar verblendet sind (verzeihe mir wen es antrifft) [...]."[20] Ausgerechnet bei den Deutschen, die von sich behaupteten, sie „förchten auff gantzer Erden nichts denn das der himmel hin ab falle", sei es so weit gekommen, „das man auch die alten/ arbeitseligen/ kümerlich kriehenden Vetreln/ ja ihre besen/ häfen/ vnd alten krachbeltz (ich hätte schier etwas anders gesagt) förcht. Pfu dich/ pfu dich/ pfu dich der blutigen schand. [...] Die Zeuber/ Gifftsüppler/ etc. so mit vorbedachtem rhat des Teuffels Bundtsgenossen sind last man bassiern/ die ellenden alten Vetteln

---

19. Ibid., Vorred. Von Wier (+Vir).
20. Ibid., Vored. Von Füglin (iijr–iiijv).

aber/ Hexen genant/ so in der phatasey geäffet/ müssen ein scheiterbeigen für ein todtenbaum haben."[21]

Mit Johannes Weyer empörte sich demnach der Basler Pfarrer Johannes Füglin über Schwarzkünstler, die vorsätzlich als Teufels Bundesgenossen durch allerlei Kunststücke den Menschen etwas vorgaukelten, und richtete sich gegen Giftmischer, hielt aber vermeintlichen Zauberkräfte und Hexenflüge für reine Phantasiegebilde und die Angst vor den zahlreich in Europa verurteilten Hexen für schändlich.

Die Mahnungen Weyers und Füglins fielen in Basel auf fruchtbaren Boden, der bereits von Basler Humanistenkreisen und Basels Reformator Johannes Oekolampad aufgelockert war. Darauf ist zurückzukommen.

Der Antistes Simon Sulzer, der die Übersetzung von Weyers Werk gefördert hatte, konnte für dessen Ideen unter den Basler Ratsherren seinen beträchtlichen Einfluss geltend machen, einen Einfluss, den Heinrich Bullinger und Jean Calvin in den Auseinandersetzungen um den Straßburger Consensus (1563) und das zweite Helvetische Bekenntnis (1566) bitter beklagten.[22] Einzelnachweise für ein Wirken Sulzers gegen den Hexenwahn kann ich nicht beibringen, aber die Sache spricht für sich. Noch weit über seinen Tod im Jahre 1585 hinaus, hat der Basler Rat keine Hexereivorwürfe mehr aufgegriffen.

Um so spektakulärer wirkt der erste wieder vom Rat durchgeführte Prozess von 1602, der sich zunächst kaum von den üblichen Hexereiverfahren unterschied, die etwa im verbündeten Zürich um 1600 fast Jahr für Jahr zu Hinrichtungen führten. Wie verliefen solche Prozesse?

DER EINFLUSS VON TENGLERS *LAYENSPIEGEL* AUF DEN PROZESS VON 1602

Das Hexereiverbrechen galt nach heutigen Begriffen als Offizialdelikt und jeder Verdächtigung war nachzugehen. Wie andernorts auch hatte sich in Basel im Laufe des 16. Jahrhunderts das inquisitorische Prozessverfahren durchgesetzt. Im viel gedruckten *Layenspiegel* (Erstausgabe 1509), einem für Laienrichter entworfenen, ausführlichen allgemeinen Rechtsbuch, hatte der Autor Ulrich Tengler 1511 einen Paragraphen zu Hexenprozessen aufgenommen,

---

21. Ibid., iijr–iijv.
22. *Amy Nelson Burnett*, Bucers letzter Jünger. Simon Sulzer und Basels konfessionelle Identität zwischen 1550 und 1570, in: Basler Zeitschrift für Geschichte und Altertumskunde 107 (2007), 137–172, bes. 163–169.

der sich, wenn auch nicht sklavisch, doch stark an die berüchtigten Anweisungen des 1486 gedruckten *Malleus Maleficarum* von Heinrich Kramer anlehnte. Der *Malleus* wurde erst im 20. Jhd. als *Hexenhammer* ins Deutsche übersetzt. Das Handbuch Tenglers aber bot Laienrichtern ein übersichtliches deutsches Nachschlagewerk auch für Hexenprozesse.

Der *Layenspiegel* war in Basel verbreitet. Der Rechtsprofessor und Rechtskonsulent der Stadt, Bonifacius Amerbach (1495–1562), Erasmusverehrer und enger Freund des älteren Humanisten, besaß eine Ausgabe von 1527. In einer weiteren der vier Ausgaben, die aus Basler altem Bibliotheksbesitz erhalten sind, hat ein Unbekannter im 16. Jahrhundert ein ausführliches Register eingetragen.[23] Nach dem *Layenspiegel* fiel Zauberei unter die Rubrik Ketzerei. Zauberer oder Magier übten nach Tengler ihre Kunst „durch offenbar anruffen der bösen gaist".[24] Sie seien durch Verbrennen zu strafen.[25] Amerbach hat nur zwei kleine Notizen in den dicken Folianten geschrieben, eine bezieht sich auf den Abschnitt, der für die Hexenprozesse das überkommene Akkusationsrecht mit „der peen Talionis" aussetzt. Die Beweislast lag demnach bei den Angeklagten und das Strafmaß musste nicht mehr dem Schaden, den der Verbrecher zugefügt hatte, entsprechen. Galt Hexerei doch als „crimen exceptum". Bei einem so schweren Verbrechen gegen den christlichen Glauben, in Heimlichkeit und mit Hilfe des bösen Geistes verübt, sei es, mahnt Tengler, gefährlich nach den üblichen Regeln vorzugehen. Er forderte also ein Sonderverfahren für Ausnahmeverbrechen. Die weltlichen Richter sollten allein auf Verleumdung und Gerücht hin den Prozess beginnen.[26] Amerbach notierte dazu die Begriffe „Accusatio, Denuntiatio, Inquisitio". Er gibt keine Auskunft darüber, was er von der vorgeschlagenen Art, die Hexenprozesse einzuleiten, hielt.

Sicher aber ist: Zusammen mit dem damaligen Basler Antistes Oswald Mykonius, dem Pfarrer zu St. Leonhard Markus Bertschi und dem Medizinprofessor Oswald Bär setzte er sich 1545 ein für die der Hexerei verleumdete alte Lehrerin Catharina Leiderin. Der Rat verurteilte sie zwar nicht als Hexe, glaub-

---

23. Ulrich Tengler, Der Neü Layenspiegel von rechtmässigen ordnungen in Burgerlichen und peinlichen Regimenten. Mit Addition. Auch der Güldin Bulla, Künigklich Reformation, landtfrieden. Auch bewärung gemainer recht und andern antzaigen [Mit Vorrede von Sebastian Brant], Straßburg 1527, Signatur UBH Nd II 8 (ein entsprechender Druck in VD 16 T 345) mit Besitzvermerk Amerbachs und Eintragungen auf folio 43v und 125v. Die Ausgabe mit den Registereintragungen von 1521 hat die Signatur UBH Nm I 10. Ich danke Lorenz Heiligensetzer für die Bestätigung meiner Zuweisung ins 16. Jahrhundert. Vgl. auch Signaturen: UBH Nm I 4 und UBH Nm I 5.
24. *Tengler*, Layenspiegel, 1527 (wie Anm. 23), 124v.
25. Vgl. ibid., 124v–125v, bes. 124v.
26. Ibid., 125v.

te aber die aus St. Gallen stammende Frau aus der Stadt weisen zu müssen, weil die Angst vor ihrer vermeintlichen Hexerei sie unhaltbar mache. Sie habe, begründete er sein Urteil, sich selbst „mit jrem unbehuotsamen mundt" in eine so üble Lage gebracht, „das sich menglichs dorumb beclagt".[27] Mykonius, Bertschi, Amerbach und Bär suchten ihr, freilich ziemlich erfolglos, beizustehen. Mykonius schrieb in ihrer aller Namen einen Brief an Vadian, den Bürgermeister St. Gallens, „pro ipsa multa egimus; nihil peregimus vel certe parum".[28] Die Vier bezeugten, die Leiderin habe in Basel „fromm und ernst" den Mädchen Schreiben und Lesen beigebracht und sich bei vielen Lob erworben. Wegen der Rücksichtslosigkeit des Volkes habe sie fortziehen müssen. Sie bitten Vadian, sich ihrer anzunehmen. Amerbach notierte zu einer seiner Geldspenden für die Verbannte aus dem Erasmuslegat: „der armen wyslosen [hilflosen] lerfrawen [...], eine arme gottselige liebe fraw, die [vss] böser lüt geschrey halben nitt platz mag hie haben (gott geb, das wir das nit ettwan gegen gott engelten miessen, das wir der sinen so wenig achten), dormitt sy wider hervff gen Sant Gallen kummen mag, geben 1 krönen."[29]

Das Einleiten des Hexereiprozesses auf Verleumdung hin war nicht die einzige fragwürdige Praxis, die der *Layenspiegel* empfahl. Tengler schlug vor, nach der Verhaftung so vorzugehen: Zeugen sind bei Androhung der Pein zur Aussage zu verpflichten. Sie sollen straffrei bleiben, wenn ihre Verleumdungen sich nicht bewahrheiten.[30] Nicht die Ankläger, müssen die Schuld, nein, die Angeklagten müssen ihre Unschuld beweisen. Die Beweislast wurde also umgekehrt in einem Verfahren, das den Verdächtigten kaum eine Chance ließ. Die vermeintlichen „Hexen" – der *Layenspiegel* spricht wie der *Malleus Maleficarum* fast nur von weiblichen „Unholdinnen"[31] – sollten nicht erfahren, was gegen sie vorlag, sollten aber gezielt nach den Anklagepunkten befragt werden, zunächst gütlich, dann unter Folter. Streite die vermeintliche Hexe die Vorwürfe ab, „so mag der richter vermuotten, sy sey verzaubert [...]",[32] mit anderen Worten, der Teufel stehe ihr bei. Allerlei Vorsichtsmaßnahmen werden den Richtern ans Herz gelegt. „Sie mögen auch die vnholden rügkling zuo solcher

---

27. *Guggenbühl*, Mit Tieren (wie Anm. 10), 220.
28. Vadianische Briefsammlung, hg. von *Emil Arbenz*, 7 Bde., St. Gallen 1890–1913, Bd. 6, Nr. 1403.
29. Die Amerbachkorrespondenz, hg. von *Alfred Hartmann* et al., 11 Bde., Basel 1942–2010, Bd. 6, Ep. 2749 mit Einleitung; vgl. *Guggenbühl*, Mit Tieren (wie Anm. 10), 220.
30. *Tengler*, Layenspiegel, 1527 (wie Anm. 23), 126r.
31. Zum Geschlechteraspekt vgl. *Claudia Opitz-Belakhal*, Böse Weiber. Wissen und Geschlecht in der Dämonologie der frühen Neuzeit, Sulzbach 2017.
32. *Tengler*, Layenspiegel, 1527 (wie Anm. 23), 126v.

frag fürfaren lassen" und das Kreuz schlagen, „damitt der alten schlangen ir boßhait und gifft mit götlicher hilff abgelait werden mög". Vor der Folter sollten den Verdächtigten Haupt und Schamhaare geschoren werden, weil sie darin Zauberwerk verstecken könnten, und die Richter sollten sich hüten, die vermeintlichen Zauberinnen zu berühren.[33]

Offenbar ließen sich die „Siebnerherren", die in Basel im Auftrag ihrer Ratskollegen die Untersuchungen im Kerker und in der Folterkammer durchführten, 1545 bei Catharina Leiderin von solch rücksichtslosem Vorgehen zurückhalten, richteten sich aber 1602 nach Tenglers Empfehlungen.

Die von Zeugen aus Riehen des Schadenzaubers verdächtigte Margreth Vögtlin wurde nach einer Dorsalnotiz zuerst gütlich befragt. Sie leugnete die Anklagepunkte ab und beteuerte bei Gott, sie habe „weder einem noch dem anderen Menschen, einich Leidts beschuldigtermaßen, nicht angefüegt, Vil wenigers mit dem bösen geist was zethun gehept".[34] Sie wurde also offensichtlich von den Richtern nach einem Teufelspakt befragt. Obwohl auch entlastende Zeugenaussagen vorlagen, glaubten die Ratsherren, sie der Tortur unterziehen zu dürfen, was das Reichsrecht nur erlaubte, wenn die Tat als „bewiesen angenommen" werden konnte.[35] Die Basler Obrigkeit war allerdings nicht ans Reichsrecht gebunden. Die Ratsherren haben denn auch, wie der *Layenspiegel* vorschlug, „gleichwol sie an die Torturen gschlagen". Margreth Vögtlin habe die außerordentlich harten Martern „one soderparn geschrey erlitten, Allerdings nichts bekhennen, noch auf beschehen zuspruch was antworten wöllen."[36] Auf das beharrliche Beteuern ihrer Unschuld hin hat der Rat theologische und juristische Gutachten eingefordert.

DAS THEOLOGISCHE GUTACHTEN VON 1602

Die Pfarrer und Theologieprofessoren unter dem Vorsitz von Professor und Antistes Johann Jakob Grynäus waren über das Vorgehen des Rates empört. Sie räumten nach der üblichen höflichen Einleitung gleichsam als captatio benevolentiae ein: „Erstlich, so tragend wir gar keinen zweyfel, daß E. G. uß dem heiligen Gsatz und Wort Gottes, gar wol bekanndt seye, daß ein iede Christliche Oberkeit, vor Gott, auch guotter gewissne halben, verbunden und schul-

---

33. Ibid., 126v–127r.
34. *Guggenbühl*, Mit Tieren (wie Anm. 10), 233.
35. CCC: Constitutio criminalis Carolina: peinliche Gerichtsordnung Kaiser Karls V., Osnabrück 1973, § 45.
36. *Guggenbühl*, Mit Tieren (wie Anm. 10), 233 mit Anm. 341.

dig seye, die erschrockenliche Sünd der Zauberey, des veruntrewens an menschen und viehe, sampt allem, was diesem erschrockenlichenn laster verwandt sein mag, nach rechtmässiger gepüer (Damit wie Gott selber spricht: Das übel wider seinem Volckh ausgerüttet werde) zestraffen, Wie dann die Wort des Gesatzes Gottes außtruckenlichen befelch gebend. Du solt die Zauberinnen nit leben lassen."[37]

Dieser Bibelvers nach Ex 22,18(17) war das am häufigsten zitierte Schriftwort, um die Todesstrafe bei Hexereidelikten zu legitimieren. Meist wurde „m^{e^-}kaššefā lō'; t^echajjäh" mit seinem grammatisch offenen Subjekt, lateinisch als „Maleficos", so die Vulgata, oder auch als „Maleficam non patieris vivere" wiedergegeben. Die Zürcher Bibel von 1531 und Martin Luthers Text von 1545 haben: „Die zeuberinen soltu nicht läben [Luther: leben] lassen". Luther, Calvin, Bullinger und Johannes Brenz, aber auch Jean Bodin und viele andere haben mit dem Wort die Todesstrafe für Zauberei gefordert und oft wird betont, sie entspreche auch dem weltlichen Recht.[38]

Wie gingen die Basler mit dem Text um? Wie Weyer in *De praestigiis,* so zitierten Basler Theologen 1602 den Text, ohne eine Todesstrafe zu fordern. Die Theologische Fakultät und die Pfarrerschaft kritisierten dagegen, dass der Rat auf die Hexereiverdächtigungen überhaupt eingegangen war und ein peinliches Verfahren eingeleitet hatte. Sie gestanden mit dem Hinweis auf Ex 22 dem Rat nur grundsätzlich zu, gegen Zaubereidelikte und Aberglauben vorzugehen.[39]

Die Gutachter sprechen des Weiteren der Obrigkeit ihr Vertrauen aus, fordern aber keineswegs, die Ratsherren sollten Zauberei als crimen exeptum behandeln und nach den Richtlinien des *Layenspiegels* vorgehen, sie sollten vielmehr „in erforschung sollicher bösen Sachen, aller Abergleubischer und dem

---

37. StA Basel, Gutachten der Theologischen Fakultät und der städtischen Pfarrer von 1602 betr. M. Vögtlin, Criminalia 4,6 (6). Teiltranskription bei *Guggenbühl*, Mit Tieren (wie Anm. 10), 234–236, hier 234.

38. WA: D. Martin Luthers Werke. Kritische Gesamtausgabe, 73 Bde., Weimar 1883–2009, Bd. 16, 551b; CO: Joannis Calvini opera quae supersunt omnia, hg. von *Wilhelm Baum, Eduard Cunitz, Eduard Reuss*, 59 Bde. (= Corpus Reformatorum 29–87], Braunschweig, Berlin 1863–1900, Bd. 24 (= CR 52), 365 f. Calvin geht dort nicht auf das weltliche Recht ein; *Johannes Brenz*, In Exodvm Mosi commentarij, Halle 1544, 100v; *Heinrich Bullinger*, Gegen die schwarzen Künste. Transkription der Handschrift ZB Zürich, Ms. F 63, 356r-363v, bearb. von *Rainer Henrich*, in: *Hans Ulrich Bächtold, Ruth Jörg* et al. (Hg.), *Heinrich Bullinger*, Schriften zum Tage, Zug 2006, 304; *Jean Bodin*, De Magorum Daemonomania libri IV, Hildesheim 2003 (ND der Basler Ausgabe von 1581), 383, vgl. auch in der Praaefatio * jiiiv.

39. StA Basel, Criminalia 4,6 (6).

heiligen Wort Gottes widerwärtiger mittlen, aller dings sich entschlagen".[40] Zu den gemeinten abergläubischen Mitteln bzw. Rechtspraktiken, deren sich die Obrigkeit enthalten sollte, nennen sie den Brauch, Verdächtigte auf freiem Erdreich zu fangen und in einem Wagen ins Gefängnis zu fahren, um einen vermeintlichen Schweigezauber zu brechen, und das Rasieren vor der Folter, wie sie im *Malleus Maleficarum* und im *Layenspiegel* vorgeschlagen wurden oder auch 1580 vom bekannten Juristen und Staatstheoretiker Jean Bodin.[41] In den Augen der Geistlichen waren das Praktiken, die „im Bapstumb mit großem Aberglauben und unloblicher leichtfertigkeit, so Christenlicher dapfferkeit zewider, geüebet" werden.[42] Die vom Rat angestellten Theologen werfen also ziemlich unverhohlen den Ratsherren und nicht der Verdächtigten Aberglauben vor oder befürchten ihn zumindest bei den Ratsherren.

Die Geistlichen bezweifeln obendrein den Wahrheitsgehalt der belastenden Zeugenaussagen, denn sie widersprächen sich. Einige brächten zwar Sachen vor, „die des tods wärdt seindt"[43] – Zeugen beschuldigten Margreth Vögtlin, Unfälle, Krankheiten und auch den Tod eines Kindes vorsätzlich verursacht zu haben, also Verbrechen, die damals in jedem Fall (ob mit oder ohne teuflische Zauberei bewirkt) mit dem Tode bestraft wurden. Aber andere entlasteten die angebliche Hexe: „etliche sagend sye aller dingen ledig".[44] Zudem redeten die Belastungszeugen „mehrtheils in iren eignen Sachen: in welchen doch niemandt gebüeret, nach der Sag, des allgemeinen Rechtens, weder Richter noch Zeug zesein". Die Theologen gehen in ihrer Kritik noch weiter. Sie halten fest: Wären die Belastungszeugen „mit solcher scherpffe befragt", also gefoltert worden, wie „die gefangne ist befragt worden, so soltend, die inen selber Zeugnus geben, villeicht anders reden".[45] Damit stellten die Geistlichen Basels implizit das angewandte Rechtsverfahren mit Folteranwendung infrage. Insbesondere bei Hexereiverfahren spielte die Folter die alles entscheidende Rolle und entsprechend war der entscheidende Einspruch gegen die Hexenprozesse ein Kampf gegen die Folter, während Versuche, das magische Weltbild und den weit herum geteilten Hexenglauben infrage zu stellen, erfolglos blieben.

In diesem Fall hatte die Verdächtigte Margreth Vögtlin allerdings trotz wiederholter peinlicher Befragung nicht gestanden,[46] was nach Tenglers *Layen-*

---

40. Ibid., bei *Guggenbühl*, Mit Tieren (wie Anm. 10), 235.
41. *Bodin*, De Daemonomania (wie Anm. 38), 316.
42. StA Basel, Criminalia 4,6 (6), bei *Guggenbühl*, Mit Tieren (wie Anm. 10), 235.
43. StA Basel, Criminalia 4,6 (6).
44. Ibid.
45. Ibid.
46. Ibid., bei *Guggenbühl*, Mit Tieren (wie Anm. 10), 236.

spiegel, im Gegensatz zur *Halsgerichtsordnung* Kaiser Karls V., keineswegs ihre Unschuld bewies. Tengler warnte, wie gesagt: Wenn sie mit Schweigen oder Leugnen reagiere, „so mag der richter vermuotten, sy sey verzaubert", mit anderen Worten, der Teufel schütze sie vor den Schmerzen, ein Indiz gerade für ihre vermeintliche Schuld. Dagegen erklärten die Geistlichen: „Anderntheils, betreffendt die gefangene und ir antwort, auff die strenge und ernstliche Fragen, daß sy so gar nüth andtwortet, mag villicht irer unschuldt anzeigung und gemerck sein."[47]

Die Theologen sind von der Unschuld, dieser, wie sie beteuern, frommen Frau überzeugt und bitten um die Erlaubnis, ihr seelsorgerlichen Trost spenden zu dürfen, was auch der Wahrheitsfindung förderlich sein könnte.[48]

DAS JURISTISCHE GUTACHTEN VON 1602

Auch den gleichzeitig angefragten juristischen Gutachtern genügten die Zeugenaussagen nicht, um Margreth Vögtlin zu verurteilen, und auch sie bezogen sich auf Ex 22,18. Sie betonten wie Luther, Brenz und Bullinger, Ex 22,18 stimme mit dem weltlichen Recht überein: „Als ist erstlich, ihn gemeine, gnugsamen bewusst, gleich wie Gott der Herr dem Jsraelitischen Volck bevolhen, die Zauberinnen nicht leben zulassen, das also auch die Gemeinen Geschribnen Recht ausweissen."[49] Bevor die Juristen zu einer Rechtsbelehrung aus der *Carolina* kommen, definieren sie die Zauberei, wobei sie auf einen Teufelsbund Bezug nehmen. Sie zählen, wie der *Layenspiegel,*[50] dreierlei Sorten von Zauberern auf: „Dan ettliche (leider) von Gott gar abfallen, sich auß desselbigen bundt, darein sie, bei, und durch den Heiligen Tauff aufgenommen worden, thunt, ihren Christenlichen glauben, darauf sie getaufft, fürsetzlicher weiße verlaugnen, und mitt dem Sathan, [...] wüssentliche bündtnuß aufrichten, mitt demselben umbgehen, und zuschaffen haben, hiemit zauberei üben, und treiben, auch gemeinlich nitt allein viehe, sonder auch menschen, mit, oder ohne gifft beschedigen."[51] Andere würden keinen Teufelsbund abschließen, aber dennoch Schadenzauber betreiben und wieder andere würden mit teuflischen Künsten wahrsagen, aber niemand schädigen und auch keinen Teu-

---

47. *Tengler*, Layenspiegel, 1527 (wie Anm. 23), 126v. Vgl. CCC, § 109.
48. StA Basel, Criminalia 4,6 (6).
49. StA Basel, Gutachten der juristischen Fakultät von 1602 betr. M. Vögtlin, Criminalia 4,6 (7). Teiltranskription bei *Guggenbühl*, Mit Tieren (wie Anm. 10), 236–238, hier 237.
50. *Tengler*, Layenspiegel, 1527 (wie Anm. 23), 124v–125r.
51. StA Basel, Criminalia 4,6 (7), bei *Guggenbühl*, Mit Tieren (wie Anm. 10), 237 f.

felsbund abschließen, aber „auß fürwitz, mitt dem Sathan gesprech zu halten sich understehen".[52] Nur die beiden ersten Arten von Zauberern sollen nach Römischem und Reichsrecht hingerichtet werden.[53] Die *Carolina* stellte in der Tat nur Schadenzauber unter Todesstrafe durch Verbrennen, einen Teufelsbund aber nannte das Reichsrecht, anders als der *Layenspiegel*, nicht.[54]

Die Verbindung von Zauberei mit einem Teufelsbund beruht auf antiken und volkstümlichen Zauberei- und Magievorstellungen in Kombination mit spätantiker und mittelalterlicher christlicher Theologie. Augustinus hat wohl als erster Zauberei auf einen Vertrag mit Dämonen zurückgeführt. Teuflische Kräfte erlaubten den Magiern, so erklärte er, sich, sofern Gott das zulasse, übermenschlicher Kräfte zu bedienen.[55] Die Scholastik hat Augustins Lehre weiter ausgebaut. Nach Thomas von Aquin beruht Zauberei und Wahrsagerei auf einem Teufelspakt.[56] Im 15. Jahrhundert war die Vorstellung voll ausgereift: Danach ging für viele Theologen und Juristen jede Form von Magie, also auch heilende Magie, auf teuflische Kräfte zurück. Alle, die mit Zauberei umgingen, galten als Ketzer und Apostaten. Ihnen wurde unterstellt, sie verschrieben sich dem Teufel, der den Bund durch einen Beischlaf mit einem je nachdem weiblichen oder männlichen Dämon besiegle. Entsprechend wurden die Verdächtigen, so in zahlreichen Prozessakten in Europa und eben auch Margreth Vögtlin 1602 in Basel, nach einem Teufelspakt und Teufelskoitus ausgefragt, den die meisten hart Gefolterten schließlich auch bekannten – was den Glauben daran weiter befestigte.

Die Vorstellung der „christlichen Hexe" (Harmening)[57], die einen Bund mit dem leiblich erscheinenden und sie beschlafenden Teufel eingeht, war so allgemein verbreitet, dass auch die Professoren der juristischen Fakultät sie vertraten, obwohl das Römische Recht, auf das sie sich beriefen, diese Vorstellung nicht kannte und auch die *Carolina* jeden Bezug auf den Teufel bei Zauberei vermied. Wie die Juristen, die die *Carolina* Anfang des 16. Jahrhunderts entworfen hatten, haben offenbar auch die Basler Theologen um 1600 diese Vorstellung nicht geteilt. Denn in ihrem Gutachten kommt kein Teufelsbund vor. Der Teufel wird überhaupt nicht genannt.

---

52. Ibid.
53. StA Basel, Criminalia 4,6 (7), bei *Guggenbühl*, Mit Tieren (wie Anm. 10), 237–238.
54. CCC, § 109.
55. *Augustinus*, De doctrina christiana, II, 20 und 23 f.
56. *Thomas von Aquin*, Summa theol II. II. 92–96 (Busa, Bd. 2, 646–652); vgl. *Dieter Harmening*, Zauberei (wie Anm. 1), 27–31.
57. Ibid., 21.

JOHANN JAKOB GRYNÄUS' EINSTELLUNG ZUM HEXENDELIKT IM VERGLEICH

Ist das eine Überinterpretation der theologischen Expertise? Kaum. Der Antistes Grynäus jedenfalls hat auch in allen von mir konsultierten Schriften nie von einem Teufelsbund gesprochen, ja, wo immer möglich, vermieden, von Zauberei überhaupt zu reden. 1577 gab er seine *Epitomes Sacrorum Biblion* heraus. Sie sollten jungen Theologen einen Abriss der Heiligen Schrift bieten, ihnen dunkle Stellen des Alten Testamentes durch das Neue erklären und ihnen das Verständnis des Gotteswortes als Ganzes eröffnen.[58]

Danach waren die Bestimmungen in Exodus 22 mit dem Vers 18 „Du sollst die Zauberin nicht leben lassen" nur „praecepta", also nicht von derselben Bedeutung wie die Zehn Gebote. Während Calvin Ex 22,18 ohne irgendeinen Vorbehalt zum 1. Gebot zog,[59] geht Grynäus gar nicht darauf ein.

Grynäus fasst die dreißig Verse des Kapitels 22 so zusammen: „Du sollst nicht stehlen. Gott will nämlich, dass wir weder dem Nächsten durch böse List noch durch offene Gewalt, noch durch unsere Nachlässigkeit Schaden zufügen. Du sollst nicht ehebrechen. Du sollst nicht töten. Ich beziehe mich auf die Vorschrift, die über die Menschlichkeit, die gegen Waisen, Witwen und Fremdlingen geübt werden soll, geboten wird. Ehre die Eltern. Gott befiehlt nämlich, dass niemand den Magistrat schmähen soll."[60] Hexerei war ihm offenbar kein Wort wert.

Es lohnt sich auch noch seine Bemerkungen zu Ex 7 und 8 anzusehen. Dort befiehlt Gott Mose, den Pharao zu bitten, das Volk Israel fortziehen zu lassen und durch Aaron Wunder, bzw. Plagen zu wirken, um der göttlichen Forderung Nachdruck zu verleihen. Drei der Wunder, die Aaron auf Geheiß Gottes wirkt, können die Magier am Pharaonenhof nachahmen. Auch sie verwandeln das Nilwasser in Blut und ihre Stäbe in Schlangen und lassen Frösche aus dem Nil steigen.

Grynäus erklärt zum Schlangenwunder in Kapitel 7: „Wie Jannes und Jambres [nach 2. Tim 3,8 die Namen der ägyptischen Magier am Pharaonenhof] Mose widerstanden, so widerstehen gewisse Menschen, die den Glauben verwerfen, der Wahrheit durch einen verdorbenen Verstand [...]. Alle Elemente dienen Gott zur Strafe der Gottlosen."[61] Grynäus interessieren also die Verse

---

58. *Johann Jakob Grynäus*, Epitomes sacrorum Biblion pars prima complectens Veteris Testamenti tum librorum, tum capitum argumenta [...], Basel 1577, ß2r.
59. CO, Bd. 24 (= CR 52), 364, vgl. auch 265–268 zu Dt 18.
60. *Grynäus*, Epitomes (wie Anm. 58), 189f.
61. Ibid., 179f.

nicht als Hinweis auf Zauberei, sondern nur als Hinweis auf den Unglauben der Menschen, den der Timotheusbrief herstellte.

Zu 2. Mos 8 nennt Grynäus nur kurz die Frösche: „Primo Ranas, Ciniphes, et noxia insecta, affligendis Aegyptijs, Dominus immisit." Gott sandte also Frösche und Insekten, die wie er versichert, nur Ägypter stachen, wodurch Gott seine Gerechtigkeit und Vergeltung gegenüber den Ungläubigen und sein Erbarmen über die Gläubigen bewies. Er fährt fort: „Die Magier und Astrologen waren unfähig, die kleinen Tiere zu produzieren (Magi & Genethliaci deficientes in minimi animalculi productione)." Er betonte, nur „permittente Domino" konnten die Zauberer etwas ausrichten. Kein ernst zu nehmender Theologe hätte das bestritten, aber die meisten Zeitgenossen schoben mit Luther zwischen die Magier und Gottes Allmacht Teufelsmächte ein, deren sich die Zauberer bedienten. Grynäus aber verzichtete darauf.[62] Anders sein Basler Kollege Amandus Polanus, er erklärt zu Ex 7: Dämonen hätten die Stöcke der Magier schnell weggeräumt und Schlangen herbeigeschafft, also kein wirkliches Wunder supra naturam bewirkt.[63] Polanus blieb im Rahmen der gängigen Dämonologie. Er gestand Dämonen eine Wirkung, aber kein echtes Wunder zu. Seine Auslegung zeigt, welchen Schwierigkeiten Theologen sich damals gegenüber sahen, die wohl die Wirkmacht von Zauberern anzweifelten, aber die allgemein akzeptierte magische Weltsicht, in der Teufel und Dämonen Teil der Natur waren, nicht infrage stellen konnten oder wollten.[64]

Für Heinrich Bullinger in Zürich waren hingegen die vollbrachten Wunder der ägyptischen Magier 1571 Beweis, dass Zauberei wirksam sei. „Hie wird aber gefraget, ob die zauberer, schwarzkünstler und häxen öttwz der dingen vermögind, die geachtet werdent, als ob sy von innen beschähind? Dan vil wöllend achten, es sye ein whon, ytele ynbildung und fantasy, und vermögind nüt, weder mit dem wätter noch wider lüth noch vych. Dargegen aber die erfarung, darzuo die h. gschrift zügend, das sy ein würkung der dingen habind, die sy thuond, und menklich sicht und befindt, dz es nütt im whon ist, sonder warlich bschicht, wz sy thuond. Als Exod. [Ex 7,11.22; 8,7.18 f.; 9,11] die zauberer pharaonis vil der zeichen wurktend mit der that, die vorhin Mose

---

62. Ibid., 180; WA, Bd. 16, 552b.
63. *Polanus*, De miraculis (wie Anm. 9), § 56.
64. Vgl. *Stuart Clark*, Thinking with Demons: The Idea of Witchcraft in Early Modern Europe, Oxford 1997, 156, 161–166; *Wolfgang Behringer*, Meinungsbildende Befürworter und Gegner der Hexenverfolgung (15. bis 18. Jahrhundert), in: *Helfried Valentinitsch* (Hg.), Hexen und Zauberer, Graz 1987, 219–236, bes. 233.

und Aaron durch gottes krafft thon hattend, doch allwägen von den göttlichen zeichen zuo schanden gmacht wurdent."[65]

Dass Grynäus in seinen kurzen Hinweisen zum Exodus kein Wort zur zeitgenössischen Zauberei verlor, war kaum ein Zufall. 1614 gab er seine bereits 1588 vorgestellten Thesen *De Apostasia, quae est peccatum ad mortem* neu heraus. Darin kommen zwar mit Hinweis auf 1 Kor 10,20 und Apk 13,8.17 „Daemoniorum consortes" und Anbeter der „Bestie" vor, aber auch dort, wie im ganzen Werk, geht Grynäus nicht auf Zauberei ein, obwohl Hexen und Zauberer in erster Linie als Apostaten und Teufelsanbeter verurteilt wurden. Die Apostaten und consortes Daemoniorum sind nach Grynäus „Pseudochristen", die den Antichrist anbeten. Sie drehen ihre Lehren nach dem Wind, vergehen sich gegen ihr Gewissen, lassen sich von der Wahrheit abbringen und werden abergläubisch. Sie sind falsche Lehrer, Epikureer, betreiben Idolatrie, und leben ein fleischliches Leben. Sie lieben Geld, vermischen die kanonischen mit apokryphen und nachgeordneten Schriften, die sie als gleichwertig behandeln, sie hängen einem falschen Abendmahlsritus an, sind Heuchler und Sektierer:[66] Kurz – die Apostaten sind Sektierer und vor allem Anhänger der „Papstkirche", für welche vom benachbarten bischöflichen und vorderösterreichischen Gebiet aus Jesuiten und Kapuziner bedrohlich warben. Gegen sie kämpfte Grynäus verbissen, Hexerei aber war für ihn offenbar kein nennenswertes Problem. Er spricht sie in seiner Schrift über die Apostasie gar nicht an.

Entsprechendes gilt für seine Schrift *Character Christianorvm. Seu de fidei, spei et charitatis doctrina* von 1578. Darin kommt Grynäus auf Simon den Magier nach Apg 8. Von irgendwelcher Zauberei des Magiers ist keine Rede; er ist ein „homo auarus et malitiosus", der die Taufe um weltlicher Güter willen begehrte.[67] Die Schrift enthält auch Thesen zum Apostolikum, Nicänum und den Zehn Geboten.

---

65. *Bullinger*, Gegen die schwarzen Künste (wie Anm. 38), 301. Für Luther vgl. *Haustein*, Martin Luthers Stellung (wie Anm. 1), 74–76.

66. *Johann Jakob Grynäus*, De Apostasia, quae est peccatum ad mortem, Basel 1614, 10–21. Vgl. auch Grynäus' *Didaskalia de Apostasia,* Basel 1588.

67. *Johann Jakob Grynäus*, Character Christianorvm. Seu de fidei, spei et charitatis doctrina [...], Basel 1578, 26.

DIE AUSLEGUNG DES DEKALOGS

Insbesondere die erste Dekalogtafel war der Ort, an dem die spätmittelalterliche katechetische Literatur Zauberei behandelte.[68] Das gilt auch für die Frühe Neuzeit. Ich erinnere hier nur an den Großen und den Kleinen Katechismus von Luther. Da heißt es: „Daher [zu den Gesetzesübertretern] gehoeren auch, die es gar zu grob treiben und mit dem Teuffel ein bund machen, das er yhn gelt gnug gebe odder zur bulschafft helffe, yhr viech beware, verloren gut widderschaffe etc., Als die zeuberer und schwartzkuenstige. Denn diese alle setzen yhr hertz und vertrawen anders wo denn auff den warhafftigen Gott, versehen sich kein guts zu yhm, suchens auch nicht bey yhm."[69] Oder: „So verstehestu nu, was Gottes namen misbrauchen heisse, nemlich (auffs kuertzt zuwidderholen) entweder blos zu luegen und etwas unter dem namenausgeben das nicht ist, odder zufluchen, schweren, zeubern und Summa, wie man mag, bosheit auszurichten", so im Großen Katechismus[70] und im Kleinen: „Wir sollen Gott fuerchten und lieben, das wir bey seinem namen nicht Fluchen, Schweren, Zaubern, Liegen odder Triegen, sondern den selbigen ynn allen noeten Anruffen, Beten, Loben unnd dancken."[71]

In Grynäus' aufgestellten Thesen von 1587, findet sich bei der Diskussion der ersten Tafel kein Wort zur Zauberei, dagegen richtet sich die Erklärung zum ersten Gebot gegen Marien- und Heiligenkult, zum zweiten gegen Idolatrie und zum dritten gegen Exorzismen und eine Fülle von Weiheriten und Frömmigkeitsformen der katholischen Kirche, die als magisch verdammt werden. Da heißt es: „E diametro autem aduersantur tertio praecepto, Exorcismi, quibus profanatur Baptismus. Consecratio Magica panis, lardi, olei, ouorum et c. Baptismus Campanarum. Coemeteriorum consecrationes. Ridiculi exorcismi, quibus stolidi quidam Exorcistae, illudente eis Satana, ad energumenos curandos, ad spectra fuganda, utuntur. Rosaria, horae Canonica, *patrologias* in precibus. Inuocatio Sanctorum, qui e uiuis excesserunt. Iusjurandum in nomine creaturarum praestitum etc."[72]

Das entsprach einer weit verbreiteten reformatorischen Sicht. Auch Luther, Zwingli, Brenz und Calvin setzten katholische Riten mit Magie gleich[73] und

---

68. *Harmening*, Zauberei (wie Anm. 1), 50–59.
69. WA, Bd. 30.1, 134.
70. Ibid., 141.
71. Ibid., 282a.
72. *Grynäus*, Character Christianorvm (wie Anm. 67), 108 f.
73. WA, Bd. 30.1, 134 und Bd. 50, 644 f.; Z: Huldrych Zwinglis sämtliche Werke im Corpus Reformatorum, 21 Bde., Berlin, Leipzig et. al. 1905–2015, Bd. 3, 740, 791. *Brenz*,

das entsprach auch guter Basler Tradition. Oekolampad hatte in seinen *Conciones aliquot populares*, im Sermo septimus gepredigt: „So täuscht auch der Satan die Menschen mit geweihtem Wasser, Kräutern, Wachs und dem Kreuzeszeichen. Was, obwohl wir wissen sollten, dass diese Dinge zu verachten sind, geduldet wird, so dass die Magier und Segner (incantatores) sie benutzen. Was sonst begehrt der Dämon, als dass die Hoffnung auf Kreatürliches gesetzt wird, oder auf unsere Bitten. So sorgt er dafür, das für die in den Krieg Ziehenden Messen gelesen werden." Der Teufel verführe zum teuren Messelesen, um den rechten Gebrauch des Glaubens und der Liebe zu zerstören.[74]

Oekolampad dürfte mit seinen Hinweisen auf die „incantatores" neben katholischen Priestern auch noch volkstümliche Segner und Heilerinnen im Blick gehabt haben, die christliche Versatzstücke als Zaubersprüche benutzten, um Krankheiten zu besprechen, etwa das Vaterunser, das Ave-Maria oder die trinitarische Formel. 1530 schrieb er zuhanden der Bannherren: „Zum andern seind zuo warnen und zuo bannen die warsager, versegner, schwartzkünstler, zauberer, die ein heimlichen oder offentlichen pundt mit dem teufel haben, deszgleichen die davon räht suochen."[75] Oekolampad hat also im Zusammenhang mit dem Bann – wie üblich – Zauberei und Teufelsbund noch genannt. Anders Grynäus. Grynäus ging auch in seiner Epitome zu den Zehn Geboten nach Ex 20 nicht auf Zauberei ein. Dort interessieren ihn die einzelnen Gebote gar nicht. Er behandelt nur die Grundsatzfrage: Was das Gesetz sei, die er mit Galater 3 beantwortet. Das Gesetz sei nicht aufgehoben. Gott habe schon zuvor dem Abraham den Erben [Jesus Christus] versprochen.[76]

Dass Grynäus in seinen Auslegungen zum Exodus nicht auf Zauberei eingeht, mag noch nicht viel heißen, behandelt er doch die Kapitel nur kursorisch. Aber auch in den Basler Katechismen wird Zauberei nicht erwähnt.

In Exodvm (wie Anm. 38), benutzt Kapitel 7, um die katholische Kirche mit ihren Wundern als häretisch zu verunglimpfen, so 39v–40v, und zu Kap. 8: 43vf; zurückhaltender Calvin, CO, Bd. 24 [= CR 52], 105 f. und Bd. 1 [= CR 29], 35.

74. *Johannes Oekolampad*, Conciones aliquot populares (Anhang zu Enarratio in Evangelivm Matthaei, Basel 1536], Sermo septimus,170r–172r.

75. Die handschriftliche Anweisung ist abgedruckt in: *Ernst Staehelin* (Hg.), Briefe und Akten zum Leben Oekolampads, 2 Bde., Basel 1927 und 1934, Bd. 2, 544.

76. *Grynäus*, Epitomes pars prima (wie Anm. 58), 188.

REFORMATIONSORDNUNGEN

Ebenso wenig wie in den *Frag- und Antwortstücken* Oekolampads bezieht sich das Glaubensbekenntnis von 1534, das Grynäus 1590 neu herausgab, auf Zauberei. Sowohl der Artikel zu den Geboten, als auch der Artikel zum Bann schweigt sich darüber aus: Dort setzt sich die Basler Kirche ab gegenüber der überkommenen Kirche und – wie schon in der Reformationsordnung von 1529 – gegenüber den Wiedertäufern: Was Christus nicht geboten habe, dürfe niemand gebieten, und niemand verbieten, was er nicht verboten habe. So seien „ongeboten" Feiertag, Ohrenbeichte, Fasten und die Priesterehe sei erlaubt. Aber noch weniger dürfe jemand erlauben, was Gott verboten habe, so Heiligenkult, Bilder und dergleichen. Das verwerfe die Basler Kirche. Die Lehren der „Widerteuffer" seien „grewel und lesterung".[77] Volkstümliche Zauberei oder gelehrte Magie kommen im Glaubensbekenntnis nicht vor.

In der Basler Reformationsordnung von 1529 ist jedoch Zauberei noch unter dem Bann genannt: „Es mögend in diesem Nachtmal nit gemeinschafft haben/ die offentliche abgötterer / zouberer / Gots lästerer / durchachter des wort Gottes / und der heyligen Sacrament des Touffs und des Herren nachtmals"[78], aber eigene Zaubereiparagraphen oder Zaubereimandate verabschiedete Basel lange Zeit nicht.

Anders Zürich. Zwar hatte sich Zwingli zur Zauberei ausgeschwiegen, aber der Zürcher Rat erließ bereits 1533 ein Mandat gegen Aberglauben, Wahrsagerei und Zauberei, das er 1550 wiederholte, 1580 neu fasste und 1616, 1619 und 1627 erneut einschärfte.[79] Der Basler Rat veröffentlichte erstmals 1595 ein einschlägiges Mandat, das aber nur von Wahrsagern spricht und zwar von nicht Einheimischen, es mahnt: „Demnach sollen jr auch gewarnet sein/ ewern Weibern / Töchtern unnd gesinde/ dz sie deß wahrsagens von Heiden [sic]/ so sich etwan zun zeiten / under / oder vor der Statt thoren finden lassen/ müssigend und enthaltend."[80] Die Basler Verantwortlichen nahmen offenbar in der Stadt keine Hellseher wahr, die verbotene Praxis werde nur von Fahrenden vor den Toren betrieben.

---

77. Bekanntnus vnsers Heyligen Christenlichen glaubens/ wie es die Kilch zuo Basel haltet, [Basel 1534], Aiiijv, Bijr und v; Das Geistliche vnd herrliche Kleinot der Kirchen Gottes in Statt und Landschafft Basel, [Basel 1590], 13, 16, 17.
78. *Emidio Campi, Philipp Wälchli* (Hg.), Basler Kirchenordnungen 1528–1675, Zürich 2012, 25.
79. *Emidio Campi, Philipp Wälchli* (Hg.), Zürcher Kirchenordnungen 1520–1675, Zürich, 2 Bde., Zürich 2011, Bd. 1, 158, 259, 263, 520, 533 f.
80. Basler Kirchenordnungen (wie Anm. 78), 125.

Das ändert sich erst mit der großen neuen *Reformation* von 1637. Auf dem Höhepunkt des Dreißigjährigen Krieges glaubte der Rat in einem längeren Passus, ernstlich vorgehen zu müssen gegen „teuffelische Zauberey / Wahrsageery / Beschweerung / Versegnung" und namentlich der eben erst aufgekommenen „Passawischen Kunst", die versprach mit Zauberzetteln Schüsse abzuwehren.[81] Sie spielte in Basler Prozessen damals eine Rolle, auch schon in dem Prozess mit Todesurteil von 1624.[82] Das Mandat von 1637 richtet sich also gegen magische Praktiken, die auch Weyer grundsätzlich als teuflisch ablehnte und bestraft wissen wollte, allerdings nicht mit der Todesstrafe. Das Mandat, ebenso seine Wiederholung von 1660, drohte zwar mit der Todesstrafe bei Zaubereidelikten, ließ den Richtern aber einen Spielraum „je nach gestalt und befindung jhres übertretens/ ohne Gnad" abzustrafen.[83] Die Richter machten davon Gebrauch. Nur die genannte des dreizehnfachen Giftmordes Angeklagte wurde nach 1637 in Zusammenhang mit Zauberei zum Tode verurteilt. Von 1665 an ließ der Rat die Zaubereiartikel wieder fallen.[84]

OEKOLAMPADS SICHT AUF ZAUBEREI UND SEINE TEUFELSLEHRE

Wohl hat Oekolampad im Rahmen der Kirchenzucht traditionell noch von Zauberei und einem zu bekämpfenden Teufelspakt gesprochen, aber er hat in seinen Kommentaren doch schon einen neuen Weg beschritten. Exodusauslegungen sind von ihm nicht überliefert, aber aus Kommentaren zu Jeremia und Jesaja und aus seinen Exegesen zu Hiob und zur Versuchungsgeschichte lässt sich seine Sicht auf Zauberei und sein Teufelsbild ablesen.

Zu Jes 8, 19–20 „Befragt die Totengeister und die Wahrsager, die wispernden und murmelnden (mussitantes et disertantes)" erklärt Oekolampad: „Einst (olim) habe er [der Teufel] die Menschen auf verschiedene Weise verführt, durch Götzenbilder, Vogelschau und Vorzeichen. […] So ersinnt er [der Teufel] auch heute durch wunderbare Künste dasselbe. Nichts ist ihm so unerträglich wie die evangelische Wahrheit und das Hören des Gotteswortes. Daher bemüht er sich eifrig, uns zu den menschlichen Traditionen zu be-

---

81. Ibid., 319.
82. *Schnyder*, Zauberei (wie Anm. 12), 74f., 111
83. Basler Kirchenordnungen (wie Anm. 78), 319f., vgl. entsprechend nochmals 1660, ibid., 413.
84. Ibid., Nr. 108, 441–446.

kehren."⁸⁵ Die Pythonici würden Dämonen herauf beschwören und die Wahrsager betrieben Künste wie Handlesen, Astrologie oder Eingeweideschau. „Unter den Murmelnden könntest du richtig die Dekretalisten und Kanonisten verstehen [...] unter den Beredten (disertos) aber die modernen Scholastiker [...]."⁸⁶ Der Exeget Oekolampad scheute sich nicht, zu aktualisieren, aber er bezog den Text nicht auf vermeintliche zeitgenössische Hexerei oder Teufelsbünde.

Dass Zauberei für ihn nur eine vermeintliche war, deutet er mehr als nur an in seiner Auslegung zu Jer 27,9 „Und ihr, hört doch nicht auf eure Propheten und eure Zeichendeuter und auf eure Zauberer [...]". Da charakterisiert Oekolampad die Zauberer so: „fascinant praestigiis aciem oculorum, ut existimetur aliud uideri, quam revera coram fit." Sie betörten also die Augenschärfe durch Gaukeleien, sodass vermeintlich anderes gesehen wurde, als was in Wahrheit vor ihren Augen geschah. Mit anderen Worten, ihre Zauberei war nicht real, sondern ein Wahn der betörten Menschen.⁸⁷

Was hielt Oekolampad von der vermeintlichen Inkarnation des Teufels, von der Vorstellung eines leibhaftig erscheinenden Teufels oder eines teuflischen Dämonen? Wie verstand er die Bibelstellen, in denen der Teufel auftrat? Zur Rahmenerzählung des Hiobbuches, wo die Gottessöhne und unter ihnen der Satan sich im Himmel über den frommen Hiob besprechen (Hiob 1,6), erklärte Oekolampad: Der Satan „kam, aber nicht augenblicklich, nicht indem er sich näherte oder eintrat, sondern er kam gedanklich (cogitatione), mit dem Plan und übelsten Wunsch, den Gerechten vor Gott zu verklagen. [...] Auch später kam er nicht selbst, sondern durch nichtswürdigste Gedanken. [...] Jener Nichtsnutzigste erschien nicht vor dem Angesicht des guten Gottes, sondern seine grausamen und üblen Absichten kamen vor Gottes Augen. Und so kommt der Teufel auch heute mit jenen [üblen Absichten], um anzuklagen, herabzuziehen, zu hemmen, zu quälen, zu verfolgen und den Frommen Lasten aufzuerlegen."⁸⁸ Die Teufelserscheinung, jedenfalls im Himmel, ist also rein

---

85. *Johannes Oekolampad*, In Iesaiam prophetam Hypomnematon, hoc est, Commentariorum, Libri 6, Basel 1525, 77v.

86. Ibid, 77vf., vgl. auch die Kommentierung von Jesaja 47,8 f., wo von Babels Zaubereien und Beschwörungen die Rede ist, über die nach Oekolampad Gott spottet, und wo Oekolampad nicht auf zeitgenössische magische Praktiken oder Hexerei eingeht. Ibid., 242r.

87. *Johannes Oekolampad*, In Hieremiam prophetam commentariorvm Lib. Tres, Straßburg 1533, 141v.

88. *Johannes Oecolampad*, In librum Iob exegemata, Basel 1532, 8rf.

spirituell gedacht und Oekolampad aktualisiert die Pläne des Teufels, ohne auf Zauberei einzugehen.[89]

Zum Umherschweifen des Teufels auf der Erde nach Hiob 2,2 fasst sich Oekolampad kurz. Er erklärt die Erde zum Teufelsreich, um dann sofort zu falschen Propheten überzugehen, die wie der Teufel sich auch als Besiegte gern rühmen: „Insinuatur interim impudentia satanae qui etiam uictus gloriatur de uagatione et uenatione sua super terram, hoc est de imperio suo. In quo imitantur illum falsi prophetae, electa eius membra, [...]."[90]

Und wie versteht Oekolampad die Erscheinung des Teufels in der Versuchungsgeschichte? Oekolampad behandelt die Versuchung Jesu in der *Enarratio in Evangelivm Mattaei*, die Mykonius posthum herausgab, hinter der also auch Oekolampads Nachfolger grundsätzlich stand. Wie aber erscheint da der Teufel? Für Oekolampad war die Versuchung eine spirituelle. Da geht der Basler Reformator noch über Erasmus von Rotterdam hinaus, der sie zwar implizit auch als rein spirituelle – also als innerseelisches Geschehen – ausgelegt hatte.[91] Aber Oekolampad betonte explizit: Dass der Teufel Jesus wegtrug, sei unwahrscheinlich. Christus sei nur geistig nicht körperlich versucht worden, er habe wie die Propheten Visionen gehabt. „Verum quemadmodum prophetae uarias uisiones habuerunt, in quibus multa paßi sunt, ita et Christus spiritualiter tentatus est. [...] istae visiones uel res non sunt factae corporaliter."[92] Mit anderen Worten, der Teufel sei ihm nicht körperlich erschienen.

Oekolampads Teufelsbild als einer rein spirituellen Macht des Bösen entsprach kaum der gängigen Vorstellung eines leibhaftig erscheinenden Teufels und Beischläfers von Hexen. Sie war denn auch so ungewöhnlich, dass Oekolampad befürchten musste, falsch verstanden zu werden. Wenn der Teufel nicht leibhaftig erschien, dann, so könnte gefolgert werden, sei auch Christus nur als ein Geistwesen zu verstehen. Gegen eine solche Auslegung wehrte sich Oekolampad: Nein Christus dürfen wir nicht zu einem Luftgebilde machen, er wurde durch Hunger körperlich versucht. „Non propterea facimus Christum phantasticum. Certum etiam corporaliter tentatum per famem."[93]

---

89. Ibid., 11r.
90. Ibid., 14r.
91. LB: Desiderii Erasmi Roterodami opera omnia, hg. von *Johannes Clericus*, 11 Bde., Leiden 1703–1706, Bd. 7, 18–20; vgl. insbesondere die Auslegung zu Lk 4: Ibid., 318–323, bes. 319F und 322. *Erasmus von Rotterdam*, Opera omnia Desiderii Erasmi Roterodami, Bd. VII-2, Amsterdam 2017, 165–176.
92. *Johannes Oekolampad*, Enarratio in Evangelivm Matthaei [...] et alia nonnulla quae sequens pagella indicabit, Basel 1536, 44v–48v, bes. 47r f.
93. Ibid., 47v.

Calvin hat dazu zu sagen: Ob Jesus tatsächlich vom Teufel auf die Zinne des Tempels entführt worden sei oder eine Vision hatte, „c'est une question qui est plus curieuse qu'utile". Vieles deutet für Calvin zwar auf eine Vision, aber er ziehe vor, die Frage offen zu lassen. „Mais pource que cela ne vaut point d'esmouvoir grand noise et dispute, il vaut mieux le laisser là à part [...]."[94] Tatsächlich drohten theologische Streitigkeiten dazu, hatte Luther doch betont, dass der Teufel Gottes Sohn leibhaftig erschien, und ihm folgten andere wie Heinrich Bullinger und Rudolph Gwalther, die sich zudem die Gelegenheit nicht entgehen ließen, an dieser Stelle zeitgenössische Hexerei anzuprangern.[95]

GRYNÄUS' TEUFELSLEHRE IM VERGLEICH MIT BULLINGERS

Grynäus quält sich in seinen *S. Evangelistarvm Mattaei, Marci, Lvcae et Johannis demonstrationes* von 1587 nicht mit solchen Fragen. Für eine Teufelslehre zeigt er keinerlei Interesse. Mt 4 dient ihm als solide Tröstung, weil Christus nicht nur als Gott, sondern auch als Mensch die Versuchungen des Teufels überwunden habe und zugleich in seinen Gläubigen überwinden werde.[96]

Zu Lk 4 behandelt er auch Jesus als Dämonenaustreiber und erklärt zu Vers 28–37, die Dämonen sprächen je nachdem die Wahrheit. Die Lehre daraus sei: „Daemones non audiendos nobis esse, etiam quum vera dicunt."[97] Am Besten, so ist zu folgern, wird das ganze Thema gemieden und Grynäus benutzte denn auch die Gelegenheit nicht, um eine Dämonenlehre zu entfalten oder Teufelserscheinungen, Teufelspakte oder Hexerei zu thematisieren, genauso wenig wie bei naheliegenden Texten aus der Apostelgeschichte. Weder die Erzählung über Simon Magus (Apg 8,9–24) noch über Barjesus Apg 13,6–12 werden von ihm ausgeschlachtet.[98] Etwas mehr Worte verliert Grynäus zur Austreibung des Wahrsagegeistes in Philippi (Apg 16,16–18) und zur freiwilligen Abgabe der Zauberbücher und Amulette in Ephesus (Apg 19,18–20). Zu Apg 16 mahnt er,

---

94. CO, Bd. 46 [= CR 74], 619f.
95. WA, Bd. 17.2, 196; *Heinrich Bullinger*, In sancrosanctvm Iesu Christi Domini nostri Euangelium secundum Matthaeum, Commentariorum libri XII, Zürich 1542, 42v; *Heinrich Bullinger*, In Lvcvlentvm et sacrosanctum Euangelium domini nostri Iesu Christi secundum Lucam, Commentariorum lib. IX, Zürich 1546, 50r; *Rudolph Gwalther*, Von Versuochung und Anfächtungen: nün Predigen über die History unsers Herren Jesu Christi, Zürich 1577, 175r–176v.
96. *Johann Jakob Grynäus*, S. Evangelistarvm Matthaei, Marci, Lvcae et Iohannis Demonstrationes [...] et [...] quae in Actis Apostolorum descripta extat [...], Basel 1588, 14f.
97. Ibid., 171–173, bes. 171.
98. Ibid., 257–259 und 267–270.

auch wenn wir damit den Hass der Welt auf uns ziehen und viele Leiden zu tragen haben, seien die Zeugnisse Satans zurückzuweisen.[99] Zu Apg 19,18–20 fordert er auf: „Das aber wollen wir betreiben, dass wir, denen die Möglichkeit Wunder zu wirken mangelt, durch Reinheit des Lebens unsern heiligen Beruf schmücken. Dieser Trost soll uns bleiben, weil wir unterdessen den Satan und seine Komplizen durch Gottes Eingreifen bekämpft wissen (quod interdum Sathanam cum suis complicibus ita diuinitus comitti animaduertimus), sodass sie den traurigen Lohn von ihrem Meister ertragen müssen. Auch freuen wir uns, weil wir sehen, dass Christus durch das Bekenntnis der Sünder und die Abschaffung der Zauberbücher und Zauberkunststücke in der Kirche Gericht hält (per peccatorum confessionem et magicorum Scriptorum ac praestigiarum abolitionem, Christum in Ecclesia iudicium exercere videmus)."[100] Für Grynäus ist der Teufel mit seinen Komplizen bereits bekämpft und Christus selbst hält in der Kirche Gericht, indem er wie in Ephesus zur freiwilligen Abgabe der Zauberbücher antreibt.

Ganz anders interpretiert Bullinger, der nicht nur in seinem Kommentar zur Apostelgeschichte ausgiebig auf teuflische Magie einging,[101] sondern die beiden Episoden in Philippi und Ephesus 1571 auch als Fundament benutzte für sein schon genanntes Gutachten gegen die Schwarze Kunst und Hexerei zuhanden des Zürcher Rates.[102] Danach verpflichten sich die Hexen dem leibhaftigen Teufel, der ihnen, nachdem sie die heilige Taufe verleugnet haben, ein Teufelszeichen zufügt, sich auf Hochzeiten, Gastmählern und Tänzen mit ihnen vergnügt und sie beschläft.[103] Wie in seinem Kommentar zur Apostelgeschichte verbindet er auch dort die Erzählungen mit Versen aus dem mosaischen Gesetz, welche die Tötung der Zauberer fordern: „Und zum bschluss wöllend wir hören, was gott in sinem gsaz von disen künsten gsezt hatt, wz auch andere gsazte und rächte darvon geurtheylt, und wil doch nun ettliche wort melden. Ein yeder gange über gottes gsazt und die rächte und läse es selbs." Er zieht Deut 18,9–12. Lev 20,6 und 27 und zuletzt Ex 22,18 heran: „Die zeuberinen solt du nütt läben lassen. Die keyserlichen rächte heyssends auch töden wie dz göttlich rächt. Darum luogind die, wz sy sagind, die wider dise rächte disputierend und schliessend, man sölle die häxen, die nun mit

---

99. Ibid., 275.
100. Ibid., 281–283, bes, 282 f.
101. *Heinrich Bullinger*, In Acta Apostolorvm [...] libri IV, Zürich 1533, 197r–198r und 238r–239v; vgl. auch die außerordentlich langen Ausführungen über teuflische Magie zu Simon Magus: ibid, 94v–97v und 99v–101v.
102. *Bullinger*, Gegen die schwarzen Künste (wie Anm. 38), 291–293.
103. Ibid., 300.

fantasy umbgond, nüt verbrennen oder töden." So fragt er drohend und mahnt eindringlich gegen Hexerei und Magie mit der Todesstrafe vorzugehen.[104]

DIE ANHALTENDE ZURÜCKHALTUNG UND MILDE DER BASLER GEISTLICHKEIT

Dass Grynäus in seinen exegetischen Werken so beharrlich vermied, über Hexerei zu sprechen, während in Europa große Hexenjagden zahlreiche Opfer auch in Basels nächster Nachbarschaft forderten, kann kein Zufall gewesen sein. Sein Schweigen ist ein beredtes. Wer Hexerei für einen Wahn hält, der wird sich für der Hexerei Verdächtigte einsetzen, aber er hat keinen Grund, in seiner Exegese mit Ex 22,18 und ähnlichen Stellen die Todesstrafe für Hexerei zu fordern oder in Auslegungen der Versuchung Christi oder der einschlägigen Stellen aus der Apostelgeschichte vermeintliches Hexenunwesen anzuprangern.

Nicht, dass der Glaube an übernatürliche Zauberkräfte, Teufelsbeschwörungen und Teufelspakte in Basel ausgerottet gewesen wäre. 1602 musste sich Margreth Vögtlin vor den Siebnerherren gegen den Vorwurf verteidigen, mit dem Teufel etwas zu tun gehabt zu haben, und in den beiden genannten außerordentlichen Prozessen von 1624 und 1680 kam am Rande das Thema des Teufelspaktes auf. So wurde 1624 im Fall Reinhard Ruggraff festgehalten, er habe nicht gestanden, „mit dem bösen feind" ein „bündnuß aufgericht" zu haben und ein Pfarrherr, wohl Johannes Groß von St. Leonhard, bezichtigte ihn, er habe auf dem Kirchhof den Teufel beschworen.[105] Aber Grynäus schwieg sich über Zauberei und Teufelspakte aus, obwohl auch in der akademischen Elite das Thema präsent gewesen sein muss. Bodins *Daemonomania* war 1581 in Basel erschienen, allerdings nicht wie Weyers Werk in einem der angesehensten Verlage der Stadt, sondern beim Glaubensflüchtling Thomas Guarinus, der in die kleine Isengrinsche Druckerei eingeheiratet hatte. Der große Staatstheoretiker Bodin versuchte bekanntlich, Weyer zu widerlegen, und mahnte, Hexerei und Teufelspakte mit allen Mitteln zu verfolgen. Die Juristen der Universität thematisierten denn auch 1602 den Teufelsbund, forderten aber – anders als Bodin – eine zurückhaltende Jurisdiktion nach der *Carolina*.

Die Basler Theologen standen 1602 dem Hexenwahn noch wesentlich kritischer gegenüber. Aber auch sie konnten den Prozess nicht verhindern und

---

104. Ibid., 304 f.
105. Befragung vom 24./25. April, StA Basel, Criminalia 4,8 (9); vgl. auch die am 7. Mai 1624 verlesene Befragung, StA Basel, Criminalia 4,8 (15).

auch keinen Freispruch der Verdächtigen erwirken, doch ein Todesurteil wurde abgewendet. Der Rat ließ Margreth Vögtlin in einer elenden Hütte beim Spital wegsperren. Auf Ansuchen ihrer Tochter und des Riehener Pfarrers, Johannes Müller, wird sie immerhin zwar nicht, wie erbeten, bald wieder freigelassen, aber doch in eine nicht ganz so elende Spitalstube verlegt. Ein Jahr später setzt sich Antistes Johann Jakob Grynäus nochmals für die alte Frau ein. Er schreibt am 26. März 1603 an den Rat: „Wiewol Jch erkennen mag, das wer die sachen mit der elenden, gfangnen frauen jm Spital […] treibt, nachred und ungunst auf sich ladet […]."[106] Also auf die Gefahr hin sich unbeliebt zu machen, bittet er, dass die Gefangene zu ihrer Familie zurückkehren dürfe. Der bewegende Brief beruft sich auf die Gutachten und das kaiserliche Recht sowie auf Menschlichkeit gegenüber der Gemarterten und Gefangenen, die in einer Kammer zusammen mit Mäusen und Ratten hausen müsse und als gläubige Christin nicht einmal die Predigt hören könne. Der Rat erteilt darauf dem Riehener Vogt den Auftrag: „mit der Gmeind zerreden, dz man sie wider hinuß lassen wolle, doch dz sie nit uß huß [aus dem Haus ihrer Tochter] gelossen werde".[107] Leider sind bisher keine Akten zur Gemeindeversammlung bekannt. Die Gemeinde muss sich vehement gegen einen Hausarrest der Verdächtigen in ihrer Mitte gewehrt haben. Abscheu und Angst vor der vermeintlichen Hexe scheinen im Dorf so groß gewesen zu sein, dass der Rat wohl einen Aufstand oder gar Lynchjustiz befürchtete, wie sie aus anderen Regionen zahlreich überliefert sind, wenn die Obrigkeit nicht gegen angebliche Hexen durchgriff.[108] Jedenfalls blieb Margreth Vögtlin im Spital, allerdings nicht mehr in Einzelhaft. Sie wurde „in der Lohnstuben by and[ern] Wyben" untergebracht und durfte die Predigt besuchen.[109] So viel hat Grynäus doch erreicht.

Keine drei Wochen nach dem Tod des schon seit Jahren erblindeten Antistes Grynäus gibt ein weiteres Gutachten der Theologischen Fakultät und der Pfarrerschaft vom 17. September 1617 nochmals Auskunft über deren Umgang mit der alttestamentlichen Vorschrift, Zauberer auszurotten. Die Geistlichen erhielten den Auftrag, zu berichten, „was vermög heiliger göttlicher Schrift, als Kaiserlichen Rechten", von der Zauberei und von lästerlichem Fluchen und Schwören, sowie von Schriftfälschungen und Schriftenunterschlagungen, deren das Ratsmitglied Adalbert Meyer angeklagt war, zu halten und wie sie zu bestrafen seien. Adalbert Meyer gehörte als Enkel des Bürgermeisters Adalbert

---

106. Nach *Guggenbühl*, Mit Tieren (wie Anm. 10), 240.
107. Ibid., 242.
108. Vgl. *Behringer*, Hexen (wie Anm. 1), 34 f. und 71; *Rita Voltmer*, Hexen. Wissen was stimmt (wie Anm. 1), 19, 83, 96.
109. Nach *Guggenbühl*, Mit Tieren (wie Anm. 10), 242.

Meyer zum Pfeil, der die Reformation durchzusetzen half, zur Elite Basels und war seit Jahren in einen hässlichen Erbschaftsstreit verwickelt, der ihn schwer belastete. Als schließlich sein Haus konfisziert wurde, um seine Schulden zu bezahlen, kamen unerwartet allerlei Zaubermittel zum Vorschein: „Spiegel, Ringe, silberne Bixlein, hebräische Sägenschrift, Zauberbüchlein und Zaubersprüchlein".[110]

Die Geistlichen haben auch in diesem heiklen Fall Ex 22,18 zitiert. Sie hätten auch gar nicht darauf verzichten können, denn das Schriftwort war weitherum bekannt. Daneben beziehen sie sich nur summarisch auf Lev 19 und Deut 18. Am Schluss führen sie interessanterweise noch Lev 20,6 an, wonach Gott selbst Wahrsagerei bestraft: Verlangt ein Mensch danach, sich an die Wahrsager und Zeichendeuter zu wenden, fassen sie zusammen, „so will ich [Gott] ihn abhauen aus seinem Volk".[111] Das Alte Testament bedrohe also, macht das Gutachten klar, die Zauberer selbst und diejenigen, die sich bei ihnen Rat holten, mit dem Tode. Dennoch sprechen sich die Geistlichen gegen die Todesstrafe für Adalbert Meyer aus, obwohl der, wenn auch nicht eindeutig als Zauberer und ausdrücklich auch nicht des Teufelsbundes überführt sei, doch unbestreitbar bei Zauberern Rat eingeholt und selbst Zaubermittel gebraucht habe: „jedoch ist aus den ermelten Zeugensagen und beigelegten Käpslein, Zedelein und ring, offenbar daß gedachter Meyer bei einem verschreiten Zauberer rat und hülf' gesucht und den gegebenen Rat nach seiner Nächsten Hab' und Gut zu ervorteilen und betrügen, den Richter selbst zu erblenden, unterstanden und solcher Künsten fürsetzlich nachgesetzt habe. Wollte man dem Göttlichen Gesetz strenge nachfragen, müßte er diese Mißhandlungen verbessern müssen. Sie können aber diese Strafe nicht zugeben, da andere vor ihm milder und ringer gestraft worden sind, so daß sie an dieser Person nicht solch' schwere Straf anfangen wollten."[112]

Die Geistlichen wollen also explizit nicht „strenge" dem göttlichen Gesetz nachfragen, mahnen indessen die Obrigkeit grundsätzlich Aberglauben und Zauberei „mit größerem Ernst" zu bestrafen, damit „sich niemand der Unwissenheit zu entschuldigen habe".[113]

Hier lag also, anders als im Fall von Margreth Vögtlin, nach Sicht der Geistlichen schwerer Aberglauben und versuchte Zauberei vor, die nach der Thora

---

110. Nach *Eduard Eckenstein Schröter*, Der Erb- Und Güterrechts-Prozess zwischen den Eckhenstein'schen und Adalbert Meyer zum Pfeil, Zunftmeister und Ratsherr der Zunft zu Fischern, Basel 1905, 76–81, bes. 76.
111. Ibid., 79.
112. Ibid., 80.
113. Ibid., 80 f.

mit dem Tod zu bestrafen wären. Das bedeutete für die Basler Theologieprofessoren und Pfarrer aber im Jahre 1617 nach Christus nicht zwingend, dass der Delinquent hinzurichten sei. Sie hielten sich offenbar an die seinerzeit in Basel formulierten und publizierten kritischen Einsichten des Humanisten Erasmus, der die Bibel mit seinem historischen Ansatz ausgelegt hatte und auch die sogenannten göttlichen Gesetze den Zeitläufen anpassen wollte. Er hatte erklärt, den Juden des Alten Testamentes sei manches erlaubt, was den Christen verboten sei, und von Todesstrafen abgeraten.[114] Die Basler Theologen fassten 1617 nicht einmal einen dauerhaften Ausschluss aus der christlichen Gemeinde ins Auge. Nachdem die Geistlichen ihr Urteil über Meyers gotteslästerlichen Reden und seine Betrügereien abgegeben hatten, bitten sie den Rat: „Schließlichen, sinthemalen Adalbert Meyer mit seiner Mißhandlung allß welche nicht mehr verborgen, sondern allbereith außgebrochen, auch die Kirche Gottes schwerlich geärgert, hoffen wir, es werde ein Gottseelig undt weyse Obrigkeit dahin bedacht sein, daß er sich zu seiner Zeit (wofern solches der Straf so ihm würd aufgelegt werden, nicht verhindern würde) offentlich wiederumb mit dero versühne."[115] Adalbert Meyer sollte sich also nach seiner Strafe einem öffentlichen Reueritual unterziehen und danach wieder als anerkanntes Glied der Kirchgemeinde gelten. In einem Fall von 1622 versuchten die Geistlichen, einen Zaubereifall gar zunächst nur kirchendisziplinarisch zu regeln.[116]

Wie Weyer plädierten die Theologen im Jahre 1617 auch bei offensichtlichem Gebrauch von zauberischen Mitteln für Milde und hofften, den Delinquenten wieder auf den rechten Weg zu bringen.

Grundsätzlich blieben die Basler Theologen bei dieser Sicht. An die Wirksamkeit von Zauberkünsten zu glauben und Zaubersprüche anzuwenden, insbesondere „gotteslästerlich" unter Anrufung Gottes im Zusammenhang mit Zauberei zu „segnen", war für die Theologen nach den Gesetzen des Alten Testamentes todeswürdig. So sind sie im Fall von Johann Reinhard Ruggraff von 1624 entsetzt über sein Zauberbüchlein, das lehrte Liebeszauber mit der Anrufung der Dreifaltigkeit zu vollbringen. Aber auch da fordern sie Milde,

---

114. LB, Bd. 9, 842B; ibid., Bd. 7, 79. *Erasmus von Rotterdam*, Opera omnia Desiderii Erasmi Roterodami, Bd. IV-1, Amsterdam 1974, 196f. Vgl. *Christine Christ-von Wedel*, Erasmus of Rotterdam: Advocate of a New Christianity, Toronto 2013, bes. 7–10, 81–88, 97–112, 207–223 und kürzer: Erasmus of Rotterdam: A Portrait, Basel 2020, 60f., 131, 152.
115. *Eduard Eckenstein Schröter*, Der Erb- Und Güterrechts-Prozess (wie Anm. 110), 82.
116. Universitätsbibliothek Basel, Hss, Kirchen Archiv 22c, Faszikel 108. Ich danke Beat von Scarpatetti für Entzifferungshilfe. Vgl. zur Wiederaufnahme in die Gemeinde nach Zaubereidelikten u. Anm. 119.

wenn auch nicht ausdrücklich gegenüber dem Ehebrecher und Magier Ruggraff selbst, der aus ihrer Sicht überführt war, ihn sollte der Rat „gebührlich" strafen, so doch gegenüber allen, die bei Ruggraff Rat suchten und von dem Ehebrecher verführt wurden. Aber auch, wie der Täter selbst gebührlich zu strafen sei, lassen sie offen.[117]

In einem Gutachten von 1647 zweifeln Antistes Theodor Zwinger und Stadtsyndikus Johann Jakob Faesch grundsätzlich an dem freiwillig, ohne Folter abgegebenen Bekenntnis einer halbseitig gelähmten jungen Frau über ihren Umgang mit Geistern: Der Teufel würde bekanntlich „einfältige Leüth betriegen. [...] auch dz der Sathan viel leüth in dem Schlaff dergestalten verblendet, alls wan sie Leibhafftig mit Jemandem hetten zethun gehabt, daran aber nichts gewesen."[118] 1681 hält Antistes Peter Werenfels Teufelserscheinungen für „phantastey", will aber Aberglauben abschreckend bestraft wissen. 1696 erklärt er zum immer wieder zitierten alttestamentlichen Gebot, Zauberei mit dem Tode zu bestrafen, es habe „auf die jüdische Polizei gezielt" sei in Abgang geraten und „nicht recht verbindlich".[119]

---

117. Der Pastoren Bedenken vom 15.4.1624, StA Basel, Criminalia 4,8 (6). Vgl. *Schnyder*, Zauberei (wie Anm. 12), 85f. Schnyder sieht die Rolle der Pfarrerschaft sehr negativ, so schon den Fall von 1622 (wie Anm. 116), wo er unterstellt, die Geistlichen hätten Lese- und Schreibfähigkeiten von Laien kritisch gesehen (67–72). Im Fall Ruggraff hätten sie den Zaubereiverdacht überhaupt erst aufgebracht, weil sie das ihnen zur Begutachtung übergebene Zauberbuch aus dem Besitz des Angeklagten als solches beurteilten und erklärten, der Gebrauch von Liebeszauber im Namen der Dreifaltigkeit sei nach alttestamentlichen Vorschriften todeswürdig. Sie wären allerdings kaum zugezogen worden, hätte der Verdacht nicht schon bestanden. In dem Bedenken erklären sie am Ende: „Wie nun mit den von ihm vermutlich verblenten und verfürten ein mitleiden zu haben, alß verhoffen obgemelte he[rren] pastores, es werde ein christliche oberkeit auß tragenden eyffer für Gottes so hoch gelesterten Ehr, wol müssen ihn Ruggraffen zur bekenntnis der warheit und gebührlichen straff zuziehen, damit unser Kirchen nicht bey den nachparten des Namens habe, als theten sie der Zauberey sünd nicht achten." Daraus zu folgern, die Gutachter hätten auf die Todesstrafe gepocht, halte ich für fragwürdig. Sie sprechen von einer gebührlichen, nicht von einer Todesstrafe.
118. StA Basel, Criminalia 4,12, bei *Guggenbühl*, Mit Tieren (wie Anm. 10), 311–314, bes. 312f.
119. StA Basel, Criminalia 4,12; 4,17 (1) und 4,19. Vgl. auch zu dem Zaubereiprozess von 1696: *Alexander Wolleb*, Christliche Warnungs-Predigt/Wider allerhand Zauberey vnd Aber-Glaub, uber die Wort des H. Propheten Esaj Cap VIII, 19.20. [...], Basel [1696]. Der Rat hatte die Predigt angeordnet, die der Pfarrer von St. Martin nach Zaubereidelikten im in der Basler Herrschaft gelegenen Bubendorf zu halten hatte anlässlich der Wiederaufnahme der reuigen Verurteilten in die christliche Gemeinde. Eindringlich warnte er mit den einschlägigen Stellen aus dem Alten Testament vor dem todeswürdigen Verbrechen der Zauberei und Teufelsbeschwörung, um dann zu erklären: Dank Christi Freikauf von unseren Sünden werden dem Reuigen auch diese grässlichen Untaten vergeben.

DER UNTERSCHIEDLICHE UMGANG MIT DER HEXENTHEMATIK IN REFORMIERTEN GEBIETEN

Ist Basel mit dem Eintreten seiner Geistlichkeit für Milde in Zaubereiprozessen, wie Weyer sie gefordert hatte, ein typisches Beispiel für eine reformierte Stadt? Kaum. Die eingangs zusammengefassten Thesen zum Anteil der Reformation an der Hexenpanik umzukehren und in Bausch und Bogen zu behaupten, *die* Reformation habe den Hexenwahn zurückgedrängt, ist ebenso unhaltbar, wie die These, *die* Reformation habe sie gefördert. Nicht jede reformatorische Obrigkeit und nicht jede Geistlichkeit handelten gleich.

Bekanntlich hieß Martin Luther in Wittenberg trotz gelegentlichen Eintretens für Milde und Hoffen auf Reue Hexenverbrennungen grundsätzlich gut.[120] Er widmete Ex 22,18 eine ganze Predigt, worin er sich keineswegs von der üblichen Hexenpanik abhebt. Er sagte zum Beispiel nach einer Predigtnachschrift: „Die Zauberinnen sollen getötet werden (occidantur magae), weil sie Schurken, Ehebrecher, Räuber und Mörder sind. Einige verachten sie, als ob die Hexen keine Fähigkeiten besäßen, aber sie besitzen sie tatsächlich (sed re vera possunt)." Luther erzählte: Ein gewisser Prediger habe die Zauberkraft der Hexen verachtet, um dann selbst an ihrem Gift zu verderben. „Also ist gegen sie nicht Verachtung angebracht, sondern mit Schwert und festen Glauben gegen sie fortzufahren. Sie schaden auf verschiedene Weise, also sind sie zu töten, nicht nur weil sie schaden, sondern auch weil sie Umgang mit dem Satan haben."[121]

Oskar Pfister mag Calvins Beitrag an den großen Genfer Hexenprozessen überinterpretiert haben,[122] sicher ist indessen, dass Calvin glaubte, Hexerei sei real, denn sonst hätte, so erklärte er, Gott sie nicht verboten. Zu leugnen, magische Künste seien in Gebrauch gewesen, hält er für ein Sakrileg. Wohl glaubt er mit zeitgenössischen Humanisten wie Andrea Alciato, die Versammlungen am Hexensabbat seien erträumt, aber er spricht von einer Übergabe an den Teufel in Zusammenhang mit Hexerei. Die Erfahrung aller Zeiten, so Calvin,

---

120. *Günter Jerouschek*, Luthers Hexenglaube und die Hexenverfolgung, in: *Markus Hirte* (Hg.), Mit dem Schwert (wie Anm. 1), 111–122; *Jörg Haustein*, Martin Luthers Stellung (wie Anm. 1), bes. 127; *Beatrice Frank*, Zauberei und Hexenwerk, in: *Gerhard Hammer, Karl-Heinz zur Mühlen* (Hg.), Lutheriana. Zum 500. Geburtstag Martin Luthers von den Mitarbeitern der Weimarer Ausgabe im Auftrag der Kommission zur Herausgabe der Werke Martin Luthers, Köln u. a. 1984, 292–297, bes. 297.

121. WA, Bd. 16, 551bf., bes. 552b, Zeile 14–23.

122. *Oskar Pfister*, Calvins Eingreifen in die Hexer- & Hexenprozesse von Peney 1545 nach seiner Bedeutung für Geschichte & Gegenwart, Zürich 1947.

überzeuge davon, dass Menschen oft vom Teufel durch Magier gelernt hätten, was von Menschen nicht erkundet werden könnte. Umso mehr sei Gott anzuflehen, den Feind, der mit tödlichen Künsten gegen uns in Stellung steht, zu bändigen.[123] Ohne wenn und aber fordert Calvin mit Ex 22,18 die Todesstrafe für Hexen.[124]

Ganz anders Zwingli.[125] Zwingli selbst glaubte sicher nicht an die Wirksamkeit von Hexerei. Bei dem einzigen Zitat, aufgrund dessen Zwingli bisher Hexenglauben zugeschrieben wurde, handelt es sich um eine nichtssagende metaphorische Redeweise. Zwingli hat dagegen die einschlägigen Bibelstellen zur Magie am Pharaonenhof nach Exodus 7 und 8 wie Grynäus, als Täuschungen und heidnischen Wahn kommentiert. Ex 22,18 zitierte er gar kühn unpersönlich mit „Veneficium aut maleficium, non pacieris uiuere", als fordere der Vers nicht auf, Zauberer oder Hexen zu töten, sondern Verbrechen auszurotten. Das Wirken des Teufels ist in seinen Werken unpersönlich als *das* Böse gedacht und Zwingli vermeidet von Teufelserscheinungen oder einem Teufelsbund zu sprechen. In Zürich gingen die Hexenprozesse wie andernorts auch nach 1519 deutlich zurück. Solange Zwingli wirkte, sprach der Zürcher Rat dennoch ein Todesurteil aus, das Zwingli zumindest nicht verhindert hat oder wohl besser: nicht verhindern konnte. Denn der Prozess fand 1525 während der Bauernunruhen und täuferischer Umtriebe im Kyburger Amt statt, nachdem der amtierende Vogt gerade gestorben und der neue noch nicht eingesetzt war. Die Lage vor Ort war äußerst fragil. Der Rat wird nicht gewagt haben, die Bevölkerung noch weiter gegen sich aufzubringen, die forderte, das Dorf von der gefürchteten vermeintlichen Giftmischerin zu befreien.

Zwinglis Nachfolger, Heinrich Bullinger, hingegen vertrat die übliche auf Augustinus zurückgehende Hexenlehre, die in der Spätscholastik theologisch ausgefeilt wurde. Für ihn verfügten zwar nur Teufel und Dämonen über Zauberkräfte, die aber „der böse Feind", sofern Gott es zuließ, dem Menschen nach einem Pakt mit einem leibhaftig erschienenen Dämon oder dem Teufel selbst übertragen konnte. Alle Arten von Magie, schädliche sowie nutzbringende waren nach Bullinger teuflisch und mit dem Tod zu bestrafen. Schon 1552 hatte sich der Zürcher Antistes öffentlich zu Hexerei und Teufelsbund geäußert und forderte 1571 in seinem ausführlichen Gutachten die Todesstrafe für jede Form von Magie und Zauberei sowie für das volksmedizinische Segnen mit

---

123. CO, Bd. 24 [= CR 52], 267–269.
124. Ibid., 364–367; vgl. auch CO, Bd. 8 (= CR 30), Braunschweig 1886, 630–634.
125. Zum ganzen Abschnitt über Zwingli, Bullinger und Zürich: *Christ-von Wedel*, Die Zürcher Hexenprozesse (wie Anm. 6).

christlichen Texten. Im gleichen Jahr 1571 setzten in Zürich wieder vermehrt Hexenprozesse mit Folteranwendung ein, die mit Verbrennungen endeten. Zwischen 1571 und 1629 verurteilte das Zürcher Malefizgericht sechsundfünfzig Menschen wegen Hexerei zum Tode. Danach erst begannen Zürcher Theologen gegen die Folteranwendung und die fragwürdige inquisitorische Prozessführung aufzubegehren, stellten aber vor dem 18. Jahrhundert die übliche Hexenlehre kaum infrage. Die Prozesse gingen zurück, hörten aber nicht auf. Noch 1701 forderte der größte Hexenprozess Zürichs acht Todesopfer. Erst danach verurteilte der Zürcher Rat keine Verdächtigen mehr zum Tode und trat 1714 ein letztes Mal überhaupt auf Hexereiverdächtigungen ein.

Bullingers Gutachten von 1571 reihte sich in zahlreiche theologische und juristische Verlautbarungen von Autoren ein, die der Hexenpanik verfallen waren – ich erinnere nur nochmals an Bodins *Daemonomania*. Die Angst vor Zauberei und mit dem Teufel verbündeten Hexen erfasste damals weite Teile Europas, und auch das zuvor zurückhaltende reformierte Zürich erlag ihr, genauso wie das reformierte Berner Gebiet. Allein in der Waadt, die seit 1536 zu Bern gehörte, wurden zwischen 1580 und 1655 tausendsiebenhundert Hexen und Zauberer verurteilt.[126] Wie in Bern klagten auch in Zürich vornehmlich die Untertanen auf der Landschaft die vermeintlichen Hexen an. Basel hatte ein viel kleineres Territorium als Bern und Zürich. Dennoch ist der Unterschied zu den nahe gelegenen und mit ihm verbündeten protestantischen Städten verblüffend.

In Basel hat der Rat lange der 1560 in Europa neu einsetzenden Hexenpanik ganz widerstanden und erst seit 1602 ausnahmsweise Folter aufgrund von Hexereiverdächtigungen wieder angewendet. Offenbar waren die Ratsherren sich ihrer Sache nicht sicher und baten darum ihre Theologen und Juristen um Gutachten. Die konnten zwar 1602 einen Freispruch nicht durchsetzten, aber doch weiteres Foltern und ein Todesurteil abwenden. Auch später trat der Rat wieder auf Zaubereianklagen ein, was auch seine Theologen guthießen, sprach aber allein auf Grund von Zaubereidelikten keine Todesurteile aus. Bei den beiden Hinrichtungen von 1624 und 1680 standen Delikte wie Ehebruch und Mord im Vordergrund. Dagegen verurteilte der Rat Verleumder, die andere der Hexerei verdächtigt hatten. Die reformierte Pfarrerschaft hat den Hexenglauben in Basel nicht ausrotten, aber eindämmen können, und mahnte erfolgreich zu Milde.

---

126. *Ulrich Pfister*, Artikel Hexenwesen, § 2. Frühe Neuzeit, in: Historisches Lexikon der Schweiz (https://hls-dhs-dss.ch/de/articles/011450/2014–10–16/, abgerufen 22.6.2021).

SCHLUSSBETRACHTUNG

Hat das humanistische Erbe, das in Basel insbesondere im 16. Jahrhundert lebendig blieb, die Rheinstadt vor Hexenpanik bewahrt? Hat humanistische Prägung vor Hexenwahn gefeit? Das pauschal zu formulieren, scheint unsinnig. Müssen doch Ulrich Tengler, der Autor des *Layenspiegel,* (wenn auch mit Vorbehalten), jedoch ganz sicher sein Freund und Verfasser des lobenden Vorwortes, Sebastian Brant, als Frühhumanisten bezeichnet werden[127] sowie als Späthumanisten Bodin und sein Übersetzer Johann Fischart, der in Basel seinen Doktortitel erwarb, und im Basel benachbarten Elsass mit seinen humanistischen Zentren in Schlettstadt und Straßburg wurden Hexen „mit besonderer Heftigkeit" (Soldan-Heppe) hingerichtet.[128]

Ich habe kein Zeugnis gefunden, dass die Basler reformierten Theologen wie Erasmus Teufelserscheinungen und Hexenglauben kühn der Lächerlichkeit preisgegeben oder mit dem humanistischen Juristen Andrea Alciato Hexereivorwürfe grundsätzlich als Fiktionen abgetan[129] und so dem von Magie durchdrungenen Zeitgeist offen getrotzt hätten. Sie schweigen sich, wo immer möglich, vornehm und vorsichtig über Hexerei aus. Aber sie haben mit dem berühmten in ihrer Stadt begrabenen Bibelhumanisten Erasmus die alttestamentlichen Aufrufe, Zauberer zu töten, als historische Anweisungen gelesen, die nicht eins zu eins im 16. oder 17. Jahrhundert n. Chr. anzuwenden seien. Dieser humanistische Ansatz hat ihre Gutachten geprägt. Sie haben für die Verbreitung der Kampfschrift des Humanisten Weyer gegen den Hexenwahn gesorgt, in ihren Gutachten in seinem und Erasmus' Sinn Teufelserscheinungen als Fiktion entlarvt sowie die inquisitorische Prozessführung mit Folteranwendung vorsichtig infrage gestellt.

---

127. Vgl. *Joachim Knappe,* Der humanistische Geleittext als Paratext – am Beispiel von Brants. Beigaben zu Tenglers Layen Spiegel, in: *Andreas Deutsch* (Hg.), Ulrich Tenglers Laienspiegel. Ein Rechtsbuch, Heidelberg 2011, 117–137.

128. *Soldan-Heppe,* Geschichte der Hexenprozesse, neu bearb. und hg. von *Max Bauer,* München 1912, Bd. 1, 528. Die oft wiederholte Behauptung Soldans, in Straßburg seien 1582 134 Hexen verbrannt worden, beruht zwar fälschlich auf einer Flugschrift, die in Straßburg erschien, aber Hexenhinrichtungen in ganz Süddeutschland samt dem Elsass aufzählt, darunter jedoch keine aus Straßburg, aber 36 aus „Dürcken im Elsaß", womit wohl Türckheim gemeint ist. Vgl. Warhaffte vnd glaubwirdige Zeyttung. Von Hundert vnd vier vnd dreyssig Vnholden, So […] 1582 […] zum Fewer verdampt und verbrennet worden […], Straßburg 1583. Aber die Zeugnisse zum Elsass sind auch abzüglich der fälschlichen Angabe „heftig" genug.

129. *Erasmus von Rotterdam,* Opera omnia Desiderii Erasmi Roterodami, Bd. I-3, Amsterdam 1972, 417–423; *Andrea Alciatus,* Parergon Iuris, Basel 1543, 484–488.

Dr. phil. Christine Christ-von Wedel
Research fellow
Theologische Fakultät der Universität Basel und
Institut für Schweizerische Reformationsgeschichte an der Universität Zürich
Mühlenberg 10
CH-4052 Basel
Schweiz
Christine.christ@unibas.ch

ABSTRACT

Only a few sorcery trials were held, and only two death sentences passed, in the Reformed city of Basel in the sixteenth and early seventeenth century. Moreover, the Protestant clergy in Basel were astonishingly reluctant to speak about witches or magicians in their theological publications. When judges asked for advisory opinions, the theological faculty and the reverends recommended clemency. Conceding that the divine law prescribed capital punishment in the Old Testament, the clergy nevertheless advocated for Christian charity in line with an Erasmian method of exegesis and Johann Weyer's campaign against witch-hunts. Not only was Weyer's controversial *De praestigiis daemonum* repeatedly printed in Basel, it was also Johannes Füglin, a Basel minister, who, at the suggestion of Antistes Simon Sulzer, propagated a German translation of the text amongst lay persons.

Möglichkeiten und Grenzen konfessioneller Koexistenz. Briefwechsel, Studien- und Druckorte Oberlausitzer Geistlicher in der zweiten Hälfte des 16. Jahrhunderts

Von Saskia Limbach und Martin Christ

Denkt man an Verbindungen zwischen der Lausitz und den Städten des Heiligen Römischen Reiches, würde einem wohl nicht gerade die kleine, freie Reichsstadt Schwäbisch Gmünd, die knapp 500 Kilometer entfernt lag, als offensichtliche Kandidatin einfallen. Doch sind aus dieser Stadt zwei Briefe an den Kanoniker Wolfgang Hulbeck, der aus Schwäbisch Gmünd stammte, erhalten.[1] Hulbeck war von 1551 bis 1569 Kanoniker in Bautzen, Pfarrer von Jauernick und Propst des Laubaner Magdalenerinnenklosters.[2] Bemerkenswert sind die beiden Briefe aus mehreren Gründen, von denen uns einer hier besonders interessieren soll. Schwäbisch Gmünd war eine der wenigen katholischen freien Reichsstädte und somit sind die Schreiben ein Hinweis darauf, dass sich die Lausitzer Katholiken aufgrund ihrer Isolation immer wieder an weiter entfernte Glaubensgenossen wenden mussten. Dabei wirkte sich die periphere Lage der Oberlausitz auch auf die Schnelligkeit des Austauschs aus: Der erste Brief wurde am 5. März 1570 verschickt und ging ziemlich genau zwei Monate später, am 4. Mai, in Bautzen ein. Der zweite Brief ist auf den 15. Oktober datiert und erreichte sein Ziel drei Wochen später, am 8. November. Da ein berittener Bote zu dieser Zeit etwa 50–60 Kilometer am Tag zurücklegen konnte, hätten die Briefe auch in 10 Tagen zugestellt werden können.[3] Doch war die

---

1. Domstiftsarchiv Bautzen, Loc. 7107, Acta allerlei protestantische Pfarrer und Pfarreien betrf: 1547–1902, I. Konvolut 1547–1593, Brief 8. Im Schwäbisch Gmünder Stadtarchiv haben sich nach bisherigen Erkenntnissen keine Briefe aus Bautzen erhalten.
2. *Hermann Kinne*, Die Bistümer der Kirchenprovinz Magdeburg. Das (exemte) Bistum Meißen 1. Das Kollegiatstift St. Petri zu Bautzen von der Gründung bis 1569, Berlin 2014, 1004–1005; *Paul Skobel*, Das Jungfräuliche Klosterstift zur Heiligen Maria Magdalena von der Buße zu Lauban in Schlesien von 1320–1821, hg. und ergänzt bis zur Gegenwart von *Edmund Piekorz*, Aalen und Stuttgart 1970, 208–209.
3. Zum Postwesen, siehe *Wolfgang Behringer*, Im Zeichen des Merkur. Reichspost und Kommunikationsrevolution in der Frühen Neuzeit, Göttingen 2003; vgl. auch *Peter H. Wilson*, The Holy Roman Empire. A Thousand Years of Europe's History, London 2016; bzgl. der Tagesleistung eines Botens, siehe *Robert Walser*, Lasst mich ohne nachricht nit: Botenwesen und Informationsbeschaffung unter der Regierung des Markgrafen Albrecht Achilles von Brandenburg. Dissertation, LMU München 2004, online: https://edoc.ub.uni-muenchen.de/2796/ (Zugriffsdatum: 14.06.2022).

Oberlausitz nur mäßig an die großen Handelszentren im Reich angebunden, sodass Briefe häufig nur als Beiladung auf dem Weg nach Prag oder bei regional bedeutenden Ereignissen, wie der Leipziger Buchmesse, zugestellt wurden.

Die briefliche Kommunikation illustriert somit die Möglichkeiten und Grenzen des intellektuellen Transfer zwischen Lausitzer Geistlichen und anderen Gebieten in Zentraleuropa.[4] Dabei umfasste die Verbindung nach Schwäbisch Gmünd nicht nur eine bloße Informationsübermittlung, sondern auch den Austausch von Geschenken.[5] Der Gmünder Rat schickte 1570 Wein, sowohl vom Rhein als auch aus dem Remstal, in die Oberlausitz, was in der Stadt üblich war, wie Listen im Gmünder Stadtarchiv zeigen.[6] Im Begleitschreiben bedankt sich der Stadtrat im Gegenzug für das Geld, das Hulbeck nach Schwaben geschickt hatte und das u. a. für Bücher und Kleider für die Armen verwendet wurde. Dabei nennt der Stadtrat auch namentlich die Personen, denen die Bautzener Spende zugutekommen würde.

Wie die Quellen nahelegen, beruhte die Verbindung zwischen dem Stadtrat und Hulbeck nicht nur auf seinen persönlichen Beziehungen zu seiner Heimatstadt, sondern wurde auch von konfessionellen Faktoren geprägt. So schreibt der Gmünder Stadtrat beispielsweise „der Allmechtige wolle uns vor falscher Leer gnedig bewaren".[7] Gemeint war damit die protestantische Lehre, die zu diesem Zeitpunkt in der Oberlausitz sowie im Süden des Reiches fest etabliert war. Schwäbisch Gmünd und das Bautzener Domstift befanden sich in einer ähnlichen Situation. Beide waren innerhalb ihrer jeweiligen regionalen Konfessionstopographie Ausnahmefälle, die letzten katholischen Vertreter in

---

4. Zu Schwäbisch Gmünd, siehe allgemein *Klaus Jürgen Herrmann, Ulrich Müller*, Kleine Geschichte der Stadt Schwäbisch Gmünd, Leinfelden-Echterdingen 2006; vgl. auch *Klaus Graf*, Gmünder Chroniken im 16. Jahrhundert. Texte und Untersuchungen zur Geschichtsschreibung der Reichsstadt Schwäbisch Gmünd, Schwäbisch Gmünd 1984.

5. Zu Geschenken in der Frühen Neuzeit, siehe *Harriet Rudolph*, „Fürstliche Gaben? Schenkakte als Elemente der politischen Kultur im Alten Reich", in: *Mark Häberlein, Christof Jeggle* (Hg.), Materielle Grundlagen der Diplomatie. Schenken, Sammeln und Verhandeln in Spätmittelalter und Früher Neuzeit, Konstanz 2012, 79–102; *Maurice Godelier*, Das Rätsel der Gabe. Geld, Geschenke, heilige Objekte, München 1999. Siehe auch für einen englischen Vergleich, *Felicity Heal*, The Power of Gifts: Gift Exchange in Early Modern England, Oxford 2014; und im französischen Kontext: *Natalie Zemon Davis*, Die schenkende Gesellschaft. Zur Kultur der französischen Renaissance, München 2000.

6. Für 1570 befindet sich die Rechnung mit insgesamt 17 Posten im Stadtarchiv Schwäbisch Gmünd, XIV/1, Stadtrechnung 1570, Vl. 133r–133v.

7. Domstiftsarchiv Bautzen, Loc. 7107, Acta allerlei protestantische Pfarrer und Pfarreien betrf: 1547–1902, I. Konvolut 1547–1593, Brief 8.

einer evangelisch geprägten Umgebung.[8] Dies band die beiden Korrespondenzpartner enger aneinander.

Hulbecks Vita zeigt weitere interessante Verbindungen auf. Zunächst immatrikulierte er sich 1517 an der Universität Leipzig. Zu dieser Zeit war Leipzig eine attraktive Anlaufstelle für katholische Geistliche, während sich Wittenberg in den folgenden Jahren schnell als Ausbildungszentrum für Lutheraner etablierte. In einigen Fällen blieben auch über die Studienzeit hinaus persönliche Kontakte zu Professoren oder Kommilitonen bestehen. Somit kann die Auswahl des Studienortes selbst wichtige Auskünfte über konfessionelle Präferenzen und Verbindungen geben. Schließlich zeigt das Beispiel Hulbeck auch einen weiteren Indikator, der die Möglichkeiten und Verbindungen Lausitzer Geistlicher illustriert, nämlich die Druckorte ihrer Werke. Der Druck *Devotae et piae preces,* dessen Hauptautor der Bautzener Domdechant Johann Leisentrit ist, beinhaltet auch einen gedruckten Brief Hulbecks.[9] Während die erste Ausgabe 1559 ohne Drucker und Druckort herausgegeben wurde, existiert eine zweite Ausgabe, die in Köln gedruckt wurde.[10] Die Auswahl dieses Druckzentrums, welches weit von der Oberlausitz entfernt lag, deutet bereits auf Probleme bei der Drucklegung hin, die vor allem Katholiken spürten.

Im Nachfolgenden sollen die Verbindungen von lutherischen und katholischen Geistlichen der Oberlausitz anhand dieser drei Indikatoren nachgezeichnet werden: den Briefwechseln, den Studienorten und den Druckorten ihrer Werke. Die Besonderheiten der konfessionellen Situation in der Oberlausitz beeinflussten die Austauschprozesse auf vielfältige Weise.[11] Bei einigen dieser Prozesse trat die Konfession in den Hintergrund, während in anderen Fällen Verbindungen nur aufgrund der Konfession entstehen bzw. genutzt werden konnten.

Besonders lohnenswert ist eine solche Analyse aus drei Gründen. Zum einen ist die frühneuzeitliche Oberlausitz eine außergewöhnlich passende Fallstudie für Netzwerke in der Frühen Neuzeit, weil durch die Bikonfessionalität ein

---

8. Vgl. zur Einführung der Reformation in Südwestdeutschland, *Martin Brecht, Hermann Ehmer,* Südwestdeutsche Reformationsgeschichte. Zur Einführung der Reformation im Herzogtum Württemberg 1534, Stuttgart 1984.
9. *Johann Leisentrit,* Devotae et piae preces, Köln: Horst (1564), 3–7.
10. VD16 ZV 26137 (1559), VD16 L 1059 (1564).
11. Für einen Überblick über diese Besonderheiten, siehe *Joachim Bahlcke* (Hg.), Geschichte der Oberlausitz. Herrschaft, Gesellschaft und Kultur vom Mittelalter bis zum Ende des 20. Jahrhunderts, Leipzig 2004; und zur frühneuzeitlichen Oberlausitz, *Joachim Bahlcke* (Hg.), Die Oberlausitz im frühneuzeitlichen Mitteleuropa. Beziehungen, Strukturen, Prozesse, Stuttgart 2007.

direkter Vergleich zwischen Lutheranern und Katholiken möglich ist.¹² Auch wenn die Katholiken lange nicht so zahlreich und wichtig wie die Lutheraner waren, ermöglicht ein Blick auf die Briefwechsel, Studien- und Druckorte Lausitzer Theologen, wichtige Unterschiede aufzuzeigen. Dies ist besonders der Fall, weil die Lausitzen als böhmische Nebenländer einem katholischen Landesherren unterstellt waren.

Zum anderen zeigt eine Analyse der Verbindungen von Theologen, dass sich diese sowohl an den Nachbarregionen Schlesien, Niederlausitz und Sachsen orientierten, sich aber auch andere Verbindungen zunutze machten, beispielsweise durch die Drucklegung Lausitzer Werke in Köln oder den Besuch der Universität Frankfurt/Oder. Die Oberlausitzer richteten sich selektiv an bestimmte Orte, abhängig von konfessionellen, wirtschaftlichen und persönlichen Kriterien. Die Anbindung an Böhmen spielte zwar für persönliche Kontakte eine wichtige Rolle, aber in Bezug auf Studien und Druck-Erzeugnisse wird deutlich, dass Prag unter diesen Gesichtspunkten verhältnismäßig unwichtig war.¹³ Daneben zeigen die Referenzpunkte im Heiligen Römischen Reich, dass die Oberlausitz als Grenzregion, oder „Integrationslandschaft", auch bei der Ausbildung der Geistlichen eine wichtige Rolle spielte.¹⁴

Drittens ermöglicht ein Blick auf die Oberlausitz die Durchsetzung wichtiger Aspekte des Luthertums bzw. des nach-tridentinischen Katholizismus zu analysieren. Der Aufsatz geht somit auch der Frage nach, ob ein Studienaufenthalt in Wittenberg per se dazu geführt hat, dass Prediger das Luthertum strikt durchsetzten, oder ob es danach auch noch möglich war, mit Katholiken zu verhandeln und sogar Aspekte des Katholizismus in die lutherische Theologie zu integrieren. Aus diesem Grund fokussiert der Aufsatz besonders die zweite Hälfte des sechzehnten Jahrhunderts, da zu diesem Zeitpunkt die konfessionellen Grenzen klarer erkennbar werden.¹⁵

---

12. Zum bikonfesionellen Milieu in Bautzen, siehe *Friedrich Hermann Baumgärtel*, Die kirchlichen Zustände Bautzens im 16. und 17. Jahrhundert, Bautzen 1889; für das ebenfalls bikonfessionelle Augsburg, vgl. *Emily Fisher Grey*, „‚Good Neighborhood' and Confessional Coexistence in Augsburg's Holy Cross Quarter, 1548–1629", in: Archiv für Reformationsgeschichte 107 (2016), 62–82; allgemein, *Joachim Bahlcke, Karen Lambrecht, Hans-Christian Maner* (Hg.), Konfessionelle Pluralität als Herausforderung. Koexistenz und Konflikt in Spätmittelalter und Früher Neuzeit. Winfried Eberhard zum 65. Geburtstag, Leipzig 2006.
13. Anders verhielt sich dies bei anderen Berufsgruppen, beispielsweise Juristen. Vgl. *Norbert Kersken*, „Intellektuelle Raumbeziehungen der Oberlausitz", in *Bahlcke* (Hg.), Die Oberlausitz im frühneuzeitlichen Mitteleuropa (wie Anm. 11), 256–288, hier 287.
14. *Heinz-Dieter Heimann, Klaus Neitmann, Uwe Tresp* (Hg.), Die Nieder- und Oberlausitz: Konturen einer Integrationslandschaft, Bd. II: Frühe Neuzeit, Leipzig 2014.
15. Vgl. dazu, *Thomas Kaufmann*, Konfession und Kultur. Lutherischer Protestantismus

DIE REFORMATION IN DER FRÜHNEUZEITLICHEN OBERLAUSITZ

Die Oberlausitz war von 1319 bis 1635 als Markgraftum gleichzeitig ein Nebenland der böhmischen Krone. Aufgrund dieser politischen Situation war die Oberlausitz bei wichtigen politischen Entscheidungen auch von Prag abhängig und wurde wiederholt von den Ereignissen in Böhmen beeinflusst. Die Privilegien der Städte, wie z. B. die Ausrichtung von Märkten, die Gerichtsbarkeit und das Recht auf Besteuerung wurden normalerweise vom König in Prag verliehen.[16] Diese Ausgangslage konnte auch immer wieder zu Beschwerden und Konflikten führen. Als z. B. Görlitz 1433 das Stadtwappen von Kaiser Sigismund erhielt, äußerte sich ein Ratsmitglied abfällig darüber: „ein esel mit gulden hoden, als ein backoffen gros, der were vns viel angenemer gewest, den das wappen".[17] Privilegien konnten auch durch den König wieder zurückgenommen werden, wie dies im so genannten „Pönfall" 1547 geschah, bei dem die Oberlausitzer Städte wegen Gefolgschaftsverweigerung durch den böhmischen König bestraft wurden.[18]

Von 1526 bis 1635 wurde die Oberlausitz vom katholischen Geschlecht der Habsburger regiert, als die böhmische Krone in ihren Besitz kam. Als Markgraftum wurde die Oberlausitz nominell von Prag aus verwaltet, welches den Landvogt als lokalen Repräsentanten beauftragte. Daneben konnten Kommis-

---

in der zweiten Hälfte des Reformationsjahrhunderts, Tübingen 2006; *Thomas Kirchner*, Katholiken, Lutheraner und Reformierte in Aachen 1555–1618. Konfessionskulturen im Zusammenspiel, Tübingen 2015. Siehe auch die umfangreiche Literatur zur Konfessionalisierung, z. B. *Ute Lotz-Heumann*, „Confessionalization is Dead, Long Live the Reformation? Reflections on Historiographical Paradigm Shifts on the Occasion of the 500th Anniversary of the Protestant Reformation" in: *Jan Stievermann, Randall C. Zachman* (Hg.), Multiple Reformations? The Many Faces and Legacies of the Reformation, Tübingen 2018, 127–137; Helga Schnabel-Schüle, „Vierzig Jahre Konfessionalisierungsforschung – eine Standortbestimmung", in: *Peer Friess, Rolf Kiessling* (Hg.), Konfessionalisierung und Region, Konstanz 1999, 23–40; *Kaspar von Greyerz, Manfred Jakubowski-Tiessen, Thomas Kaufmann, Hartmut Lehmann* (Hg.), Interkonfessionalität – Transkonfessionalität – binnenkonfessionelle Pluralität. Neue Forschungen zur Konfessionalisierungsthese, Gütersloh 2003.

16. Vgl. *Norbert Kersken*, „Die Oberlausitz von der Gründung des Sechsstädtebundes bis zum Übergang an das Kurfürstentum Sachsen (1346–1635)" in: *Bahlcke*, Geschichte der Oberlausitz (wie Anm. 11), 99–142, hier 99–112.

17. *Johannes Hass, E. E. Struve* (Hg.), Magister Johannes Hass, Bürgermeisters zu Görlitz, Görlitzer Rathsannalen. Bd. 3 (1521–1542), Görlitz 1870, 131.

18. Zum Pönfall, vgl. *Matthias Herrmann* (Hg.), Pönfall der Oberlausitzer Sechsstädte. 1547–1997, Kamenz 1999; *ders.*, „Der Pönfall der oberlausitzischen Sechsstädte und seine überregionale Einordnung", in: *Joachim Bahlcke, Volker Dudeck* (Hg.), Welt – Macht – Geist. Das Haus Habsburg und die Oberlausitz 1526 bis 1635, Görlitz und Zittau 2002, 97–110.

sare und böhmische Beamte bei Bedarf in die Lausitz kommen. In der Oberlausitz breitete sich reformatorisches Gedankengut in den 1520er Jahren aus, allerdings wurden wichtige Elemente erst später oder gar nicht umgesetzt. Diese Tatsache ist auch mit der politischen Konstellation zu erklären, in der ein größtenteils lutherisch geprägtes Gebiet von einem katholischen König regiert wurde. Dies machte es möglich, dass die Klöster Marienthal und Marienstern, sowie das Magdalenerinnenkloster in Lauban die Reformation überstanden.[19] Daneben blieben auch das Bautzener Domstift katholisch sowie einige Dörfer, die zu den Klöstern gehörten.[20] Besonders wichtig war für die politische Situation und Verwaltung der Oberlausitz der 1346 gegründete Sechsstädtebund, der aus den relativ kleinen Städten Kamenz und Löbau, dem heute in Polen gelegenen Lauban und den wichtigen Handelszentren Görlitz, Bautzen und Zittau bestand. Treffen des Bundes fanden oft wöchentlich und normalerweise in Löbau statt. In Bautzen führte die Koexistenz von Lutheranern und Katholiken auch dazu, dass sich die beiden Gruppen die Hauptkirche, den Dom St. Petri, teilten. Damit ist die Kirche eine der ältesten und größten Simultankirchen im Heiligen Römischen Reich.[21] Aufgrund solcher räumlicher Kompromisse kam es auch zu einem verstärkten Austausch zwischen den Konfessionen. In Lauban gab es zusätzlich eine zweite Simultankirche.[22] Bei Streitigkeiten konnten die Katholiken zusammen mit den Lutheranern Briefe an den böhmischen König schicken, der durch die Amtshauptmänner und Landvögte vor Ort seine Antworten mitteilen ließ.[23] Außerdem waren die Lausitzer Stände, neben den Sechsstädten, den Klöstern und dem Adel, auch an Treffen beteiligt, bei denen königliche Repräsentanten anwesend waren.[24] Die Lutheraner waren darauf bedacht, den böhmischen König nicht zu sehr herauszufordern, auch

---

19. Zu den Frauenklöstern, siehe *Jan Zdichynec*, Les abbayes féminines de la Haute-Lusace aux XVIe et XVIIe siècles. Les Religieuses Entre Pouvoir Temporel et Spirituel au Temps des Réformes, Paris 2014.

20. Zum Domstift, siehe *Kinne*, Die Bistümer der Kirchenprovinz Magdeburg (wie Anm. 2); vgl. auch *Petr Hrachovec, Gerd Schwerhoff, Winfried Müller, Martina Schattkowsky* (Hg.), Reformation als Kommunikationsprozess. Die böhmischen Kronländer und Sachsen, Köln und Wien 2021.

21. Siehe *Kai Wenzel, Birgit Mitzscherlich, Nicole Wohlfarth*, Der Dom St. Petri zu Bautzen, Bautzen 2016; *Richard Vötig*, Die simultankirchlichen Beziehungen zwischen Katholiken und Protestanten zu St. Peter in Bautzen, Leipzig 1911.

22. *Skobel*, Das Jungfräuliche Klosterstift zur Heiligen Maria Magdalena (wie Anm. 2).

23. Zur Rolle der böhmischen Nebenländer allgemein, vgl. *Joachim Bahlcke*, Regionalismus und Staatsintegration im Widerstreit. Die Länder der böhmischen Krone im ersten Jahrhundert der Habsburgerherrschaft (1526–1619), München 1994.

24. *Lars Behrisch*, Städtische Obrigkeit und Soziale Kontrolle. Görlitz 1450–1600, Epfendorf am Neckar 2005.

wenn eine Stadt lutherisch wurde. Konsistorien gab es deshalb in der Oberlausitz keine und Kirchenordnungen wurden verhältnismäßig spät gedruckt.[25] Zittau stellte in diesem konfessionellen Geflecht eine Ausnahme dar, weil es hier zwischen ca. 1530 und 1560 eine signifikante zwinglianische Minderheit gab.[26]

Einige Elemente des Luthertums, wie die Kommunion in beiderlei Gestalt, setzten sich bereits in den frühen 1520er-Jahren in den wichtigen Städten der Oberlausitz durch, aber wegen der komplexen politischen und konfessionellen Gemengelage war die Einführung der Reformation ein langsamer Prozess, der auch von einem intrakonfessionellen Austausch geprägt war.[27] In den ländlichen Gegenden konnte es Jahrzehnte dauern, bis wichtige Elemente des Luthertums eingeführt wurden.[28] Doch auch in den Städten dauerte es über 20 Jahre bis wichtige Elemente der lutherischen Lehre umgesetzt wurden, wie beispielsweise die Aufhebung des Zölibats. So wurde Franz Rotbart als erster evangelischer Prediger von Görlitz noch 1530 aus der Neißestadt vertrieben, weil er die Tochter eines Tuchmachers heiratete.[29] Ähnliches widerfuhr Lorenz Heidenreich in Zittau.[30] Besonders in Bautzen behielten die Katholiken weiterhin Privilegien, wie die Predigt auf Sorbisch oder die Ehegerichtsbarkeit. In einigen Fällen führte das konfessionelle Nebeneinander zu Mischformen, bei

---

25. *Christian Speer*, Strategien des Machterhalts in Zeiten des Umbruchs. Der Görlitzer Rat zu Beginn des 16. Jahrhunderts, in *Heimann, Neitmann, Tresp*, Die Nieder- und Oberlausitz (wie Anm. 14), 46–55, 51–52; *Petr Hrachovec*, Die Zittauer und ihre Kirchen (1300–1600). Zum Wandel religiöser Stiftungen während der Reformation. Leipzig 2020, 379 und 380–385.
26. Siehe *Hrachovec*, Zittauer und ihre Kirchen (wie Anm. 25), 339–367.
27. Siehe dazu, *Martin Christ*, Biographies of a Reformation. Religious Change and Confessional Coexistence in Upper Lusatia, c. 1520–1635, Oxford 2021.
28. Vgl. *Jens Bulisch*, Die gebremste Reformation. Beobachtungen zur Einführung eines evangelischen Kirchenwesens in der Oberlausitz, in: *Lars-Arne Dannenberg, Dietrich Scholze* (Hg.), Stätten und Stationen religiösen Wirkens Studien zur Kirchengeschichte der zweisprachigen Oberlausitz, Bautzen 2009, 253–267.
29. *Christian Speer*, Frömmigkeit und Politik. Städtische Eliten in Görlitz zwischen 1300 und 1550, Berlin 2011, 363–392. Zu dieser Thematik allgemein, vgl. *Marjorie Elizabeth Plummer*, From Priest's Whore to Pastor's Wife: Clerical Marriage and the Process of Reform in the Early German Reformation, Burlington, VT, 2012.
30. *Petr Hrachovec*, „Von feindlichen Ketzern zu Glaubensgenossen und wieder zurück. Das Bild der böhmischen Reformation in Zittauer Quellen des Spätmittelalters und der Frühneuzeit", in: *Marius Winzeler* (Hg.), Jan Hus, Wege der Wahrheit: Das Erbe des böhmischen Reformators in der Oberlausitz und in Nordböhmen, Zittau 2015, 131–156; siehe auch *Johann Benedict Carpzov*, Memoria Heidenreichiana oder Historischer Bericht von dem Leben, Lehre, Wandel, Reformation und Aembtern M. Laurentii Heidenreichs, Leipzig 1717, 30–36.

denen z. B. katholische Priester die Einsetzungsworte bei der Kommunion auf Deutsch sprachen und wahrscheinlich auch die Kommunion in beiderlei Gestalt ausgaben.[31] In Zittau wurden ebenfalls viele vorreformatorische Bräuche, wie das Totengeläut, beibehalten.[32] In Einzelfällen, beispielsweise wenn der böhmische König in die Oberlausitz kam, waren die Lutheraner auch bereit alte Gegenstände und Rituale weiterhin zu verwenden.[33]

DIE BRIEFKOMMUNIKATION ZWISCHEN REFORMATOREN, LAUSITZER THEOLOGEN UND STADTRÄTEN

Im Nachfolgenden soll der erste Indikator für Verbindungen der Lausitzer Geistlichen, ihr Briefwechsel und die daran abzulesenden Kontakte, näher dargestellt werden. Die Quellenlage hierfür ist besonders für die 1520er- und 1530er-Jahre gut, weil größere Editionsprojekte und Vorarbeiten es ermöglichen, die Kommunikation von Lausitzer Stadträten mit wichtigen Reformatoren nachzuzeichnen, die wiederum einen wichtigen Einfluss auf die Auswahl und Anstellung lutherischer Prediger hatten und die Briefe auch Hinweise auf die persönlichen Verbindungen dieser geben. Die Korrespondenz von Lausitzer Geistlichen selber ist unterdessen schwieriger nachzuvollziehen, weil wenige Briefe, besonders von lutherischer Seite, vorhanden sind.

Den Umständen entsprechend mussten sich auch Katholiken in den Städten mit Lutheranern arrangieren, da diese oft höhere Stellungen bekleideten. Viele solcher Kommunikationen zwischen Lutheranern und Katholiken fanden neben persönlichen Treffen auch durch Briefe statt. Nachdem lutherische Neuerungen auf das Wohlgefallen der Bevölkerung stießen, mussten die Katholiken ebenfalls Kompromisse eingehen und tauften beispielsweise nach Luthers kleinem Taufbüchlein oder sangen lutherische Lieder.[34] Selbstverständlich gab es auch Grenzen, die nicht überschritten wurden, und zahlreiche Konflikte zwischen den Religionsparteien, die allerdings nur selten gewaltsam ausgetragen wurden.[35] Ein solcher Fall war der Versuch, in Görlitz einen katho-

---

31. Vgl. *Christ*, Biographies of a Reformation (wie Anm. 27), 118–137. Siehe auch *Kinne*, Die Bistümer der Kirchenprovinz Magdeburg (wie Anm. 2), 1006, für den Ostritzer Pleban Wolfgang Hempel, der beim Prager Erzbischof nach der Erlaubnis fragte, die Kommunion *sub utraque* durchführen zu dürfen.
32. *Hrachovec*, Zittauer und ihre Kirchen (wie Anm. 25), 682–705. Siehe auch 619–629.
33. *Christ*, Biographies of a Reformation (wie Anm. 27), 1–5.
34. *Walther Lipphardt*, Leisentrits Gesangbuch von 1567, Leipzig 1964.
35. Für spätere Beispiele, vgl. *Jan Zdichynec*, „Konfessionsstreitigkeiten unter dem Mi-

lischen Priester einzustellen. Dieser wurde jedoch letztendlich aus der Stadt gejagt und der bisher amtierende lutherische Geistliche von den Bürgern weiterhin unterstützt.[36] Katholiken versicherten sich dabei auch durch Kontakt zu anderen Würdenträgern, wie weit sie mit solchen Kompromissen gehen konnten. Neben konfessionsübergreifenden Briefen, z. B. zwischen lutherischen Stadträten und katholischen Priestern, existieren auch Briefe, die ein klar konfessionelles Profil erkennen lassen, wenn beispielsweise die Bautzener apostolischen Administratoren ihre kirchliche Politik und liturgische Neuerungen von päpstlicher Seite genehmigen lassen wollten, um Konflikte zu vermeiden.[37]

Wie in anderen Teilen Zentraleuropas, spielte Wittenberg auch als Referenzort bei theologischen und politischen Fragen eine wichtige Rolle. Sowohl 1527 als auch 1530 wandte sich der Görlitzer Stadtrat nach Wittenberg, um Martin Luther um Hilfe zu bitten bzw. Philipp Melanchthon nach einem neuen Prediger zu ersuchen. Luther verfasste einige wenige Briefe an die Stadträte der Oberlausitz, in denen er sich aber nicht zu der Kirchenpolitik in den Städten selbst äußert.[38] Der 1525 in Wittenberg immatrikulierte Konrad Nesen aus Zittau stand mit Melanchthon in Kontakt und wurde von ihm als Prediger empfohlen.[39] Melanchthon verfasste 1539 auch einen Empfehlungsbrief für den ebenfalls aus Zittau stammenden Martin Tectander, der an den Reformator Johann Brenz adressiert war.[40] Daneben ist der Besuch Melanchthons, dessen Kontakte in die Oberlausitz insgesamt intensiver waren als die Luthers, in Bautzen 1559 bei der Familie seines Schwiegersohnes Kaspar Peucer ein weiteres Zeugnis der engen Verbindungen zwischen Wittenberg und Bautzen.[41]

Eine ähnliche Rolle wie Wittenberg für die Lutheraner erfüllte Zürich für eine Gruppe von Zwinglianern in Zittau. Wie Petr Hrachovec in seinen Arbei-

---

kroskop. Beispiele aus der Oberlausitz vor und nach 1600", in *Hrachovec, Schwerhoff, Müller, Schattkowsky,* Reformation als Kommunikationsprozess (wie Anm. 20), 511–539.

36. Vgl. *Hass, Struve,* Görlitzer Rathsannalen (wie Anm. 17).
37. Domstiftsarchiv Bautzen, Loc. 213, Briefwechsel Johann Leisentritts, 1553–1584, Brief 27.
38. D. Martin Luthers Werke: Kritische Gesamtausgabe, 73 Bde., Weimar 1883–2009, Bd. 9, Nr. 3639 und Bd. 6, Nr. 1956.
39. *Petr Hrachovec,* „Die Reformation der langen Distanz. Der Zittauer Stadtschreiber Oswald Pergener († 1546) und sein zwinglianischer deutsch-böhmischer Lesezirkel", in *Hrachovec, Schwerhoff, Müller, Schattkowsky,* Reformation als Kommunikationsprozess (wie Anm. 20), 449–510, hier 456–460.
40. Siehe die Abbildung des Originals in *Bahlcke, Dudeck,* Welt – Macht – Geist (wie Anm. 18), 306–307.
41. Vgl. *Hans-Peter Hasse, Günther Wartenberg* (Hg.), Caspar Peucer (1525–1602). Wissenschaft, Glaube und Politik im konfessionellen Zeitalter, Leipzig 2004.

ten gezeigt hat, gab es eine signifikante zwinglianische Minderheit im Stadtrat Zittaus.⁴² Diese korrespondierte ab ca. 1533 mit Züricher Reformatoren und Geistlichen und unterhielt auch Kontakte zu den böhmischen Utraquisten und der Brüderunität. Die genaue Anzahl der Briefe ist schwierig zu schätzen, da nur Teile der Korrespondenz noch vorhanden sind und mindestens ein Brief an Martin Bucer komplett verschollen ist, schätzungsweise existierten aber mehr als 50 Briefe.⁴³ Besonders wichtig war Heinrich Bullinger, dessen Korrespondenznetzwerk ganz Europa umspannte. Diesem und anderen Züricher Gelehrten ließen die Zittauer Zwinglianer Informationen zukommen und tauschten sich über eine Vielzahl von politischen und religiösen Ereignissen aus. So diskutierten die Korrespondenten beispielsweise das zwinglianische Abendmahlsverständnis, das Tragen von Kirchengewändern oder die Beschaffenheit liturgischer Gegenstände. Doch auch größere Zusammenhänge fanden Erwähnung, beispielsweise die Vertreibung der Juden aus den böhmischen Ländern.⁴⁴ Oswald Pergener, der wohl wichtigste Zittauer Korrespondent, teilte dabei Briefe und Bücher mit weiteren Glaubensgenossen in der Oberlausitz und Böhmen, sodass man von einer zwinglianischen Glaubensgemeinschaft in Zittau ausgehen kann. Die Zittauer wollten regelmäßig mehr Bücher der Schweizer erhalten, doch logistische Probleme verhinderten dies.⁴⁵ Die Briefe und Bücher wurden auf den Leipziger und Frankfurter Buchmessen ausgetauscht und auch nach Pergeners Tod wurde die Korrespondenz fortgeführt. Nach 1560 sind keine Briefe mehr erhalten und es ist nicht klar, was mit den Zwinglianern geschah. Es gibt aber keine Hinweise, dass sie vertrieben oder verfolgt wurden, vielmehr scheint es, als hätten sie mit den Lutheranern friedlich zusammengelebt, denn Pergener unterhielt auch freundschaftliche und familiäre Verbindungen zu Lutheranern und den Böhmischen Brüdern.⁴⁶

Für die zweite Hälfte des sechzehnten Jahrhunderts lassen sich insgesamt schwieriger Korrespondenznetzwerke finden, weil die Quellenlage kaum stichhaltige Rückschlüsse zulässt. Einige wenige Hinweise lassen sich jedoch ausmachen. Das Kloster der Magdalenerinnen in Lauban unterhielt Verbindun-

---

42. Im Folgenden: *Hrachovec*, „Von feindlichen Ketzern zu Glaubensgenossen und wieder zurück" (wie Anm. 30), 131–156. Vgl. auch, *ders.*, „Reformation der langen Distanz" (wie Anm. 39), 449–510.
43. *Hrachovec*, Zittauer und ihre Kirchen (wie Anm. 25), 351.
44. *Hrachovec*, „Reformation der langen Distanz" (wie Anm. 39), 486–499.
45. *Hrachovec*, „Reformation der langen Distanz" (wie Anm. 39), 449–510.
46. *Hrachovec*, „Von feindlichen Ketzern zu Glaubensgenossen und wieder zurück" (wie Anm. 30), 131–156.

gen zu anderen mitteleuropäischen Klöstern, u. a. in Schlesien, Böhmen und der Niederlausitz.[47] Die Lausitzer Klöster standen aber auch mit lutherischen Stadträten in ständigem Austausch.[48] Die Görlitzer Briefbücher (*Libri Missivarum*), die bisher noch nicht systematisch ausgewertet wurden, geben weitere Indizien. Sie zeigen, dass die Stadträte immer wieder mit Geistlichen korrespondierten, besonders wenn es um die Anstellung von neuen Predigern ging. Ein Brief vom 26. September 1561 beinhaltet beispielsweise eine Einladung für Samuel Jauch aus Lauban, die Frühpredigt in Görlitz zu halten.[49] In einigen Fällen wurden auch Briefe über praktische Belange ausgetauscht. So bat beispielsweise der Zittauer Prediger Martin Hofmann am 11. September 1574 den Görlitzer Stadtrat um einen Aufschub bei der Rückzahlung eines Darlehens.[50] Genauso sind aber Briefe an das Bautzener Domstift erhalten, wie ein Brief vom 11. August 1592 an den Dechant in Bautzen Gregor Leisentrit den Pfarrer Georg Rosenberger betreffend oder ein Schreiben vom 11. März 1603 an den Dechant Christoph Blöbel über einen ausstehenden Dezem für den Schönauer Pfarrer.[51] In den meisten Fällen handelt es sich bei diesen Briefen allerdings eher um Einzelfälle, als um längerfristige Briefwechsel.

Von wichtigen lausitzischen Geistlichen sind kaum Briefe bekannt, die über die Grenzen der Oberlausitz hinausreichten. Wie der oben beschriebene Briefwechsel nach Zürich illustriert, bedeutet dies nicht zwangsläufig, dass ein solcher Briefverkehr nicht existierte, sondern kann auch Überlieferungszufällen geschuldet sein. In einigen Fällen legen Verweise in gedruckten Werken nahe, dass weitere Kontakte zu Lausitzer Geistlichen bestanden.[52] Ob diese allerdings aufgrund persönlicher Treffen, der Zirkulation von Werken Lausitzer Geistlicher oder Briefen zustande kamen, lässt sich oft nicht mehr nachvollziehen.

---

47. *Skobel*, Das Jungfräuliche Klosterstift zur Heiligen Maria Magdalena (wie Anm. 2), 210, 213–214 und 224.
48. Vgl. Stadtarchiv Kamenz, 5613, Wahrnehmung des Patronatsrechtes durch die Äbtissin des Klosters St. Marienstern (1533–1687); *Christ*, Biographies of a Reformation, 103–104.
49. Stadtarchiv/ Ratsarchiv Görlitz, Liber Missivarum 1561–66, folio 77v. Wir danken Steffen Menzel für die Bereitstellung seiner Übersicht der Görlitzer Briefbücher.
50. Stadtarchiv/ Ratsarchiv Görlitz, Liber Missivarum 1574–1576, folio 69r.
51. Stadtarchiv/ Ratsarchiv Görlitz, Liber Missivarum 1591–1595, folio 167 und Liber Missivarum 1603–1605, folio 26.
52. Das von dem Laubaner Pastor Primarius Sigismund Suevus 1578 in Görlitz herausgegebene „Cometen. Was sie für grosse Wunder vnd schreckliche ding zu bedeuten" (VD16 S 4536) beinhaltet beispielsweise auch Texte von Balthasar Dietrich, Paulus Bernavus, Laurentius Ludovicus und Martin Mylius.

Die eingeschränkten Verbindungen der Oberlausitz waren für umfangreiche epistolarische Netzwerke dabei nicht förderlich.[53]

Eine wichtige Ausnahme zur spärlichen Überlieferung von Lausitzer Briefwechseln stellen die Briefe Johann Leisentrits dar, die im Domstiftsarchiv Bautzen erhalten sind. Leisentrit tauschte sich regelmäßig mit Angehörigen beider Konfessionen in den beiden Lausitzen, Böhmen und Schlesien aus.[54] Daneben unterhielt er auch konfessionsübergreifende freundschaftliche Netzwerke, z. B. mit dem Görlitzer Bürgermeister und Astronom Bartholomäus Scultetus (1540–1614).[55] Die Überlieferung beinhaltet 121 Briefe von und an Leisentrit oder das Domstift von 1553 bis 1584. Die Briefe zeigen, dass Leisentrit sich sowohl an katholische Institutionen in der Nähe Bautzens, wie z. B. Klöster und Stifte, als auch an Rezipienten, die in größerer Entfernung residierten, beispielsweise den fürstlichen Rat Johannes Rauchdorn in Bamberg, richtete.[56] Leisentrit stand auch mit päpstlichen Nuntien, besonders in Wien und Prag in Kontakt.[57] Im Fall des zum Katholizismus konvertierten Laubaner Bürgermeisters Scheufler war Leisentrit ebenfalls ein wichtiger Ansprechpartner, was verdeutlicht, dass in der Oberlausitz weiterhin katholische Akteure zur Verfügung standen, was auch zum Fortbestehen des Katholizismus in der Region beitrug.[58] Insgesamt werden aber auch hier besonders die lokalen und regionalen Bezugspunkte deutlich. Die meisten Briefe entfallen auf die Korrespondenz mit dem Bischof von Meißen. In einigen Fällen waren die Briefe noch stärker auf Bautzen zentriert, als etwa der Seiler Michael Karl Leisentrit um ein Darlehen von 30 Talern bat.[59]

---

53. Zu den Problemen der Zittauer ‚Zwinglianer' Briefe und Bücher auszutauschen, vgl. Hrachovec, „Reformation der langen Distanz" (wie Anm. 39), 481–486.

54. Vgl. Domstiftsarchiv Bautzen, Loc. 213, Briefwechsel Johann Leisentritts, 1553–1584. Die Briefe lassen sich anhand der Nummerierung eines beiliegenden Inhaltsverzeichnisses identifizieren.

55. Vgl. *Heinrich Gottlob Gräve*, „M. Bartholomäus Scultetus, Bürgermeister zu Görlitz", in: Neues Lausitzisches Magazin 3 (1824), 455–505; *Joachim Bahlcke*, „Scultetus, Bartholomäus", in Neue Deutsche Biographie 24, Berlin 2010.

56. Domstiftsarchiv Bautzen, Loc. 213, Briefwechsel Johann Leisentritts, 1553–1584, vgl. Briefe 21, 61, 94, 95.

57. Z. B. Domstiftsarchiv Bautzen, Loc. 213, Briefwechsel Johann Leisentritts, 1553–1584, Brief 85.

58. *Zdichynec*, „Konfessionsstreitigkeiten unter dem Mikroskop", in *Hrachovec, Schwerhoff, Müller, Schattkowsky*, Reformation als Kommunikationsprozess (wie Anm. 20), 511–512 und 516–527.

59. Domstiftsarchiv Bautzen, Loc. 213, Briefwechsel Johann Leisentritts, 1553–1584, Brief 52.

Die Korrespondenz mit Leisentrit und seinen Nachfolgern im Amt des apostolischen Administrators zeigt, dass auf Grund der besonderen konfessionellen Lage in der Oberlausitz, Briefwechsel über konfessionelle Grenzen hinweg möglich waren. So konsultierten die lutherisch geprägten Stadträte bei Ehestreitigkeiten und theologischen Fragen zum richtigen Umgang bei fraglichen Eheschließungen das katholische Domstift, wie Briefe der Stadträte der Sechsstädte an die Bautzener Administratoren belegen.[60]

DIE STUDIENORTE DER LAUSITZER GEISTLICHEN

Für die persönlichen Verbindungen der Oberlausitzer Geistlichen lassen die Quellen im Untersuchungszeitraum nicht immer stichhaltige Rückschlüsse zu. Einige der Männer, die als Geistliche in die Oberlausitz kamen, unterhielten weiterhin Verbindungen in ihre Geburtsorte. Allerdings stammten viele Geistliche, besonders diejenigen, die niedriger in der kirchlichen Hierarchie angesiedelt waren, ohnehin aus der Lausitz, wobei einige von ihnen auch in weiter entfernte Schulen, z. B. in Goldberg, gingen und dann in die Oberlausitz zurückkehrten.[61] Viele der Geistlichen besuchten deshalb auch Schulen direkt im Markgraftum, die nach den Idealen Melanchthons reformiert waren.[62]

Wie bereits Norbert Kersken für Oberlausitzer allgemein gezeigt hat, sind die Studienorte Lausitzer Geistlicher hingegen ein aussagekräftiges Indiz für intellektuelle Verbindungen.[63] Die meisten lutherischen Theologen wurden im nahe liegenden Wittenberg ausgebildet, wo einige von ihnen auch Melan-

---

60. *Lars Behrisch*, Protestantische Sittenzucht und katholisches Ehegericht: Die Stadt Görlitz und das Bautzener Domkapitel im 16. Jahrhundert, in: *Vera Isaiasz, Ute Lotz-Heumann, Monika Mommertz, Matthias Pohlig* (Hg.), Stadt und Religion in der frühen Neuzeit. Soziale Ordnungen und ihre Repräsentationen, Frankfurt, New York 2007, 33–66. Siehe auch *Speer*, Strategien des Machterhalts in Zeiten des Umbruchs (wie Anm. 25), 50–54.
61. *Kersken*, „Intellektuelle Raumbeziehungen" (wie Anm. 13), 258.
62. Vgl. *Joachim Bahlcke*, „Das Görlitzer Gymnasium Augustum. Entwicklung, Struktur und regionale Ausstrahlung einer höheren Schule im konfessionellen Zeitalter", in *Bahlcke*, Die Oberlausitz im frühneuzeitlichen Mitteleuropa (wie Anm. 11), 289–310; *Winfried Müller*, „Die Reformation als Impuls für den Strukturwandel im höheren Schulwesen", in *Hrachovec, Schwerhoff, Müller, Schattkowsky*, Reformation als Kommunikationsprozess (wie Anm. 20), 247–259.
63. *Kersken*, „Intellektuelle Raumbeziehungen" (wie Anm. 13), 258–262.

chthon, Luther oder Johannes Bugenhagen persönlich kennenlernten.[64] Daneben gingen einige Geistliche auch an die Universität Frankfurt/Oder.[65] Später im sechzehnten Jahrhundert spielte die Universität Leipzig als Ausbildungsort ebenfalls eine wesentliche Rolle. Die beiden wichtigen Bautzener Prediger Martin Tectander und Friedrich Fischer besuchten beispielsweise die Universität Leipzig.[66] Joachim Pascha, der in Zittau im frühen siebzehnten Jahrhundert *Pastor Primarius* war, besuchte sogar alle drei Universitäten.[67] Dieses Bild deckt sich mit den Befunden, die für die Universitätsbesuche von Oberlausitzern allgemein gemacht wurden. Die drei Universitäten bildeten bis 1650 jeweils über 1.000 Personen aus dem Markgraftum aus.[68]

Auch wenn zum Ende des sechzehnten Jahrhunderts hin viele Oberlausitzer die Universität Leipzig besuchten, spielte Wittenberg nach wie vor die wichtigste Rolle. Diese anhaltende Präferenz ist vermutlich auch ein Grund für die Nähe vieler Lausitzer Theologen zum Philippismus und den damit verbundenen Anschuldigungen des „Kryptocalvinismus" am Ende des sechzehnten und zu Beginn des siebzehnten Jahrhunderts.[69] Solche Anschuldigungen führten letztendlich sogar zu Verhören von Stadträten, Lehrern und Predigern in Bautzen. Die hervorgehobene Stellung Wittenbergs um 1600 ist auch ein Indiz, dass dies mit der Ausbildung an der philippistisch geprägten Leucorea zusammenhing. Seltener kam es vor, dass Männer andere Universitäten als Wittenberg, Leipzig oder Frankfurt/Oder besuchten. Ein solches Beispiel ist Martin Behm, der in Wien und Straßburg ausgebildet wurde.[70]

Normalerweise gingen die aus der Oberlausitz stammenden Geistlichen zurück in das Markgraftum und nahmen dort eine Position als Prediger oder

---

64. Vor der Gründung Wittenbergs wurden zunächst Prag und ab 1410 Leipzig von den Theologiestudenten präferiert. *Kersken*, „Intellektuelle Raumbeziehungen", (wie Anm. 13) 256–288. In Zittau waren diese Tendenzen insgesamt weniger ausgeprägt, vgl. *Hrachovec*, Zittauer und ihre Kirchen (wie Anm. 25), 375–376.

65. Vgl. *Michael Höhle*, Universität und Reformation. Die Universität Frankfurt (Oder) von 1506 bis 1550. Köln, Weimar, Wien 2002; *Paul Pfotenhauer*, „Sechsstädter auf der Universität Frankfurt a. O. in der Zeit von 1506–1606", in: Neues Lausitzisches Magazin 62 (1886), 181–205.

66. *Karl Gottlob Dietmann*, Die gesamte der ungeänderten Augsb. Confeßion zugethane Priesterschaft in dem Marggrafthum Oberlausitz, Lauban, Leipzig 1777, 33–36.

67. *Dietmann*, Augsb. Confeßion (wie Anm. 66), 342–343.

68. *Kersken*, „Intellektuelle Raumbeziehungen" (wie Anm. 13), 260.

69. *Christian Adolph Pescheck*, „Zur Geschichte des Krypto-Calvinismus in der Lausitz", in: Neues Lausitzisches Magazin 22 (1844), 353–378; *Christ*, Biographies of a Reformation (wie Anm. 27), 181–189.

70. *Dietmann*, Augsb. Confeßion (wie Anm. 66), 505–518.

Lehrer an.⁷¹ Wie auch bei den Briefwechseln lässt sich damit auch hier ein starker regionaler Fokus konstatieren. Seltener gingen die Oberlausitzer nicht mehr in ihre Heimat zurück und wurden anderswo als Geistliche angestellt. Schlesien, besonders Breslau, Liegnitz, Löwenberg und Schweidnitz, spielten als Zielorte einiger Oberlausitzer eine hervorgehobene Rolle. Daneben blieben einige Oberlausitzer auch als Geistliche in Sachsen, besonders nachdem sie in Leipzig oder Wittenberg ausgebildet wurden. Außerdem war auch die Niederlausitz ein wichtiges Ziel für Oberlausitzer Geistliche. So gingen Joachim Hosemann aus Lauban und Daniel Römer aus Bautzen nach Lübben oder Urban Schmolke aus Bautzen nach Sorau.⁷² Dabei lässt sich auch immer wieder feststellen, dass die geographische Nähe eine wichtige Rolle spielte und beispielsweise Personen aus Lauban besonders häufig in das nahe gelegene Löwenberg gingen.⁷³ Wechsel nach Böhmen beschränkten sich normalerweise auf die nordböhmische Grenzregion und den Zeitraum 1550 bis 1620.⁷⁴ In Einzelfällen zog es Oberlausitzer auch in andere Städte. Matthias Zeidler aus Kamenz wurde nach seiner Ausbildung in Jena Pfarrer in Sörnewitz bei Meißen, der Görlitzer Pastor Primarius Othmar Epplin ging nach Frankfurt/Oder und Johannes Schmidt aus Bautzen wurde zwar in Wittenberg ausgebildet, wurde dann aber Theologieprofessor an der Universität von Straßburg.⁷⁵

Der Universitätsbesuch war allerdings nicht in allen Fällen eine Voraussetzung für die Anstellung als Geistlicher. Besonders verbreitet war dies bei Sorben, die wegen ihrer sprachlichen Kenntnisse eingestellt wurden.⁷⁶ Einige von ihnen wurden von Luther oder Melanchthon selber ordiniert. Auch für die Sorben war Wittenberg als Ausbildungsort von besonderer Wichtigkeit und die meisten sorbischen, evangelischen Prediger wurden dort ausgebildet.⁷⁷ Wesentlich seltener war es für deutschsprachige Geistliche, die keine Universität besucht hatten, als Prediger angestellt zu werden. Das bedeutendste Beispiel hierfür ist der wichtige Lieddichter und Pastoraltheologe Martin Moller, der

---

71. *Kersken*, „Intellektuelle Raumbeziehungen der Oberlausitz" (wie Anm. 13), 263.
72. *Kersken*, „Intellektuelle Raumbeziehungen der Oberlausitz" (wie Anm. 13), 274.
73. *Kersken*, „Intellektuelle Raumbeziehungen der Oberlausitz" (wie Anm. 13), 273.
74. *Kersken*, „Intellektuelle Raumbeziehungen der Oberlausitz" (wie Anm. 13), 274.
75. *Kersken*, „Intellektuelle Raumbeziehungen der Oberlausitz" (wie Anm. 13), 266–268.
76. *Friedrich Pollack*, Kirche – Sprache – Nation. Eine Kollektivbiografie der sorbischen evangelischen Geistlichkeit in der frühneuzeitlichen Oberlausitz, Bautzen 2018; vgl. auch *Peter Kunze*, „Geschichte und Kultur der Sorben in der Oberlausitz. Ein kulturgeschichtlicher Abriß", in: *Bahlcke*, Geschichte der Oberlausitz (wie Anm. 11), 267–316, hier 278–287.
77. *Kunze*, „Geschichte und Kultur der Sorben in der Oberlausitz" (wie Anm. 76), hier 204.

von 1600 bis 1606 *Pastor Primarius* in Görlitz war.[78] Da im Laufe des sechzehnten Jahrhunderts allerdings die Ausbildung der Geistlichen kontinuierlich verbessert wurde, waren solche Fälle bereits im siebzehnten Jahrhundert eine Ausnahme.

Die Ausbildung der Oberlausitzer Geistlichen war stark konfessionell geprägt; protestantische Geistliche besuchten z. B. auch die Straßburger Universität nach ihrer Gründung 1621, während altgläubige Geistliche traditionell katholische Universitäten besuchten.[79] Im früheren sechzehnten Jahrhundert besuchten die Domdekane meistens die Universität in Leipzig.[80] Besonders reichhaltig ist die Überlieferung einmal mehr für den Bautzener Domdekan Johann Leisentrit, den ersten apostolischen Administrator der Lausitz. Er wurde 1527 in Olmütz als Handwerkersohn geboren.[81] Danach studierte er wahrscheinlich in Krakau und 1549 erhielt er seine Priesterweihe. Nach einem Aufenthalt in Prag kam er 1551 als Kanoniker nach Bautzen. 1559 wurde er zum Dekan ernannt und schließlich 1560 zum apostolischen Administrator erhoben. Er starb 1586 in Bautzen. Leisentrits Ausbildung in Krakau stellt dabei eine Besonderheit dar, auch wenn sie zu der generellen Auswahl traditionellkatholischer Ausbildungsorte passt. Gleichzeitig ist Leisentrit ein besonders gutes Beispiel für die Akzeptanz lutherischer Positionen durch einen Katholiken. So beinhaltet sein Gesangbuch Lieder von Luther, er verwendete deutsche Einsetzungsworte bei der Kommunion und viele seiner Werke beinhalteten nur wenige Verweise auf Heilige.[82]

In einigen Fällen studierten die katholischen Geistlichen auch an Universitäten, die weiter entfernt waren. Der Kanoniker Johannes Cyrus erwarb in Padua den Grad des Doktors beider Rechte und wurde 1551 Kanoniker in Bautzen, war allerdings nicht in Bautzen präsent.[83] Zwei weitere Bautzener Kanoniker studierten an derselben Universität.[84] Allerdings lassen sich hier,

---

78. *Elke Axmacher*, Praxis Evangeliorum. Theologie und Frömmigkeit bei Martin Moller (1547–1606), Göttingen 1989.

79. *Kersken*, „Intellektuelle Raumbeziehungen der Oberlausitz" (wie Anm. 13), 262.

80. Vgl. *Kinne*, Die Bistümer der Kirchenprovinz Magdeburg (wie Anm. 2), 834–839.

81. Zur Biographie Leisentrits, siehe *Siegfried Seifert*, Johann Leisentrit 1527–1586. Zum vierhundertsten Todestag, Leipzig 1987; *Walter Gerblich*, Johann Leisentrit und die Administratur des Bistums Meißen in den Lausitzen, Leipzig 1959; *Josef Gülden*, Johann Leisentrits Pastoralliturgische Schriften, Leipzig 1963.

82. Vgl. *Christ*, Biographies of a Reformation (wie Anm. 27), 115–152.

83. *Kinne*, Die Bistümer der Kirchenprovinz Magdeburg (wie Anm. 2), 1003–1004.

84. Heinrich Reibisch und Georg von Logau. Vgl. *Kinne*, Die Bistümer der Kirchenprovinz Magdeburg (wie Anm. 2), 995–997.

aufgrund der insgesamt kleineren Anzahl an katholischen Geistlichen, in erster Linie nur Einzelbefunde machen.

Eine Betrachtung der Studienorte von katholischen und lutherischen Geistlichen zeigt deutlich, wie stark sich die beiden Konfessionen in ihrer Universitätswahl unterschieden. Gerade in konfessionell gemischten Gebieten gab es somit Grenzen, die Angehörige einer bestimmten Religion nicht gewillt waren zu überschreiten. Die universitäre Ausbildung war zweifelsfrei eine davon. Aber sogar bei der klar konfessionell geprägten Wahl der Universitäten gab es interessante Ausnahmen. Der oben erwähnte Oswald Pergener, der sich eher zur schweizerischen Reformation hin orientierte, empfahl seinem Schwager 1542 an der Universität von Wittenberg zu studieren.[85] Allgemein zeigt die eingangs diskutierte Durchmischung konfessioneller Praktiken, dass die insgesamt klar getrennte Ausbildung nicht bedeutet hat, dass die Theologie und der tägliche Umgang monokonfessionell geprägt sein mussten.

DER BUCHDRUCK ALS ZEUGNIS FÜR KULTURBEZIEHUNGEN

Da der Buchdruck während der Reformationszeit eine wichtige Rolle für beide Konfessionen spielte, ist ein Blick auf die Druckstädte bzw. auf die Drucker, die in der Oberlausitz agierten, besonders ergiebig. Das Potenzial des Buchdrucks ist hinreichend bekannt, besonders in Bezug auf seine Schnelligkeit: vor allem kleinere Werke, die nur einige Seiten beinhalteten, konnten innerhalb von wenigen Stunden produziert und noch am Herstellungstag genutzt werden. So verfasste Melanchthon, zum Beispiel, am 13. April 1560 eine Universitätsschrift, die im Rahmen des Osterfestes öffentlich ausgehangen werden sollte. Dazu brachte er sie morgens zum Drucker, korrigierte den Probedruck nach dem Gottesdienst und erhielt bereits am Nachmittag um 14 Uhr die fertigen Exemplare.[86] Diese konnten daraufhin zeitnah in der Stadt verteilt und auch an Auswärtige versendet werden, was zusätzlich durch den voranschreitenden Ausbau der Kommunikations-Infrastruktur im Reich – allen voran der Post – beschleunigt wurde.[87] Diese bis dahin unerreichte Geschwindigkeit der Produktion und der Verbreitung machten sich Oberlausitzer Geistliche zunehmend im Verlauf des 16. und 17. Jahrhunderts zunutze.

---

85. *Hrachovec*, Zittauer und ihre Kirchen (wie Anm. 25), 360.
86. *Christiane Domtera-Schleichardt*, Die Wittenberger „Scripta Publice Proposita" (1540–1569). Universitätsbekanntmachungen im Umfeld des späten Melanchthons, Leipzig 2021, 37, mit dem lateinischen Zitat der Originalquelle.
87. *Behringer*, Reichspost und Kommunikationsrevolution (wie Anm. 3).

Die rasche geographische Ausbreitung der neuen Technologie ist ebenfalls weitestgehend bekannt. Bereits im 15. Jahrhundert fasste der Buchdruck in zahlreichen Städten Fuß, vor allem die traditionellen Handelszentren Köln, Nürnberg und Augsburg wurden zu wichtigen Druckzentren. Einer der ersten Druckorte nahe der Oberlausitz war Leipzig, wo bereits seit Mitte der 1480er Jahre gedruckte Werke hergestellt wurden. Die Stadt etablierte sich nach und nach zu einem weiteren Druckzentrum, welches um 1500 bereits vier verschiedene Druckoffizine beherbergte.[88] Etwa zur gleichen Zeit wurde in Magdeburg und später auch in Dresden begonnen, Bücher durch den Druck zu vervielfältigen.

Doch nach einem anfänglichen Druck-Boom, vor allem in den ersten beiden Jahrzehnten des 16. Jahrhunderts, wurde es nach 1530 deutlich schwieriger Druckereien in weniger zentralen Orten einzurichten bzw. diese länger zu betreiben.[89] Es gibt zahlreiche Beispiele von Ortschaften, in denen Buchdrucker gezwungen waren nach einigen unproduktiven Jahren ihre Offizin aufzugeben. So auch in der Oberlausitz, in der die erste Druckwerkstatt erst Mitte des 16. Jahrhunderts eröffnet wurde.[90] Der erste Drucker war 1545 in Görlitz tätig, doch er produzierte nur wenig: Das Verzeichnis der im deutschen Sprachbereich erschienenen Drucke des 16. Jahrhunderts (VD 16) beinhaltet nur zwei kleine Oktavbände für seine Görlitzer Offizin.[91] Schließlich verließ der Drucker die Stadt nach nur wenigen Jahren wieder. Kurz danach wurde in Bautzen eine Offizin eröffnet, jedoch gab es auch hier Schwierigkeiten, wie wir noch sehen werden. In den anderen Sechsstädten fand der Buchdruck erst deutlich später Einzug. In Zittau wurde 1586 eine Offizin eröffnet, die sich allerdings nur zwei Jahre halten konnte. Erst ab 1610 fand sich hier durchgehend ein Buchdrucker und in Lauban wurde sogar erst ab 1661 eine Druckerei betrieben.

Die Gründe hierfür sind in den ökonomischen Bedingungen des Handwerkes zu sehen. Schließlich verlangte die Drucklegung von Büchern enormes

---

88. *Christoph Reske*, Die Buchdrucker des 16. und 17. Jahrhunderts im deutschen Sprachgebiet: Auf der Grundlage des gleichnamigen Werkes von Josef Benzing, Wiesbaden 2015, 514–517.

89. *Thomas Kaufmann*, Die Mitte der Reformation. Eine Studie zu Buchdruck und Publizistik im deutschen Sprachgebiet, zu ihren Akteuren und deren Strategien, Inszenierungs- und Ausdrucksformen, Tübingen 2019, 447.

90. Vgl. *Hagen Schulz*, „„Gedruckt zu Budissin sonst Bautzen genant/In der Hauptstadt des Marggraffenthumbs Ober Laußnitz'. Leben und Werk des Buchdruckers Michael Wolrab", in: Jahresschrift – Stadtmuseum Bautzen 7 (2001), 115–184.

91. VD16 M 435, VD16 ZV 11458.

Startkapital, welches für die Maschinerie, die Ausstattung, die Arbeiter und die Miete aufgebracht werden musste. Des Weiteren benötigten die Drucker Farbe, Transportmöglichkeiten und selbstverständlich Papier, welches häufig den größten Kostenfaktor bei der Druckherstellung von Büchern in der Frühen Neuzeit darstellte. Dadurch waren die Drucker mit hohen laufenden Kosten konfrontiert, die sie allerdings erst nach Fertigstellung der kompletten Auflage decken konnten. Diese Fertigstellung der meist mehreren hundert, zum Teil auch Tausenden, Exemplaren einer Auflage konnte jedoch unter Umständen Monate in Anspruch nehmen.

Für Buchdrucker war die Oberlausitz als Produktionsstandort eher unattraktiv, da sie von bereits etablierten Zentren umgeben war. Somit waren die Oberlausitzer Autoren, die ihre Werke in den Druck geben wollten, zunächst auf diese auswärtigen Druckzentren angewiesen. Dabei hatten sie mehrere Städte in ihrer unmittelbaren Nähe zur Auswahl, wie zum Beispiel das rasch wachsende Druckzentrum Wittenberg. Obwohl der Ort weder zu den größten Handelszentren im Reich gehörte, noch ein Hauptverkehrsplatz für Händler darstellte, konnte er sich dennoch als eines der führenden Zentren für die Publikation von gedruckten Büchern etablieren. Grund dafür war die Präsenz Luthers und seiner Anhänger, die eine immer größer werdende Anzahl von Schriften veröffentlichten.[92] Auch Melanchthon hatte gute Beziehungen zu den vielen Buchdruckern und Verlegern in Wittenberg, was unter anderem auch dazu führte, dass dem Reformator zahlreiche Manuskripte von Autoren aus dem Umland zugeschickt wurden, mit der Bitte für diese einen geeigneten Drucker in Wittenberg (aber auch in anderen Druckzentren) zu finden.[93] Diese Bitten rührten sicherlich auch von der verbreiteten Kenntnis her, dass Wittenberger Drucke erstaunlich hohe Auflagen erreichen und einen reißenden Absatz finden konnten: Wenn wir Melanchthons Äußerung in seinem Brief

---

92. Vgl. *Andrew Pettegree*, Brand Luther: How an Unheralded Monk Turned His Small Town into a Center of Publishing, Made Himself the Most Famous Man in Europe – and Started the Protestant Reformation, New York 2015, hier 143–167; zu Luthers Nutzung des Buchdrucks, siehe auch *Lyndal Roper*, Martin Luther. Renegade and Prophet, London 2016, 156–160, und jüngst *Thomas Kaufmann*, „Buchdruck und Reformation. Buchkulturgeschichtliche Beobachtungen, insbesondere zu Innovationen in der Wittenberger Produktion der Jahre 1517 und 1520", in: *Hrachovec, Schwerhoff, Müller, Schattkowsky*, Reformation als Kommunikationsprozess (wie Anm. 20), der Luther treffend als „printing native" bezeichnet.

93. *Saskia Limbach*, „Scholars, Printers and the Sphere: New Evidence for the Challenging Production of Academic Books in Wittenberg, 1531–1550", in: *Matteo Valleriani, Andrea Ottone* (Hg.), The Sphere. Knowledge System Evolution and the Shared Scientific Identity of Europe, Cham, 2022, 147–185.

vom 18. Oktober 1547 Glauben schenken dürfen, dann waren die 3.000 Exemplare seiner Dialektik in nur 6 ½ Wochen ausverkauft.[94]

Die Wittenberger Drucker waren nicht nur besonders schnell – sie waren auch zahlreich: Zeitweise arbeiteten bis zu 12 Offizine gleichzeitig.[95] Obwohl freilich auch hier einige Schriften erfolglos den Druckern angeboten wurden, konnte sich Wittenberg mit dieser hohen Zahl an Druckwerkstätten durchaus mit den größten Zentren der Buchproduktion im Reich Köln, Nürnberg und Augsburg messen.[96]

Viele Lausitzer Theologen nutzten die gut ausgeprägte Buchdruckindustrie Wittenbergs. Sigismund Suevus, der 1566 in Lauban angestellt wurde, ließ seine *Computua Ecclesiasticus* in Wittenberg drucken.[97] Allerdings erschienen seine Werke nicht nur in Wittenberg, sondern auch in Breslau, Eisleben, Leipzig, Görlitz, Frankfurt/Oder und Freiberg.[98] Dieser häufige Ortswechsel bei den Druck-Erzeugnissen hängt vermutlich einerseits mit der Tatsache zusammen, dass Suevus selbst oft seine Stellen wechseln musste, andererseits könnte es auch damit zu erklären sein, dass seine Schriften nicht immer direkt von einem Drucker angenommen wurden und er somit gezwungen war, einen neuen zu finden. Auch etliche Schriften von Johann Agricola, der ab 1577 als Prediger in Bautzen arbeitete, wurden in Wittenberg gedruckt. Der evangelische Theologe hatte selbst an der dortigen Universität studiert, wo er von seinen Kommilitonen und Kollegen auch „deutscher Poet" genannt wurde, weil er seine Werke zum Teil in Reimen verfasste, um den Text einprägsamer zu machen. So enthält eines seiner Werke den Zusatz, dass er es durch die Verwendung der Reime den „Leien und Einfältigen" zugänglich machen wolle.[99]

Obwohl die Wittenberger Drucker häufig die Werke der dortigen Reformatoren herstellten, war die Stadt als Druckzentrum so bedeutend, dass es auch Katholiken möglich war, dort zu publizieren. Christoph von Haugwitz ließ so

---

94. Philipp Melanchthon: Briefwechsel. Kritische und kommentierte Gesamtausgabe, Regesten, 16 Bde., Stuttgart, Bad Cannstatt 1977 f., 4875, online: https://www.hadw-bw.de/forschung/forschungsstelle/melanchthon-briefwechsel-mbw (Zugriffsdatum: 14.06.2022).

95. *Hans E. Braun*, „Von der Handschrift zum gedruckten Buch", in: *Michael Stolz, Adrian Mettauer* (Hg.), Buchkultur im Mittelalter. Schrift – Bild – Kommunikation, Berlin 2005, 239.

96. *Limbach*, „Scholars, Printers and the Sphere" (wie Anm. 93).

97. *Sigismund Suevus*, Computua Ecclesiasticus. Gewisse Kirchenrechnung. Aus den Schrifften der Heiligen Propheten vnd Apostel, Wittenberg 1574 (VD16 S 4527).

98. Siehe die Einträge für *Sigismund Suevus* im VD16.

99. *Johann Agricola*, Die zwelff Artickel vnsers Christlichen glaubens, Wittenberg 1564 (VD16 A 1043).

zum Beispiel 1536 eine Schrift in Wittenberg drucken.[100] Dies stellte für Katholiken jedoch einige der wenigen Ausnahmen dar, denn Wittenberg wurde bereits seit der frühen Reformation stark mit der Person Luthers assoziiert.[101] Allerdings waren in dieser Frühphase der Reformation auch die Konfessionen noch nicht vollständig als solche erkennbar, was Austauschprozesse erleichterte.

Im Verlauf des 16. Jahrhunderts wurde es jedoch zunehmend schwieriger für katholische Autoren aus dem Sechsstädtebund ihre Schriften durch den Druck zu vervielfältigen. Dies lässt sich zunächst auf die prominente Stellung Wittenbergs und die u. a. auch daraus resultierenden unattraktiven Voraussetzungen für das Druckhandwerk in der Oberlausitz zurückführen. Ein weiteres Hindernis war die fehlende Patronage. Während manche, v. a. reformatorisch gesinnten, Obrigkeiten zunehmend den Buchdruck nutzten und nicht nur Verlautbarungen und Ordnungen herstellen ließen, sondern zum Teil sogar die Drucklegung von theologischen Werken, Streitschriften und Gebeten gänzlich finanzierten, war dies in der Oberlausitz nicht der Fall.[102] Die Katholiken wurden in Bezug auf die Drucklegung ihrer Werke nicht durch ihren gleichgesinnten Landesherren, den böhmischen König, unterstützt, weder durch finanzielle Zuwendungen noch durch die Einrichtung einer Druckerei. Auch wurde den Altgläubigen in der Oberlausitz nicht die Unterstützung katholischer Orden, wie den Jesuiten, zuteil, die in anderen Regionen stark mit den Buchdruckern vor Ort zusammenarbeiteten oder zumindest ein Augenmerk auf die Buchproduktion gerichtet hatten.[103] In Posen bewirkten die Jesuiten zum Beispiel, dass die einzige Druckerei geschlossen wurde, nachdem sich der Drucker nicht an das Verbot der Herstellung protestantischer Schriften gehalten hatte. In der Oberlausitz siedelten sich die Jesuiten zwar 1556 in dem ehemaligen Cölestinerkloster auf dem Berg Oybin in der Nähe von Zittau an, doch gaben sie bereits nach kurzer Zeit im Jahr 1563 ihren Sitz wieder auf,

---

100. *Johann von Haugwitz*, Woher Thumherrn Canonici heissen Vnd was jr vnd etlicher anderer jrer Thumpfaffen vrsprüngliche Empter gewesen sind, Wittenberg 1536 (VD16 H 786).

101. *Pettegree*, Brand Luther (wie Anm. 92), 143–167.

102. Zum Vergleich, siehe *Saskia Limbach*, „Life and Production of Magdalena Morhart. A Successful Business Woman in Sixteenth-Century Germany", in: Gutenberg-Jahrbuch 94 (2019), 151–172, in dem die Werke und Auflagenhöhen, die vom württembergischen Herzog zwischen 1554–1572 in Auftrag gegeben und durch den Kirchenkasten bezahlt wurden, aufgeschlüsselt werden.

103. So zum Beispiel in Köln, wo die Jesuiten mit dem Buchdrucker Maternus Cholinus arbeiteten, siehe *Wolfgang Schmitz*, Die Überlieferung deutscher Texte im Kölner Buchdruck des 15. und 16. Jahrhunderts, Köln 1990, 148.

weil ihnen die Oberlausitz zu abgelegen war.[104] Dadurch konnten sie in der Oberlausitz weder die Drucklegung überblicken noch finanzieren.

Die fehlende Unterstützung von institutioneller Seite isolierte die katholischen Autoren in der Oberlausitz, wodurch sie gezwungen waren, selbstständig die Drucklegung ihrer Bücher voranzutreiben. Ein Vertragsentwurf zwischen Johan Leisentrit und dem Drucker Michael Wolrab vom 14. August 1574 veranschaulicht dies in außergewöhnlich detaillierter Form.[105] Im Entwurf werden die Modalitäten der Publikation, welche in 500 Exemplaren erscheinen und vom Autor komplett bezahlt werden sollte, dezidiert beschlossen und auch offene Posten aus vorherigen Kooperationen verrechnet.[106] Offensichtlich schuldete die Offizin dem Domdechanten noch etliche Gulden, unter anderem weil Leisentrit selbst im Vorfeld zwei Ballen Papier in die Druckerei hatte liefern lassen, wodurch sich die Gesamtsumme des Vertrages neu errechnete und der Drucker Leisentrit versprach, zusätzlich einhundert Exemplare kostenfrei herzustellen. Die Kosten für die Drucklegung seiner Werke werden von Leisentrit auch im Vorwort zum 2. Teil seines Gesangbuches thematisiert, welches insgesamt über 900 Seiten zählt und zahlreiche Illustrationen beinhaltet.[107] Darin bemerkt der Geistliche, dass er „mit gar grosser müh, arbeit, und unkosten, das Deutsche Gesangbuch de tempore zusammen bracht, und durch den druck zu tag kommen lassen [hat]". Obwohl Autoren zu dieser Zeit des Öfteren ihre Arbeitsmühen in den Vorworten ihrer Werke betonten, handelte es sich hier nicht um einen bloßen Topos. Das Werk ist dem Erzbischof von Prag gewidmet und wird aller Wahrscheinlichkeit nach ein kluger Schachzug Leisentrits gewesen sein, eine finanzielle Entlohnung, wenn auch nur teilweise, durch den Erzbischof zu erlangen. Interessanterweise wurden Auszüge aus Leisentrits *Geistliche Lieder* 1576 dank der Bestrebungen des Bambergers Bischof

---

104. *Hrachovec*, Zittauer und ihre Kirchen (wie Anm. 25), 495–516. Siehe auch *ders.*, „Der Untergang des Oybiner Cölestinerklosters während der Reformation", in: Neues Archiv für sächsische Geschichte 88 (2017), 3–53.

105. *Schulz*, „Leben und Werk des Buchdruckers Michael Wolrab" (wie Anm. 90), 121.

106. *Schulz*, „Leben und Werk des Buchdruckers Michael Wolrab" (wie Anm. 90), 128 ff., enthält eine Transkription des Vertrages. Allerdings handelt es sich hier um ein Werk (Kurze Fragstücke) welches letztendlich in Köln gedruckt wurde (VD16 L 1068), da sich der Autor wohl nicht mit dem Bautzener Drucker einig werden konnte.

107. *Johann Leisentritt*, Geistliche Lieder vnd Psalmen/ der alten Apostolischer recht vnd warglaubiger Christlicher Kirchen, Bautzen 1567 (VD16 L 1061); zum Gesangbuch, siehe *Erika Heitmayer*, Das Gesangbuch von Johann Leisentrit 1567. Adaption als Merkmal von Struktur und Genese früher deutscher Gesangbuchlieder, St. Ottilien 1988; *Erika Heitmayer*, *Richard Wetzel*, Johann Leisentrits Geistliche Lieder und Psalmen, 1567. Hymnody of the Counter-Reformation in Germany, Madison 2013.

in Dillingen nachgedruckt.[108] Dies verdeutlicht, wie wichtig gedruckte Werke für die Herausbildung von Netzwerken sein konnten. Die herausragende Bedeutung des Gesangbuches für das Bamberger Bistum zeigt sich anhand der Tatsache, dass der Bischof in einer Proklamation seine Untertanen daran erinnerte, nur solche Weihnachtslieder zu singen, welche aus dem Auszug des Leisentritschen Gesangbuches stammten. Bemerkenswert ist dabei, dass die Liste der erlaubten Lieder auch Luthers „Vom Himmel Hoch da Komm ich her" beinhaltete, da Leisentrits Gesangbuch Lieder beider Konfessionen enthielt.[109]

Zusätzlich zu den Kosten für die Druckproduktion, die altgläubige Geistliche aufgrund der fehlenden Patronage selbst tragen mussten, war zudem auch noch mit Transportkosten sowie Zeitverzug zu rechnen, die je nach Druckort und Umfang des Druckes erheblich sein konnten. Anhand des o. g. Buches lässt sich veranschaulichen, wie viel Papier für die gesamte Auflage eines einzigen Buches benötigt wurde. Die *Geistlichen Lieder* erschienen zwar als kleiner Oktavband allerdings bedeuteten die über 900 Seiten, dass die Produktion nur eines einzigen Exemplars 59 Bögen Papier umfasste.[110] Wenn hier ebenfalls eine Auflage von 500 Exemplaren produziert wurde, erforderte dies folglich über 29.500 Bögen Papier. Der Transport konnte Tage, wenn nicht Wochen, in Anspruch nehmen: Die Papierbögen wurden häufig in großen hölzernen Bottichen verpackt, um sie so gegen Wind und Wetter zu schützen.[111] Allerdings waren sie dadurch auch sperrig und mussten – auf einen Wagen gespannt – langsam kutschiert werden. Durch diese Umstände akkumulierten sich beachtliche Kosten. Hinzu kommt, dass ganz wie bei Melanchthons Druck, das Buch zunächst als Probedruck erscheinen und korrigiert werden musste. Die Abstimmungswege zwischen den Autoren in der Oberlausitz und den Druckern in den zum Teil weit entfernten Städten nahmen somit weiteres Geld und Zeit in Anspruch.

Die Drucklegung der Werke, die in der Oberlausitz verfasst wurden, wurde zum Teil erheblich beschleunigt, als in dem Markgrafum die ersten Druck-

---

108. *Dieter J. Weiss*, Das exemte Bistum Bamberg 3. Die Bischofsreihe von 1522 bis 1693, Berlin, New York 2000, 191; *Christ*, Biographies of a Reformation, 104.

109. Staatsarchiv Bamberg, Bamberger Verordnungen, B 26 c 1V, 120v–122v. Vgl. auch *Heitmeyer, Wetzel*, Johann Leisentrits Geistliche Lieder und Psalmen (wie Anm. 107).

110. Zu der Berechnung von den benötigen Papierbögen, siehe *Jean-Francois Gilmont*, „Printing at the Dawn of the Sixteenth Century" (übersetzt von Karin Maag), in: *Jean-Francois Gilmont* (Hg.), The Reformation and the Book, Aldershot 1998, 17.

111. Siehe hierzu zum Beispiel die Abbildung in den Hausbüchern der Nürnberger Zwölfbrüderstiftung, https://hausbuecher.nuernberg.de/75-Amb-2-279-31-v (Zugriffsdatum: 14.06.2022).

werkstätten eröffnet wurden. Doch, wie bereits oben erwähnt, gab es zunächst Schwierigkeiten. Erst im Jahre 1545 wurde die erste Offizin in Görlitz eingerichtet und von Crispin Scharffenberg betrieben, der das Druckerhandwerk zuvor in Krakau gelernt hatte.[112] Er war 1543 nach Görlitz gekommen und hatte zwei Jahre später das Bürgerrecht erworben. Als ersten Druck publiziert er *Ein schön geistlich lied, der new lentz genant*.[113] Das Werk erschien ohne Angaben zum Autor, der im Buch nur als ein frommer und gottesfürchtiger Pfarrer in Schlesien bezeichnet wird. Allerdings scheint die Dominanz der Zentren Wittenberg und Leipzig zu groß gewesen zu sein, denn Crispin Scharffenberg verließ Görlitz bereits nach ein paar unproduktiven Jahren.[114] Somit war die Oberlausitz wieder ohne einen Drucker und auf die Drucklegung von Werken in umliegenden Städten angewiesen. Die Dominanz der Druckzentren in der Nähe der Oberlausitz war damit nicht immer der Verbreitung von Schriften auf einem lokalen Level zuträglich, weil regional tätige Prediger in dieser Frühphase der Reformation mehr Kosten und logistischen Aufwand hatten, als dies der Fall gewesen wäre, wenn es eine Offizin in der Oberlausitz gegeben hätte. Damit kann das Fehlen einer Oberlausitzer Offizin während dieser Zeit auch als ein Grund für die unvollständige Durchsetzung der Reformation angesehen werden.[115]

Mehr Erfolg hatte der Betreiber der zweiten Druckerei in der Oberlausitz, die drei Jahre nach Scharffenbergs Verlassen im Markgraftum eingerichtet wurde. Der aus Leipzig kommende Nikolas Wolrab ließ sich 1554 in Bautzen nieder, wo bereits seit den frühen 1550er Jahren sein Sohn Johannes als Buchhändler und Verleger tätig war.[116] Über seine religiöse Gesinnung können wir nur spekulieren, denn zunächst hatte Wolrab in Leipzig eng mit dem altgläubigen Theologen Johann Cochläus zusammengearbeitet, der die Offizin

---

112. *Reske*, Die Buchdrucker (wie Anm. 88), 322.
113. *Anonym*, Ein schön geistlich lied, der new lentz genant, so man auff die Osterliche zeit pfleget zu singenn, Görlitz 1545 (VD16 ZV 11458).
114. Vgl. auch *Gustav Köhler*, Zur Geschichte der Buchdruckerei in Görlitz. Eine Festschrift, Görlitz 1840.
115. Jens Bulisch spricht in diesem Zusammenhang von einer „gebremsten Reformation". Siehe *Bulisch*, Die gebremste Reformation, in: *Dannenberg, Scholze*, Stätten und Stationen religiösen Wirkens (wie Anm. 28), 253–267.
116. *Mark Lehmstedt*, Buchstadt Leipzig. Biographisches Lexikon des Leipziger Buchgewerbes. Bd. 1 (1420–1538), Leipzig 2019, 211; Reske sieht VD16 ZV 24099 nur als Verlagswerk, also ein von Johannes Wolrab finanziertes, jedoch nicht von ihm gedrucktes Werk *Reske*, Die Buchdrucker (wie Anm. 88), 102; zu Wolrab vgl. auch *Christian Knauthe*, Annales typographici Lusatiae superioris oder Geschichte der Ober-Lausitzischen Buchdruckereyen, Lauban 1740, 1–9.

auch finanziell unterstützte. Doch später produzierte Wolrab auch lutherische Schriften. Es ist daher anzunehmen, dass er – wie so viele Handwerker und Künstler seiner Zeit – seine religiöse Überzeugung dem Verdienst unterordnete und vornehmlich die Bücher druckte, die den Erhalt seiner Druckerei sicherten.[117]

In der nun eröffneten Druckerei in Bautzen erschien Leisentrits umfangreiches Werk *Christianae adeoque piae precationes ex orthodoxae & catholicae ecclesiae doctoribus*, welches über 200 Seiten umfasst.[118] Die Zusammenarbeit des Geistlichen mit den Handwerkern führte nicht nur zu der Vervielfältigung seiner eigenen Werke, sondern auch zu der seiner Schüler. So erschien 1559 ein Werk des Johannes Lactantius Codicus.[119] Im selben Jahr verstarb Nikolas Wohlrab und sein Sohn Johannes übernahm die Leitung der Offizin. Als Johannes Wolrab später finanzielle Schwierigkeiten hatte, half Leisentrit ihm sogar und ermöglichte ihm seine Offizin in einem der Kapitelhäuser unterzubringen.[120]

Allerdings reichten die Aufträge des katholischen Geistlichen und seiner Schüler auf Dauer nicht aus, um eine Offizin in der Hauptstadt der Oberlausitz zu führen und sich gegen die Konkurrenz in anderen Städten zu behaupten. Es ist möglich, dass zudem der Stadtrat von Bautzen im Jahre 1575 die Drucklegung von katholischen Büchern sogar verboten hat, jedoch ist dies nicht sicher überliefert.[121] Somit verlor Michael Wolrab, der die Offizin in dritter Generation weiterführte, vielleicht auch noch diese wenigen Aufträge, sodass seine Produktion 1576 einbrach.[122] Erschwerend kam hinzu, dass seit

---

117. Auch im Bezug auf andere Drucker lässt sich diese Priorisierung beobachten. So druckte zum Beispiel Ulrich Morhart in Tübingen zunächst für seine katholischen und nach deren Vertreibung ausschließlich für seine evangelischen Auftraggeber, siehe *Saskia Limbach*, Government Use of Print. Official Publications in the Holy Roman Empire, 1500–1600, Frankfurt/Main 2021, 84–86. Dies wird auch für zeitgenössische Künstler, wie Cranach und Dürer, angenommen, siehe zum Beispiel *Wolfgang Schmid*, Dürer als Unternehmer: Kunst, Humanismus und Ökonomie in Nürnberg um 1500, Trier 2003.

118. *Johann Leisentrit*, Christianae Adeoque Piae Precationes, Bautzen 1557 (VD16 ZV 9539).

119. *Jan Laktanc Codicius*, De Reverendo Atque Celebrrimo Viro Ioanne Leisentrittio, Bautzen 1559 (VD16 ZV 3743).

120. *Schulz*, „Leben und Werk des Buchdruckers Michael Wolrab" (wie Anm. 90), 122.

121. *Schulz*, „Leben und Werk des Buchdruckers Michael Wolrab" (wie Anm. 90), 130, jedoch stützt sich der Autor nur auf eine Annahme von *Gerblich*, Johann Leisentritt (wie Anm. 81), 52. Eine Primärquelle, die diese Annahme unterstützen würde, ist jedoch noch nicht gefunden worden.

122. *Schulz*, „Leben und Werk des Buchdruckers Michael Wolrab" (wie Anm. 90), 131.

1565 Ambrosius Fritsch eine Druckerwerkstatt in Görlitz betrieb.[123] Um ihre Offizin nicht gänzlich aufgeben zu müssen, konzentrierte sich die Wolrabsche Druckerei in Bautzen daher zunehmend auf die Werke evangelischer Gelehrter und ordnete eventuelle persönliche religiöse Überzeugungen den ökonomischen Interessen unter. So wurden in der Bautzener Offizin in den folgenden Jahren auch die Schriften von Luther, Melanchthon, Nicolaus Selnecker, Urbanus Rhegius, Johannes Heune und David Chytraeus veröffentlicht. Michael Wolrab druckte auch das *Wendische Gesangbuch* des sorbischen Geistlichen Albin Moller.[124] Dabei lag das Augenmerk des Druckers in den folgenden Jahren vor allem auf Hochzeitsgedichten, theologischen Schriften und Leichenpredigten.[125]

Mit dieser Umorientierung wurde es für die Katholiken in der Oberlausitz zunehmend schwieriger einen Drucker zu finden, der sich für ihre Sache gewinnen ließ. In den umliegenden Orten, welche die Reformation einführten, wurde der Büchermarkt zum Teil sehr streng kontrolliert. Die Strafen für die Veröffentlichung von katholischen Schriften konnten weitreichende Konsequenzen haben, wie Nikolaus Wolrab bereits in seiner früheren Wirkungsstätte Leipzig zu spüren bekommen hatte. Als die Stadt sich zur Reformation bekannte, wurden Wolrabs Bücher konfisziert und er selbst sogar für einen Monat gefangen genommen.[126] Für einen Geschäftsmann im 16. Jahrhundert konnte solch eine Inhaftierung schwerwiegende Folgen nach sich ziehen – von Verdienstausfall bis zum schlechten Ruf – und so konzentrierte sich Wolrab nur noch auf evangelische Werke, während er sich in Leipzig aufhielt.

Die Suche nach einem geeigneten Drucker für katholische Werke wurde zudem durch den Umstand erschwert, dass der Drucker nicht nur rechtlich abgesichert sein musste, sondern auch das nötige Geschick und Wissen besaß – vor allem wenn es sich um die Herstellung lateinischer Werke handelte. Aber auch Noten waren vergleichsweise schwierig zu drucken. In der Frühen Neuzeit beschwerten sich viele Gelehrte über die Leichtfertigkeit und Einfältigkeit der Handwerker in den Offizinen. Luther bezeichnete die Drucker als „Schmutzfinken" und „Geldmacher", die nur den eigenen Profit im Sinn hat-

---

123. *Ernst Köhler*, Die Geschichte der Oberlausitz von den ältesten Zeiten bis zum Jahre 1815, Görlitz 1867, 195–196; *Knauthe*, Annales typographici (wie Anm. 116), 37–47.

124. *Albin Moller*, Wendisches Gesangbuch Bautzen 1574 (VD16 ZV 11095); vgl. auch *Knauthe*, Annales typographici (wie Anm. 116), 19–29.

125. Für eine statistische Auswertung des Druckprogramms von Michael Wolrab (1573–1601), siehe *Schulz*, „Leben und Werk des Buchdruckers Michael Wolrab" (wie Anm. 90), 164.

126. *Lehmstedt*, Buchstadt Leipzig (wie Anm. 116), 204.

ten und sich nicht um die Korrektheit des Textes scherten. Luther war einmal sogar so erbost, dass er behauptete, der Setzer habe sein Werk so abgeändert, dass er, als Autor, seine eigenen Worte nicht mehr erkennen könne.[127] Für die Drucklegung katholischer Werke, die in der Oberlausitz konzipiert wurden, war es daher vonnöten sich an Drucker in weiter entfernten Städten zu wenden. Damit waren die Katholiken in der Oberlausitz nicht allein, denn selbst im bikonfessionellen Augsburg war es schwierig einen Drucker zu finden, der altgläubige Schriften produzierte.[128] Sogar in gänzlich katholischen Städten, oder dem nahe gelegenen gemischtkonfessionellen Prag, war es nicht leicht die Werke der Oberlausitzer zu publizieren, obwohl in der Hauptstadt des Königreich Böhmens bereits seit dem ausgehenden 15. Jahrhundert gedruckt wurde. Hier waren die Anfänge des Druckhandwerkes jedoch zunächst bescheiden, da die handschriftliche Tradition noch tief verankert war und fremdsprachige Drucke aus dem Ausland importiert werden konnten. Die Prager Drucker spezialisierten sich daher hauptsächlich auf tschechische Drucke, vor allem während der Hussitenzeit.[129] Ebenfalls fand sich wenig Gelegenheit im schlesischen Breslau (Wrocław), denn die Stadt beherbergte nur eine in einem längeren Zeitraum tätige Druckerfamilie im 16. Jahrhundert: die Scharffenbergs. Nach seinem Misserfolg in Görlitz ließ sich Crispin Scharffenberg in der Bischofsstadt nieder und seine Erben führten ab 1576 das Geschäft weiter. Doch florierte das Buchwesen in Breslau nur bedingt, da sich hier weder eine Universität noch der Hof befand. So sahen sich selbst die Bischöfe in Breslau und in Olmütz gezwungen, ihre Bücher in einer anderen Stadt produzieren zu lassen.[130] Als katholischer Druckort etablierte sich schließlich Nei-

---

127. *Hans Widmann* (Hg.), Der deutsche Buchhandel in Urkunden und Quellen, Bd. 2, Hamburg 1965, 16, 327.
128. *Kaufmann*, Die Mitte der Reformation (wie Anm. 89), 427–428.
129. In Prag lassen sich bisher zwischen 1501 und 1600 2.764 gedruckte bibliographische Einheiten belegen. Die meisten Drucke bis 1550 waren auf Tschechisch verfasst, seit 1550 stieg der Anteil der lateinischen Druckproduktion sprunghaft an (vor allem des poetischen Gelegenheitsschrifttums anlässlich Begräbnissen, Hochzeiten, usw.). Die deutsche Druckproduktion, die sich in Prag seit 1541 belegen lässt, war bis zur Schlacht am Weißen Berg 1620 unbedeutend. Siehe *Petr Voit*, Die Utraquisten und der Buchdruck (bis ca. 1526), in: *Hrachovec, Schwerhoff, Müller, Schattkowsky*, Reformation als Kommunikationsprozess (wie Anm. 20), 127–154; im Universal Short Title Catalogue (USTC), dem Katalog für Europäische Drucke bis 1650 sind bisher für „Prag" als „place of printing" für den Zeitraum 1500–1600 etwa 1.300 Werke verzeichnet, https://www.ustc.ac.uk (Zugriffsdatum: 14.06.2022).
130. *Karen Lambrecht*, „Die Funktion der bischöflichen Zentren Breslau und Olmütz im Zeitalter des Humanismus", in: *Klaus Graber* (Hg.), Kulturgeschichte Schlesiens in der Frühen Neuzeit, Tübingen 2005, 49–68, hier 63.

sse, der Residenzort des Bischofs von Breslau, in dem bis 1600 über 250 Drucke hergestellt wurden.[131] Dabei wurde die Etablierung einer Druckerei maßgeblich auf Empfehlung des Rektors der dortigen Pfarrschule angeregt, welcher der Bischof Folge leistete und 1555 eine Druckerei einrichten ließ.[132] Zwar ist die anschließende Produktion für den kleinen Ort beachtlich, doch konnte Neisse trotzdem nicht mit den größeren Druckzentren mithalten.

In Bautzen richtete Leisentrit sein Augenmerk auf eines der größten Druckzentren im Alten Reich: Köln.[133] Hier wurde bereits seit 1474 gedruckt und die Stadt wurde – aufgrund ihrer hervorragenden Absatzmöglichkeiten – schnell zu einem wichtigen Druckzentrum. Doch das wichtigste Argument für Leisentrit war der Umstand, dass die Stadt, trotz Reformationsversuchen, dem alten Glauben treu blieb und somit das Druckzentrum der Katholiken war.[134] Wie das eingangs erwähnte Beispiel der Briefe aus Schwäbisch Gmünd zeigt, war es Katholiken in anderen Teilen des Reiches durchaus bewusst, wie sie Kontakte zu weiteren Glaubensgenossen schließen und halten konnten.

Einer der größten Produzenten für katholische Werke in Köln war Maternus Cholinus, ein sehr findiger Geschäftsmann, der in wenigen Jahren aus bescheidenen Verhältnissen in die Führungselite der Stadt aufstieg.[135] Sein Erfolg beruhte u. a. auf der Tatsache, dass er seine Expertise ganz in den Dienst der Gegenreformation stellte und vorwiegend für zahlreiche katholische Auftraggeber produzierte. Hierzu gehörten besonders die Karthäuser und Jesuiten, die fast ausschließlich Cholinus mit der Drucklegung ihrer Werke betrauten. Seine

---

131. *Detlef Haberland*, „Der Buchdruck in Schlesien und die Reformation", in: *Andrea Seidler, István Monok* (Hg.), Reformation und Bücher: Zentren der Ideen – Zentren der Buchproduktion, Wiesbaden 2020, 173–194, hier 193. Die Zahl der Drucke basiert auf den Forschungen des Autors, der viele Quellen, die nicht im VD16 enthalten sind, ausgewertet hat.

132. *Reske*, Die Buchdrucker (wie Anm. 88), 695.

133. Einige wenige Werke werden auch ohne Angabe des Druckortes veröffentlich. Für ein Werk wird angenommen, dass es evtl. sogar in Prag gedruckt wurde: VD16 ZV 26137 (Digitalisat der Nationalbibliothek in Prag unter http://www.manuscriptorium.com/apps/index.php?direct=record&pid=NKCR__-NKCR__46_E_000066_09HVR32-cs). Gerblich nimmt jedoch an, dass es sich hierbei um einen Bautzener Druck handelt, *Gerblich*, Johann Leisentritt (wie Anm. 81), 45.

134. Die Gründe hierfür legt *Robert W. Scribner* dar in „Why was there no Reformation in Cologne?", in: Bulletin of the Institute for Historical Research, volume 49/120 (1976), 217–241. Siehe auch *Manfred Groten*, „Die nächste Generation: Scribners Thesen aus heutiger Sicht", in *Gerd Schwerhoff, Georg Mölich* (Hg.), Köln als Kommunikationszentrum. Studien zur frühneuzeitlichen Stadtgeschichte, Köln 1999, 110–113.

135. *Wolfgang Schmitz*, Die Überlieferung deutscher Texte im Kölner Buchdruck des 15. und 16. Jahrhunderts, Köln 1990, 402.

guten Dienste veranlassten weitere Glaubensgenossen aus dem ganzen Reich dazu, ihn mit Aufträgen zu versehen. So stellte der Drucker ein Brevarium in 1.600 Exemplaren für den Bischof von Würzburg her.[136] Das Buch wurde sehr sorgfältig erstellt und mit zahlreichen Illustrationen versehen, wofür der Bischof insgesamt die stolze Summe von 1.800 Gulden bezahlte (zum Vergleich: ein Stadtschreiber verdiente in Köln 110 Gulden im gesamten Jahr).[137]

Nachdem zuerst der Kölner Drucker Peter Horst 1564 ein Werk für den Lausitzer Geistlichen Leisentrit druckte, stellte Cholinus ab der Mitte der 1570er Jahre zahlreiche Publikationen des apostolischen Administrators her. So entstand 1575 seine Schrift über das Altarssakrament, welche im handlichen Quartformat gedruckt wurde.[138] Einige Zeit später erschien das katholische Pfarrbuch, das zwar im gleichen Format hergestellt wurde, allerdings deutlich umfangreicher war.[139] Das Werk richtete sich an katholische Priester und gab ihnen Instruktionen, wie sie mit Sterbenden und dem Tod umgehen sollten. Cholinus war jedoch nicht der einzige Hersteller von Leisentrits Werken. Sie sind auch bei anderen Kölner Druckern erschienen, beispielsweise druckte Heinrich Falckenburg eine weitere Ausgabe des *Catholisch Pfarbuchs*.[140]

Trotz der offensichtlich fruchtbaren Zusammenarbeit zwischen dem Geistlichen Leisentrit und den Kölner Druckern, wurden Leisentrits Schriften später jedoch wieder in Bautzen hergestellt – eine Tatsache, die der Forschung (bis auf einige Ausnahmen)[141] bisher verborgen geblieben ist.[142] Dies weist auf zwei

---

136. *Anton Ruland*, „Zur Druckgeschichte des vom Fürstbishof Julius zu Würzburg herausgegebenem Brevarium secundum usum ecclesiae Herbibolensis von 1575", in: Serapeum 24 (1863), 222–223.
137. *Limbach*, Government Use of Print (wie Anm. 117), 168, 207.
138. *Johann Leisentritt*, Kurtze Fragstücke Von dem Hochwirdigen Sacrament des Altars, Köln 1575 (VD16 L 1068).
139. Zu dem Pfarrbuch, vgl. *Radmila Prchal Pavlíčková*, „‚Unter den Ketzern zu leben und zu sterben ist gar schwerlich und geferlich.' Das Sterbebuch des Johann Leisentritt im Kontext der katholischen Sterbebücher des 16. Jahrhunderts", in: Archiv für Reformationsgeschichte, 107/1 (2016), 193–216; *Martin Christ*, „Between Domestic and Public: Johann Leisentritt's (1527–1586) Instructions for the Sick and Dying of Upper Lusatia", in *Marco Faini, Alessia Meneghin* (Hg.), Domestic Devotions in the Early Modern World, Leiden 2019, 82–106.
140. VD16 L 1067.
141. Gerblich ging noch davon aus, dass nach 1575 alle Schriften Leisentrits in Köln erschienen sind, siehe *Gerblich*, Johann Leisentritt (wie Anm. 81), 52–53. Schulz widerlegt diese Annahme, *Schulz*, „Leben und Werk des Buchdruckers Michael Wolrab" (wie Anm. 90), 128.
142. So zum Beispiel im Jahre 1578 (VD16 ZV 20872) und 1580 (VD16 ZV 9540).

interessante Aspekte hin: Zum einen wurde das vermutlich vom Stadtrat ausgegebene Verbot katholische Schriften zu drucken, nur bedingt (falls überhaupt) beachtet. Zum anderen sah es die Druckerei Wolrab, nachdem sie sich von ihren finanziellen Problemen erholt hatte, offensichtlich wieder als lohnenswert an, auch katholische Werke herzustellen. Allerdings waren die späteren Schriften Leisentrits, die nach der Veröffentlichung des Pfarrbuchs erschienen, deutlich weniger umfangreich und somit auch attraktiver für die Offizin in Bautzen.

FAZIT

Die Studien- und Druckorte protestantischer und katholischer Geistlicher aus der Oberlausitz folgen insgesamt klaren Linien. Die Lutheraner orientierten sich vor allem nach Wittenberg, während sich die Katholiken auch an päpstliche Repräsentanten wandten. Die Verbindungen nach Wittenberg ermöglichten es Protestanten auch, von dort Informationen zu erfragen und sich mit Reformatoren abzustimmen. Die Zittauer Zwinglianer hingegen orientierten sich bis ca. 1560 vor allem nach Zürich. Lutherische Geistliche studierten in Wittenberg, nach 1540 in Leipzig oder in Frankfurt/Oder. Katholische Geistliche hingegen studierten vor 1540 in Leipzig, danach besonders an anderen katholischen Universitäten. Allerdings muss hier nochmals betont werden, dass die katholischen Beispiele insgesamt nicht so zahlreich sind, wie die protestantischen. Wittenberg war ebenfalls der attraktivste Druckort für Lutheraner, während Katholiken, besonders der produktivste lausitzische Katholik des 16. Jahrhunderts, Johann Leisentrit, zum Teil auf Druckorte, die weiter entfernt lagen, zurückgreifen mussten. Die Briefwechsel zeigen aber, dass nicht alle Verbindungen stark konfessionell geprägt waren. Es gab auch Briefe lutherisch geprägter Stadträte an den apostolischen Administrator in Bautzen und dieser Indikator ist von denen drei hier ausgewählten derjenige, der am stärksten supraconfessionell war. Für alle drei Indikatoren lassen die Quellen nur erste Schlussfolgerungen zu, die im Zuge weiterer Forschungen noch durch andere Faktoren und systematische Analysen zu den Lausitzer Netzwerken ergänzt werden können.[143]

---

143. Ein weiterer Faktor, der für die intellektuellen Netzwerke relevant sind, sind Patronagenetzwerke, die hier aus Platzgründen nur am Rande erwähnt werden konnten. Für ein mittelalterliches Beispiel, das ebenfalls eine auf den ersten Blick überraschende Verbindung skizziert, siehe *Christian Speer*, „Wirtschaftsbeziehungen zwischen Lübeck und Görlitz 1390.

Immer wieder spielte die Isolation und verhältnismäßig schlechte Anbindung der Oberlausitz eine wichtige Rolle. So beschwerten sich beispielsweise die Zittauer Zwinglianer über Probleme bei der Lieferung von Büchern und Briefen. Diese Tatsache erklärt auch den stark regionalen Fokus bei Korrespondenzen und der Ausbildung von Geistlichen, macht allerdings die Ausnahmefälle, in denen in Städten, die weiter weg von der Oberlausitz waren (Köln als Druckzentrum oder das eingangs erwähnte Schwäbisch Gmünd) umso bemerkenswerter. Die schlechte Ausgangslage für katholische Druckwerke war auch ein Grund, warum die oberlausitzischen Katholiken im Laufe des 16. Jahrhunderts zunehmend an Einfluss einbüßen und immer wieder Kompromisse mit den Lutheranern eingehen mussten. Ähnlich verhielt es sich mit den Lutheranern in der ersten Hälfte des sechzehnten Jahrhunderts.

In einem oberlausitzischen Kontext ist die klare konfessionelle Kodierung bei Studien- und Druckorten bemerkenswert, weil die konfessionelle Aufteilung wesentlich stärker ausgeprägt war, als dies die allgemeine, religiöse Ausrichtung der Region nahelegen würde. Wie bereits eingangs betont wurde, war die Reformation in der Oberlausitz von Kompromissen geprägt. Die Zwinglianer waren gewillt an lutherischen Gottesdiensten teilzunehmen, die Lutheraner Taufen von Katholiken zu empfangen und die Katholiken sprachen die Einsetzungsworte bei der Eucharistie auf Deutsch, um nur einige wenige Beispiele zu nennen.[144] Die Studienorte aber blieben besonders stark konfessionell konnotiert. Obwohl Geistliche eine lutherische Ausbildung genossen, schlossen sie dennoch viele Kompromisse mit den Katholiken, was verdeutlicht, dass die Reformation in der Oberlausitz sich auch von Institutionen wie Universitäten absetzte und diese auf einer individuellen Ebene verhandelt werden konnte.

Außerdem ist bemerkenswert, dass weder für Lutheraner noch für Katholiken die bohemikale Anbindung bei der Wahl von Studien- und Druckorten eine zentrale Rolle spielte. Teilweise war dies aus praktischen Überlegungen zu erklären, weil sich die Prager Drucker beispielsweise auf tschechische Drucke spezialisierten. Es sollte auch nicht unterschlagen werden, dass es zahlreiche persönliche Kontakte nach Böhmen und Schlesien gab. Die Zittauer Zwinglianer unterhielten beispielsweise einen regen Kontakt zur böhmischen Brüderunität.[145] Betrachtet man aber die Druck- und Studienorte orientierten sich die frühneuzeitlichen Oberlausitzer wesentlich häufiger nach Westen. Die bi-

---

Ein Zinskauf Hermann Warendorps von Peter dem Schulmeister", in: Schlesische Geschichtsblätter. Zeitschrift für Regionalgeschichte Schlesiens 47 (2020), 125–127.
144. Vgl. *Christ*, Biographies of a Reformation (wie Anm. 27).
145. Siehe *Hrachovec*, „Von feindlichen Ketzern zu Glaubensgenossen und wieder zurück" (wie Anm. 30), 131–156.

konfessionelle Aufteilung der Oberlausitz blieb dabei anderen Städten nicht verborgen und so konnte sich auch ein katholischer Stadtrat, wie der Schwäbisch Gmünds, an ein Mitglied des Bautzener Domstifts, und nicht an den lutherischen Stadtrat, wenden.

Dr. Saskia Limbach
Wissenschaftliche Mitarbeiterin
Lehrstuhl für Kirchengeschichte
Georg-August-Universität Göttingen
Platz der Göttinger Sieben 2
D-37073 Göttingen
saskia.limbach@theologie.uni-goettingen.de

Dr. Martin Christ
Junior Fellow
Max-Weber-Kolleg für kultur- und sozialwissenschaftliche Studien
Universität Erfurt
Postfach 90 02 21
D-99105 Erfurt
martin.christ@uni-erfurt.de

ABSTRACT

This essay explores connections of clerics in Upper Lusatia focusing on three factors: their correspondence, which universities they attended, and where they published their works. On the one hand, the network of correspondence reflects the region's character as a center of confessional coexistence. Confessional divisions, on the other hand, are clearly visible with regard to the places the clerics chose for their studies and those they chose for their publications. This posed particular challenges for Catholic authors, who had to find a suitable printer to reproduce their texts in distant territories.

"Holy Handkerchiefs!"
A Study of St. Lawrence of Brindisi's Eucharistic Spirituality and Mass Handkerchiefs

By Andrew J. G. Drenas

Frederick McGinness has established that after the Council of Trent, the Eucharist moved well beyond its traditional settings and uses in masses and liturgical processions to become a focal point of Catholic reform. The sacrament served to reorganize society as people communicated more frequently, participated in activities such as the Forty Hours' Devotion, and joined eucharistic confraternities. Moreover, it shaped the age's saints, who were avid promoters of frequent communion, the belief in transubstantiation, and the elevation of the priesthood.[1] Among these champions of the Eucharist, we must number the Capuchin priest, and now doctor of the church, St. Lawrence of Brindisi (1559–1619). He stands out among his contemporary eucharistic devotees due to the utter extravagance with which he celebrated his daily private masses and because they engendered a cult of highly coveted relics. As for his manner of celebration, his coreligionists witnessed him say extremely long masses, usually in honor of the Virgin Mary, in secret locations every night; he insisted on celebrating even while suffering from agonizing gout. These masses were supposedly the scenes of paramystical phenomena, including levitation. Lawrence wept profusely while saying mass, which caused him to need multiple handkerchiefs to dry his face. His lachrymosity and use of these handkerchiefs are depicted vividly in an eighteenth-century painting of him at the Franciscan Mu-

---

1. Frederick McGinness, "*Roma Sancta* and the Saint: Eucharist, Chastity, and the Logic of Catholic Reform," *Historical Reflections/Réflexions Historiques* 15 (1988): 99–116. This present article began as a paper given for the "New Approaches to Sanctity: Holy Bodies" panel at the 2019 Renaissance Society of America Conference. I am grateful to the following people who, through their guidance and assistance, helped make it possible: Michele Camaioni, Vittorio Casalino, Christopher Carlsmith, Jonathan Greenwood, Simonetta Ottani, Rose Paton, Joyce Penniston, Christian Washburn, Paolino Zilio, Mario Zocca, and the two anonymous reviewers. Abbreviations –AAV, CR: Archivio Apostolico Vaticano, Congregazione dei Riti; Arturo: Arturo da Carmignano di Brenta, *San Lorenzo da Brindisi, Dottore della Chiesa Universale (1559–1619)*, 4 vols. (Venice-Mestre: Curia Provinciale dei FF. MM. Cappuccini, 1960–1963); *Opera*: Lawrence of Brindisi, *S. Laurentii a Brundusio opera omnia a Patribus Minoribus Capuccinis Provinciae Venetae e textu originali nunc primum in lucem edita notisque illustrata* (Padua: Officina Typographica Seminarii, 1928–1956).

seum in Rome (see fig. 1). Since Lawrence's contemporaries deemed him a living saint, they believed that these cloths that had come into physical contact with his body were no longer mere handkerchiefs, but had become potential thaumaturgic relics.[2] They were "living holy matter," as Caroline Walker Bynum designates it.[3] Devout Catholics throughout Italy, therefore, eagerly pursued Lawrence's confreres to acquire what we shall call "Lawrence-handkerchiefs," which they circulated zealously in their spheres of influence. The first part of this article will consider the dramatic masses Lawrence celebrated, and the second part will analyze the consequent distribution of his handkerchiefs. In so doing, it will further elucidate Lawrence and the early Capuchins, early modern eucharistic spirituality and emotions, and post-Tridentine conceptions of sanctity and Christian materiality.[4]

Before examining Lawrence's masses and holy handkerchiefs, we must first consider his career and why he remains significant. This Apulian-born, Venetian-reared friar was the towering figure of the early Capuchins, the reformed branch of the Franciscan Order that sought to live in strict observance of the Rule of St. Francis of Assisi (1181/82–1226). Lawrence played a leading role in many of the activities that made the Capuchins so instrumental to devotional reform. Besides being a dynamic vernacular preacher, Lawrence was also a formidable biblical scholar who had a magisterial knowledge of the text's original languages: Hebrew, Aramaic, and Greek. He functioned as one of the Capuchins' chief administrators, supervising the order at the provincial level in Tuscany (1589–1592), Venice (1594–1597), and Genoa (1613–1616), and universally as its vicar general (1602–1605). Lawrence was one of the era's notable Catholic missionaries. He preached to the Jews of Italy, most notably to those in Rome from 1592 to 1594. In 1599, he led the Capuchins' first mission into the religiously divided kingdom of Bohemia, where he spent years in Prague defending the beleaguered Catholic community and opposing Protestantism. While in central Europe, Lawrence also served as a military chaplain in October 1601, during the Long Turkish War (1593–1606), when he preached and

---

2. For more regarding early modern living saints, see Gabriella Zarri, "Living Saints: A Typology of Female Sanctity in the Early Sixteenth Century," in *Women and Religion in Medieval and Renaissance Italy*, ed. Daniel Bornstein and Roberto Rusconi (Chicago: University of Chicago Press, 1996), 219–303.

3. Caroline Walker Bynum, *Christian Materiality: An Essay on Religion in Late Medieval Europe* (New York: Zone Books, 2015), 20–21.

4. Fr. Cuthbert, *The Capuchins: A Contribution to the History of the Counter-Reformation*, 2 vols. (London: Sheed and Ward, 1928); Arturo. Despite its age, Fr. Cuthbert's work is still the major study of Lawrence of Brindisi, and Arturo da Carmignano di Brenta's biography of the Capuchin, although dated, is still the major biography of him.

ministered spiritedly to the Christian soldiers engaging the Turks at Székesfehérvár, Hungary. Lawrence played an important role in early modern diplomacy, too. In June 1609, he journeyed to Spain to obtain the favor and aid of King Philip III (r. 1598–1621) as the Catholic princes of the Holy Roman Empire were forming the Catholic League against the Protestant Union. To promote greater unity among Europe's Catholic powers, he was sent to Munich in 1610, where, through April 1613, he operated as a diplomatic intermediary between the papal nuncio and the Spanish ambassador in Prague and Duke Maximilian of Bavaria (r. 1598–1651). It was in an ambassadorial role that Lawrence spent his last days, after being commissioned in 1618 by the Neapolitan nobility to present to Philip III their grievances with the kingdom of Naples's Spanish viceroy. The Roman church beatified Lawrence in 1783 and canonized him in 1881. This took such a long time largely due to the reforms of the 1620s–1630s that made the canonization process more stringent, and consequently more competitive. After the publication of Lawrence's writings, Pope John XXIII proclaimed him a doctor of the church—the "Apostolic Doctor"—in 1959.[5]

How do we know about Lawrence's masses? It is not through his own writings. Although they do provide important insight into his gout condition (his letters), his understanding of devotional tears (his sermon plans), and his Tridentine eucharistology (the aggregate of his works), one will search these texts in vain for reflection on personal mystical experiences. In this respect, he was quite unlike spiritual masters of the age, such as Teresa of Avila (1515–1582) and Ignatius of Loyola (1491–1556), who included such details in their autobiographical writings. Rather, in typical Franciscan fashion, Lawrence was usually reticent about himself.[6] To learn more about his eucharistic spirituality, we

---

5. Andrew Drenas, *The Standard Bearer of the Roman Church: Lawrence of Brindisi and Capuchin Missions in the Holy Roman Empire (1599–1613)* (Washington, D.C.: Catholic University of America Press, 2018), 21–50. For more on canonization reform, see Simon Ditchfield, "'Coping with the *beati moderni*' : Canonization Procedure in the Aftermath of the Council of Trent," in *Ite inflammate omnia: Selected Historical Papers from Conferences Held at Loyola and Rome in 2006*, ed. Thomas McCoog (Rome: IInstitutum Historicum Societatis Iesu, 2010), 413–440, here 413–439.

6. The *Commentariolum de rebus Austriae et Bohemiae* (1612) is Lawrence's sole autobiographical work, a terse yet colorful account of his central European activities. The Capuchin procurator general ordered him to write it. For the text in its original Italian, see *Opera*, 10.2:353–415. For an English translation and analysis of the *Commentariolum*, see Andrew Drenas, "Lorenzo da Brindisi's *Commentariolum de rebus Austriae et Bohemiae*: An Introduction to, and Translation of, the Document in English," *Collectanea Franciscana* 85 (2015): 595–629.

must instead refer to the records of his beatification process. During its earliest stages in the 1620s–1630s, numerous investigations into Lawrence's life, virtues, and supposed miracles were conducted throughout Italy (in Naples, Brindisi, Genoa, Albenga, Milan, Venice, Vicenza, Verona, and Bassano) as well as in Munich and Villafranca del Bierzo, his final resting place in Spain. The people who could report on these subjects were summoned to testify first for the informative process (the initial inquiry carried out at the local level, under the authority of a bishop or ordinary) and then for the apostolic process (conducted under papal authority).[7] It is these witness depositions that inform us about Lawrence's masses and handkerchiefs. Most are preserved among the records of the Congregation of Sacred Rites at the Vatican Archives; many were reproduced in the fourth volume of Arturo da Carmignano's major twentieth-century biography of Lawrence, *San Lorenzo da Brindisi: Dottore della Chiesa Universale*. These documents provide valuable insight into Lawrence and his spirituality—but must be treated with caution. As Laura Smoller and David Gentilcore remind us, canonization testimonies as sources present historians with multiple problems through which they must sift.[8] For our present study, we must be mindful especially of witnesses' exaggerations, pious fictions, and omission of details that might make Lawrence seem less supernatural and holy.

LAWRENCE'S MASSES

Lawrence's sacerdotal duties began in December 1582, when the patriarch of Venice ordained him at the age of twenty-three.[9] By the early seventeenth century, it had become his practice to say Mass daily. One of several attesting witnesses was John Mary of Monteforte. He had first met Lawrence in the 1590s as a newly professed Capuchin during the latter's Venetian provincialate. John Mary would eventually work with Lawrence in Prague, accompanied him as he traversed Italy and Iberia during the last three and a half years of his life, and regularly served during his private masses. Notwithstanding Lawrence's many cares and travel obligations, John Mary remembered that his superior "always

---

7. Clare Copeland, *Maria Maddalena de' Pazzi: The Making of a Counter-Reformation Saint* (New York: Oxford University Press, 2016), 9, 103–105.

8. Laura Smoller, "Defining the Boundaries of the Natural in Fifteenth-Century Brittany: The Inquest into the Miracles of Saint Vincent Ferrer (d. 1419)," *Viator* 28 (1997): 333–360, here 335–338; David Gentilcore, *From Bishop to Witch: The System of the Sacred in Early Modern Terra d'Otranto* (New York: Manchester University Press, 1992), 164–165.

9. Arturo 4.1:106.

celebrated Holy Mass every day" (*sempre ogni giorno celebrò la santa Messa*).[10] That a Capuchin would adopt such a custom should not be surprising: as H. Outram Evennett notes, saying Mass daily or several times a week was a mark of this period's reformed and new religious orders.[11] What is more remarkable is that Lawrence could maintain this practice despite his oppressive schedule.

Lawrence said most of his daily private masses in honor of the Virgin Mary.[12] He was an ardent devotee to the Madonna all his life and must be numbered among the prominent Marian thinkers of the Reformation era.[13] Lawrence felt a special gratitude to Mary that can be traced to his youth in the Veneto, when he believed she had healed him of a stomach illness that interrupted his studies in 1580. He would fast in her honor every Saturday for the rest of his life.[14] Perhaps stemming from this same experience, shortly after his ordination two years later, he began to take a strong interest in the votive Mass of the Virgin, the mass one can celebrate in her honor that is not in the liturgical calendar for a particular day.[15] From that time through the first decade of the seventeenth century, that is what he said when it was not a Sunday or double feast day, as high-ranking feasts were then identified.[16] While in Rome in early 1610 after his first mission to Spain, Pope Paul V (r. 1605–1621) granted Lawrence an indult, or dispensation, to celebrate the Mass of the Madonna as often as he liked, except on the church's principal solemnities. Lawrence therefore refrained from saying the Marian Mass on holy days like Christmas, Easter, and Pentecost.[17] When he celebrated, he looked to his serv-

---

10. Arturo 4.2:281. See also Arturo 4.2:292, 310, 327, 368.

11. H. Outram Evennett, *The Spirit of the Counter-Reformation: The Birkbeck Lectures in Ecclesiastical History Given in the University of Cambridge in May 1951* (Cambridge: Cambridge University Press, 1968), 38.

12. Arturo 4.2:191, 208, 228, 234, 240, 252, 258, 262, 277, 281, 286, 292, 299, 310, 327, 361, 368.

13. Donna Spivey Ellington, *From Sacred Body to Angelic Soul: Understanding Mary in Late Medieval and Early Modern Europe* (Washington, D.C.: The Catholic University of America Press, 2001). For Lawrence's Mariology, see his *Mariale*, the eighty-four sermon plans on the Virgin Mary that make up volume 1 of his *Opera*. Lawrence is one of the Marian thinkers treated in Donna Spivey Ellington's work.

14. Arturo 1:170–173.

15. Arturo 4.2:208, 277, 286; John Hardon, *Catholic Dictionary: An Abridged and Updated Edition of Modern Catholic Dictionary* (New York: Image, 2013), 527–528.

16. Arturo 4.2:252, 277. For the church's former categorization of holy days into double, semi-double, and simple feasts, see Edward J. Quigley, *The Divine Office: A Study of the Roman Breviary* (1920; repr., St. Albans: Wentworth Press, 2019), 38–42.

17. Arturo 2:587–609; 3:454; 4.2:228, 234, 258, 262, 286, 309–310, 327, 361–362.

ers or the sacristans where he was staying to ensure that a picture of the Virgin Mary was present. It would be placed in the middle of the altar where the *Gloria* card stood. According to Adam of Rovigo, his server in Munich, the image's presence facilitated his contemplation of Mary.[18]

Another aspect of Lawrence's eucharistic spirituality that witnesses emphasized was the unusually long duration of his private masses. Through his term as vicar general, they took approximately half an hour; and when required to celebrate publicly for congregations later in life, these, too, he kept brief.[19] However, his private masses started to become longer after his generalate and upon returning to the Capuchin mission in Prague in 1606. John Mary, serving as infirmarian there, reported that Lawrence was now sometimes spending three to four hours at the altar.[20] That was just the beginning. As time passed, when Lawrence was not traveling or entangled in administrative tasks, these masses supposedly began to last six, eight, ten, twelve, and even sixteen hours.[21] John Mary, who frequently served on these occasions, explained when Lawrence required such lengths of time. Most days, he would spend seven to eight hours saying Mass. On Fridays and Saturdays, the days of the week associated with Christ's Passion and the Virgin Mary, he usually needed nine hours. It was solely on the solemnities of Christ, the Madonna, and the saints to whom he was devoted—such as Saints Joseph, Lawrence of Rome, and Mary Magdalene —that he required more than nine hours.[22] He took so long because there were points during the liturgy when he slowed down to meditate. John Mary remembered this deceleration commencing after the offertory. Bernard of Grottaminarda in Naples elaborated: "While saying Mass, [Lawrence] was very fast in the readings and in the actions; but all of his delay was in the secret prayers,

---

18. Arturo 4.2:191, 227, 262, 286, 289, 292, 299, 327, 362. Among those mentioning Lawrence's image of Mary was Angelo of Montesarchio, sacristan at the Immaculate Conception friary in Naples: "Io so che per quel tempo, che stette Padre Fra Lorenzo in detto luogo della Concettione [...]. Io come Sacristano vedeva, che Brindisi celebrava sempre Messa della Madonna per la gran divotione che l'havea; e sempre si faceva trasportare un certo quadretto, dov'era ritratto la Madonna santissima. Com'io a sua istanza accomodai detto quadro sopra l'Altare, dove celebrava." AAV, CR, processus 379, fol. 59r (57v–61r, Angelo's 19 December 1626 deposition). The manuscripts cited in this article are from documents not reproduced in Arturo. For altar cards, see Adrian Fortescue, J. B. O'Connell, and Alcuin Reid, *The Ceremonies of the Roman Rite Described*, 15th ed. (New York: Bloomsbury, 2009), 42.

19. Arturo 4.2:209, 300, 304, 326–327.

20. Arturo 4.2:181. For Lawrence's role in establishing the Prague friary (1600), see Drenas, *Standard Bearer* (see note 5), 56–76.

21. Arturo 4.2:190, 208, 219, 228–229, 234, 240, 244, 261, 277, 281, 286, 289, 292, 299, 304, 310, 316, 324–325, 328, 353, 362, 367–369.

22. Arturo 4.2:327–328.

and particularly when he began the offertory and all the way through the memento, consecration, and communion."[23]

The testimonies contain numerous descriptions of some of Lawrence's lengthiest masses. Several of the other Capuchins in Naples, including the sacristans Philip of Soragna and Angelo of Montesarchio, were witness to more than one in the summer of 1618, before Lawrence's departure for Spain. On 10 August, the feast of St. Lawrence, his namesake, it took him twelve to thirteen hours to say Mass. The feast of the Assumption a few days later, on 15 August, saw him occupied for twelve to fourteen hours.[24] Bernard of Grottaminarda recalled clocking another mass at eleven hours using an hourglass; it was possibly for Lawrence's celebration of the Nativity of the Virgin on 8 September.[25] Lawrence's Christmas masses, the supreme opportunity for him to meditate on Christ's incarnation, are the longest on record. His companion in Genoa, John of Fossombrone, related that on one Christmas Day, he began a mass at 5 a.m. and did not finish until 8 p.m.—approximately fifteen hours. John Mary spoke of another Christmas when Lawrence spent sixteen unbroken hours at the altar.[26] Admittedly, were these details the testimony of one informant or a few from a single location, we should justly suspect overenthusiastic exaggeration. Instead, these astonishing lengths of time are recorded repeatedly in depositions given by many witnesses scattered throughout Italy and the Holy Roman Empire, making the evidence more difficult to dismiss.

Lawrence was not the only early modern Catholic to spend a remarkably long time celebrating private masses. There was also Ruffino of Santorso (ca. 1525–1575), the Capuchin who served as Verona's master of novices after joining the order around 1555. Besides spending much of his day in church meditating and praying before the tabernacle, he was also keen to say Mass daily,

---

23. "Nel dire la Messa lui era velocissimo nel leggere, e nell'attioni; ma tutto il suo trattenimento era negli secreti, et in particolare da che cominciava l'offertorio per tutto il decorso del memento, consecratione, e communione […]."AAV, CR, processus 379, fol. 93v (92v–95r, Bernard's 28 September 1627 deposition). See also Arturo 4.2:338. For the secret prayers, see Fortescue, *Roman Rite* (see note 18), 74, 143.

24. "Il giorno dell'Assuntione disse Messa, e viddi, che durò quattordici hore. E nella festività di San Lorenzo durò altre hore dodici." AAV, CR, processus 379, fol. 59v. See also Arturo 4.2:234, 244, 261.

25. "Osservai, che nel celebrare la sua Messa stava sopra l'altare l'otto, e le dieci hore sino all'undeci […]. E questo l'osservai in particolare la festa di San Lorenzo Martire, santo del suo nome, e non me ricordo bene se in questo giorno, o'vero nello giorno dell'Assunta, o Natività della Beata Vergine io feci questa sperienza particolare di voltar l'ampollina dell'hora, et osservai, che la durò undeci hore, havendo voltato detta ampollina undeci volte." AAV, CR, processus 379, fol. 93v.

26. Arturo 4.2:190, 229, 328.

and could take one to two hours. As Arturo notes, Lawrence was likely under Ruffino's spiritual direction during the first few months of his novitiate, which began in February 1575; it may be that Ruffino's example influenced Lawrence's own spirituality.[27] The Oratorians' founder, Philip Neri (1515–1595), whom Lawrence might have encountered while preaching to Rome's Jewish population, was also a passionate devotee of the Eucharist. He, too, was loath to let a day pass without saying Mass and might require more than two hours to complete it.[28] But surpassing both Neri and Ruffino was Roman Catholicism's famous "flying friar," the Conventual Franciscan Joseph of Copertino (1603–1663). His masses were known to last between three and four hours.[29] While Lawrence might not have been alone in celebrating unusually long masses, it seems that he eclipsed by far his kindred spirits. Also, we must remember that such extravagant piety was not found solely among eucharistic devotees, but was manifested multifariously by those early modern people who were considered holy. For example, the Capuchin Felix of Cantalice (1515–1587) was so dedicated to poverty that, when he begged daily for the brothers in Rome, whether in summer or winter, he always went barefoot without the sandals permitted to weaker friars. He refused to wear a cloak even on frigid days, though the Rule allowed it.[30] And Charles Borromeo (1538–1584), the reforming cardinal-archbishop of Milan, revered sacred scripture so much that he reportedly read it continually on bare knees, with his head uncovered, crying as he meditated on its contents. He was also wont to kneel through his recitation of the divine office.[31]

To prevent distractions and obstacles to his eucharistic devotion, Lawrence celebrated secretly and in hidden locations. Public ecclesiastical space was not suitable, given the constant presence of congregations. That was the case, for example, in spring 1618, while Lawrence was in Milan advising the Spanish governor, Pedro de Toledo, during his territorial conflict with the duke of Savoy. When Lawrence said Mass in the cathedral at Borromeo's tomb, he had to

---

27. Davide da Portogruaro and Arturo da Carmignano, *Storia dei cappuccini veneti* (Venice-Mestre: Curia Provinciale dei FF. MM. Cappuccini, 1941–1979), 2:478, 482; Arturo 1:135, 3:413; Drenas, *Standard Bearer* (see note 5), 20.

28. Antonio Gallonio, *The Life of St. Philip Neri*, trans. Jerome Bertram (San Francisco: Ignatius Press, 2005), 30, 169.

29. Michael Grosso, *The Man Who Could Fly: St. Joseph of Copertino and the Mystery of Levitation* (New York: Rowman and Littlefield, 2016), 72.

30. Cuthbert, *The Capuchins* (see note 4), 1:174.

31. Giovanni Pietro Giussano, *Vita di s. Carlo Borromeo, Prete Cardinale del titolo di Santa Prassede, Arcivescovo di Milano* (Rome: Stamperia della Camera Apostolica, 1610), 484–487, 527, 616.

keep it short; Milan's faithful and visiting pilgrims were also anxious to be in the saint's presence.[32] Moreover, since the time of Lawrence's generalate, the Catholic faithful everywhere had been thronging him to receive his blessing. Reports of his "miraculous" thwarting of the Turks with his relic-filled cross in Hungary inspired Europe's Catholics to pursue him for healing.[33] For Lawrence to savor the sacrament without this ever-present nuisance, secret celebrations were essential. Therefore, while in Munich, he opted to use an oratory near his cell at the friary rather than the church. He sought out similar places in Genoa and Pavia during his Genoan provincialate; in fact, his fifteen-hour Christmas Mass in Genoa was celebrated in the chapel under the choir of the Capuchins' Santissima Concezione Church. In Mantua, where he gave the Lenten discourses at the ducal church of Santa Barbara in 1615, he made use of an oratory in the duke's palace. Seeking tranquility after his term in Genoa, he relocated to the Veneto, where he sojourned in Verona (December 1616 to April 1617), Venice (April to June 1617), and Bassano (June 1617 to February 1618). According to Capuchin tradition, while in Venice, Lawrence became fond of the little chapel of St. John the Baptist concealed behind the magnificent Redentore church. And while residing at the Capuchin friaries near the Eastern Gate in Milan and the Immaculate Conception in Naples, he frequented their infirmary oratories.[34] Several of these locations would serve as matrices of Lawrence-handkerchiefs.

But these secret chapels could not prevent Lawrence's chronic gout condition from threatening the amount of time he could spend at the altar. That he suffered later in life from debilitating gout is another subject witnesses discussed repeatedly.[35] Lawrence himself even mentioned his condition in three letters he composed at Bassano in 1618.[36] His hands, feet, and knees were all afflicted. In Naples, one of his knees was so swollen, Philip of Soragna recalled, that it looked like "a big ball" (*una grossa palla*). Simply touching these areas caused Lawrence excruciating pain. He confessed that the gout was so awful that "it made me scream" (*mi faceva gridare*). He referred to it as his own "little

---

32. Arturo 3:327–348; 4.2:308, 310. See also Copeland, *Pazzi* (see note 7), 216. Borromeo had been canonized in 1610.

33. For a sense of what these crowds were like, see the testimony of Gaspar de' Gasparotti of Cassano, the assistant to one of Lawrence's companions during his generalate, in Arturo 4.2:306–308.

34. Arturo 3:301–332, 435–436; 4.2:198–199, 208, 229, 237, 286, 310, 316, 325, 352, 362.

35. Arturo 4.2:181, 190, 198, 208, 219, 229, 235, 240, 251, 253, 261–262, 277–278, 281, 287, 289, 292, 299, 310, 312, 317, 325, 328, 341, 362, 368–369.

36. Arturo 4.1:74–76.

cross" (*puoca croce*).³⁷ Despite the agony, he remained adamant in his desire still to say Mass.

A consistent picture emerges from the testimonies, giving us a sense of how Lawrence celebrated while unwell. An infirmarian who tended him in the Veneto, Francis of Valdobbiadene (ca. 1560–1640), provided a vivid description:

> [Lawrence's] companion and I [...] bore him up in our arms because he could in no way touch the floor with his feet [...]. We carried him from the infirmary, bringing him to the little chapel. We sat him on a chair. While he put on his vestments, he would raise himself to his feet, leaning on the altar. And he stood, that is, he persevered through the mass for at least four and even five hours. And when the mass was completed, again we brought him back to the infirmary in our arms [...]. In my judgment, after having associated with so many people sick with gout, humanly speaking it was not possible that the father could endure such pains, and especially stand on his feet as he did, unless he had been aided by the Lord's hand. So to me it seems like it was a miracle and supernatural gift.³⁸

Indeed, these masses must have been astonishing to behold—though they were not quite as supernatural as Francis and others believed. Rather than always standing uninterruptedly, two witnesses spoke of times Lawrence had to sit down to rest. Philip of Costozza, another Capuchin who helped carry him, admitted this, yet downplayed it. He claimed that it happened only two or three times when Lawrence was gravely ill, and did not last long. Victor of Udine, the guardian of Venice, agreed that it was only necessary when Lawrence was very sick. On these occasions, a seat would be brought for him; he would sit while reciting quietly the secret prayers or the memento.³⁹ Surely Lawrence being seated was a far more regular, lengthy ocurrence than the depositions would have us believe, whether due to witnesses' exaggeration or their inability to observe him every minute.

Understandably, Lawrence's "gout masses" were shorter in duration. Some informants reported that they lasted two to four hours, while others claimed between five and eight hours. Francis of Valdobbiadene was clearly somewhere

---

37. Arturo 4.1:74–75; 4.2:261. See also, Arturo 4.2: 190, 198, 229, 251, 299, 328, 341.

38. "Io con il suo compagno [...] lo portavimo soso in braccio, perchè in modo alcuno non poteva toccar terra con li piedi [...]. Lo solevavimo dall'infermaria, portandolo alla capellina [...]. Lo sentavimo sopra di un scagno. Mentre si parava, si levava in piedi, appoggiandosi all'altare, et stava, cioè durava la Messa, almeno quattro et anco cinque hore; et, fornita la Messa, lo riportavimo di novo in braccio all'infermaria [...]. A giuditio mio, havendo pratticato tanti infermi di podraga, humanamente parlando non era possibile che il padre potesse soportar tali dolori, et massime star in piedi come stava, se dalla mano del Signore non era agiutato; sì che a me par un miracolo et dono sopranaturale." Arturo 4.2:289. For more on Francis, see Davide, *Storia dei cappuccini veneti* (see note 27), 2:442–444.

39. Arturo 4.2:292, 368.

in the middle. John Mary and Adam of Rovigo, two servers, were among the more conservative witnesses and stated that these celebrations might last between three and four hours—roughly half the time of Lawrence's ferial masses. Given these friars' constant presence with Lawrence, their testimonies presumably point more accurately, and less hyperbolically, toward the reality.[40] Whatever the truth, that Lawrence would even celebrate Mass while racked with gout pain is a reminder both of his personal stamina and his profound devotion to the sacrament of the altar.

Whether in good health or suffering from severe pain, once Lawrence was sealed off from the world in his chapel, he normally wanted no one admitted except the server.[41] Neri's masses in Rome were comparable; he had received papal permission to celebrate privately in the chapel adjacent to his room at the Chiesa Nuova. After saying, "Lord, I am not worthy," Neri would ask those in attendance, including the server, to exit so that he might meditate alone. Upon consuming the elements, he would readmit the server and complete the ceremony.[42] Lawrence did not have his servers leave, and even occasionally allowed special guests to be present. While in Munich, Duke Maximilian and his wife Elisabeth of Lorraine were welcome to attend his masses, and frequently did. They, too, were known for their eucharistic piety: Elisabeth communicated weekly, and Maximilian had the reputation for attending two to three masses a day—on his knees.[43] During Lawrence's stay in Mantua, he likewise permitted Duke Ferdinand Gonzaga (r. 1612–1626) to hear a mass, although the duke was unable to perservere to the end. The duke's pages did not fare so well either; impatient that the mass was taking so long, they exited the oratory one by one.[44]

Lawrence could fit such long masses into his already crammed schedule by adapting to celebrate at night. While Lawrence's confreres were assembled in choir for matins, he would head to his oratory of choice to say Mass. These celebrations might commence around midnight and continue uninterrupted into the morning.[45] This was of course a highly unusual arrangement, considering clerics did not say Mass after midnight or any earlier than dawn. The Venetian apostolic process called attention to this as it heard Adam of Rovigo's

---

40. Arturo 4.2:190, 208, 229, 240, 251, 253, 289, 328, 362, 368.
41. Arturo 4.2:316, 325.
42. Gallonio, *Neri* (see note 28), 169.
43. Arturo 4.2:198, 362. See also Dieter Albrecht, *Maximilian I. von Bayern 1573–1651* (Munich: Oldenbourg Verlag, 1998), 130–131, 287.
44. Arturo 4.2:209, 286.
45. Arturo 4.2:183, 208, 292, 298, 324–325, 337, 352, 362.

testimony. After the investigators reminded him that nocturnal masses were prohibited, Adam informed them that Lawrence had told him that he had papal permission.[46] Although Adam did not explain when and how Lawrence had received it, it seems reasonable to conclude that Paul V would have granted him this additional liturgical indult during Lawrence's aforementioned 1610 visit to Rome, before he was transferred to Munich.

Some witnesses reported paramystical phenomena as Lawrence practiced his eucharistic devotion. Adam insisted that during one of Lawrence's masses in Munich, the Christ Child appeared with radiance on the altar, where he played cheerfully with Lawrence, putting his hands in the friar's beard.[47] Moreover, as Lawrence sought to cross the threshold between the terrestrial and celestial realms, it resulted, people said, in his own visage becoming radiant. According to Francis of Valdobbiadene, when Lawrence finished saying Mass, his face would appear "transformed" (*transformata*) and as if it were "very hot" (*che havesse un gran calore*). John of Fossombrone elaborated: while at the altar, sometimes Lawrence's face was "transformed" and looked "like fire" (*trasformarsi in faccia come di fuoco*).[48] Other deponents described Lawrence as becoming ecstatic. John Mary, for one, reported seeing his superior in ecstasy at the altar some twenty times. He recounted: "While [Lawrence] was celebrating Holy Mass, he stood upright on his feet, completely immobile as if he were dead. And I, on all fours, went inspecting him everywhere, and saw that he was completely abstracted. And he stood there like that, like a dead man, for hours on end. The only conclusion I can draw is that he was rapt in ecstasy."[49]

Concerning these paramystical phenomena, Lawrence is comparable to another daily communicant, the Capuchiness mystic and convent foundress Passitea Crogi of Siena (1564–1615). Simply to read or hear mention of, say, heaven or Jesus could supposedly launch her into ecstasies. She, too, would become immobile, like a statue, in whatever position she had been, and might appear fiery and luminous. One story relates that while she was at a table with a full cup in hand reading about a saint going into ecstasy, the mere mention of

---

46. *Missale romanum: editio princeps (1570)*, ed. Manlio Sodi and Achille Maria Triacca, 2nd ed. (Vatican City: Libreria Editrice Vaticana, 2012), 25; Fortescue, *Roman Rite* (see note 18), 63; Arturo 4.2:362.

47. Arturo 4.2:362.

48. Arturo 4.2:229, 289.

49. "Da circa venti volte io viddi et osservai che, mentre celebrava la santa Messa, restò dritto in piedi, tutto immobile come se fosse morto; et io, così a gattolone, andai guardandolo da ogni parte, e viddi che era tutto astratto; e così restava le hore intiere come morto; nè posso fare altro giuditio, se non che fosse rapito in estasi." Arturo 4.2:341.

ecstasy propelled her into an ecstatic state of her own. She remained thus for hours yet spilled none of the contents of the cup.[50]

One of Lawrence's ecstatic experiences in Munich allegedly gave way to levitation. The witness claiming this was the baron and mercenary captain Francesco Visconti. After having confessed to Lawrence in early April 1611, the friar imposed on him a harsh penance. He would have to hear on his bare knees, and serve at, one of Lawrence's nocturnal masses—one that would last ten to twelve hours! After Lawrence had come to the memento of the living before the elevation of the host, the exhausted captain looked in his direction only to discover something shocking: "[Lawrence] was elevated in the air with his body [...]. He stood high, about an arm's length, off the ground and all the floor." Not believing his eyes, Visconti, much like the curious John Mary, arose to investigate, feeling beneath Lawrence's feet and searching near the altar. He could detect nothing propping him up. As he examined Lawrence's countenance, he discovered that the Capuchin "was holding both his arms and his hands joined in the act of praying, as is the habit of priests during the memento, and that he kept his eyes raised toward heaven, and that he was rapt in ecstasy." Lawrence remained thus for approximately ninety minutes before returning to his senses and continuing the mass.[51]

Lawrence is not the only early modern Catholic reputed to have levitated while practicing eucharistic devotion. Teresa of Avila confessed in her *Life* that there were times, however rare, when her body was raised from the ground. It happened once, she said, while she and her fellow nuns were together in the convent choir preparing to receive communion, and she was kneeling. Moreover, Joseph of Copertino goes down in history as the ultimate example of a Catholic levitator. We read that Joseph might levitate three or four times during a single mass, with these flights lasting ten or thirty minutes. Upon going into ecstasy at the altar, his body would assume a cruciform shape, become immobile, and then rise and float in the air, with his toes often hovering inches above the floor.[52] Levitation, then, whether fact or fiction, was clearly associ-

---

50. Lodovico Marracci, *Vita della venerabile madre Passitea Crogi senese Fondatrice del Monasterio delle Religiose Cappuccine nella Città di Siena* (Rome: Filippo Maria Mancini, 1669), 216–220, 223–224; Gianfranco Formichetti, "Crogi, Passitea," in *Dizionario biografico degli italiani* (Rome: Istituto della Enciclopedia Italiana, 1985), 31:227–229.

51. "Viddi che egli era elevato in aria col corpo [...]. Stava alto da terra et da tutto il pavimento per l'altezza d'un braccio in circa [...]. Viddi et ritrovai che esso teneva amendue le braccia et mani sue gionte in atto di fare oratione, come si costuma da sacerdoti nel Memento, et che teneva gl'occhi sollevati al cielo et che era rapito in estasi." Arturo 4.2:351–353.

52. Teresa de Jesus, *Libro de la Vida*, 20.4–5, in *Obras completas: edición manual*, ed. Efren de la Madre de Dios and Otger Steggink (1967; repr., Madrid: Biblioteca de Autores

ated with some of early modern Catholicism's fervent devotees to the Eucharist, including Lawrence.

HOLY HANDKERCHIEFS!

There is another aspect of Lawrence's masses described repeatedly: he wept profusely.[53] Indeed, he was a man of intense emotion known especially for his lachrymosity. His friend Andrew of Venice knew this well. He said that when Lawrence prepared sermons as a young preacher in the Veneto, he would study scripture on his knees before an image of the Virgin Mary, and would cry, sob, and sigh. When preaching, his face would be "all soaked with tears" (*tutta bagnata di lacrime*). Francis of Valdobbiadene described Lawrence's appearance as he preached on Good Friday 1615 in Mantua. He cried so much that the audience doubted he could finish the sermon. When he finally did, he took up the crucifix for veneration "with his eyes ablaze and weeping" (*con li occhi sì infiamati et lacrimanti*), moving everyone to devotion.[54] According to Ambrose of Florence, Lawrence's confessor and secretary during his Venetian provincialate, Lawrence's tears literally spilled over into his administrative work: "Many times, after I had given him many letters to sign, as the office required, he would soak them with his tears to such an extent that sometimes I would say to him, laughing, 'How do you expect me to serve these letters?'"[55] Moreover, while at the altar Lawrence's groans and sighs were so doleful, John Mary said, that "they were like daggers piercing the heart of whoever heard them" (*parevano stiletti con i quali trapassava il cuore di chi lo sentiva*). "A flood of tears" (*un profluvio di lagrime*) would follow.[56] Allowing for exaggeration, these testimonies nonetheless demonstrate that Lawrence's contemporaries experienced him as a man who wept constantly, openly, and abundantly.

But why did Lawrence cry so much during Mass? John Mary believed it stemmed from his contemplation of Christ's Passion, the Virgin Mary's suffer-

---

Cristianos, 2012), 109; Grosso, *The Man Who Could Fly* (see note 29), 29, 71–72, 80. For Passitea also reportedly as a levitator, see Marracci, *Vita* (see note 50), 217, 223–224.

53. Arturo 4.2:190, 198, 208, 219, 229, 234–235, 240, 244, 251, 253, 261, 277–278, 281, 286, 289, 292, 298–299, 317, 325, 337–338, 362, 368–369.

54. Arturo 4.2:206–207, 291.

55. "Et molte volte, dandogli io molte lettere da sottoscrivere, come l'offitio portava, le bagnava con le lagrime, talmente che qualche volta, così ridendo, gli dicevo: 'Come volete che servi queste lettere?'" Arturo 4.2:210.

56. Arturo 4.2:327.

ing, and worldly people's ingratitude and offenses against heaven.[57] That should not be surprising: Susan Karant-Nunn reminds us that Lawrence's world was one in which the faithful were expected to be moved to tears as they viewed art and heard sermons about these themes.[58] Fortunately for us, Lawrence himself reveals what devotional tears meant to him in his Lenten sermon plans. For example, while reflecting on love for God, he said this about the bride in the Song of Songs: "Her heart melts with the flame of love just as wax melts near fire. Accordingly, because of love, a person often totally melts in tears." While exhorting listeners to work diligently in imitation of Christ, he wrote: "The time of the present life is the time for sowing in tears with Christ, so that afterward we may reap with him in joy." Lastly, while considering true penitence, he stated: "Tears are the most sweet drink of Christ; love and devotion, his food."[59] For Lawrence, then, these tears were a mystical expression of ardent love, toilsome spiritual labor, and authentic penitence.

Despite its intensity, Lawrence's tearfulness was not unique to him. He was one of the early modern Catholics to possess the "gift of tears" (*donum lacrimarum*). Joseph Imorde explains that this charism, manifest in those who weep while performing devotions, had been recognized in holy people since patristic times and through the Middle Ages. Early modern Catholics who aspired to sanctity had to imitate these men and women.[60] Among these exemplars was Francis of Assisi. According to St. Bonaventure, Francis shed floods of contrite tears and wept so much that it threatened his eyesight—a "danger" Ambrose of Florence would warn Lawrence of centuries later.[61] Lawrence presumably considered his own crying a way he could emulate Francis. Ignatius of Loyola likewise had the gift of tears. He apparently wept almost daily, especially while celebrating Mass, and sometimes with such intensity that he could not speak. As one reads his *Spiritual Diary*, a record of almost thirteen months' worth of

---

57. Arturo 4.2:327.

58. Susan C. Karant-Nunn, "The Reformations," in *Early Modern Emotions: An Introduction*, ed. Susan Broomhall (New York: Routledge, 2017), 280–283, here 280–281.

59. "Liquescit cor ad flammam amoris sicut cera ad ignem, hinc saepe homo prae amore in lacrimis totus resolvitur." *Opera* 4:399. See also "Tempus autem praesentis vitae est tempus seminandi in lacrimis cum Christo, ut postea cum eo in gaudio metamus." *Opera* 5.3:81; "Lacrimae sunt potus Christi suavissimus, caritas et devotio cibi […]." *Opera* 6:591.

60. Joseph Imorde, "Tasting God: The Sweetness of Crying in the Counter Reformation," in *Religion and the Senses in Early Modern Europe*, ed. Wietse de Boer and Christine Göttler (Brill: Boston, 2013), 257–269, here 258–259.

61. For St. Bonaventure's description of St. Francis, see *Doctoris Seraphici S. Bonaventurae S. R. E. Cardinalis opera omnia* (Quaracchi: Collegium S. Bonaventurae, 1898), 8:318. For the warning to Lawrence, see Arturo 4.2:210.

mystical experiences, one might imagine the pages to be as moist as Lawrence's Venetian correspondence.[62] Philip Neri was no stranger to profuse weeping either. He was reportedly so full of the love and grace of God that he could not help but to be consumed in tears and constantly sob.[63] Also possessing this charism was Pope Clement VIII (r. 1592–1605), who commissioned the Capuchins' aforementioned first mission to Bohemia. Clement used to cry openly during holy rites, particularly while in the presence of the host. As he led his first Corpus Christi procession as pope, there were reportedly so many tears streaming down his cheeks that some of the auditors of the Rota accompanying him found themselves having to dry his face continually with towels.[64]

Lawrence needed something like Clement VIII's towels to dry his tears. He used "fazzoletti," which we might translate generically as "handkerchiefs." Because he cried so much, he supposedly required two, three, and even up to six per mass. He did not sprinkle these cloths with tears; we are told that he "soaked" (*bagnava*) them.[65] Do we know whether Lawrence used specific kinds of handkerchiefs? John of Fossombrone recalled his usage of "il fazzoletto del lavabo," indicating that Lawrence was accustomed to using the manutergium, the small linen cloth with which celebrants dried their fingers after washing them in preparation for communion.[66] But not all of Lawrence's *fazzoletti* were manutergia. After his return to Italy from Munich in 1613, fellow Catholics started to give their own *fazzoletti* to his associates for his use during Mass.[67] This implies that these must not have been liturgical cloths but rather were common handkerchiefs. It seems reasonable to conclude, then, that Lawrence's initial *fazzoletti* were the manutergia readily available to him at the altar, with large numbers of regular handkerchiefs supplementing them as more people learned of his emotional masses.

The faithful gave Lawrence their handkerchiefs because they desired their return—after this "living saint" had touched them. For these people, objects that had come into contact with his body would serve as relics they could use to cure illnesses. Lawrence's confreres were the intermediaries in this exchange

---

62. Ignatius of Loyola, *Ephemeris Sancti Ignatii*, in *Monumenta ignatiana ex autographis vel antiquioribus exemplis collecta* (Rome: Pontificia Universitas Gregoriana, 1934), 1:86–158.

63. Gallonio, *Neri* (see note 28), 31, 169.

64. Imorde, "Tasting God" (see note 60), 257; Drenas, *Standard Bearer* (see note 5), 59–60. Imorde also discusses Lawrence (265–266).

65. Arturo 4.2:190, 198, 208, 229, 235, 240, 244, 261, 277, 281, 286, 289, 292, 299, 317, 337–338, 362, 368–369.

66. Arturo 4.2:229. See Fortescue, *Roman Rite* (see note 18), 36, 73–74.

67. Arturo 4.2:190, 292.

that developed. Philip of Costozza, for one, was diligent to return the cloths to their original owners; but this was all done, he stated, without Lawrence's knowledge. The Capuchins presumably feared that Lawrence would not cooperate for humility's sake or might have found offensive people's efforts to capitalize on his devotion. John Mary, therefore, would surreptitiously remove wet handkerchiefs from the altar, replace them, and return the used ones to their owners. As a sacristan in Naples, many handkerchiefs passed through Philip of Soragna's hands, too. The handkerchiefs were so highly coveted, he said, that the faithful had to "compete" (*concorrevano*) for them; those who obtained even a fragment considered themselves lucky.[68] One Lawrence-handkerchief, a manutergium whose provenance was the Capuchins' Veronese house, is extant and preserved at the order's provincial archive in Mestre (see fig. 2).[69]

Lawrence's handkerchiefs are comparable to other contact relics disseminated by past Christians. St. Paul's handkerchiefs (σουδάρια/*soudaria*) and aprons (σιμικίνθια/*simikinthia*) are obvious examples. The Acts of the Apostles records that God was acting miraculously through Paul as he sought to persuade the Ephesians to embrace Christianity. These objects that had touched his skin were taken and brought to the sick, whose diseases were healed and from whom evil spirits were expelled (Acts 19:11–12). Clare Copeland describes an example contemporary to Lawrence: the flowers adorning the body of the Florentine Carmelite mystic Maria Maddalena de' Pazzi (1566–1607) after her death. There was so much competition for these flowers among relic seekers who had come to view her body in the church that it became necessary to redecorate the corpse. Many Florentines who had acquired flowers shared them with sick people in their social circles. The miraculous healing of a desperately ill woman was reported less than a week after the Carmelite's passing.[70] And Giulia Calvi discusses additional contact relics circulated in early seventeenth-century Florence, particularly bread taken from the tomb of the Dominican tertiary and mystic Domenica of Paradiso (1473–1553). During

---

68. Arturo 4.2:190, 235, 261, 292.

69. For this handkerchief's history, see Archivio Provinciale dei Cappuccini Veneti, Chancellery of the Episcopal Curia of Verona (under Bishop Girolamo Cardinale), certificate of authenticity for relics of St. Lawrence of Brindisi, 5 July 1935; Giuseppe Carraro, certificates of authenticity for relics of St. Lawrence of Brindisi, 26 January 1960; Fernando da Riese Pio X, description of the relics of St. Lawrence of Brindisi in Verona, ca. 19 March 1959. The handkerchief is preserved with Lawrence's cord, an amice he used, and a slipper he wore while afflicted by gout.

70. Copeland, *Pazzi* (see note 7), 66–67, 72–73, 76–79.

the 1620s and 1630s, people used it to combat plague and other illnesses, often making bread soup with it.[71]

Lawrence's handkerchiefs should also be numbered among Christendom's significant effluvial relics, since they were sacralized primarily by his tears. Collecting holy peoples' tears, specifically, was nothing new: that practice originated, Kimberly-Joy Knight explains, during the High Middle Ages. In fact, one of the relics most sought-after by Christians had been Christ's "Holy Tear" (*La Sainte Larme*), supposedly shed at Lazarus's tomb, and preserved at the Benedictine Abbey of La Trinité in Vendôme, France.[72] There were also the sacred liquids that exuded from some saints' bodies in their tombs. In her groundbreaking study of medieval women who practiced extreme fasting often as part of their eucharistic devotion, Bynum identifies several who were myroblytes (oil-producing saints), including the widowed princess and Franciscan tertiary Elizabeth of Hungary (1207–1231).[73] And at the Apulian port of Bari, near Brindisi, visitors to St. Nicholas's tomb were keen to obtain "manna," the water that his bones exuded. Whether by drinking it or being anointed with it, the faithful trusted that it would heal them of their illnesses. Lawrence himself participated enthusiastically in the circulation of manna.[74] Across the peninsula, the people of Naples took great interest in the purported blood of the city's patron, the martyr-bishop St. Januarius († ca. 305). This hard, dark substance would liquefy and become red during certain liturgical celebrations each year.[75] Moreover, in high demand in Jesuit spheres of influence were Ignatius-Water and Xavier-Water, holy water in which relics or medals of Ignatius of Loyola and the missionary Francis Xavier (1506–1552) had been immersed. People used these liquids to combat illnesses like plague and fever, and to protect their fields and livestock from harm.[76]

---

71. Giulia Calvi, *Histories of a Plague Year: The Social and the Imaginary in Baroque Florence*, trans. Dario Biocca and Bryant Ragan (Berkeley: University of California Press, 1989), 228–243.

72. Kimberly-Joy Knight, "Droplets of Heaven: Tear Relics in the High and Later Middle Ages," *The Medieval Journal* 6, no. 2 (2016): 45–80, here 48–75.

73. Caroline Walker Bynum, *Holy Feast and Holy Fast: The Religious Significance of Food to Medieval Women* (Berkeley: University of California Press, 1987), 89, 135–136.

74. Gerardo Cioffari, "La Manna di S. Nicola: Testimonianze storiche di una devozione," *Nicolaus: studi storici* 15 (2004): 209–248, here 223–227, 245–248; Arturo 4.1:21.

75. Francesco Paolo de Ceglia, *Il segreto di san Gennaro* (Turin: Giulio Einaudi, 2016).

76. Estanislao Olivares, "Agua de San Francisco Javier," in *Diccionario histórico de la Compañía de Jesús: Biográfico-temático*, ed. Charles O'Neill and Joaquín Domínguez (Rome: Institutum Historicum, S.I., 2001), 1:20; Jerome Aixalá, "Agua de San Ignacio," in O'Neill, Domínguez, *Diccionario histórico* 1:20; Trevor Johnson, "Blood, Tears and Xavier-Water: Jesuit Missionaries and Popular Religion in the Eighteenth-century Upper Palatinate," in

Lawrence's beatification records contain many depositions revealing who came to possess his handkerchiefs and how they were deemed thaumaturgic. One handkerchief was circulated at the Dominican convent of St. Dominic in Verona. Its owner was Francesco Turco, the doctor who regularly visited the convent's sick sisters. He testified for the Veronese apostolic process between 7 and 12 December 1628 that he had associated with Lawrence in Mantua and Verona as a friend and as one of the physicians to examine his gout. Turco believed that his wife Bianca had been healed of a terrible fever upon receiving the friar's blessing in December 1616. Furthermore, Turco had been aware of Lawrence's handkerchiefs, and saw several on an altar one night in January 1617. The one in his possession, which was sprinkled with blood stains, had been among them.[77] How he acquired it is not explained.

One of the nuns to whom Turco lent his Lawrence-handkerchief was Brigida Nichesola. She testified for the Veronese process on 15 May 1629, when about seventy years old (the same age Lawrence would have been). Since the age of thirty-six, her left breast had suffered from painful mastitis and a discharge. The doctors and knowledgeable women recommended treatments; none worked. Around 1614–1615, Nichesola was confined to bed because her condition might become cancerous. There she remained for eight months, until she could take it no longer—an experience she likened to martyrdom. But when Lawrence was in town in 1617, Turco told her about him, and asked the Capuchin to visit her. One morning several days later, perhaps after recovering from a gout attack, Lawrence arrived and found Nichesola behind the convent church's communion window. After praying quietly with her, he made the sign of the cross over her and touched her breast through the window. She felt immediate relief, though the pain did not disappear completely. Eventually, news of Lawrence's death in 1619 reached the convent; Nichesola was grieved, as he had been her only source of alleviation. Turco urged her not to doubt, because he had Lawrence's stained handkerchief, which he was certain would help her. Around 1624, Nichesola borrowed it. She said that when in her cell,

---

Popular Religion in Germany and Central Europe, 1400–1800, ed. Robert Scribner and Trevor Johnson (Basingstoke, UK: St. Martin's Press, 1996), 183–202, here 185, 195–198.

77. "[Lawrence] ha […] fatto gratia alla Signora Bianca mia moglie l'anno 1616 a 26 Decembre […]. Era oppressa da febra maligna con straordinario delirio, et prostrattion di virtù […]. Padre Brindesi fu condotto a casa nostra […] et gionto nella camera di detta inferma […] dopo haverla visitata gli mise le mani sopra il capo, la benedì due volte, et dopo la benedittione levò in piedi, et disse eh guarirà bene […]. Ogni giorno cominciò a migliorare in fine ricuperò la sua sanità." AAV, CR, processus 373, fols. 65r–v (61r–67v, Turco's full testimony). For the partial reproduction of Turco's testimony, see Arturo 4.2:298–299,

"I made use of it with much devotion, making the sign of the cross over the diseased part of my body. Sometimes I also put it there and kept it there for entire nights, from which I received the greatest relief." The result, she averred, was that she had been healed, though she still felt a little pain while tossing and turning in bed at night and took medication. By 1629, she had not used the handkerchief for a long time. The grateful nun asserted, "I live devoted to Father Lawrence of Brindisi!"[78]

What can we glean from Nichesola's account? The person sharing the Lawrence-handkerchief was a pious doctor. Inspired by his own experience with Lawrence the thaumaturge, Turco, when not actually able to bring his saint-friend to his desperate patients, would instead produce for them this relic. In Nichesola's case, physical contact with Lawrence himself had not been enough to heal her (unlike Turco's wife); rather, frequent handling of the handkerchief after Lawrence's death proved necessary. So, what Turco had effectively done was bring both this handkerchief and knowledge of Lawrence across "religious order boundaries" from Verona's Capuchin friary to the Dominican convent. Copeland discusses a similar dynamic concerning the spread of Maria Maddalena de' Pazzi's cult to Lucca after her death. Relics of this Carmelite, including the aforementioned flowers, were circulated enthusiastically in the city's Dominican, Benedictine, and Jesuatess convents. In Lucca, too, doctors played a significant role in sharing devotions and devotional objects among cloistered religious.[79] Because of Turco, one of the early modern Catholics most excitedly anticipating the Capuchin Lawrence's beatification was a Dominican nun.

Turco might have owned only one Lawrence-handkerchief; another witness, the thirty-five-year-old priest Giovanni Stefano Ferrari, possessed two. He testified for the Genoan apostolic process on 29 January 1627. He was then a novice in another of the new religious orders, the Piarists, who were devoted to educating poor boys, and who had established their school in Genoa only three years prior. Ferrari had interacted with Lawrence in his Piedmontese village, Voltaggio, around 1613–1614, during Lawrence's Genoan provincialate.

---

78. "Me ne son valsa con molta devotione segnandomi la parte offesa, et anco qualche volta ponendovelo, et tenendovelo sopra le notti intiere, per il che ho ricevuto grandissimo sollievo […]. […]Vivo devota del Padre Lorenzo Brindesi" AAV, CR, processus 373, fol. 117r (115r–117v, Nichesola's full deposition). Turco also lent his handkerchief to Sister Justina Lombarda, who claimed healing of a painful stomach illness, also around 1624. For Lombarda's deposition of 5 and 15 May 1629, see AAV, CR, processus 373, fols. 109v–112r, 114r–115r. For the corroborating 19 May testimonies of the convent nurses Maximilla Maza, Cintia Spolverina, and Margarita Pellegrina, see AAV, CR, processus 373, fols. 119r–124r.

79. Copeland, *Pazzi* (see note 7), 80.

Lawrence had stopped there while conducting the visitation of the friary and traveling to other locations. Lawrence's reputation for sanctity had preceded him: Ferrari was eager to associate with him. Ferrari claimed that he was always present for Lawrence's seven-to-eight-hour masses at San Michele, the Capuchins' church. He observed how the server would have to hand Lawrence one or two handkerchiefs for his tears. Ferrari wanted one. While in Genoa a short time later, he approached one of Lawrence's companions at the friary, a Veronese Capuchin, to make his request. The friar explained that he could not give away property of the Capuchin Order. If Ferrari brought back his own handkerchief, however, the friar would have Lawrence use it during a mass. Ferrari returned with not one, but two new handkerchiefs! A little over a week later, he collected his prizes from his contact, who confirmed that Lawrence had used them, and returned to Voltaggio.[80]

According to Ferrari, these handkerchiefs proved a boon for not only those around him in Voltaggio but also for him. Regarding himself, he recounted this experience from a few years before 1627: "Since I was suffering in those times from a terrible migraine, when I was overtaken by the pain, I put one of the handkerchiefs on my head, and the pain ceased immediately. And it has been at least two years since I have felt the migraine pain." Around that same time, one of the people in Voltaggio with whom Ferrari shared his Lawrence-handkerchiefs was the organist Timoteo Boido, who had had a bad case of edema. His legs were so swollen that his skin was cracking in multiple places. Ferrari decided to visit him. Boido informed him that despite the doctors' and barbers' efforts, no treatments had worked. The pain was terrible. Feeling compassion, Ferrari went home to fetch his handkerchiefs and immediately returned to Boido's house. After explaining what they were, Boido gave him permission to use them. Ferrari narrated, "I took one of the two handkerchiefs and placed it over his legs and left it there for the space of a creed. And then the organist told me that the pain ceased, and that the handkerchief seemed to have been the Magdalene's ointment." Within two or three days, the edema cleared up completely.[81]

---

80. AAV, CR, processus 376, part 2, fols. 1r–2r (1r–3r, Ferrari's full deposition). For an introduction to the Piarists and the locations of their first schools, see Paul Grendler, "The Piarists of the Pious Schools," in *Religious Orders of the Catholic Reformation: In Honor of John C. Olin on His Seventy-fifth Birthday*, ed. Richard De Molen (New York: Fordham University Press, 1994), 252–278.

81. "Presi uno di detti dui fassoleti, et glielo steti sopra esse gambe, e glielo lasciai per spatio di un credo, et in quell mentre detto organista mi disse, che le cessava il dolore, et che pareva, che fusse stato l'unguento della Madalena [...]. Patendo io in quei tempi un gran

What do we learn from Ferrari? His testimony confirms that ecclesiastics, too, made use of Capuchin connections to obtain Lawrence-handkerchiefs. Ferrari, a young priest and future novice of another new religious order, was the one to acquire the relics and propagate devotion to Lawrence. His handkerchiefs were undoubtedly products of a mass Lawrence celebrated in his secret chapel at the Santissima Concezione in Genoa. While the evidence indicates that Turco was keen to lend his handkerchief to his cloistered patients, Ferrari was zealous to share his two with people out in the community. Here, also, postmortem miracles are described. But while Nichesola's and Boido's healings were gradual, Ferrari claimed that his own was instantaneous.

Another instantaneous postmortem Lawrence-handkerchief miracle story is that of the Neapolitan widow Eugenia d'Apuzzo. She testified for the apostolic process of Naples on 14 December 1627 and 15 January 1628. Around 1620, when about forty-three, her doctors told her to have some blood drawn; why exactly is not explained. She sent for the barber, Pietro Cioffo. As he made the incision to draw from the "hepatic vein" (*la vena del fegato*), as the vein within the muscle tissue surrounding the right humerus was then called, his hand slipped, cutting the arteries. Before they knew it, the wound was gushing blood. It would not stop. D'Apuzzo's clothes were drenched. Blood was all over the floor. Frantically, they tried to stanch the bleeding by soaking the wound with cold water, dressing it with wadding, and Cioffo taking his hand and applying pressure to it. Nothing worked. An hour had already passed. The debilitated D'Apuzzo inched ever closer to death. Then she remembered that she had a piece of one of Lawrence's handkerchiefs. Isabella Grieco, her neighbor, had given it to her after obtaining it from a Capuchin sacristan—presumably Philip of Soragna. D'Apuzzo had Grieco fetch it. Feeling confident that Lawrence's intercession would save her, D'Apuzzo ordered Cioffo to remove his hand and the dressing beneath it. "Immediately," she said, "the blood gushed up like a fountain. The barber and I put that piece of cloth on the wound, and immediately the flow stopped without leaving any blood stain in the handkerchief." All signs of the lesion had vanished. Since D'Apuzzo was convinced that her partial Lawrence-handkerchief had thaumaturgic power,

---

dolore di magrania di capo, quando io ero soprapreso da detto dolore mi mettevo in capo uno di detti fassoleti, et il dolore subito mi cessava, et sono almeno dui anni, che non sento più di detto dolore di magrania di capo." AAV, CR, processus 376, part 2, fol. 2v. For Ferrari's narration of how a handkerchief had supposedly saved the life of the cleric Giulio Scorza, who fell down some stairs and smashed his head, causing him to lose his ability to speak, as attested by the cleric Francesco Scortia on 14 June 1627, see AAV, CR, processus 376, part 2, fols. 2v, 9r–v.

she would eventually lend it to people she knew and give additional fragments to others.[82]

In D'Apuzzo's case, it was not a doctor or priest who acquired and gave her the Lawrence-handkerchief, but her neighbor, Isabella Grieco. This time, the miracle took place not through a whole handkerchief, like those in Verona and Voltaggio, but a mere fragment—one of the pieces Philip of Soragna referred to that had generated such enthusiasm in Naples. The Neapolitan Capuchins apparently adopted this strategy of circulating fractions of individual handkerchiefs to share their spiritual wealth more readily and to satisfy demand. D'Apuzzo would eventually do the same as she gave away pieces of her own fragment. As Gentilcore aptly expresses it, relics "could be cut up and divided into the smallest pieces without losing their efficacy."[83] Interestingly, the church found D'Apuzzo's dramatic account convincing enough that in 1775 her miracle became the first confirmed on the long and tedious road to Lawrence's beatification in 1783.[84]

CONCLUSION

Studying Lawrence of Brindisi's private masses and holy handkerchiefs enriches our knowledge of the Capuchin Order, early modern eucharistic piety and emotionality, and post-Tridentine conceptions of sanctity and "holy matter." We now have a fuller understanding of Lawrence, the early Capuchins' preeminent figure. We have also learned more about other Capuchins with whom he can be compared, including Ruffino of Santorso, Felix of Cantalice, and Passitea of Siena, contemporaries even more obscure to us than he is. Like Lawrence, all merit additional academic scrutiny for how they educate us about the history of their order.

---

82. "Subito sbottò in alto detto sangue come una fontana, et io, e detto Barbiero ponemmo detta pezza sopra detta ferita, e subito si stagnò immediatamente senza lasciar macchia alcuna di sangue in detto faccioletto [...]." AAV, CR, processus 379, fols. 128r–129r, 130r (127v–130v, D'Apuzzo's full deposition). For the 1 February 1628 depositions of Isabella Grieco and Antonia Buonvino, another neighbor, see also AAV, CR, processus 379, fols. 143v–147v. Grieco was the one to note that the lesion had disappeared (145v: "Nè all'hora, nè mai vi rimase lesione alcuna"). Concerning the hepatic vein, see Giovanni Valverde, *La anatomia del corpo umano* (Venice: Stamperia de Giunti, 1586), fols. 124r, 132v.

83. Gentilcore, *From Bishop to Witch* (see note 8), 188.

84. Silvinus a Nadro, ed., *Acta et decreta causarum beatificationis et canonizationis O.F.M. Cap.: ex regestis manuscriptis SS. Rituum Congregationis ab anno 1592 ad annum 1964* (Rome: Postulatio Generalis O.F.M. Cap., 1964), 1010.

Regarding Lawrence's spirituality and mysticism, he was among his era's many fervent eucharistic devotees. Being a priest in one of the new religious orders, it is unsurprising that he said Mass daily; however, so much else about his celebrations was extraordinary. He almost always said the votive Mass of the Virgin, for which he had received papal permission. Although he was not alone in celebrating long masses, the evidence indicates that his were extremely long, with the number of hours eventually varying from seven to sixteen depending on the day of the week, the liturgical calendar, and his struggle with gout. To fit such lengthy celebrations into his already full schedule, saying nocturnal masses, again with papal permission, became vital. To keep the crowds and other distractions at bay, he celebrated in the most isolated oratories possible, which supposedly became the scenes of paramystical experiences like celestial apparitions, luminosity, ecstasies, and levitation. Indeed, Lawrence manifests the considerable extent to which early modern saints might go to express their eucharistic devotion and the extravagance with which they might celebrate.

Furthermore, as someone possessing the gift of tears, Lawrence wept copiously as he celebrated. His contemporaries emphasized repeatedly this lachrymosity that stemmed from his own melodramatic nature and the intensity with which he meditated on the sorrowful mysteries of his faith. Such emotional piety was characteristic of this period during which many others, mystical authorities and ecclesiastical administrators alike, had this charism and felt so profoundly about their devotional practices. But as we have established, the gift of tears was not exclusive to the Reformation era, so those early modern figures such as Lawrence who possessed it were imitating holy people of the past. Nowhere was Lawrence's gift of tears more evident than at the altar, where he needed multiple handkerchiefs to dry his tear-drenched face.

Moreover, as we observed, Lawrence's eucharistic devotion and sacred tears proved impactful beyond his secret chapels. Perhaps unbeknownst to him, they generated one of the noteworthy early modern relic cults, which his Capuchin companions mediated. Throughout Italy, doctors, priests, and laywomen alike all sought these Lawrence-handkerchiefs, which were simultaneously contact relics and effluvial relics. Believing that these cloths possessed miraculous power, people used them on themselves and shared them in their spheres of influence, which included monastic communities, their villages, and their neighbors. Used stained handkerchiefs, brand-new handkerchiefs, and even pieces of handkerchief were deemed responsible for healing maladies like migraines, seemingly hopeless cases of mastitis and edema, and even a lethal phlebotomy accident. Indeed, in the early decades of the seventeenth century, Lawrence-handkerchiefs were a sensation. Yet, this was all a result of one

Capuchin's ardent pursuit of personal spiritual satisfaction and much needed solitude and serenity.

Andrew J. G. Drenas
Visiting Lecturer
Department of History
University of Massachusetts Lowell
Dugan Hall 106
883 Broadway Street
Lowell, MA. 01854
USA
Andrew_Drenas@uml.edu

ZUSAMMENFASSUNG

Zu den vielen begeisterten Anhängern der Eucharistie im Katholizismus der frühen Neuzeit gehörte der Kapuzinerpater und Kirchenlehrer Laurentius von Brindisi (1559–1619). Er zeichnete sich durch die massive zeitliche Ausdehnung seiner Messen, die bis zu sechzehn Stunden dauerten, aus, und durch die Tatsache, dass seine Messen einen Reliquienkult hervorbrachten. Seinen Glaubensbrüdern zufolge hielt er jeden Tag extrem lange, dramatische Privatmessen ab, währenddessen er ausgiebig weinte und mehrere Taschentücher benötigte, um seine Tränen zu trocknen. Da er als lebender Heiliger galt, waren die Gläubigen in Italien sehr daran interessiert, in den Besitz dieser Taschentücher, die mit Laurentius' Körper in Berührung gekommen waren, zu gelangen, um sie als potenzielle thaumaturgische Reliquien zu verwenden. Auf der Grundlage von Laurentius' eigenen Schriften und den Akten seines Seligsprechungsprozesses aus dem frühen 17. Jahrhundert wirft dieser Artikel zusätzliches Licht auf die frühen Kapuziner, die frühneuzeitliche eucharistische Spiritualität sowie das nachtridentinische Verständnis von Heiligkeit.

Figure 1: Unknown painter, *San Lorenzo da Brindisi, asciugandosi le lagrime* (St. Lawrence of Brindisi Drying His Tears), eighteenth century. With permission from the Museo Francescano, Rome.

Figure 2: Lawrence-handkerchief (*linteolum*) preserved among relics of St. Lawrence of Brindisi. With permission from the Archivio Provinciale dei Cappuccini Veneti, Mestre, Italy.

„der erst, der das Euangelium den von kitzingen
zu den letzten Zeiten bracht":
Der Weg des Christoph Hoffmann (um 1495–1553)
vom Promovenden Karlstadts zum kursächsischen Hofprediger

Von Wolfgang Huber

Ein kleines, aber eigenes Reformationsjubiläum könnte im Jahr 2022 die unterfränkische Kreisstadt Kitzingen begehen. Vor genau 500 Jahren zeigten sich in ihr – im Zusammenhang mit der Anstellung eines neuen Prädikanten – nach jahrelangen Bestrebungen erste Erfolge, die in die nachhaltige „evangelische" Neuordnung des kommunalen Kirchenwesens einmündeten. Das trotz aller Gefährdungen stabile Fortbestehen dieser „Reformation", im Unterschied etwa zur nahe gelegenen Reichsstadt Rothenburg auch über den Bauernkrieg hinweg, verdankt Kitzingen zwei bemerkenswerten Theologen, die mit dem Rückhalt des städtischen Rates das Leben der Kirchengemeinde fundamental nach alleiniger Maßgabe des Evangeliums umgestalteten: Christoph Hoffmann, eben jener 1522 neu angestellte Ratsprädikant, und Martin Meglin, von März 1525 bis zu seinem Tod 1533 der erste evangelische Stadtpfarrer. Deren Namen sind bekannt, ihre Lebenswege, soweit sie sich noch erhellen lassen, haben aber bisher keine eingehende Darstellung gefunden. Eine solche will vorliegender Beitrag für Christoph Hoffmann zumindest als Skizze in Angriff nehmen. Nicht nur vor dem Hintergrund eines Kitzinger Jubiläums, sondern vor allem auch weil Hoffmanns Person in der Forschungsliteratur bei der Behandlung einzelner Phasen der Reformationsgeschichte immer wieder, jedoch nur schlaglichtartig auftaucht, ist es durchaus reizvoll, seine Spuren als früher gemeinsamer Wittenberger Schüler von Luther und Karlstadt nachzuverfolgen und seine facettenreiche Reformatoren-Biographie einmal umfassender zu betrachten.[1]

---

1. Zur „biographischen Zugangsweise zur Reformationsgeschichte" vgl. *Thomas Kaufmann*, Reformatoren, Göttingen 1998, 6–39, sowie *ders.*, „Reformatoren als Konvertiten", in: Zeitschrift für Theologie und Kirche 114 (2017), 149–176. Zu Hoffmann, von dem keine Selbstzeugnisse und persönlichen Briefe erhalten sind und dessen Werke auch nichts über seine Biographie preisgeben, vgl. die prägnanten Einträge in: *Matthias Simon*, Ansbachisches Pfarrerbuch. Die evangelisch-lutherische Geistlichkeit des Fürstentums Brandenburg-Ansbach 1528–1806, Nürnberg 1955, Nr. 1242; Pfarrerbuch der Kirchenprovinz Sachsen, Bd. 4: Biogramme He–Kl), Leipzig 2006, 251 f., und Bd. 10: Series Pastorum, Leip-

HERKUNFT UND STUDIUM

Christoph Hoffmann kam aus Ansbach, der Residenzstadt der fränkischen Hohenzollern, der Burggrafen von Nürnberg, die als vornehmsten Titel den der Markgrafen von Brandenburg führten. Sein Herkunftsort ist überliefert durch den Eintrag am 7. November 1513 in die Matrikel der Universität Freiburg im Breisgau: Cristopherus Hofman de Anspach Herbipolens.⟨is⟩ dioc.⟨esis⟩.[2] Über sein Elternhaus ist nichts bekannt. Vermutlich hat er in Ansbach die Stiftsschule bei St. Gumbertus besucht, wie gut ein Jahrzehnt später auch der aus Kitzingen stammende nachmalige Wittenberger Theologieprofessor Paul Eber (1511–1569).[3] An der Universität Freiburg hat Christoph Hoffmann die Artes studiert und wohl einen akademischen Abschluss erworben. Er ist dann in sein Heimatbistum zurückgekehrt: am 2. Juni 1520 empfing er in Würzburg durch Weihbischof Johann Pettendorfer (um 1470–1533) die Priesterweihe.[4] Da das vorgeschriebene, übliche Mindestalter für die Weihe 25 Jahre betrug,[5] deutet dies auf ein Geburtsjahr um 1495 hin. Zugleich ist ein viel früheres Geburtsjahr, etwa im Blick auf den üblichen Studienanfang, schwer vorstellbar, es finden sich auch keine Hinweise darauf.[6] Damit war Hoffmann etwa gleichaltrig mit den bedeutenden süddeutschen Reformatoren

---

zig 2009, 325 (s.v. Archidiakonat); *Kurt Zahn*, Die Pfarrer der Superintendentur Jena von den Anfängen bis zum Ausgang des 18. Jahrhunderts, 5. Aufl., Kleve 2005, 59 f.; Melanchthons Briefwechsel. Kritische und kommentierte Gesamtausgabe, hg. von *Heinz Scheible*, Stuttgart/Bad Cannstatt 1977 (im Folgenden: MBW), Bd. 12 (2005): Personen F–K, 310 f. Mit dem Ansbacher Hoffmann nicht zu verwechseln ist – bei beiden kommt auch die Schreibung „Hoffman" vor – der Pädagoge Christoph Hofmann (1519–1576) aus Altenburg, der um 1550 kurzzeitig an der neu gegründeten Hohen Schule Jena lehrte; zu diesem vgl. unten Anm. 79.

2. *Hermann Mayer*, Die Matrikel der Universität Freiburg im Breisgau 1460–1656, Bd. 1, Freiburg 1907, 210, Nr. 2.

3. Vgl. *Hermann Jordan*, Reformation und gelehrte Bildung in der Markgrafschaft Ansbach-Bayreuth. Eine Vorgeschichte der Universität Erlangen, Leipzig 1917, 77 f.

4. *Theobald Freudenberger*, Die Würzburger Weihematrikel der Jahre 1520 bis 1552, Würzburg 1990, 88, Nr. 29 („Accoliti seculares"), 95, Nr. 160 („Subdiaconi saeculares"), 99, Nr. 247 („Diaconi saeculares") und 103, Nr. 346 („Presbyteri saeculares"). Zum später ebenfalls evangelisch gewordenen Weihbischof Johann Pettendorfer vgl. Biographisch-Bibliographisches Kirchenlexikon 35 (2014), 1097–1099.

5. Vgl. *Harald Müller*, „Die Pfarrei im Normengefüge der mittelalterlichen Kirche", in: *Enno Bünz, Gerhard Fouquet* (Hg.), Die Pfarrei im späten Mittelalter. Vorträge und Forschungen 77, Ostfildern 2013, 61–96, hier 70.

6. *Daniel Gehrt*, Ernestinische Konfessionspolitik. Bekenntnisbildung, Herrschaftskonsolidierung und dynastische Identitätsstiftung vom Augsburger Interim 1548 bis zur Konkordienformel 1577, Leipzig 2011, 684, nennt (ohne Beleg) das Geburtsjahr 1502.

Andreas Osiander (1496–1552)[7] und Erhard Schnepf (1495–1558), dem späteren Theologieprofessor und Nachfolger Hoffmanns als Stadtpfarrer in Jena. Offenbar strebte Christoph Hoffmann die typische Laufbahn eines gelehrten Geistlichen an, denn bereits kurz danach, am 7. August 1520, immatrikulierte er sich zum Studium der Theologie an der durch Luther in die größte öffentliche Aufmerksamkeit gerückte Universität Wittenberg.[8]

Bereits im Jahr darauf, am 19. Juli 1521 – Luther befand sich auf der Wartburg –, erwarb Christoph Hoffmann an der Leucorea den theologischen Grad eines Baccalaureus biblicus.[9] Seine Promotion erfolgte unter dem Dekanat von Professor Andreas Bodenstein von Karlstadt (1486–1541), und zwar auf der Grundlage einer Disputation über 24 von Karlstadt selbst formulierten Thesen „De perfecta sanitate animae, de participibus mensae Domini, de delicto operum".[10] An den Thesen 9 bis 14 dieser Reihe, in denen Karlstadt den Abendmahlsempfang *sub una specie,* wie ihn die römische Kirche verpflichtend vorschrieb, als Sünde bezeichnete, übte Luther in einem Brief an Melanchthon vom 1. August 1521 scharfe Kritik.[11] Er verteidigte gegen Karlstadt den Freiraum, den Christus nach dem Zeugnis der Heiligen Schrift gelassen habe. Luther wollte, anders als Karlstadt, nicht die Sakramentsempfänger für die dem biblischen Wortlaut zuwiderlaufende Austeilung verantwortlich machen. Er sah die Schuld vielmehr bei denjenigen, die eine solche Spendung willkürlich vorschrieben. In diesem Dissens zwischen Karlstadt und Luther deutete sich bereits der spätere Konflikt um die Gestaltung der evangelischen Abend-

---

7. Das vorgeschriebene und übliche Mindestalter bei der Priesterweihe spricht im Fall Osianders sehr für die Annahme des früheren der beiden erwogenen möglichen Geburtsjahre, also für 1496; vgl. zuletzt dazu *Gerhard Simon,* „Das Geburtsjahr Andreas Osianders", in: Zeitschrift für bayerische Kirchengeschichte 84 (2015), 101–113.

8. Immatrikulationseintrag: „Christophorus Hoffmann Anolspachius Herbi: dio. 7 augustj"; *Karl Eduard Förstemann,* Album Academiae Vitebergensis ab a. Ch. MDII usque ad a. MDLX [1502–1560], Leipzig 1841, 96 b, Nr. 13.

9. Promotionsnotiz: „anno MDXXI sub ẹstiuo Decanatu-Andree Carolstadij […] D. Christophorus Hoffman Onolczpachus die 19 Iulij respondit pro biblijs et promotus est in baccalaureum Biblię"; *Karl Eduard Förstemann, Liber Decanorum* facultatis theologicae Academiae Vitebergensis, Leipzig 1838, 25. Das Nachschlagewerk *Daniel Bohnert, Markus Wriedt,* Theologiae Alumni Vitebergenses (TAV). Die graduierten Absolventen der Wittenberger Theologischen Fakultät (1502–1648), Leipzig 2020, übergeht bedauerlicherweise die (zahlenmäßig geringen) Graduierungen der Baccalaurei.

10. Edition: *Andreas Bodenstein von Karlstadt,* Kritische Gesamtausgabe der Schriften und Briefe, hg. von *Thomas Kaufmann,* Gütersloh 2017 ff., hier Bd. 4, Nr. 186; vgl. *Hermann Barge,* Andreas Bodenstein von Karlstadt, 2 Bde., Leipzig 1905, hier Bd. 1, 290 f. und 479 f.

11. D. Martin Luthers Werke. Kritische Gesamtausgabe, 73 Bde., Weimar 1883–2009 (im Folgenden: WA); hier Briefwechsel (im Folgenden: WA.B), Bd. 2, 371,51–372,64, Nr. 424, sowie MBW 157 (MBW.T 1), 322–326.

mahlspraxis in Wittenberg an, der um die Jahreswende 1521/1522 ausbrach – ein Vorbote des späteren Abendmahlsstreits, den Karlstadt mit seinen Publikationen im Jahr 1524 entfesseln sollte.

Im Frühjahr 1522 war es vermutlich Christoph Hoffmann – die Identität des Fragestellers ist allerdings nicht ganz sicher –, der Karlstadt um Auskunft zu verschiedenen aktuell diskutierten theologischen Streitpunkten bat. Es ging um Themen wie das Wissen des Gläubigen um seine Prädestination, den Sündenfall und die Auferstehung des Gerechtfertigten. Angesprochen war auch die „fides aliena" und die Kindertaufe sowie der Punkt der wirksamen Perseveranz des Geistes in den „Heiligen". Dieser Brief, mit dem bei Karlstadt angefragt worden war, ist selbst nicht erhalten. Er lässt sich nur über einen lateinischen Brief Luthers, der inzwischen von der Wartburg zurückgekehrt war, an einen sich nun nicht (mehr) in Wittenberg befindlichen Empfänger erschließen, den er mit dem Vornamen „Christophore" anredete.[12] Bei diesem Adressaten handelte es sich aller Wahrscheinlichkeit nach um Christoph Hoffmann, der an der Leucorea studiert hatte und Luther daher wohl auch persönlich bekannt war.[13] Vor dem Hintergrund seiner Erfahrungen mit den sog. Zwickauer Propheten ermahnte Luther seinen Korrespondenzpartner freundlich, sich vor solchen neuen dogmatischen Streitpunkten in Acht zu nehmen.

Dass Hoffmann theologischen Debatten nicht aus dem Weg ging, zeigt auch die Notiz des Chronisten Beringer: In einer Disputation mit dem Kitzinger Lateinschulmeister Christoph Flurheim, der beweisen wollte, dass der

---

12. WA.B Bd. 2, 550, 1–5: „Ex iis, qui tibi bene volunt, amicis, optime Christophore, intellexi quaestiones tuas, quas Doctori Andreae Carlstadio proposuisti de scientia praedestinationis, de lapsu et resurrectione iusti, de fide aliena, de baptismo parvulorum, de perseverantia spiritus in sanctis etc." Der Brief (WA.B Bd. 2, 549–551, Nr. 502) ist nur durch seinen Erstdruck im Rahmen der Jenaer Lutherausgabe überliefert; vgl. Verzeichnis der im deutschen Sprachbereich erschienenen Drucke des 16. Jahrhunderts (im Folgenden: VD16), VD16 L 4652, hier: Bl. 308r/v. Dieser 1565 erschienene Briefband geht zurück auf die Sammlung von Johannes Aurifaber (um 1519–1575), dem späteren Nachfolger Hoffmanns als Weimarer Hofprediger. Eine Datierung des Luther-Briefs ist nur vom Inhalt her ungefähr möglich. Luther hatte, wie sein Schreiben zu erkennen gibt, von der theologischen Anfrage des Christoph bei Karlstadt erfahren. Auch ein Antwortbrief Karlstadts, wenn es ihn überhaupt gegeben hat, ist nicht überliefert; vgl. dazu ausführlich *Karlstadt*, Gesamtausgabe (wie Anm. 10), Bd. 5, Nr. 230.

13. Die briefliche Anrede mit „optime Christophore" deutet auf eine gewisse Vertrautheit Luthers mit dem Adressaten hin und könnte gut an ein an der Universität entstandenes Lehrer-Schüler-Verhältnis zum Ausdruck bringen. Über das im Zusammenhang mit *Bohnert, Wriedt*, Theologiae Alumni Vitebergenses (wie Anm. 9) erarbeitete Datenbankprojekt Corpus Inscriptorum Witebergense (www.civ-online.org) lassen sich bequem alle eingeschriebenen Wittenberger Studenten mit dem Vornamen Christoph ermitteln: unter diesen ist Hoffmann aus Ansbach mit Abstand der plausibelste Korrespondenzpartner.

Mensch einen freien Wille besitze, dass es das Fegefeuer gebe und dass man die Heiligen anrufen solle, habe sich Christoph Hoffmann als tief in der Heiligen Schrift gegründeter Theologe behauptet. Überlegen habe er seinen Kontrahenten zum Schweigen gebracht.[14] Insgesamt ist allerdings zu konstatieren, dass sich eigene Texte und briefliche Äußerungen Hoffmanns allein aus seinen Wirkungszeiten in Jena und Weimar bzw. in Augsburg überliefert finden, also nur aus den Lebensjahren von 1536 bis 1549. Besonders mag man das Fehlen sämtlicher authentischer Zeugnisse aus Hoffmanns früheren Jahren, den Zeiten seines Studiums und seiner Tätigkeit als Prädikant und Reformator in Kitzingen bedauern. Seine theologische Positionierung lässt sich daher nur indirekt erschließen. Dies betrifft insbesondere auch die Einschätzung seiner Haltung zu Luther und Karlstadt. Hoffmann hat Luthers Warnung vor irreführenden theologischen Fragen offenbar beherzigt. Es finden sich jedenfalls keine anderslautenden Quellenhinweise dazu und ebenso wenig Hinweise auf weitere persönliche Kontakte Hoffmanns mit Karlstadt. Vielmehr deutet alles darauf hin, dass sich Hoffmann in seiner weiteren theologischen Entwicklung eng Luther angeschlossen hat.

RATSPRÄDIKANT UND REFORMATOR IN KITZINGEN, 1522–1527

Wo Christoph Hoffmann tätig war, bevor er im Hochsommer 1522 nach Kitzingen kam, liegt im Dunkeln. Möglicherweise bewegte er sich in Würzburg im Umfeld der evangelisch gesinnten Domprediger Paul Speratus (1484–1551) und Johann Gramann (1487–1541) oder in seiner Heimatstadt Ansbach.[15] Am Hof der Markgrafen waren mit Kaplan Johann Rurer (um 1485–1542) und Kanzleisekretär Georg Vogler (1486/7–1550) entschiedene Luther-Anhänger am Werk.[16] Sicher bezeugt ist allerdings, dass Christoph Hoffmann durch die Vermittlung von Konrad Gutmann, dem markgräflichen Kastner

---

14. Vgl. *Hans-Christoph Rublack* (Bearb.), „Quellen zur Reformationsgeschichte Kitzingens", in: *Dieter Demandt, Hans-Christoph Rublack* (Hg.), Stadt und Kirche in Kitzingen. Darstellung und Quellen zu Spätmittelalter und Reformation, Stuttgart 1978, 101–321, hier 287.

15. Zum Kreis früh in Würzburg präsenter evangelisch gesinnter Kleriker vgl. *Hans-Christoph Rublack*, Geschreiterte Reformation. Frühreformatorische und protestantische Bewegungen in süd- und westdeutschen geistlichen Residenzen, Stuttgart 1978, 10–29.

16. Vgl. *Wolfgang Huber, „Georg Vogler (1486/87–1550). Kanzler der Markgrafen von Brandenburg-Ansbach und Vorkämpfer der Reformation", in: *Zeitschrift für bayerische Kirchengeschichte* 77 (2008), 52–82; vgl. Rurer, Johann (um 1485–1542), in: Biographisch-Bi-

und Zentgrafen,[17] die Anstellung als Ratsprädikant in Kitzingen erhielt. Der Rat nahm Hoffmann am 10. August 1522 in seinen Dienst.[18] Große Teile des Rates und der Einwohnerschaft hatten sich offenbar schon früh der Theologie Luthers geöffnet. Kitzingen, das seit 1443 vom Fürstbischof von Würzburg an die Markgrafen von Brandenburg-Ansbach verpfändet war, lebte von seiner günstigen Lage am Main, und zwar vor allem vom Weinhandel. Mit einer Einwohnerzahl von an die 3.000 gehörte es zu den größten und wohlhabendsten Städten des Fürstentums Ansbach.[19] Dem Kitzinger Rat, der sich auch in diesem Bereich in der Verantwortung sah, lag erkennbar an einer Reform des kommunalen Kirchenwesens, insbesondere einer zuverlässigen und schriftgemäßen Seelsorge sowie an einer gelehrten und sachgemäßen „verkundigung der Euangelischenn ler vnnd wort gottes".[20] Unter dieser Prämisse begann der in Wittenberg ausgebildete Theologe Christoph Hoffmann seinen Dienst als Ratsprädikant. Hoffmann darf noch vor Johann Schenk von Siemau, einem ehemaligen Franziskaner, angestellt im Februar 1523 als Pfarrverweser,[21] und mindestens neben dessen seit März 1525 amtierenden Nachfolger Martin Meglin als bedeutendster reformatorischer Theologe Kitzingens gelten.[22] Mit großem Einsatz und Überzeugungskraft hat Hoffmann die evangelische Be-

---

bliographisches Kirchenlexikon, hg. von *Friedrich Wilhelm Bautz, Traugott Bautz*, Hamm 1975 ff., hier Band 33 (2012), 1149–1159.

17. Zu Konrad Gutmann (gest. 20. Juli 1526) vgl. *Erdmann Weyrauch*, „Die politische Führungsschicht Kitzingens vornehmlich im 16. Jahrhundert", in: *Erdmann Weyrauch, Ingrid Bátory* (Hg.), Die bürgerliche Elite der Stadt Kitzingen. Studien zur Sozial- und Wirtschaftsgeschichte einer landesherrlichen Stadt im 16. Jahrhundert, Stuttgart 1982, 205–879, hier 816–818.

18. Vgl. *Hans-Christoph Rublack*, „Die Reformation in Kitzingen", in: *Demandt, Rublack*, Stadt (wie Anm. 14), 34–96, hier 39 mit Anm. 16 und 46–50 zur Auseinandersetzung um die „Aneignung der Pfründe der Alten Frühmesse" durch den Rat, die die Grundlage der Finanzierung der Prädikatur Hoffmanns war.

19. Vgl. *Klaus Arnold*, „Spätmittelalterliche Sozialstruktur, Bürgeropposition und Bauernkrieg in der Stadt Kitzingen", in: Jahrbuch für fränkische Landesforschung 36 (1976), 173–214, hier 176.

20. *Rublack*, Quellen (wie Anm. 14), 204 (Brief des Kitzinger Rates an Markgraf Kasimir von Brandenburg-Ansbach, 9. Oktober 1522).

21. Vgl. *Rublack*, Reformation (wie Anm. 18), 44 f. mit Anm. 33, und *Rublack*, Quellen (wie Anm. 14), 288 (Beringer-Chronik). Über Herkunft und den weiteren Weg des „Johannes Schencke von Synaw" – so die Schreibung beim zeitgenössischen Kitzinger Chronisten Hans Beringer – vgl. *Simon*, Ansbachisches Pfarrerbuch (wie Anm. 1), Nr. 2570, sowie den in Anm. 22 genannten Beitrag.

22. Zu Meglin vgl. *Wolfgang Huber*, „Martin Meglin und sein Vorgänger Johann Schenk von Siemau. Die beiden ersten evangelischen Pfarrer von Kitzingen (1523–1533)", in: Zeitschrift für bayerische Kirchengeschichte 90 (2021), 41–69.

wegung in Kitzingen und den frühen reformatorischen Kurs der Stadt entscheidend vorangebracht, oder wie der zeitgenössische Chronist seine Rolle kennzeichnet: „der war der erst, der das Euangelium den von kitzingen zu den letzten Zeiten bracht".[23]

Erstmals konkret sichtbar wird der eingeschlagene Reformationskurs an der Neuordnung der kommunalen Armenfürsorge, die der Kitzinger Rat nach dem Vorbild Wittenbergs und Nürnbergs im Jahr 1523 durchführte. Dem Projekt des sog. „Gemeinen Kastens"[24] zugrunde gelegt wurde die aus der Bibel gewonnene Erkenntnis, dass Christenmenschen zur Liebe Gottes und des Nächsten verpflichtet seien und darum niemand zum Betteln gezwungen sein dürfe. Die gebotene brüderliche Liebe zeige sich in der Fürsorge für die Mitmenschen, die mit ihrer Hände Arbeit ohne eigene Schuld nicht genügend für ihren Lebensunterhalt verdienen können. Im Gegenzug erwartete man von Armen ein frommes, ehrliches Verhalten. Auswärtige Bedürftige wurden von den Leistungen des Gemeinen Kastens ausgeschlossen. Christoph Hoffmann setzte sich stark für die Sache des Gemeinen Kastens ein, wofür ihm der Chronist Beringer besondere Anerkennung zollte.[25] Er hat sehr wahrscheinlich bei dessen Konzeption mitgewirkt. Ihre Formulierungen erinnern im übrigen stellenweise an die Wittenberger Beutelordnung,[26] was Hoffmann, der Beziehungen an die Leucorea unterhielt, eingebracht haben könnte. Dass in den Jahren 1523 und 1524 neben Nürnberg auch in der Reichsstadt Windsheim sowie in den markgräflichen Städten Ansbach und Schwabach neue Armenordnungen erlassen wurden,[27] spricht für eine konzertierte Aktion, die sich insgesamt an Wittenberg ausrichtete und vermutlich über Georg Vogler in der Ansbacher Regie-

---

23. Vgl. die Darstellung der Chronik von Hans Beringer, in: *Rublack*, Quellen (wie Anm. 14), 310 (Beringer-Chronik): Im Jahr 1522 „gab der Almechtig ewig gott durch seine mittel ein gelerten trefflichen man Inn dreien sprachen mit namen Cristoff Hoffman von Onoltzbach gen kitzing das heilig lauter Euangelium zu predigen das er dann unstrefflich und unthadelich mit grossem geist thet. wiewol er deshalben grossen anstos erstlich litte und seer von den Bepstischen pfaffen geneidt und verhasset ward etc. und der war der erst, der das Euangelium den von kitzingen zu den letzten Zeiten bracht".

24. Die zugrundeliegende Ordnung wurde in Nürnberg zum Druck gebracht: Ein christliche Ordnung der Bettler halben über den aufgerichteten Gemeinen Kasten in der Stadt Kitzingen zu Franken, am Tag Martini angangen 1523; VD16 K 1115; Edition: *Emil Sehling* (Hg.), Die evangelischen Kirchenordnungen des XVI. Jahrhunderts. Bd. 11/I: Bayern: (Franken), Tübingen 1961, 72–76; vgl. *Rublack*, Reformation (wie Anm. 18), 51–57.

25. Vgl. *Rublack*, Quellen (wie Anm. 14), 288f.

26. Vgl. *Barge*, Karlstadt (wie Anm. 10), Bd. 1, 498–500 mit einem synoptischen Vergleich.

27. Vgl. *Jürgen Wolfgang Hansen*, Almosenordnungen im 16. Jahrhundert. Anfänge einer Sozialpolitik, insbesondere in süddeutschen Städten, Diss. phil. masch. Passau 2007, passim.

rungskanzlei vermittelt wurde. Überhaupt waren innerhalb der beiden brandenburgischen Fürstentümer Ansbach und Kulmbach/Bayreuth die Städte sozusagen die Schrittmacher für den Eingang und die Ausbreitung der Reformation.[28]

Mit dem Rückhalt des Rates nahmen Hoffmann und Pfarreiverweser Schenk von Siemau erste Änderungen in den Zeremonien vor.[29] Gegen dieses Vorgehen, der evangelischen Predigt entsprechende Reformmaßnahmen folgen zu lassen, regte sich auch Widerstand von romtreuen Klerikern und einzelnen Ratsmitgliedern.[30] Namentlich Hoffmann wurde als Protagonist der Wittenberger Theologie in Kitzingen wahrgenommen und – nach dem Zeugnis des Chronisten Hans Beringer, der mit Hoffmann sogar gemeinsam in Wittenberg studiert hatte[31] – in der Kitzinger Bevölkerung gelegentlich gar als „der junge Luther" bezeichnet.[32] Eine alles dominierende Rolle als evangelischer Theologe hat Christoph Hoffmann, wie es scheint, wiederum auch nicht gespielt. Ein frei herumziehender Prediger, der vorher aus Nürnberg ausgewiesen worden war und schlicht der „Bauer von Wöhrd" genannt wurde,[33] hielt Ende Mai 1524 Predigten unter freiem Himmel. Er übte vor allem Kritik an der überkommenen Heiligenverehrung und erzielte überwältigende Resonanz bei der Bevölkerung. Auch der Kitzinger Rat ließ sich von seiner charismatischen Predigttätigkeit beeindrucken und fand sich bereit, diese ganz praktisch zu fördern. Dies wiederum provozierte das Eingreifen des um die öffentliche Ordnung besorgten Landesherrn: Markgraf Kasimir verbot das Treiben dieses „Bauern" in seinem Herrschaftsgebiet und verfügte dessen Ausweisung. Der Markgraf bzw. dessen Kanzlei verband diesen Befehl mit dem Hinweis, dass

---

28. Vgl. *Martin G. Meier*, Systembruch und Neuordnung. Reformation und Konfessionsbildung in den Markgraftümern Brandenburg-Ansbach-Kulmbach 1520–1594, Frankfurt/M. 1999, 48–95.

29. Vgl. *Rublack*, Reformation (wie Anm. 18), 44 f. mit Anm. 32–35, sowie *Rublack*, Quellen (wie Anm. 14), 288 (Beringer-Chronik).

30. Zum Problem der Identifizierung der Gegner vgl. *Weyrauch*, Führungsschicht (wie Anm. 17), 268 f.

31. Zu Johann Beringer (1496–1558) vgl. *Weyrauch*, Führungsschicht (wie Anm. 17), 337–342.

32. *Rublack*, Quellen (wie Anm. 14), 287 f. (Beringer-Chronik): „Es wart auch gedachter prediger vonn dem gemaynen man nit annderß dann der Jung Luther genannt."

33. Zu Diepold Peringer, dem „Bauern von Wöhrd", vgl. *Günter Vogler*, Nürnberg 1524/25. Studien zur Geschichte der reformatorischen und sozialen Bewegung in der Reichsstadt, Berlin 1982, 135–151 u. ö.; neuerdings *Martin Keßler*, „Kirchengeschichtliche Epochenkonzepte und Endzeiterwartungen in der frühen Reformation zwischen gemessener und erlebbarer Zeit", in: Berliner Theologische Zeitschrift 37 (2020), 119–139, hier 134–138.

Kitzingen an Predigern des Wortes Gottes – gemeint waren natürlich zuerst Christoph Hoffmann und Johann Schenk von Siemau – doch offenkundig keinen Mangel leide.[34] So blieb das Auftreten des „Bauern von Wöhrd" auch in Kitzingen eine Episode. Sie zeigte jedoch, dass neben Hoffmann noch Raum blieb für das Agieren einer weiteren für die Reformation engagierten Persönlichkeit. Diesen Raum besetzte, wie es scheint, seit März 1525 der neue, von den bischöflichen Behörden regulär bestellte Verweser der Stadtpfarrei Martin Meglin. Bis zu seinem Tod im Jahr 1533 hatte er zweifellos die Führungsposition in der Kitzinger Reformation inne.

Vorher noch war – wie Beringer in seinem „Zeitbüchlein" berichtet – Andreas Karlstadt, Hoffmanns vormaliger Wittenberger Professor, im Herbst 1524 nach Kitzingen gekommen. Zu Luther in erbitterte Gegnerschaft geraten und aus Kursachsen ausgewiesen, suchte er offenbar in seiner fränkischen Heimat nach einer neuen Anstellung und Bleibe für sich und seine junge Familie. In Kitzingen stellte freilich nicht der vormalige Wittenberger Promovend Hoffmann die erste Bezugsperson dar, sondern vielmehr der markgräfliche Kastner Gutmann, dem Karlstadt 1521 seine Schrift über die Mönchsgelübde gewidmet hatte.[35] Karlstadt blieb nach der Chronik Beringers „etlich tag alda konnt aber nit vnnter khomen Dann es hatten etlich ein schewen vor Ime".[36] Karlstadt hielt sich also nur kurz in Kitzingen auf, spürte hier wohl die Scheu, sich mit ihm einzulassen, und wandte sich weiter nach Rothenburg ob der Tauber.[37] Möglicherweise war es sogar Hoffmann gewesen, der wegen seiner Verbindungen nach Wittenberg und Ansbach Karlstadts längeren Aufenthalt in der Stadt Kitzingen verhinderte. Ein paar Wochen später, nämlich Ende Januar 1525, war es wiederum Gutmann, der das Schreiben Karlstadts an Markgraf Kasimir von Brandenburg-Ansbach (1481–1527) weiterleitete, in dem er um die Aufenthaltserlaubnis in seinem Territorium bat. Der Ansbacher Hof schlug dieses Ansinnen ab.[38] Karlstadt musste sich weiter in Rothenburg verborgen halten, bis ihn die katastrophalen Niederlagen der aufständischen

---

34. Zu Peringers Auftreten in Kitzingen vgl. *Rublack*, Reformation (wie Anm. 18), 58–63, und (populärwissenschaftlich) *Hans-Christoph Rublack*, Hat die Nonne den Pfarrer geküßt? Aus dem Alltag der Reformationszeit, Gütersloh 1991, 24–31.
35. Vgl. *Karlstadt*, Gesamtausgabe (wie Anm. 10), Bd. 4, Nr. 203.
36. Vgl. *Rublack*, Quellen (wie Anm. 14), 284f. (Beringer-Chronik).
37. Zu den Karlstadts Reisen im Herbst 1524 nach seiner Ausweisung aus Orlamünde zwischen Mainfranken, Zürich, Basel, Heidelberg, Straßburg und Rothenburg vgl. künftig *Karlstadt*, Gesamtausgabe (wie Anm. 10), Bd. 6.
38. Vgl. *Rublack*, Reformation (wie Anm. 18), 61 mit Anm. 20; *Barge*, Karlstadt (wie Anm. 10) Bd. 2, 297f., 310f.

Bauern in Franken und Thüringen zwangen, für sich und seine Familie bei Luther selbst Schutz zu suchen, den ihm dieser auch gewährte.[39]

Unter dem evangelischen Theologen Christoph Hoffmann, dem Ratsprädikanten, und Johann Schenk von Siemau, dem Pfarrverweser, fanden die ersten evangelischen Reformen in Kitzingen statt:[40] irreführende Zeremonien wurden von ihnen abgestellt. Offenbar begannen Hoffmann und Schenk von Siemau damit, in der Stadtpfarrkirche – nach dem Rat Luthers in der Adelsschrift – täglich nur noch eine „Messe" zu feiern und das Abendmahl auch unter beiderlei Gestalt auszuteilen, wenn das die Empfänger so begehrten. Sie strebten also frühzeitig danach, die Feier der Abendmahlsgottesdienste eng an der biblischen Einsetzung auszurichten, und gebrauchten in ihnen sicher auch die deutsche Sprache. Im August 1523 sandte Moritz Marschalk von Ostheim, zu Wallbach und Waltershausen (1474–1523) – der designierte, doch schon bald darauf verstorbene Amtmann von Kitzingen, der von der evangelischen Bewegung um Hoffmann und Schenk von Siemau mit „Wohlgefallen" und „Freude" gehört hatte – der Stadt „vir deutzsche messen" zu.[41] Gemeint sind damit vermutlich vier Exemplare des von dem evangelisch gesinnten Adeligen besorgten Drucks der Übersetzung der Messordnung, die Johannes Oekolampad als Hofkaplan auf Sickingens Ebernburg angefertigt hatte.[42] Moritz Marschalk von Ostheim ließ sie, wie er den Kitzingern mitteilte, in den Kirchen seiner Herrschaft so „mit verkundigen des worts Gottes offentlich alle sontag halten und brauchen".[43] Praktisch orientierten Hoffmann und Schenk von Siemau sich

---

39. Vgl. *Barge*, Karlstadt (wie Anm. 10), 297–372.

40. Vgl. *Rublack*, Reformation (wie Anm. 18), S. 45 mit Anm. 35 und S. 64. Nach Auskunft der Beringer-Chronik wurden unter anderem abgeschafft: das Weihwasser, das geweihte Salz und die Weihe von Gewürzen und Fladen, die Prozessionen in den Fastenzeiten, die Palmenweihen, die Hungertücher und die Verhüllung der Altäre, die Fronleichnamsbegängnisse, das Gewitterläuten sowie das Singen des „Salve Regina" und anderer „gottloser" Gesänge; *Rublack*, Quellen (wie Anm. 14), 288.

41. Vgl. *Rublack*, Quellen (wie Anm. 14), S. 221 f. Zu Moritz Marschalk von Ostheim vgl. *Ernst Staehelin* (Bearb.): Briefe und Akten zum Leben Oekolampads 1, Leipzig 1927, 248 f., Anm. 2–5; *Ernst Staehelin,* Das theologische Lebenswerk Johannes Oekolampads, Leipzig 1939, 165–169.

42. Zu Oekolampads Zeit auf der Ebernburg vgl. *Thomas Kaufmann,* „Sickingen, Hutten, der Ebernburg-Kreis und die reformatorische Bewegung", in: Blätter für pfälzische Kirchengeschichte 82 (2015), 235–290, hier 273–280; auch gedruckt als Ebernburg-Hefte 49/2015, 35–90.

43. Druck: Das Testament Jesu Christi, das man bisher hat genannt die Messe, verdeutscht durch Dr. Johann Oekolampad, Ecclesiasten zu Adelnburg, zu Heil allen Evangelischen, nämlich Herr Moritz Marschalk, Ritter zu Waltershausen, 1523. – Dieses deutschsprachige, evangelische Messformular wurde allem Anschein nach in Bamberg zuerst zum Druck gebracht und in typischen Mess-Lettern gesetzt (VD 16, M 4862 und ZV 31674).

gewiss am Fortgang der Gottesdienstreformen in Wittenberg und Nürnberg. Wie es scheint, strebten sie auch mit der Äbtissin, der Inhaberin des Patronats, die Verständigung darüber an. Allerdings wich diese offenbar einer Entscheidung aus, verhielt sich in den Auseinandersetzungen eher passiv und versuchte sich mit der Entwicklung in der Stadt zu arrangieren.[44]

Bei aller grundsätzlich notwendigen Rücksicht auf die landesfürstliche Haltung in der Religionspolitik wurden vermutlich in Kitzingen früher als in der Residenzstadt Ansbach öffentlich evangelische Abendmahlsgottesdienste gefeiert. Wann genau und unter wessen Leitung solche Gottesdienste erstmals stattfanden, im Spätjahr 1523 oder erst im Lauf des Jahres 1524, ist nicht überliefert.[45] Die Feier nach dem überkommenen römischen Messkanon wurde freilich auch in Kitzingen zunächst nicht völlig abgestellt. Die Abschaffung der Feier nach dem römischen Messkanon erfolgte erst im Jahr 1528 auf der Grundlage der Anordnungen des neuen Landesherrn Markgraf Georg von Brandenburg-Ansbach (1484–1543). Die Eintracht zwischen dem Ratsprädikanten Hoffmann und dem Stadtpfarrer bestand unter Martin Meglin, der im März 1525, am Vorabend des Bauernkriegs das Amt des Stadtpfarrers antrat, weiter. Beide arbeiteten offenbar gedeihlich zusammen.[46] Hoffmann war insbesondere für die Gottesdienste an Sonn- und Feiertagen „nach mittemtag" in der Stadtpfarrkirche zuständig.[47] Bei den gottesdienstlichen Reformen wurde – auch hier wird die Orientierung an Wittenberg und Nürnberg spürbar – behutsam vorgegangen. Man behielt ganz offensichtlich die Form der evangeli-

---

Ein sprachlich leicht überarbeiteter Nachdruck erschien noch im selben Jahr 1523 in Nürnberg (VD16 M 4864) und dann diesem Nürnberger Druck jeweils folgend in Augsburg (VD16 4861), Erfurt (VD16 4863), Zwickau (VD16 M 4866 und ZV 3863). 1524 erschien in Nürnberg ein neuer Nachdruck (VD16 M 4867). Vgl. die gründliche erste Analyse und Edition (nach dem Erfurter Druck, VD16 M 4863) bei: *Julius Smend*, Die evangelischen deutschen Messen bis zu Luthers Deutscher Messe, Göttingen 1896, 49–71.

44. Der seit 1522 amtierenden Äbtissin Katharina von Fronhofen (gest. 1529) wurden von der romtreuen Seite deswegen Vorhaltungen gemacht; vgl. *Rublack*, Reformation (wie Anm. 18), 63 mit Anm. 1. Das im Bauernkrieg geplünderte und zerstörte Benediktinerinnenkloster wurde danach wieder aufgebaut, im Jahr 1544 jedoch endgültig aufgelöst. In seine Gebäude zog 1558 ein evangelisches Damenstift ein. Nach der Gegenreformation errichtete man an seiner Stelle 1686 bis 1693 ein neues Ursulinenkloster, das bis 1804 bestand. Seit 1817 dient die vormalige Klosterkirche, erworben im Tausch gegen die St. Michaelskirche Etwashausens, als Evangelische Stadtkirche Kitzingens.

45. Vgl. *Rublack*, Reformation (wie Anm. 18), 64 mit Anm. 4.

46. Vgl. *Rublack*, Quellen (wie Anm. 14), 288 (Beringer-Chronik).

47. Vgl. den Bericht der Kitzinger Amtleute und des Rates an den Hof vom 8. August 1528, ediert bei *Karl Schornbaum*, Aktenstücke zur ersten Brandenburgischen Kirchenvisitation 1528, München 1928, 41–46, hier: 43.

schen, deutschsprachigen Messe bei und führte gemeinsam Gemeindegesänge ein wie die von Luther übersetzten Hymnen „Komm, Heiliger Geist, Herre Gott" oder „Wir glauben all an einen Gott".

Kitzingen wurde tief hineingezogen in die katastrophalen Ereignisse des fränkischen Bauernkrieges. Die Aufständischen nahmen die Stadt ein und zwangen sie zum Bündnis, das Benediktinerinnenkloster wurde geplündert und zerstört. Hoffmann hat sich sicher, wie wohl auch Meglin, distanziert-kritisch zum Aufstand verhalten. Ansonsten hätte er persönliche Konsequenzen erleiden müssen, als Markgraf Kasimir die Stadt einnahm und ein grausames Strafgericht hielt.[48] Hoffmann dagegen leistete seine Unterschrift unter die von Meglin verfasste Petition an Markgraf Kasimir, in der die evangelischen Theologen der Stadt um Gnade für die vom Landesherrn bereits genügend gestraften Kitzinger Bürger baten. Dies stellte eine mutige Tat dar angesichts der allseits gefürchteten Bereitschaft des Fürsten auch zu brutaler Herrschaftsausübung.

Am 5. November 1526 vollzog Pfarrer Meglin in aller „Ehrbarkeit" die Trauung Hoffmanns mit der Tochter eines Kitzinger Bürgers.[49] Der Ehe entsprangen sieben Kinder. Als verheirateter Geistlicher musste Hoffmann am 22. April 1527 aufgrund der Repressionen Markgraf Kasimirs, der nach der neuen vermittelnden Religionsregelung die Protagonisten der reformatorischen Bewegung in seinem Fürstentum verfolgen ließ, Kitzingen verlassen.[50] Dass die Bedrohung real war, zeigte sich etwa am Ansbacher Stadtpfarrer Johann Rurer, der im Februar 1527 nach Schlesien fliehen musste, und besonders tragisch am Schicksal des Bayreuther Reformators Georg Schmalzing (1491–1554). Dieser war bereits im November 1526 von den markgräflichen Behörden verhaftet und an den Bamberger Fürstbischof ausgeliefert worden. Erst im Februar 1530 sollte er die Freiheit wieder erlangen. Schmalzing kam dann – in den Markgraftümern Ansbach und Kulmbach hatte mit dem Regierungsantritt Markgraf Georgs von Brandenburg die Reformation Einzug gehalten – aber noch in den Genuss eines dreisemestrigen Theologiestudiums in Wittenberg, wo er den Magistergrad erwarb.[51] Als im Jahr 1533 der Kitzinger

---

48. Vgl. (überhaupt pointiert zur Geschichte der Reformation in Kitzingen) *Peter Blickle*, Gemeindereformation. Die Menschen des 16. Jahrhunderts auf dem Weg zum Heil, München 1987, 82–85, besonders 82.
49. Vgl. *Rublack*, Quellen (wie Anm. 14), 289 (Beringer-Chronik).
50. Vgl. *Rublack*, Reformation (wie Anm. 18), 82 mit Anm. 49.
51. Vgl. *Friedrich Lippert*, „Die 400jährige Reformation im Markgrafentum Bayreuth und Georg Schmalzing", in: Archiv für Geschichte und Altertumskunde von Oberfranken 30 (1928), Heft 2, 1–172 (bes. 132–172).

Stadtpfarrer Martin Meglin allzu früh starb, wurden von Luther und Melanchthon, die um Empfehlungen für einen Nachfolger gebeten wurden, die Namen Christoph Hoffmanns und Georg Schmalzings genannt.[52] Das Amt übernahm schließlich Georg Schmalzing. Dass der evangelische Prädikant Hoffmann die Bedrohung seiner Person und die Flucht mit seiner jungen Familie aus ihrer Heimat in eine unsichere Zukunft als existenzielle Erschütterung erfuhr, darf man annehmen. Möglicherweise ist hierin auch seine später dokumentierte apokalyptische Geschichtswahrnehmung in diesem persönlichen Erleben zumindest mitmotiviert. Allerdings liegen dazu keine Selbstzeugnisse vor.

PFARRER UND SUPERINTENDENT IN HERZBERG UND JENA, 1527–1544

Nach seiner Flucht aus den fränkischen Markgrafentümern wandte sich Christoph Hoffmann bezeichnenderweise zuerst an seinen früheren Studienort zu Luther und Melanchthon, um von dort aus nach neuen Lebens- und Arbeitsmöglichkeiten für sich und seine Familie Ausschau zu halten.[53] Noch im Jahr 1527 erreichte ihn die Berufung in die kursächsische Amtsstadt Herzberg an der Elster, ungefähr 50 Kilometer südöstlich von Wittenberg gelegen, an der Fernstraße von Leipzig nach Frankfurt an der Oder. Hier übernahm Hoffmann am 12. April 1528 das Amt des Archidiakons an der Seite von Andreas Wagener (vor 1495–1561), der seit 1522 als Ortspfarrer amtierte und als letzter Beichtvater Friedrichs des Weisen diesem auf dem Sterbebett das evangelische Abendmahl gereicht hatte.[54] Möglicherweise war es die Nähe zwischen Herzberg und dem kürfürstlichen Jagdschloss Lochau, das den Herzberger Archidiakon mit dem ernestinischen Fürstenhaus in persönliche Bekanntschaft brachte. Im Pfarrdienst in Herzberg, nach dem Studium und dem knapp fünfjährigen Wirken als evangelischer Prediger in Kitzingen, dem dritten Abschnitt seiner theologischen Laufbahn, bewährte sich Hoffmann offenbar, denn nach

---

52. Vgl. WA.B 7, 3.
53. „Der Prediger Herr Christof Hoffman raißet wiederumb hinein gein Wittemberg Zum Doctor Mart[ino] Luther vnnd Zum Philippo Melanch[thoni] (Die Ine wol kanten vnnd sehr lieb Hetten) Gottes Rath bey Innen Zu suchen vnnd Zuge von den von Kitzingen am letsten ostertag [...]"; *Rublack*, Quellen (wie Anm. 14), 291.
54. Vgl. *Ingetraut Ludolphy*, Friedrich der Weise, Kurfürst von Sachsen, Göttingen 1984, 483; zu Wagener vgl. Pfarrerbuch Kirchenprovinz Sachsen (wie Anm. 1), Bd. 9, 181, und Bd. 10, 325 (s. v. Herzberg/Elster).

wiederum gut acht Jahren erfolgte der Ruf in eine weitere verantwortungsvolle Position: Er trat am 23. April 1536 als Nachfolger des Anton Musa (um 1485–1547) das Amt des leitenden Pfarrers und kursächsischen Superintendenten in Jena an.[55] Die Universität war zwar noch nicht gegründet, aber die prosperierende Stadt an der Saale stellte das Zentrum der Region dar, in der Karlstadt etwa gut zehn Jahre zuvor als Reformator gewirkt hatte, wo es besonders wichtig war, ein stabiles evangelisches Kirchenwesen aufrecht zu erhalten. Hoffmann und seine Familie kamen zunächst im vormaligen Dominikanerkloster unter, da das Jenenser Pfarrhaus noch durch vormalige Zisterziensernonnen des Michaelisklosters belegt war.[56] Über die pastorale Tätigkeit Hoffmanns in Herzberg liegen keine Quellenhinweise vor. Von seinem Wirken in Jena ist lediglich überliefert, dass Hoffmann wie sein Vorgänger und seine Nachfolger „abgöttische Schnitzwerke aus der Kirche, besonders die abgöttischen Bilder vom großen Altare hinwegnehmen" ließ.[57]

BIBELEXEGETISCH-THEOLOGISCHE PUBLIKATIONEN, 1540–1546

Christoph Hoffmann brachte lediglich in den Jahren 1540 bis 1546 Schriften zum Druck. Aus den Jahren vorher und nachher sind keine Texte von ihm bekannt, die zur Veröffentlichung kamen. Spätestens seit seinem Amtsantritt in Jena stand Hoffmann wegen seiner theologischen Publikationsprojekte, die er neben seinen pastoralen und ephoralen Aufgaben in Herzberg und Jena betrieb, mit Philipp Melanchthon in Kontakt. Hoffmann sandte seine lateinischen Texte vor deren Veröffentlichung Melanchthon und Luther zur Begutachtung zu.[58] Melanchthon wiederum vermittelte die Drucklegung bei dem zunächst in Schwäbisch Hall, dann in Frankfurt ansässigen Buchdrucker Georg Braubach.[59] Die Wittenberger Drucker hatten nämlich kein Interesse

---

55. Zu seiner Berufung durch Kurfürst Johann Friedrich vgl. *Ernst Devrient* (Hg.), Urkundenbuch der Stadt Jena und ihrer geistlichen Anstalten, Bd. 3, Jena 1936, 345. Zu Musa vgl. *Michael Wetzel*, „Anton Musa" in: Sächsische Biografie, 5.4.2018, https://saebi.isgv.de/biografie/2965 (Zugriffsdatum 16.02.2022).
56. Vgl. *Zahn*, Pfarrer (wie Anm. 1), 59.
57. *Gottlieb Albin von Wette*, Evangelisches Jena, oder gesamlete Nachrichten von den sämtlichen Predigern ..., Jena 1756, 68–79.
58. Vgl. MBW 1980 (MBW.T 8), 29 f.
59. Zum Drucker Peter Braubach (um 1500–1567) vgl. *Christoph Reske*, Die Buchdrucker des 16. und 17. Jahrhunderts im deutschen Sprachgebiet, Wiesbaden 2007, 227 f. 322 f. 830 f.

an lateinischen Publikationen, die sich ausschließlich an die Gelehrtenwelt richteten. Nach eigenem Bekunden standen Hoffmann zuerst die Pfarrer der evangelischen Gemeinden als Leser seiner Schriften vor Augen. Möglicherweise wollte er sich mit diesen lateinischen Kommentaren auch für eine akademische Anstellung empfehlen, so anspruchsvoll zeigt sich ihr theologisches und sprachliches Niveau. Kurfürst Johann Friedrich jedenfalls entwickelte Interesse an Hoffmanns Arbeiten und förderte ihre Veröffentlichung.[60]

Angesichts der Auseinandersetzungen um Johann Agricola, der Melanchthons Lehre von der Notwendigkeit guter Werke bestritt, veröffentlichte Hoffmann im Jahr 1540 ein umfangreiches Kommentarwerk „De poenitentia".[61] Erkennbare Resonanz hat dieses Werk, dessen Vorbereitung er freilich schon längere Zeit begonnen haben muss, anscheinend nicht gefunden. Gleichwohl kam es in Hoffmanns Todesjahr 1553 in neuer Auflage heraus.[62] Von 1541 bis 1545 legte Hoffmann weitere Kommentare vor: zum Titusbrief,[63] zum Phi-

---

60. Kurfürst Johann Friedrich ließ 1542/43 „j^c fl dem pfarher zu Jhene Christoffero Hoffmann, nemlichen 1 gulden zu einer bawsteur seines wonhauses zu Jhene und 1 gulden zu einer vorehrung von wegen eins lateinischen und deutzschen buches (dem Kurfürsten zugeschrieben)" zukommen: *Georg Buchwald*, „Kleine Notizen aus Rechnungsbüchern des Thüringischen Staatsarchivs (Weimar)", in: Archiv für Reformationsgeschichte 31 (1934), 82–100, hier 100.

61. Titel: De poenitentia commentariorum libri tres. – Impressum: Schwäbisch Hall: Peter Braubach, 1540; Umfang: 232 Bl., 2°; Nachweise: VD16 H 4128; Vorrede Melanchthons: MBW 2342 (MBW.T 9), 44 f.; Widmungsvorrede an Brück: MBW 2350 (MBW. T 9), 61–63; *Helmut Claus*, Melanchthon-Bibliographie 1510–1560, Gütersloh 2014, 1540.76. Die drei Kommentarbücher über die Buße hat Hoffmann, wie der Briefwechsel mit Melanchthon zeigt, im wesentlichen bereits in seiner Herzberger Zeit verfasst; vgl. MBW 1980 (MBW.T 8), 29 f. Melanchthon lobte auch die Überarbeitung; MBW 1987 (MBW.T 8), 37 f.

62. Titel: Contra theologiam scholasticam De poenitentia libri. – Impressum: Frankfurt/ Main: Peter Braubach, 1553; Umfang: 244 Bl., 2°; Nachweis: VD16 H 4129 bzw. M 3075; *Claus*, Melanchthon-Bibliographie (wie Anm. 61), 1553.15. Die Neuausgabe ersetzte das kürzere Vorwort der ersten Ausgabe von 1540 durch Melanchthons ausführlichere „Doctrina poenitentiae", welche dieser zu Jahresbeginn 1549 in Wittenberg als Antwort an Flacius im Druck veröffentlicht hatte: Corpus Reformatorum 23, 647–666 bzw. Melanchthons Werke in Auswahl. Studienausgabe, Bd. 6, Gütersloh 1955, 429–451.

63. Titel: Commentarii in epistolam Pauli apostoli ad Titum. – Impressum: Frankfurt/ Main: Peter Braubach, 1541; Umfang: 243 Bl., 8°; Nachweis: VD16 B 5181. Der Titusbrief-Kommentar ist dem jungen Herzog August von Sachsen (1526–1586), dem späteren Kurfürsten, gewidmet. Den Kommentar hatte Melanchthon ebenfalls vorher für den Druck genehmigt; vgl. MBW 2340 (MBW.T 9), 38 f. (Melanchthon an Hoffmann, 2. Januar 1540). Zugleich hatte Kurfürst Johann Friedrich selbst Luther angewiesen, den Kommentar begutachten lassen; vgl. WA.B 8, 545 f., Nr. 3382.

lipperbrief,[64] und zum 2. Thessalonicherbrief.[65] Seine exegetisch-theologische Arbeit an den kleineren Paulusbriefen verstand Hoffmann offenbar als Ergänzung zu den bereits vorliegenden verschiedenen Paulus-Kommentaren der Wittenberger. Neben den Widmungsbriefen und den Vorreden zur Kommentierung lässt auch die besondere Auswahl der Apostelbriefe das spezifische Interesse Hoffmanns greifbar werden. In diesen Paulusbriefen geht es thematisch um die Bekämpfung von Irrlehre, die Verantwortung der Hirten und der Obrigkeit, die Leidensgemeinschaft und die Freude mit Christus, die endzeitliche Bedrängung der Kirche durch den hinter inneren und äußeren Feinden sein Unwesen treibenden Antichrist und das notwendige Beharren der Christen bei der Wahrheit des Evangeliums. Aktuelle Ereignisse und Bedrohungssituationen erschlossen sich, indem sie anhand biblisch-apokalyptischer Motive und Bilder gedeutet wurden, als sinnvoll. Der von Melanchthon verfasste Widmungsbrief zum Philipperbrief-Kommentar[66] warnte – mit Blick auf die aktuellen Religionsverhandlungen auf Reichsebene – vor unbedacht in Kauf genommener Verfälschung der Lehre um der Eintracht willen. Gemeinsam mit dem Kommentar zum 2. Thessalonicherbrief entstand die Abhandlung „De christiana religione et de regno Antichristi", die offenbar zunächst separat in einem eigenen Druck erscheinen sollte, dann aber doch, wie das Titelblatt zeigt, dem weniger umfangreichen Kommentar angebunden wurde.[67]

Diese Abhandlung wurde noch in demselben Jahr ins Deutsche übertragen und erschien in dieser Version als eigenständige Schrift: „Von der christlichen Religion Sachen und endechristischem Reiche".[68] Die von Mitte Oktober 1544 datierte Vorrede an Kurfürst Johann Friedrich erinnerte zunächst an die Grundlage der Lehre im Glauben an das Evangelium von Jesus Christus, der allein zum Vater führe. Vor allem ging es Hoffmann – offenbar mit Blick auf

---

64. Titel: Commentarius in epistolam Pauli ad Philippenses. – Impressum: Frankfurt/Main: Peter Braubach, 1541; Umfang: 243 Bl., 8°; Nachweis: VD16 B 5122.

65. Titel: Commentarius in posteriorem D. Pauli ad Thessal⟨onicenses⟩. – Impressum: Frankfurt/Main: Peter Braubach, 1545. – Umfang: 158 Bl. und 2 leere Bl., 8°; Nachweis VD16 H 4131 und B 5156.

66. Widmungsbrief vom Februar 1541, MBW 2627 (MBW.T 10), 64f.; vgl. *Claus*, Melanchthon-Bibliographie (wie Anm. 61), 1541.25. Zum Adressaten Glüenspieß vgl. MBW Bd. 12 (Personen F-K), 155f.

67. Nachweis: VD16 H 4130. Sie weist innerhalb des gesamten Drucks ein eigenes Titelblatt und eine wieder neu beginnende Blätter-Zählung auf.

68. Impressum: Frankfurt/Main: Peter Braubach, 1545; Umfang: 158 Bl. und 2 leere Bl., 8°; Nachweis: VD16 H 4130. Die spätere Neuausgabe von *Robert Barnes*, Vitae Romanorum pontificum, Basel 1555 (VD16 B 410) zitiert (Bl. β2v) Hoffmanns ausdrückliche Zustimmung zu Barnes historischen Befund über Papst Silvester.

das einberufene Konzil von Trient – darum, die auftretenden antichristlichen Irrlehren, insbesondere die des römischen Papsttums, gegenüber den rechten christlichen Lehren zu kennzeichnen. Hoffmann hob hervor: „die ware Religion und Christenlehre ist einig und an allen orten ir selbs gleich/ und leret von warer forchte Gottes/ von rechtem glauben an Gott/ und der nötigen buß und besserung unsers lebens".[69] Mohammed und der römische Papst hätten dagegen mit selbstherrlichem Machtanspruch „ein new gesetz geschriben" und tyrannisierten die Menschen damit. Hoffmann möchte den „Endechrist" freilich nicht mit einer Person identifizieren, vielmehr handle es sich bei diesem um „ein rottierung viler böser und ungerechten menschen". Das Grundbefinden, in endzeitlich-apokalyptischen Kämpfen zu stehen, in denen der christliche Glaube sich durch treues Festhalten am Wort Gottes zu bewähren habe, zeichnete diese und alle anderen Schriften Hoffmanns besonders aus. Im Vorwort zu seiner Abhandlung ging Hoffmann näher auf das Problem der Apostasie von dem „im Evangelium gepredigten Glauben" ein, genauer den „abfall im bapstum". Exemplarisch nannte er dafür den scholastischen Lehrbetrieb, der im Grunde die Heilige Schrift verachtete. Dagegen nahm für ihn der Artikel von der Rechtfertigung des Gläubigen durch die Vergebung aus Gnaden um Christi willen entscheidende Bedeutung ein und konnte niemals zur Disposition gestellt werden.

Noch im Todesjahr Luthers gab Hoffmann auf Wunsch des Kurfürsten die erstmals im Jahr 1541 erschienene „Vermahnung an alle Pfarrherrn zum Gebet wider den Türken" des Reformators neu heraus.[70] In seinem Vorwort, das auf den aktuellen Hintergrund der Neuausgabe einging, beschwor Hoffmann die apokalyptische Bedrohung des wieder aufgegangenen hellen Lichts des Evangeliums durch die Heere der Türken und der „Bepstischen unauffhörlich böse tück, mörderische practicken und grewlich Tyranney". Nachdrücklich erinnerte er dabei – angesprochen sind wiederum zuerst die evangelischen Seelsorger – an Luthers, „unsers lieben Vaters in Christo", Vermahnung zu „emsigem, steten Gebete" und zu „rech[t]schaffener Buesse gegen Gott und beserung unsers lebens".

---

69. „Von der christlichen Religion Sachen und endechristischem Reiche" (wie Anm. 68), Bl. A4v; das folgende Zitat: Bl. A6r.

70. WA 51, (577) 585–625. Von der durch Hoffmann besorgten Neuausgabe liegen drei Drucke vor, deren Vergleich zeigt: Er erschien zunächst in Wittenberg (VD16 L 6914), erfuhr einen Nachdruck in Erfurt (VD16 L 6912), welcher wiederum die Vorlage bildete für den Nürnberger Druck (VD16 L 6913). Die folgenden Zitate entstammen dem Wittenberger Druck, Bl. A2b und Bl. A3a.

HOFPREDIGER UND BERATER DES KURFÜRSTEN IN WEIMAR, AUGSBURG UND JENA, 1544–1553

Kurfürst Johann Friedrich von Sachsen (1503–1554) bestellte Christoph Hoffmann – nach acht Jahren Tätigkeit als Pfarrer und Superintendent in Jena – am 25. Juni 1544 zu seinem Hofprediger in Weimar. Gut zwei Jahre später folgte Hoffmann seinem Herrn dann auch als Feldprediger in den Schmalkaldischen Krieg. Und nach der Niederlage in der Schlacht auf der Lochauer Heide bei Mühlberg an der Elbe am 24. April 1547 begleitete er den Kurfürsten als persönlichen Gefangenen Kaiser Karls V. nach Augsburg, wo auf dem Reichstag die Verhältnisse des Reiches unter Einschluss der Religionsfrage neu geordnet werden sollten. Auf den militärisch geschlagenen Herzog Johann Friedrich, dem die Kurwürde entzogen wurde, lastete großer Druck, den universalpolitischen Absichten des siegreichen Monarchen nachzugeben. Die deutsche Öffentlichkeit wartete gespannt darauf, wie der Herzog sich vor allem in Sachen der Religion verhalten würde. Hofprediger Hoffmann appellierte in seinem „Bekenntnis" vom Juni 1548 programmatisch an seinen Herrn, die große reformatorische Tradition der ernestinischen Regenten fortzusetzen.[71] Hoffmann rief dazu auf, am evangelischen Bekenntnis standhaft festzuhalten. Dessen klaren Ausdruck erkannte man in der Folge in den von Luther selbst formulierten Schmalkaldischen Artikeln von 1537. In einem Gutachten vom 15. Juni 1548 beurteilte Hoffmann die Regelungen des Augsburger Interims als inakzeptabel, sah er doch dahinter, ganz auf der Linie seiner bisherigen theologischen Veröffentlichungen, den Teufel am Werk.[72] Gegen alle Anfechtungen mahnte er zum geduldigen Beharren im Glauben. Seinem Schreiben legte Hoffmann „Ein schöne form einer bekentnis unsers heiligen Christenlichen glaubens aus einer schrifft D.M.L. aus gezogen und zusamen getragen" bei.[73] Hoffmann verband diese aktualisierende Luther-Bearbeitung mit schar-

---

71. Vgl. *Volker Leppin*, „Bekenntnisbildung als Katastrophenverarbeitung. Das Konfutationsbuch als ernestinische Ortsbestimmung nach dem Todes Johann Friedrichs I.", in: *Volker Leppin, Georg Schmidt, Sabine Wefers* (Hg.), Johann Friedrich I., der lutherische Kurfürst, Gütersloh 2006, 295–306, hier 302 mit Anm. 26.

72. Die hier gegebene Darstellung folgt *Volker Leppin*, „‚... und das Ichs nicht fur gotlich sonder fur eine lauter teufels lehr halte und achte'. Die theologische Verarbeitung des Interims durch Johann Friedrich d. Ä.", in: *Irene Dingel, Günther Wartenberg* (Hg.), Politik und Bekenntnis. Die Reaktionen auf das Interim von 1548, Leipzig 2006, 111–123, hier 121 f. (mit Quellennachweisen); vgl. daneben *Ernst Koch*, „Theologische Aspekte der ernestinischen Reaktionen auf das Interim", in: *Luise Schorn-Schütte* (Hg.), Das Interim 1548/50. Herrschaftskrise und Glaubenskonflikt, Gütersloh 2005, 312–330, hier 312 f.

73. Bei dieser Luther-Schrift handelt es sich nach *Leppin* um den Traktat „Vom Anbeten

fen Angriffen auf die religionspolitischen Ziele des Kaisers. Diesem warf er vor, den wahren Glauben zu verfolgen und durch einen „hispanischen Glauben" zu ersetzen. Hoffmann musste aus Augsburg fliehen, weil ihm zu Recht der Vorwurf gemacht wurde, Herzog Johann Friedrich in der Ablehnung des Interim zu bestärken.[74] Gemeinsam mit Nikolaus von Amsdorff (1483–1565) und weiteren lutherischen Theologen unterzeichnete der nach Weimar zurückgekehrte vormalige Hofprediger dann am 28. Juli 1548 eine Erklärung gegen das Augsburger Interim.[75] Auf Anordnung Herzog Johann Friedrichs beriet Hoffmann im Februar 1549 mit anderen Räten und Theologen über die Leipziger Artikel zum Interim. Dieses „Leipziger Interim" erklärten sie für unannehmbar und beteuerten, sie könnten „von der reynen Lere des Euangelij nicht ein har breit weichen, Ob auch himel vnd Erden druber solten zu boden gehn".[76] Dem protestantischen Verhandlungsführer Philipp Melanchthon wurden schwere Vorwürfe wegen seiner Nachgiebigkeit gemacht. Auch Christoph Hoffmann übte theologische Kritik an den Kompromissen, zu denen Melanchthon bereit war.[77] Er tat dies freilich sachlich und enthielt sich persönlicher Attacken.

Seine letzten Lebensjahre verbrachte Hoffmann wieder in Jena, vermutlich in der Stellung eines geheimen herzoglichen Rates. Seine Wiederverwendung als Pfarrer und Superintendent, die Herzog Johann Friedrich unterstützte, stieß freilich in Jena wegen Hoffmans unverträglichen Charakters und seiner weichen Stimme auf Widerspruch und kam nicht mehr zustande.[78] Das Amt

---

des Sakraments des heiligen Leichnams Christi" aus dem Jahr 1523, WA 11, (417) 431–456. Von inhaltlichen Gesichtspunkten her weist *Koch,* Aspekte (wie Anm. 72), 312f., zu Recht auf die von Luther mit einer Vorrede versehene „Rechenschaft des Glaubens" der Böhmischen Brüder von 1533 (VD16 A 4140) hin als Grundlage für die von Hoffmann hergestellte Bearbeitung des Luther'schen Glaubensbekenntnisses.

74. Vgl. *Georg Mentz,* Johann Friedrich der Grossmütige 1503–1554, Teil III, Jena 1908, 284–289, bes. 285 mit Anm. 1.

75. Vgl. *Irene Dingel* (Hg.), Controversia et Confessio 1: Der interimistische Streit (1548), 201,4. – Zu den Zusammenhängen vgl. *Koch,* Aspekte (wie Anm. 72), 320–322; *Gehrt,* Ernestinische Konfessionspolitik (wie Anm. 6), 35–50; *Anja Moritz,* Interim und Apokalypse. Die religiösen Vereinheitlichungsversuche Karls V. im Spiegel der magdeburgischen Publizistik 1548–1551/52, Tübingen 2010, 47f.

76. Zitatwiedergabe bei *Ernst Koch,* „Der Ausbruch des adiaphoristischen Streits und seine Folgewirkungen", in: *Dingel, Wartenberg,* Politik und Bekenntnis (wie Anm. 72), 179–190, hier Zitat 186f. Edition des Leipziger Interim in: MBW 5387 (MBW.T 19), 115–125; vgl. auch die Darstellung bei *Koch,* Aspekte (wie Anm. 72), 316–319.

77. Vgl. *Beate Kobler,* Die Entstehung eines negativen Melanchthonbildes. Protestantische Melanchthonkritik bis 1560, Tübingen 2014, 546.

78. Vgl. *Zahn,* Pfarrer (wie Anm. 1), 60.

des Superintendenten übte etwa seit 1550 faktisch der seit 1549 an der neugegründeten Hohen Schule Jena als Theologieprofessor lehrende Erhard Schnepf aus. Eine engere persönliche Verbindung unterhielt Hoffmann offenbar weiter mit Altkanzler Gregor Brück aufrecht. Dass Hoffmann tatsächlich um das Jahr 1550 herum an der späteren Universität selbst gelehrt hat, wie gelegentlich angenommen wird,[79] ist wenig wahrscheinlich. Der lutherische Theologe und Reformator, der noch in der spätmittelalterlichen Kirche aufgewachsen war, starb im Jahr 1553 in Jena.[80]

Christoph Hoffmann gehörte noch zur ersten Generation der Reformatoren und unter diesen zu den jüngeren. In seiner 30 Jahre umfassenden beruflichen Laufbahn als Geistlicher hat er sich in seinen unterschiedlichen Stationen mit ihren Aufgaben an der Wittenberger Theologie ausgerichtet. Obwohl unter Karlstadt promoviert, scheint er dennoch von diesem nicht nachhaltig beeinflusst worden zu sein. Vielmehr war es die Theologie Luthers, die den Ratsprädikanten Christoph Hoffmann dazu befähigte, seit 1522 in der kleinen fränki-

---

79. Vgl. MBW Band 12 (Personen F–K), 310, oder auch *Julius Hartmann*, Erhard Schnepff, der Reformator in Schwaben, Nassau, Hessen und Tübingen, Tübingen 1870, 69. Christoph Hoffmanns Name ist freilich weder erwähnt bei *Karl Heussi*, Geschichte der Theologischen Fakultät Jena, Weimar 1954, noch bei *Thomas Kaufmann*, „Die Anfänge der Theologischen Fakultät in Jena im Kontext der ‚innerlutherischen' Kontroversen zwischen 1548 und 1561", in: *Leppin*, Kurfürst (wie Anm. 71), 209–258, und auch nicht bei *Bärbel Schneider*, Die Anfänge der Universität Jena. Johann Stigels Briefwechsel im ersten Jahrfünft der Hohen Schule (12. März 1548–31. Mai 1553). Edition, Übersetzung und Kommentar, Diss. Leipzig 2002, Neuried 2002. Der namensgleiche „paedagogus", den im Juli 1548 die beiden Gründungsprofessoren Victorinus Strigel (1524–1569) und Johann Stigel (1515–1562) zur Anstellung an der Hohen Schule Jena vorschlugen, war der vormalige Wittenberger Stipendiat Christoph Hofmann d. J. (1519–1576) aus Altenburg; vgl. *Förstemann*, Album (wie Anm. 8), 178b; *Schneider*, Anfänge, 73. Hofmann fungierte später als Hofprediger in Altenburg, Superintendent in Penig (1561) und Hofprediger in Schwerin (1566); vgl. *Ernst Koch*, „Mitteldeutsche Wurzeln des österreichischen Flacianismus", in: Jahrbuch für die Geschichte des Protestantismus in Österreich 131 (2015), 17–29, hier 23–25. Zum Altenburger Hofmann vgl. auch MBW Band 12 (Personen F–K), 312, und neuerdings *Ulrike Ludwig*, Das landesherrliche Stipendienwesen an der Universität Wittenberg, Leipzig 2019, 336–340, Nr. 88. Zu dem wiederum namensgleichen Chr. H. (1815–1885), von der negativen Zeitdiagnostik und der Endzeiterwartung des Württembergischen Pietismus bestimmten Theologen, Politiker, Sektengründer, der aus einer Württembergischen Pfarrer- und Beamtenfamilie stammte und als Siedler in Palästina bei Jerusalem verstarb (NDB 9, 392 f.), gibt es keine genealogisch erkennbare Verbindung.

80. Den 13. September 1553 als genaues Todesdatum bietet auf der Basis entlegener ortsgeschichtlicher Forschungen *Zahn*, Pfarrer (wie Anm. 1), 59 f.; der Hinweis darauf verdankt sich *Friedrich Meinhof*, Thüringer Pfarrerbuch, Bd. 8: Großherzogtum Sachsen (-Weimar-Eisenach), Landesteil Weimar mit Jena und Neustadt/Orla, Heiligstadt 2017 [Internetpublikation], Verzeichnis der Pfarrer (Biogramme) A–H, 469 f.

schen Landstadt Kitzingen sozusagen als Pionier die Reformation theologisch vorzubereiten und orientiert an Wittenberg und Nürnberg praktisch durchzuführen. Durch die Vermittlung der Wittenberger gelangte der aus Kitzingen Geflohene 1527 nach Herzberg an der Elster, wo er als Gemeindepfarrer anscheinend auch die nötige Ruhe zur Vorbereitung seiner später veröffentlichten theologischen Werke fand. Seit 1536 amtierte er als Pfarrer in Jena, dann von 1544 bis etwa 1548 als Hofprediger in Weimar. Seine anspruchsvollen Publikationsprojekte verfolgte Hoffmann in Zusammenarbeit mit Philipp Melanchthon. Von Luthers Theologie herkommend versuchte er, der allgemeinen Leserschaft, besonders den sächsischen Herzögen, denen er mehrere Schriften widmete, in unsicheren Zeiten Orientierung zu geben. Hoffmann deutete vor dem Hintergrund der endzeitlich-apokalyptischen Grundstimmung seiner Zeit die gegenwärtigen äußeren Bedrohungen der Christenheit (durch die türkische Expansion) und ihre inneren Streitigkeiten (verursacht durch den Herrschaftsanspruch des Papsttums) anhand der einschlägigen biblischen Aussagen. In den „antichristlichen" Bedrängungen mahnte er, am Evangelium, in dessen Zentrum er die paulinische Lehre von der Rechtfertigung sah, unbedingt festzuhalten. Als Seelsorger des geschlagenen Kurfürsten Johann Friedrich konnte Hoffmann in der Situation der Bewährung nur diesen konkreten Rat geben: das Interim abzulehnen, dem unverfälschten lutherischen Bekenntnis treu zu bleiben und so in der Krise neue Kraft aus dem evangelischen Glauben zu schöpfen. Nicht zuletzt gehörte der aus Ansbach stammende evangelische Geistliche zur stattlichen Riege der Kirchenleute der Reformationszeit, die für die starke theologische Verbindung zwischen Franken und Kursachsen stehen. Diese entfaltete eine Jahrhunderte lange, bis heute wirkende konfessionskulturelle Prägewirkung – sinnigerweise trotz des dominierenden Endzeitbewusstseins, welches das frühe Luthertum so charakteristisch auszeichnete.

Wolfgang Huber
Pfarrer und Wissenschaftl. Mitarbeiter (Karlstadt-Edition)
Über der Kirch 1 d
D-35041 Marburg
wolfgang.huber@theologie.uni-goettingen.de

ABSTRACT

Christoph Hoffmann was the first to preach "the gospel" in Kitzingen starting in 1522. Although he graduated from Wittenberg under Karlstadt, Hoffmann showed little inclination to cooperate at a theological or personal level with his mentor, but remained closely allied with Luther. In 1527 Hoffmann was appointed pastor in Herzberg, before going on to serve as superintendent in Jena after 1536 and as court preacher in Weimar after 1544. His theological publications reveal a strong interest in an eschatological interpretation of history, which shaped his perception of the present: Hoffmann saw the Antichrist at work in the afflictions of the evangelical church—whose members now had to prove themselves through repentance, correctness of lifestyle, and perseverance in the right faith. This view also led him to vehemently reject the Augsburg Interim, and to encourage the imprisoned Duke John Frederick I (the Magnanimous) of Saxony to do the same.

Brieffunde in einer Sammelhandschrift aus dem Hamburger Geistlichen Ministerium

Von Thomas Gerhard Wilhelmi

Unbekannte oder im vollständigen Wortlaut noch nicht bekannte Briefe von Philipp Melanchthon oder gar Martin Luther findet man heutzutage in Archiven und Bibliotheken nur noch selten. Zum Vorschein kommen hin und wieder lediglich Abschriften bereits bekannter Briefe. Durchaus unerwartet waren somit die Funde in einer 1276 Seiten umfassenden Sammelhandschrift, die sich unter der Signatur S/849 im historischen Safebestand der Commerzbibliothek in der Stiftung Hanseatisches Wirtschaftsarchiv in Hamburg befindet.[1] Diese Handschrift und zahlreiche weitere Handschriften und Drucke – die meisten zur Kirchengeschichte und auch Stadtgeschichte Hamburgs im 16., 17. und frühen 18. Jahrhundert – gelangten im Januar 1794 in den Bestand der Hamburger Commerzbibliothek und fanden seither zumeist keine größere Beachtung.

Diese Handschriften und Drucke wurden aufgrund eines Beschlusses der Commerzdeputation am 18. Januar 1794 von dem Hamburger Privatgelehrten und Sammler Arnold Schuback (1762–1826)[2] für „1987 Mark Courant 30 Schilling" für die Commerzbibliothek angekauft.[3] Für die Bibliothek war der „Protokollist" Friedrich Surland zuständig (im Amt 1765–1797).[4] Die Handschriften und Drucke entstammten der Sammlung des Hamburger Kauf-

---

1. Für die Identifizierung einiger Briefe und wertvolle Hinweise danke ich Christine Mundhenk von der Melanchthon-Forschungsstelle der Heidelberger Akademie der Wissenschaften. Kathrin Enzel, der Geschäftsführerin der Stiftung Hanseatisches Wirtschaftsarchiv, danke ich für manche Informationen zur Geschichte der Bibliothek und für Ihr Interesse und Entgegenkommen.
2. Zu Arnold Schuback, vgl. *Otto Beneke*, „Schuback, Arnold", in: Allgemeine Deutsche Biographie 32 (1891), 585. Neuer Nekrolog der Deutschen 4 (1826), 272–278.
3. Im „Unkostenbuch der Commerzdeputation" (Stiftung Hanseatisches Wirtschaftsarchiv, Safebestand der Commerzbibliothek, S/599 21 blau) ist auf S. 260 für den 18. Januar 1794 die Zahlung an Arnold Schuback für Bücher aus der Behrmannischen Auktion vermerkt.
4. *Bertha Backe-Dietrich*, 250 Jahre Commerzbibliothek der Handelskammer Hamburg 1735–1985, Hamburg 1985, 111. Zu Surland vgl. auch *Friedrich Lorenz Hoffmann*, „Die Commerz-Bibliothek in Hamburg", in: Serapeum 10 (1849), 129–153, hier 133f. (1849 in Leipzig auch separat erschienen).

manns und Literaten Georg Behrmann (1704–1756).[5] Behrmanns sehr große Bibliothek wurde am 14. Oktober 1793 in einem „bekannten Hause" am Hamburger Gänsemarkt versteigert. Der 1793 von Johann Peter Treder in Hamburg gedruckte Auktionskatalog trägt den Titel „Verzeichniß der von dem sel. Herrn Georg Behrmann hinterlassenen merkwürdigen und sehr vollständigen Sammlung gedruckter und geschriebener Hamburgensien und anderer Bücher, welche den 14ten October 1793 in einem bekannten Hause am Gänsemarkt durch den Auctionarius verkauft werden sollen".[6]

Schuback dürfte die Handschriften und Drucke an der Versteigerung im Auftrag der Commerzdeputation erworben haben. Er erhielt am 18. Januar 1794 den genannten Betrag „für die auf der Behrmannischen Auction gekauften Bücher, laut Nota No. 6". Aus dem Protokollbuch der Commerzdeputation 1756/57[7] geht hervor, dass die Commerzdeputation am 2. Dezember 1756 entschied, auf Behrmanns Erben zuzugehen und über die Erwerbung von Hamburgensien aus dem Nachlass zu verhandeln. Im Februar 1757 informierte die Witwe die Commerzdeputation darüber, dass die Hamburgensien aus dem Nachlass katalogisiert seien und gesichtet werden könnten. Die Commerzdeputation beauftragte daraufhin zunächst Prof. Michael Richey und dann nach dessen Erkrankung den Justizrat Paschen Ritter von Cossel mit dieser Sichtung. Am 30. März und abschließend am 7. Juni wurden die beiden Gutachten verlesen, die Justizrat von Cossel über diese Sichtungen erstellt hatte. Die Entscheidung über den Ankauf scheint am 7. Juni 1757 zunächst vertagt worden zu sein, bis ein geeigneter Raum für die Aufstellung gefunden werden konnte. Bisher konnte noch nicht ermittelt werden, ob es in den Jahren zwischen 1757 und 1793 zu einem Ankauf von Teilen der Sammlung kam oder ob die Hamburgensien alle erst bei der Auktion 1793 erworben wurden. Herrn von Cossel wurden 1757 für seine Bemühungen fünf Portugaleser geschenkt.[8]

Woher Georg Behrmann diese zum überwiegenden Teil aus dem 17. Jahrhundert stammenden Handschriften hatte, bleibt vorerst ungeklärt. Ein Teil der Handschriften – oft sind es auch Hamburgische Kirchenakten – muss sich

---

5. Zu Georg Behrmann, vgl. *Eckehard Catholy*, „Behrmann, Friedrich Georg", in: Neue Deutsche Biographie 2 (1955), 16f. *Jürgen Rathje/Red.*, „Behrmann, Georg", in: Killy Literaturlexikon 1, Berlin ²2008, 423f. *Ferdinand Heitmüller*, Hamburgische Dramatiker zur Zeit Gottscheds, Diss. Universität Jena, Wandsbeck 1890, 4–34.
6. Exemplar im Staatsarchiv der Freien und Hansestadt Hamburg. Signatur: A 572/109.
7. Commerzbibliothek, S/599, 1756–1757.
8. *Backe-Dietrich*, Commerzbibliothek (wie Anm. 4), 18f.; wesentlich ergänzt von Kathrin Enzel.

im Besitz des Hamburger Geistlichen Ministeriums befunden haben, später vielleicht in der Obhut oder im Besitz des Pastors und Seniorrates Johann Friedrich Winckler.[9]

An der Auktion sicherte sich möglicherweise die Hamburger Stadtbibliothek einen Teil der Drucke und auch einige Handschriften, sei es direkt an der Auktion oder über den Mittelsmann Schuback oder aus dessen Nachlass. Richard Gerecke erwähnt in seinem bibliotheksgeschichtlichen Abriss die Behrmann-Auktion vom 14. November 1793 nicht, wohl aber die sehr große Büchersammlung von Arnold Schuback, die nach dessen Tod teilweise in die Stadtbibliothek kam (und wohl zahlreiche 1793 ersteigerte Drucke aus Behrmanns Bibliothek enthielt).[10]

Die 1735 gegründete Commerzbibliothek befand sich damals im Obergeschoss der Ratswaage, dem Nebenhaus der alten Börse (Commercium).[11] Sie erfuhr durch diese Zugänge eine wesentliche Erweiterung. In der Einleitung zum gedruckten Katalog von 1841 wird erwähnt, dass Bücherauktionen Anlass für die Erweiterung des Anschaffungsprofils durch den Erwerb von Hamburgensien gegeben hätten und namentlich aus der Sammlung von Georg Behrmann wertvolle handschriftliche Aufzeichnungen erworben worden seien.[12] Der wesentliche Teil der in der Commerzbibliothek aufbewahrten Hamburgensia aus dem 16., 17. und frühen 18. Jahrhundert stammt aus der erwähnten Auktion.

Vor dem großen Hamburger Stadtbrand im Mai 1842 blieb die Commerzbibliothek glücklicherweise verschont. In der Nacht vom 24. auf den 25. Juli 1943 hingegen verlor die Bibliothek, die seit 1919 in Räumlichkeiten des Johanneums untergebracht war, etwa 92% ihres Bestandes an gedruckten Büchern in dem durch die Bombardierung entstandenen Feuersturm. Zum guten Glück waren aber sämtliche Handschriften und Inkunabeln und etliche wertvolle Drucke aus der Zeit nach 1500 im Keller der Börse und auch im Tresorraum des Bankhauses Brinckmann-Wirtz & Co. ausgelagert und blieben unbe-

---

9. Zu Johann Friedrich Winckler, vgl. *Carl Bertheau*, „Winckler, Johann Friedrich", in: Allgemeine Deutsche Biographie 43 (1898), 375 f.

10. *Richard Gerecke*, „Staats- und Universitätsbibliothek Hamburg Carl von Ossietzky", in: Handbuch der historischen Buchbestände in Deutschland, Bd. 1, Hildesheim 1996, 189–194.

11. Zur Commerzbibliothek: *Hoffmann*, Commerz-Bibliothek (wie Anm. 4). *Backe-Dietrich* (wie Anm. 4), 15–27. Bertha Backe-Dietrich, Eva Lembcke, „Commerzbibliothek der Handelskammer", in: Handbuch der historischen Buchbestände in Deutschland, Bd. 1, Hildesheim 1996, 218–222.

12. Katalog der Commerz-Bibliothek in Hamburg, Hamburg 1841, [III]-IV.

schädigt.[13] Bei der Flutkatastrophe am 16./17. Februar 1962 allerdings erlitten große Teile dieser Bestände, darunter auch manche Handschriften, zum Teil erhebliche Schäden.[14]

Die Sammelhandschrift S/849 findet sich auf der Seite 23 des Auktionskataloges vom 14. Oktober 1793 als Los unter der Nummer 173: „eine Sammlung von mehr als 150 merkwürdigen, und zum Theil Original-Briefen und Urkunden zur Hamburgischen Kirchengeschichte, mit vorgeschriebnen Registern, 1276 Seiten".

In diesem 1276 Seiten umfassenden, 22 × 34,5 × 11 cm großen Konvolut,[15] das vermutlich bis 1962 in der Commerzbibliothek unter der Signatur H 665/1 aufbewahrt wurde, befinden sich zahlreiche Abschriften, aber auch manche Originale theologischer Abhandlungen, Berichte und Briefe sowie historische Aufzeichnungen und Akten, zu einem guten Teil Hamburgensia, insgesamt etwa zweihundert heterogene Dokumente verschiedenen Umfanges, alles aus der Zeit von 1533 bis 1733 und in halbwegs chronologischer Reihenfolge.

Der heute vorliegende Band dürfte in der Mitte des 19. Jahrhunderts hergestellt worden sein. Er trägt den Rückentitel: „Sammlung von Briefen etc. zur Hamb. Kirchengeschichte". Diese Bindung ersetzte die frühere, die mit ziemlicher Sicherheit in der Zeit von 1733 bis Oktober 1738 erfolgt sein muss. Die neuesten Aktenstücke in S/849 datieren aus dem Jahr 1733. Johann Friedrich Winckler (1679–1738), der seit 1712 Hauptpastor zu St. Nicolai und seit 1730 zudem Senior des Geistlichen Ministeriums war,[16] fertigte ein von Anfang an mitgebundenes fünfseitiges Inhaltsverzeichnis („Contenta dieses Bandes") und ein fünfseitiges Sachwortverzeichnis („Index der Vornehmsten Materien") an.[17] Die Paginierung (Seiten 1–1276) stammt aus dem 18. Jahrhundert, vielleicht aus denselben Jahren. Etliche Blätter der Handschrift sind bei der Bindung – vermutlich der ersten – beschnitten worden; dies hat da und dort zu Textverlusten geführt.

---

13. *Backe-Dietrich*, Commerzbibliothek (wie Anm. 4), 79–86.
14. *Backe-Dietrich*, Commerzbibliothek (wie Anm. 4), 100–102. *Backe-Dietrich/Lembcke*, Commerzbibliothek (wie Anm. 11), 220.
15. Maße des Einbandes. Die Blätter der Sammelhandschrift weisen ganz verschiedene Formate auf.
16. S. oben Anm. 9.
17. Die insgesamt zehn nicht paginierten Seiten stehen am Anfang des Bandes. Gemäß der vielleicht etwa um 1800 gemachten Eintragung am oberen Rand von Seite [I] stammen diese Verzeichnisse von der Hand Johann Friedrich Wincklers.

Einige der im Folgenden genannten, in der Handschrift S/849 enthaltenen Briefe sollen voraussichtlich im nächsten Jahrgang des ARG kritisch ediert werden.

Martin Bucer an Martin Luther, Straßburg, 22. Juli 1536, lateinisch, Abschrift 17. Jh.
Der Brief ist aufgrund einer Abschrift von Johann Wilhelm Baum (Mitte 19. Jh.), BNU Straßburg, MS. 0.668 (Thesaurus Baumianus IX), S. 171, in der Weimarer Briefwechsel-Edition[18] und ebenso von Theodor Kolde[19] ediert worden. Der für diese Editionen benutzten Abschrift von Baum liegt eine Abschrift aus der Zeit um 1600 zugrunde, die sich im Stadtarchiv Straßburg befindet: 1 AST 173, fol. 96v-97r.[20] Enders hat den Brief aus einer Abschrift aus der Zeit um 1600, HAB Wolfenbüttel, Cod. Guelf. 85 Helmst., fol. 1v, und aus der Abschrift von Baum ediert.[21] Bei der in S/849 auf S. 3, 5 und 7 enthaltenen Abschrift handelt es sich um eine eigenständige Überlieferung.

Martin Luther an die Hamburger Bürgerinnen Hileke Rheders (Elike Reders), Gesche Huige (Geske Hugeske), Wonelcke Tonagels (Womelke Thunagels), Abeleke Schelhovedes (Apelke Skölhoves), s. l., Montag nach Petri et Pauli 1533 (= 30. Juni 1533), deutsch, Abschrift Mitte 16. Jh. (S. 19) und Abschrift 17. Jh. (S. 9). – Abbildung 1.
Der Brief wird in Otto Sperlings „Collectio Inscriptionum Hamburgensium"[22] erwähnt, entsprechend bei Enders unter der Nummer 2100b[23] und in der Folge ohne eigene Nummer in WA Br 6, 499. Den Wortlaut des Briefes bieten nun die in S/849 auf S. 19 (mit Textverlusten am Rand infolge Beschneidung) und auf S. 9 enthaltenen Abschriften.

---

18. D. Martin Luthers Werke. Kritische Gesamtausgabe. Briefwechsel (im Folgenden mit WA Br bezeichnet), Bd. 7, 471–473 (Nr. 3050).
19. *Theodor Kolde*, Analecta Lutherana, Gotha 1883, 240 f.
20. Die Briefhandschrift ist in der Datenbank „Theologenbriefwechsel im Südwesten des Reichs in der Frühen Neuzeit (1550–1620)" https://thbw.hadw-bw.de als 68689 erfasst (Brief 70874).
21. Dr. Martin Luthers Briefwechsel, Bd. 11, hg. von *Ernst Ludwig Enders*, Leipzig 1907, 6–9 (Nr. 2416).
22. Manuskript in der Kgl. Bibliothek Kopenhagen, GKS 2308 quarto, fol. 691.
23. Dr. Martin Luthers Briefwechsel, Bd. 17, hg. von *Ernst Ludwig Enders*, *Gustav Kawerau* und *Paul Flemming*, Bd. 17, Leipzig 1920, 319 f.

Philipp Melanchthon an die Hamburger Bürgerin Abeleke Schelhovedes (Abelke Schölhoves), Wittenberg, Montag nach Petri et Pauli 1533 (= 30. Juni 1533), deutsch, Abschrift Mitte des 16. Jh.

Der Brief wird Otto Sperlings Chronik „Collectio Inscriptionum Hamburgensium"[24] erwähnt, entsprechend in WA Br 6, 499 und daraus übernommen in MBW[25] 1340. Den Wortlaut des Briefes an Abeleke Schelhovedes, die Melanchthon offenbar ein Geschenk geschickt hatte und von ihm nun ermuntert wird, bei der in Hamburg erfolgreich verbreiteten neuen Lehre zu bleiben, bietet nun die in S/849 auf S. 19 (mit Textverlusten am Rand infolge Beschneidung) enthaltene Abschrift.

„Fragmentum Epistolae D. Lutheri, ex eius autographo descriptum agens de duobus casibus: 1. si quis non revelet coniurationem contra Principem, an incurrat crimen laesae Maiestatis. 2 si quis vulneratum magis vulnerat, ur prior reus liberetur." Empfänger unbekannt, s. l. et a., lateinisch, Abschrift aus Luthers Autograph aus dem 17. Jh. – Abbildung 2.

Der Text beginnt mit der Überschrift „Omnis homo mendax" und weist dann diese Abschnitte auf: „II. Pone quod aliquis machinetur contra Principem, puta, quod faciat ... me in tales causas intromittere" und „III. Quemadmodum est calamitas humani generis, quod unus insidiatur ... tales Advocati debuerant suspendi." Der nicht datierte Brief, der sich unvollständig in S/849 auf S. 11 befindet (S. 12 ist leer), ist vorerst nicht nachgewiesen.

Martin Luther an Jakob Probst, Bischof der Kirche in Bremen, s. l., Dominica Judica 1542 (= 26. März 1542), lateinisch, Abschrift aus Luthers Autograph aus dem 17. Jh., deutsch, Abschrift um 1700.

Enders und Kawerau haben diesen Brief aufgrund einer Abschrift aus dem 16. Jh., Wolfenbüttel, Cod. Guelf. 108 Helmst., fol. 320v und 396r, lateinisch und deutsch ediert.[26]

In Klammern genannt wird die in der Edition nicht benutzte lateinische Abschrift (18. Jh.), Hamburg SUB, Sup. ep. 4, 2.

S/849, S. 13–15 (lateinisch), S. 59–61 (deutsch).

---

24. Manuskript (wie Anm. 22), fol. 692.
25. Melanchthons Briefwechsel. Kritische und kommentierte Gesamtausgabe, Stuttgart 1977 ff. (im Folgenden MBW).
26. Dr. Martin Luthers Briefwechsel, Bd. 14, hg. von *Ernst Ludwig Enders* und *Gustav Kawerau*, Leipzig 1912, 218–220 (Nr. 3120); entsprechend WA Br 10, 23–25 (Nr. 2728).

N. N. an Anna Münster in Nürnberg, Wittenberg, 24. Juni 1546, deutsch, Ausfertigung. – Abbildung 3.

Der Brief gibt Rätsel auf. Als Verfasser konnte man Philipp Melanchthon in Betracht ziehen, da er mit der als „Jungfrau Anna" und „liebe mum" angesprochenen Anna Münster (auch: Münsterer) verwandt war. Anna Münster d. J. war die Tochter von Melanchthons Schwägerin Anna Krapp, der Schwester seiner Frau Katharina Krapp.[27] Melanchthon erwähnt Anna Münster mehrfach in seinen Briefen. Die im Text erwähnte „Großmutter" der Anna Münster wäre dann Melanchthons Schwiegermutter Katharina Müntzer, die am 2. Mai 1548 in Wittenberg gestorben ist,[28] was zu der Briefpassage „und die großmutter wolt dich gern noch vor yhrem end sehen" durchaus passen würde. Der vorliegende Brief, in dem Anna Münster um die Zusendung einer Goldborte gebeten wird, dürfte zusammen mit anderen Briefen (u. a. MBW 4296 und 4297, beide ebenfalls vom 24. Juni) nach Nürnberg geschickt worden sein.[29] Der im Brief zunächst erwähnte Bote ist der Melanchthon vertraute Bote Andreas [Zencker]. Sein Name wurde aber im Text gestrichen, weil er als Bote (u. a. mit dem Brief MBW 4291 vom 20. Juni) am 24. Juni bereits auf dem Wege nach Nürnberg war. Der vorliegende Brief dürfte somit zusammen mit den Briefen MBW 4296 und 4297 von Franciscus Dryander nach Nürnberg mitgenommen worden sein. Der Brief, eine manche Korrekturen aufweisende Ausfertigung, die aus nicht ersichtlichem Grund nach Hamburg gelangt ist, ist aber nicht von Melanchthon geschrieben worden.[30]

S/849, S. 17 f.

Johannes Bugenhagen an Abeleke Schelhovedes (Abelke Schölhoves), Wittenberg, Mittwoch vor Luciae 1533 (= 10. Dezember 1533), niederdeutsch, Abschrift 16. Jh. In der Edition des Briefwechsels von Johannes Bugenhagen[31] ist dieser Brief nicht enthalten.

S/849, S. 20.

---

27. Vgl. MBW, Bd. 12, S. 458.
28. MBW, Bd. 13 (Regesten – Personen), S. 455.
29. Für diese Hinweise danke ich Matthias Dall'Asta von der Melanchthon-Forschungsstelle der Heidelberger Akademie der Wissenschaften.
30. Heinz Scheible danke ich für die eindeutige Beurteilung.
31. Dr. Johannes Bugenhagens Briefwechsel, hg. von *Otto Vogt*. Neuausgabe mit Vorwort und Ergänzungen von Eike Wolgast, Hildesheim 1966.

Philipp Melanchthon, Johannes Bugenhagen und Georg Maior an die Hamburger Pastoren, [Wittenberg], 14. April 1549, lateinisch, unvollständige Abschrift, 17. Jh.

Der Brief ist in MBW 5501a aufgrund von Abschriften ediert. In S/849 auf S. 55 unten wird angegeben „inter Epistolas Melanchthonianas Basileae in 8 pag. 462". Damit gemeint ist nicht die 1565 in Basel erschienene Briefausgabe von Manlius, sondern die 1565 in Wittenberg erschienene von Caspar Peucer.[32] Es ist noch nicht geklärt, ob es sich bei der unvollständigen Abschrift (etwa erstes Viertel des Textes) um eine Abschrift aus Peucers Edition von 1565 oder aus der nicht mehr nachzuweisenden Ausfertigung des Briefes in den Akten des Hamburger Ministeriums handelt.

S/849, S. 55 f.

Peter von Spreckelsen, Hamburger Bürgermeister, und die Ratsherren Jürgen Plate, Matthias Reder (Reders) und Dithmar Kohl an Johannes Bugenhagen, Philipp Melanchthon und die ganze theologische Fakultät der Universität Wittenberg, [Hamburg], Mittwoch nach Mariae Magdalenae 1550 (= 23. Juli 1550), deutsch, Abschrift um 1700.

Der Wortlaut dieses Briefes, mit dem der Hamburger Bürgermeister und drei Ratsherren die Wittenberger Theologen um ein Urteil in der Auseinandersetzung der Hamburger Pastoren um die Höllenfahrt Christi bitten, um eine Spaltung in der Stadt abzuwenden, war durch die Edition von Arnold Greve bekannt.[33] Diese diente MBW 5860 als Vorlage. In der Edition von Bugenhagens Briefwechsel wird der Brief nur erwähnt.[34] Greve nennt die Vorlage seiner Edition: „Descripsi ex tabellario Rev. Ministerii litteras supplices",[35] ein Manuskript, das sich im Archiv des Hamburger Ministeriums befand. Ob es sich dabei um S/849, S. 63–68 handelt oder um eine hierfür benutzte Vorlage, bleibt vorerst ungeklärt.

Johann Bugenhagen, Caspar Cruciger und Philipp Melanchthon an den Hamburger Senat, September 1550, lateinisch, Abschrift frühes 17. Jh.

Der Brief, in dem Senat auf dessen Anfrage vom 23. Juli 1550 geraten wird, wie er sich im Hamburger Lehrstreit um die Höllenfahrt Christi am besten verhalten sollte, ist in MBW 5911 aufgrund von Abschriften, die ausdrücklich

---

32. *Philipp Melanchthon*, Epistolae selectiores, hg. von *Caspar Peucer*, Wittenberg 1565 (VD16 M 3221), 461–468.
33. *Arnold Greve*, Memoria Aepini […] instaurata, Hamburg 1736, 179–184.
34. Bugenhagens Briefwechsel (wie Anm. 31), 616.
35. *Greve*, Memoria Aepini (wie Anm. 33), 95, Anm. 1.

auf Melanchthons Autograph – vielleicht das Konzept oder eine von ihm angefertigte Abschrift? – basieren, ediert. Dabei werden als Verfasser Bugenhagen und Melanchthon genannt. In den diversen Abschriften und auch in der Melanchthon-Briefwechsel-Edition von Manlius[36] ist von mehreren, namentlich nicht genannten Wittenberger Theologen als Verfasser die Rede. In der bislang nicht bekannten Überlieferung in S/849, S. 69 f. werden Bugenhagen, Cruciger, Melanchthon, in dieser Reihenfolge, als Unterzeichner ausgeführt. Es ist davon auszugehen, dass diese Abschrift auf der nach Hamburg geschickten Ausfertigung des Briefes beruht.

Was sich in S/849 sonst an zumeist kaum erschlossenen Materialien befindet, kann hier nur kurz und in geringer Auswahl mitgeteilt werden:

S. 21 Urbanus Rhegius an die Hamburger Bürgerinnen Hileke Rheders (Elike Reders), Gesche Huige (Geske Hugeske), Wonelcke Tonagels (Womelke Thunagels), Lüneburg, 20. Juli 1533, deutsch, Abschrift 16. Jh.[37]

S. 22 Hamburger Ministerium an Jakob Andreae, [Hamburg] 1570, lateinisch, Abschrift [wohl 1570]. Die Hamburger Pastoren reagieren auf Andreaes Konkordienbemühungen.[38]

S. 23–26 Friedrich Henninges, Stadtsuperintendent in Lüneburg, an Joachim Westphal, Pastor an der Hamburger Katharinenkirche, Lüneburg, 21. August 1556, lateinisch, autographe Ausfertigung

S. 27–54 Johannes Aepinus (Johann Hoeck), Ad regem Angliae, 1548

S. 57 Melanchthon [und andere] an den Hamburger Superintendenten Johannes Aepinus (Johann Hoeck), [Wittenberg], 10. Juli 1549, lateinisch, unvollständige Abschrift 17. Jh. (nur MBW 5585, Z. 1–7), übernommen aus der Melanchthon-Briefwechsel-Edition von Manlius[39]

S. 62 Martin Luther an „fürsichtige Herren" [Rat der Stadt Kiel], s. l, Montag nach Visitationis Mariae 1544 (= 7. Juli 1544), deutsch, Abschrift um 1700[40]

---

36. *Philipp Melanchthon*, Epistolarum Farrago, hg. von *Johannes Manlius*, Basel 1565 (VD16 M 3220), 373–376.

37. Auf S. 21 mit Textverlusten am Rand infolge Bescheidung; weitere Abschrift um 1700 auf S. 58. Der Brief ist als Abschrift (18. Jh.) auch in der SUB Hamburg, Sup. ep. 4, 1 überliefert.

38. Beschreibung und Transkription: Datenbank „Theologenbriefwechsel im Südwesten des Reichs in der Frühen Neuzeit (1550–1620)"; https://thbw.hadw-bw.de (Brief 51360).

39. *Melanchthon*, Epistolarum Farrago (wie Anm. 36), 220–222.

40. Editionen aus dem Autograph (Hamburg SUB, Sup. ep. 1, 13): Enders und Kawerau

S. 71 Philipp Melanchthon, Aufzeichnungen über die Höllenfahrt Christi [von Ende Februar/Anfang März 1550], lateinisch, Abschrift frühes 17. Jh.[41]

S. 75–80 Paul von Eitzen an den König von Dänemark (Christian VII.), Schleswig, Januar 1579

S. 81 f. Zwei Briefe von Hugo Grotius an Johann Quistorp, 1645

S. 89–95 Calvinisten, Begräbnisse in Hamburg, 1617/1622

S. 97–104 Auszug aus dem Protokoll des Hamburger Ministeriums, 1617

S. 107–110 Mandat des Hamburger Senats betreffend Häresie, Anfang 17. Jh.

S. 111–117 Vom Zehen pffenig [sic!], Anfang 17. Jh.

S. 143–158 Begräbnisse von Calvinisten, 1636

S. 443–462 Traum Friedrichs des Weisen, dazu Auslegung

S. 463–465 König Ferdinand I. an Martin Luther, Innsbruck, 1. Februar 1537 (Fälschung), deutsch, Abschrift 17. Jh.[42]

S. 467–506 betreffend Stade und u. a. Joachim Neander, 1619, 1622, 1625

S. 507–1276 diverse Dokumente, 1626–1733

Die ohne Zweifel anspruchsvolle und zeitraubende Erschließung der vorliegenden Sammelhandschrift und der weiteren ca. 23 ebenfalls noch weitgehend unerschlossenen Hamburgensien aus derselben Periode im Bestand der Hamburger Commerzbibliothek stellt ein wichtiges Desiderat dar. Genannt seien hier insbesondere die Sammelhandschriften S/847 (Hamburgische Kirchensachen 17./18. Jh.), S/850 (Kempe, Acta Hamburgensia und Ergänzungen dazu), S/855 (Kirchenwesen Hamburg 1529–1849), S/872 (Kirchenwesen Hamburg 17./18. Jh.), S/893 (Hamburgisches Ministerium 1610–1749). Hinzu kommen noch die Mandate und Verordnungen aus dem Nachlass des 1768 verstorbenen Hamburger Orientalisten Hermann Samuel Reimarus und eine Sammlung von Gelegenheitsgedichten aus dem Nachlass des 1761 verstorbenen Hamburger Historikers und Philologen Michael Richey.[43] Die sämtlichen Akten- und Handschrifteneinheiten sind anhand ihrer Beschriftungen auf den Einbänden und den entsprechenden Angaben im Katalog von 1841

Dr. Martin Luthers Briefwechsel, Bd. 16, hg. von *Ernst Ludwig Enders* und *Gustav Kawerau*, Leipzig 1915, 47 f. (Nr. 3413); WA Br 10, 603 (Nr. 4008).

41. Edition: MBW 5742 (aus Abschriften). Am Rand wird erwähnt, dass der Wortlaut mit demjenigen im Druck *Melanchthon*, Epistolarum Farrago (wie Anm. 36), 547 f. übereinstimmt. Möglicherweise war die Abschrift, die sich heute in Hamburg SUB, Sup. ep. fol. 92, fol. 57r–58r befindet, die Vorlage der Abschrift in S/849.

42. Edition: WA Br 8, 31–33 (Nr. 3132).

43. *Backe-Dietrich/Lembcke*, Commerzbibliothek (wie Anm. 11), 220.

knapp beschrieben. Diese Angaben wurden in den vor Ort benutzbaren Online-Katalog der Handschriften übernommen.

Prof. Dr. Thomas Gerhard Wilhelmi
Forschungsstelle „Briefwechsel südwestdeutscher Theologen"
Heidelberger Akademie der Wissenschaften
Karlstraße 5
D-69117 Heidelberg
Thomas.Wilhelmi@gs.uni-heidelberg.de

ABSTRACT

Unknown letters from Philipp Melanchthon or Martin Luther—or letters whose complete wording is not already known from other sources—are rarely found anymore. An extensive handwritten collection in the Commerzbibliothek in Hamburg has been found to contain an as yet unknown letter and a letter the wording of which was not previously known from Martin Luther as well as two letters from Philipp Melanchthon the wording of which was thus far unknown, along with relevant copies of several letters from Luther and Melanchthon that were known from other sources and an unknown letter from Johannes Bugenhagen. The 1,276 pages of the mixed volume include further letters (among others from Urbanus Rhegius) and numerous documents about local church history in Hamburg during the period from 1533 to 1733.

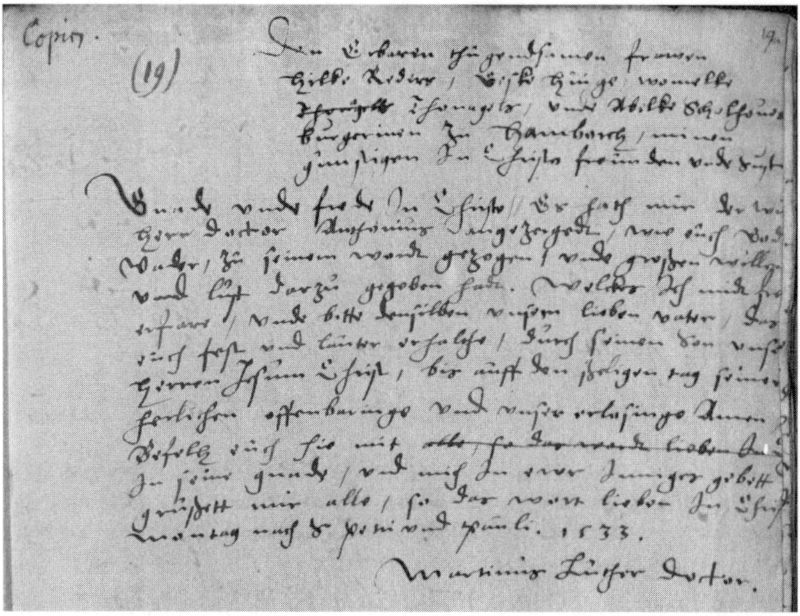

Abbildung 1: Martin Luther an Hamburger Bürgerinnen, 30. Juni 1533.
Abschrift Mitte 16. Jh. Commerzbibliothek Hamburg, S/849, S. 19 (obere Hälfte).

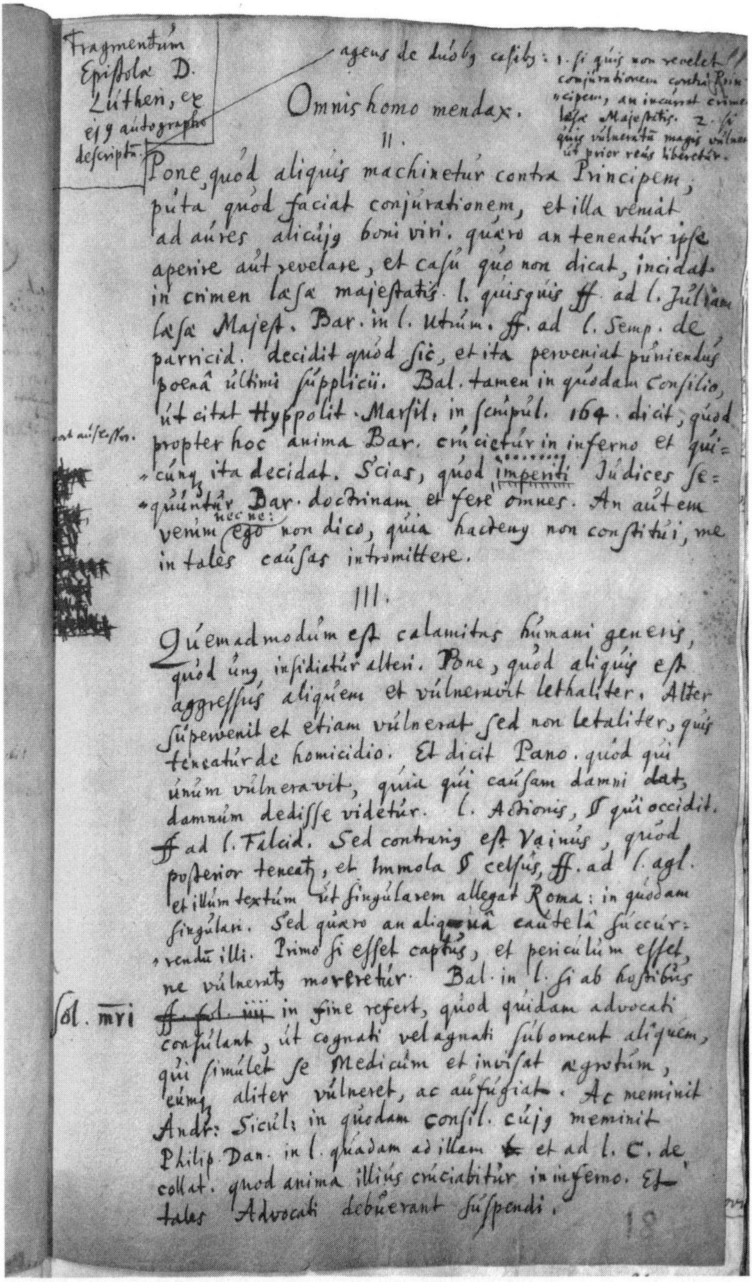
Fragmentum Epistolæ D. Lutheri, ex ejus autographo descripti.

agens de duobus casibus: 1. si quis non revelet conjurationem contra Principem, an incurrat crimen læsæ Majestatis. 2. si quis vulneratum magis vulneret ut prior reus liberetur.

Omnis homo mendax.

II.

Pone, quod aliquis machinetur contra Principem, puta quod faciat conjurationem, et illa veniat ad aures alicujus boni viri. quæro an teneatur ipse aperire aut revelare, et casu quo non dicat, incidat in crimen læsæ majestatis. l. quisquis ff. ad l. Juliam læsæ Majest. Bar. in l. utrum. ff. ad l. Semp. de parricid. decidit quod sic, et ita perveniat puniendus poenâ ultimi supplicii. Bal. tamen in quodam consilio, ut citat Hyppolit. Marsil. in singul. 164. dicit, quod propter hoc anima Bar. cruciatur in inferno et quicunque ita decidat. Scias, quod imperiti Judices sequuntur Bar. doctrinam et fere omnes. An autem verum nec ne: ego non dico, quia hactenus non constitui, me in tales causas intromittere.

III.

Quemadmodum est calamitas humani generis, quod unus insidiatur alteri. Pone, quod aliquis est aggressus aliquem et vulneravit lethaliter. Alter supervenit et etiam vulnerat sed non letaliter, quis teneatur de homicidio. Et dicit Pano. quod qui unum vulneravit, quia qui causam damni dat, damnum dedisse videtur. l. Actionis, § qui occidit. ff ad l. Falcid. Sed contrarius est Vainus, quod posterior teneatur, et Immola § celsus, ff. ad l. agl. et illum textum ut singularem allegat Roma: in quodam singulari. Sed quæro an aliqua cautela succurrendum illi. Primo si esset captus, et periculum esset, ne vulneratus moreretur. Bal. in l. si ab hostibus in fine refert, quod quidam advocati consulant, ut cognati vel agnati suboment aliquem, qui simulet se Medicum et invisat ægrotum, eumque aliter vulneret, ac aufugiat. Ac meminit Andr: Sicul: in quodam consil. cujus meminit Philip. Dec. in l. quadam ad illam et ad l. C. de collat. quod anima illius cruciatur in inferno. Et tales Advocati debuerant suspendi.

fol. mri

18

Abbildung 2: Martin Luther an N. N., s. l. et a. („Fragmentum Epistolae D. Lutheri, ex eius autographo descriptum"), Abschrift 17. Jh. Commerzbibliothek Hamburg, S/849, S. 11.

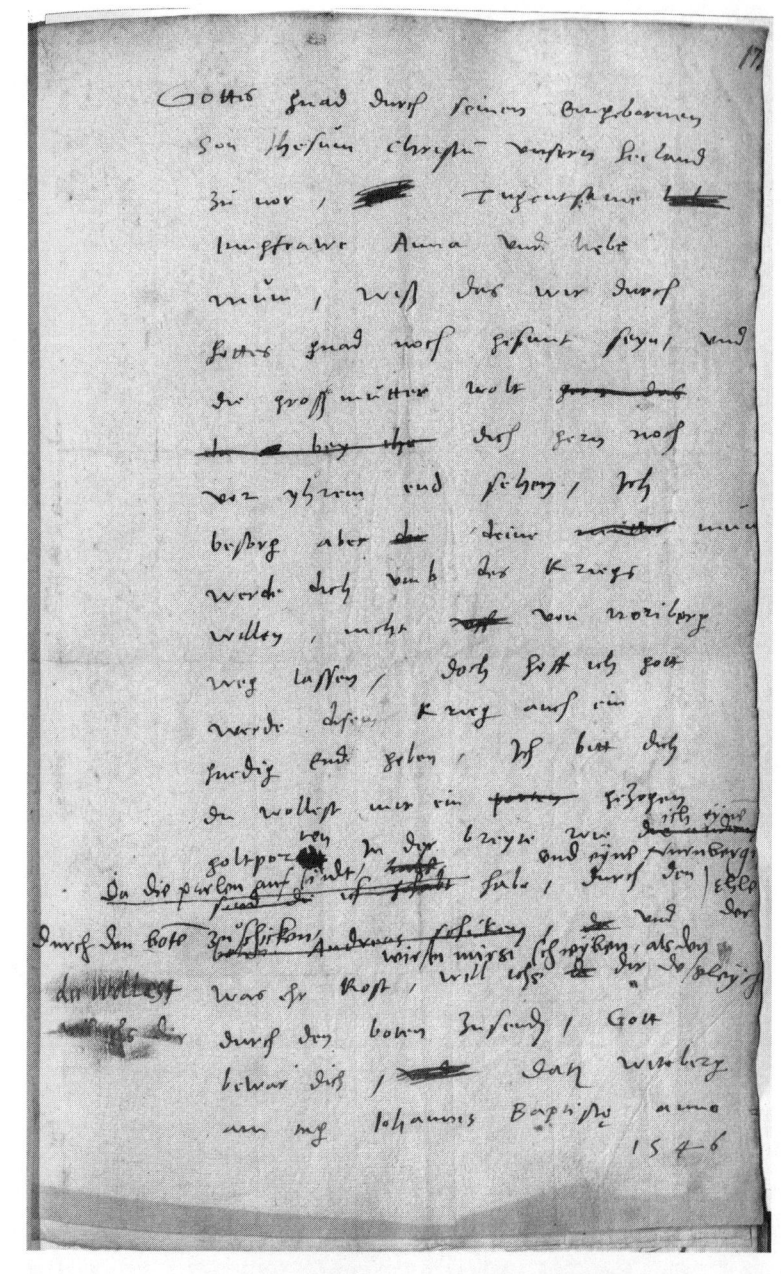

Abbildung 3: N. N. an Anna Münster(er) in Nürnberg, Wittenberg, 24. Juni 1546. Ausfertigung. Commerzbibliothek Hamburg, S/849, S. 17f., hier S. 17.